PSYCHOLOGY
IN TEACHING READING
SECOND EDITION

EMERALD V. DECHANT

Professor of Education
Fort Hays Kansas State College

HENRY P. SMITH

Prentice-Hall, Inc., Englewood Cliffs, New Jersey   07632

Library of Congress Cataloging in Publication Data

DECHANT, EMERALD V
Psychology in teaching reading.

Authors' names in inverse order on t.p. of 1st ed.
Includes bibliographies and index.
1. Reading, Psychology of. I. Smith, Henry
Peter, 1910–1968 joint author. II. Title.
BF456.R2S57 1977   372.4'01'9   76–30298
ISBN 0-13-736686-8

© 1977 by Prentice-Hall, Inc., Englewood Cliffs, N.J. 07632

Printed in the United States of America

10 9 8 7 6 5 4 3 2 1

Prentice-Hall International, Inc., *London*
Prentice-Hall of Australia Pty. Limited, *Sydney*
Prentice-Hall of Canada, Ltd., *Toronto*
Prentice-Hall of India Private Limited, *New Delhi*
Prentice-Hall of Japan, Inc., *Tokyo*
Prentice-Hall of Southeast Asia Pte. Ltd., *Singapore*
Whitehall Books Limited, *Wellington, New Zealand*

To

HENRY P. SMITH

Dr. Smith was my adviser while I worked towards my Ph.D. at the University of Kansas. His untimely death left me and many of his students and colleagues, but especially his family, with a deep sense of loss. It was his inspiration and guidance that led me into the study of reading. For this I will always be grateful. It is an honor and pleasure to dedicate this revised edition to him.

Contents

preface, ix

1 INTRODUCTION, 1

Research in Reading, *1*
The Content of the Book, *3*
Summary, *6*
Questions for Discussion, *6*
Bibliography, *7*

2 THE PSYCHOLOGY OF READING, 8

The Nature of the Reading Process, *8*
Theoretical Models of Reading, *14*
Recent Research, *22*
A Synthesis, *22*
Summary, *27*
Questions for Discussion, *27*
Bibliography, *28*

3 THE PERCEPTUAL NATURE OF READING, 32

The Perceptual Process, *32*
The Major Determinants of Meaning, *36*
Concept Formation, *39*
Summary, *46*
Questions for Discussion, *47*
Bibliography, *47*

4 LEARNING PRINCIPLES
AND THE READING PROCESS, 50

Stimulus-Response Theories of Learning: An Overview, *50*
Field Theories: An Overview, *52*
Thorndike's Connectionism, *54*
Guthrie's Contiguous Association, *62*
Skinner's Operant Conditioning, *64*
Hull's Habit Theory, *66*
Field Theory, *68*
The Field Concept, *72*
Differentiation, *73*
Kurt Lewin and Edward Tolman, *77*
A Synthesis, *78*
Questions for Discussion, *82*
Bibliography, *83*

5 THE PSYCHOLOGICAL BASES OF READINESS, 87

The Nature of Reading Readiness, *87*
The Correlates of Reading Readiness, *88*
When Is the Child Ready?, *110*
Summary, *113*
Questions for Discussion, *114*
Bibliography, *114*

6 THE SENSORY BASES OF READING, 121

Vision and Reading, *121*
Types of Defective Vision, *129*
Eye Defects and Reading Proficiency, *133*
Visual Screening Tests, *135*
Hearing and Reading, *136*
Listening and Reading Proficiency, *140*
Summary, *143*
Questions for Discussion, *143*
Bibliography, *144*

7 THE PHYSIOLOGICAL CORRELATES OF READING, 148

General Physical Conditions, *148*
Language and Reading Readiness, *149*
Neural Adequacy and Reading, *155*
Reversals and Reading, *167*
Summary, *170*

Questions for Discussion, *170*
Bibliography, *171*

8 INTEREST AND PERSONALITY FACTORS IN THE READING PROCESS, 176

The Framework of Motivation, *176*
Interest in Reading, *178*
Determinants of Reading Interest, *180*
Developing Interests and Tastes, *185*
Summary, *187*
Personal and Social Development of the Learner, *188*
Personal Adjustment and Reading Achievement, *189*
Maladjustment and Reading Achievement, *193*
Types of Treatment, *196*
Summary, *197*
Questions for Discussion, *198*
Bibliography, *198*

9 BASIC READING SKILLS: IDENTIFICATION AND ASSOCIATION, 202

Oral Reading, *202*
Reading as an Associative Process, *206*
Methods of Teaching Word Recognition, *208*
Introducing the Pupil to Linguistic Phonics, *222*
Summary, *231*
Questions for Discussion, *232*
Bibliography, *233*

10 BASIC READING SKILLS: COMPREHENSION SKILLS, 237

The Nature of Comprehension, *238*
Developing Comprehension Skills, *239*
Reading for Evaluation (Critical Reading), *259*
Reading for Learning, *262*
Reading Maps, Graphs, Tables, and Charts, *267*
Summary, *270*
Questions for Discussion, *270*
Bibliography, *271*

11 RATE OF COMPREHENSION,
     READABILITY AND LEGIBILITY, 276

Rate of Comprehension, *276*
Readability, *289*
Legibility, *299*
Summary, *304*
Questions for Discussion, *305*
Bibliography, *305*

12 READING IN THE CONTENT AREAS, 314

Knowledge of Vocabulary and Concepts, *316*
Comprehension in a Specific Content Area, *317*
The Teacher and the Content Areas, *328*
Summary, *328*
Questions for Discussion, *328*
Bibliography, *329*

13 PROVIDING FOR INDIVIDUAL DIFFERENCES, 332

The Developmental Program, *336*
Grouping, *341*
The Slow Learner, *352*
The Gifted Learner, *354*
The Disadvantaged Learner, *357*
Summary, *362*
Bibliography, *362*
Questions for Discussion, *362*

14 DIAGNOSIS AND REMEDIATION, 368

Definition of Diagnosis, *369*
Principles of Diagnosis, *370*
Steps in Diagnosis, *371*
Instruments Useful in Identifying Mode of Learning, *390*
Characteristics of the Corrective Reader, *395*
Characteristics of the Remedial Reader, *396*
Summary, *425*
Questions for Discussion, *425*
Bibliography, *426*

Index, **433**

Preface

The purpose of this book is to provide teachers with an understanding of the psychological bases of the reading process. As teachers, we need to know the facts and principles behind our classroom methods. But facts and principles presented in isolation are difficult to understand and unlikely to be used; we must see how they apply to the teaching of boys and girls. Psychologists have made numerous attempts to systematize what is known about behavior. In this work, we seek to identify and organize the facts concerning *reading behavior*. In order effectively to guide the child who is learning to read, the teacher should understand both those general principles that govern all learning and those special principles that govern learning to read.

Just what is a psychology of reading? There is a vast amount of data and carefully considered theory to be found in psychology and related fields. But frequently it is expressed in technical language and those portions of it that have educational implications are interwoven with much that has little or no direct application to education. Out of this wealth of information, a psychology of reading selects what is relevant to the teaching of reading and attempts to organize it in logical form. But it must do more than this. It must suggest applications of the findings and theories of the psychologist to classroom situations.

In a very real sense this book is an introduction to educational methods and materials as well as a basic course in the psychology of the reading-learning process. However, the methods and materials discussed are used primarily to illustrate the application of psychological principles. We cannot hope to include in one book both a psychology of reading and an account of all the numerous and complex methods and materials of teaching reading. We have therefore emphasized the essential psychological data and introduced only those applications that are needed for an understanding of the place of psychology in the reading process.

This book was not written for the *reading* teacher alone. It is rather for all teachers, because *all* share the responsibility for improving reading. It is for the prospective teacher, the active teacher, and, indeed, for the administrator who wishes to gain a better understanding of the psychology of reading. In a broad sense, it is a psychology of teaching directed specifically toward reading. At all levels of development, reading is perhaps our best example of the effective teaching-learning process and, at the same time, one of its most important products. This book therefore has four major goals:

1. To *select* those data that are most relevant to the teacher's understanding of the reading process.
2. To *interpret* these data in terms of the problems that the teacher will encounter.
3. To *apply* the interpretations to the specific classroom problems that teachers meet.
4. To *identify* at least a portion of those problems that require further investigation.

This revision of our 1961 edition differs from the first edition. We have emphasized the basic difference between *learning to read* and *proficient* or *fluent reading;* between *word identification* and *reading for comprehension;* and between *word identification* and *word recognition.* The good reader is still one who can deal efficiently with both the surface structure (written representation of language) and the deep structure which gives meaning. *And,* the surface and deep structure are related in a complex way through the system of rules that is grammar or syntax.

This second edition also provides a better understanding of the importance of the sign system, of decoding, and of language structures in reading. It points out that the good reader makes use of graphic information, semantic information, and syntactic information. It explores various models of reading and emphasizes one with a strong psycholinguistic base. It presents a view of reading as both a complex cognitive skill aimed at obtaining information and a complex language system.

Finally, this addition has added some 750 new references. We have not discarded or substituted for pre-1960 references simply to make the book appear up to date. In fact, in numerous instances where subsequent research has only tended to corroborate earlier research, we often have chosen to report the earlier research.

EMERALD DECHANT

1

Introduction

For the child, reading is a key to success in school, to the development of out-of-school interests, to the enjoyment of leisure time, and to personal and social adjustment. It helps him to adjust to his age mates, to become independent of parents and teachers, to select and prepare for an occupation, and to achieve social responsibilities. As our culture becomes more complex, reading plays an increasingly greater role in satisfying personal needs and in promoting social awareness and growth. Through reading we acquire many of our standards of behavior and morality; we may broaden our interests, our tastes, and our understanding of others. As Aldous Huxley points out, "Every man who knows how to read has it in his power to magnify himself, to multiply the ways in which he exists, to make his life full, significant and interesting." But, above all, in the modern school, effective reading is the most important avenue to effective learning.

Reading is so interrelated with the total educational process that educational success requires successful reading. Experience has taught us that those who fail in school usually have failed first in reading. Giordano Bruno pointed out that if the first button of a man's coat is wrongly buttoned, all the rest are certain to be crooked. Reading is that first button in the garment of education.

RESEARCH IN READING

Reading's importance in our modern schools is indicated by the amount of research that has been devoted to it. Over the past seventy years no single problem has received more attention from the educational and psychological laboratories than the problem of understanding the reading process. Both teachers and research specialists have sought to understand what reading is; how reading facility may be developed; and what adjustments in method and material must be made in order that all pupils may profit optimally from reading instruction.

Unfortunately, most of the comprehensive reviews of research are

1

written for the benefit of research workers. They are not in a form particularly usable by the teacher. A purpose of this book is to identify and organize the findings of the researchers in such a way that the teacher can become acquainted with the most useful facts and principles.

Although most of us, reading specialists as well as classroom teachers, are much more interested in the practical problems of developmental and remedial reading than in the philosophical and psychological bases for these applications, it is worthwhile for us to consider those data upon which we must depend for sound applications. Professionalism is based on sound theory and experimental research. The physician anchors his art in biology, anatomy, and chemistry. The engineer anchors his art in mathematical and physical theory and research. The teacher cannot be merely a practitioner; he must anchor his teaching art in psychological, physiological, and educational research.

New concepts and theories give meaning and direction to our professional activities. They help us to see the reasons for our methodology and to predict its success. For example, theories form the basis for hypotheses about the child's deficiencies; they help us to identify causes, choose remediation, and make prognoses.

We have made every attempt throughout the book to relate psychological theory and research to practice. Sometimes, the results are rather frustrating, but this should not keep us either from theorizing and engaging in research or from making applications.

Psychology does not consist of a catalogue of educational formulae that tell the teacher how to teach, the administrator how to administer, and the parent how to be a parent. It would be nice if psychology had attained this degree of refinement, but there are no ready-made pills available for educational ills.

Psychology, in a sense, may even make the answers come less easy. This should not discourage the teacher. It is worthwhile to work a little harder at a solution if the solution tends to be correct. Frequently, those who have the quickest answers are in error. Psychology should help the teacher to avoid making errors because it will open up for him more alternatives of action. Before acting, he will consider more possibilities. The average layman would have little difficulty in deciding whether to retain or not to retain a pupil. The trained teacher may find it not as easy, but he may make fewer errors.

There are few questions in education that have clearcut answers. Furthermore, there is no automatic, one-to-one relationship between theory and practice or application. The theorist, even the learning theorist, cannot replace the educator. The theorist offers advice, gives direction, and prevents errors, but in the final analysis the educational programs must emerge from "the distillation of theoretical principles with practical 'know how' (Kendler, 1961)." William James, writing in 1899, pointed out that:

> . . . you make a great, a very great mistake, if you think that psychology, being the science of the mind's laws, is something from which you can deduce definite programmes and schemes and methods of instruction for

immediate schoolroom use. Psychology is a science, and teaching is an art; and sciences never generate arts directly out of themselves. An intermediary inventive mind must make the application, by using its originality. The science of logic never made a man reason rightly and the science of ethics . . . never made a man behave rightly. The most such sciences can do is to help us catch ourselves up and check ourselves if we start to reason or to behave wrongly; and to criticize ourselves more articulately after we have made mistakes. . . . Everywhere teaching must *agree* with psychology, but need not necessarily be the only kind of teaching that would so agree; for many diverse methods of teaching may equally well agree with psychological laws. . . .

But, if the use of psychological principles thus be negative rather than positive, it does not follow that it may not be of great use, all the same. It certainly narrows the path for experiments and trials. We know in advance, if we are psychologists, that certain methods will be wrong, so our psychology saves us from mistakes. It makes us, moreover, more clear as to what we are about. (James, 1920, pp. 7–11).

Nevertheless, if psychology is to have a significant effect upon teaching procedures and techniques, theory and practice must be tied up in a very definite way. We simply can't be an "ammunition wagon" loaded with knowledge which we don't know how to use; we must be a rifle (Rogers, 1961, p. 281).

The transition from what we know as individuals to what we do is always a great leap. Perhaps an even greater transition exists between what researchers, as a group, have learned and the individual teacher's practices in the classroom. The challenge facing teachers today is the improvement of classroom practice in the light of present knowledge. This is particularly true in reading where research has been above the ordinary.

THE CONTENT OF THE BOOK

Because this book is intended for both the active and the prospective teacher, it is only reasonable that the informational needs of the teacher should guide the selection of the topics that are discussed. This book is built around thirteen areas of content, with a chapter being devoted to each area:

Chapter II: *The Psychology of Reading.* The student of the psychology of reading needs to have an overall view of the reading process, of the importance of the sign system, of decoding, and of language structures. He needs to see how the various models designed to help us understand reading are interrelated. And, before studying the vast amount of research about reading, he should have a model that attempts to help him relate the research to the actual teaching and learning of reading.

Chapter III: *The Perceptual Nature of Reading.* The teacher must understand the basic nature of reading. Reading is a perceptual rather than merely a sensory process and, as such, it includes more than mere recognition of words. Neither printed pages nor orally spoken words transmit meaning. The essence of meaning comes from the reader's fund of experience. Reading includes thinking as well as understanding. We are concerned with what the psychologist has discovered about the general nature of perception and how perceptual abilities are developed.

Chapter IV: *Learning Principles and the Reading Process.* Reading is a process that must be learned. The laws of learning and the facts concerning such topics as motivation, reinforcement, practice, interference, transfer, and conditioning apply to learning to read. The tremendous body of knowledge on the learning process must *not* be reserved for specialized books on learning, but must become a part of the reading teacher's professional equipment.

Chapter V: *The Psychological Bases of Readiness.* As teachers, we are intimately concerned with the readiness of individuals for learning. As teachers of reading, we wish to know the most favorable moment for beginning to teach a child to read and for the teaching of each specific reading skill. The readiness concept is not reserved for the period of beginning reading; it applies to all levels of reading development.

Chapter VI: *The Sensory Bases of Reading.* The reading teacher needs to understand the sensory processes of reading. Efficiency in reading frequently depends on the oculo-motor habits of the reader. Reading begins with visual stimuli; the eyes bring the stimuli to the reader. Auditory factors, though perhaps not as significant as visual factors, under certain conditions also are determinants of reading success.

Chapter VII: *The Physiological Correlates of Reading.* There are numerous physiological factors in addition to vision and hearing that play significant roles in the reading process. Thus, general physical health, speech development, and glandular and neurological functioning become of professional interest to the teacher.

Chapter VIII: *Interest and Personality Factors in the Reading Process.* We know that performance is closely dependent upon motivation. Without motivation learning seldom, if ever, occurs. The reading teacher employs his knowledge of motivated learning to direct children first toward learning to read and later toward reading to learn. Interests are closely related to motivation: they develop from attempts to satisfy basic motives. The teacher wants to know the factors that direct interest toward reading and that attract the child to specific reading content.

Chapter IX: *Basic Reading Skills: Identification and Association.* To a large extent at least, the development of reading ability is the acquisition of a series of skills. The reading teacher is interested in how these skills meet the specific demands of both oral and silent reading and how they may best be fostered. The first of these are the word-recognition skills.

Chapter X: *Basic Reading Skills: Comprehension Skills.* Word recognition is but one of the basic reading skills. Comprehension is at least as important. Meaning is the *sine qua non* of reading.

Chapter XI: *Rate of Comprehension, Readability and Legibility.* Effective reading emphasizes economy which includes comprehension *and* rate. These two skills are so interrelated that we speak of rate of comprehension. We also wish to put the right book in the right hands at the right time. To accomplish this we need to know how to recognize the materials that best fit the needs of each child. A knowledge of readability will be useful to us. We also need to know the legibility factors which either promote or hinder reading.

Chapter XII: *Reading in the Content Areas.* In reading for learning each content area requires its own specific skills. The teacher must know the unique reading needs of social studies, science, mathematics, and the language arts. Special problems are posed by the vocabulary, symbolism, and concepts of each area.

Chapter XIII: *Providing for Individual Differences.* Reading and the entire process of growth and development are interdependent. Data concerning the typical patterns of development of boys and girls, as well as individual differences among members of the same sex, are of particular interest to teachers. Differences among children of the same age in physical, social, emotional, and attitudinal development guarantee that we cannot successfully use a patent-medicine approach to teaching children to read. When we add to the problems stemming from differences in intellectual development, we see why the teaching of reading at all grade levels is so extremely complex and why we must make individual diagnoses and prescriptions for each child.

Chapter XIV: *Diagnosis and Remediation.* We know that, in learning to read, all children do not progress at the same rate. Even among those of adequate ability some meet problems that delay or block their learning. We must strive constantly to discover these deterrents to learning and plan individual work to further each child's development. An effective developmental reading program is built on a foundation of early diagnosis of inadequacies, careful evaluation of needs and abilities, and the utilization of professionally designed materials and methods.

There will be wide variations in purpose among the users of this book. Yet, unfortunately, it cannot be all things to all people. Many of its readers will be teachers, but some teachers are most concerned with the elementary level whereas others are most concerned with the secondary level. And even among its teacher-readers, some will come to it for a first view of the psychological bases of the reading process and others will have a background of numerous courses in psychology, educational psychology, and teaching methods. Thus, some will find it desirable to review principles and theory commonly found in early courses in a teacher-preparation program; others will wish to pursue certain topics in a depth or detail greater than can be provided by a single book.

SUMMARY

The major purpose of this chapter has been to outline the scope and goals of this book. We cannot be content to find out merely what is known about the psychological bases of the reading process. We must go further and learn how such knowledge may be applied to the teaching that we do in our classrooms. Although we must become acquainted with facts, opinions, and principles, we will be equally concerned with applications. The challenge to improve the reading skills of our children is an important one. Reading proficiency is important to all ages. Both the teacher who has reading as a specific responsibility and the teacher of the content areas must be capable of helping children to progress in reading. It is hoped that this book will help you in the successful performance of your professional task.

QUESTIONS FOR DISCUSSION

---

1. How would you define reading?
2. What are the elements of professionalism? What makes one a professional teacher?
3. What portion of a teacher's knowledge may be classed as professional? How would you classify his general cultural background and his knowledge of subject matter?
4. What uses do we have for reading? Are different kinds of reading required for different purposes? Explain.
5. What are some of the possible reasons for failing to learn to read?
6. Is it possible that reading instruction in the elementary grades is far better than it was thirty years ago even though we may have far more poor readers in our high schools? Explain.
7. Is excellent instruction in reading during the elementary school years likely to result in an increase or a decrease in the range of differences in reading ability among high school students? Explain.
8. List as many as you can of the questions that a study of the psychology of reading should help you to answer.

BIBLIOGRAPHY

JAMES, WILLIAM. *Talks to Teachers on Psychology.* New York: Holt, Rinehart and Winston, 1920.

KENDLER, HOWARD H. "Stimulus-Response Psychology and Audio-Visual Education." *AV Communication Review* 9, No. 5, (1961); 33–41.

ROGERS, CARL. *On Becoming a Person.* Boston: Houghton Mifflin, 1961.

2

The Psychology
of Reading

This chapter in capsule form presents the topics and ideas that will be dealt with in greater detail in the remaining twelve chapters of the book. It gives an overview of recent contributions of cognitive psychology and psycholinguistics and presents a theoretical model that should help you to tie together the many bits of research in the chapters that follow. The discussion of reading models is preceded by comments on the sign system in reading, the importance of coding and language structures, and the significance of cue systems.

Reading is a most complex process, requiring very specialized skills on the part of the reader. Einstein noted that it is the most difficult of tasks. It is a form of human behavior that we would expect to be studied and analyzed by psychologists with great precision, but perhaps because it is a form of covert behavior (Weaver, 1964), it has not been given the attention by learning theorists that it deserves. It is for this reason that Kingston (1968) feels that at present there does not exist a systematic, well-formulated psychology of reading and that what is available is too inadequately structured to be of much value to the classroom teacher.

Psychology has nonetheless had a profound effect on such concepts as readiness, intelligence, developmental reading, practice, sensation, readability and legibility, and evaluation of student progress and on our understanding of perception, cognition, learning, comprehension, and cognitive styles.

Kingston (1968) keynotes the purpose of this chapter. He states that the one major contribution which psychology can make to reading is to provide the impetus needed to develop a more adequate theory of reading. We do believe that we are at least on the verge of some significant movement in this direction.

THE NATURE OF THE READING PROCESS

Definitions of reading have one element in common: they all note that reading is an interpretation of graphic symbols. Reading is thus perceived as a two-fold process: it requires identification of the symbols and the association of appropriate meanings with them. Reading requires identification *and* comprehension. A second aspect of reading is that it is a language and communication process. It is the process of putting the reader in contact and communication with ideas. It is the culminating act of the communication process, initiated by the thoughts of the writer and expressed through the symbols on the page. Without the reader, communication via the printed page is impossible. Reading always involves an interaction between the writer and the reader. Reading requires the communication of a message and it requires a language system—a sign system—in which messages are formulated or encoded.

Let us briefly examine the significance of the sign system in reading which the reader must be able to identify and recognize. Let us also look at the decoding or the comprehension process. We will explore particularly the role that semantic or experientially-derived meanings and language structures play in decoding.

The Sign System

The purpose of all communication is the sharing of meanings. But, it is the sign system or symbol that must carry the burden of meaning between the communicators. In reading, the sign system is the graphic symbols. They are the writer's tools for awakening meaning in the reader. James (1890, p. 356) noted that language is "a system of signs, different from the things signified, but able to suggest them."

The focus for many years in the thinking and research about reading has been on the habit-forming practices needed to develop high speed recognition responses to the sign system, the alphabetic writing (the graphic input) or the graphic language system. The purpose of these practices was to develop the ability to perceive the significant contrastive features of the separate letters (Cooper, 1965). Research thus focused on feature analysis (analysis of the written symbols) or on the analysis of the surface structure of the language. The reading teacher spent most of his time and energy on the perceptual aspects of word identification.

This research was not without value. After all, reading is a sensory process. The reader must make discriminative visual responses to the graphic symbols. The reader coordinates his eyes as he moves them along the lines of print in a left-to-right fashion, stopping to perceive words or word parts.

Reading is also a word-identification process, and one aspect of the beginning reader's problem is to discover the critical differences between two letters or two words. He needs to learn what the distinctive features of written language are. The raw material, therefore, of reading is the distinctive features, the visual configuration, or the visual array of letters and words.

It is a common observation that the beginning reader has to rely on the visual information much more than the fluent reader because he is unable to make full use of the nonvisual sources of information, both syntactic and semantic. He must deduce meaning from the surface structure or the visual array of letters on the page. Unfortunately, he often becomes so engrossed with the mechanical aspects of reading, with word identification and pronunciation, that he fails to understand the need for comprehension. The good reader, on the other hand, processes only a part of the available information, attending selectively to the more important words (Willows, 1974). Good readers concentrate most of their processing capacity on the extraction of meanings, and seem to employ an analysis-by-synthesis strategy of reading for meaning. They sample the text to validate linguistic expectancies of the information content of the text rather than analyzing the passage in a word-by-word manner (Hochberg, 1970).

The Importance of Decoding

Reading is much more than simple recognition of the graphic symbols. It is even more than the mere ability to pronounce the words on the printed page, than simply matching the written word with the spoken code, or going from the graphic code to the oral code. It is more than a matching of phoneme and grapheme. This is *recoding*, but it is not *decoding*. Decoding occurs only when meaning is associated with the written symbol and only when the meaning that the writer wanted to share with the reader has been received by him.

A team of experts, under the sponsorship of the United States Office of Education, thus tentatively defined reading as "a term used to refer to an interaction by which meaning encoded in visual stimuli by an author becomes meaning in the mind of the reader."

Communication in reading happens through a process of encoding, recoding, and decoding. Reading is always a two-fold process: the identification of the symbols and the association of meaning with them.

Reading as decoding focuses on the semantic information or cues. Semantic cues are meaning-bearing cues based on experience. Meaning is supplied by the reader as he processes the symbols by relating them to experience.

Obviously, reading of graphic symbols consists of two processes: the mechanical processes involved in bringing the stimuli to the brain and the mental processes involved in interpreting the stimuli or the graphic symbols after they get to the brain. When the light rays from the printed page hit the retinal cells of the eyes, signals are sent along the optic nerve to the visual centers of the brain. The reader must give significance to the graphic symbols. He must bring meaning to the graphic symbol. The critical element in reading often is not what is on the page, but, rather, what the graphic symbols signify to the reader. Reading thus might in a general way be described as the process of giving the significance intended by the writer to the graphic symbols by relating them to one's own fund of experiences (Dechant, 1970, p. 19).

Reading is thus also a perceptual process, an interpretative process, a conceptual and thinking process. Conceptual thought is required to react with meaning. The reader interprets what he reads, associates it with his past experience, and projects beyond it in terms of ideas, relations, and categorizations. Reading is a process of forming tentative judgments and interpretations, and verifying, correcting, and confirming guesses. Since the words on the printed page have no meaning of their own, reading always must go beyond the information given or beyond what is seen. The reader does not see the object, person, or experience of which the author writes. His eyes are in contact with a word, in fact, with the light rays that are reflected by the word, and so it is impossible for him to see meaning. And yet, the pupil takes meaning to the word.

What determines the reader's reaction? Clearly, his reactions to the printed word are determined by the experiences that he has had with those objects or events for which the symbol stands. This is what is meant by perception (Hebb, 1958). Perception is a consciousness or awareness of the experiences evoked by a symbol. It is a process whereby sensory stimulation is translated into organized experience. It is through perception that the graphic symbol achieves meaning. And yet, we cannot forget that the constructions of our imaging or perceptual processes are clearly dependent upon the stimulus information received through the eyes (Smith, 1971, p. 83).

In reading, there simply is not a one-to-one correspondence between the stimulus (the graphic input) and the response. Concepts and perceptions include a reading of the past experience. That which the person adds is the sum total of the retained and organized effects of past experience. The individual perceives his world in terms of "what he is" as much as "what it is." (Hurvich and Jameson, 1974).

William James (1890, p. 103) pointed out years ago that "Whilst part of what we perceive comes through our senses from the object before us, another part always comes . . . out of our head."

Horn (1937, p. 154) points out that the writer does not really convey ideas to the reader; he merely stimulates him to construct them out of his own experience. And, the one who takes the most to the printed page gains the most. Chall (1947) gave an information test about tuberculosis to about one hundred sixth and eighth graders. She then had them read a selection on tuberculosis and gave them a test on the selection. Those children who already knew the most about tuberculosis also made the best comprehension scores on the reading selection. Chall (1947, p. 230) noted that we read in order to gain experience, and yet it is also true that we get more out of reading if we have more experience. Thus, reading typically is the bringing of meaning *to* rather than the gaining of meaning *from* the printed page.

Emerging from cognitive research is a picture of a reader as an active and selective information-gathering individual. The brain is an input-output device producing perceptions and changes of behavior. The human being both gains and creates knowledge. His brain is constantly processing information, and incoming information is continually being tested, reformulated, and acted upon. Meaning is both output (what the reader brings by way of past experience to the printed page), and also input (the new meanings that the reader gets from the printed page).

The Importance of Language Structures

Recent discussions of the nature of the reading process have broadened the description of reading and have focused on language structures. Thus Birkley (1970) defines reading as "the recognition and perception of language structures as wholes in order to comprehend both the surface and deep meaning which these structures communicate." The advocates of this view generally agree on what reading is not. They point out that their view is different from one which perceives reading as a precise process, consisting of exact, detailed, sequential perception and identification of letters, words, and spelling patterns. It is not at all clear that the view is essentially different from those who emphasize the perceptual nature of the reading process. Perhaps, it is different in its specific emphasis on how meaning is acquired and how meaning is conveyed through the "deep structures" of language.

Goodman (1967) notes that reading is a selective process, involving partial use of available minimal language clues (graphic, semantic, and syntactic) selected from perceptual input on the basis of the reader's expectation. The reader, as he processes this partial information, confirms, rejects, or refines his tentative decisions as reading progresses. Goodman notes that readers utilize three kinds of information simultaneously. Certainly without the graphic input there would be no reading, but the reader uses syntactic and semantic information as well.

Reading as a sensory process focuses on the graphic input or information, the letters used in printing and their sequencing in words; reading as a perceptual process focuses on the semantic information or cues, the lexical information or bundles of experience which have been given vocabulary tags by an author (Hoskisson and Krohm, 1974); reading as a language process is concerned with the syntactic information, or structure, the word order, word categories, and patterns of sentences.

Smith (1971) points out that a fluent reader maximizes his use of cues contained in printed language and minimizes his dependence on feature analysis or the surface structure. He operates at a deep structure level, predicts as he reads, sampling the surface structure as he tests out his predictions. When his predictions are not confirmed, he then engages in greater visual analysis.

Smith (1971, p. 44) criticizes the perception of reading as a matter of "decoding" printed symbols into sounds and then extracting meaning from sound. He suggests that the fluent reader generally is unable to do so because fluent reading is accomplished too fast for the translation into sound to occur. The decoding that the reader does transforms the visual representation of language into meaning. Decoding is effected through syntax; syntax mediates between the visual surface structure and meaning (Smith, 1971, p. 222).

Wardhaugh (1969) notes that the processing in reading is not just a matter of processing visual signals in order to convert these signals into some kind of covert speech. This conversion is merely the beginning of the process, because semantic and syntactic processing are necessary in addition to the processing of the visual signs. He notes that one cannot read a foreign language by simply being able to vocalize the print. This is more in the nature of barking at print.

Structure, as used in the above descriptions, refers to the patterned regularities among the elements of a language (Weener, 1971). The presumption is that increasing knowledge of syntax (rules for ordering words in sentences) in addition to increasing knowledge of semantics (knowledge of word meanings) will reflect in improved ability to process sentences (Frasure and Entwisle, 1973).

The import of all this is that the reader will do a better job of decoding if he understands language structures. It is not enough to focus on the semantic or referential meaning (what the symbol "steeple" represents or in other words, its referend); the good reader also uses structure to decode meaning. The language structure, the syntax, the word order, the inflectional endings, and the intonation patterns all redundantly define the meaning of a symbol. Language structures communicate meanings and the better one's knowledge of language structure is, the less need the reader has for visual information.

The good reader can deal with both surface and deep structure; he can use both the semantic and the syntactic contexts in reading. Words get meaning as a consequence of occurring in sentences. And, for this reason, it is almost impossible to read a sentence correctly without mastery of the grammar of a language. *Syntax determines how the semantic associations are to be interpreted.*

The Cue Systems in Reading

Our discussion thus far has identified three basic cue systems operating in reading that can cue meaning: the sign system itself, experience, and syntax. There are, however, many specific cues that the reader of this book should become familiar with at an early stage. We therefore reproduce here with some modification a listing by Smith, Goodman, and Meredith (1970):

1. **Cue systems within words.**
    a. Letter-sound relationships or grapheme-phoneme correspondences
    b. Shape or word configuration or word's physiognomy
    c. Known little words in new words or comparison to known words
    d. Affixes, prefixes and suffixes
    e. Recurrent spelling patterns, phonograms
    f. Diacritical marking systems, color coding
    g. Legibility factors
2. **Cue systems in the flow of language.**
    a. Patterns of word order or function order (subject, predicate)
    b. Inflectional endings (ed, s, es, ing)
    c. Function words (articles, auxiliary verbs, prepositions, conjunctions)

    d. Intonation patterns (pitch, stress, juncture)
    e. Verbal or grammatical context in which the word or words are placed
    f. Redundancy cues (In the sentence, "The boys eat their lunches," there are at least four cues that the subject is plural).
    g. Grammatical and syntactical patterns
    h. Punctuation marks

3. **Cues external to the reader or to language.**
    a. Pictures, art activities, dramatization, tracing, etc.
    b. Prompting (telling the child what the word is)
    c. Concrete objects

4. **Cues within the reader.**
    a. Language facility (especially innate rules of language)
    b. Dialect differences (cultural factors)
    c. Physiology (biological-neurological and maturational factors)
    d. Learned responses to graphic cues or the perceptual skill of the learner
    e. Experiential and socio-economic background of the learner
    f. Intellectual and conceptual development of the learner
    g. Physicial, social, and emotional factors

Reading is message reconstruction (like reading a map) and for the most part comprehension of meaning depends on using all the cues available.

THEORETICAL MODELS OF READING

In the preceding pages we have looked at the various aspects that seem related to the nature of the reading process: reading always requires a sign system—the symbols on the page; it involves decoding—the association of meaning with the symbols; and it also involves language structures—a syntax that mediates between the surface structure and the deep structure, both semantic and syntactic meaning.

In this section, we will take a look at some theoretical models of reading, hoping thereby to attain an even better understanding of the reading process and perhaps offer some guidelines for a synthesis of the nature of the reading process.

Theories and models of reading instruction include the following (Williams 1973):

  I. Taxonomic Models
  II. Psychometric Models
 III. Psychological Models
    A. Behavioral
    B. Cognitive
 IV. Information Processing Models
  V. Linguistic Models
    A. Early Formulations
    B. Transformational-Generative Grammar Models

Taxonomic Models

A characteristic taxonomic model is the descriptive model of Gray (1950; 1960). He described reading as consisting of four skills: word recognition, comprehension, reaction, and assimilation. Robinson (1966) broadened the model to include rate of reading.

Psychometric Models

The statistically-determined models of Holmes and Singer (Holmes, 1953, 1960, 1965; Singer, 1962, 1965, 1968, 1969; Holmes and Singer, 1961, 1964, 1966), constructed by the use of substrata analysis, are designed to determine the combination of hierarchically-organized subsystems that form a working system for attaining speed and power of reading. Models have been developed for college, high school, and elementary levels. The four systems, accounting for 89 percent of the variance in power of reading, are word recognition, word meaning, morphemic analysis, and reasoning in context. Three subtests (reasoning in context, auditory vocabulary-word meaning, and phrase perception discrimination) accounted for 77 percent of the variance in speed of reading.

The model suggests that silent reading ability is divisible into two major interrelated components, speed and power of reading. As the reader changes from speed to power of reading he reorganizes his set of systems (and subsystems) from emphasizing the visuomotor perceptual system to one stressing morphemic and word recognition systems.

Psychological Models

Behavioral Models. Learning theories generally are divided into Stimulus Response Theories and Field Theories. Learning to read cannot be explained if only one of the theories of learning is adopted.

The behaviorist model holds that all learning is habit formation, a connection between a stimulus and a response. The connection is referred to as an S-R bond. The S-R theorist focuses on the response or the observable action; the learner learns an action or a response. The S-R theorist asserts his predilection for conditioning, which to him is the clearest and most simple instance of a response to a stimulus. Learning is defined as the acquisition of new behavior patterns or the changing of behavior either by strengthening or weakening of old patterns as a result of practice or training.

The best contemporary exponent of behaviorism is B. F. Skinner. In Skinnerian terminology, all behavior can be understood, predicted and controlled in terms of habits established or shaped by a process of successive approximation by the reinforcement of a response in the presence of ·
a particular stimulus.

Reinforcement determines whether conditioning in fact takes place. A particular S-R bond will be established only if the behaving organism is reinforced in a particular way while responding in the presence of a stimulus. This type of conditioning in Skinner's experiments is called operant conditioning in contrast to classical conditioning. In this type of conditioning, the reinforcement occurs after the behavior that is to be conditioned. For Skinner, the behavior had first to be emitted before reinforcement would occur. The process of setting up the type of behavior that it is desired to reinforce is known as shaping. Shaping of behavior does not wait until the learner makes the desired response exactly correct. Operant learning may be quite gradual. At first, it may be necessary to reinforce gross approximations to the final response. Behavior thus is molded into shape by a process of successive approximation. It is through shaping that the very fine discriminations required in reading are produced. Through a process of chaining, elaborate sequences of behavior, such as are required in reading, are built up.

The behaviorist view explains why learning takes place (by reinforcement), and once the habit is established, we find that habits have their own momentum. The very exercise of the habit (reading) reinforces and consolidates the habit. The simple opportunity to engage in this habit is an effective reinforcer.

Cognitive Models. The cognitive model, representing as it does the second significant explanation of learning, perceives the learner as a gatherer, processor, and consumer of information (Smith, 1971, pp. 68–79) rather than as a simple reactor to stimuli (Boneau, 1974). The cognitive theorist does not believe that language skills can be explained as habits established by the conditioning of S-R bonds. Rather, he points out that the reader extracts meaning from what he reads on the basis of the visual information (the surface structure of the language) but also on the basis of all the deep structure of language and the knowledge and experiences contained within his brain. Language and what is read cannot be comprehended unless the reader (listener) makes this critical, active contribution. Thus, one of the principal tenets of the cognitive theorist is that perception is a constructive process, adding something to the stimulus aspects. Cognition is defined as the integrative activity of the brain, overriding reflex response behavior and freeing behavior from sense dominance (Hebb, 1974). It refers to all the processes by which the sensory input is transformed, reduced, elaborated, stored, recovered, and used (Neisser, 1967, p. 4).

Recently, Boneau (1974) has proposed a decision theory/ information-processing approach which emphasizes that behavior is determined primarily by events within the organism and which allows behavior to be based on cognitive processes. The theory assumes that through commerce with the environment the individual internalizes information about the external world and develops an internal model of the environment (IME). The IME is unique to the individual, being based on the individual's history of interaction with the world and with biological potential in a very personal way. The cognitive theorist speaks of restructuring of perceptions or relationships. Thus, the pupil is taught and in fact learns a system of attacking new words and he uses this system to make an insightful response to a new word. He does not have to be conditioned to come up with the correct response.

Information Processing Model

One of the best descriptions of reading as information processing is offered by Smith (1971, pp. 12–27).

A key principle in the psychology of reading is that reading is an act of communication in which information is transferred from a transmitter to a receiver and for this reason a knowledge of theories of communication and information and signal detection theory are relevant to a study of the psychology of reading and the terminology of communication theory is especially useful in describing a theory of reading. Terms from communication theory that have special significance in understanding reading are: communication channel, noise, limited channel capacity, information, and redundancy.

Communication Channel. The writer (transmitter) and the reader (receiver) are two ends of a communication channel along which information flows. As a message passes through the communication channel, it takes on a variety of forms. At each part of the communication process, there is possibility that the message will be changed in some way.

Limited Channel Capacity. Just as in a communication system, there also is a limit of channel capacity in the communication system of the reader. There is a limit to the speed at which the eye can travel over a passage of text making information-gathering fixations and to the amount of information that can be acquired in a single fixation.

Noise. A message or communication may be confused or made less clear by extraneous signals called noise. Because all communication channels have limited capacities, noise may overload the system and prevent the transmission of informative signals. In reading, these may be difficult-to-read type face, poor illumination, distraction of the reader's attention, etc. Smith (1971, p. 16) notes that because of noise, reading is intrinsically more difficult for the beginning reader than for the experienced reader. Everything is much noisier for the beginner. Anything that one lacks the skill or knowledge to understand automatically becomes noise.

Information. This is defined as a reduction of uncertainty. In reading, information exists when the reader can reduce the number of alternative possibilities and can discriminate a given letter from the other 25 possibilities. If he can eliminate all alternatives except one, then the amount of information transmitted is equal to the amount of uncertainty that existed.

Redundancy. Redundancy exists whenever information is duplicated by more than one source or, putting it in another way, redundancy exists whenever the same alternatives (26 letters or multiple meanings for a sentence) can be eliminated in more than one way. The reason for presenting a word both visually and auditorily is that it is a form of redundancy that helps the learner. In reading, it is immediately apparent that the larger the context, the greater is the redundancy. And, the more redundancy there is, the less visual information the skilled reader requires.

The application of redundancy to reading, of course, suggests that the skilled reader does not need a fixed amount of information to identify a word or to ascertain the meaning. The amount of information he will need depends on the difficulty of the passage, on the reader's skill, and the reader's decision-making criterion. Does he demand absolute certainty before venturing a guess? Is he willing to take a chance? Setting his criterion too high for word identification may mean that he can't identify the word quickly enough to comprehend. The beginning reader may not venture a guess for fear of being wrong and so becomes a very inefficient reader.

The Physiology of Reading

The concepts of communication theory applied to reading help us to put physiological factors in reading in proper perspective.

As we already noted, reading of graphic symbols consists of two processes: the mechanical processes involved in bringing the stimuli to the brain and the mental processes involved in interpreting the stimuli after they get to the brain. When the light rays from the printed page hit the retinal cells of the eyes, signals are sent along the optic nerve to the visual centers of the brain. This is not yet reading. The signals must be interpreted. The reader must give significance to the graphic symbols. He must bring meaning to the graphic symbol.

Unfortunately, there are numerous possibilities for noise within the communication channel. There also is the prospect of limited channel capacity; and the learner may not be able to take advantage of redundancy.

Lack of experience (with life itself, with the materials and their content, with words and their identification) is a major determinant of poor reading. The experiential deficiencies that plague the beginning reader are: (1) his lack of experience in processing letters, words, and meanings; (2) lack of experience in grouping letters into words and words into meanings; (3) his lack of knowledge of redundant features in words (patterns of letter features can occur only in certain combinations—there is an orthographic or spelling redundancy that he has not mastered); (4)

inability to use the syntactic and semantic redundancy that exists across sequences of words—certain combinations of words cannot occur in the English language; and (5) lack of knowledge of the sources of redundancy in written language. The beginning reader must overcome these deficiencies so that he can overcome the channel capacity limitations of the visual system. When the reader must get enough visual information to identify every single letter or even every word, he will be a slow reader and rarely will be able to read for meaning. The reader gains the above information only by doing a lot of reading. The child learning to read needs the opportunity to examine a large sample of language, to generate hypotheses about the regularities underlying it, and to modify these hypotheses on the basis of feedback (Smith and Goodman, 1971).

Reading is an act, a performance, or a response that the reader makes to the printed page. Certain physiological factors may prohibit making the response. We have already alluded to the channel capacity limitations of the visual system. Here are others:

One. The reader must first see and identify the words before he can take meaning to them. Among the inhibitory factors are inadequate vision, lack of single vision or clear vision, lack of visual coordination or muscular imbalance, the restrictions of the visual-information processing system, or tunnel vision.

Tunnel vision means that the amount of information that can be picked up in a single glance is limited. There is a limitation on the rate at which information can be processed from a sensory store or from the number of distinctive features required to identify four or five unrelated letters three or four times every second. The output from a single fixation may be four or five letters, two unrelated words, or four or five words in a meaningful sequence.

The simple fact is that the more difficulty a reader experiences with reading the more he must rely on visual information. He is forced to analyze all the constituents of the surface representation in order to be able to apply his syntactic skills (Smith, 1971, pp. 218–222).

Two. The reader must have adequate auditory acuity, auditory discrimination, auditory blending, and auditory comprehension. Inhibitory factors are intensity deafness and tone deafness (as from a conductive hearing loss stemming from a punctured eardrum or malfunction of the three small bones in the middle ear or from a nerve loss resulting from an impairment of the auditory nerve and causing difficulty with sounds represented by f, v, s, sh, zh, th, t, d, b, p, k, and g). The pupil will have difficulty with phonics and with oral reading.

Most children possess the visual and auditory acuity needed for successful reading. What they need is visual and auditory discrimination skills. They need to know where to look for distinctive features. They need to know what makes a difference in reading.

Most physiological deficits make it difficult to read fluently and at an appropriate rate. Rate is important apart from its economy because it helps the pupil to comprehend by discovering the syntactic rules.

Linguistic Models

Early Formulations. The early linguistic models were developed by Bloomfield, Fries, and Lefevre. In general, Bloomfield (1942) (1961) emphasized that beginning reading should present only regular correspondences between orthography and speech; Fries (1963) stressed letter-sound relationships; and Lefevre stressed syntactical cues both intra-word (such as inflections) and interword (such as sentence structure). Lefevre (1962; 1964, p. 68) noted that the "Grasp of meaning is integrally linked to grasp of structure—intonation gives the unifying configuration." Genuine reading proficiency is described as the ability to read language structure. The best reader is one mentally aware of the stresses, elongations of words, changes of pitch, intonation, and rhythms of the sentences that he reads. If he reads the way the writer would like it to have been said, true communication of meaning may be possible. Fries and Bloomfield concentrated on letters, sounds, and words as the prime units in reading; Lefevre makes the sentence the key unit in reading.

Bloomfield and Fries define reading as the act of turning the stimulus of graphic shape on a surface back into speech (Edwards, 1966). Bloomfield differentiated between the act of reading (recognition of grapheme-phoneme correspondences) and the goal of reading (comprehension).

The central thesis of the Bloomfield-Barnhart method is that there is an inseparable relationship between the words as printed and the sounds for which the letters are conventional signs, and that converting letters to meaning requires from the beginning a concentration upon letter and sound to bring about as rapidly as possible an automatic association between them. Bloomfield's system is a linguistic system of teaching reading which separates the problem of the study of word-form from the study of word-meaning. He notes that children come to school knowing how to speak the English language, but they do not know how to read the form of words.

Lefevre, having a different emphasis than Bloomfield, adapted linguistic ideas to meaningful reading. He suggests an analytical method of teaching reading emphasizing language patterns. He emphasized that meaning comes only through the grasping of the language structure exemplified in a sentence. Meaning thus depends on the intonation, the word and sentence order, the grammatical inflections, and certain key function words. Only by reading structures can full meaning be attained. Or, to put it another way, unless the reader translates correctly the printed text into the intonation pattern of the writer, he may not be getting the meaning intended.

Walcutt, Lamport, and McCracken (1974, pp. 41–42), noting that syntax concerns itself with meaning-bearing patterns, point out that the word *dogs* is easily understood on a surface level as two morphemes expressing a recognized relationship among certain animals. There are however very noticeable differences among "Dogs make good pets," "It's a dog's life," and "He's gone to the dogs," all of which incidentally employ the same two morphemes. The illustrations clearly show that meaning comes through syntax by intonation patterns, word form changes, and the use of structure and function words.

Bloomfield felt that initial teaching of reading for meaning is incorrect, and that meaning will come quite naturally as the alphabetic code or principle is discovered. Lefevre is critical of Bloomfield's approach, criticizing him for confining himself largely to phonemic analysis and for neglecting intonation and syntax.

Reading is thus bascially described by Fries and Bloomfield as decoding printed symbols into sound and then extracting meaning from sound.

The early linguists focused primarily on the problems of beginning reading and more specifically on the problems of word recognition (Chall, 1969).

Transformational-Generative Grammar. The theorists in this group (Chomsky, 1957, 1965, 1968, 1969, 1970; Chomsky and Halle, 1968; Goodman, 1966, 1970; Ruddell, 1974) reject the notion that reading is simply sequential word recognition. Reading is perceived as a psycholinguistic process, only superficially different from the comprehension of speech. The beginning reader is thought to use abstract rules about language structure to arrive at comprehension.

This approach emphasizes that all languages and hence sentences have a surface structure and a deep structure. Sounds or written words are the surface representation of a message; meaning, syntactic and semantic interpretation are the deep level. The deep structure gives the meaning of the sentence; the surface structure gives the form of a sentence (Jacobs and Rosenbaum, 1968)

The Transformational-Generative grammar model suggests that grammar or the rules of syntax are a set of rules by which sense is made out of language, or by which words are arranged into sentences. Grammar is the link between sound and meaning.

Chomsky hypothesized that there is an innate rational ability in humans which permits them to generate the underlying rules or syntax of their language after having been sufficiently exposed to it. The rules are identified as deep structures which are transformed to surface structures while being given phonological and semantic flesh (Vogel, 1974).

Children even at an early age appear to be rule-producing learners. They can construct sentences they have never heard but which are nevertheless well-formed in terms of general rules. They can produce novel sentences.

Grammatical transformations are special ways of translating the deep structure of a sentence into a variety of surface representations; transformational rules, conversely, permit the reader to move from surface structure to the meaning.

The role of syntax to mediate between the visual surface structure and meaning is precisely the function that generative-transformational grammarians attribute to it (Smith, 1971, p. 222).

RECENT RESEARCH

The position of the psycholinguistic school is supported by recent research and by the observations of other reading specialists. Denner (1970) found that problem readers (grades three to four) and children expected to be poor readers (grade one) performed more poorly than normal children on tasks requiring representational and syntactic competence.

Steiner, Wiener, and Cromer (1971) found that poor readers fail to extract contextual cues essential for identification, and they fail to utilize such cues in identification even when they are presented with them. "They seem to be identifying words as if the words were unrelated items unaffected by syntactical or contextual relationships."

Bever and Bower (1966) report that the best readers among able college students do not read sentences in linear fashion, but in terms of their deep syntactic structure.

Weber (1967) found that an analysis of errors on the syntactic and semantic level suggests that even early readers can successfully make use of preceding verbal context. It is apparent that they do not depend solely on graphic representation to make a response.

Burke and Goodman, (1971) using Goodman's *Taxonomy of Cues and Miscues in Reading,* analyzed the reading of a boy named Daniel and concluded that there was little relationship between the miscues and comprehension. Some miscues simply did not result in changed meaning and they were usually corrected if they did. Miscues tended to be corrected when the resulting syntax was unacceptable.

Vogel (1974) found that dyslexic children with reading comprehension difficulties are deficient in oral syntax.

A SYNTHESIS

The theoretical model that the writer began developing in the first edition of *Psychology in Teaching Reading* and which we lean toward today is basically a psycholinguistic model, but it is surely eclectic in that it has some elements of the taxonomic model, the psychological model, both behavioral and cognitive, the information processing model, and the linguistic models, both the early formations and the transformational-generative grammar models.

There probably is no pure model. Every model seems to have many elements in common with other models. Singer (1969) notes that probably a series of models is necessary to explain and predict reading performance.

We agree with the observations of Williams (1973) that there is a growing rapproachement among theorists toward a view of reading as both a complex cognitive skill aimed at obtaining information and a complex language system. The psycholinguistic approach has perhaps the most to offer in reading instruction. It suggests that reading involves a basic knowledge of language as well as the utilization of complex active perceptual and cognitive strategies of information selection and processing. Reading is an active cognitive skill; it is not merely a simple associative learning process; it is not a passive process "with the graphic input cueing directly and automatically the already learned and therefore instantly meaningful speech code."

Psycholinguistics was developed about twenty years ago and according to Miller (1964, 1965) its central task is to describe the psychological processes that go on when children use language (read).

The dynamics of reading clearly point to a basic difference between learning to read and proficient or fluent reading. The beginning reader puts most of his energy into identifying words, but word recognition is not reading and, although the fluent reader is a competent word identifier, he normally does not need to identify individual words in fluent reading (Smith, 1971, p. 125).

Similarly, there is also a basic distinction between word identification and reading for comprehension. And, there is a difference between word identification and word recognition.

Some basic observations about the nature of the reading process are the following:

One. Reading involves some sort of interaction between writer and reader (communication must take place). Reading thus is a language and communication process. Reading is a process by which a person reconstructs a message encoded graphically by a writer (Goodman, 1970). The reader goes from the written language, visually perceived, to a reconstruction of the message encoded in the written language by the writer. Comprehension and hence communication occur when the reconstruction agrees with the writer's intended message.

Two. Reading requires that the reader make visual contact with the stimulus or graphic cues and that he form a perceptual image of the graphic stimulus. Reading thus is a sensory process and a word identification process.

   a. The reader picks up graphic cues (stimulus input). This is the signal in reading. Reading requires a sign system in which messages are formulated (the graphic system). Without graphic input there would be no reading. Reading thus is a sensory process, requiring discriminative visual responses to graphic symbols.

   b. The reader forms a perceptual image. This is the process of visual perception. Reading is a word-identification process.

Three. Language has a surface structure (the sounds and written representations of language) and a deep structure which gives meaning

(Smith and Goodman, 1971). The basic requirement for reading is for the learner to be able to deal efficiently with both the surface and the deep structure. Let us make a few observations about the surface structure:

a. The child's problem is to discover the critical differences between two letters or words, which is not so much a matter of knowing how to look as knowing what to look for. The beginning reader must learn to look for the distinctive features, those elements of the visual aspects of words, the visual stimuli, the visual configuration, or the visual array that distinguishes one letter of the word from another. Letter and word identification are alike in that they both involve the discrimination and categorization of a visual configuration. Goodman (1970) notes that perception as it functions in language teaches us what to pay attention to and what not to pay attention to. The reader has to learn to ignore the non-significant differences or he would be constantly distracted.

b. The three principal avenues for word identification (phonics, the letter-cluster approach, and identification by analogy as when a word is identified by putting together the sounds of bits of words) are useful only in that they show where a significant difference or association lies.

c. Smith (1971, p. 4) distinguishes between mediated and immediate word identification. In mediated word identification, the learner makes use of additional non-visual processes of word synthesis such as the use of phonics or asking someone what the word is.

   In immediate word identification the learner goes directly to word identification. I have used "word recognition" to refer to the same process.

Four. Reading usually requires recoding—going from the written code to the spoken code, but it is not absolutely necessary to go from graphic symbol to meaning through the auditory-vocal counterparts of the printed symbol. The beginning reader does so more frequently; the fluent reader less often. Reading is not only the processing of visual signals into sound. It requires, as we shall note later, the processing of semantic and syntactic information as well.

a. A common model for reading (Carroll, 1964, 1970) has been based on the reconstruction of a spoken message from a printed text and making the same meaning responses to the printed text that one would make to the spoken message.

   Thus for many teachers, the most natural way for teaching reading has been to go through the spoken word. The teacher says to the child: "Look at this word. This word says (spells) cat." The spoken word is the familiar stimulus; the written word is the novel stimulus. Gradually, with repeated associations between the written and the spoken word, the child brings to the written word the same meaning he previously attached to the spoken word.

   Bannatyne (1973) notes that visual symbols (graphemes) represent sounds (phonemes), not concepts or meanings except in ideographic languages such as Chinese. The printed word is a phonetic code for our auditory-vocal language. Meaning is always the property of the spoken word, not the printed word. "Only the sounds strung together in auditory-vocal words and sentences represent meaning." Reading should become fully automatic so that the reader can concentrate on the auditory-vocal language which is the communicative vehicle for meaning.

b. Goodman (1967) notes that the reader searches his memory for related graphophonological, syntactic, and semantic cues on the basis of which the reader comes up with reconstruction of the message.

Good readers, according to Goodman, tend to decode directly from the graphic stimulus. The graphophonic coding or cues system refers to the perception of printed cues (letters, words, punctuation marks) and to a knowledge of spelling-sound patterns. It refers to the use of cues within words.

The syntactic decoding or cues system consists of a knowledge of sentence patterns that signal information or redundantly confirm the use of a word.

The semantic decoding or cues system consists of the concept and experiences elicted by the message which lead to tentative meaning choices that are tested, and if not correct, are modified by going back to get more information.

Five. Reading is a perceptual process, a conceptual and thinking process—conceptual thought is required to react with meaning. Reading has as its central purpose the effective communication of meaning. Meaning is a part of the deep structure, the semantic, cognitive level. Because reading is a perceptual process:

a. A sentence, written or spoken, has no meaning as such; its meaning is peculiar to the listener or reader. Meaning is not a property of language (the words themselves have no intrinsic meaning). There is no direct or invariable connection between the symbol and the referend, the datum, object, event, or sensation. Meaning is supplied by the reader as he processes the symbolic system by relating it to experiences and conceptual structures.

b. The meaning of a sentence is not the sum total of the meanings of the individual words of that sentence. Reading is not a process of combining individual letters into words and strings of words into sentences from which meanings spring automatically.

c. Words get meaning as a consequence of occurring in sentences.

d. While word identification and reading for comprehension are distinctive processes, it is possible to read for comprehension without actually identifying all individual words.

The fluent reader can go directly to meaning through the process of redundancy. He uses the words around a given word, in other words the context, to identify the word. The beginning reader must put letters together to form words; the skilled reader only rarely does this. In comprehending, the bigger the learner's knowledge of language, the less need exists for visual information from the printed page.

e. Comprehension, or the extraction of meaning from text, is the reduction of uncertainty (Smith, 1971, p. 185). Reduction of uncertainty occurs when the reader can eliminate all the alternate meanings that the particular visual configurations might convey. A principal technique for achieving better comprehension is the application of syntactic and semantic sequential redundancy. The fluent reader is one who can make optimal use of all the redundancy available in a passage of text. He merely samples the visual information to confirm his expectations. He decodes not from visual symbols into sound, but from visual symbol to meaning.[1] He is predicting his way through a passage of text. Reading may begin with almost total dependence upon speech, but it can be freed from this dependence. The fluent reader is not so stimulus bound. Thus, the beginning reader uses a technique—that of going through the auditory-vocal counterparts of the printed symbol—a technique which may be of relatively less use to him once he becomes a fluent reader.

Six. The two levels of language (surface and deep structure) are related in a complex way through the system of rules that is grammar or syntax (Smith and Goodman, 1971). It is almost impossible to read a sentence without mastery of the grammar of the language. Grammar is the link between sound and meaning. The rules of syntax determine how the particular visual-semantic associations should be interpreted for a cognitive re-organization (Smith, 1971, p. 216).

a. Children develop the rules rapidly between the age of eighteen months and four years.

b. The pattern of development of these rules is so systematic and invariant that it is believed that children have an innate predisposition for discovering the rules of language (Chomsky, 1969). They have an innate preprogrammed ability to create language. Innate in language are "the capacity for language" and the "structures of language" (Hansen, 1974).

Seven. The reader makes a meaning choice or a guess consistent with the graphic cues. Semantic analysis leads to partial decoding. If he can make a decodable choice, he tests it for semantic and grammatical acceptability. If the choice is semantically and grammatically acceptable, he assimilates a new meaning or integrates it with prior meanings.

a. Reading is a receptive psycholinguistic process. It is a spiral of predict, sample, select, guess, and confirm activities. The good reader uses the least amount of information to make the best possible first guesses (Goodman, 1970). As this partial information is processed, tentative decisions are made to be confirmed, rejected, or refined as reading progresses.

b. The reader checks the validity of his guesses by asking himself whether they produced language structures as he knows them and whether they make sense (Goodman, 1970). There are two contexts in reading: one is syntactic, the language structure; the other is semantic, the meaning or message.

c. No two persons will have exactly the same perceptions of the same word or sentence. Perception rarely is totally veridical. Herrick (1956, p. 340) suggested that the validity of a perception is its predictive value as a guide for action. "The perceiver calls upon his previous experiences and generally assumes that the perception that was successful in the past is most likely to be correct now." He interprets the sensory data on the basis of his past experience. When he finds his perception to be in error, he must change his interpretation.

[1]The apparent contradiction between Smith and Bannatyne (referred to in 4a above) probably stems from their differences of emphasis; beginning reading vs. fluent reading.

d. It is not enough to put one's own stamp of meaning on the words. The reader must follow the thought of the writer (Langman, 1960, pp. 19–23). The reader may and even must gain meaning from the printed page. This occurs when the writer's symbols stimulate the reader to combine or reconstruct his own experiences in a novel way.

SUMMARY

In this chapter we have looked at three aspects of the reading process: the sign system, decoding, and the role of language structures in reading. We looked at various reading models and developed a personal synthesis.

We have seen that a reader can be a good reader only if his past experience has furnished him with a cognitive base relevant to the information contained in a particular written communication (Hollander, 1975). We have also noted that the reader's level of experience with language itself, with syntactics and idiomatic usage, will play a significant role in determining the level of his comprehension.

As we look at individual differences in Chapters 5 through 8, it will become even clearer that comprehension depends upon more than simple phonemic reproduction. All the cues to meaning have relevance—the cultural experiences of the reader, the reader's cognitive style, his purpose for reading, his general health, his visual abilities, his experience with similar materials, etc.

Finally, the basic theme of the chapter is that reading is clearly a process which is complete only when comprehension is attained.

QUESTIONS FOR DISCUSSION

1. Explain what is meant when we say that reading is a language and a communication process.
2. What is the importance of vision in reading? What is the key visual skill needed by the beginning reader?
3. What is meant by recoding, decoding, encoding?
4. Is it absolutely necessary to identify individual words? Substantiate your answer.
5. Distinguish between the surface and deep structure of language.
6. Explain the sentence: *Decoding is effected through syntax; syntax mediates between the visual surface structure and meaning.*
7. Compare and contrast the cue systems in reading.
8. Compare and contrast two of the models of the reading process discussed in this chapter.

BIBLIOGRAPHY

BANNATYNE, ALEX. "Reading: An Auditory-Vocal Process." *Academic Therapy* (Summer, 1973): 429–31.

BEVER, THOMAS and THOMAS BOWER. "How to Read Without Listening." Ithaca: Cornell University, 1966.

BIRKLEY, MARILYN. "Effecting Reading Improvement in the Classroom Through Teacher Self-Improvement Programs." *Journal of Reading* 14 (1970): 94–100.

BLOOMFIELD, LEONARD and BARNHART, CLARENCE L. *Let's Read: A Linguistic Approach.* Detroit: Wayne State University Press, 1961.

BONEAU, C. ALAN. "Paradigm Regained? Cognitive Behaviorism Restated." *American Psychologist* 29 (1974): 297–309.

BURKE, CAROLYN L. and KENNETH S. GOODMAN. "When a Child Reads: A Psycholinguistic Analysis." *Elementary English* (January, 1970).

CARROLL, JOHN B. *Language and Thought.* Englewood Cliffs, N.J.: Prentice-Hall, 1964.

CARROLL, JOHN B. "The Nature of the Reading Process." *Theoretical Models and Processes of Reading,* ed. by Harry Singer and R. B. Ruddell. International Reading Association. Newark, Del.: 1970, 292–303.

CHALL, JEANNE. "The Influence of Previous Knowledge on Reading Ability." *Educational Research Bulletin,* Ohio State University, 26 (1947): 225–30.

CHALL, JEANNE. "Research in Linguistics and Reading Instruction: For Further Research and Practice." In J. Allen Figurel, ed., *Reading and Realism.* Volume 13, International Reading Association Conference Proceedings, 1969, pp. 560–71.

CHOMSKY, N. *Syntactic Structures.* The Hague: Mouton, 1957.

CHOMSKY, N. *Aspects of the Theory of Syntax.* Cambridge: MIT Press, 1965.

CHOMSKY, N. *Language and Mind.* New York: Harcourt Brace Jovanovich, 1968.

CHOMSKY, N. "Form and Meaning in Natural Language." In J. D. Roslansky, ed., *Communication.* Amsterdam: North Holland, 1969, pp. 63–86.

CHOMSKY, N. "Phonology and Reading." In Harry Levin and Joanna P. Williams, eds., *Basic Studies in Reading.* New York: Basic Books, 1970.

CHOMSKY, N. & HALLE, M. *Sound Patterns of English.* New York: Harper & Row, 1968.

COOPER, BERNICE. "Contributions of Linguistics in Teaching Reading." *Education* 85 (1965): 529–32.

DECHANT, EMERALD. "The Philosophy and Sociology of Reading." *The Philosophical and Sociological Bases of Reading.* National Reading Conference Yearbook, Milwaukee, 1965, pp. 9–20.

DECHANT, EMERALD. *Improving the Teaching of Reading.* Englewood Cliffs, N.J.: Prentice-Hall, 1970.

EDWARDS, THOMAS J. "Teaching Reading: A Critique." In John Money, ed., *The Disabled Reader.* Baltimore: John Hopkins Press, 1966, pp. 349–62.

FRIES, C. C. *Linguistics and Reading.* New York: Holt, Rinehart and Winston, 1963.

FRASURE, NANCY E. and ENTWISLE, DORIS R. "Semantic and Syntactic Development in Children." *Developmental Psychology* 9 (1973): 236–45.

GOODMAN, KENNETH S. "Reading: A Psycholinguistic Guessing Game." *Journal of the Reading Specialist* 4 (1967): 126–35.

GOODMAN, KENNETH S. "Comprehension-Centered Reading." *Claremont Reading Conference Yearbook* 34 (1970): 125–35.

GOODMAN, KENNETH S. "Decoding—From Code to What?" *Journal of Reading* 14 (1971): 455–62, 498.

GRAY, W. S. "Growth in Understanding of Reading and Its Development Among Youth." *Keeping Reading Programs Abreast of the Times,* Supplementary Educational Monographs, No. 72, pp. 8–13, Chicago: Chicago University Press, 1950.

GRAY, W. S. "Reading and Physiology and Psychology of Reading." In E. W. Harris, ed., *Encyclopedia of Educational Research.* New York: Macmillan, 1960, pp. 1086–88.

HANSEN, HALVOR P. "Language Acquisition and Development in the Child: A Teacher-Child Verbal Interaction." *Elementary English* 51 (1974): 276–85, 290.

HEBB, D. O. "What Psychology is About." *American Psychologist* 29 (1974): 71–79.

HERRICK, JUDSON. *The Evolution of Human Nature.* Austin: University of Texas Press, 1956.

HOLLANDER, SHEILA, K. "Reading: Process or Product." *The Reading Teacher* 28 (1975): 550–54.

HOLMES, JACK A. *The Substrata-Factor Theory of Reading.* Berkeley: California Book Company, 1953.

HOLMES, JACK A. "The Substrata-Factor Theory of Reading: Some New Experimental Evidence." *New Frontiers in Reading.* International Reading Association Conference Proceedings, Vol. 5, 1960. (Edited by J. Allen Figurel.) New York: Scholastic Magazines, 1960, pp. 115–21.

HOLMES, JACK A. "Basic Assumptions Underlying the Substrata-Factor Theory." *Reading Research Quarterly 1* (1965): 5–28.

HOLMES, JACK A. and SINGER, HARRY. *The Substrata-Factor Theory: The Substrata-Factor Differences Underlying Reading Ability in Known Groups.* Final report. Contracts 538 and 538A, Office of Education, U.S. Department of Health, Education, and Welfare, Washington, D.C.: 1961.

HOLMES, JACK A. and SINGER, HARRY. "Theoretical Models and Trends Toward More Basic Research in Reading." *Review of Educational Research* 34 (1964): 127–55.

HOLMES, JACK A. and SINGER, HARRY. *Speed and Power in Reading in High School.* Office of Education, U.S. Department of Health, Education, and Welfare. A publication of the Bureau of Educational Research and Development. Washington, D.C.: U.S. Government Printing Office, 1966.

HORN, ERNEST. *Methods of Instruction in the Social Studies.* New York: Charles Scribners' Sons, 1937.

HURVICH, LEO M. and JAMESON, DOROTHEA. "Opponent Processes as a Model of Neural Organization." *American Psychologist* 29 (1974): 88–102.

HOSKISSON, KENNETH and KROHM, BERNADETTE. "Reading by Immersion: Assisted Reading." *Elementary English* 51 (1974): 832–36.

JACOBS, RODERICK A. and ROSENBAUM, PETER S. *English Transformational Grammar,* Waltham, Mass.: Blaisdell Publishing Co., 1968.

JAMES, WILLIAM. *Principles of Psychology.* New York: Holt, Rinehart and Winston, 1890.

KINGSTON, ALBERT J. "The Psychology of Reading." *Forging Ahead in Reading.* International Reading Association Conference Proceedings. Newark, Del.: 1968, pp. 425–32.

LANGMAN, MURIEL POTTER. "The Reading Process: A Descriptive, Interdisciplinary Approach." *Genetic Psychology Monographs* 62 (1960): 1–40.

LEFEVRE, CARL A. *Linguistics and the Teaching of Reading.* New York: McGraw-Hill, New York, 1964.

LEFEVRE, CARL A. "Reading Our Language Patterns: A Linguistic View—Contributions to a Theory of Reading." *Challenge and Experiment in Reading.* International Reading Association Conference Proceedings, Vol. 7 1962: pp. 66–70.

MILLER, G. A. "Psycholinguistics." *Encounter* 23 (1964): 29–37.

MILLER, G. A. "Some Preliminaries to Psycholinguistics." *American Psychologist* 20 (1965): 15–20.

NEISSER, U. *Cognitive Psychology.* New York: Appleton-Century Crofts, 1967.

ROBINSON, H. M. "The Major Aspects of Reading." In H. S. Robinson, ed., *Reading: Seventy-Five Years of Progress.* Chicago: University of Chicago Press, 1966, pp. 22–32.

RUDDELL, R. B. *Reading-Language Instruction: Innovative Practices.* Englewood Cliffs, N.J.: Prentice-Hall, 1974.

SINGER, HARRY. "Substrata-Factor Theory of Reading: Theoretical Design for Teaching Reading." *Challenge and Experiment in Reading.* International Reading Association Conference Proceedings, Vol. 7, 1962. (Edited by J. Allen Figurel) New York: Scholastic Magazines, 1962, pp. 226–32.

SINGER, HARRY. "Symposium on the Substrata-Factor Theory of Reading: Research and Evaluation of Critiques." *Reading and Inquiry.* International Reading Association Proceedings, Vol. 10, 1965 (Edited by J. Allen Figurel). Newark, Del.: International Reading Association, 1965, pp. 325–31.

SINGER, HARRY. "Stimulus Models for Teaching Reading." *Proceedings of the Fifth Annual Conference of the United Kingdom Reading Association.* Edinburgh, Scotland, 1968.

SINGER, HARRY. "Theoretical Models of Reading." *Journal of Communication* 19 (1969): 134–56.

SMITH, E. BROOKS; GOODMAN, KENNETH S.; and MEREDITH, ROBERT. *Language Thinking in the Elementary School.* New York: Holt, Rinehart and Winston, 1970.

SMITH, FRANK. *Understanding Reading: A Psycholinguistic Analysis of Reading and Learning to Read.* Holt, Rinehart and Winston, New York, 1971.

SMITH, FRANK and GOODMAN, KENNETH S. "On the Psycholinguistic Method of Teaching Reading." *Elementary School Journal* 71 (1971): 177–81.

STEINER, ROLLIN; WIENER, MORTON; and CROMER, WARD. "Comprehension Training and Identification for Poor and Good Readers." *Journal of Educational Psychology* 62 (1971): 506–13.

VOGEL, SUSAN A. "Syntactic Abilities in Normal and Dyslexic Children." *Journal of Learning Disabilities* 7 (1974): 103–9.

WALCUTT, CHARLES C.; LAMPORT, JOAN; and GLEN MCCRACKEN. *Teaching Reading.* New York: Macmillan, 1974.

WARDHAUGH, RONALD. "Reading: A New Perspective." *A Linguistic Perspective.* New York: Harcourt Brace Jovanovich, 1969.

WEAVER, WENDELL W. "On the Psychology of Reading." In E. Thurston and L. E. Hagner, ed., *New Concepts in College-Adult Reading.* Thirteenth Yearbook.

WEBER, ROSE-MARIE. *A Linguistic Analysis of First-Grade Reading Errors.* Ithaca, N.Y.: Cornell University Press, 1967.

WEENER, P. "Language Structure and Free Recall of Verbal Messages by Children." *Developmental Psychology* 5 (1971): 237–43.

WILLIAMS, JOANNA P. "Learning to Read: A Review of Theories and Models." *Reading Research Quarterly* 8 (1973): 121–46.

WILLOWS, DALE M. "Reading between the Lines: Selective Attention in Good and Poor Readers." *Child Development* 45 (1974): 408–15.

3

The Perceptual
Nature of Reading

The teacher must understand the basic nature of reading. Reading is a perceptual rather than merely a sensory process and, as such, it includes more than mere recognition of words. Neither printed page nor orally spoken words transmit meaning. In the previous chapter we noted that the reader must be able to use graphic, semantic, and syntactic cues to be a good reader. This chapter focuses on the importance of semantic cues. The essence of meaning comes from the reader's fund of experience.

As indicated earlier, reading certainly involves much more than recognition of the graphic symbol; it includes even more than the arousal of meaning or the gaining of meaning from printed symbols. Effective reading includes experiencing, learning, and thinking. The reader is stimulated by the author's printed words, but in turn he vests the author's words with his own meaning.

Reading may be described as: ". . . a perfect interaction between ocular functions and interpretive factors. The reader coordinates his eyes as he moves them along the lines of print in a left-to-right fashion, stopping to perceive words or word-parts which he continuously adds up into thought units. He interprets what he reads in light of his background, associates it with past experience, and projects beyond it in terms of ideas, judgments, applications, and conclusions" (Taylor, 1960, p. 1).

Dr. Spencer's (1946) definition of reading shows the clear relation of experience to reading. He pointed out that in the broadest sense reading is performed whenever one experiences sensory stimulation. Benjamin Franklin in *Poor Richard's Almanac* had such a definition in mind when he wrote: "Read much, but not too many books."

THE PERCEPTUAL PROCESS

Surely, the critical element in the reading act is the organism's meaningful response to the stimulus (the written symbol). Such a response requires perception. From first to last, perception includes initiation by a stimulus, preparation for a response (perception itself), and culmination in a response. Reading, in its simplest form, conforms to this same pattern. It includes the stimulus (graphic symbol), the meanings and interpretations drawn from the reader's past experiences, and the response of relating meaning to the symbol.

In reading, as in all perception, the arousal of meaning is an integral portion of the process, and the selection of an appropriate meaning forms the basis for an adequate response. The critical element is not what is seen on the page, but, rather, what is signified by the written symbol. The ancient Greeks interpreted the perceptual process as one in which "copies" of objects passed down sensory tubes. In the early 1700s Berkeley interpreted perception as habit involving both the sensory experience and memories. In later years the phenomenon of apparent movement, generally called the phi-phenomenon, gave impetus to other interpretations of the nature of perception. Motion pictures are an excellent example of apparent movement. The projected images from the individual frames of the film have no movement; the movement is only apparent. Certainly what is apprehended by the viewer involves sensory data not presently available to the senses. There is an implication here that, in some way, the incoming sensory data are retained, processed, and reorganized by the viewer. Some intermediary step takes place between the sensory input and the response.

Although the phi-phenomenon emphasizes perception in its relation to visual stimulation only, perception may be generated through other sensory avenues such as hearing, taste, and touch as well. Perception refers to the interpretation of everything that we sense. In the previous chapter we defined perception after Hebb as a consciousness or awareness of the experiences evoked by a symbol or as a process whereby sensory stimulation is translated into organized experience. Atkinson (1971, p. 106) notes that perception involves "the interaction of the sensory systems with those parts of the brain that are concerned with storage and retrieval of past experiences."

Our percepts (the end-products of perceiving) may vary in their complexity as well as in their origins. An elementary percept such as from a black dot on white paper is dependent almost entirely on the physical characteristics of the stimulus plus the perceiver's physiological functioning which includes brain function and the properties of the receptors. This simple process goes little beyond sensation. The more complex processes in which percepts involve values, word connotations, estimation of character and definition of complex ambiguous stimulations, frequently are called apperception, or cognition.

Perception obviously involves more than the transmission of nerve impulses by the sensory systems. The information must be interpreted by the brain. The brain constructs its image from a composite of information extracted from the retinal pattern and from information from past visual inputs. Vision is nothing more than the transformation of the retinal image into a perception (Hubel, 1971). The inner image or mental experience is not an exact copy of the optical pattern thrown on the retina by an object. Thus, the comparison of the eye to a camera made first by Johannes Kepler in 1604 and supported by René Descartes' observation of the eye of an ox[1] is not an entirely accurate analogy. The fact is that one does not see the retinal image; one sees with the aid of the retinal image (Neisser, 1971, p. 124) and with this information constructs the internal representations of objects called "conscious experience." In our study of eye movement we find that because of the narrowness of foveal vision and because the eye movements or saccades occur every twentieth of a second, the inner visual world is somehow constructed on the basis of information taken in during many distinct fixations. During a series of fixations the perceiver synthesizes a schema of the scene before him, using information from each successive fixation to construct a whole or in short what he sees. The most significant fact is that mental images are constructs and not copies.

Terminology

Hammill (1972, p. 553), studying thirty-three definitions of perception, summarized thinking as follows:

1. Some theorists term the entire receptive process as perception.
2. Others draw a distinction between sensation (the passive reaction of the receptor cells, not involving memory) and perception (the remainder of the receptive process).
3. Still others write only of sensation and cognition and subsume perception under cognition.
4. Some distinguish between sensation, perception, and cognition. (Here thinking, meaningful language, problem solving, etc. are assigned to cognition while the non-symbolic processes or non-abstract properties such as size, color, shape, are relegated to perception.)

In our discussion of concept formation in a latter portion of this chapter, we have accepted the latter explanation.

Theories of Perception

The Gestalt psychologists (field theorists) used the phi-phenomenon to demonstrate that the individual's response is not determined directly by the stimulus. They emphasize that a central process is a codeterminer of behavior (Scheerer, 1953). This central cerebral process is a representational process. Leeper (1953, p. 36) pointed out these cerebral processes represent properties which may not be present in the immediate stimulus-situation at all, and which are now represented merely because of past learning experiences.

In Gestalt psychology two points are emphasized: (1) a central proc-

---

[1]Descartes set the eye of an ox in a hole in a window shutter in the exact position it would have had if the ox would have been peering out. Looking at the back of the eye (which he had scraped to make it transparent) he saw a small inverted image of the scene outside the window.

ess intervenes between the stimulus and the response; (2) this process modifies the incoming sensory data. The important point is that the organization given to the sensation comes from within the organism.[2] Other psychologists of the stimulus-response (S-R) school tend to emphasize habit formation as a basis of perception. They suggest that when the afferent neural materials come into the brain, each discriminable aspect of this material tends to keep its independent and separate existence, and gets habit-linkages with the response (Leeper, 1953, p. 33).

Hebb (1958), though admitting to speculation, based his discussion of mediatiating processes on physiological hypotheses. He theorized (p. 103) that the mediating process consists of activity in neuron groups or in a series of such groups. He refers to the neuron groups, arranged as a set of closed pathways, as cell-assemblies and to a series of such groups as a phase sequence and he uses these terms in discussing the physiological aspects of the mediating process. He suggested that each time an impulse crosses a synapse it becomes increasingly easy for later impulses to accomplish that crossing. He indicated that the increasing ease may be due to enlargement of synaptic knobs or to some chemical change.

This discussion of the general nature of the perceptual process and some of the theories of perception cannot pretend to be either comprehensive or conclusive. It is presented only for the purpose of giving an overview of the subject to serve as a background for discussing perception in reading. The various viewpoints of perception emphasizing, as they do, the roles of representation, intervention of a central cerebral process, organization and modification of sensory data, and individualization of understandings and meanings do seem to be in agreement with what we know of the nature of the reading process. The perception of a graphic symbol must, of necessity, involve simple perception of certain forms (the printed word) as a means of learning to read. But the more complex perception of the word must come to include the organization and modification of various sensory data in order that a particular series of printed letters (the word) may evoke meaning.

Although the earlier psychologists used somewhat different terminology than those writing in recent years, they noted similar characteristics of perception. Lange (1902, p. 8) wrote: "The mind apprehends outer impressions in accordance with its wealth of knowledge gained through former activity." William James (1890, p. 103) noted that "Whilst part of what we perceive comes through our senses from the object before us, another (and it may be the greater part) always comes . . . out of our head." Lange (1902, p. 21) added that "we see and hear not only with the eye and ear, but quite as much with the help of our present knowledge, with the apperceiving content of the mind."

Personal Nature of Perception

Perception is a very personal thing. If a group of persons were to look at the same object, there would be as many different interpretations (perceptions) of that object as there were viewers. Lange (1902, p. 3)

---

[2]The Gestalt view is described in greater detail in Chapter 4.

noted that of the same landscape the poet's image would differ greatly from that of the botanist, the painter's from that of the geologist or the farmer, the stranger's from that of him who calls it home. Each perceptual experience may have, also, its affective aspects. We not only see an object and perhaps have images of former sensory stimulation, but the object impresses us as pleasant, unpleasant, or perhaps neither. The nature of the impression made upon us depends upon the tenor of our past experiences.

It is easy to understand that, due to the personal nature of perception, there are many possibilities for faulty communication between writer and reader, and there is little likelihood that any two readers ever will give exactly the same interpretation to any given paragraph. The simple fact is that our perceptions are determined almost exclusively by our experiences. And everything that has contributed to making the organism what it is influences its response to the printed page.

THE MAJOR DETERMINANTS OF MEANING

To this point we have concluded that reading is a perceptual process and that without perception there is no true reading. It is through perception that the graphic symbol achieves meaning. We have discussed the personalized pattern of perception and have considered some of the theories of the perceptual process. The evidence suggests that perception is a form of behavior that results in an organization of incoming sensory data. Perception has biological predeterminants but its personalized characteristics are due in great part to the individual's past experiences.

It seems appropriate, then, that we discuss further some of the factors which influence perception. What are some determinants of the meanings which the individual will bring to the graphic symbol? Are there ways in which we can help a group of persons to have similar understandings of the materials they read? And how can we reduce "discommunication" between reader and writer? It may be worth noting at this point that much of the discussion of the determinants of meaning pertains almost equally well to the formation of concepts which will be discussed later in the chapter.

Before discussing in detail some of the various cue systems that operate in reading to cue meaning, we refer the reader back to Chapter 2 for a complete listing of these cues.

Physiological, Biological-Neurological Factors

Although meaning must develop from experience, the process is "rooted in biology" (Anderson, 1952, p. 1). And, if the organism lacks the ability to organize the stimuli (Gestaltists), or to develop habit linkages (S-R Theorists), or if there is a breakdown in the "phase cycle" (Hebb), or if no "trace" or "record" is left by the neural activities, there is little hope that perception will reach a level adequate for thinking, reasoning, reading, or even for simple recall or rote memorization.

Culture

The culture in which one has lived surely is another major determinant of what a word will mean to him. Smith (1956, p. 23) noted that "... our interpretation of what we read, in fact our very readiness to learn to read, is largely a function of those human groups and institutions with which we have been associated." Stroud (1956, p. 189) points out that both our thoughts and our everyday perceptions have a social origin. Language and culture are closely related. Sapir (1957, p. 69), for example, noted that the understanding of a simple poem involves an understanding of the single words but also a full comprehension of the whole life of the community as it is mirrored in the words, or as it is suggested by their overtones.

Past Experiences

The individual's specific life experiences are, as we have noted, a major determinant of the nature of the interpretation that he will give to a stimulus. The individual is a storehouse of his past experiences. Each new experience relates to and becomes a part of previous experiences which, in turn, are the bases for interpretation of the new experiences or stimuli.

The backwoods boy who has known a "road" to be the painfully rocky mule-path along a gullied hillside might give an unusual interpretation of the sentence, "All roads lead to Rome." And, the child who has lived all his life in the city or near a superhighway is likely to take to the lines of the poem, "Let me live in my house by the side of the road and be a friend to man" numerous memories of the roar of speeding vehicles and the odors of gas fumes and speed-heated tires. This is hardly the peaceful atmosphere the poet intended to project.

Although each child's interpretation of the two quotations will become more accurate as his experiences, real or vicarious, become more extensive, there will always remain some elements of his original perceptions.

Porter (1958) points out that each human being represents literally billions of varied experiences which have been assimilated and ordered in specific ways and each attempt at communication, at understanding or being understood, bears the mark of this prodigious personal context. He adds that no word or gesture can ever mean precisely the same thing to any two individuals.

Physical and Emotional Factors

The physical state of the individual also influences his perceptions and meanings. The child who is ill and the healthy, normally hungry youngster will have quite different reactions to such phrases as "hot dogs and mustard" or "turkey stuffed with dressing."

Earlier we referred to the affective aspects of perception. Perception also may be dependent on the emotive quality of our past experiences.

The word "cave," for example, will be interpreted differently by the boy who has enjoyed security while digging or exploring caves and by the boy whose experience with a cave was one of terror and panic. Leeper (1953, p. 37) points out that our representational mechanisms create a psychological environment or apparent reality which seems so real to us that we do not dream that *we* are actually producing such effects. In fact, the emotional state of the reader may distort, color, or completely change meaning to such an extent that communication becomes impossible.

Perceptual Veridicality

The discussion of factors which influence perception and hence reading indicates that no two persons will have exactly the same perceptions of the same object, or, as applied to reading, of the same word. However, the individual does seem to strive to achieve the closest possible agreement between the realities of his environment and his own perceptions of them. In other words, the individual is striving for perceptual veridicality. Perception, unfortunately, rarely is totally veridical. Due to the various and varying factors which influence it, perception is, at best, an inadequate and approximate representation of concrete reality.

As noted in Chapter 2, Herrick (1956, p. 340) suggested that the validity of a perception is its predictive value as a guide for action. The perceiver calls upon his previous experience and generally assumes that the perception that was most successful in the past is most likely to be correct now. He interprets the sensory data on the basis of his past experience. When he finds his perception to be in error, he must change his interpretation even though his retinal image has not changed. Weiner (1956), for example, demonstrated that through experience individuals learn how to perceive. A cigarette box was moved away from the subject along a distorted wall and was perceived as shrinking in size instead of as receding into distance. As the subject became familiar with the room, he gradually began to see the cigarette box in proper perspective and, when he was tested in another experimental room, he did not make his former error.

In reading, veridicality generally is difficult to attain. Words are abstractions that have acquired their meaning from specific experiences. And if the symbolic or affective processes of perceiving have caused inaccuracies or have left deeply entrenched inaccurate interpretation, a high degree of veridicality will be even more difficult to attain.

Words permit the writer to share experiences with the reader. The reader does not see nor experience directly the object, person, place, sensation, or event of which the author writes. He sees or experiences them through the symbols that stand for them and evoke his perception of them. There is no direct or invariable connection between the symbol and the referend, the datum, object, event, or sensation. Verbal symbols at best are inadequate substitutes for direct experience. In fact, language does not represent objects but, rather, concepts that the mind has formed of them. Communication through reading is most difficult when the reader's experience is inadequate. And the degree of accuracy of perceptions depends greatly upon the number and variety of experiences that the reader has had.

CONCEPT FORMATION

We recommend that the reader become familiar with the section "Problems in Developing Meaning," in Dechant, *Improving the Teaching of Reading*, pp. 363–74 before proceeding to the following material. There we describe the process of concept formation or the individual's experience-based understanding as a growth from sensation (the basic experiences) to perception, and to cognition. Perception can range from the concrete and specific to the abstract and generic. At the latter extreme it is properly called conceptualization and may involve categorization, generalization, analysis and synthesis, and insight—all of which are dependent upon experience.

Jean Piaget

We will restrict ourselves in this section essentially to the research and thinking of Piaget. His model of cognitive development is particularly significant because it supports the scientific approach which linguists have offered to explain the reading process.

Piaget, as we do above, draws a distinction between perceptual and conceptual processes. He does not lump together, as the Gestaltists did, all cognitive processes. A concept keeps its character irrespective of the context or pattern into which it is put. The concepts "number" or "mile" are stable from one time to the next. Not so with perceptions. They vary from person to person and are determined by the pattern of which they are a common component.

Piaget's hypothesis (Avdul, 1974; Piaget, 1952, 1957, 1961, 1969; Inhelder, 1963; Inhelder and Piaget, 1958) simply is that cognitive development, and by extension the concrete operations of cognition including language development, is "an integrated process of successive equilibrations of cognitive structures, each structure . . . deriving logically and inevitably from the preceding one" (Flavell, 1963).

Piaget, positing four interrelated stages of cognitive development, perceived the process of development as structured or sequentialized. Organisms develop and evolve in a patterned fashion. The process of change is neither cyclic nor linear; it is spiral. In a linear order it is possible to jump over one stage and still get to the next one. For Piaget, each stage integrates the preceding stage and prepares the way for the following one (Jennings, 1967).

Development thus is a series of different plateaus of complex behaviors related in a continuous progression (Svoboda, 1973). The stages are *lawful* in that they are invariant in their developmental sequence from sensori-motor to formal operations; *hierarchical,* in that each successive stage is dependent upon prior development and integration of each preceding stage (Laurita, 1973).

Piaget focused his research on cognition, that one function which distinguishes behavior as human. Like other developmental functions, cognition was perceived as developing in a logical, dialectically patterned process. Piaget sees the individual as learning about patterns, growing in knowledge, and building in his own mind the structures of thought which the Gestaltists believe are innately acquired (Emans, 1973). He suggested that children at different ages have different ways of thinking about the world. The child is perceived as a constructor who acts on the world, not as passive reactor to the environment (Gardner, 1973).

Piaget suggests that mental acts reflect structures or coherent systems of actions that evolve at certain points in a child's development (Gardner, 1973). His cognitive theory starts from the central postulate that motor action is the source from which mental operations emerge (Tuddenham, 1966). Intelligence is born of action. The action of the organism is central to the acquisition of operations (ideas) that are needed in order to cope with the world.

A second central postulate, as indicated earlier, is that intellectual operations, which are acquired by interaction between the organism and the environment, are acquired in a lawful sequence. Piaget's concern has been more with elucidating the sequence rather than establishing exact age norms for the stages of development. He has tried to write an ontogenetic history of cognition (Tuddenham, 1966).

In the first stage, the *Sensory-Motor Period*, from about birth to age two, the child adapts to his environment and manifests his intelligence through sensori-motor action rather than through symbolic means. This stage carries the child from inborn reflexes to acquired behavior patterns, from a body-centered or self-centered world to an object-centered one. The child's mental activity during this stage consists of establishing relationships between sensory experiences and action by physically manipulating the world. The child's sensori-motor actions on objects and his interaction with the environment thus results in knowledge of the perceptual invariants of his environment. The objects he perceives tend to stay within him even when not in view. If the appropriate linguistic forms are associated with these perceptual invariants, he begins to use these linguistic forms to identify objects and to represent his actions on them. At about twelve months he can say two words.

The *Preoperational Period*, from approximately age two to seven, covers the important period when rapid growth of language occurs. During the pre-conceptual period (age two—four), the child rapidly learns to represent objects and the world by symbolic means such as language and mental images. For example, fifty percent of children age two can identify common objects, such as a cup or the parts on the body of a doll and he can repeat two numbers. However, the child tends to orient his activities on the basis of appearances. He is easily misled by what he sees. Language is not something apart from objects and experience. The name of the thing inheres in the thing itself. A chair is called a chair; a rocker is something else entirely (Raven and Salzer, 1971). Every event is new. At age four, children can repeat a nine to ten word sentence, and name a variety of objects.

In the latter part of stage two, age four to seven, the *intuitive period*, the child moves from near-total dependence on sensation and perception to the initial stages of logical thought. He can now group objects into classes by noting similarities and differences, but he still pays attention to one aspect of an object to the neglect of other aspects. This tendency is termed centration. He can also form the concept of "fruit," relating "orange" and "apple." He has intuitively learned and uses the grammar of the language spoken in his environment. He uses all the parts of speech and can transform his vocabulary into a variety of utterances. He has a vocabulary of from 2,500 to 7,500 words, by a process of decentering has learned the physical relationships of time and space, and has some idea of causality. His causal reasoning, however, is dependent upon his perceptions and therefore is often in error because his attention is centered on irrelevant or insufficient attributes. For example, he concludes that a narrow, higher glass contains more liquid than a large and low glass, even though he has seen the liquid poured from one vessel into the other.

Piaget feels that a mental age of four is all that is required to manage reading skills (Furth, 1970), and in fact most children experience initial reading instruction during this period. By age seven, the child is capable of producing simple-active declarative sentences and can apply inflectional rules. However, the child during this period will still experience difficulty with (1) sounds that occur in the middle or final position of a word; (2) with certain consonant sounds; and (3) with such clusters of consonants as *lfth* (twelfth). The child is gradually consolidating language structures and is just beginning to comprehend the passive construction. He seldom uses the passive in his own spontaneous speech (Palermo and Molfese, 1972).

Beginning about age seven *(Concrete Operational Period)*, the child develops the capability of carrying out logical operations. He can classify according to one or more criteria, order in series, and can number. In fact, because the child has developed the logical structure of groups, he can organize his cognitive activities much better. He develops some concept of linear measure and weights about age nine. He is less dependent upon his own perceptions and motor actions and shows a capacity for reasoning. He can internalize actions that represent physical objects and relationships. For example, the child can use his imagination to mentally reverse actions; he can break a candy bar in half and he can mentally put the parts together. He also can now make transformations. He will notice that, in pouring liquid from a short glass into a tall glass, nothing is added and nothing has been taken away. He can also transform and manipulate sentences. Such operations suggest that in this period thought and language are freed from dependence upon sensation and perception, but the child's mental activity is still tied to concrete or physical situations or experiences.

At about age eleven to fifteen (the *Formal Operations Period*), a child attains the fourth and mature stage of mental development. He can imagine possible and potential relationships, can intellectually manipulate the purely hypothetical, and can think in terms of formal propositions. He can deal with abstract relationships instead of just with things. Whereas the concrete-operational child reasons only from directly observed data, his older counterpart is freed from dependence on directly experienced events and begins to deal with conditional, suppositional, and hypothetical statements and propositions.

Although the sequence of these stages of cognitive development and the overall order of the stages is the same for all individuals, not all children pass through the stages of intellectual growth in exactly the same way or exactly at the same rate. As a child acquires more experience, his concepts broaden, become clearer, and are hierarchically organized. They also are less egocentric and take on conventionalized significance. In his own way, each person passes from a sensori-motor stage to a preoperational stage, to a concrete operational stage, to an abstract operational stage. As the concepts of individuals become consistent with the concepts of their culture, they can and do communicate more effectively and efficiently.

Children whose experience is more limited, who have less verbal interchange with adults, or who are asked to deal with content that is unfamiliar to them are less likely to attain the information, linguistic forms, and syntax for organizing and communicating new experiences. Their understanding will not go much deeper than the making of a few verbal associations. Because of some gaps in the materials, in their experience, or in their thinking, they often cannot communicate effectively in certain content areas, even though they have the requisite general mental capabilities.

Palermo and Molfese (1972) noted that the research data in fact reflect a steady development of linguistic form from age five to adolescence, with the periods of five to eight and ten to thirteen being special transitional points in which significant development occurs. These are precisely the periods in cognitive development that are reported by Piaget to be transition points from pre-operational to concrete operations (between five and eight) and from concrete operations to formal operations (between ten and thirteen). It is during these periods that we note large increases in grammatical constructions and high error rates on some constructions. Because cognitive development precedes expression in language and because numerous studies have shown that cognitive development (mental age) is closely related to reading achievement, particularly at the upper grade levels, with the correlation rising from about .35 at first-grade level to about .65 at the sixth-grade level, it becomes increasingly clear that a theory of language development must be embedded within the larger context of a theory of cognitive development.

The further implication is that for best teaching of reading skills and indeed, for best diagnosis of the child's needs, it becomes imperative that the teacher identify the child's perceptual and cognitive development.

These latter will identify for the teacher the learning style of the child and have major significance for the type of educational strategies that should be employed. An article by Cohen and Schwartz (1975) offers some ideas on this point.

The child's perceptual and cognitive behavior reflect the developmental mode in which the child finds himself. Thus, perceptual activities develop with age. Initially the child perceives only a vague impression of the object. This is identified as the global stage (Werner, 1948). At this stage figures do not stand out clearly against background. One detail often becomes the signal for recognition of the whole.

Analogous to global perception is the "blob" stage or holistic approach to word recognition. At this level the child recognizes only gross characteristics. The child does not yet understand that a one-to-one correspondence exists between a discrete written word and its oral counterpart. He cannot differentiate a specific word from the rest of the words in a sentence. Such a pupil will substitute "winter" for "snow" or "little" for "big." He will also confuse letters like *b* and *d,* or *l* and *i.* He obviously has not learned to distinguish the salient features of these letters, or of words. He will readily confuse similar-appearing words.

At this stage of a child's development, it is common for children to experience reversals but it is also common to explain them developmentally.

The second stage is identified as the analytic stage (Werner, 1948). At this point the pupil often prefers not to make any response. In the beginning reader, this may indicate deficiency in letter-sound knowledge; in the dyslexic it may mean an unwillingness to take a risk, to be wrong again.

He is becoming aware of letter function but he cannot effectively express it. He begins to differentiate words on the basis of letter features. He still is not aware of the perceptual scheme inherent in word recognition, but now his substitutions have something in common with the stimulus word: he now substitutes a word that begins or ends with the same letter; "over" for "other." At this stage he may know "in" and "to," but cannot identify "into." He may know "walk" and "ing," but "walking" is a new perceptual element. He may know "cat," but can't use the "at" in "cat" to identify "bat."

The child is responding to the first dominant stimulus and thus is unable to use the most salient features which distinguish words from one another. The pupil cannot delay or inhibit his first response. Such a child may know the letter-sound discriminations in isolation, but his cognitive style does not permit him to consider alternatives. He impulsively selects the first solution that comes to mind. He needs to learn to scan the word, looking for salient features. These often are larger chunks than a single letter. They more commonly are phonograms.

Cohen and Schwartz (1975) add that at the synthetic or third stage word recognition functions at its most mature level. He now can explore unfamiliar words and can use regularities found in words in perceiving new words. He can identify those graphic features which are distinctive and those which remain variant. He now can differentiate "walking," "into," or "happiness."

Abstract Thinking in Concept Formation

Individuals differ in ability to handle the events they encounter. They differ in their ability to react to symbols and their interpretations have varying degrees of adequacy. Some typically seek to form conceptual groupings whereas others deal with events in simple categories. They think of words in their general or specific sense. Those taking the first approach tend to think on an abstract level and the latter on a concrete level.

The difference in approach is not dependent entirely upon the maturity and experiences of the individuals. There is evidence that not all individuals, though mentally capable, achieve concept development commensurate to their maturity and experiences. Then, too, there are those who are victims of either structural or functional disturbances such as brain lesions and emotional blockings. For example, studies with aphasics indicate that frequently they are able to use symbols in a concrete sense but are unable to categorize and thus, to abstract. An aphasic may call a knife a knife only when it is presented with a fork. If the knife is presented with an apple he may call it an apple peeler; with a pencil he may call it a pencil sharpener. When asked to give the names of the animals he saw at the zoo, he may reply, "a polar bear, a brown bear, a black bear, a lion, and a monkey." Each name represents a specific animal and he is unable to generalize "bears" (Goldstein, 1936).

In their monograph, *Abstract and Concrete Behavior,* Goldstein and Scheerer (1941) suggest that the aphasic is incapable of abstracting, of planning ahead, and of symbolizing. He cannot use a word in its generic sense. Young children and frequently poor readers tend to be like aphasics in the level of their interpretations. Liublinskaya (1957, p. 201) notes that only as his experience becomes richer does the child relate one and the same word to many different objects of the same kind or perceive one object as a representative of a whole known group of objects.

Thus the research indicates: (1) that the lower the mental age of the child, the more specific his reaction to a word tends to be; and (2) that the development of facility in conceptualization is a function of previous experience in concept formation. Younger children or less mature readers tend to perceive words as concrete and older or more mature children turn more to the abstract features of word meaning (Lundsteen, 1974).

Specific reactions to symbols also are observable with older children. They find abstract words especially difficult, and identify them with specific experiences: "Beauty is when you comb your hair neatly." "Sportsmanship is when you do not kick somebody." Children easily give meaning to a book, a building, a car, but not to the more complex concepts represented by the words beauty, democracy, and truth.

Jan Tausch (1962), studying 170 children in the fourth to the seventh grade, found that good readers were characterized by abstract thinking and that poor readers demonstrated concreteness in behavior. The relationship is more significant in the upper grades, suggesting perhaps that reading comprehension at the upper grade levels is more abstract in nature. Other studies show that intelligence is more closely related to reading comprehension at the upper grade levels than at the lower levels. Thus intelligence may become a more important determinant of reading success as the abstractness of the materials read increases. Another example may be taken from reading itself. Pupils frequently make substitutions when they read. The good reader tends to substitute words that harmonize with the context. The poor reader, on the other hand, substitutes words that do not fit the context. He may not have had sufficient experience to bring the appropriate meaning to the printed page, and communication between writer and reader does not occur. He cannot see the relationships between the various words and the various ideas communicated.

Generally, the writer and the reader communicate only if they are capable of assigning some common meaning to a symbol. This means that they must have had some commonality of experience. And usually they must be able to make generic responses to their experience. Thus, Bruner (1957b, p. 125) notes: "If perceptual experience is ever had raw, that is, free of categorical identity, it is doomed to be a gem serene, locked in the silence of private experience."

With experience the person makes the word generic in meaning. He abstracts, forms concepts, learns to associate these concepts with printed symbols, and identifies the word with a category or a class of objects. When perception is on an abstract level, when the reader associates a concept with a word, then, indeed, perception is a kind of summing up of the meanings of numerous sensory impingements (Norberg, 1953). The reader then is capable of bringing sufficient meaning to the printed page to permit him to obtain from the page an approximation of the experience that the writer is trying to convey. The reader attains an understanding of the writer's experience and hence his perceptions. Only then is communication via reading taking place.

Thorndike (1917, p. 331) suggested that reading a textbook paragraph and, to a lesser extent, reading a narrative involve the same sort of organization and analytic action as that which occurs in thinking of "supposedly higher sorts." We may assume, then, that the effective reader will employ most or all of the elements of perception, conceptualization, abstract and concrete thinking, selection, integration, generalization, analysis—in fact, all of the elements which are included in "thinking of supposedly higher sorts." It seems logical to assume, also, that the readers who employ these elements to the greatest extent will be the most effective readers.

The evidence concerning concept formation suggests certain general conclusions:

1. The greater the number of concepts that the reader has fixed through words, the better tends to be his understanding of what he reads.
2. The more specific the reader's reaction to printed words, the less effective tends to be the communication between writer and reader; and the more generic the reaction, the more effective tends to be the communication.
3. Differences in abstracting ability or in the ability to think in categories generally differentiate the superior reader from the poor reader.

As we examined the topic of concept formation considerable point was made of the differences between concrete and abstract levels of interpretation. The ability to form categories and thus to conceptualize seems essential for effective reading. The written word cannot awaken a generic meaning within the reader who is unable to conceptualize. Although such a reader takes a meaning to the printed symbol, too frequently it is an incorrect or inadequate meaning.

SUMMARY

This chapter has sought to define the nature of the reading process by expanding on the nature of perception and its significance for reading and by emphasizing semantic aspects. Furthermore it identified the significance of the cognitive style of the child. The stress has been on perception rather than sensation and on meaning rather than on the symbol.

Our recognition of the perceptual nature of the reading process has a number of applications to our understanding of reading. We know that the printed word itself possesses no meaning. And we know that the perceiver's reaction to the word depends on the quality and number of his prior experiences, his ability to reconstruct and combine these experiences, and the general nature of the culture in which he has lived.

Perception always involves an interpretation. This is so because words can only "stand for" experiences; they are substitutes that must be interpreted in terms of the perceiver's experiences. Rarely do words communicate perfectly.

We have seen that reading involves meaningful interpretation of sensory data; that this interpretation is greatly influenced by one's culture and one's experiences; and that the interpretation has degrees of accuracy. Interpretation that is consistently on a concrete level and interpretation that is restricted by lack of experience are not adequate for meaningful reading.

The teacher needs to become especially familiar with the levels of interpretation made by any given child. To a great extent, a child's understanding of what he reads depends on his level of concept development.

QUESTIONS FOR DISCUSSION

1. What is meant by culture? How does culture influence perception? Illustrate.
2. What are the implications of the statement "Reading is the bringing of meaning to the printed page?" (In regard to the beginning reader, the slow reader, reading rate increase, and the reading of technical material.)
3. What is the difference between sensation, recognition, and perception?
4. Illustrate from your own experience the personal nature of perception.
5. Who gets most from a single reading about a topic? One who already knows much or one who knows little?
6. What is meant by "apparent movement"?
7. What do we mean by veridicality?

BIBLIOGRAPHY

ANDERSON, IRVING H., and DEARBORN, WALTER F. *The Psychology of Teaching Reading.* New York: Ronald Press, 1952.

ATKINSON, RICHARD C. *Contemporary Psychology.* San Francisco: W. H. Freeman and Company, 1971.

AVDUL, RICHARD. "Piaget was a Quarterback." *Teacher* 91 (1974): 10–12.

BRUNER, JEROME S. "Going Beyond the Information Given." *Contemporary Approaches to Cognition.* Cambridge: Harvard University Press, 1957a.

BRUNER, JEROME S. "On Perceptual Readiness." *Psychological Review* 64 (1957b): 123–52.

COHEN, ALICE SHEFF and SCHWARTZ, ELAINE. "Interpreting Errors in Word Recognition." *The Reading Teacher* 28 (1975): 534–37.

DECHANT, EMERALD. *Improving the Teaching of Reading,* Second Edition. Englewood Cliffs, N.J.: Prentice-Hall, 1970.

EMANS, ROBERT. "Oral Language and Learning to Read." *Elementary English* 50 (1973): 929–34.

FLAVELL, J. H. *The Developmental Psychology of Jean Piaget.* Princeton, N.J.: Van Nostrand, 1963, pp. 36–37.

FURTH, HAUS G. *Piaget for Teachers.* Englewood Cliffs, N.J.: Prentice-Hall, 1970.

GARDNER, HOWARD. "France and the Modern Mind." *Psychology Today* 7 (1973): 59–62, 104.

GOLDSTEIN, KURT. "The Problem of the Meaning of Words Based Upon Observation of Aphasic Patients." *Journal of Psychology* 2 (1936): 301–16.

HAMMILL, D. "Training Visual Perception Processes." *Journal of Learning Disabilities* 5 (1972): 552–59.

HEBB, DONALD OLDING. *A Textbook of Psychology*. Philadelphia: W. B. Saunders Company, 1958.

HERRICK, JUDSON. *The Evolution of Human Nature*. Austin: University of Texas Press, 1956.

HUBEL, DAVID H. "The Visual Cortex of the Brain." In *Contemporary Psychology: Readings from Scientific American*. San Francisco: W. H. Freeman, 1971, pp. 132–40.

INHELDER, BARBEL. "Criteria of the Stages of Mental Development." In R. Kuhlen and G. J. Thompson, eds., *Psychological Studies of Human Development*, 2nd edition. New York: Appleton-Century-Crofts, 1963, pp. 28–48.

INHELDER, BARBEL and PIAGET, JEAN. *The Growth of Logical Thinking from Childhood to Adolescence*. New York: Basic Books, 1958.

JAMES, WILLIAM. *Principles of Psychology*. New York: Holt, Rinehart and Winston, 1890.

JENNINGS, F. "Jean Piaget: Notes on Learning." *Saturday Review*, May 20, 1967.

LANGE, KARL. *Apperception: A Monograph on Psychology and Pedagogy*. Edited by Charles De Garmo. Boston: Heath, 1902.

LAURITA, RAYMOND E. "Bringing Order to the Teaching of Reading and Writing." *Education* 93 (1973): 254–61.

LEEPER, ROBERT W. "What Contributions Might Cognitive Learning Theory Make to Our Understanding of Personality." *Journal of Personality* 22 (1953): 32–40.

LIUBLINSKAYA, A. A. "The Development of Children's Speech and Thought." In Brian Simon, ed., *Psychology in the Soviet Union*. London: Routledge & Kegan Paul, 1957, 197–204.

LUNDSTEEN, SARA W. "Levels of Meaning in Reading." *The Reading Teacher* 28 (1974): 268–72.

NEISSER, ULRIC. "The Processes of Vision." In *Contemporary Psychology: Readings from Scientific American*. San Francisco: W. H. Freeman, 1971, pp. 124–31.

NORBERG, KENNETH. "Perception Research and Audio-Visual Education." *Audio-Visual Communication Review* 1 (1953): 18–29.

PALERMO, DAVID S. and MOLFESE, DENNIS L. "Language Acquisition from Age Five Onward." *Psychological Bulletin* 78 (1972): 409–28.

PIAGET, J. *The Origins of Intelligence in Children*. New York: International Universities Press, 1952.

PIAGET, J. *Logic and Psychology*. New York: Basic Books, 1957.

PIAGET, JEAN. "The Genetic Approach to the Psychology of Thought." *Journal of Educational Psychology* 52 (1961): 271–76.

PIAGET, JEAN. *The Mechanisms of Perception*. New York: Basic Books, 1969.

PORTER, WILLIAM E. "Mass Communication and Education." *The National Elementary Principal* 37 (1958): 12–16.

RAVEN, RONALD J. and SALZER, RICHARD T. "Piaget and Reading Instruction." *Reading Teacher* (April, 1971).

SAPIR, EDWARD. "The Status of Linguistics as a Science." *Culture, Language and Personality: Selected Essays*. Berkeley: University of California Press, 1957, pp. 65–77.

SCHEERER, MARTIN, "Personality Functioning and Cognitive Psychology." *Journal of Personality* 22 (1953): 1–16.

SCHEERER, MARTIN. "Spheres of Meaning: An Analysis of Stages from Perception to Abstract Thinking." *Journal of Individual Psychology* 15 (1959): 50–61.

SMITH, HENRY P. "The Sociology of Reading." *Exploring the Goals of College Reading Programs.* Fifth Yearbook of the Southwest Reading Conference for Colleges and Universities, Texas Christian University Press, Fort Worth, 1956, pp. 23–28.

SPENCER, L. PETER. "The Reading Process and Types of Reading." *Claremont College Reading Conference,* Eleventh Yearbook, 1946, pp. 19–20.

STROUD, JAMES B. *Psychology in Education.* New York: Longmans, Green and Company, 1956.

SVOBODA, CYRIL P. "Sources and Characteristics of Piaget's Stage Concept of Development: A Historical Perspective." *Journal of Education, 155* (1973): 28–39.

TAUSCH, JAN-, JAMES. "Concrete Thinking as a Factor in Reading Comprehension." *Challenge and Experiment in Reading.* International Reading Association Conference Proceedings. Newark, Delaware, 1962, pp. 161–64.

TAYLOR, STANFORD E.; and FRACKENPOHL, HELEN; and PETTEE, JAMES L. *Grade Level Norms for the Components of the Fundamental Reading Skill* (Huntington, New York: Educational Developmental Laboratories, Inc.), Bulletin No. 3, 1960.

THORNDIKE, EDWARD L. "Reading as Reasoning: A Study of Mistakes in Paragraph Reading." *Journal of Educational Psychology* 8 (1917): 323–32.

TUDDENHAM, READ D. "Jean Piaget and the World of the Child." *American Psychologist* 21 (1966): 207–17.

WEINER, MELVIN. "Perceptual Development in a Distorted Room: A Phenomenological Study." *Psychological Monographs* 70, No. 423 (1956): 1–38.

WERNER, H. *Comparative Psychology of Mental Development.* New York: International Universities Press, 1948.

4

Learning Principles and the Reading Process

Reading is a process that must be learned. The laws of learning and the facts concerning such topics as motivation, reinforcement, practice, interference, transfer, and conditioning apply to learning to read. The tremendous body of knowledge on the learning process must not be reserved for specialized books on learning, but must become a part of the reading teacher's professional equipment.

In chapter one, while discussing the various theoretical models of reading, we noted that learning theories are a proper content for a psychology of reading because learning to read is representative of learning in general. We also noted that learning to read cannot be explained if only one of the two major theories of learning, namely either the S-R theories or the Field theories, is adopted. Let us then study carefully both theories, looking constantly for explanations of learning as it relates to learning to read.

Theory, especially learning theory, must provide the unifying concept of this book. Theory gives direction and helps to evaluate practice. Learning is what the teacher is trying to promote. Only by knowing what learning is and how it must be encouraged and promoted can he hope to provide effective teaching. Only in this way can the teacher know and understand how the child learns to read.

STIMULUS-RESPONSE THEORIES OF LEARNING: AN OVERVIEW

Learning theories can be divided into Stimulus-Response Theories and Field Theories. Each of these major divisions has its supporters, and each may be subdivided into numerous segments. Figure 4-1 illustrates this.

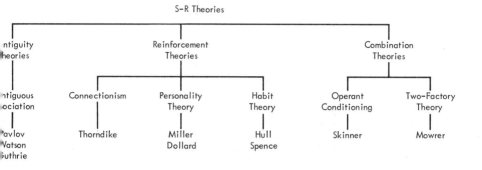

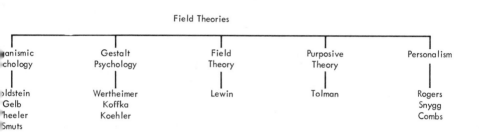

FIGURE 4–1 *Theories of learning*

   S-R theorists suggest that in any activity there are three basic elements: the situation or stimulus, the response that a given person makes to the situation or stimulus, and the connection or association between the stimulus and the response. This connection is referred to as an S-R bond. The S-R theorist focuses on the response or the observable action or behavior as the basic data of his science and suggests that what the organism learns is the response. For example, the pupil learns to type words; he learns to read a word; or he learns to kick a football. The pupil is learning an action or a response.

   All definitions of learning embody the idea that it requires some interaction of the organism and its environment. In short, experience is a necessary condition for learning.

   The S-R theorist defines learning as: "The acquisition of new behavior patterns or the strengthening or weakening of old behavior patterns as a result of practice" (Smith, 1954). Such a definition of learning suggests that we learn by doing something or by experiencing. Thompson and De Bold (1976, p. 232) note that what is learned is the potential to perform a particular response under appropriate conditions and define learning as "a relatively permanent change in behavior potential which occurs as a result of practice."

S-R theorists generally assert their predilection for conditioning, which to them is the clearest and most simple instance of a response to a stimulus. This is the simplest form of learning in S-R theory.

FIELD THEORIES: AN OVERVIEW

The field theorists, on the other hand, emphasize ideations, thoughts, mental or cognitive processes and structures, purposive behavior, the organizational nature of the learning process, contemporary experience, and wholes rather than parts.

Emphasis on Cognitive Processes

Whereas S-R theorists emphasize the observable response or the peripheral events, field theorists emphasize the perceptual process or understanding, conscious experience, and meaning. Gestaltists took issue with the proposition that all learning consisted of simple connections of responses to stimuli, without recourse to ideas or thought processes. The Gestalt psychologist is more interested in what the child understands than in what he does; he is more interested in man's ability to conceptualize, reason, and form judgments.

The field theorist suggests that the meaning that an experience has for the person experiencing may be as significant as the experience itself. He studies the effect that a change in the structure of meanings or perceptions may have on behavior. He is a firm believer that psychology is enriched when it finds the lawful relationships between inner meanings and external behavior.

The field theorist thus stresses that learning is both a perceptual as well as an associative process. He suggests that learning is guided by intervening mental processes which may be labelled cognition, thought, or perception.

Hebb (1974) suggests that psychology is about the mind. He defines mind as the capacity for thought and thought as the integrative activity of the brain. Hebb notes that most behavior of man is under the joint guidance of sense input and the immediately prior pattern of cortical activity.

Emphasis on Purposive Behavior

Field theorists also emphasize that man is purposive and not subject entirely to instincts, as Freudianism would lead us to believe, nor is he an entirely passive being who is the prey of stimuli, as some S-R thinking might suggest. There are stable, central processes which integrate behavior and give purpose to it. Man lives a life which is not entirely explained by previous conditionings or the unconscious. He is interested in inner meanings (Rogers, 1964), in purposes, goals, values, choice, perceptions of self, and in man as a self-determining and self-actualizing system.

Emphasis on Learning as an Organizational Process

In field theories, learning is defined as a change in perception and is the result of a new organization of experience. Learning is an organizational response to a stimulus, an active process resulting in a new organization. The field theorist maintains that man is constantly acting upon the environment, structuring it, and bettering his perception of it, not simply reacting to it.

Learning thus proceeds by reorganization rather than by accretion. When the pupil suddenly realizes that multiplication is simply another form of addition, the flash of understanding that comes at this single trial is not simply the result of adding up S-R connections. The learner now perceives previously acquired learning in a better way. The differentiations result from a change in perceptual structure either through a new organization of past experiences or by the addition of novel experiences.

What is learned? The field theorist maintains that the learner discovers and understands relationships between the various elements of the present stimulus situation or between those of the present and the past.

The meaning that the learner assigns to the stimulus is an indication of how he has organized experience. It is a sign of his peculiar organization. The meaning that he takes to a word, such as beauty, comes from within him more than from the stimulus situation, and while determined by his previous experiences, to be sure, it is not entirely so. It is also determined by the learner's constitutional makeup, the quality and organization of his experiences, by his affective state, and by his culture. The learner reacts as an organized whole.

The stages in perception are, then: (1) a pattern of stimulation, (2) an organization, and (3) a response to the product of organization. Yanoff (1972) separates the cognitive process into four major functions: input, integration, output, and feedback. Cognition begins with appropriate perception and perception begins with sensory stimulation. The brain is perceived as an information processing system.

Emphasis on the Contemporary Experience

The field-theoretical approach to learning emphasizes the primacy of the contemporary pattern, organization, field, or Gestalt rather than the past history or experiences of the organism. The S-R theorist endorses a historical viewpoint and suggests that responses and response patterns are the accumulation of numerous trials. When a new problem is met, in his view, the learner calls upon his previous habits and responds to the new situation in terms of previous responses to similar aspects or elements, or he varies his response, using a trial-and-error approach, until he achieves a correct response.

The field theorist believes that the learner comes up with an organization fit to meet the demands of the present situation. He admits that in solving problems past experience is useful, but suggests that the present structuring of the problem may prevent or enhance the possibilities of a solution.

Emphasis on Wholes Rather Than Parts

Field theorists all maintain that one can deal better with organisms by observing the total organism. In this sense all are organismic psychologists, who emphasize the functional belongingness of parts to the whole and suggest that organismic events are best understood if they are examined in the pattern into which they belong.

THORNDIKE'S CONNECTIONISM

Learning theory for years was associated with the name of Edward L. Thorndike (1874–1949). He initiated systematic laboratory investigations of animal learning and produced the first formalized associationistic learning theory. Most of Thorndike's experiments were done with cats. Usually a hungry cat was placed in a box or cage which had a loop or string hanging from the top or that contained a latch which, if operated by the cat, would open the door and the way to escape. The cat was rewarded with food or fish if it learned to manipulate the latch or to pull the string that opened the door. Thorndike noted that initially in such a situation the cat will walk around, claw, bite, and dash back and forth. It will usually take a long time before the cat either pulls the string or operates the latch, freeing it from the cage.

With repeated exposure to the box, the cat becomes more proficient in performing the response that immediately precedes the opening of the door and the attainment of food and gets out of the box much more quickly. Thorndike suggested that the cat gradually stamped in the correct responses and stamped out the incorrect ones. He pointed out that the cat, when confronted with the problem of getting out of the cage, selects the proper response from a series of possible responses and connects it with the appropriate stimulus. He termed such learning trial-and-error learning.

Thorndike believed that complex learning should be broken into more simple learning and that human learning could be essentially explained by animal or trial-and-error learning.

The Law of Readiness

Thorndike developed various "laws" to explain the learning of the cat and the learning of the pupil in the classroom. One of these was the Law of Readiness. Thorndike gave readiness a physiological interpretation, suggesting that when a tendency to act is aroused through preparatory adjustments, sets, or attitudes, carrying out the act is satisfying and not acting is annoying. Readiness thus is a preparation for action. Thorndike's concept of readiness is roughly analogous to attention or motivation for learning. All of us have watched a cat readying itself to pounce upon its prey. We also have seen many children who come to school with a set to read. They are psychologically ready. They have the proper attitudes and sets to attend to the reading task. Sometimes, however, the learner does not have a "felt need to learn," and not much learning occurs. Teachers then must prepare the pupil for learning. They must arouse curiosity and in other ways appeal to the needs of the child.

Bugelski (1964, pp. 460–61) points out that the teacher functions in the classroom as a motivator of learning. Motivation does not necessarily mean that the student consciously desires to learn. Rather it implies that he is "set" to react to stimuli. The first obligation of the teacher is to create "an appropriate level of anxiety" or curiosity within the student. The learner must come to feel uneasy or distressed in situations where his knowledge is inadequate. Bugelski suggests that the teacher must develop "controlled degrees of anxiety or curiosity" even by artificial means, if necessary. In this way he employs the learner's attention and interest as positive forces to foster learning.

Readiness also has acquired a maturational interpretation. In this connection it means that the organism should be mature enough to make the responses required for learning. Readiness then is defined as the developmental stage at which constitutional factors have prepared the pupil for instruction. Learning readiness for a given task also may be described as the teachable moment for that task.

The Law of Exercise

A second law formulated by Thorndike is the Law of Exercise. Thorndike recognized the need for practice when he first proposed the Law of Exercise. Later in his *Educational Psychology*, he discussed the place of exercise:

> When a modifiable connection is made between a situation and a response, that connection's strength is, other things being equal, increased. . . . When a modifiable connection is not made between a situation and response during a length of time, that connection's strength is decreased (1930, pp. 2–4).

The Law of Exercise is sometimes termed the law of use and disuse and asserts that practice is necessary for learning and that when practice is discontinued, learning deteriorates. To learn, the organism must do something. And whenever a response is made to a given stimulus, the response becomes associated with that stimulus, and the more frequently that response is made to the stimulus the stronger the association becomes. The learner must make at least one response to a stimulus. To this extent practice is necessary for all learning.

Thorndike found that the more frequently the cat was put into the cage and managed to escape, the more quickly it was able to solve the problem when again put into the cage. Pupils generally become better in word recognition the more frequently they see the word.

Learning was conceived by Thorndike as a gradual process. The initial response to a stimulus might be likened to the birth of a new association; practice or repetition, to its maturation. Learning thus involves both a stimulus and a response.

All theories of learning have to find some place for practice. The child looks at the word for the seventy-fifth time for the same reason that he did the first time. In fact, sometimes the learner breaks a bad habit such as typing *the* as *hte* by actually practicing the habit (Dunlap, 1932) or by engaging in negative practice (Schubert, 1972). Our suggestions on how to overcome reversals include this technique.

Learning is basically a perceptual or psychological process. Learning to read is basically a perceptual process. But, reading also is a skill that is learned, and skills are learned best through practice.

This means that the teacher must find ways and means of developing the skills to be learned. He must guide pupils through the processes and provide them with the materials that are necessary for the attainment of the objective.

Motivation and Learning

Thorndike recognized that practice is not the sole determinant of learning; it does not in itself cause learning. He found that a blindfolded person did not improve in his ability to draw a line three inches long regardless of the number of practices. Practice is important only because of the conditions that operate during practice.

Thorndike recognized that improvement in performance requires certain motivations. The learner improved his performance only if he was interested in his work, if he was interested in improving himself, if the material to be learned had special significance for him, if he was attentive to the situation, and if he had a problem-solving attitude. Motivation is the *why* of human behavior. It initiates, sustains, and directs behavior toward a goal (Lindsley, 1957, p. 48). It arouses the learner, moves him, wakes him up as it were, and tenses him just enough for action. In discussing motivation, the problem of terminology is immediately apparent. What is the need? What is the goal? What is the motive? What is an incentive?

Needs are a want or a lack, whether it be a mineral, vitamin, or dietary component or even an environmental condition (Nelson, 1961, p. 2). They may exist apart from motive or drive. If a rat lacks Vitamin D, it will develop rickets. The rat needs Vitamin D, but may have no drive to seek the vitamins. Needs might also be described as more or less stable tendencies to be motivated in specific ways (MacDonald, 1959, p. 84). They are the underlying states out of which specific motivations arise (MacDonald, 1959, p. 125).

Motives or drives are within the person. They initiate activity in the direction of a goal—an object or condition that satisfies the need that gave rise to the drive or motive in the first place. Motives are internal conditions, energies, or forces that impel the learner toward a goal. The motive is inferred from the behavior and is an outgrowth of a need. A child who has a need for recognition may be motivated to do well in school. A boy who has a need for aggression may be motivated to show his hostile feelings by giving someone a black eye. Need seems to be a broader concept than motive. Motives imply a specific mode of satisfying a need. The person who has a need for affection may on a given occasion be motivated to behave in one way; on another occasion, in another. Each time he is trying to satisfy the same need.

Incentives are also an important determinant of behavior. Behavior that leads to a need-satisfying goal or to a goal that is reinforced externally is more likely to reoccur when the need arises again.

Incentives sometimes refer simply to the object that satisfies the motive. In this sense it is an environmental and an external element that stimulates a drive in the direction of a goal. Food thus may be termed an incentive if the person seeking it is hungry. In this instance goal and incentive are the same. Incentive can also mean a secondary goal that encourages and elicits behavior in the direction of the primary goal or toward the satisfaction of a basic need. Thus a child may be given candy for getting good grades.

A discussion of motivation seeks to answer two questions (Hunt, 1960, p. 490): (1) Why does a person act? (2) Why does a person act the way he does? Traditionally, psychologists have believed that the motivated person is constantly concerned with reducing tension within the nervous system. Thus, in answer to the question, "Why does a person act?" psychologists have said: "The person either is *driven* by primary, internal stimuli which arise when there is a homeostatic or organic imbalance or he is *driven* by external stimuli of a painful nature." These two forms of stimuli make the organism active. They bring the organism into the state of excitation that has been labelled drive. Drives or motives thus are conditions within the organism that initiate activity in the direction of a goal—tension or pain reduction. *Need* is a state of tension created by organic deficiencies or by painful external stimuli. Figure 4-2 summarizes the drive-reduction theory.

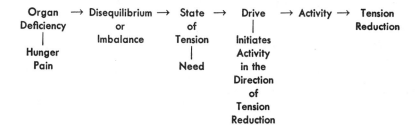

FIGURE 4–2 *Drive-Reduction Theory*

The drive-reduction theory presumes that the organism is essentially inactive when not motivated by internal or external stimuli. However, experience shows that persons are active when neither homeostatic drive nor painful external stimuli are present. This is explained thus: Certain innocuous stimuli acquire the capacity to "motivate" by being associated with either painful or homeostatic needs. Conditioned or learned drives do in fact motivate behavior. Thus rats shocked in a white box will attempt to escape when returned to the white box even though no shocking occurs.

Hunt (1960, pp. 489–92), after outlining the traditional approach to motivation, calls for certain reinterpretations. He questions the assumptions that all behavior is motivated by homeostatic need, painful stimulation, or conditioned stimuli for these. He notes that children play most when they are homeostatically satisfied. Well-fed monkeys solve problems. Man characteristically is unable to resign himself to rest and equilibrium. The tension—the need to act and to learn—seems to be in the brain rather than in the stomach. The electroencephalograms (EEGs) indicate that the brain cells are constantly active. Hunt (1960, p. 493) concludes that organisms characteristically show intrinsic activity and that to live means to act. Furthermore, the needs for self-esteem, esteem of others, curiosity, security, and aggression seem to motivate behavior in their own right and function like the physiological drives of hunger, pain, thirst, and sex. To be human means to yearn for the esteem of others, for self-realization, and for personal adequacy.

Nissen (1954, p. 300) suggests that there is a biogenic drive to explore, to perceive, and to want to know. "Capacity is its own motivation." If one can see, one wants to see. If one can know, one wants to know. Manipulative behavior is a type of functioning for which the body is designed.

The import of all this is that the motivating condition frequently seems to be psychological. Pupils strive for self-enhancement, self-realization, and self-actualization. They seek for personal adequacy. Motives, it seems, need not always be pleasurable or reduce physiological tension.

The theory of cognitive dissonance (Festinger, 1957, 1962) suggests that if a person knows something that is not psychologically consistent with another event he will try to make them consistent or congruent. Changes in items of information that restore consistency are termed dissonance-reducing changes. Cognitive dissonance thus is a motivator causing people to change their opinions or their behavior. Hunt (1960, pp. 499–500) notes that an individual constantly strives for consistency; when a stimulus is perceived as not belonging with existing cognitions, tension is aroused, and the organism will attempt to restore the system to balance. When his expectations are not fulfilled, dissonance occurs.

Whenever the pupil realizes that there is a disparity between what he is or can do and what he wants to be or could do, a cognitive dissonance results. The pupil is then motivated to become more adequate and to reduce the dissonance. Thus, learning may be motivated not so much by what the teacher does or by after-the-learning events such as rewards and punishments, as by what the learner wants, is interested in, or by what he feels will enhance his self-esteem and personal worth. The motivating condition begins within and is more psychological than physiological.

Motivation then is the end-product of having a goal and being prevented from the attainment of that goal by some barrier, whether physiological or psychological. Not being able to attain one's goal creates tension and results in cognitive dissonance.

When the incongruity or dissonance is slight, it is accommodated or may be tackled as a problem to be solved; when the dissonance is too great, when it is so great that the person cannot accommodate it, the person may become fearful, defensive, or avoid it. A pupil who fears failure in learning to read may not apply himself at all, thereby preserving his self-concept. He reasons thus: "I could learn to read if I really wanted to."

The learner learns more readily and retention is more permanent when he *wants* to learn, when he actively participates in the learning task, when he perceives the meaningfulness of the task, or when he is moving toward a goal. The goal-directed movements of the learner must be interpreted as his attempts to secure for himself what he interprets as success. Success may be simply the desire to do a good job or to meet a challenge.

Objects also have motivating powers. Ice cream, for example, has qualities other than hunger satisfaction which attract the little child. Learning tasks have varying degrees of attraction and challenge. Reading materials are more or less interesting and children are more motivated by comprehensible and interesting subject matter. The key to human learning may be motivation aroused by external stimuli.

Hull had tied motivation to physiological imbalance or need reduction. Miller (Dollard and Miller, 1950) reduced drive to stimulus intensity and motivation to drive reduction or to a reduction in intensity of the stimulus. The focus in cognitive circles is not on stimulus intensity but on the organism's internal response to stimulation. The key variable is arousal intensity with drives defined as states of high arousal and rewards as reductions in arousal level (December, 1974, p. 164). Exploration and curiosity are perceived as behaviors that reduce high arousal that accompanies sensory deprivation or boredom. Similar cognitive models focus on the motivational force of "events as perceived," the "informational value of events," or as we noted above "cognitive dissonance" reduction.

It is of course necessary that the teacher remember that children from different status levels in society will be characterized by different motivational systems, will have different goal expectancies, and will be motivated by different kinds of rewards. Since the average American school typically has children from practically all levels of society, the teacher is faced with the complex problem of motivating children who have different need systems.

The Law of Effect

Thorndike also developed the Law of Effect (1932, p. 176). It reads:

> When a modifiable connection between a situation and a response is made and is accompanied or followed by a satisfying state of affairs, that connection's strength is increased; when made and accompanied or followed by an annoying state of affairs, its strength is decreased.

Thorndike suggested that the learner uses a trial-and-error approach until he hits upon the correct response, which tends to be repeated because of the operation of the Law of Effect. When after a series of exploratory movements the cat pulls the string or operates the latch, it is able to escape and is rewarded with food for having solved the problem. This successful event intensifies the association between the stimulus and the response.

Learning frequently requires the accompaniment of a rewarding situation. As indicated in Chapter 3, each perceptual experience has its emotional matrix. All experiences tend to involve feeling. They may be accompanied by "satisfying" feelings or by "feelings of annoyance." The learner will turn to experiences that satisfy and turn away from those that annoy. In either case, the individual is said to have been "rewarded" or the behavior to have been reinforced.

Secondary Reinforcement

Psychologists have tried repeatedly to explain how drives can become attached to objects. Wolfe (1936) trained chimpanzees to obtain grapes by inserting a poker chip in a vending machine. The chimps learned to value the chips and, in a later experiment, Cowles (1937) found that the chips alone could be used to motivate learning. The poker chips had indeed taken on some of the qualities of primary motivation and reinforcement. A chimp, for example, would learn "position habits"[1] for tokens.

These and other experiments have demonstrated that when a stimulus has been associated with a primary reinforcer, the stimulus may itself become a reinforcer. Whenever this occurs, it is customary to speak of secondary reinforcement.

Reinforcement certainly offers some explanation of the child's learning to read. In the beginning he wishes to read because he wants to know how, because his brothers and sisters read, because his parents want him to learn to read, or because learning to read is the acceptable group activity of his class. For the motivating condition to be satisfied, he reads.

---

[1] In two-position learning the chimp must locate a token in one of two cups. The cups themselves are in separate wooden boxes closed by a horizontal lid. In five-position learning there are five wooden boxes. The tokens apparently are adequate incentives. The chimps learn not only the rather simple right and left position of the box containing the token, but also the much more complicated problem required in the five-box arrangement.

Gradually, reading may become a secondary reinforcer. When it does so, reading becomes an interest, in itself. Although a later chapter discusses reading as an interest, we can see here that a part of the process by which it becomes an interest is secondary reinforcement.

The various learning theorists differ somewhat in their explanations of the exact nature of reinforcement. Hull identified reinforcement with physiological drive reduction; Guthrie, with the termination of stimulation; Tolman, with the confirmation of expectancies; and Sheffield, with consummatory responses. Stroud (1956, p. 346) notes that the satisfaction of a motivating condition is, of necessity, rewarding. Hebb and Bugelski base their explanation on the findings of neurology and physiology. In fact, Bugelski defines motivation as a disturbance of the normal rhythms of the brain (1964, p. 260). When this neural disturbance is terminated, the drive or motivation dissipates and reinforcement occurs.

Rewarding situations are usually referred to as incentives. These are goal objects toward which a behavior sequence is directed. There are many reinforcers of human behavior: rewards, punishments, praise, blame, group recognition, knowledge of progress, friendly conferences, or encouragement. Just as not all children are similarly motivated, so also what is rewarding to one child may not be rewarding to another.

All pupils are motivated. Sometimes the major problem is to pry it loose. The good teacher uses kindness, recognition, praise, a friendly conference, or a pat on the shoulder. He tries to make the learning of reading a satisfying experience. He capitalizes on the pupil's curiosity and on his desire for improvement. He uses the pupil's identification with him to lead the pupil to greater accomplishment. He encourages excellence. He upsets the pupil's equilibrium and enlarges his expectations. But above all, he makes education something that the pupil wants. *Good entertainment is educational and good education is entertaining.*

When education becomes entertaining, the teacher does not have to threaten the pupil with punishment, with failure, or with a slip to be taken home to his parents. A pupil so threatened will work just hard enough and long enough to get the teacher off his back. Having accomplished this he falls back to his normal way of behaving.

The Law of Belongingness

Thorndike likewise developed the Law of Belongingness. According to this principle, an association is more easily learned if the response belongs to the situation. Hilgard (1956, pp. 28–29) gives an illustration. He notes that in the sentences "John is a butcher. Henry is a carpenter," the association between the words, "John" and "butcher," is a stronger one than the association between "butcher" and "Henry," even though the latter two words are more contiguous. The reason is that the subject and the predicate have a more natural belongingness one with the other than has the end of one sentence with the beginning of another.

The Law of Belongingness has application to teaching. For example, it stresses the importance of context. The child will learn and remember words better if he can immediately use them in meaningful reading or writing. A child learns a word more readily when he needs to know the word in order to understand a passage that he is reading than when it is given as an isolated word to be learned by rote. Stroud (1956, pp. 340–41) points out that belonging may be thought of as the seeing of relationships; the noting that one event is caused by or belongs with another. Although belonging is not essential to all learning, it is extremely important for most of the learning that is done in school situations.

GUTHRIE'S CONTIGUOUS ASSOCIATION

By the time Guthrie made his presence felt, Watson had already developed behaviorism and Pavlov had discovered conditioning. To understand Guthrie's contribution, it is useful to take a look at the contributions of Watson and Pavlov.

The Behaviorism of Watson

John B. Watson (1878–1958) laid the ground work for S-R theories. His behavioristic emphasis led him away from a study of what people "think" and "feel" to what people "do." He insisted on an objective study of behavior. In 1913 in "Psychology as the Behaviorist Views It" (Watson, 1913) Watson defined behavior as movements of muscles. Speech was movements of the muscles of the throat, thought was "sub-vocal speech," and behavior was learned through conditioning and could be subdivided into a series of conditioned reflexes.

Watson's view of conditioning was based on Pavlov, and complex and new behaviors represented for him a combination of simple reflexes.

Watson felt that when a rat learns to run to the goal box at the end of a maze, it simply learns the series of mechanical leg and body movements involved in turning left or right. He suggested that all differences in ability and personality were learned through conditioning. This concept easily fit in with "traditional American pragmatic bias in favor of action rather than thought or feeling"; in the United States it still is "what a man does that counts, not what he says or thinks or feels" (McClelland, 1955, p. 297).

Pavlov's Classical Conditioning

Let us review Pavlov's classical conditioning experiment, which is an example of stimulus selection learning and which helps us to understand association. Pavlov (1927) found that a dog salivated immediately when food was placed in its mouth. This he termed the unconditioned reflex (UR). In a simple experiment, a tuning fork was sounded (conditioned stimulus or CS) and about 7 or 8 seconds later the dog was presented with a plate of powdered meat (unconditioned stimulus or US). Initially the tone did not arouse a salivary response, but after 30 associations or pairings between tone and food, the sound alone caused the dog to salivate 60 drops (conditioned response or CR). The dog had become conditioned to the tone.

The meat powder served as a reinforcement because it produced a much greater flow of saliva than did the tuning fork. It had about the same function as Thorndike's reward. The meat (US) reinforced the association between the tuning fork and the salivary response much as the food in Thorndike's experiments reinforced the association between the string and the clawing or pulling. Conditioning historically is a term used ". . . to denote the behavioral fact that a stimulus inadequate for some response could become adequate by virtue of being combined one or more times with a stimulus adequate for the response. . . ." (Razran, 1955, p. 173). This definition presupposes that all conditioning requires some association.

The Law of Contiguity

Guthrie had only one law: "A combination of stimuli which has accompanied a movement will on its recurrence tend to be followed by that movement." (1952, p. 23) This law has been termed the Law of Contiguity and has been paraphrased in many ways. Kingsley and Garry (1957, p. 98) suggest that it might mean: "We repeat what we learn and we learn what we do." It might also mean that if you do something in a given situation, when that situation occurs again, you will do the same thing. Contiguity simply means that if stimuli act at the same time that a response occurs, the response will tend to recur on subsequent occasions whenever the stimuli are present. The pupil, who responds to *was* with *saw*, will on the next presentation of the stimulus *was* tend to respond again with *saw*.

Guthrie rejected the Law of Relative Frequency, which suggested that the strength of the stimulus-response connection increased with practice. For Guthrie, it was either all or nothing on the occasion of the first pairing between the stimulus and the response. He believed in one-trial learning. He felt that the stimulus pattern gains its full associative strength on the occasion of its first pairing with a response. Guthrie (1952, pp. 79–80, 88) notes, for example, that sometimes a habit is established with one repetition, that a person can recall a name after hearing it only once, that fear is born out of one experience, that one doesn't have to practice getting up at eight when he has gotten up at 7:30 for years, and that a man may stop smoking all at once after smoking for years. Frequently, learning that is occasioned by one experience seems to be accompanied by strong emotional response.

Guthrie, however, did not completely reject the value of practice. He gave reasons why practice and repetition lead to improvement. Guthrie notes (1952, pp. 85–86) that practice is necessary to break a habit because numerous stimuli usually can elicit the response and that each of these must be inhibited. Thus the smoking habit may be elicited by the sight of tobacco, the aroma of another's pipe, finishing of a meal, or sitting on a bank fishing. Each of these in the past became signals for smoking.

He suggested that whereas Thorndike was concerned with end results (scores on tests or correct response made), he himself was concerned only with movements. Each activity (swinging of a bat) consists of a complex of individual movements, and improvement and learning are not attained by frequent swinging of a bat, but rather by increasing the number of correct movements in swinging the bat (balance of the body, position of the feet, position of the hands, keeping one's eye on the ball) and by reducing the number of incorrect movements in the total complex of movements comprising the total activity. Each time a person swings a bat, if new learning is to occur, there will be movement more correct than before. Improvement occurs because the learner gradually replaces the erroneous movements that he still is making with correct ones (e.g., he may improve his stance). Thus, additional practice gives more opportunity to master the myriad of movements comprising a complex stimulus-response situation. And the end result is improvement in the total performance.

Skills thus represent a population or complex of habits but each habit, of the hundreds comprising a single skill, is learned completely at full strength in a single performance. The learner does not learn the skill with the first pairing of a stimulus and a response because the skill is a complex of many stimulus-response pairings. But the strength of the stimulus-response bond is at its maximum at its first pairing. Guthrie thus drew a distinction between the acts and movements and noted that, although acts, such as swinging a bat, are usually measured, it is the movements that are actually conditioned as response.

Guthrie suggested that "What is learned" are movements. Other theorists suggested that we learn habits or relationships. Which is correct?

In an experimental study Logan (1963) asked the following question. Does the organism learn a fast or a slow response? When reinforcement is delayed, a rat will run the maze more slowly than if it is rewarded immediately. Is the rat learning the molar response of running or the micro-molar response of running at a particular speed?

Could it be that when the teacher tells the child, "Take your time in doing these addition problems but be right," that the child is being taught to "behave more slowly when adding"?

Logan found that students tend to repeat information at the same rate as it was learned and that performance deteriorates when the required speed of performance is increased.

SKINNER'S OPERANT CONDITIONING

Skinner's major contribution perhaps is his distinction between respondent and operant behavior.[2] Previous theories had suggested that all responses were to some specific stimulus, and when no external stim-

[2]Some major works of Skinner are: *The Behavior of Organisms: An Experimental Analysis,* 1938; *Science and Human Behavior,* 1953; "Are Theories of Learning Necessary?" *Psychological Review* 57 (1950): 193–216; *Verbal Behavior,* 1957.

ulation was observed, internal stimuli were postulated. Skinner felt this was begging the question and suggested that some behaviors simply do not have an identifiable stimulus. Responses which have a known stimulus are termed *respondents* (knee jerk after a blow on the patellar tendon, an eyeblink that follows a loud noise, fear that accompanies the sight of a vicious animal, or an answer to a teacher's specific question); those responses whose stimulus is not known are termed *operants*. Operant conditioning is frequently termed instrumental conditioning because the organism must make a response, and the response makes possible or is instrumental in the achievement of the goal or reward. In the Skinner box, depressing of the lever by the rat or pecking of a key by the pigeon leads to food; pulling the plunger of a vending machine does so in the case of humans. Reinforcement is dependent upon making the correct response.

Skinner has devoted much effort to developing operant behavior or to shaping behavior. He has trained pigeons to play a type of Ping-Pong, with the pigeon pecking a ball back and forth across a table. When the ball gets by one pigeon, the behavior of the other pigeon is reinforced. In another experiment Skinner taught a pigeon to bowl.

Shaping of behavior thus does not wait until the learner makes the desired response exactly correct. Operant learning may be quite gradual. At first, it may be necessary to reinforce gross approximations to the final response. These successive approximations gradually result in making the correct response.

According to Skinner, the first task of the teacher is to get the pupil to express himself in some observable way so that it will be possible to reinforce his behavior in some way. Skinner suggests that any activity that is to be learned must be divided into numerous small steps and that reinforcement must accompany the learning of each discrete step. The entire process of teaching beginning readers is based on a continuous or partial reinforcement schedule used by the teacher to keep the child going, to keep him motivated (Gargiulo, 1971). Skinner's thinking has led to programmed materials.

Skinner (1958) emphasized the importance for teachers of analyzing the reinforcing contingencies in the classroom. What reinforcers are available? He notes that a teacher may be tempted to dismiss a class when discipline has broken down. This simply reinforces what the teacher is trying to prevent. A teacher might more profitably dismiss the class a few minutes early when all are working well. A few repetitions of this may lead to fewer discipline problems. Skinner felt that every reinforcement counts. He suggests that we should reinforce even if the child doesn't know what he is doing.

Skinner outlines the steps to be taken in teaching or in shaping behavior:

1. Analyze the skill to be learned; know what it requires the learner to do and make certain that it is within the learner's capacity.
2. Prepare the learner for learning. Create a psychological readiness for learning.

3. Use immediate rewards. Reward each successful movement in the sequence.
4. Provide an opportunity for learning.

The experimenter may want to train the learner to respond to a stimulus only when another stimulus is also present. He may reinforce the bar-pressing response only when a light is on and may not reinforce bar pressing when the light is off. The light is termed the discriminative stimulus or the cue stimulus. Darkness is termed a delta stimulus.

This principle is very useful in the classroom. A child, learning to read, sees many word symbols on a page. To only one word, perhaps, he must learn to respond with something like "this word says cat." The teacher is constantly reinforcing the *cat* response to one given word. The word then becomes a discriminative stimulus for one specific sound.

HULL'S HABIT THEORY

Clark L. Hull (1884–1952) was concerned with the stimulus (the input), the response (the output), and the organism. His was an S-O-R theory rather than an S-R theory. This simply means that the stimulus (S) affects the organism (O), and the resultant response (R) is the product of both the stimulus and the organism. In his equations Hull sought to account for the activity of the organism.

Hull was not simply concerned with the stimulus and the response, but wanted to know the factors within the individual that affect the response. Hull sought to quantify all the variables in learning. This attempt of Hull has special meaning for the teacher, for the practitioner in the classroom will make fewer mistakes if he considers all possible variables.

Reaction Potential

Hull's theory focuses on performance, and so reaction potential (sEr) assumes a major role. sEr is the total tendency to make a given response to a given stimulus. It is an active readiness to make the response, to perform. It is dependent upon a previous habit strength, drive, incentive motivation or reinforcement, and intensity of the stimulus.

For Hull, learning involves the strengthening or establishment of connections or habits. As learning occurs, an internal factor, which was termed habit strength (sHr), is strengthened. The tendency to respond (sEr) thus depends upon habit strength or on previous learning. It might be said that a pupil's tendency to read, since reading is a performance or a response, is dependent at least partially on previous habits of reading. The pupil who has read a lot in the past will tend to read more than the pupil who has read only infrequently.

Habit strength is the strength of the bond between a stimulus and a response, a bond which is built up through reinforced practice. Habit strength, designated sHr, with *s* referring to stimulus, *r* to response, and

H for habit, increases with practice. As the number of reinforced trials or responses increases, so also will habit strength. The first association between *s* and *r* leads to the development of a strong connection or habit. The tendency to respond is dependent also on drive *(D)* and incentive motivation *(K)*. When a rat has eaten its fill, it will tend to fall asleep in a maze. This illustrates that performance depends on learning but also on drive and incentive motivation. Their interaction thus is multiplicative rather than additive. Reduce any one of them to zero and there is no performance. To determine what behavior will occur in a given situation, it is necessary to multiply the drive level of the organism by the level of learning attained. In other words, sEr is the product of $D \times K \times$ sHr. Reaction potential (sEr) is also a function of stimulus intensity *(V)*. The person tends to react to the stimulus of greatest intensity. When there is excessive stimulation, minor stimuli are usually not detected. The noise of a locomotive moving by the classroom forces the teacher to raise his voice, but the pupil frequently will still concentrate on the loudest noise or stimulus.

Let us apply these ideas to reading. Reading is a response. The ability to respond through reading is dependent on the many variables that affect performance. The tendency to read (sEr) is a function of previous habits of reading, of motivation, of the reinforcement value of reading, and of the proximity with which reinforcement follows reading.

We find that the more reading the child did before instruction starts (sHr), the greater the desire to read, and the better reading satisfies personal motives, the more interesting reading becomes and thus the closer it comes to being a motive in its own right. The greater the reinforcement value of reading or the closer reinforcement follows actual reading, the greater is the tendency to read.

Some children do not read even though they profess a great desire to do so. Perhaps reading constantly conflicts with television, and television may be the stronger stimulus, thus preventing reading. Perhaps reading has never been made meaningful because it has not been followed by satisfying aftereffects. The habit of reading thus may never have been learned.

Effective Reaction Potential

Hull also spoke of an organism's effective reaction potential (s$\bar{\text{E}}$r). The effective reaction potential is equivalent to sEr—$\bar{\text{I}}$r or the inhibitory factors, which Hull termed reactive inhibition (Ir) and conditioned inhibition (sIr). When the inhibitory factors are stronger than sEr, no reaction will occur. The total inhibitory tendency ($\bar{\text{I}}$r) is equal to Ir plus sIr.

The factors that inhibit performance are numerous, the most obvious of which is fatigue (Ir). As an organism continues to perform, as a student continues to read, for example, the tendency to read is gradually lessened. Reactive inhibition or Ir is generated each time a response is made. The greater the number of responses, and hence the greater the effort needed to make a response, the greater is the reactive inhibition. When the organism ceases to make responses, naturally Ir is reduced. Otto (1963, 1965, 1966) found that poor achievers accumulate reactive inhibition more rapidly than good achievers and that poor readers accumulate it more rapidly than good readers.

sIr is the conditioned nonactivity that is brought on by Ir. If the organism rests too long, it gradually develops the habit of not responding, becomes lazy, and avoids work. This is especially so when the organism is in the presence of stimuli normally associated with "not working." A comfortable easy chair or a beautiful green lawn may become a conditioned stimulus for resting.

If the inhibitory factors are too great, even a well-established habit may not show up in performance. The same occurs in the absence of drive or incentives.

The effective tendency to read $(s\bar{E}r)$ is equal to the total tendency to read minus the inhibitory factors (Ir) that tend to block performance. Among the more obvious inhibitory factors in reading are poor health, fatigue, low physical energy, and the number of unreinforced reading experiences. The greater the amount of energy the reader must expend in reading, the less he tends to read. The more difficult the materials, the quicker the student becomes fatigued, and the less reading will be done. The more frequently reading is unrewarded, the less the pupil tends to read. A pupil who reads but does not understand tends to lose interest in reading. And we find that the pupil who does not read gradually develops the habit of "not reading."

Momentary Reaction Potential

Hull likewise spoke of momentary reaction potential $(s\dot{\bar{E}}r)$. This is equivalent to $s\bar{E}r$-sOr or the organisms's oscillation potential; it serves as another way of describing variability in behavior. The organism generally may have a tendency to perform well, but at a given moment cannot do so.

A person's tendency to respond through reading is subject to a certain amount of variability. On certain days a child may not care to read or to play piano regardless of the fact that the class schedule calls for reading or that it is time for practice on the piano. A child does not and, in fact, cannot respond in the same way or with equal proficiency every day. He may bring the appropriate meaning to a word 99 out of 100 times, but once in a while he cannot do so. Thus perfect prediction of behavior is not possible.

The diagram in Figure 4-3 summarizes Hull's theory.

FIELD THEORY

A second major group of learning theories are the field theories. Numerous psychologies representing variant shades of approach might be included in this group. We will concern ourselves primarily with three

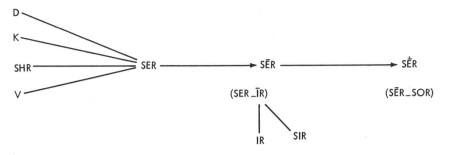

FIGURE 4–3 *A summary of Hull's Theory*

branches, namely Gestalt Psychology, Field Theory per se as seen in the writings of Kurt Lewin, and the Purposivism of Tolman. Field Theory began with Gestalt Psychology, and Gestalt Psychology was primarily concerned with perception. Gestalt psychology developed out of the work and writings of Max Wertheimer (1880–1943), Kurt Koffka (1886–1941), and Wolfgang Koehler (1887–1967).[3]

The Perceptual Process

The phenomenon of apparent movement, generally called the phi-phenomenon, gave impetus to the field interpretations of the nature of perception. Motion pictures are an excellent example of apparent movement. The projected images from the individual frames of the film have no movement; the movement is only apparent. The light in the neon advertising signs is perceived as moving from one place to another, but actually as the light in one place is turned off, another light goes on.

Certainly in these instances what is apprehended by the viewer involves sensory data not presently available to the senses. There is an implication here that the incoming sensory data are in some way retained, processed, and reorganized by the viewer. Some intermediary step takes place between the sensory input and the response.

Going Beyond the Sensory Data

A study of perception emphasizes two facts: (1) that we can come to know the external world and (2) that we go beyond what the senses provide. Perception has characteristics which cannot be derived from sensation alone.

Here, we wish to explore this last concept more fully. In looking at a chair the senses are not really in contact with the chair at all. What hits the rods and the cones of the retina is a series of light rays that are reflected

[3]The reader should refer back to Chapter 2 for more recent cognitive approaches, especially the sections on "Psychological Models: Cognitive Models" and "Information Processing Models."

from the chair. In looking at a circle the person organizes the incoming impulses into a circle even though the pattern (the Gestalt) on the retina is not circular. This presents the perceiver with a peculiar difficulty. Although the light rays are the cause of his perceptions, he perceives not the light rays, but the geographical object (Koffka, 1935, p. 79). His behavior is determined by the object and not by the light rays.

Because of the above situation the field theorist draws a distinction between the light rays—the proximal stimuli, and the object—the distal stimulus. Generally, psychologists refer to the proximal stimulus as simply the stimulus. Figure 4-4 illustrates the various steps in perception.

The problem has always been: how do the proximal stimuli come to signify the distal stimulus? This, the field theorist identifies as the problem of cognition.

The field theorist is not particularly concerned with the "knowability" of external reality. He accepts the validity of the senses. He assumes that he can know the external world, even though he realizes that many errors may creep into his perceptions.

As a matter of fact, because the perceiver masters the outer world through his perceptions, he rarely ever knows the true nature of things. His perceptions commonly attain only partial truth because he responds to outer reality in his own way.

The Central Intermediary

To explain *what* (not necessarily *how*) occurs when the person perceives, for example, a chair, cognitive theorists have suggested that the organism's response is determined not only by the proximal stimuli (the light rays) or even the geographical object or experience but also, and perhaps chiefly, by a central process within the organism. This central process influences the person's reactions to the stimulus and provides him with a representation of the distal stimulus or environmental-geographical object or experience (Scheerer, 1954). Field theorists refer to this representational process as cognition.

That in reality there is a central intermediary is indicated by experimental data. Hebb (1958, pp. 48, 52–57) gives a few examples.

Pavlov's dog salivated to the sound of the bell only when he was hungry. When he was satisfied he was not "set" to respond. The same

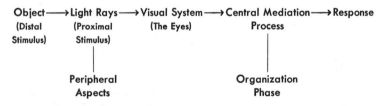

FIGURE 4–4 *The Perceptual Process*

stimulus pattern 8, 2 may lead to the response 10, 4, 6, 16 depending upon the particular "set" to respond. The response will change as the learner is told to add, divide, subtract, or multiply. A monkey that likes both lettuce and bananas will reject lettuce if he is expecting bananas as the reward for successful completion of a task (Tinklepaugh, 1928).

These data indicate that "set" depends on a neural trace of one kind or another that gradually develops activity of its own without the benefit of an immediate sensory stimulation. Set is analogous to closing a switch in the switchboard of the central nervous system, thus getting the organism "set" to respond in a predetermined way to the incoming data (Hebb, 1958, p. 64). Some sets depend on the blood chemistry (hunger or lack of it in the dog); others depend on neural processes (the lettuce and the banana).

It is most common to hear the pupil say: "I can't concentrate. My attention is constantly wandering." In a sense he is not set to respond to the learning task. Langman (1960, p. 31) notes that poor readers cannot attend to the significant visual stimuli in word recognition situations. Furthermore, they become distracted by less pertinent stimuli. Poor readers do not perceive the importance of particular details in letter shapes and of their relationships to one another. We also note that the poor reader has a special set in responding to words. He tends to think of them in their specific rather than their generic sense.

Set results in the imposition of an organization or meaning upon all incoming sensory data. And each learner is "set" to respond in one way or another; he is set or physiologically and psychologically ready to respond to some details rather than to others. Langman (1960, p. 32) notes that set makes the difference between the nonreader's observation of a multiplicity of irregular marks and the reader's recognition of combinations of letters composing familiar and meaning-associated patterns.

The Role of Experience and Organization

One of our first observations is that the cognitive representation (for example, of the meaning of the word democracy) has many characteristics which are not in the immediate stimulus-situation at all, but are to be found in the past experiences of the organism (environmental) and/or in its organizational (biological) response characteristics.

The organizational response characteristics of the organism are especially interesting. Studies show that "higher" animals perceive relationships which "lower" animals cannot. The spider monkey, for example, cannot grasp the principle of similarity, but the chimpanzee does so very readily.

Lashley (1949) notes that all animals learn but not all can learn the same thing. What is learned differentiates their organizational ability and this essentially seems to be biologically determined. It frequently is not the experience that guarantees the solution of the problem, but rather the organizational pattern or the biological inheritance into which the experience is fitted.

Perceptions and the Reading Process

Up to this point, we have identified two basic facts: (1) A central process intervenes between the stimulus and the response; (2) This process modifies the stimulus or afferent materials. Cognition organizes the incoming data into a meaningful pattern. William James (1890, p. 103) noted that "whilst part of what we perceive comes through our senses from the object before us, another part (and it may be the greater part) always comes . . . out of our head."

Our definition of reading, given in Chapter 2, emphasizes the perceptual nature of reading. Reading was described as the process of giving significance to graphic symbols by relating them to one's own fund of experience. Thus, the meaning is not something inherent in a word; meaning at least partly comes from within the reader.

The definition didn't stop there. It indicated that the meaning of a word is a function of experience. The meaning of a perception generally is based on the perceiver's previous experiences. Thus, Lange (1902, p. 21) notes that "we see and hear not only with the eye and ear, but quite as much with the help of our present knowledge, with the apperceiving content of the mind."

The concept is really a creation of an individual mind and cannot be shared directly. Teachers sometimes behave as though they could share concepts; all they can do is to transmit the words that symbolize the concept. Words sometimes do not convey accurately what is intended and what is intended may not represent accurately the event or experience.

Brunswik (1957, p. 10) refers to the degree of distal-proximal similarity as "ecological validity." [4] Generally, the perceiver (as also the reader) calls upon his previous experiences and assumes that the perception that was most successful in the past is the most likely to be correct now. However, numerous experiments have shown that since the perceiver interprets sense data on the basis of his past experience, his interpretation at times is in error.

Generally, the greater the number of experiences and the richer their quality, the greater are the chances for veridicality, but even the most veridical perception may be an inadequate representation of the concrete object or experience. Perception normally remains a representation.

THE FIELD CONCEPT

To explain the facts of perceptual organization, psychologists have introduced the field concept. The field, sometimes labelled the perceptual or phenomenal field, refers to the "more or less fluid organization of meanings existing for every individual at any instant" (Combs and Snygg,

[4] Ecology here means the environmental realities that surround the organism (Brunswik, 1957, p. 6).

1959, p. 20). Combs and Snygg add that the perceptual field is "the entire universe, including himself, as it is experienced by the individual at the instant of action" (p. 20).

Since no two individuals have had the same experiences, they cannot have the same perceptual field. Thus the fields of others often seem to us full of error and inadequacy in meaning. We refer to another as prejudiced and bigoted and he in turn may think the same of us. Two children playing in a sand box may live in entirely different worlds.

The significant fact is that the perceptual field is a major determinant of the individual's reactions to external reality or to a word. Wife and husband see completely different realities in looking at a sink full of dishes. Two readers see the word democracy and take completely different meanings to the term. Each one's behavior is determined by his own perceptual field. Each behaves according to how things *seem* to him. He may not actually be responding to the external reality. He more characteristically responds to the *meanings* that each bit of reality has for him.

The child's response to a word may or may not be adequate. He will react on the basis of his past experience, and if this has been inadequate, his response of necessity must be inadequate. His meaning for the word will be inadequate.

DIFFERENTIATION

The emergence of a new figure from the ground, or the process by which certain aspects of the perceptual field become figure, is called differentiation. The child gradually differentiates "Daddy" (figure) from all other men (ground). The learner, faced with the problem of multiple meaning of words, differentiates one specific meaning from a number of meanings.

The field theorist has to explain how the specific figure is selected from all the possible alternative organizations. Why does the learner take one specific meaning to the word, for example, democracy? We have here, according to Gestalt psychologists, an instance, not of stimulus nor indeed of response selection, but rather a case of perceptual selection. The organism is stimulated, and of all the possible perceptual organizations that might be made of the incoming sensory data one eventually emerges. This organization then becomes a determinant of the response. Figure 4-5 illustrates the process.

Selection is not a good term to describe perceptual organization. The Gestaltists spoke of how the organization *emerged*. The laws of organization likewise are not principles of connection, but rather state which structures will arise or emerge.

The reader may assume that individual differentiations and hence the perceptual field are completely private. At times this may be true, but usually it is not. Individuals of the same culture, whose contacts with the external reality are similar and indeed where the objects are essentially similar, have many things in common. Human beings living in the same environment generally make similar differentiations.

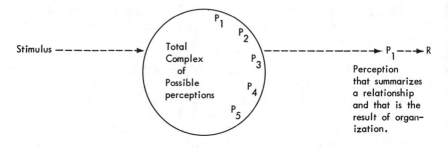

Perceptual Selection

Only because of this are we capable of communicating with one another. We already noted that the major determinants of meaning are: culture, experience, ability to reconstruct experience, previous experience in concept formation, one's native endowment, one's affective state, and the context in which the word occurs. The more alike the above elements are in both communicator and perceiver, the better the communication tends to be.

Persons with similar experience both make similar differentiations and have similar perceptual fields. Unfortunately, the learner's differentiations often are quite limited. Chapters 5 and 6 contain much evidence concerning the inhibitory factors in learning to read. Reading retardation results because the child cannot make the proper differentiations required for mastery of the reading task.

Differentiations take time and the teacher must constantly make adjustments for this. The application of white paint at the choice points in an otherwise completely black maze leads to quicker and more accurate learning by the rat. In reading, the method of teaching can be simplified or made unnecessarily difficult. The teacher can arrange the learning situation in such a way that the differentiations come easily or are immediately obvious.

Learning is a change in performance whether physiological or psychological as a result of a differentiation within the perceptual field. It is an active process resulting in a new organization. It is an emergence of new figures, entities, and characteristics from an undifferentiated ground. Hull's concept of the habit hierarchy is an analogous one. Learning thus may be an increasing or raising of the strength of a specific response in a hierarchy of responses. The differentiations result from a change in the figure-group structure either through a new organization of past experiences or by the addition of novel experiences.

To the question, "What is learned?," the S-R theorist answered, "habit"; the field psychologist, on the other hand, says it is a differentiation. The theories are perhaps closer than they seem.

For the S-R theorist, the end result of practice is *habit*. Thus, the pupil with repeated practice learns to respond automatically to the words on the page. He doesn't have to figure out the pronunciation of each word. For the field theorist, habit is more than a fixed sequence of acts that are neurologically determined; it more frequently is the result of learned insights. Habits, although they seem automatic and occur without awareness, are low-level perceptual differentiations. The person performs them with minimum or no awareness. They are more ground than figure. As already noted, Dunlap (1932) overcame the habit of typing *hte* for *the* only after he actually brought back into figure the *hte* by typing it. The differentiation now was clear and he could break the habit. Emphasizing *the* would not have removed from the ground (conscious or unconscious) the previously-learned *hte*.

According to Gestalt psychologists, a restructuring of the perceptual field frequently results in sudden solutions to problems. Behaviorists, so the Gestaltists maintained, placed animals in situations entirely foreign to them. It was not the animal that was behaving stupidly; rather, the situation itself was stupid. The levers and mechanical devices were usually above the animal's level of comprehension. Naturally, confronted with such situations the animal could not engage in genuine problem-solving activity, and the S-R theorist could falsely conclude that learning is a simple trial-and-error process.

Koehler, in experiments with chimps in 1913–1917 at Tenerife, in the Canary Islands, set about to devise experiments which permitted the organism to show insightful learning. Young chimpanzees were placed in a room to the ceiling of which was fastened a banana. The banana served as a lure. Some distance from the banana and on the floor was a wooden box. Initially all chimpanzees jumped repeatedly toward the banana, but could not reach it. One of the chimps, Sultan by name, soon ceased his jumping and paced back and forth across the room. He stopped for a moment in front of the box. He moved the box under the banana, climbed on top of the box, and jumped from the box toward the banana, which he now was able to get. Sultan apparently grasped a relationship between box and "getting the banana." He had "learned" and then made the appropriate response.

The type of behavior exhibited by the chimp was termed *insightful learning*. Insight, however, is not an explanation of learning. It is not correct to define learning as a change in performance as a result of insight. Insight does not cause learning any more than practice causes learning. Insight occurs when the differentiation of a relationship is made as a result of the restructuring of the field. Insight is an end-product of having perceived a relationship. It is a combination and reorganization of preexistent perceptions. In such instances we find that the child readily repeats the correct solution and applies what he has learned to new situations.

In most "insightful situations" the learner has a relatively high degree of awareness of "what leads to what" or of what leads to the correct solution. This perception of relationships may be encouraged in the classroom through either inductive or deductive teaching methods. Thus the pupil may be shown the principle or relationship directly (deductive method—the principle is stated for him) or he may learn the relationship by reasoning from specific fact to the generalization (inductive method).

The pupil quite frequently develops a system of attacking words. It is better if the pupil is taught such a system and if teaching procedure prepares for it. This will lead more readily to insightful response by the pupil in attacking new words.

Hilgard (1956, pp. 234–37) notes that insight or the perception of relationships is more readily attained by the more intelligent and more experienced person. These persons can make sharper differentiations in the field. Hilgard also points out that some experimental arrangements are more favorable to insightful behavior than others. Hilgard (1964, pp. 61–62) notes that a problem can be structured in such a way that relationships are perceived and a sensible solution is attained.

The experimenter in the laboratory and the teacher in the classroom can arrange the situation in such a way that the subject or the child cannot behave insightfully. Thus it has been demonstrated that with proper materials and with proper levels of difficulty the five-year-old can learn to read; with less well-prepared materials even the seven-year-old may not learn. Children, no less than animals, can be put in situations in which they can show only trial-and-error learning.

Past experiences, and the transfer that is made from the past situation to the present, surely play a major role in the development of insight. These experiences and transfer are a necessary condition, for it is only by seeing relationships among events that the pupil can generalize. Thus, materials are meaningful or insightful because they are partially learned materials (Stroud, 1956, p. 437). Insight occurs only when transfer is made from one situation to another.

No educator questions the importance of transfer of learning. If transfer were not possible, the learner would have to acquire new behavior for each new situation. The important questions are how, when, where, and why transfer occurs. Unfortunately too often the learnings of the classroom seem designed only for use within the classroom. They do not appear to fit directly into life situations. In short, they lack *belongingness*. Transfer is said to have occurred when something that is learned affects later relearning of the same thing or the acquisition of new responses. When one utilizes his past experience in reacting to a situation that has in it some element of newness, we conclude that there has been transfer of learning.

The learner originally makes specific responses to specific stimuli. When he learns to apply these responses in other situations, he has generalized his behavior. This generalization of behavior is a most important kind of transfer. Frequently generalization and transfer are used synonymously.

Generalizations require that differences as well as likenesses be discriminated. The decoding process in reading requires discrimination of similar, yet different stimuli (Gargiulo, 1971). When a teacher says to a child, "Look at the word" he is asking the learner to discriminate, by the shape and arrangement of letters, just what word is represented. In short, abstraction of relationship is involved.

KURT LEWIN AND EDWARD TOLMAN

Lewin's chief point of emphasis, in the Gestaltist tradition, was perhaps his insistence that analysis of behavior should begin with the total situation. He felt that theory should be multidimensional in scope, embracing a network of interacting variables rather than simply a pair of variables.

Lewin emphasized the need for a psychological analysis of behavior. For example, typing is not simply the accretion of S-R connections or even movements, as Guthrie suggested. Lewin pointed out that what the beginner is doing and what the proficient typist is doing are distinct. In Chapter 2 we pointed out that the child who is just beginning to learn to read and the skilled reader are identifying the word and reading in completely different ways.

Tolman's theory put major emphasis on the development of expectancies. Expectancy is represented by $S_1R_1S_2$ much as an association is represented by S-R; S_1 refers to the elicitor of an expectancy; R_1, to the response following this perception; and S_2, to the expectandum or significate, that something which is expected or the goal of the expectancy. The following example illustrates how an expectancy is formed. "When this *button* (S_1) is pressed (R_1), I *expect* to hear the ringing *doorbell* (S_2)" (Hilgard, 1956, p. 446). An expectancy refers to this process, prior to any occurrence of action. When the bell rings, my expectancy is confirmed and the attractiveness of the button is increased. The next time I wish to ring the doorbell, I push the button. Thus the incentive power of the doorbell will depend on my need to ring the doorbell as well as on the attractiveness of the button.

Tolman says that the learner follows signs to a goal, is getting a "feel" of the situation, and is learning meanings rather than movements. He learns sign-significate relationships or means-end relationships, that is, means to the goal. Learning involves the formation of a relationship between stimuli. In terms of Tolman's thinking, if S_1 occurs, we expect S_2. This is another way of saying, Given S_1, I judge or assert or suppose that S_2 will follow. This is cognition. An illusion results when S_1 is not followed by S_2. An error of omission occurs when S_1 is judged to be S_2 alone when in reality it is also S_3, S_4, etc.

Tolman's expectancy theory posits that in the presence of certain signs the learner expects to find a certain goal or goal object if he follows the customary behavior route.

Thorndike had said in answer to the question, "What is learned?," that we learn S-R bonds and that reward explains how we learn. Tolman insisted that we learn the whole sequence-the connection and the reward. The rat in essence learns the "good path with food at the end" better than the "bad path without food." It learns the relationship between what it does and the reward. The animal learns a path "as one where it expects to find food," and another path as "one where it does not expect to find food." The animal learns an expectancy.

A SYNTHESIS

We are now in a position to make some summary observations about S-R and Field Theories of Learning. Learning theorists in common have sought to discover and specify the experimental variables that control and determine behavioral changes that occur with practice, experience, or perception, and furthermore they have tried to formulate the functional interrelationships or laws that hold between these variables. (Bigge, 1966).

All theorists agree that the observable response is a function of the physical and social world and the condition of the organism. Furthermore, as we observe responses, we note changes in response and infer that these are accompanied by certain internal changes. These internal changes or hypothetical learning factors in turn affect present performance. Theorists agree that these internal events have their character partly determined by the impinging stimulus and partly by various organic states and past experience, but they disagree as to their conception of these hypothetical learning factors.

Psychologists today maintain that behavior is lawfully related to antecedent events, that phenomena are lawful, that the relationships can be quantitatively described (Immergluck, 1964) and that "science is concerned with the formulation of general, invariant functional relations between antecedent events and consequents." (Sells, 1963, p. 696) Behavior is lawful. Some call it deterministic.

Behaviorists assert that all behavior can be predicted and controlled in terms of habits established or shaped by a process of successive approximation by the reinforcement of a response in the presence of a particular stimulus.

Cognitive psychologists, on the other hand, see human beings as consumers of information (Smith, 1971, p. 68). To the cognitive psychologist what is interesting is the unobservable manner in which information is acquired and organized by the brain (Smith, 1971, p. 60). Reinforcement means people scale mountains, not from force of habit, but to see what is on the other side. They read books to find out what is in them. A reader extracts meaning from a sentence on the basis of the visual information (the surface structure of the language) and of the deep structure of the language and the knowledge in his brain.

Smith (1971, pp. 68–80) rejects the behaviorist view because:

1. There is no simple correspondence between sound (writing) and meaning.
2. Skill in language production and comprehension cannot have developed through the establishment of S-R bonds because practically all the sentences we speak or read are novel ones.

3. Perception is a constructive process, adding something to the stimulus aspects. A reader extracts meaning on the basis of the visual information (the surface structure of the language) and of the deep structure of the language and the knowledge in the brain. The reader makes decisions on the basis of two kinds of evidence: current information received from the environment by his receptor systems and the stored information that is available in memory. Writing cannot be comprehended unless the reader makes this critical, active contribution. Our fund of knowledge about the world is given a variety of technical names (cognitive schemata, cognitive structures, cognitive maps).

4. Since sentence meaning cannot be determined on a sequential word-by-word basis, information from several printed words has to be held in short term memory. The load on short term memory is reduced by "chunking" information into larger units (by storing words rather than letters, or meanings rather than words) (Smith, 1971, pp. 78–79).

For the field theorist the inner world of the individual is a significant datum and it sometimes has a more significant influence upon behavior than the external environmental stimulus.

In general, all theorists agree on the following points: learning situations involve stimuli and responses; motives initiate and direct behavior; responses are organized for the attainment of goals or ends; and goals, when attained and leading to the satisfaction of motives, also lead to the establishment of responses or expectancies. Hull spoke of drive, stimulus, response, and reinforcement; Lewin spoke of tension, path, vector, and valence; and Tolman, of demand, sign, expectancy, and goal object.

Hebb (1960) notes that Gestalt psychology is not an alternative to S-R learning theory; it has had rather a complementary and a corrective influence. It called for more adequate statement of the problem and for more adequate consideration of cognitive and innate factors.

The reading-learning process involves usually two persons: the teacher and the pupil. The teacher commonly is an indispensable ingredient of the learning process, but hardly any more so than the pupil. Education is essentially the internal process of learning and this occurs within a pupil. Learning is individual and until the teacher understands the nature of this individualness, he may not be able to teach the pupil in an optimum way.

When the teacher and child meet, a major part of the teacher's armament must be knowledge of principles of learning.

The following statements summarize learning principles discussed in this chapter that are particularly applicable in dealing with learning problems in the classroom.

1. All learning involves a stimulus (S), response (R), and a connection between the stimulus and the response. The pupil is stimulated by a book (S) and reads words, sentences, and paragraphs (R).

2. Learning proceeds best when the learner understands what he is doing.
   a. Teachers need to be aware that sometimes the pupil comes up with the

correct response by accident or by guessing, *without understanding why his answer is correct.*

b. The teacher needs to determine whether to reward the correct response, the correct process, or only the correct response when it is accompanied by the correct process. The pupil is not best served when the teacher simply feeds phonogram-phoneme relationships to children and cares only if the right response comes back. The child is not best served when the teacher rewards guesses or accidental solutions.

3. Learning is an associative process, but also a perceptual process.

4. The pupil learns by doing, learning occurs under conditions of practice, and overlearning is of crucial importance to poor readers. Children generally become better in word recognition the more frequently they see the word. However, practice or repetition per se does not cause learning. The pupil's practice must be both motivated and rewarded and it should be slightly varied from session to session. The reconditioning should have a creative aspect; it should not degenerate into drudgery (Steinkellner, 1967).

5. The learner learns best when he is psychologically and physiologically ready to respond to the stimulus. The learner will not respond unless he is motivated and he cannot learn unless he responds. The reader's performance will improve only if he is interested in his work, if he is interested in improving himself, if the material to be learned has special significance for himself, and if he is attentive to the situation. The student must recognize his reading problem as one he wants to solve (Steinkellner, 1967). Reduce motivations to zero, and there is no performance and, hence, no learning.

6. The learner cannot learn without doing, but he won't do anything without being rewarded. The best rewards in the reading setting are often pleasant pupil-teacher relationships, permissiveness on the part of the teacher, and feelings of success. The teacher must divide the learning situation into numerous small steps and must reward the learning of each discrete step.

7. Learning is often a matter of present organization and reorganization, not simply past accretion.

8. Letters might best be taught to most children as parts of a whole word, but the perceptual whole for the retarded reader often is the single letter. The size of the unit of instruction depends on the nature of the pupil, and many retarded readers benefit greatly from a synthetic-phonetic approach.

9. The teacher needs to ask himself whether he is trying to get the pupil to substitute one stimulus for another or whether he wants to elicit the correct response. In teaching the child to read, we obviously have a case of stimulus substitution. In essence we are asking the child to bring to the written word the same meanings that he previously attached to the spoken word.

10. Reading also involves response selection. A child who can read *the* and *there* may not be too sure of *their*. He makes provisional tries at the word and when he comes up with the correct pronunciational response the teacher reinforces this response, thus gradually stamping it in. Thus, from a series of possible responses the child gradually learns to select the correct response.

11. Each activity (reading of a sentence, for example) consists of a complex of individual movements, and improvement and learning are not necessarily attained by *much* reading but rather by increasing the number of correct movements in reading (moving from left to right, proper identification of the word, association of the proper meaning with the word, development of proper eye movements) and by reducing the number of incorrect movements (excessive regressions, improper word attack, etc.) in the total com-

plex of movements comprising the total capacity. Improvement occurs because the learner gradually replaces the erroneous movements that he still is making with correct ones. Thus additional practice gives more opportunity to master the myriad of movements comprising a complex total performance.

This view of the learning of a skill certainly emphasizes the need for the teaching of specific habits. Telling a retarded reader "to read" is not specific enough. We need to teach specific habits in specific situations. This requires careful job analysis, leading to an identification of all specific movements. The curriculum, methods and materials must be so specific that they will serve as proper stimuli to call forth appropriate responses. It is not enough to identify large, all-embracing abilities such as "gaining a sight vocabulary." It is necessary to break the broad area into basic subskills, such as the ability to discriminate between sounds, to see elements within a word, and to blend the elements into the total word.

12. When a stimulus is followed by a response, there is a tendency for the same response to occur when the stimulus recurs (Law of Contiguity). The pupil who responds to *was* with *saw,* on the next presentation of the stimulus *was,* tends to respond again with *saw.* In the classroom, much teaching follows this contiguity principle. The teacher shows the child a card containing the word "cat" and says "cat," and the assumption is that the child will, upon subsequent occasions, say the word "cat" when the same printed stimulus is presented alone.

It is important, especially when learning is a one-shot or a one-trial affair, that the teacher not permit the learner to leave a learning situation without performing the response correctly. A pupil should read the word correctly before going on to another word. Bugelski (1964, p. 104) decries that teachers allow children to do homework without having the answers supplied. He notes that such homework is not training or practice. It is a *test.*

The reader should not "get by" with approximations of the correct answer (Bugelski, 1964, p. 103). The pupil should not be permitted simply to get a "general idea." Teachers frequently give partial credit for partially correct answers. Partially correct answers such as reading *their* for *them* are in fact totally wrong. Bugelski (1964, p. 103) notes that "Too many students are rated as 'knowing what to do' without being able to do."

It may well be that when the teacher says to the reader, "read with care," the pupil is not learning the molar response of reading but rather the micromolar response "when you read, read slowly."

13. If the learner tends to repeat the response that was made most recently in the presence of the stimulus (Law of Relative Recency), the teacher should exercise great care, especially with the retarded reader, in not permitting extraneous materials to come between the stimulus and response. The teacher must see to it that when the response is made, it is made to the proper stimulus and not to any of many other possible stimuli that may have intervened. Too frequently in teaching, by the time the proper response occurs, the original stimulus situation has disappeared. The teacher must take great care that the necessary stimuli are so distinct for the pupil that he cannot help but see the connection between a given stimulus and the objective of teaching.

We have already suggested that learning is also a psychological and perceptual process. The incoming data (stimuli) are retained, processed, and reorganized by the viewer. This intermediary step, which is initiated by a stimulus and culminates in a response, is termed perception. This process modifies the stimulus data.

The facts of perception as they apply to the teaching of reading are essentially these:

1. Perception goes beyond sensation. Recognition of a word is not reading. The pupil must react with meaning and this frequently requires the organization of previous experiences. This is perception.

2. Perception of a word or the meaning taken to a word or series of words is usually representational, neither representing wholly or completely the meaning intended.

   The meanings taken to a word usually are many more than one, but also far fewer than they could be. The greater the number of meanings that are associable with a word, the more difficult it is to understand such a word and the less reliable the individual learner's meaning for such a word tends to be. This is why pupils have difficulty with multiple meanings of words.

3. The meaning comes from the learner rather than from the word and is determined primarily by the learner's previous experiences but also by his own constitutional make-up, by the number, quality, and organization of his experiences, by his ability to reconstruct his own experiences, by his affective state, and by his culture. The learner reacts as an organized whole.

4. The reaction to a word, the meaning in other words, is an indication that the learner has organized his experiences in a specific way.

5. The process whereby a figure arises from a ground is called differentiation. The pupil must be taught to use his experience and the context to differentiate the correct meaning from a series of meanings.

6. The child's differentiations are prevented or inhibited by such factors as visual or auditory inadequacies, brain injuries, lack of intelligence, lack of experience, etc. Learning retardation frequently results because the pupil cannot make the proper differentiations required for mastery of the learning task.

   Differentiations take time, and the teacher must constantly make adjustments for this. In classroom learning, the method of teaching can be simplified or made unnecessarily difficult. The teacher can arrange the learning situation in such a way that the differentiations come easily or are more difficult. With the retarded reader in particular, the learning task needs to be presented in structured, carefully-planned steps.

   The manner in which a problem is presented determines at least in some way whether past experiences can be used appropriately or not. Some classroom arrangements are more conducive than others to the elicitation of insightful solutions. The evidence indicates that with retarded readers, who often are weak in the visual association-memory area, materials should be presented through the auditory and kinesthetic channels.

QUESTIONS FOR DISCUSSION

---

1. What is the role of attention in perception?
2. What is the nature of perception?
3. What is the meaning of set? Discuss its implications in reading.

4. What is the significance of Hebb's physiological and Smith's chemical emphasis?

5. Is it possible to share directly one's concepts with another person?

6. Illustrate how the "perceptual field" influences the meaning content that the pupil takes to a word, sentence, or paragraph.

7. Explain: What is perceived frequently is not what actually is seen but what the perceiver believes he saw.

8. Define differentiation, learning, insight, communication, and transfer.

9. Discuss:
   a. All learning requires at least one performance, one association between a stimulus and a response.
   b. The good reader is differentiated from the poor reader in that he has made more distinct associative connections and he needs fewer cues to arouse responses. (He requires less and less stimulation to make more and more responses. This applies both to the perception as well as the recognition of words. Each word suggests a wider range of meaning, and he needs fewer cues to recognize a word).

BIBLIOGRAPHY

BIGGE, MORRIS L. "Theories of Learning." *Today's Education: NEA Journal* 55 (1966): 18–19.

BLANK, MARION; HIGGINS, THOMAS J.; and BRIDGER, WAGNER H. "Stimulus Complexity and Intramodal Reaction Time in Retarded Readers." *Journal of Educational Psychology* 62 (1971): 117–22.

BRUNSWIK, EGON. "Scope and Aspects of the Cognitive Problem." *Contemporary Approaches to Cognition.* Cambridge: Harvard University Press, 1957, pp. 5–31.

BUGELSKI, B. R. *The Psychology of Learning Applied to Teaching.* Indianapolis: Bobbs-Merrill, 1964.

COMBS, ARTHUR W., and SNYGG, DONALD. *Individual Behavior,* Revised edition. New York: Harper & Row, 1959.

COWLES, JOHN T. "Food Tokens as Incentives for Learning by Chimpanzees." *Comparative Psychology Monographs* 14 (1937): 1–96.

DEMBER, WILLIAM N. "Motivation and the Cognitive Revolution." *American Psychologist* 29 (1974): 161–68.

DOLLARD, J., and MILLER, N. E. *Personality and Psychotherapy.* New York: McGraw-Hill, 1950.

DUNLAP, K. *Habits: Their Making and Unmaking.* New York: Liveright, 1932.

FESTINGER, LEON. "The Relation Between Behavior and Cognition." *Contemporary Approaches to Cognition.* Cambridge: Harvard University Press, 1957, pp. 127–50.

FESTINGER, LEON. "Cognitive Dissonance." *Scientific American* 207 (1962): 93–102.

GARGIULO, RAYMOND J. "Applying Learning Theory to the Reading Process." *The Reading Teacher* 25 (1971): 20–23.

GUTHRIE, EDWIN R. *The Psychology of Learning,* New York: Harper and Brothers, 1952.

HEBB, DONALD OLDING. *A Textbook of Psychology.* Philadelphia: W. B. Saunders Co., 1958, p. 276 ff.

HEBB, DONALD OLDING. "The American Revolution." *American Psychologist* 15 (1960): 735–45.

HEBB, DONALD OLDING. "What Psychology Is About." *American Psychologist* 29 (1974): 71–78.

HILGARD, ERNEST R. *Theories of Learning,* 2nd. edition. New York: Appleton-Century-Crofts, 1956.

HILGARD, ERNEST R. "The Place of Gestalt Psychology and Field Theories in Contemporary Learning Theory." *Theories of Learning and Instruction.* Sixty-third Yearbook of the National Society of the Study of Education. University of Chicago Press, 1964, pp. 54–77.

HUNT, J. MCVICKER., "Experience and the Development of Motivation: Some Reinterpretations." *Child Development* 31 (1960): 489–504.

IMMERGLUCK, LUDWIG. "Determinism: Freedom in Contemporary Psychology." *American Psychologist* 19 (1964): 270–81.

JAMES, WILLIAM. *Principles of Psychology.* New York: Holt, Rinehart and Winston, 1890.

KINGSLEY, HOWARD L. and GARRY, RALPH. *The Nature and Conditions of Learning.* Englewood Cliffs, N. J.: Prentice-Hall, 1957.

LANGE, K. *Apperception: A Monograph on Psychology and Pedagogy,* edited by Charles De Garma. Boston: Heath, 1902.

LANGMAN, MURIEL POTTER. "The Reading Process: A Descriptive, Interdisciplinary Approach." *Genetic Psychology Monographs* 62 (1960): 1–40.

LASHLEY, K. S. "Persistent Problems in the Evolution of Mind." *Quarterly Review of Biology* 24 (1949): 28–42.

LINDSLEY, DONALD B. "Psychophysiology and Motivation." In Marshall R. Jones, ed., *Nebraska Symposium on Motivation.* Lincoln: University of Nebraska Press, 1957, pp. 44–105.

LOGAN, FRANK A. "Micromolar Behavior Theory and Performance Speed in Education." *Harvard Educational Review* 33 (1963): 178–85.

MCCLELLAND, DAVID C. "The Psychology of Mental Content Reconsidered." *Psychological Review* 62 (1955): 297–302.

MCDONALD, FREDERICK J. *Educational Psychology.* San Francisco: Wadsworth Publishing Company, 1959.

NELSON, FREDERIC. "How Well are We Teaching Reading?: Reply." *Controversial Issues in Reading* 1 (1961): 1–3. Tenth Annual Reading Conference, Lehigh University.

NISSEN, HENRY W. "The Nature of the Drive as Innate Determinant of Behavioral Organization." In Marshall R. Jones, ed., *Nebraska Symposium on Motivation.* Lincoln: University of Nebraska Press, 1954, pp. 281–321.

NOBLE, CLYDE E. "An Analysis of Meaning." *Psychological Review* 59 (1952): 421–30.

OTTO, WAYNE. "Inhibitory Potential in Good and Poor Achievers." *Journal of Educational Psychology* 56 (1965): 200–207.

OTTO, W. and FREDERICKS, R. C. "Relationship of Reactive Inhibition to Reading Skill Attainment." *Journal of Educational Psychology* 54 (1963): 227–30.

OTTO, WAYNE. "Reactive Inhibition (The Hullian Construct) and Achievement in Reading." *New Frontiers in College: Adult Reading.* Milwaukee: National Reading Conference, 1966.

OVERLINE, HARRY M. and QUAYLE, SUZANNE K. "Learning Disabilities from an Ecological Perspective." *Education* 92 (1971): 28–33.

PAVLOV, I. P. *Conditioned Reflexes.* London: Oxford University Press, 1927.

RAZRAN, GREGORY. "A Note on the Use of the Terms *Conditioning* and *Reinforcement.*" *American Psychologist* 10 (1955): 173–74.

ROGERS, CARL. *Client Centered Therapy.* New York: Houghton Mifflin, 1951.

ROGERS, CARL. "Toward a Science of the Person." In T. W. Wann, ed., *Behaviorism and Phenomenology.* Chicago: University of Chicago Press, 1964, pp. 109–49.

SCHEERER, MARTIN. "Cognitive Theory." In Garner Lindzey, ed., *Handbook of Social Psychology,* Vol. I. Cambridge: Addison-Wesley, 1954, pp. 91–142.

SCHUBERT, DELWYN G. "Negative Practice: Why Not Give It a Try?" *Education* 93 (1972): 80–81.

SELLS, S. B. "An Interactionist Looks at the Environment," *American Psychologist,* 18 (1963): 696–702.

SKINNER, B. F. "Reinforcement Today." *The American Psychologist* 13 (1958): 94–99.

SMITH, HENRY P. *Psychology in Teaching,* Revised edition. Englewood Cliffs, N.J.: Prentice-Hall, 1954, p. 210.

SMITH, FRANK. *Understanding Reading: A Psycholinguistic Analysis of Reading and Learning to Read.* New York: Holt, Rinehart and Winston, 1971.

STEINKELLNER, ROBERT H. "Reading Improvement Needs in High School." *Reading Improvement* 4 (1967): 77–79.

STROUD, JAMES B. *Psychology in Education.* New York: David McKay Company, 1956.

THOMPSON, WILLIAM R., and DEBOLD, RICHARD C. *Psychology: A Systematic Introduction.* New York: McGraw-Hill Book Co., 1971.

THORNDIKE, E. L. *Animal Intelligence.* New York: Macmillan, 1911.

THORNDIKE, E. L. *The Original Nature of Man.* Educational Psychology, Vol. I, Teachers College, Columbia University, 1913a.

THORNDIKE, E. L. *Psychology of Learning.* Educational Psychology, Vol. II, Teachers College, Columbia University, 1913b, 1930.

THORNDIKE, E. L. *Educational Psychology,* Teachers College, Columbia University, 1932.

THORNDIKE, E. L. *Man and His Works.* Cambridge: Harvard University Press, 1943.

TINKLEPAUGH, OTTO LEIF. "An Experimental Study of Representative Factors in Monkeys." *Journal of Comparative Psychology* 8 (1928): 197–236.

WATSON, JOHN B. "Psychology as the Behaviorist Views It." *Psychological Review* 20 (1913): 158–77.

WATSON, JOHN B. and RAYNER, ROSALIE. "Conditioned Emotional Reactions." *Journal of Experimental Psychology* 3 (1920): 1–14.

WOLFE, JOHN B., "Effectiveness of Token Rewards for Chimpanzees." *Comparative Psychology Monographs* 12 (1936): 1–72.

YANOFF, JAY M. "The Functions of the Mind in the Learning Process." In Melvin L. Silberman, Jerome S. Allender, and Jay M. Yanoff, eds., *The Psychology of Open Teaching and Learning.* Boston: Little Brown and Company, 1972, pp. 114–21.

5

The Psychological
Bases of Readiness

As teachers, we are intimately concerned with the readiness of individuals for learning. As teachers of reading, we wish to know the most favorable moment for beginning to teach a child to read and for the teaching of each specific reading skill. The readiness concept is not reserved for the period of beginning reading; it applies to all levels of reading development.

In the three previous chapters we have been concerned with the significance and importance of reading, the basic nature of the reading process, and the learning principles that should guide us in the teaching of reading. Here we wish to identify the determinants of reading readiness at all levels. Our basic question is: When is the child ready to learn to read and to learn each subsequent reading skill?

We know that in our culture all children must attempt to learn to read. Society demands that the child be a reader. A child who cannot read risks insecurity, loss of self-esteem, and an inability to pursue his future interests to fullest satisfaction.

THE NATURE OF READING READINESS

Havighurst has proposed that there are certain tasks that every child needs to accomplish. These he calls developmental tasks. He (1953, p. 2) identifies a developmental task as a task which arises during a certain period in the life of the individual, successful achievement of which leads to success with later tasks while failure leads to disapproval by the society and difficulty with later tasks.

Certainly reading qualifies as a developmental task. It is a task that the child must perform to satisfy his own needs and the demands of society. And reading readiness commonly is understood to be a developmental stage at which constitutional and environmental factors have prepared the child for reading.

Originally, the concept of readiness was reserved for readiness for initial reading. Lamoreaux and Lee, however, emphasized that each stage of reading is a step toward readiness for further reading (1943, p. 1). And Betts (1957, p. 104) pointed out that mental, emotional, and physical readiness for sustained reading activities has as much significance in a modern secondary school as it does in a modern primary school. Thus the reading readiness concept applies not only to initital reading instruction but to the teaching of every specific reading skill. And our interest in readiness continues throughout the developmental reading program. A child may become ready for learning to read by age six; most children will not become ready to read to learn until much later.

What are the factors that determine or characterize the teachable moment of reading? And which of these factors are most significant?

In attempting to answer the first question, authorities generally have suggested that a child's readiness for reading is dependent upon the following eleven factors:

1. Perceptual development
2. Intellectual development
3. Maturational adequacy, including the reader's sex
4. Background of personal experience
5. Auditory and visual discrimination skills
6. Language development
7. Sensory development
8. Health and freedom from neurological disturbances
9. Attitudes and motivation: interest in and desire for reading
10. Social and emotional development
11. Instructional methods and procedures

In this chapter our emphasis will be on factors two through six, namely the child's intellectual, maturational, and experiential readiness and his growth in sensory discrimination and language facility. Factors seven through eleven are discussed in later chapters. Chapter 3 emphasized the importance of perceptual readiness.

THE CORRELATES OF READING READINESS

A psychology of reading has to be concerned with child development. Reading cannot be completely understood until there is an understanding of the perceptual, cognitive, and developmental aspects of living and learning in general. The research tends to point to the acquisition of language and reading in some developmental fashion.

There thus has been a great deal of research on maturational and environmental and/or learning influences. In general, we have found that the human system can be programmed in three ways: structurally (genetically and through hereditary endowment); environmentally (by the environment with which it interacts); and by learning processes, (Blake, 1970, p. 94).

The determinants of learning and achievement are inextricably interrelated. Obviously, no one single factor determines a learner's success. It is rarely a single variable that accounts for reading disability. It is the pattern, the complex of correlates, with which we must be concerned. Lambert (1967) notes that we need to look for a multivariate rather than a single-variable cause for reading and achievement differences. The student must have a certain degree of readiness in each of the areas because each in its own way may contribute to reading disability or prevent future growth. It is illogical to expect to produce a successful reader by promoting growth and development in a few specifics while ignoring others. The teacher must examine the composite of interacting elements, and on the basis of them must identify each student's overall readiness for reading and learning.

Nevertheless, some factors contribute more to achievement than do others. They are relatively more important than others; they have a higher weight value in the correlate pattern. A student might be ready for reading in all areas except motivation. The absence of motivation alone may keep the student from learning. If the student does not want to read, no reading will occur.

The teacher must thus ascertain the student's readiness in each of the specifics. If some one element interferes with learning to read, it needs to be identified. The effect of inhibitory factors is multiplicative rather than additive.

Too often we look for the reason for reading success or failure in the wrong place. It is so easy to overplay the role of some of the correlates of reading disability that sometimes we may overlook the significant. Too often we look for and find a single cause in all reading disability cases. It is far too easy to assume that something is a cause when it may not be so. The measurable and the observable simply are not identical at times with the significant, and Pascal notes that "we should not judge the truth of things by our capacity to conceive them." A cause may well be shared in common by reading disability and by its correlates.

The causes of reading disability are so varied that the poor reader becomes the object of inquiry of many people, not always to his own advantage. The optometrist may discover an instance of exophoria and immediately conclude that this is the chief cause. The psychiatrist notices the pupil's anxiety and may conclude that this is the chief problem. Daddy and Mamma simply notice the boy's laziness.

And yet, proceeding as though correlation meant causation is not entirely without its heuristic values. Perhaps this is why it is so easy to equate the two. Correcting the visual problem, removing the anxiety, or motivating the student may be the best that we can do, and it is often better than nothing.

As we examine possible causal factors in reading achievement and disability, it is necessary to remember that sometimes the same behavioral characteristic may be both symptom and cause. A poor reader generally develops anxiety and perhaps even a dislike for reading. In this instance, anxiety and dislike for reading are symptoms. Anxiety may also initiate the reading disability by prohibiting the use of the student's intellectual energies. In the latter instance, anxiety may be the cause.

The student reads with his biology and his geography, with his nature and his nurture. He is a product of the interaction of heredity and environment, and these forces are accountable for the vast differences between students. No two students develop to the same point at the same time in any given characteristic. The uniqueness of the individual is a fundamental principle of human life (Tyler, 1969, p. 639). Growth and development are variable, and so is achievement in reading.

Four differing assumptions are today adduced to account for reading difficulty (Weiner and Cromer, 1967): Reading difficulty is attributed to some malfunction, preventing the student from benefiting from experience (damage to left cerebral hemisphere); to the absence of some function, which needs to be added (lack of phonic skills); to something that is present but must be removed (dislike for reading); or to mismatches between student and task (improper material, mode of instruction).

In evaluating causal factors in reading disability, the teacher needs to remember that when significant adults in a student's life believe the pupil can learn and achieve, he tends to do so (Ladd, 1967). In Russian schools children *do* learn to read and Durr and Hickman (1974) intimate that at least a partial explanation of this may be that in Russian schools parents and teachers and hence the children are convinced that the child *will* learn; in American schools the emphasis often is on why the child cannot or will not learn. In their diagnostic efforts teachers also must come to see that all mistakes in reading are significant. There simply is no such thing as a meaningless mistake (Ladd, 1967). Each mistake assists the teacher in planning correction and remediation.

The premises of this and the subsequent chapter are simply the following:

1. Reading is a response made by a learner and must be learned by a learner. The major element in any learning process is the learner. We must understand him.
2. Reading achievement is interrelated with the learner's total growth and development.
3. Growth and development of the learner are variable, and so is achievement in reading.
4. It is imperative that the teacher understand the causes for this variability in achievement.
5. Those variables (adequate experience, etc.) that are associated with good achievement in reading, if absent (lack of experience), may become causes for reading deficiency.
6. There is for each student a teachable moment for learning each of the reading skills. This teachable moment depends on those elements with which this chapter deals.

Let us now examine more closely some of the factors that make for achievement or lack of achievement in reading.

Intellectual Readiness

Numerous writers have emphasized that intelligence is an extremely important determinant of reading readiness and general reading achievement. We should expect this to be true. Reading is a thinking process. Essentially intelligence implies the ability to learn and to apply what is learned. Both the reading skill itself and the background necessary for the reading-thinking process must be learned.

Harrison (1939, pp. 8–9) has suggested that the successful reader must see likenesses and differences, remember word forms, must have a memory span of ideas, must be able to do abstract thinking, and he must be able to correlate abstractions with definite modes of response as this ability is related to the reading process.

The child must be able to tell stories in proper sequence, to interpret pictures, to associate symbols or language with pictures, objects and facts, to anticipate what may happen in a story or poem, to express his thoughts in his own words, and to think on an abstract level. He must be able to give identity and meaning to objects, events, and symbols. He must be able to categorize or to associate the particular object or experience with the appropriate class or category.

Intellectual development is a function of both biology and environment. Biology sets the limits to the child's mental development, and how close the child comes to attaining his potential depends upon the environment and the use that he makes of that environment. It depends also upon other factors, among which are opportunity, challenge, desire, nutrition, rest, self-discipline, aggressiveness, and the need to achieve. Thus, biology provides the potential and the environment converts it into abilities. "Native ability" actually is the potential to become able; ability is realized potential.

Intelligence always has been difficult to define. Surely one of the reasons for this is the removal of intelligence from the realm of time. A child's potential for intellectual activity at the moment of conception may not be the same as his potential at birth or indeed at any given moment of life.

At conception the child possesses what might be described as native intellectual endowment. Biology has set a limit at that time to the child's intellectual capacity. In a later portion of this book we discuss the human brain. The brain is biologically determined and the "mind," "intellect," "cognition," or "perception" must operate through this brain. In a very real sense, man's potential for intellectual behavior is completely dependent upon the proper functioning of the brain.

Aphasia is an instance of improper brain functioning. As a result of cerebral injury, the aphasic is unable to deal with symbols. He can think only on a concrete or specific level. He cannot think abstractly, he cannot categorize, and he is unable to think of the individual object as a member of a class. He cannot, for example, see that a polar bear and a brown bear are bears. These have an individuality for him that does not allow for categorization.

If brain injury can so limit human thought, biology can do likewise. Inadequacy in the genes is a very real cause of inadequate brain development. Nervoid idiocy, amaurotic idiocy, gargoylism (grotesque bone structure), phenylpyruvic idiocy, and primary microcephaly, to mention a few, are caused by gene disturbances.

Intelligence in this sense is, according to Eames (1960, p. 16), the functional manifestation of the integrity of the central nervous system. Thus the intelligence manifested by a person bears a relationship to the structural and functional state of his brain. Damage or failure of development of a part of it is likely to produce corresponding variations in the capacity to perform the functions affected by the part (Eames, 1960, p. 16).

Intelligence can be viewed in another way. At the moment of birth the child has an intellectual potential that has been limited and defined by biology but now also is conditioned by environment. The child's intrauterine existence may have been favorable, or it may have been unfavorable for the realization of the child's full intellectual potential at the moment of conception.

Experience has shown repeatedly that the brain, and hence the intellectual functioning of the child, may be damaged by infection, by birth trauma, by toxic agents, or by endocrine disorders. It may be damaged by pressure upon the fetus, by faulty position of the fetus, by temperature changes, by overexposure to X-rays, by premature separation from the placenta, by umbilical-cord complications, by an overdosage of the mother with drugs, by delayed breathing of the infant, or by forceps delivery. Barbiturates may produce asphyxiation in the fetus. The mother also can pass diseases on to the child that interfere with normal brain development. Some common ones are: smallpox, German measles, scarlet fever, syphilis, and tuberculosis.

Finally, intelligence may be viewed as the child's present functioning level. This is essentially what scholastic aptitude tests measure. However, if the child's environment or experience is defective, it frequently happens that a measure of the pupil's present functioning level is not a good indicator of his true potential. It is not uncommon to have a pupil obtain scores like the following on a group intelligence test: linguistic IQ–85; quantitative IQ–115; and total IQ–100. The linguistic score and the total score probably are the best predictors of the child's present scholastic functioning level. Scholastic functioning depends most on the child's ability to deal with symbols, and the linguistic score measures this ability. The quantitative score may be closer to the pupil's true potential. The chances are that a pupil with such discrepancies between linguistic and quantitative scores is from a poor cultural environment, has a reading problem, and/or is bilingual. If the causative factor is removed, it is not uncommon to find that the IQ score of such a pupil will rise from fifteen to twenty points.

The teacher essentially is an environmentalist. Even though he cannot add to the child's basic capacity, he can do much to encourage the child to develop his potential. The child commonly has a much greater mental capacity than he is willing to use. As teachers, our task is to challenge the existent capacity of the pupil rather than to try to add increments to his native endowment.

In the light of the above discussion the biological-environmental[1] controversy, despite the controversy centering around Arthur B. Jensen and William Schockley, seems to be a pseudo-conflict. The relative contribution of biology, for example, depends on the trait under consideration, upon the individual possessing the trait, and upon the environment. Thus, in some environments, the principal cause of reading inadequacy may be biological in origin; in others, where there is inadequate teaching, it may be environmental. Anastasi and Foley (1958, p. 11) point out that most hereditary-or-environmental discussions are actually concerned with structural or functional factors. Teachers are more concerned with the following: "Is reading failure caused by structural or functional conditions?"   •

Blatt and Garfunkel (1967) note that it just could be that whatever intelligence tests measure (ability to learn, capacity to profit from experience, innate potential) may not be malleable, but it also may not be intelligence. Boyer and Walsh (1968), on the other hand, *a la* John Locke feel that intelligence is merely the sum total of environmental input. Gaudia (1973) advocates, like we have above, a position between extreme environmentalism and biological determinism.

Mental Age

Mental age (M.A.) refers to the level of mental growth that has been achieved. It is the pupil's score on an intelligence test expressed in age units, or put another way, it is the average age of the individuals who attained that score in the standardization process (Stroud, 1956, pp. 216–217). An average six-year-old child will have a mental age of six; an average child of ten, a mental age of 10; an average youth of fifteen, a mental age of fifteen. And any child making the same score on the test that was made by the average child of any given age is assumed to have that mental age. Mental growth has been assumed to continue at a fairly constant pace until about age fifteen or sixteen after which time scores on intelligence tests on an average no longer increase significantly. Thus an average youth of twenty will still have a mental age of but 15 or 16.[2]

Intelligence Quotient. Another term, the intelligence quotient, (IQ) is a statement of the rate of mental growth. We all remember the simple rate, time, and distance formulas: distance equals rate multiplied by time (D = R × T) and rate equals distance divided by time (R = D ÷ T).

---

[1] We prefer the term biological-environmental to hereditary-environmental.

[2] Some studies indicate that mental age scores may continue to increase beyond the chronological ages of fifteen or sixteen.

We may use an analogous formula in thinking about mental age and IQ: thus, MA = IQ × CA. In the formula MA refers to the distance that the pupil has traveled mentally; the IQ refers to the rate at which he has been going; and the CA refers to the length of time that he has been at it.

If we think of an IQ of 120 as meaning that the person has advanced at the rate of 1.2 years mentally for each year of chronological life (up to the age of fifteen or sixteen), and of an IQ of 80 as meaning that he has advanced 0.8 of a year mentally for each year of chronological life, the formula (MA = IQ × CA) is easy to understand and to use. A ten-year-old boy with an IQ of 120 has a mental age of twelve (MA = IQ × CA—1.2 × 10). Another ten-year-old with an IQ of 80 has a mental age of 8 (MA = IQ × CA—0.8 × 10). The first boy has attained the mental level of the average twelve-year-old; the second, the mental level of the average eight-year-old.

There are four statements that we can make about the IQ:

1. IQ is the rate of mental development
2. $IQ = \dfrac{MA}{CA} \times 100$
3. An IQ of 120 means that the individual has developed 1.2 years mentally for each year of chronoligical life
4. An IQ of a given magnitude also describes the percentage of children in the general population that possess that IQ

Let us give some consideration to this last point. IQ also may be defined in terms of a relative position among a defined group of persons. An IQ tells how much above or below the average an individual is when comparing himself with persons of his own age. It measures the person's ability relative to persons of his own age group.

Mental age scores have been found to be closely related both to reading readiness and to reading achievement. Generally, mental age scores correlate highly with reading-readiness test scores. In numerous studies and summaries of research the correlation between these two sets of scores has been found to range from about .35 to .80. We know that reading-achievement test scores also correlate highly with intelligence-test scores. This leads us to conclude that to a large extent reading-achievement and reading-readiness tests measure the same factors that are measured by intelligence tests.

Bond and Tinker (1967) report that by the end of the first grade the correlation between intelligence and reading ability (achievement) is generally around .35, but by the sixth grade it increases to .65. Cohen and Glass (1968) found no significant relationship between IQ scores and reading ability in first grade; in the fourth grade, IQ and reading ability were significantly related. De Hirsch and Jansky (1970) and Slobodzian (1970) also report low correlations between reading achievement and intelligence test scores on the kindergarten-primary level. These findings suggest that mental age actually is a more basic determinant of reading success when children have reached the stage at which they *read to learn* than it is when they are *learning to read.*

Although there is a high relationship between mental age scores and reading test scores, it also is true that a high correlation is quite different from a perfect correlation. So long as the interrelation between two factors is imperfect, we expect to find that other factors are operating. Clearly, we cannot expect to predict reading readiness on the basis of intellectual development or mental age scores alone.

There are many possible reasons for poor reading. A child's desire and will to learn, his attentiveness, his habits of work, and his persistence are important variables. Various problems of emotional and physiological development also may contribute to reading failure. We also realize that the age for learning to read under one program or with the method employed by one teacher may be entirely different from that required under other circumstances. And, the mental age required for learning to read is directly related to the provisions for individual differences that are made within the classroom. It seems likely that in those instances in which very young children learn to read there is a combination of favorable circumstances and that both high intelligence and extreme individualization of instruction are most important factors.[3]

In general, the evidence concerning intellectual development and readiness to read cautions us that no single index can guarantee success in reading. The child's wants, interests, and attitudes, and his levels of physiological maturation may be at least as important as his level of mental development in determining whether or not he will learn to read.

Maturational Factors

Even though maturational factors might more logically be discussed in Chapter 7, we include a discussion of them here because the pupil's achievement depends on both maturation and experience. Baller and Charles (1961, p. 22) note that "Maturation is an unfolding or 'ripening' of potentials that an individual possesses by virtue of his being a member of a given species and by virtue, more specifically, of his biological inheritance from a particular heritage." [4]

We generally assume that the child receives his biological inheritance through maturation, while he acquires his social inheritance through learning. Maturation, however, is a prerequisite to much learning, and environment and experience are prerequisite to maturation. Gesell and Ilg (1949) suggest that readiness for learning results more from internal unfolding rather than from external stimulation. Nevertheless readiness is dependent upon appropriate stimulation, relevant learn-

---

[3]We will look at this matter in greater detail in the latter part of this chapter under the heading "When Is the Child Ready?"

[4]Baller, Warren R., and Charles, Don C. *The Psychology of Human Growth and Development.* Holt, Rinehart and Winston, Inc., New York, 1961.

ing experiences, practice, and integration of information. And, certain patterns of growth of neural structures must occur before certain experiential factors can effectively contribute to development.

Bruner (1962) adds a slightly different dimension when he observes that readiness for learning depends more on our ability to translate ideas into the language and concepts at the age level we are teaching than on maturation.

The pupil's achievement is certainly affected by inadequacies and delays in maturation or in development of the physical-physiological functions. There is a difference between maturational delays and developmental delays (Belmont, 1964). Developmental delays are delays in progress in which the experiential factors play a predominant role; in maturational delays physical-physiological factors are of primary importance.

Belmont (1964) notes that the stage as well as the rate of physical maturation influence and probably are influenced by the nature of the child's experience. And Harris (1962, p. 3) writes: "Without maturation the child cannot learn; without experience he has nothing to learn."

Belmont adds that just as it is very difficult for a seven-month-old child to establish voluntary control over bowel function for biological reasons (the nerve pathways necessary for this function are not yet completely myelinated, and, hence, are not voluntarily operational) so there are varying degrees of biological maturational preparedness to undertake learning.

Maturational changes usually are orderly and sequential. Wide variations of environmental conditions seem to have little effect on maturation. The nervous system develops regularly according to its own intrinsic pattern. There thus seems to be very little benefit in rushing the maturation process. For example, we don't teach the child to swing a bat before he is capable of lifting a bat. The child learns to talk only after he is old enough. Practice needs to wait for maturation.

However, teaching and other environmental stimulations are not useless. Children need appropriate environmental stimulation if maturational development is to progress at an appropriate rate. In many instances the child has inadequacies in his experiential background. The teacher cannot overemphasize either maturation or experience-learning. Too much emphasis on maturation may lead to useless postponing of what could be learned; too much emphasis on learning or experience may lead to futile attempts at teaching that for which the child is not ready. Nevertheless, instruction must march slightly ahead of development. "It must be aimed not so much at the ripe as at the ripening function" (Vygotsky, 1952, p. 104).

In summary:

1. Students generally become ready for specific learning tasks at different ages.
2. Students develop reading skills most readily if they are built upon the natural foundation of maturational development. They put most effort into

tasks that are neither too difficult nor too easy, that are within their "range of challenge"—that are possible for them but not necessarily easy.

3. Students should not be forced into readiness for either beginning reading or for any subsequent reading skill before maturational development is adequate. Such premature training may lead to no improvement, to only temporary improvement, or to actual harm. Premature training may destroy the student's natural enthusiasm for a given activity, and it is doubtful that drill and exercises will ever be a substitute for maturation.

4. Generally, the more mature the student is, the less training is needed to develop a given proficiency.

5. The teacher can promote the student's readiness for a given learning task by filling the gaps in his experience.

6. Readiness may refer to an intrinsic state of the organism, but also to the extrinsic acculturation of the organism (Beckett, 1964). The latter is often referred to as building readiness, but some note that readiness comes with age, not with special drills or practice. It may be that both concepts have meaning in that a student is more or less ready dependent upon the method and materials used in teaching and that building readiness comes to mean such things as removing blocks to learning and filling gaps of experience. Readiness may depend more on our ability to translate ideas into the language and concepts of the age level we are teaching than on maturation (Bruner, 1962). Pestalozzi in 1802 said it very beautifully when he wrote: "To instruct man is nothing more than to help nature develop in its own way, and the art of instruction depends primarily on harmonizing our messages, and the demands we make upon the child, with his powers at the moment."

Sex and Readiness

Teachers have always been concerned with differences in achievement between boys and girls. One of the more obvious differences is in achievement in reading. Girls as a group achieve better than boys in reading. They learn to read earlier, and fewer of them are significantly retarded in reading. They generally seem to perform better than boys in English usage, spelling, and handwriting.

Girls and boys exhibit differences also in other areas. For example, the incidence of stuttering and brain damage is substantially greater among boys. Boys also tend to lisp and lall more. Girls tend to be better than boys in visual discrimination and boys have poorer listening habits and greater difficulty with auditory discrimination (Stanchfield, 1971; Dykstra, 1966). The incidence of left-handedness, ambidexterity, and high-frequency hearing loss is greater among boys.

Males show greater susceptibility to stress (Bentzen, 1966) as indicated by higher mortality rate from conception and higher morbidity rates, being affected to a greater degree than girls by albinism, congenital, night and color blindness, hemophilia, shortsightedness and retinal detachment. The incidence is greater also for epilepsy, schizophrenia, infantile autism, and feeblemindedness. The brain control center is on the same side as the dominant hand five times more frequently among boys than among girls (Sexton, 1969). The fontanelle closes earlier in girls and the bones and muscles of girls develop their strength earlier. Female superiority is shown also in wrist movement, fine finger movement, and manual dexterity, clerical aptitude, verbal fluency, and rote memory. Boys show superiority in spatial relationships, problem solving, and mechanical aptitude.

Numerous attempts have been made to explain the differences in reading achievement. In general, the explanations have emphasized either heredity or environment. It has been suggested that girls have an inherited language advantage or that they reach maturity about a year and a half earlier than boys. Bentzen (1963) advances the hypothesis that the boy's problems stem from the stresses put on his immature organism by a society that fails to make appropriate provisions for the biological age differential between boys and girls. Since attainment of a skill or neuromuscular maturation seems to depend upon the myelination of the motor and association tracts, myelination may be completed earlier in girls than in boys.

The evidence also seems to indicate that there are sex differences in general educational achievement. In general, the girls establish a definite superiority in educational achievement during the elementary grades, but much if not all of their advantage disappears by the time high school is reached. Perhaps this is because different elements are emphasized in high school. History and science tend to replace some subjects such as spelling and handwriting in which girls generally excel. However, girls do maintain their superiority in English usage throughout the high-school years.

The differences between girls and boys in reading readiness and achievement seem genuine and we must look for reasons. An examination of certain related data may help us to come to a better understanding of the problem as well as to arrive at useful conclusions.

Generally, by the twentieth month of life, girls show some superiority in the production of speech sounds. McCarthy (1935) states that in the prelinguistic or babbling stage no appreciable differences are noticeable, but she cites evidence that differences appear in the second year of life. Durrell (1940, p. 281) found that even when children are equated on oral language achievement there are still twice as many reading disability cases among boys as among girls. Gallagher (1948) indicates that the difference might be explained on the basis of heredity and suggests that a substantial deviation in the language mechanism may be a primary cause of reading disability. Sheridan (1948, p. 8) also suggests that girls, even those of lesser intelligence, have a superior language sense. Some writers stress maturational differences, particularly in emotional and intellectual development. Others intimate that girls possess a natural advantage of interest in verbal rather than mechanical or athletic activities.

It has been suggested that the prevalance of women teachers may be a determining factor. Back in 1909 Ayres (p. 158) concluded that schools were better fitted to the needs and natures of girls than of boys. He felt that the poorer showing of the boys was the result of over-feminization.

St. John (1932, p. 668), studying some 500 boys and 450 girls in Grade One to Six, suggested that the difference was due chiefly to a maladjustment between the boys and their teachers. A study by Davis and Slobodian (1967), however, indicated that teachers showed no differences in verbal behavior toward boys and girls. They report that teachers did not call on girls with greater frequency, did not direct more negative comments toward boys, and did not treat boy-responses differently during reading instruction. Apparently, on the basis of this study, differential teacher behavior is not a significant cause of sex differences in reading achievement.

Betts (1957, p. 137) observed that girls are promoted on lower standards of achievement than boys are and girls use reading activities for recreation more often than boys do.

The expectations of society require boys and girls to play distinctly different roles. Girls are supposed to be good, feminine, and to achieve in school. On the other hand, boys are expected to be active and to excel in sports rather than in books. Girls, in addition, before coming to school engage in numerous activities that may better prepare them for reading. In their weaving, sewing, and doll playing they have more opportunity to develop near vision and motor coordination (Durkin, 1966b, p. 27). Girls use reading more frequently for recreation than do boys. Reading materials generally are more in accordance with the interests of girls. Firester and Firester (1974) stress that strong social forces (excessively feminine atmosphere especially) within the school, make it difficult for boys to cope. Retention rates are higher for boys, boys exhibit more behavior problems, and boys often suffer decrease in self-esteem.

Certainly, not all reading disability cases are referred to the reading clinic. And of those who are referred not all of them may be referred for reading disability alone. It is quite possible that boys more frequently than girls tend to manifest their reading problems through aggressive tendencies, and as a result more of them are referred to the clinic. Boys are clearly more openly aggressive (Storr, 1968). The reading problems of well-behaved tractable girls may go undetected, or may be taken care of in the classroom (Vernon, 1957, p. 114).

A recent study by Naiden (1976) of 14,700 students or the entire fourth, sixth and eighth grade school population in the Seattle Public Schools, found that the ratio of boys to girls with significant deficit in reading was three to two, not the three or four to one reported in most studies of reading clinic populations. Naiden added that her data indicate that there are large numbers of female students with serious reading deficits who are not finding their way to the reading diagnostician.

Some studies have indicated that intelligence is more variable among boys than among girls—more boys than girls have extremely low as well as extremely high intelligence quotients. This would lead us to expect that the reading ability of boys might also be more variable and that a larger number of boys would be poor readers (Vernon, 1957, p. 112).

A comparative study (Preston, 1961) of reading in Germany and the United States revealed that the mean reading scores of fourth- and sixth-grade German boys exceeded those of German girls and that the variability of scores was greater among the girls than among the boys. These findings are just the reverse of those in this country and suggest that sex differences may best be explained by cultural and environmental factors. It is interesting to note that the teaching staffs in Germany, even in elementary school, are predominantly male. Gentile (1975) found that at least in one grade, male tutorship was associated with greater gains in the reading achievement of Mexican-American boys.

However, Orlow (1976) reports that German reading authors such as Kowarik (1973) state that three to four times as many boys as girls have reading difficulty in Germany and Orlow's own experience in Germany tended to bear this out. There is an indication even here, however, that a disproportionate number of boys are placed in remedial classes because of personality factors.

That there are sex differences in readiness and reading achievement in favor of the girls in this country can hardly be questioned. There also are vast differences among boys themselves, and many six-year-old boys are more mature than the average six-year-old girl. What educational implications do these differences have? Two educational recommendations have been based on these differences. Some have suggested that boys begin first grade later than girls; other have suggested that separate mental age norms be devised for girls and boys.

Clark (1959), in a study of third, fifth, and eighth graders, found no significant differences between the sexes in reading vocabulary, reading comprehension, and arithmetic reasoning. In mechanics of English, however, the fifth- and eighth-grade girls did better than the boys. In spelling, the girls had better scores at all three grade levels. Thus, even when differences that are attributable to age and mental age are held constant, the girls still excelled in spelling and English mechanics.

Educational provisions must ultimately be for the individual pupil. It is not enough to know what is best for the group. It is not enough to know what type of reading program would benefit most boys or girls. The teacher must prescribe for the individual boy and girl, and as soon as he attempts this, he realizes that differences between boys and girls and between one boy and another—differences other than sex—play a significant role in reading achievement.

Nevertheless, the variations among children in readiness for reading demand that educational adjustments be made. Delayed entrance to school would be a negative approach whether the variations are due primarily to differences in rate of maturation or to differences in the cultural stimulation of the home. The school must somehow offer a planned program of experiences that will build a framework of readiness as rapidly as possible on whatever abilities the child possesses. The solution probably lies in a delay of formal reading instruction until the child is ready for it and in an early provision of experiences that will prepare him for reading.

Experiential Readiness

In Chapter 3 we discussed the importance of experience as a determinant of perceptual readiness. Experience is the basis for all educational development. Concepts develop from experience, and their richness and scope are in direct proportion to the richness and scope of the individual's experience. One of the more naive beliefs is that a student's academic performance is a simple function of innate ability. The most important reason for the difference between the adult's concepts and the child's concepts is the differential in experience and knowledge. And, frequently, the significant reason for differences in reading achievement is the differential in experience, and opportunity for experience often depends on whether or not one is favored by socioeconomic status. Callaway (1972), studying 408 fourth-grade children and 400 seventh-grade children, found that the amount of reading materials in the home was a significant determinant of reading achievement. A study of reading comprehension in fifteen countries (Thorndike, 1973) showed a very large difference in reading level between the developed and developing countries. The difference was so large that by the standards of the developed countries, the fourteen-year-olds in the developing countries seemed almost illiterate. In the developed countries the home and family backgrounds of the children were the principal determinant of reading achievement. When the children come from homes in which the parents are well-educated, economically advantaged, and provide reading materials, the children generally show a superior level of reading achievement. The clear result of this study was that good home environmental backgrounds provide strong differentiation between countries and, within countries, between students.

Benson (1969, p. 266) suggests that in middle class communities the number of children retarded in reading is between 10 and 20 percent whereas in low socioeconomic areas the range is as high as 80 percent.

Frasure and Entwisle (1973), studying kindergarten, first, and third grade children, found evidence for significant semantic development between the ages of five and eight for all children with rates of growth decreasing for white middle class children and increasing for black lower class children. The rate for white lower class children was fairly constant. Performance based on syntax improved more with age, with the middle class children making use of syntactic information earlier (Kindergarten-grade one) than lower class children (between first and third grade).

Montagu (1971) points to social malnutrition resulting from exposure to inadequate and confusing stimuli in early years, preventing some children from realizing their genetic potential. Vilscek (1964) found a functional relationship between socioeconomic class and mental age. The lower the mental age of the pupil, the higher the socioeconomic level had to be for initial learning to read; and conversely, the lower the socioeconomic level, the higher the mental age had to be. However, Callaway (1972) found that income of the family and occupations of the parent were not significantly related to reading achievement.

Socioeconomic status is an individual's position in a given society, as determined by wealth, occupation, and social class. Social class in turn is a grouping or division of a society, made up of persons having certain common social characteristics and usually formed on a combination of criteria: similarities in education, vocation, value systems, custom, family, and wealth. It is an aggregate of individuals who occupy broadly similar positions on the scale of prestige.

Social class provides certain economic advantages for the student, but it also determines what goals the student will seek, what attitudes he will hold, how motivated toward school he will be, his interest in school and its curricular offerings, and the friends he will choose, and it is positively related to intelligence, adjustment, achievement, educational level attained, church activity, interests, age of marriage, work adjustment, educational aspiration, and language experience and skills. Social class is one of the chief factors that helps to account for the individual differences among students and as such is a determinant of individual differences in behavior, learning, and achievement.

Most studies show that pupils from upper-socioeconomic homes come to school more ready than those from lower-socioeconomic homes to learn the tasks needed for success The middle class home contains "a hidden curriculum" (Henry, 1963) which permits the pupil to deal appropriately with school experiences. Even the amount and kinds of reading are different in different sections of the country, among various occupational groups, and among individuals of various socioeconomic groups. Barton (1962) found in a survey of twelve hundred teachers that the most important single determinant of success in reading in school is socioeconomic class. When he divided classrooms according to the socioeconomic status of the pupil's parents (using a combination of income and occupation), he found that reading retardation rose steadily through the first six grades for working class children and especially for the lower skilled. Worley and Story (1967) found that the language facility of first-grade children from low socioeconomic groups was over a year below that of children from high socioeconomic status. The evidence shows that black children do not read as well as white children on an average, not because of an absence of symbolic activity, but because the black student, especially from lower socioeconomic groups, has a different cultural base in which the language is different from that of the middle class white person. It may also well be that students from lower-socioeconomic homes are at a distinct disadvantage in learning to read because they have spoken and heard language patterns that interfere with the comprehension of both oral and written materials. It is important to point out that the socially deprived do not lack the capacity to develop the cerebral functions upon which advanced learning is based. They simply have not had the opportunity to do so.

Although socioeconomic status is not a completely accurate indicator of reading achievement, it generally goes hand in hand with broadness of experience and with language facility (Worley and Story, 1967). This broadness of experience and the added language facility result in superior achievement in reading by equipping the pupil with the tools for meaningful reaction to the printed page. The symbols on the page are empty unless the reader endows them with meaning. For this the reader needs the appropriate experience. Smith (1974) after summarizing the research concluded that low self-concepts, health defects, and impoverished environment all interfere with reading achievement.

The following statements summarize the importance of experience and, indirectly, of socioeconomic status for reading achievement:

1. Experience is one factor that accounts for differences in reading achievement, and lack of experience may be a cause of reading disability.
2. Experience and maturation are the basis of all educational development. To predict behavior, both the person and the environment must be considered as a constellation of interdependent factors.
3. Differences in learning ability of pupils are related to their biological potentials, but also to the environmental opportunities. Some pupils become reading disability cases because the environment does not call forth their potential.
4. It is impossible to predict the learning of a child without knowing the structure of his social environment, the types of behavior that are rewarded, and the types of rewards that are provided.
5. The pupil from the middle class home has an advantage because his home contains "a hidden curriculum" (Henry, 1963), which permits him to deal appropriately with school experiences.

Auditory Discrimination

Skills in auditory and visual discrimination certainly are major factors in perceptual development. Studies generally have indicated that these skills also are closely related to readiness for reading.

As early as 1886 Charcot noted that each person has a preferred modality. For some time readers have been described as visual learners, auditory learners, kinesthetic learners, or combinations of them.

Harrington and Durrell (1955) concluded from their study that auditory and visual discrimination of word elements appears to be more closely related to the acquisition of the primary-grade reading vocabulary than is mental age. The study cautions against placing too great a stress on intelligence as the major factor in reading readiness.

Nila (1953) concluded that the four chief factors related to reading readiness were auditory discrimination, visual discrimination, range of information, and mental age, in that order. Linder and Fillmer (1970) found that minority second-grade poor readers do have a preference for one modality over another. Their data also indicated that auditory factors may be a better predictor of reading achievement than visual perception.

Other studies suggest that we must give increasing consideration to auditory and visual factors in reading. Nicholson (1958), for example, concluded that a knowledge of the names of letters is the best guarantee that a child will learn to read. Tests measuring ability to associate the name of a letter with its form showed the highest correlations with learning rate for words. Olson's work (1958) suggested that while a knowledge of letter names does not always assure high reading achievement, the lack of that knowledge assures low reading achievement. De Hirsch, Jansky, and Langford (1966) found that a lack of letter-naming ability was predictive of reading failure. And Robeck (1972) noted that the value to the learner of knowing letter names appears to be a way of labeling and separating the symbols so that they can be discriminated more easily. Barrett's studies (1965, 1967) confirmed these findings.

Samuels (1971), however, found that letter-name knowledge did not facilitate word recognition. He concluded that previous correlations between letter-name knowledge and reading are the product of perhaps intelligence or socioeconomic status. For example, the kind of home background which enables a first grader to know many of the letters of the alphabet is also the kind of home in which academic achievement is stressed. And, the ability to learn to name letters is probably an index of intelligence. Letter-sound training seemed to have a facilitative effect in decoding unfamiliar words. These findings are supported by Inselberg (1972) and Johnson (1969). Ohnmacht (1969) found that knowledge of letter names had no direct beneficial effect on learning to read. Jenkins, Bausell and Jenkins (1972) report that with first graders grapheme-phoneme knowledge produced greater transfer than grapheme-name knowledge.

Walcutt, Lamport, and McCracken (1974, p. 111) reconcile the contradictory data by noting that the child who knows letter names has made the *progress in cognition* that enables him to cope with the first steps in reading when he comes to them.

Strag and Richmond (1973) report a positive correlation between auditory discrimination and reading achievement and indeed between socioeconomic status and achievement. Slobodzian (1970) found auditory-vocal association to be related significantly to reading achievement. De Hirsch and Jansky (1970) report that the ability to hear sounds is highly related to reading achievement; writing a name and ability to name letters were also predictive of reading success. Kohn and Birch (1968) report that even when IQ was held constant competence in auditory-visual functions was positively related to reading achievement through grade six.

Rosner (1973) reported correlations between first graders' beginning-of-the-year auditory analysis skills and their end-of-year reading achievement scores ranging from .50 to .65.

Hammill and Larsen (1974), however, suggest that auditory skills (auditory discrimination, memory, blending, or auditory-visual integration) are not sufficiently related to reading to be particularly useful for school practice. They did not find that auditory perceptual deficits explained reading deficiency. They caution the reader not to generalize that auditory acuity, listening comprehension, or phonic skills are similarly unrelated. Groff (1975) likewise questions the relationship between auditory discrimination and reading achievement and calls for more intensive investigation of the pros and cons of the issue.

Auditory discrimination is the ability to discriminate between the sounds or phonemes of a language. It is evident that this skill is essential to successful achievement in reading. If the child cannot hear sounds correctly, he normally cannot learn to speak them correctly. A child cannot pronounce distinctions that he cannot hear. Furthermore, if he confuses or distorts sounds in speech, it frequently is impossible for him to associate the correct sound with the visual symbol. Thus, inadequate auditory discrimination leads to improper speech and ultimately to an incorrect association of sound and printed symbol.

The Soviet psychologist, Elkonin, uses the term "phonematic hearing" to describe auditory discrimination (Ollila, 1974). He notes that beginning readers have no concept of the phoneme and do not perceive that speech can be analyzed into phonemes in a definite sequence. His research indicates that children need to know what a phoneme is if they are to understand how the alphabet works as a code for speech.

The learner must discriminate the phonetic elements that make up a word. He must make appropriate associations between the spoken and the written word. He gradually needs to realize that words that sound alike frequently look alike.

Studies (Morency, et al., 1967; Wepman, 1960) show that approximately 20 percent of the normal speaking population has poor auditory discrimination.

The ability to make auditory discriminations is greatly lessened by high frequency hearing losses. Berry and Eisenson (1956, p. 448) point out that the high frequency sounds,/f/,/v/,/s/,/z/,/sh/,/zh/,/th/,/t/,/d/,/p/, /b/, /k/, and /g/, determine the intelligibility of what is said. If these sounds are not heard correctly, interpretation of what is said becomes more difficult.

Unfortunately, many other children who have not suffered a high frequency hearing loss are unable to discriminate the sounds necessary for accurate speech. Cole (1938, p. 282), for example, notes that the average six-year-old is unable to distinguish consistently between the sounds of /g/ and /k/, /m/ and /n/, and /p/ and /b/. This makes it more difficult to learn to read. Children must learn that words consist of sounds, that the same sound may occur in more than one word, and that one word generally has different sounds than another word.

Other writers have identified additional advantages of successful auditory and visual discrimination. Cordts (1955) for example, notes that unless the child learns to differentiate between sounds in words, the foundation for phonics is inadequate. And Durrell and Murphy (1953) report that training in auditory discrimination increases general reading achievement. They note that the child who learns to read easily is usually one who notices the distinct sounds in spoken words.

The facts (Wepman, 1960) concerning auditory discrimination are these:

1. Children have varying degrees of ability in auditory discrimination.
2. The maturation of the auditory discriminatory skill is gradual and rarely is fully developed before the age of eight.
3. Poor auditory discrimination is related positively to inaccuracies in articulation and pronunciation and/or to poor achievement in reading.
4. The relationship between auditory discrimination and intelligence is essentially negative.
5. As auditory discrimination matures, the learner becomes capable of producing more and more of the sounds of the language. The child gradually learns to fashion his own speech after the speech that he hears.
6. Auditory discrimination can be developed through instruction (Silvaroli, 1966) and auditory analysis skills can be taught well in advance of reading instruction (Rosner, 1974).

Morency and Wepman (1973) add that:

1. Perceptual processes are developmental in nature, children improving in each process with age.
2. The primary modalities for learning (visual and auditory sensory pathways) develop independently (Turaids, Wepman, and Morency, 1972; Morency, 1968).
3. Within each modality, discrimination and recall have their own independent rate of development, yet they are fully mature by the age of nine (Turaids, Wepman, and Morency, 1972; Morency, 1968).

The authors' study again indicated differentiated modality development and noted that "one solution to the problem of underachievement in elementary school is early modality grouping . . . another solution is to attempt to improve the less-developed modality through direct intervention."

Some writers (Morency et al., 1967) suggest that children whose auditory discrimination is slow in developing might be separately grouped for reading. Groupings based on the pupil's best way of learning or by modality ability might facilitate the task of teaching and enhance learning. Certainly it would appear that a child with a developmental delay in articulation because of slowness in auditory discrimination development might benefit from an emphasis on visual learning until he can correct his own articulation errors as he matures.

Vandever and Neville (1974), after measuring 282 second graders, found that 72 learned significantly more or fewer words when they were presented in one method (visual, auditory, or kinesthetic) than in the other two. The students were then grouped. The conclusion, after a six-week study, was that students did not do better when taught to strengths than where taught to weakness. They further added that modality grouping was not a reasonable grouping procedure.

Visual Discrimination

Surely one of the most important skills needed for reading is the ability to visually analyze and synthesize printed words. The pupil must be able to sort out and to distinguish differences between visual stimuli (Gould, 1967). He must be able to note similarities and differences in the form of objects, pictures, geometric figures, and words. Generally children have learned to discriminate between gross figures and objects. They see the differences between a cat and a dog and between circles, triangles, and squares. They also have learned something about words. Long before they come to school they have identified signs such as "Phillips 66," "Stop," "Wichita," or "Kansas." They have noted that some words are long and others short, that some have ascending letters and others have descending letters, and that some words look alike and that others look different.

Unfortunately, it is not always possible to know whether the pupil has used the correct process in identifying a word. Unless he has identified the word through some peculiarity of the word itself, he may not have learned or at least has learned incorrectly. Children frequently learn to identify a word by a simple association process. Perhaps the word "stop" is "Stop" only when it is seen at the end of a block and appears as an octagonal-shaped figure. The word "Bob" is "Bob" only when it appears on that card with the dirt splotch in the bottom left hand corner.

Thus the question arises, "What should the teacher emphasize in visual discrimination training? Ever since there has been concern with identifying the factors that were indicative of both reading readiness and achievement, visual discrimination has been accorded a primary position. Gradually, concern focused on those specific visual discrimination tasks that are most predictive of reading readiness. Researchers identifed the importance of visual discrimination of letters or words. Some emphasized shape matching (Potter, 1949) or the ability to keep a figure in mind against distraction (Goins, 1958).

A series of studies at Boston University (Durrell, 1958) suggests that most children are able to match one capital letter with another capital letter and one lower case letter with another. It was found that the matching of nonword forms and pictures had little benefit on letter or word perception. The learning in the former did not seem to transfer to performance on the latter.

Shea (1968) found that the ability to discriminate visually between words was a significant indicator of reading readiness when the sight method of instruction was used.

Muehl and King's experiment (1967) tends to indicate that visual discrimination training from the beginning should be with word and letter stimuli. Matching of animal pictures or geometric forms does not seem to have transfer value to word discrimination.

Barrett (1965) found that being able to discriminate, recognize, and name letters and numbers was the best single predictor, but pattern copying and word matching were strongly related to first-grade reading achievement. However, other factors (auditory discrimination, language facility, story sense, etc.) still contributed as much or more to the prediction of first-grade reading.

In a later study Barrett (1967) found that recognition of letters had the highest relationship with beginning reading achievement; discrimination of beginning sounds had the next highest relationship, but ending sounds in words, shape completion, ability to copy a sentence, and discrimination of vowel sounds in words were also positively related.

Wheelock and Silvaroli (1967) found a significant difference in visual discrimination ability among kindergarten children from high and low socioeconomic groups, and their study indicated that the ability to make instant responses of recognition to the capital letters can be taught. The children from the lower extreme of the socioeconomic continuum seemed to profit most from the training.

Whipple and Kodman (1969) found that retarded readers on three tasks of perceptual learning, each involving the discrimination of visual symbols presented in sequence, were significantly poorer than normal readers in number of errors on first trial as well as in the number of total errors made in discriminating visual symbols presented in sequence.

Whisler (1974) found in a study of 295 first graders that practice in visual memory increased word discrimination skills and Word Reading scores significantly.

Reading requires the ability to distinguish each word from every other word. The pupil must be relatively more skilled in noting the differences among words than in noting the similarities.

One cannot infer that all matching is useless. Some children may not have learned this simple step. The teacher uses a matching exercise as a diagnostic device. When the pupil has not developed adequately in this regard he should stress matching of objects, signs, and words. He starts teaching at the level the child has attained. The child must learn matching to the extent that he consistently responds to *b* as *b* or to *was* as *was*.

Certain other principles should guide the teacher in his teaching of visual discrimination. He must be careful not to overdrill on any one skill. If the pupil can do a specific exercise with ease, it is imperative that with him he work on a higher-level skill. There perhaps is no quicker way to destroy interest in learning to read than to force the pupil to engage in a readiness activity that he already has mastered.

The teacher also needs to develop some sequence in teaching the letters. He must begin with simple forms and proceed to more difficult ones. Some letters are readily distinguishable, for example, *x* and *b*. Others are not so readily distinguished. Children have a tendency to confuse *b* and *d*, *p* and *b*, *p* and *d*, *p* and *q*, *u* and *n*, *m* and *w*, *o* and *e*, *o* and *c*, *e* and *c*, and *g* and *b*. These letters profitably might be introduced at different times to minimize interference.

In recent years there has been an emphasis on the use of colored symbols to differentiate the phonemes of the language. Jones (1965) found that color was a definite aid to visual perception among kindergarten children. Knafle (1973) found that color or underlining may be effectively used as cues to enhance children's learning of pattern similarities such as *cat, mat, fat.* Color cues and underlining appeared to aid the subjects in detecting structure. The study involved 636 kindergarten to third-grade subjects.

Finally, in visual discrimination exercises, the emphasis is not on reading. We do not specifically teach the pupil to associate a printed word with a spoken word or with an object or experience. The pupil must note differences in words. He should be able to verbalize the differences in words. He should be able to verbalize the difference in the initial letter, the final letter, or in the general form of the words. We expect to teach him "what to look for," so he may identify words as distinct units of language.

Language Development

The acquisition and use of language is closely related to auditory and visual discrimination. But language is more than a basis for hearing, seeing, and taking meaning to words. It is the very basis of the thinking process, and though related to auditory and visual discrimination, language development plays a significant and unique role in reading readiness.

A common cause of poor reading is inadequate language development. It is strange, but true nonetheless, that reading theory and teaching have concerned themselves largely with psychological, sociological, physical, and neurological matters but have not concerned themselves rigorously enough with language. Reading must be regarded as a language-related process; it must be studied in relation to language.

Teachers must be concerned then with the significance of language and communication for the reading process. The general assumption underyling this section is this: The first step in introducing the youngster to reading and in assuring success in reading is to provide him with an adequate development in listening and speaking.

The teacher of reading needs to understand communication and language for the following reasons:

1. The pupil's proficiency in the communication and language skills, both speaking and listening, is the best indicator of his readiness for reading. In fact, intelligence test scores may basically represent past opportunities for language experience.
2. The teacher himself cannot understand the reading process without understanding communication and oral language development.
3. The more alike the patterns of language structure in the reading material are to the patterns of language structure used in speaking, the better the student's comprehension tends to be.

Communication is the heart of the language arts. Without communication, listening or reading cannot occur. Reading takes place only when the youngster shares the ideas that the communicator intends to convey.

If reading is communication and if indeed it is a linguistic process, this has certain implications for the teaching of reading:

1. Language training should accompany reading instruction every step of the way. A linguistic background for reading lessons should be continuously built at each stage of growth.

2. Reading success depends upon the student's aural-oral experience with words. Development in reading closely parallels development in listening and speech. Reading involves the same language, the same message, and the same code as hearing of spoken words. The only difference is that in reading the contact is made on the central nervous system by light vibrations through the eyes; in hearing, it is by sound vibrations through the ears.

3. Every reading lesson should be an extension of language and a means of developing the student's linguistic skill.

4. If the student cannot sound the individual phoneme, he probably will not be a good oral reader. He will have difficulty with phonics. He may also have more difficulty in transmitting meaning.

5. Genuine reading proficiency may mean the ability to read language structure. The best reader may be one mentally aware of the stresses, elongations of words, changes of pitch and intonation, and rhythms of the sentences that he reads. If he reads the way the writer would like it to have been said, true communication of meaning may be possible.

6. The student's comprehension of speech and his oral use of language should be checked frequently. Appraisal of the linguistic competency of all slow learners and language-handicapped youth should be a part of the diagnostic and remedial program. Teachers should place emphasis, however, on being a good model for language rather than on correcting the child (Freshour, 1971). Gottesman (1968) and Baratz and Shuy (1969) point to the enormous difficulties that children, whose phonological system or dialect differs from that of the language used by teachers, have with auditory discrimination tasks and thus probably reading.

7. Some of the effort expended in teaching slow learners and particularly disadvantaged students by dint of drills and devices might better be expended in working on development in oral language and comprehension. Instruction should begin with familiar materials, *materials that represent the student's speech.*[5]

WHEN IS THE CHILD READY?

To this point we have examined seven of the factors that help to determine reading readiness. Although other factors considered in later

[5]For a complete discussion of language and its implications in the teaching of reading, see Emerald Dechant, *Improving the Teaching of Reading* (Englewood Cliffs, N. J.: Prentice-Hall, Inc.. 1970), pp. 137–61.

chapters must contribute to our final decisions, let us, on the basis of our examination of seven of the correlates of reading readiness, ask ourselves at this point: when is a child ready to read?

Durkin, (1961, 1962, 1966a, 1966b) in various and continuous studies of early and nonearly readers, found significantly higher achievement among the early readers. She reports that even after six years of instruction in reading, the early readers, as a group, achieved better than their classmates of the same mental age who did not begin to read until the first grade (1966b). The IQ of the early readers ranged from 82 to 170.

The children who learned to read early manifested an interest in learning to print either simultaneously or prior to developing an interest in reading. They eagerly responded to their word-filled world. These "pencil and paper kids" moved from scribbling and drawing to copying objects and letters of the alphabet, to questions about spelling, to ability to read. They wanted to see their name in print and used small blackboards. They were curious, conscientious, persistent, self-reliant, and became intensely interested in projects (making a calendar) for long periods of time. Their attention spans were decidedly not short, and their memories and concentration were good. They had parents or siblings who read to them. Their mothers played a key role in encouraging early achievement.

Sutton (1964) reports that children who read early tend to be girls, have siblings and parents who read to them, come from upper-socio-economic homes, have parents who are interested in school affairs and educational progress, are interested in words, are conscientious and self-reliant, have good memories and know how to concentrate, can name most of the letters of the alphabet, and have fathers who engage in mental rather than manual work. Plessas and Oakes (1964) found that early readers were taught to read by their parents or siblings; their reading was not simply a chance happening.

Brzeinski and others, (1964, 1967) in a five-year follow-up study of 4,000 Denver school children who began to read in kindergarten, noted that there was a definite advantage in the early instruction, that it did not affect visual acuity, and that it did not lead to school maladjustment, nor to a dislike for reading. Mood, (1967) however, raised questions about the research design of the Denver study, about the methods of reporting, about the different attrition rates of the experimental and control groups, and about the failure to deal adequately with the Hawthorne effect.

There is little doubt that three-, four-, and five-year-olds can be taught to read. The important question is: "Is this desirable? It would appear that children who are *ready* for an early start in reading may not suffer adverse effects when taught; they, in fact, seem to profit from activities which stimulate their interest in reading" (Karlin, 1967).

Mason and Prater (1966b) found that introducing reading teaching in the kindergarten tended to increase negative social behavior among the boys, and the teacher felt that the learning was hard work and a much slower process than with first graders. In another article, (1966a) Mason and Prater reviewed the research and concluded that:

1. Younger children make less progress than older ones of the same intelligence when they are exposed to the same program.
2. The best age for beginning reading is dependent upon the materials used, the size of the class, the pacing of the program, and teacher expectancies.

If the reading materials are suited to their level, if they are interesting, and if the teaching method is adapted to their intellectual maturity, children may learn to read at mental ages considerably below six and one-half. It appears that the younger the pupils, the lower should be the teacher-pupil ratio. A teacher needs to work more closely with younger children.

Instruction must march slightly ahead of maturation but it might be better to err by going too slowly than by going too fast. Rousseau (1899, p. 83) put it aptly when he wrote:

> I would much rather he (Emile) would never know how to read than to buy this knowledge at the price of all that can make it useful. Of what use would reading be to him after he had been disgusted with it forever?

It may be good to introduce formal reading instruction to some three-, four-, or five-year-old children, but *en masse* introduction to children may cripple the spirits of some children. It seems important that we allow the child to enjoy and to live his childhood. "Tomorrow's problems can wait. Indeed, for the best development of the child, they must wait."

It would seem that if teachers of reading are expert in reading children, they will not push children beyond their maturational level. The timing of instruction is especially important in preventing reading disability. Reading disability too often is caused by starting the child in a reading program before he is ready for it. Such a child cannot handle the day by day learning tasks and finds himself farther and farther behind as the time goes by. He becomes frustrated and develops antipathy towards reading. He actually learns *not to read*. This is quite different and far more serious than not learning to read.

Another caution seems indicated. It may be dangerous to emphasize one phase of education at the expense of another. Although we can teach very young children to read and to type, we agree with Bugelski (1964, p. 59) that "typing is not a substitute for geography, nor is reading a substitute for tying one's shoes." It may be far better to provide language background.

It would be a serious indictment of us as teachers if children became reading disability cases because we introduced them to reading too early or because we pushed them beyond their level of endurance. There is strong evidence, as we shall see later, that the eyes may be actually harmed by an emphasis on close work before the age of eight.

McCormick (1966) cautions that happiness is a child learning to read, but security is allowing him to do it when he is ready.

The question, "When are children ready to read?" has no decisive answer. There is no single criterion that applies to all children. The teacher must determine *for each child* what program would result in hurrying too much and what would result in too much delay. The facts concerning individual differences require that the teacher consider at least three different factors before he can decide on the readiness of a child for beginning reading.

First: The range of differences in level of mental development among first-grade children may be as much as four or even six years. Some who enter the first grade may need as much as three years before they are ready to learn to read, but others already may be reading second or third grade material. Differences in achievement within the same age group increase rather than decrease as children advance through school. The typical fifth grade exhibits a range of reading proficiency from second or third grade norm to secondary level.

Second: The same child may show variations in the development of his various abilities that are as great as are the differences between two children in the same grade. These vast growth differences within the child pose special problems. Readiness for reading requires that a child has achieved at least a minimum level of growth in all essential characteristics. A child may be intellectually ready for reading and have a sufficient background of experiences and yet not be emotionally or, perhaps, physiologically ready.

Third: Individual growth patterns frequently are marked by spurts and plateaus. Even children who appear to be at the same stage of development advance in reading achievement at different rates. A child may lag behind his classmates in the early stages of reading development and catch up with them later on or he may precede them and later fall behind. And variations in rate of growth and variations between boys and girls at different periods of life may be of considerable importance in determining the effectiveness of reading instruction.

SUMMARY

Certainly some aspects of readiness can be measured, but at present no single measure or known combination of measures is fully adequate. Unfortunately, as yet we have no adequate criterion for readiness and no measuring device gives us a complete answer. There is no one single basis for a *yes* or *no* answer to the question of when is a child ready for reading instruction. Thus authorities differ somewhat in their recommendations for determining reading readiness. The clinician tends to place his confidence in a case study approach; the psychometrist generally restricts his study to specific pencil and paper tests; and the teacher is preoccupied with such data as he can gather from group tests and careful observation of each child in the classroom. Lack of time for gathering data and lack of certain specialized clinical skills will bar many teachers from information they might wish to attain.

QUESTIONS FOR DISCUSSION

1. What is meant by *readiness*? Is it a concept that is of interest to the high school teacher?
2. What is a developmental task? Discuss.
3. What factors are found to be related to reading readiness?
4. What is meant by mental age? Intelligence quotient? How are they different? Which is more closely related to reading readiness?
5. Discuss the range of mental ages that you would find among a large group of unselected children of age 6. Of ages 8, 10, 12, 14. Give specific data as to the percentages of various mental age levels in each of the above groups.
6. Suggest as many reasons as you can why girls as a group are better readers than are boys.
7. Why should reading readiness be related to socioeconomic status?
8. What are some of the reasons for and against delaying reading instruction?
9. Should good teaching tend to increase or decrease the range in educational achievement in a class? Should good teaching increase or decrease the size of the correlation between mental age and educational achievement?
10. Suggest solutions to the problem presented by sex difference in readiness to read.

BIBLIOGRAPHY

ANASTASI, ANNE and FOLEY, JOHN P. JR. "A Proposed Reorientation in the Heredity-Environment Controversy." In Jerome H. Seidman, ed., *The Child: A Book of Readings.* New York: Holt, Rinehart & Winston, 1958, pp. 2–15.

AYRES, LEONARD P. *Laggards in Our Schools.* New York: Russell Sage Foundation, 1909.

BALLER, WARREN R. and CHARLES, DON C. *The Psychology of Human Growth and Development.* New York: Holt, Rinehart, and Winston, 1961.

BARATZ, J. C. and SHUY, R. W., eds. *Teaching Black Children to Read.* Washington, D.C.: Center for Applied Linguistics, 1969.

BARRETT, THOMAS C. "Visual Discrimination Tasks as Predictors of First Grade Reading Achievement." *The Reading Teacher* 18 (1965): 276–282.

BARRETT, THOMAS C. "Performance on Selected Prereading Tasks and First-Grade Reading Achievement." *Vistas in Reading.* Newark, Del.: International Reading Association, 1967, pp. 461–64.

BARTON, ALLEN. "Social Class and Instructional Procedures in the Process of Learning to Read." In *Twelfth Yearbook of the National Reading Conference,* edited by Y. Melton Culberth, and Ralph C. Staiger, Milwaukee, 1962.

BECKETT, DOROTHY B. "Philosophical Differences in Reading Concepts." *The Reading Teacher* 18 (1964): 27–32.

BELMONT, HERMAN S. "Psychological Influences on Learning." *Sociological and Psychological Factors in Reading*. Proceedings of the 21st Annual Reading Institute, Temple University, Philadelphia, 1964, pp. 15–26.

BENSON, J. "Teaching Reading to the Culturally Different Child." In Alfred R. Binter, John Diabal, and Leonard Kise, eds., *Readings on Reading*. Scranton, Pa.: International Textbook Company, 1969.

BENTZEN, FRANCIS. "Sex Ratios in Learning and Behavior Disorders." *American Journal of Ortho-psychiatry* 33 (1963): 92–98.

BERRY, MILDRED F. and EISENSON, JON. *Speech Disorders: Principles and Practices of Therapy*. New York: Appleton-Century-Crofts, 1956.

BETTS, EMMETT ALBERT. *Foundations of Reading Instruction*. New York: American Book Co., 1957.

BLAKE, JAMES NEAL. *Speech Education Activities for Children*. Springfield, Ill.: Charles C Thomas, 1970.

BLATT, BURTON and GARFUNKEL, FRANK. "Educating Intelligence: Determinants of School Behavior of Disadvantaged Children." *Exceptional Children* 33 (1967): 601–608.

BOND, GUY L. and TINKER, MILES A. *Reading Difficulties: Their Diagnosis and Correction*. New York: Appleton-Century-Crofts, Inc., 1967.

BOYER, WILLIAM H. and WALSH, PAUL. "Are Children Born Unequal?" *Saturday Review*, 51 (42) October 19, 1968, pp. 61–79.

BRUNER, JEROME S. *On Knowing*. Cambridge, Mass.: Harvard University Press, 1962.

BUGELSKI, B. R. *The Psychology of Learning Applied to Teaching*. Indianapolis: Bobbs Merrill Company, 1964.

CALLAWAY, BYRON. "Pupil and Family Characteristics Related to Reading Achievement." *Education* 92 (1972): 71–75.

CLARK, W. W., "Boys and Girls: Are There Significant Ability and Achievement Differences?" *Phi Delta Kappan* 41 (1959): 73–76.

COHEN, ALICE and GLASS, GERALD G. "Lateral Dominance and Reading Ability." *The Reading Teacher* 21 (January, 1968): 343–48.

COLE, LUELLA. *The Improvement of Reading with Special Reference to Remedial Instruction*. New York: Holt, Rinehart & Winston, 1938.

CORDTS, ANNA D. "And It's All Known as Phonics." *Elementary English* 32 (1955): 376–78, 412.

DAVIS, O. L., and SLOBODIAN, JUNE JENKINSON. "Teacher Behavior Toward Boys and Girls During First Grade Reading Instruction." *American Educational Research Journal* 4 (1967): 261–69.

DURKIN, DOLORES. "Children Who Read Before Grade One." *The Reading Teacher* 14 (1961): 163–66.

DURKIN, DOLORES. "Reading Instruction and the Five-Year-Old Child." *Challenge and Experiment in Reading*. International Reading Association Conference Proceedings, Vol. 7 (1962): 23–27.

DURKIN, DOLORES. "The Achievement of Pre-School Readers: Two Longitudinal Studies." *Reading Research Quarterly* 1 (1966a): 5–36.

DURKIN, DOLORES. *Children Who Read Early*. New York: Teachers College Press, Teachers College, Columbia University, 1966b.

DURR, WILLIAM K., and HICKMAN, ROBERTA. "Reading Instruction in Soviet Schools: Methods and Materials." *The Reading Teacher* 28 (1974): 134–40.

DURRELL, DONALD D. *The Improvement of Basic Reading Abilities.* Yonkers, N.Y.: World Book Company, 1940.

DURRELL, DONALD D. "First-Grade Reading Success Study: A Summary." *Journal of Education,* 140 (1958): 2–6.

DURRELL, DONALD D. and MURPHY, HELEN. "The Auditory Discrimination Factor in Reading Readiness and Reading Disability." *Education* 73 (1953): 556–60.

DYKSTRA, ROBERT. "Auditory Discrimination Abilities and Beginning Reading Achievement." *Reading Research Quarterly* 1 (1966): 5–34.

EAMES, THOMAS H. "Some Neural and Glandular Bases of Learning." *Journal of Education* 142 (1960): 1–36.

FIRESTER, LEE and FIRESTER, JOAN. "Wanted: A New Deal for Boys." *Elementary School Journal* 75 (1974): 28–36.

FRASURE, NANCY E. and ENTWISLE, DORIS R. "Semantic and Syntactic Development in Children." *Developmental Psychology* 9 (1973): 236–45.

FRESHOUR, FRANK W. "Dialect and the Teaching of Reading." *Education* 92 (1971): 92–94.

GALLAGHER, J. ROSWELL. "Can't Spell, Can't Read." *Atlantic* 181 (1948): 35–39.

GENTILE, LANCE M. "Effect of Tutor Sex on Learning to Read." *The Reading Teacher* 28 (1975): 726–30.

GESELL, A. and ILG, F. *Child Development. An Introduction to the Study of Human Growth.* New York: Harper & Row, 1949.

GROFF, PATRICK. "Reading Ability and Auditory Discrimination: Are They Related?" *The Reading Teacher* 28 (1975): 742–47.

GOINS, JEAN T. *Visual Perceptual Abilities and Early Reading Progress.* Supplementary Educational Monographs, No. 87. Chicago: University of Chicago Press, 1958.

GOTTESMAN, R. L. "Auditory Discrimination Ability in Standard English Speaking and Negro Dialect Speaking Children." Unpublished doctoral thesis, Columbia, 1968.

GOULD, LAWRENCE N. "Visual Perception Training." *The Elementary School Journal* 67 (1967): 381–89.

HAMMILL, DONALD D. and LARSEN, STEPHEN C. "The Relationship of Selected Auditory Perceptual Skills and Reading Ability." *Journal of Learning Disabilities* 7 (1974): 40–46.

HARRINGTON, SISTER MARY JAMES and DURRELL, DONALD D. "Mental Maturity versus Perception Abilities in Primary Reading." *Journal of Educational Psychology* 46 (1955): 375–80.

HARRIS, ALBERT J. *Effective Teaching of Reading.* New York: David McKay Company, 1962.

HARRISON, M. LUCILLE. *Reading Readiness,* rev. edition, Boston: Houghton Mifflin, 1939.

HAVIGHURST, ROBERT J. *Human Development and Education.* New York: Longmans, Green and Company, 1953.

HENRY, JULES. *Culture Against Man.* New York: Random House, 1963.

DE HIRSCH, KATRINA; JANSKY, JEANETTE and LANGFORD, WILLIAM S. *Predicting Reading Failure.* New York: Harper and Row, 1966.

DEHIRSCH, KATRINA and JANSKY, JEANETTE. "Kindergarten Protocols of Failing Readers." In Dorothy L. de Boer, ed., *Reading Diagnosis and Evaluation*, vol. 13. Newark, Del.: International Reading Association, 1970.

INSELBERG, RACHEL. "Current Issues and Research Gaps in Initial Reading Instruction." *Education* 92 (1972): 80–83.

JENKINS, JOSEPH R.; BAUSELL, R. B. and JENKINS, L. M. "Comparisons of Letter Name and Letter Sound Training as Transfer Variables." *American Educational Research Journal* 9 (1972): 75–85.

JOHNSON, R. J. "The Effect of Training in Letter Names on Success in Beginning Reading for Children of Differing Abilities." Doctoral dissertation. University of Minnesota, 1969.

JONES, J. KENNETH. "Color as an Aid to Visual Perception in Early Reading." *The British Journal of Educational Psychology* 35 (1965): 21–27.

KARLIN, ROBERT. "Research Results and Classroom Practices." *The Reading Teacher* 21 (1967): 211–26.

KNAFLE, JUNE D., "Word Perception: Cues Aiding Structure Detection." *Reading Research Quarterly* 8 (1973): 502–24.

KOHN, DALE and BIRCH, HERBERT G. "Development of Auditory-Visual Integration and Reading Achievement." *Perceptual and Motor Skills* 27 (1968): 459–68.

KOWARIK, D. and KRAFT, J. *Die Legasthenie und ihre Methodische Behandlung*. Munich: Jugend u Volk, 1973.

LADD, ELEANOR M. "Individualizing Instruction in Classroom Corrective Situations." *Vistas in Reading* Vol. 2, Part I. Newark, Del.: International Reading Association, 1967, pp. 254–56.

LAMBERT, N. "Predicting and Evaluating the Effectiveness of Children in School." In E. M. Bower and W. G. Hollister, eds., *Behavioral Science Frontiers in Education*. New York: Wiley, 1967.

LAMOREAUX, LILLIAN A. and LEE, DORRIS MAY. *Learning to Read Through Experience*. New York: Appleton-Century-Crofts, 1943.

LINDER, RONALD and FILLMER, HENRY T. "Auditory and Visual Performance of Slow Readers." *The Reading Teacher* 24 (1970): 17–22.

MASON, GEORGE E. and PRATER, NORMA JEAN. "Early Reading and Reading Instruction." Elementary English 43 (1966): 483–88, 527.

MASON, GEORGE E. and PRATER, NORMA JEAN. "Social Behavioral Aspects of Teaching Reading to Kindergartners." *Journal of Educational Research* 60 (1966b): 58–61.

MCCARTHY, DOROTHEA A. "Some Possible Explanations of Sex Differences in Language Development and Disorders." *Journal of Psychology* 35 (1935): 155–60.

MCCORMICK, NANCY. "The Countdown on Beginning Reading." *The Reading Teacher,* 20 (November, 1966) 115–120.

MONTAGU, A. "Sociogenic Brain Damage." *Developmental Medicine and Child Neurology* 13 (1971): 597–605.

MOOD, DARLENE W. "Reading in Kindergarten?" *Educational Leadership* 24 (1967): 399–403.

MORENCY, ANNE. "Auditory Modality and Reading: Research and Practice." In Helen K. Smith, ed., *Perception and Reading*. Vol. 12, Part 4. Newark, Del.: International Reading Association, 1968.

MORENCY, ANNE S.; WEPMAN, JOSEPH M.; and WEINER, PAUL S. "Studies in Speech: Developmental Articulation Inaccuracy." *Elementary School Journal* 67 (1967): 329–37.

MORENCY, ANNE and WEPMAN, JOSEPH M. "Early Perceptual Ability and Later School Achievement." *Elementary School Journal* 73 (1973): 323–27.

MUEHL, SIEGMAR and KING, ETHEL M. "Recent Research in Visual Discrimination: Significance for Beginning Reading." *Vistas in Reading.* Newark, Del.: International Reading Association, 1967, pp. 434–39.

NAIDEN, NORMA. "Ratio of Boys to Girls Among Disabled Readers." *The Reading Teacher* 29 (1976): 439–42.

NICHOLSON, ALICE. "Background Abilities Related to Reading Success in First Grade." *Journal of Education* 140 (1958): 7–24.

NILA, SISTER MARY, O.S.F. "Foundations of a Successful Reading Program." *Education* 73 (1953): 543–55.

OHNMACHT, D. D. "The Effects of Letter Knowledge on Achievement in Reading in the First Grade." Paper presented at American Educational Research Association Conference, Los Angeles, 1969.

OLLILA, LLOYD; JOHNSON, TERRY; and DOWNING, JOHN. "Adapting Russian Methods of Auditory Training for English." *Elementary English* 51 (1974): 1138–41, 1145.

OLSON, ARTHUR V. "Growth in Word Perception Abilities as It Relates to Success in Beginning Reading." *Journal of Education* 140 (1958): 25–36.

ORLOW, MARIA. "Literacy Training in West Germany and the United States." *The Reading Teacher* 29 (1976): 460–67.

PLESSAS, GUS P. and OAKES, CLIFTON R. "Prereading Experiences of Selected Early Readers." *The Reading Teacher* 17 (1964): 241–45.

POTTER, MURIEL C. *Perception of Symbol Orientation and Early Reading Success.* New York: Columbia University, Teachers College, Bureau of Publications, No. 939, 1949.

PRESTON, RALPH C. "A Comparative Study of the Reading Achievement of German and American Children." *Changing Concepts of Reading Instruction,* International Reading Association, Vol. 6, pp. 109–12.

ROBECK, MILDRED C. "An Ounce of Prevention." In Leo M. Schell and Paul C. Burns, eds., *Remedial Reading: Classroom and Clinic.* Boston: Allyn and Bacon, 1972, pp. 513–21.

ROSNER, JEROME. "Language Arts and Arithmetic Achievement and Specifically Related Perceptual Skills." *American Educational Research Journal* 10, No. 1, (1973): 59–68.

ROSNER, JEROME. "Auditory Analysis Training with Prereaders." *The Reading Teacher* 27 (1974): 379–84.

ROUSSEAU, JACQUES. *Emile.* New York: Appleton-Century-Crofts, 1899.

SAMUELS, S. JAY. "Letter-name versus Letter Sound Knowledge in Learning to Read." *The Reading Teacher* 24 (1971): 604–8.

SEXTON, PATRICIA L. *The Feminized Male: White Collars and the Decline of Manliness.* New York: Random House, 1969.

SHEA, CAROL ANN. "Visual Discrimination of Words and Reading Readiness." *The Reading Teacher* 21 (1968): 361–67.

SHERIDAN, MARY D. *The Child's Hearing for Speech.* London: Methuen & Co., Ltd., 1948.

SILVAROLI, NICKOLAS J. and WHEELOCK, WARREN B. "An Investigation of Auditory Discrimination Training for Beginning Readers." *The Reading Teacher* 20 (1966): 247–51.

SLOBODZIAN, EVELYN B. "Use of the Illinois Test of Psycholinguistic Abilities as a Readiness Measure." In D. L. de Boer, ed., *Reading Diagnosis and Evaluation*, vol. 13. Newark, Del.: International Reading Association, 1970.

SMITH, NILA B. "Some Basic Factors in Reading Difficulties of the Disadvantaged." *Reading Improvement* 11 (1974): 3–9.

ST. JOHN, CHARLES W. "The Maladjustment of Boys in Certain Elementary Grades." *Educational Administration and Supervision* 18 (1932): 659–72.

STANCHFIELD, J. M. "Development of Pre-Reading Skills in an Experimental Kindergarten Program." *The Reading Teacher* 24 (1971): 699–707.

STORR, ANTHONY. *Human Aggression.* New York: Atheneum, 1968.

STRAG, GERALD A. and RICHMOND, BERT O. "Auditory Discrimination Techniques for Young Children." *Elementary School Journal* 73 (1973): 447–54.

STROUD, JAMES B. *Psychology in Education.* New York: Longmans, Green and Company, 1956.

SUTTON, MARJORIE H. "Readiness for Reading at the Kindergarten Level." *The Reading Teacher* 17 (1964): 234–39.

THORNDIKE, ROBERT L. *Reading Comprehension Education in Fifteen Countries.* International Association for the Evaluation of Educational Achievement. New York: Halsted Press, 1973.

TURAIDS, DAINIS; WEPMAN, JOSEPH; and MORENCY, ANNE. "A Perceptual Test Battery: Development and Standardization." *Elementary School Journal* 72 (1972): 351–61.

TYLER, LEONA E. "Individual Differences." In Robert L. Ebel and Victor H. Noll, eds., *Encyclopedia of Educational Research*, 4th edition. New York: Macmillan, 1969.

VANDEVER, THOMAS R. and NEVILLE, DONALD D. "Modality Aptitude and Word Recognition." *Journal of Reading Behavior* 6 (1974): 195–201.

VERNON, M. D. *Backwardness in Reading.* London: Cambridge University Press, 1957.

VILSCEK, ELAINE C. "An Analysis of the Effect of Mental Age Levels and Socio-Economic Levels on Reading Achievement in First Grade." Unpublished doctoral thesis, University of Pittsburgh, 1964.

VYGOTSKY, LEV SEMENOVICH. *Thought and Language*, edited and translated by Eugenia Hanfmann and Gertrude Vakar. New York: John Wiley, 1952, p. 104.

WALCUTT, CHARLES C.; LAMPORT, JOAN, and MCCRACKEN, GLEN. *Teaching Reading.* New York: Macmillan, 1974.

WEINER, MORTON and WARD, CROMER. "Reading and Reading Difficulty: A Conceptual Analysis." *Harvard Educational Review* 37 (1967): 620–43.

WEPMAN, JOSEPH M. "Auditory Discrimination, Speech, and Reading." *The Elementary School Journal* 60 (1960): 325–33.

WHEELOCK, WARREN H. and SILVAROLI, NICHOLAS J. "Visual Discrimination Training for Beginning Readers." *The Reading Teacher* 21 (1967): 115–20.

WHIPPLE, CLIFFORD L. and KODMAN, FRANK, JR. "A Study of Discrimination and Perceptual Learning with Retarded Readers." *Journal of Educational Psychology* 60 (1969): 1–5.

WHISLER, NANCY G. "Visual-Memory Training in First Grade: Effects on Visual Discrimination and Reading Ability." *Elementary School Journal* 75 (1974): 51–54.

WORLEY, STINSON E. and STORY, WILLIAM E. "Socio-Economic Status and Language Facility of Beginning First Graders." *The Reading Teacher* 20 (1967): 400–403.

6

The Sensory Bases
of Reading

The reading teacher needs to understand the sensory processes of reading. Efficiency in reading frequently depends on the oculo-motor habits of the reader. Reading begins with visual stimuli; the eyes bring the stimuli to the reader. Auditory factors, though perhaps not as significant as visual factors, also are determinants of reading success. It is only through vision that the reader is able to deal with the significant contrastive features of the sign system, the graphic symbols, or the surface structure. The reader must make discriminative visual responses to the graphic symbols and he must be able to identify them. Vision is important in reading because our imaging or perceptual processes, indeed our ability to read with meaning, are clearly dependent upon the stimulus information received through the eyes.

In Chapter 5 we were concerned with seven determinants of readiness for and achievement in reading. Here we will examine the sensory bases of reading. As in Chapter 5, our concern goes far beyond readiness for beginning reading. At all levels of development reading achievement is related to sense-organ efficiency.

VISION AND READING

Obviously, reading must begin as a sensory process. Reading is a visual process and a word-identification process. Sensation is the first occurrence in all perception. The reader must react visually (in the case of Braille, kinesthetically) to the graphic symbols.

The teacher of reading is concerned with the significant facts of seeing and vision. Frequently, writers make some distinction between these two terms. Generally the term *seeing* is used to include phases of perception as well as sensation whereas *vision* refers more directly to the efficiency of the eyes. Writers, however, are not always consistent in their use of these words.

Visual Readiness

We know that a child must have attained certain levels of visual maturation before he is ready to begin reading. He should have become able to focus his eyes at distances of twenty inches or less as well as be able to focus at twenty feet or more. He should have acquired some skill in depth perception, binocular coordination, ability to center, and ability to change fixation at will. And he must see clearly, singly, and for sustained periods.

Our concern, then, is with the age at which a child achieves sufficient proficiency in these visual skills to begin reading. Our cumulative question now may be phrased: When are the child's seeing processes sufficiently mature for learning to read?

Children are born farsighted. This prevents adequate focus of the image of near objects on the retina. As the eyeball lengthens farsightedness gradually decreases and the child becomes capable of adapting to the demands of near vision.

It is possible that too early attempts to use the eyes in reading tends to produce myopia (nearsightedness). Leverett, (1957) using the Massachusetts Vision Test with some 6,000 elementary and secondary school pupils, found that vision tends to deteriorate markedly from kindergarten through grade twelve. Typically the 20/30 level of visual acuity is achieved at about age three and the 20/20 level at age five or six. At the kindergarten level 90 percent of the children passed 20/20 monocular acuity tests. Unfortunately, about the time that children attain 20/20 acuity, deterioration seems to begin. By age 17 about 39 percent are unable to demonstrate 20/20 acuity in both right and left eyes. This progressive deterioration in vision occurs among children who had achieved only the 20/30 and 20/40 levels of acuity as well as among those achieving the 20/20 level.

Whether the early introduction to reading actually is a major causal factor in the continuous loss of far-point acuity is not yet certain.

Eye-Movement Research[1]

Much of our knowledge of how the eyes react during reading has come from the work of Emile Javal who in 1878 was the first to report on the nature of eye movement during reading. He described the eyes as moving "par saccades"—by jerks or little jumps with intervening fixation pauses (Griffin, Walton, and Ives, 1974).

In reading there is no continuous sweep of the eyes across the page. The eyes proceed in quick, short movements with pauses interspersed. Eye movements are characterized by fixations, interfixation movements,

---

[1]See Gloria T. Mann, "Eye Movements During Reading: An Updated Bibliography (1966–)," *Reading Horizons* 13 (1973): 190–97.

regressions, and return sweeps. The time required for reading has two elements: fixation time and movement time.

A *fixation* is the stop the eye makes so that it *can* react to the stimuli.[2] It is the pause for reading. Because the input of visual information resulting in perception is not continuous, the material is divided into chunks that are reassembled by the brain into a spatio-temporally continuous visual world (Gaardner, 1970).

The fine discriminations of the retinal cells is possible only because the eye is constantly making tiny oscillating movements every second. Without this involuntary tremor, there can be no normal vision and the eye would be seriously damaged (Pritchard, 1971). When the image on the retina is experimentally stabilized, the image quickly fades and disappears. The movement or tremor occurs at the rate of 50 oscillations per second. It seems possible to gain information only once during a fixation (Smith, 1971, p. 99).

The fixation varies from about 220 milliseconds (.22 seconds) for easy reading material, 236 milliseconds for scientific prose, and from 270 to 324 milliseconds for reading objective test items.

Fixation time accounts for approximately 92 to 94 percent of the reading time, whereas *eye-movement time* accounts for about 6 to 8 percent of the reading time. The eyes tend to converge during the return sweeps and the interfixation movements and to diverge during the fixation that follows. The interfixation eye movements require from 10 to 23 milliseconds.

During the fixation pause the reader recognizes letters, words, or possibly phrases. The intake process is suspended and the inner process of reading occurs.

The size of the unit recognized during a single fixation depends upon the reader's facility in word recognition, his familiarity with the material being read, the physical characteristics of the material, and his ability to assimilate ideas. Perry and Whitlock (1954) emphasized vocabulary level and the familiarity with the content as determinants of the duration of the fixation pause. Each reader develops his own individual oculomotor habits and is differentiated by them from other readers.

After examining the research data Spache (1958, p. 123) concluded that while some individuals, particularly good readers, tend to show an habitual fixation pattern, fixation frequency is markedly influenced by the purposes of the reader and a number of his individual characteristics. Difficulty of the material, familiarity of the content, as well as format also influence the pattern of fixations.

To understand the role that the fixation pause plays in reading it is necessary to familiarize ourselves with three terms, namely, *visual field, perception span,* and *recognition span.* The visual field generally consists of

[2]Tinker (1933) found that photographs of eye movements record the approximate center of the field of vision. This "fixation field" is called the point of fixation. However, when "fixating" on this point, one also sees and recognizes a part of the peripheral visual field.

an horizontal arc of about 180 degrees and a vertical arc of about 60 degrees. It includes peripheral and foveal vision (spot of clearest vision) as well as depth in vision.

The perception span or the visual span is the amount (usually in terms of numbers, letters, or words) that is seen in a single fixation. This is measured by a tachistoscopic exposure and usually is larger than the amount seen in a single fixation in normal reading.

The recognition span is the amount that is seen and organized during a single fixation. It is the number of words that are recognized and understood during a single fixation. The size of the recognition span is obtained by dividing the number of words read by the number of fixations made while reading. This span varies with the difficulty of the material or with the knowledge of the reader. The less the reader knows about a stimulus situation, the less will he be able to apprehend in a single fixation.

Thought-unit reading sometimes is wrongly identified with the concept of phrase seeing or with the suggestion that it is possible or even common to read three or four words per fixation (Taylor, 1960, p. 17). Even though a child reads in thought units, he rarely comprehends more than one word per fixation.

A study (Taylor, et al., 1960) in which the writer played a small role points this out rather forcefully. Taylor, Frackenpohl, and Pettee, using the Reading Eye Camera, analyzed the eye characteristics of 12,143 subjects from grades one through college. The subjects were of average socioeconomic status, and 90 percent attended public schools. They resided in 19 different cities. They read selections that were at their grade level of difficulty. Whenever the pupil's comprehension score was 60 percent or below, he was given a new selection to read and was tested again. Table 6-1 (Taylor et al., 1960, p. 12) reports the findings.

The findings of a previous study by Taylor (1957) of the eye movements of 5000 pupils were similar.

The data in Table 6-1 certainly should lead us to reevaluate our previous assumptions. In these studies not even one student read three words per fixation. Thought units, then, must consist of a series of fixations (Taylor et al., 1960, p. 17).

A *regression* is a return to a previously fixated syllable, word, or phrase, for a repeat fixation or a return to material that was missed because the eye movement over-reached the perceptual span. It is a fixation in a right-to-left direction on the eye-movement photograph (EDL, 1958, p. 17). It is a saccade that goes in the opposite direction from the line of type—from right to left along a line (Smith, 1971, p. 99). Eye deficiencies that prevent accurate sensation often cause regressions (EDL, 1958, p. 17). Sometimes, however, the reader regresses out of habit or because he lacks confidence. He feels the need for constant rereading. Bayle (1942) reports that regressions are likely to occur when the flow of thought is interrupted or when perceptions are recognized as inaccurate. The flow of thought may be broken in a number of ways: failure to recognize the basic meaning of a word; failure to recognize the meaning

TABLE 6–1 *Averages for Measurable Components of the Fundamental Reading Skill**

Grade†	1	2	3	4	5	6	7	8	9	10	11	12	Col.
Fixations (incl. regressions) per 100 words	224	174	155	139	129	120	114	109	105	101	96	94	90
Regressions per 100 words	52	40	35	31	28	25	23	21	20	19	18	17	15
Average span of recognition (in words)	.45	.57	.65	.72	.78	.83	.88	.92	.95	.99	1.04	1.06	1.11
Average duration of fixation (in seconds)	.33	.30	.28	.27	.27	.27	.27	.27	.27	.26	.26	.25	.24
Rate with comprehension (in words per minute)	80	115	138	158	173	185	195	204	214	224	237	250	280

MALE

Grade†	1	2	3	4	5	6	7	8	9	10	11	12	Col.
Fixations (incl. regressions) per 100 words	230	178	158	143	133	123	116	111	106	102	97	94	90
Regressions per 100 words	54	42	37	32	29	26	24	22	20	19	18	17	15
Rate with comprehension (in words per minute)	75	108	132	152	168	180	190	200	210	220	234	248	280

FEMALE

Grade†	1	2	3	4	5	6	7	8	9	10	11	12	Col.
Fixations (incl. regressions) per 100 words	218	170	152	135	125	117	112	107	103	100	95	93	90
Regressions per 100 words	50	38	33	30	27	24	22	20	19	18	17	16	15
Rate comprehension (in words per minute)	85	122	146	164	178	190	200	208	218	228	240	252	280

*Stanford E. Taylor, Helen Frackenpohl, and James L. Pettee, *Grade Level Norms for the Components of the Fundamental Reading Skill.* © 1960 (Huntington, New York: Educational Developmental Laboratories, Inc.), Bulletin No. 3, p. 12. Reprinted by permission.

†First grade averages are those of pupils capable of reading silently material of 1.8 difficulty with at least 70% comprehension. Above grade 1, averages are those of students at mid-year reading silently material of mid-year difficulty with at least 70% comprehension.

suggested by the context; failure to relate the meaning of one word to that of other words; or failure to relate the meaning of a word to the conditions under which it is used.

Buswell (1922, pp. 33–36) reported that regressions result in immature reading but Bayle (1942) suggested that a certain amount of regression is desirable. Regressions for verification, for phrase analysis, and for reexamination of a previous sentence seem especially useful. Regressions thus may at times be just as productive an eye movement as a saccade in a forward direction (Smith, 1971, p. 99).

The number of regressions made per one hundred words varies from reader to reader. The average first grader makes about fifty-two; the average ninth grader about twenty; and the average college student about fifteen. (For averages for the other grades see Table 6-1.

After a line is read the eyes make a *return sweep* to the beginning of the next line. Tinker (1958) found that the return sweep takes from 40 to 54 milliseconds. Inaccuracies here may require refixation. For example, the proper line may be missed entirely or the eyes may fix on a point before or after the first word of the new line.

Buswell (1922, p. 26) reported that the average child in grade one made between 15.5 and 18.6 fixations per 3½ inch (21-pica) line. The average college student made 5.9 fixations on a line of the same length. And Taylor (1960) reports that the average first grader makes about 224 fixations per 100 words; the average college student, about 90.

Figure 6-1 illustrates the various components of the movements of the eye as recorded by the eye movement camera.

Developmental Aspects of Eye Movement

Oculo-motor behavior has come to be regarded primarily as a symptom of the underlying perceptual and assimilative processes. There is an interaction and an interdependence between the oculo-motor activity and the central processes (Taylor, 1965).

Buswell photographed the eye movements of 186 subjects ranging from the first grade to the college level. His data suggest that eye-movement skills develop rapidly during the first four grades and that after this little improvement occurs. A slight rise occurs in the sophomore and junior years of high school (Buswell, 1922, p. 27). Ballantine (1951, pp. 105–6), also noting that eye movement skills develop rapidly during the first four grades, found little improvement thereafter, with perhaps a slight improvement between grades six and ten.

Various suggestions have been made concerning the relationships between eye-movement characteristics and reading achievement. Some have suggested that eye movements are the major determinants of reading facility; some hold that they are only symptoms of good or poor reading; and still others indicate that they may be either causes or symptoms or both.

When researchers in reading first succeeded in recording eye movements, many concluded that to improve reading it was necessary

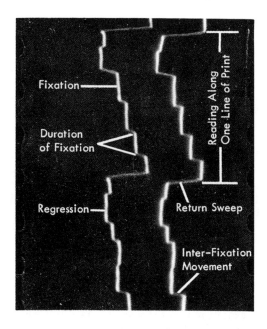

FIGURE 6–1 *Eye-Movement Photograph*

Taken from Bulletin No. P-248. (Huntington, New York: Educational Developmental Laboratories, Inc.) Reprinted by permission.

merely to improve eye movements. The reasoning was that, generally, poor readers had many more regressions and required more fixations per line than did good readers. It seemed logical that if the number of regressions and fixations could be reduced, reading would be improved. Tinker (1934) early questioned the desirability of attempting to improve reading through exercises designed to correct faulty eye movements. He believed that eye movements do not cause, but merely reflect efficient or poor reading performance. Ledbetter, (1947), studying the eye-movement records of 60 eleventh graders tested with five 300-word selections from various fields, found that eye movements varied with the nature of the material. He found that comprehension also varied and concluded that for the average student meanings are more crucial than are vocabulary, sentence length, or sentence structure.

Tinker (1947) summarized past research on this point and concluded that as the difficulty of the material increases and as the individual takes greater pains to read well, the fixation pauses become more frequent and grow longer. The difficulty of the material rather than the nature of the subject matter is the crucial element.

In a later analysis, Tinker (1958) points out that eye-movement patterns reflect the efficiency of the central processes of comprehension. He suggests that when eye movements do not vary with the difficulty of the reading matter, the readers are immature. Oculo-motor behavior is a symptom of the underlying perceptual and assimilative processes. Efficient reading results in efficient eye movements rather than vice-versa.

The immature reader generally does not vary his eye movements with the difficulty of the reading matter or with a change of purpose. The good reader, on the other hand, is distinguished from the poor reader by his better word recognition, word analysis, and comprehension and these frequently are reflected in more efficient eye movements. Thus, eye movement patterns are generally symptomatic of the reading maturity the child has achieved. The poor reader makes extra fixations and regressions because he doesn't understand, and he needs training to improve word recognition and comprehension rather than eye movement (Schubert and Torgerson, 1972, pp. 41–42). When a child makes many regressions it indicates that he is having difficulty rather than that regressions are the cause of this difficulty (Smith, 1971, p. 101). The brain moves the eye through the text as fast as it can process the incoming information (Smith, 1971, p. 104). It tells the eye when it has all the information needed and where to move next.

Under certain conditions both good and poor readers show irregularities in their eye movement. And, although eye-movement surveys indicate that a great number of children have not developed the habit of perceiving materials in a left-to-right progression, while making a minimum number of fixations and regressions (Taylor, 1959, p. 32), one must always remember that most of these surveys involve situations that are somewhat atypical. The pupil's eye movements might be different in normal reading.

The Eye-Voice and Eye-Memory Spans

Thought-unit reading, as noted previously, is not the same as interpreting an eyeful of print at a time. Because of this distinction, we speak of the eye-memory span in silent reading and the eye-voice span in oral reading.

The eye-memory span is the distance the eyes have traveled ahead of the point at which interpretation occurs. The eye-voice span is the distance the eyes have moved ahead of the point at which the pronunciation occurs. The mature reader has a wide eye-memory span and a wide eye-voice span. He does not commit himself to an interpretation until he has read a sufficient amount of material. He delays his interpretation of the visual intake until he has perceived enough material to grasp a thought unit (Hildreth, 1958, p. 75). He keeps in mind a sufficient amount of context so as to make the best interpretation. We find a similar span in listening. The good listener listens for meaning and for thought units, rather than for one word at a time.

Generally in silent reading the mature reader has a span of from fifteen to twenty letters. In oral reading it is slightly less. Rate improvement depends, to a great extent, on the shortening of the fixation pauses and on the lengthening of the eye-memory and eye-voice spans (Hildreth, 1958, p. 81).

Measuring Eye Movement

Among the most commonly used means for recording eye movements in the past were the various types of ophthalmographs, the first of which was invented by Dodge in 1901. In this process, as the individual read a selection, small beams of light were reflected from his eyes to a photographic film. The *Reading Eye Camera,* described later in this section, is the best instrument available today. A small mirror can satisfy most needs for observing eye movements. By placing a mirror on a table between the child and the examiner, the number of fixations per line can be counted. Another approach consists of punching a hole in the center of a page of reading material. As one person reads, another looks through the hole and observes the eye movement.

TYPES OF DEFECTIVE VISION

We already have spoken of the child's need for visual proficiency. There is also some indication that children often may not be visually ready for reading before the age of eight. The eye becomes structurally complete about that time. At six, the eyes frequently are too farsighted to see clearly and with ease objects as small as a word. The image of near objects does not focus adequately on the retina. Thus, the visual age of the learner may have to be given consideration in the planning of the pupil's reading program.

The ability to focus the eyes correctly during reading is part of the wider problem of motor coordination. For efficient reading the child must learn to coordinate the eyes, to move them along a line of print, and to make appropriate return sweeps. He must see clearly and distinctly both near and far, must be able to change focus and to fuse the impressions of each eye into a single image, and must have visual memory for what he has seen. He must be able to sustain visual concentration, must have good hand-eye coordination, and must be able to perceive accurately size and distance relationships (Rosenbloom, 1961, p. 91).

Even after children have become visually ready, numerous visual defects may occur. It is difficult to evaluate the specific effect of the various visual disturbances. The eyes can make amazing accommodations so words may be seen clearly. With the proper motivation the pupil may learn despite visual handicaps. He can ignore a distortion from one eye if he sees clearly with the other or if he adjusts his reading position to compensate. He may suppress the vision in one eye or alternate from one eye to another. The result is monocular vision. Generally, however, for effective vision the child must be able to use his eyes in unison.

Lack of Visual Acuity

Visual acuity does not seem to have the significance for reading achievement that some other visual factors have. First: Reading is a near-point task. One could fail the visual acuity test at 20 feet but possess good visual acuity at 16 inches. Second: To read the average book, one needs only 20/60 visual acuity.[3] Nevertheless, acuity is important. Each child should probably have at least 20/30 acuity at far point.

The emmetropic or normal eye sees with 100 percent of acuity only a very small portion of the visual field, perhaps no more than four or five letters (Feinberg, 1949).

Refractive Errors

Refractive errors are due to damage to, disease of, or weakness in the lens or other portion of one or both eyes. There is a defect in the conformation of some portion of one or both eyes. Generally refractive errors can be corrected by glasses. Glasses, however, do not increase the sensitivity of the eyes. They help the eye to focus and lower eye strain but frequently fail to provide normal vision.

Myopia or nearsightedness is perhaps the most common among the refractive errors. The myopic eyeball is too long, with the result that the light rays come into focus in front of the retina, instead of on the retina. This forces the pupil to hold the book closer than the normal 16 inches or so. Distant vision generally is blurred. Usually concave lenses are prescribed for myopic conditions.

A workshop sponsored by an advisory group to the National Institute of Neurological Diseases and Blindness and held in Washington in 1966 noted the following relevant to the etiology of myopia: "The evidence points strongly to genetic factors as the significant ones . . . but there may also be considerable environmental influence." Restricting the visual field to close objects induced myopia in monkeys. Among honor students in college, who do significantly more reading than the average college population, the incidence of myopia is 66 percent.

Eberl (1953) believes that the child may become myopic through premature attempts to adapt his eyes to the demands of close vision. Perhaps even more important, she concludes that the child who cannot adjust through becoming myopic may avoid reading (and other near-point tasks) and turn to what for him are more pleasant activities.

Kosinski (1958) suggests that myopia is symptomatic of a general weakness of connective tissue, which manifests itself also in hernias and varicose veins. The sweep in reading from the end of one line to the beginning of the next leads to congestion and pressure on the posterior pole of the eye, causing it to become myopic. Mills (1929) believes that hurried and excessive use of peripheral vision may be the causal factor. Dr. William Ludlam, professor of physiological optics at Pacific University, studied the causes of nearsightedness over a ten year period and

[3]Snellen's formula is $V = d/D$. V represents visual acuity; d is the distance at which the person is reading the letters; and D is the distance at which the person should be reading. Thus 20/60 means that the person sees at 20 feet what he should see at 60 feet. A 20/20 notation means that the pupil has 100 percent visual efficiency at far point; 20/200 means 20 percent visual efficiency.

concluded that teaching Johnny to read at an early age is a probable cause of nearsightedness.

Hyperopia or hypermetropia generally is known as farsightedness. Where the myopic eye is too long, the hyperopic eye is too short. In this case, the image falls behind the retina. To remedy this condition, convex lenses are prescribed. In testing for farsightedness, if the child reads the 20/20 test line with + 2.00 diopter lenses, he should be referred.

Another type of refractive error, *astigmatism,* is the inability to bring the light rays to a single focal point. Vision is blurred and distorted. The underlying cause is an uneven curvature of the front or cornea of the eye. The cornea is spoon-shaped rather than spherical. Unless the distorted image is corrected by the use of cylindrical lens, the child fatigues easily and usually dislikes close work or prolonged distant vision. Astigmatism is a major cause of ocular asthenopia or eyestrain (Schubert, 1968). Headaches are common, similar letters and words are confused, and the pupil experiences difficulty in sustained reading.

Coleman's study (1968) indicates that it is not enough to evaluate children's refractive errors. This will identify only about 20 percent of the children with problems. Furthermore, 30 percent of the children with more serious visual-perceptual disturbances and deficits will readily pass routine refractive evaluations.

Binocular Difficulties

Smith, Schremser, and Putz (1971), in analyzing the eye movements of three subjects, found that the left eye did the majority of the leading, suggesting that the eyes are not synchronistically moving together during saccadic movement. Presumably, when the deviations become too large, binocular difficulties occur.

The binocular difficulties have the commonality of giving the child a double image. The two eyes do not cooperate successfully. Either the two eyes do not aim correctly or they give conflicting reports. When the ocular maladjustments are minor, the individual may compensate for them. If the maladjustments are major, the child may see two of everything or the two images may be so badly blurred that he sees neither image clearly. Somehow he needs to suppress one stimulus. When he can suppress it only partially or only temporarily, he is likely to lose his place, to omit words, or to regress.

Strabismus (from the Greek word meaning to squint) or muscular imbalance stems from an incoordination of the muscles that move the eyeball. The eyes actually are aiming in different directions. One eye aims too far outward, too far inward, or in a different vertical plane from the other eye. A severe case of strabismus may result in double vision; a less severe case, in a general blurring of the image.

Each of the eyes has six muscles that must function together if the eye is to aim correctly. This is made somewhat more difficult because the eyes are set in a movable base, the head.

There are three types of strabismus or heterophoria. When the deviation is outward, it is called exophoria (wall eyes); when it is inward, esophoria (crossed eyes); and when one eye focuses higher than the other it is called hyperphoria. Hyperphoria may lead to jumping of lines or misplacement of a word to a line above or below.

Even a moderate amount of heterophoria or tendency of the eye to deviate results in fatigue. As the reader tires, his eyes tend to deviate even farther. Attempts to counteract this increase fatigue. A vicious circle is set up. The pupil becomes inattentive and irritable, loses his place, omits, and regresses. This incoordination is sometimes corrected by cutting some of the eye muscles.

Some research indicates that myopic children with phoric conditions read about as well as do children without phoria, but that children with phorias at far point have poorer reading skills.

Two additional binocular defects are *lack of fusion* and *aniseikonia*. To see clearly, the lenses of the two eyes must be in focus. The images must fuse correctly, thus giving one mental picture.

The light patterns focused on the retina generate nerve impulses that travel via the optic nerve and the visual pathways to the visual centers of the brain. On the way, the impulses from the nasal side of each eye cross, thus joining the impulses from the temporal side of the opposite eye. Each cerebral hemisphere thus receives impulses from both eyes. These impulses are then blended into one picture. (Bing, 1961).

An inability to fuse correctly is manifested by mixing of letters and words, inability to follow lines across a page, loss of place, and by slowness in reading.

Aniseikonia occurs whenever there is a difference in size or shape between the two ocular images. As a result fusion is difficult and the reader may become tense, experience fatigue, and have headaches.

Figure 6-2 illustrates the various visual defects that are present among school children. Naturally, there are other visual defects, but the incidence of these is not as great.

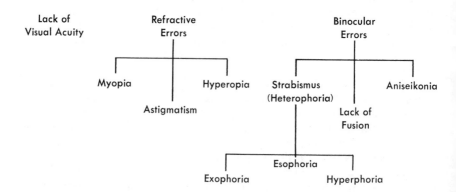

FIGURE 6–2 *Visual Deficiencies*

Symptoms of Eye Disturbances

The teacher of reading cannot be satisfied with a general knowledge of eye defects. He needs to know the individual pupil's eye condition well enough to answer a number of specific questions (Strang and Bracken, 1957, p. 163): Does the pupil need special reading materials? When should he wear his glasses? Does he require special lighting? Can he read for prolonged periods of time?

The teacher frequently must seek help from a specialist. Perhaps the teacher's chief responsibility here is to be familiar with the symptoms of eye defects. A knowledge of these will help him to detect visual problems before they have become visual defects. He should be able to identify functional problems before they have become structural problems. Bing (1961) groups symptoms into: (1) avoidance symptoms, such as in the case of the child who shuns reading tasks; (2) behavior symptoms such as squinting, fatigue, or excessive blinking; and (3) complaints such as dizziness, blurring, or double vision.[4]

Certainly the teacher should know these danger signs and look for them. Early detection of a child's visual difficulty may depend upon his alertness. The child's achievement in school generally is related to good vision. Good vision will mean more comfortable reading, and the child that sees well tends to develop favorable attitudes toward reading.

Teachers frequently are appalled by the poor concentration of some of their students. Unfortunately, in this instance "poor concentration" is not a good term. The pupil usually can concentrate, but it is on only one idea at a time. His attempt to maintain single vision or to clear blurred vision may prevent concentration on the mental task at hand. His cortical powers are directed entirely to the maintenance of basic visual skills (Dvorine, 1958). This same need for conscious control of the ocular factors may keep the child from reading as rapidly as he might.

EYE DEFECTS AND READING PROFICIENCY

Eye defects of one sort or another are rather common. These defects increase throughout the grades and may play an important role in reading inadequacy. Good readers in the elementary grades generally have fewer visual defects than have poor readers. In high school and college—possibly because by high school many of those with poor vision have left school, and those who remain have adapted their scholastic approach to their reading deficiencies—there are few indications of visual differences between good and poor readers.

Generally, the incidence of myopia does not distinguish the good reader from the poor reader. In fact, myopia may be associated with

---

[4]For listings of symptoms of visual difficulty see Knox (1953) and Diskan "Eye Problems in Children," *Postgraduate Medicine*, 34 (1963): 168–178.

better than normal progress (Farris, 1936). Although hyperopia seems to occur somewhat more frequently among poor readers (Eames, 1959, p. 7), the evidence certainly is not definitive. There also is a lack of agreement concerning the effect that astigmatism has on reading. It may be a handicap to successful reading when the learner has a severe case.

Failure of the eyes to coordinate, as in strabismus and in lack of fusion, and failure of the eyes to give images of the same size seem to have more serious impact on reading development. When the deviations are vertical, as when one eye focuses higher (hyperphoria), the reader frequently loses his place and fixates at a point either below or above the line on which he should be reading. He frequently complains of not understanding what he is reading. This condition appears to occur with equal frequency among both good and poor readers. When the deviations are lateral in nature, the convergence may be insufficient as in exophoria, or excessive as in cross eyes (esophoria). The former condition seems to occur more frequently among poor readers than does any other heterophoric condition. It leads to omissions, regressions, and loss of place.

Difficulties with fusion and aniseikonia also seem to be more common among poor readers than among good readers. Taylor (1962) reports that a survey of some 2000 children with academic difficulties showed that 95 percent of these lacked sufficient coordination and had difficulties with fusion. They failed to show the 13 to 19 diopters of convergence required to direct the eyes toward a single fixation point at 13 inches of reading distance while maintaining appropriate divergence or eye balance.

Taylor adds that deficiencies in binocular control lead to inadequate word perception and the consumption of an excessive amount of energy in maintaining single vision. The pupil will fatigue easily, experience distraction, poor comprehension, constant moving of the head, and difficulties in concentration.

Other eye movements associated with varying degrees of reading inefficiency are convergence and relative divergence, accommodation (focusing ability), compensation (compensating for head movements while reading), pursuit (smooth-movement such as used to read signs while driving or moving print on a screen) and physiological nystagmus (involuntary oscillating eye movements) (Griffin, Walton, and Ives, 1974).

Any interpretation of the relationship between visual defects and reading must consider the likelihood of multiple causation. Some children are more sensitive to visual problems than are others. Some are able to perform well in short test periods and thus escape detection through the usual methods. In fact, some eye defects may not yet have been identified. We know far too little about the syndromes or patterns of reading defects generally. Eye defects frequently may be but one of a number of factors contributing to a reading deficiency. Helvesten, Billips, and Weber (1970), comparing 310 unselected elementary school children and 67 severely disabled readers, found no laterality differences between them. The researchers concluded that controlling eye behavior has no relationship to reading ability.

The simple fact is that some children with defective vision become good readers and that others without any visual difficulty do not learn to read. However, this does not indicate that good vision is unimportant to reading. Eye defects are a handicap to both good and poor readers. And there are some interesting elements in the study by Griffin, Walton, and Ives. They found that poor readers had less efficient eye movements in spite of the fact that the decoding of words and comprehension had been eliminated; they had more regressions, and skipped and omitted more materials. They were less efficient regardless of the type of material used. Some sequenced saccadic eye movements too rapidly, thus skipping material; others sequenced too slowly, resulting in overfixation.

VISUAL SCREENING TESTS

In the past, the Snellen Chart test, designed by Snellen in Utrecht in 1862, was the acceptable screening test. It consists of rows of letters or *E*'s in varied positions. The pupil being examined stands 20 feet from the chart and names progressively smaller letters. The test identifies near-sightedness and measures visual acuity at a distance of twenty feet, but it fails to detect astigmatism and farsightedness. Since nearsightedness frequently is associated with good reading rather than with poor reading, the test is not too helpful in reading diagnosis. The *American Medical Association* (A.M.A.) *Rating Reading Card* can be used with the Snellen test. It is similar to the Snellen but is read at a distance of fourteen inches. One who fails on this test and succeeds on the Snellen Chart probably is farsighted; when the results are reversed the person probably is nearsighted.

Here are some tests commonly used in visual screening:

1. *A O Sight Screener,* American Optical Company, Kansas City, Missouri.
2. *Atlantic City Eye Test,* Freund Brothers, 1514 Pacific Avenue, Atlantic City, New Jersey.
3. *Keystone Visual Survey Telebinocular,* Mast Development Company.
4. *Massachusetts Eye Test,* Welch-Allyn Inc., Skaneateles Falls, New York or American Optical Company, 62 Mechanic, Southbridge, Massachusetts.
5. *Master Ortho-Rater Visual Efficiency Test,* Bausch and Lomb, Rochester, New York.
6. *New York School Vision Tester,* Bausch and Lomb, Inc., Rochester, New York.
7. *Prism Reader,* Educational Developmental Laboratories, Huntington, New York. (McGraw-Hill Publishing Company.)
8. *Reading Eye Camera,* Educational Developmental Laboratories, Huntington, New York. (McGraw-Hill Publishing Company).
9. *Spache Binocular Reading Test,* Mast Development Company, Davenport, Iowa.
10. *T/O Vision Testers,* Titmus Optical Company, Inc., Petersburg, Virginia.

Two simple tests which the teacher can use are the *Point of Convergence Test* and the *Muscle Balance and Suppression Test* (Brungardt and Brungardt, 1965). The *Point of Convergence Test* is administered by holding a penlight or pencil in front of the pupil. The examiner gradually moves the pencil horizontally toward the pupil's nose until the student sees two pencils. The near point of convergence is the distance in inches from that point on to the eye. Normal near-point convergence is from one to three inches. In the *Muscle Balance and Suppression Test,* a two or three foot string is held by the pupil. One end of the string is held against the bridge of the nose by the index finger, being careful so as not to block the line of sight of either eye. A knot is then tied in the string 16 inches away from the eyes. The student is instructed to look at the knot. Normally, he will see the two strings touching each other at the knot, making a V shape. If the two strings seem to cross in front of the knot, the condition is esophoria; if they cross behind the knot, it is exophoria. Orthophoria or normal muscular balance is present if the strings cross at the knot. If only one string is seen, the child is suppressing one eye. If one string is higher than the other, the condition is termed hyperophoria.

Since the vision tests suggested in this chapter are for screening purposes and frequently lack reliability, in doubtful cases the child's welfare is better served if the teacher errs in referring him to the specialist than if he errs in not referring him.

HEARING AND READING

We have already discussed the significance of auditory discrimination in reading. The child must be able to distinguish sounds so that he can learn to speak correctly and to associate the appropriate sound with the printed symbol (Carhart, 1947, p. 276). The ability to discriminate between the various phonetic elements of a word is a skill essential in reading.

The most usual way of teaching reading is still to go through the spoken word. Thus we say to the child: "Look at this word. This word says (spells) cat." The spoken word is the familiar stimulus, the written word is the novel stimulus. Gradually, with repeated associations between the written and the spoken word, the child brings to the written word the same meanings that he previously attached to one spoken word.

Some children experience much difficulty in associating the meaning that has been associated with the spoken word with the written word. Many of these difficulties stem from failure to properly identify the written word. Some may not see the word distinctly and correctly. Some may even fail to look at the word. They do not really identify the word; they learn rather that the word *cat* is on the flash card with the broken corner. Thus reading should always be a "look while you say" activity. The kinesthetic, tracing or writing method of teaching word identification may be effective precisely because it forces the child to pay close attention to the word and thus to make a proper association.

Other children are handicapped because they are not able to discriminate between the various phonetic elements of words, do not hear and do not speak the sound correctly, and thus will confuse words. No child learns to pronounce distinctions which he does not hear. The resultant confusion leads to an inability to associate the sound with the appropriate printed symbol. Hearing may bear as close a relationship to reading proficiency as does vision.

Drs. Jan Frank and Harold Levinson of Downstate Medical Center report in the *Journal of Child Psychiatry* that primary dyslexia is caused by some as yet unexplained defect in the nerve pathways that connect the inner ear, which helps control balance, with the cerebellum, the part of the brain that controls coordination. The result of this defect, they claim, is a sort of permanent motion sickness that affects a child's balance and scrambles incoming visual signals. In fact, they say, 112 out of 115 New York City children known to have primary dyslexia were tested and found to be afflicted with an inner-ear disturbance.

Frank and Levinson have devised an instrument that a school nurse can use to detect the ear disturbance, thus making it possible to diagnose primary dyslexia in preschool children. The two doctors are searching for a physiological treatment for the disorder, studying the effect of cyclizine, a motion-sickness drug, on the reading ability of dyslexic children.

Auditory adequacy includes hearing, listening, and comprehension; it encompasses auditory acuity, auditory discrimination, auditory blending, and auditory comprehension (MacGinitie, 1967; Wepman, 1961).

Hearing is the process by which sound waves are received, modified, and relayed along the nervous system by the ear (Horrworth, 1966). It is our prime concern in this section.

Auditory acuity is the recognition of discrete units of sound (Wepman, 1961). Auditory discrimination is the ability to discriminate between the sounds or phonemes of a language. Auditory blending is the ability to reproduce a word by synthesizing its component parts (Chall, Roswell, and Blumenthal, 1963). Finally, hearing is not complete until the hearer can comprehend and interpret what he has heard.

Sound waves are described as wave frequencies rather than wave lengths. Wave frequency is equivalent to the number of complete waves that pass a given point per second and is reported in cycles per second (cps). Amplitude refers to the height of the wave. High frequencies give high pitch and low frequencies result in a low pitch. By increasing the amplitude, a low pitch becomes lower and a high pitch gets higher. Intensity of the sound is expressed in decibels. The human ear is sensitive to frequencies ranging from 20 to 20,000 cps.

Normal acuity is variously defined. Some believe that a hearing loss of as little as 6 decibels[5] puts one in the hard-of-hearing group; others

---

[5]The decibel is a unit in the measure of sound intensity variation. Normal conversation has an intensity of about 60 decibels above a sound that is barely audible. Thus if an individual has a sixty decibel hearing loss in the speech range of sound, he would be aware of conversation only as a barely audible sound.

would put the cut-off point at 15 or more decibels. Because of this difference in definition, writers have reported percentages of hearing deficiencies ranging from 3 to 20 percent. Generally, it is estimated to be about 5 percent (McCabe, 1963). Other estimates are considerably higher, ranging upwards to 10 percent.

Types of Auditory Deficiency

There are two kinds of auditory deficiency: *intensity deafness* and *tone deafness.* A tone deaf person cannot discriminate between pitches. Intensity deafness is of three types: (1) *Central deafness* is caused by damage to the auditory areas of the brain or by a neurotic conversion reaction (hysteria). (2) A *conductive loss* stems from an impairment in the conductive process in the middle ear. Either the eardrum is punctured or there is a malfunction of the three small ossicles or bones in the middle ear. This reduces the person's hearing ability, affecting the loudness with which a person hears speech, but if the loudness of the sound is increased, he hears and understands. A person with a conductive loss can hear his own voice through bone conduction. Thus, the voices of others sound much softer than his own. To compensate, he frequently speaks softly so his voice conforms to the voice of others around him. (3) *Nerve loss* stems from an impairment of the auditory nerve and affects clarity and intelligibility of speech. A person with such a loss hears the speech of others, but may not understand what he hears. The high-tone nerve loss prevents him from hearing and distinguishing certain speech sounds, especially such sounds as *f, v, s, z, sh, zh, th, t, d, b, k,* and *g.* Articulation generally is affected. The pupil may speak too loudly or may develop monotony in his voice. He shows signs of frequently misunderstanding the teacher. The pupil may be thought of as mentally retarded. Figure 6-3 categorizes the various types of auditory deficiency.

Causes and Symptoms of Hearing Deficiencies

In more than 75 percent of the cases of deafness, German measles, erythroblastosis fetalis, meningitis, bilateral ear infection, fluid in the middle ear, obstructions in the ear canal, or a family history of deafness

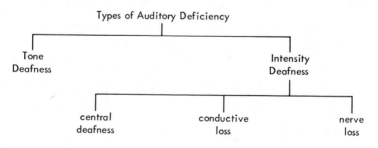

FIGURE 6-3

can be identified. In the remaining cases, the chief symptom is the inability to speak at the customary age.

Tests of Hearing

The hearing of every child showing symptoms of hearing difficulty should be tested. Bond and Tinker (1967, p. 113) suggest a number of methods for doing this. A loud ticking watch may be used as a simple test. Normally a child can hear the ticking up to a distance of about forty-eight inches. Anything below twenty inches probably indicates hearing deficiency. For a more accurate test an audiometer may be used. Audiometers produce sounds of different frequency and intensity levels for the purpose of measuring auditory sensitivity. They permit the audiologist to obtain an audiogram of an individual's hearing in terms of frequency and intensity.

The audiometer used in testing should provide for both airconduction and bone-conduction testing and for introducing masking tones (Newby, 1958, p. 39). There are two general types of audiometers: *discrete* frequency, providing tones in half- or full-octave steps; and *sweep* frequency, providing a continuous variation of frequencies. Hearing loss usually is measured in five-decibel steps. Some audiometers are similar to a portable phonograph with several connected telephone receivers that permit individual testing or the simultaneous testing of as many as ten children. For group testing with such an instrument, children must be able to write numbers, although in individual testing a teacher could record a child's answers.

A technique, called VASC (Verbal Auditory Screen for Children), permits easy testing of preschool children (Engh, 1968). VASC may be administered by non-professionals and consists of a picture chart, a modified tape recorder, and two sets of earphones. The tape uses words of two syllables rather than abstract tones. The tape plays automatically going from loud to soft, starting at 51 decibels. Children point to the pictures as they hear the words in their earphones. Each ear is tested separately. If the child can't get two of the last three words at 15 decibels, he is tested again. If he is still unable to do so, he is referred. The testing time is about five minutes.

Educational Implications

O'Connor and Streng (1950) divide the hard of hearing into four groups. Those with an average loss of 20 decibels or less in the better ear require no special treatment although it would be wise to seat them advantageously in the classroom. Children in the 25 to 55 decibel loss group may need speech training, and those with a loss of 35 decibels may need a hearing aid. A third group with losses ranging from 55 to 75 decibels usually cannot learn to speak without aid. The individuals in this group are considered educationally deaf. A fourth group consists of those who are suffering more than a 75 decibel loss. Members of this group cannot learn speech through sounds, and ordinarily the public school is unable to meet their needs. They require special treatment. Children with a 40 decibel loss across the speech range will have particular difficulty with *ch, f, k, s, sh, th,* and *z* (Frisina, 1957 p. 3ff).

Loss of hearing can aggravate a reading deficiency. Studies generally have indicated that the ability to discriminate speech sounds is important for speech and reading development. Without it, children cannot isolate the separate sounds in words and thus find phonics training incomprehensible. However, in seeking to understand the relationship between auditory deficiencies and reading disability, we again must remember that causes often are complex rather than simple, multiple rather than single. Auditory factors may be especially important when there is a severe hearing loss, when the specific hearing loss involves high-tone deafness (there is lowered acuity for sounds of high pitch) (Sheridan, 1948), or when instruction puts a premium on auditory factors. The exclusive use of the phonic method with a child who has suffered a hearing loss may prevent achievement in reading.

The child will be at a disadvantage if the teacher fails to distinguish between mistakes in reading and differences in pronunciation (Labov, 1965). The pupil, who reads "I write wif a pin," has read correctly, but may not have spoken the way the teacher would speak. Admonishing this child for poor reading may only hurt him. In fact, the child may not be able to hear the difference between *with* and *wif* or *pen* and *pin,* even under the most favorable of instructional procedures.

The teacher cannot be satisfied, however, with the mere detection of auditory deficiencies. He cannot do much about improving the child's auditory acuity. He *can* do much in developing the pupil's auditory discrimination skills. He must train the child in the awareness of sound, in making gross discriminations such as between the sounds of a bell and a horn, in making discriminations among simple speech patterns such as differences between vowels, and in the finer discriminations necessary for speech (Davis, 1947, p. 284). The latter involves the ability to distinguish the phonetic elements within words. Silvaroli and Wheelock (1966) report that auditory discrimination training helped children to discriminate more effectively thirty-three basic speech sounds.

LISTENING AND READING PROFICIENCY

In the preceding portions of this chapter we have focused our attention on the sensory processes of vision and hearing. We have discussed them at length because sensation is a first step toward perception. However, we cannot divorce the sensory phases from the perceptual phases. We must seek to integrate our knowledge of sensation with our understanding of the total process of perception.

We have already examined the perceptual aspects of vision. Let us now examine the perceptual aspects of hearing. These generally are referred to as listening.

Some writers use the term auding to refer to the "gross process of listening to, recognizing, and interpreting spoken symbols" (Horworth, 1966). Auding thus includes hearing, listening, and cognizing or comprehension of these sequences.

Communication among humans is usually though spoken symbols. However, communication may involve expression as through speaking and writing[6] or reception and comprehension as through listening or reading (Beyer, 1958). Listening is the first language art that the child develops, and so the remainder of this chapter will be devoted to it.

Listening, if it is to be learned at all, must be taught early in life. Carhart (1947, p. 279) points out that the capacity for mastering new sound discriminations diminishes with age. A child learns to speak fluently the language he hears, regardless of his race or nationality. However, when an adult learns a new language, he has what native speakers call a "foreign accent." This is so because he has fixed his habits of speech, and his habits of listening. He does not notice the subtle differences in the phonetic elements of the two languages. Furthermore, he hears his new language as though it were identical with that of his native tongue.

Unfortunately too many children are hearing but are not listening. They are apprehending and perhaps even taking notice of sound without understanding or interpreting that sound.

Listening goes beyond the mere recognition of sounds. Adequate hearing is only the first step in listening. The ability to listen evolves from hearing. An infant hears, but only after he becomes capable of directing hearing or structuring among aural stimuli does listening begin (Way, 1973).

Ross (1966) found that good listeners rated higher than poor listeners on intelligence, reading, socioeconomic status, and achievement, but not on a hearing test. Obviously listening is more than hearing. Two listeners, even with the same hearing acuity, often receive widely different messages from the same sound.

It may also well be that children from lower socioeconomic homes are at a distinct disadvantage in learning to read because they have spoken and heard language patterns that interfere with the comprehension of both oral and written materials (Deutsch, 1964). In support of this is the study by Clark and Richards (1966). They found a significant deficiency in auditory discrimination in economically disadvantaged preschool children.

There are other reasons for improving the listening skills of children. Skill in listening is closely related to proficiency in many academic areas. Some children are better listeners than readers. For children in the lower grades, for children who are poor readers, and perhaps for boys generally (Many, 1965), listening is the most important means for achievement.

Reading is not learning. It is only one of the media for learning, and

---

[6] Written words do not have a direct connection with the *object* or *event*. They are only symbols of speech. They are symbols of symbols, much as a check is a symbol of money, which itself is merely a symbol of purchasing power (Pei, 1958, p. 24). Spoken words are primary symbols; written words are secondary symbols.

for some children it is an inferior medium. In fact, some studies indicate that up to about the fifth grade (mental age of ten) children generally learn more and remember better through listening than through reading (Young, 1936). Many (1965) found that sixth-grade pupils comprehended more by reading than by listening. Generally, the lower the reading ability and the lower the scholastic aptitude, the greater is the advantage of listening over reading (Larsen and Feder, 1940). However, since reading allows the pupil to go back and reread, reading becomes more effective as the difficulty of the material increases (Larsen and Feder, 1940).

Swalm (1972), studying 108 students each in grades 2–4, found that:

1. Above-average reading ability students comprehended better when reading than when listening.
2. Average reading ability students showed the same, except the differences were not as large.
3. Below-average reading ability students comprehended best when listening.

In a later study Swalm (1974) confirmed that listening was significantly more effective than reading with the student whose reading abilities were below average. The results of the study indicated that the relationship between the student's reading ability and the readability level of the article (and not grade level) was very important and this factor should determine whether the teacher should use listening or reading for most efficient learning. Thus, it is probably inappropriate to say that listening is superior to reading for primary students.

Listening ability also is basic to the learning of reading. Coefficients of correlation between scores on listening and reading tests vary from .27 to .80 (Weintraub, 1967; Brown, 1965; Fawcett, 1966; Ruddell, 1966). Does this mean that improvement in listening will make for improvement in reading? Hollingsworth (1964) reviewed the literature on this point and concluded that listening does indeed have a positive effect on reading achievement. Listening and reading have basic similarities. Both involve the reception of ideas from others. Reading demands sight and comprehension; listening calls for hearing and comprehension.

1. Listening provides the vocabulary and the sentence structure that serve as a foundation for reading. Reading success depends upon the child's aural-oral experience with words. In a very real sense the child reads with his ears, mentally pronouncing the words to himself.
2. Listening and reading utilize similar verbal factors, but they also encompass factors unique to each skill (Ruddell, 1966).
3. Without the ability to hear and interpret sounds, the child cannot learn phonics.
4. Ability to listen to and provide an ending for a story is a good indicator of readiness for reading.
5. Words most easily read are those that have been heard and spoken.
6. Listening ability (if scores on a listening comprehension test are higher than the scores on a reading comprehension test) is an indicator of the pupil's potential ceiling in reading ability.

The child learns language by ear. The vocabulary and skills in language structure that he brings to school were learned first through listening. In fact, if it were not for these learnings the child would not, or at least only rarely, learn to read (Pooley, 1961, pp. 44–45). The teacher of reading should take advantage of these previous learnings. He should help the child to associate the visual symbols with the sounds previously learned. If the child has not learned to listen, he must be taught.

SUMMARY

Reading is a visual skill, but success in reading depends more on the underlying perceptual and assimilative processes than on visual efficiency and the peculiar oculo-motor habits of the individual reader. Faulty eye movements are not so much a cause of poor reading as a symptom of poor reading. Eye defects, even though they are of a fairly gross nature seldom are an absolute bar to a child's becoming a good reader. However, they may result in uncomfortable and inefficient reading.

Auditory defects are most likely to hinder reading success when there is a severe hearing loss, when hearing loss involves deafness for high tones, and when instruction puts a premium on auditory factors.

Closely related to auditory factors is listening. Listening requires a cultivation of auditory abilities. It involves the same basic perceptual and mental processes as reading and, indeed, in certain cases may be a more suitable method of learning than is reading. The chapter therefore suggests that reading success depends upon the child's aural-oral experience with words (Womack, 1957). Training in listening develops auditory discrimination which in turn serves as a basis for phonetic analysis in reading. Listening and speaking provide the vocabulary and the sentence patterns for reading. The instruction in grammar, usage, and composition, occurring either directly or indirectly in learning to listen and to speak, is also beneficial in learning to read. Finally, words and sentences most easily read are those that have been heard and spoken. *The language is the same in all the language arts: only the media for communication are different* (Pronovost, 1959, p. 15).

QUESTIONS FOR DISCUSSION

---

1. Discuss the question of when the child's eyes are ready for reading.
2. What are the data concerning deterioration in vision as children grow older?
3. What is known about the nature of eye movements during reading? Should training designed to improve eye movements result in reading improvement?

4. What are the general types and symptoms of defective vision?
5. What relationships have been observed between eye defects and reading proficiency?
6. What are the relationships between hearing and reading?
7. What relationships have been observed between reading and listening?
8. In what ways are reading and listening the same process? How do they differ?
9. What are the common refractive errors and binocular difficulties?

BIBLIOGRAPHY

BALLANTINE, FRANCIS A. "Age Changes in Measures of Eye-Movements in Silent Reading." *Studies in the Psychology of Reading*, Monographs in Education, No. 4. Ann Arbor: University of Michigan Press, 1951, pp. 67–111.

BAYLE, EVALYN. "The Nature and Causes of Regressive Movements in Reading." *Journal of Experimental Education* 11 (1942): 16–36.

BING, LOIS B. "Vision and Reading." *The Reading Teacher* 14 (1961): 241–44.

BOND, GUY L. and TINKER, MILES A. *Reading Difficulties: Their Diagnosis and Correction.* New York: Appleton-Century-Crofts, 1967.

BROWN, CHARLES T. "Three Studies of Listening of Children." *Speech Monographs* 32 (1965): 129–38.

BRUNGARDT, JOE B. and BRUNGARDT, MIKE J. "Let's Stop the Prevailing Injustices to Children." *Kansas Teacher* 73 (1965): 14–15, 50.

BUSWELL, GUY THOMAS. *Fundamental Reading Habits: A Study of Their Development,* Supplementary Educational Monographs, No. 21. Chicago: University of Chicago Press, 1922.

CARHART, RAYMOND. "Auditory Training" and "Conservation of Speech." In Davis, Hallowell, ed., *Hearing and Deafness: A Guide for Laymen.* New York: Murray Hill Books, 1947, pp. 276–317.

CHALL, JEANNE; ROSWELL, FLORENCE G.; and BLUMENTHAL, SUSAN H. "Auditory Blending Ability: A Factor in Success in Beginning Reading." *The Reading Teacher* 17 (1963): 113–18.

CLARK, ANN D. and RICHARDS, CHARLOTTE J. "Auditory Discrimination Among Economically Disadvantaged and Nondisadvantaged Preschool Children." *Exceptional Children* 33 (1966) 259–62.

DEUTSCH, MARTIN; MALIVER, ALMA; BROWN, BERT; and CHERRY, ESTELLE. *Communication of Information in the Elementary School Classroom.* New York: Institute for Developmental Studies, New York Medical College, 1964.

DVORINE, ISRAEL. "What You Should know About Sight—Part III—Symptoms of Abnormal Function of the Visual Process." *Education* 79 (1958): 240–46.

EBERL, MARGUERITE. "Visual Training and Reading." *Clinical Studies in Reading II.* Supplementary Educational Monographs, No. 77. Chicago: University of Chicago Press, 1953, pp. 141–48.

Educational Developmental Laboratories, Inc. *The Evolution and Growth of Controlled Reading Techniques.* Huntington, New York, 1958.

FARRIS, L. P. "Visual Defects Influencing Achievement in Reading." *Journal of Experimental Education* 5 (1936): 58–60.

FAWCETT, ANNABEL E. "Training in Listening." *Elementary English* 43 (1966): 473–76.

FEINBERG, RICHARD. "A Study of Some Aspects of Peripheral Visual Acuity." *American Journal of Optometry and Archives of American Academy of Optometry* 62 (1949): 1–23.

FRISINA, D. ROBERT. *Hearing: Its Interrelation with Speech,* Bulletin No. 1. Washington, D.C.: Gallaudet College, 1957.

GAARDNER, K. R. "Eye Movements and Perception." In F. Young and Lindsley, eds., *Early Experience and Visual Information Processing in Perceptual and Reading Disorders.* National Academy of Sciences, 1970.

GRIFFIN, DONALD C.; WALTON, HOWARD N.; and IVES, VERA. "Saccades as Related to Reading Disorders." *Journal of Learning Disabilities* 7 (1974): 52–58.

HELVESTEN, EUGENE M; BILLIPS, WILLIAM C.; and WEBER, JANET C. "Controlling Eye-Dominant Hemisphere Relationship as Factor in Reading Ability." *American Journal of Opththalmology* 70 (1970): 96–100.

HILDRETH, GERTRUDE. *Teaching Reading.* New York: Holt, Rinehart & Winston, 1958.

HOLLINGSWORTH, PAUL M. "Can Training in Listening Improve Reading?" *The Reading Teacher* 18 (1964): 121–23, 127.

HORRWORTH, GLORIA L. "Listening: A Facet of Oral Language." *Elementary English* 43 (1966): 856–64, 868.

KOSINSKI, W. 'Die Myopie als Variköses Syndrom der Augen." *Klinische Monatsblaetter fur Augenheilkunde* 130 (1957): 266–270. Quoted by Linksz, Arthur, "Optics and Visual Physiology," A.M.A. *Archives of Ophthalmology* 59 (1958): 901–969.

LABOV, W. "Linguistic Research on Non-Standard English of Negro Children." Paper read at New York Society for the Experimental Study of Education, New York, 1965.

LARSEN, ROBERT P., and FEDER, D. D. "Common and Differential Factors in Reading and Hearing Comprehension." *Journal of Educational Psychology* 31 (April, 1940) 241–52.

LEDBETTER, FRANCES GRESHAM. "Reading Reactions for Varied Types of Subject Matter: An Analytical Study of the Eye Movements of Eleventh Grade Pupils." *Journal of Educational Research* 41 (1947): 102–115.

MANY, WESLEY A. "Is There Any Difference: Reading vs. Listening?" *The Reading Teacher* 19 (1965): 110–13.

MACGINITIE, WALTER H. "Auditory Perception in Reading." *Education* 87 (1967): 532–38.

McCABE, BRIAN F. "The Etiology of Deafness." *Volta Review* 65 (1963): 471–77.

MILLS, LLOYD. "The Functions of the Eyes in the Acquisition of an Education." *Journal of the American Medical Association* 93 (1929): 841–45.

NEWBY, HAYES A. *Audiology: Principles and Practice.* New York: Appleton-Century-Crofts, 1958.

O'CONNOR, CLARENCE D. and STRENG, ALICE. "Teaching the Acoustically Handicapped." *The Education of Exceptional Children,* Forty-ninth Yearbook of the

National Society for the Study of Education, Part II, Chicago: University of Chicago Press, 1950, pp. 152–76.

PEI, MARIO. *Language for Everybody*. New York: Pocket Books, Inc., 1958.

PERRY, WILLIAM G., Jr. and WHITLOCK, CHARLES P. "A Clinical Rationale for a Reading Film." *Harvard Educational Review* 24 (1954): 6–27.

POOLEY, ROBERT C. "Reading and the Language Arts." In Nelson B. Henry, ed., *Development in and Through Reading*. National Society for the Study of Education Yearbook, No. 60. Chicago: University of Chicago Press, 1961, pp. 35–53.

PRITCHARD, ROY M. "Stabilized Images on the Retina." In Richard C. Atkinson, ed., *Contemporary Psychology*. San Francisco: W. H. Freeman and Company, 1971, pp. 117–23.

PRONOVOST, WILBERT. *The Teaching of Speaking and Listening*. New York: David McKay Company, 1959.

ROSENBLOOM, ALFRED A., JR., O. D. "Promoting Visual Readiness for Reading." *Changing Concepts of Reading Instruction*, International Reading Association Conference Proceedings. New York: Scholastic Magazines, 1961, pp. 89–93.

RUDDELL, ROBERT B. "Oral Language and the Development of Other Language Skills." *Elementary English* 43 (1966): 489–98, 517.

SCHUBERT, D. G. and TORGERSON, T. L. *Improving the Reading Program*. Dubuque, Iowa: Wm. C. Brown, 1972.

SCHUBERT, DELWYN G. and WALTON, HOWARD N. "Effects of Induced Astigmatism." *The Reading Teacher* 21 (1968): 547–51.

SHERIDAN, MARY D. *The Child's Hearing for Speech*. London: Methuen & Co., Ltd., 1948.

SMITH, FRANK. *Understanding Reading*. New York: Holt, Rinehart and Winston, 1971.

SPACHE, GEORGE D. "A Rationale for Mechanical Methods for Improving Reading." *Significant Elements in College and Adult Reading Improvement*. Seventh Yearbook of the National Reading Conference for Colleges and Adults, Fort Worth: Texas Christian University Press, 1958, pp. 115–32.

STRANG, R. and BRACKEN, D. K. *Making Better Readers*. Boston: Heath, 1957.

SWALM, JAMES E. "A Comparison of Oral Reading, Silent Reading and Listening Comprehension." *Education* 92 (1972): 111–15.

SWALM, JAMES E. "Is Listening Really More Effective for Learning in the Early Grades?" *Elementary English* 51 (1974): 1110–13.

TAYLOR, STANFORD E. *Speed Reading vs. Improved Reading Efficiency*. Huntington, N.Y.: Educational Development Laboratories, 1962.

TAYLOR, STANFORD E. "Eye Movements in Reading: Facts and Fallacies." *American Educational Research Journal* 2 (1965): 187–202.

TAYLOR, STANFORD E.; FRACKENPOHL, H.; and PETTEE, J. L. *Grade Level Norms for the Components of the Fundamental Reading Skill*. Huntington, N.Y.: Educational Developmental Laboratories, Bulletin No. 3, 1960.

TINKER, MILES A. "The Use and Limitations of Eye-Movement Measures in Reading." *Psychological Review* 40 (1933): 381–87.

TINKER, MILES A. "The Role of Eye Movements in Diagnostic and Remedial Reading," *School and Society* 39 (1934): 147–48.

TINKER, MILES A. "Time Relations for Eye-Movement Measures in Reading." *Journal of Educational Psychology* 38 (1947): 1–10.

TINKER, MILES A. "Recent Studies of Eye Movements in Reading." *Psychological Bulletin* 55 (1958): 215–31.

WEINTRAUB, SAMUEL. "Listening Comprehension." *The Reading Teacher,* 20 (April, 1967): 639–47.

WEPMAN, JOSEPH M. "The Interrelationship of Hearing, Speech, and Reading." *The Reading Teacher* 14 (1961): 245–47.

WOMACK, THURSTON. "Is English a Phonetic Language?" *Elementary English* 34 (1957): 386–88.

YOUNG, WILLIAM E. "The Relation of Reading Comprehension and Retention to Hearing Comprehension and Retention." *Journal of Experimental Education* 5 (1936): 30–39.

7

The Physiological Correlates of Reading

There are numerous physiological factors in addition to vision and hearing that play significant roles in the reading process. Thus general physical health, speech development, glandular and neurological functioning, and cerebral dominance become of professional interest to the reading teacher.

Whereas, in the previous chapter, we were most concerned with the sensory bases of the reading process, here we will examine a variety of general physical conditions—speech defects, brain injuries, and those facts concerning cerebral dominance that may have a bearing on reading readiness and achievement.

Learning requires experience. Yet defects of any kind, whether in hearing, vision, speech, or general physical health, tend to restrict experiences and hinder learning.

GENERAL PHYSICAL CONDITIONS

The child is both physical and physiological. Functions such as vision, hearing, and thought are possible only through the organs of the body, the eye, the ear, or brain. If the organ is defective, the function is likely to be impaired. This may, especially in the case of vision, hearing, and thought, lead to serious reading difficulties. In general, good health is conducive to good reading, and poor health is often associated with reading deficiency.

Numerous studies have dealt with the relationships of reading disability and glandular dysfunction, particularly underfunctioning of the pituitary glands (Mateer, 1935), thyroid deficiency (Cavanaugh, 1948), hemoglobin variations (Eames, 1953), vitamin deficiencies, endocrine disturbances, nerve disorders, nutritional and circulatory problems, and heart conditions. Other studies have stressed conditions such as adenoids, infected tonsils, poor teeth, rickets, asthma, allergies, tuberculosis, rheumatic fever, and prolonged illnesses. Eames (1962) points out that tumefaction of the pituitary gland may lead to a reduction in eye span and consequently to an increase in the number of fixations. Hypothyroid conditions may prevent normal fixation on what is being read and thus lead to daydreaming, poor attention, slow word recognition, and general fatigue. Diabetes mellitus is associated with visual defects, confusions, excessive regressions, and loss of place.

The eating habits of our children are related to a child's overall functioning and also may be a direct cause of poor learning. Far too often the elementary school child either does not eat at all or gulps down a few bites to satisfy his mother. Scrimshaw (1970) states that children with a history of early and prolonged malnutrition tend to perform poorly on intelligence and behavioral tests.

The teacher must be cautious in interpreting the relationship that these factors seemingly have to reading deficiency. Generally, physical inadequacies contribute to rather than cause reading problems. Illness keeps the child from school and causes him to miss important phases of instruction. Any physical inadequacy makes it difficult to become enthusiastic about learning and may result in lowered vitality, in depletion of energy, in slower physical development, and hence in mental retardation. Physical inadequacies cause the child to center attention on them and away from learning. The child with a smashed finger, a broken hand, a headache, or poor eyesight may be unable to concentrate on a learning task. The malnourished child does not have the energy to be an effective learner.

Sometimes a lowering of the child's basic vitality is closely related to the functions required for successful reading. For example, the basal metabolic rate, BMR, affects the convergence of the eyes. If the rate is low, the child may not be able to aim his eyes properly in binocular vision, and thus may frequently regress, omit words, lose his place, and become fatigued. And, fatigue makes it difficult to become interested in a reading task. Attention suffers and comprehension is usually lowered. As nervous tension builds up, the pupil becomes disinterested, disgusted, and may even turn from reading completely. However, Schiffman (1967) notes that there is no known relationship between errors of biochemical functioning and any *specific* reading syndrome. However, the data tell us to pay special attention to the physical health of our students and to recognize that certain physical deviations may be accompanied by educational problems.

LANGUAGE AND READING READINESS

Repeatedly in the book we have noted the importance of language, that reading is a language and communication process, and that a pupil's success in reading is intimately related to his language facility.

In Chapter 6 we stressed the significance of hearing and listening. Here our focus is more on the expressive phase of language, namely, speech. The unquestioned fact is that the child's first vocabulary, his mastery of sentence structure, and his clarity of pronunciation are each learned through listening and speaking. And, children generally must first learn the alphabet of sounds before they can be taught the alphabet of letters.

The child begins to vocalize almost immediately after birth. Generally, these vocalizations are global reactions, involving the entire bodily mechanism. There is no awareness or purpose in these responses. They arise as a column of air is expelled from the lungs. The process is reflexive in nature, and the air passes between vocal folds tense enough to produce sound. The child's first use of the physical apparatus necessary for speech occurs at birth when he takes in breath and emits the birth cry.

At this stage there are no speech organs as such. The child's grunts, gurgles, coos, snorts, cries, and hiccoughs are primarily associated with the nonlinguistic function of the organs. The child frequently is merely breathing, swallowing, or hiccoughing. He has not really begun to use the organs for speech. By exercising the physiological functions, he is conditioning the muscles for their nonspeech functions.

The child soon becomes aware of the sounds that he is making. He enjoys vocal play and in his cooing and gurgling produces a greater number and variety of sounds than are found in any given language. Some children may be able to produce a *wh, ch,* or *l* sound at this time, but unfortunately are unable to use it correctly in words for another two or three years.

The third stage occurs at about nine or ten months of age and is called lalling. The laller produces a slurred kind of half intelligible speech because he has not learned to move the tongue independently of the jaw. At this time the child repeats *heard* sounds or sound combinations (Berry, 1956, p. 20). Referred to as echolalia, the child actually echos the sounds that he or others produce. A circulatory process is now set up. The child produces a sound (oral) and hears it (aural). The first oral-aural association is being developed. At this stage, through imitation, the child may learn new groupings of sounds, but he doesn't learn new sounds. He repeats sounds which he already uses spontaneously.

Between twelve and eighteen months the child produces his first words. These frequently are quite redundant (ma-ma, da-da, bye-bye, ba-ba) and represent a complete thought unit. Thus, "ba-ba" may mean "Give me the bottle." However, the speech is undifferentiated. "Da-da" may mean anyone that looks like daddy. The word cannot be differentiated because the child's perceptions of what a daddy is are not differentiated. With experience his perceptions become more discriminative and so does his usage of words.

The child next learns that the name of an object stands for a class of things. He identifies similar objects and groups them under one word. The child is not actually abstracting. He identifies similarities in objects, but is not yet capable of seeing their differences. Children during this period feel that they know the whole of reality. They do not discriminate between the object and the word that stands for the object. To them, the word is both perception and reality.

Finally, the child learns to develop concepts and uses words to communicate his concepts. The word now is a symbol in its true sense.

Early Articulation of Sounds

Experience has shown that the child must have reached a certain amount of oral language maturity before beginning reading. The reading teacher is interested in the "speech age" of the child. He must know how many phonemes the child uses consistently and how frequently the pupil substitutes because of an inability to use a certain sound. Consonant sounds generally develop in a definite order. Hildreth (1958, p. 52) suggests that by the age of seven the average child articulates correctly the consonants and consonant blends 90 percent of the time.

Poole (1934) studied 140 preschool children over a period of three years and found that the rate of development in articulation is similar among boys and girls between the ages of two and one-half and five and one-half. After this girls develop more rapidly and attain the same degree of proficiency by six and one-half that boys attain only at seven and one-half. Poole also found that there is a regular progression in articulation development. Table 7-1 summarizes her findings and indicates at what age certain sounds had been mastered by the 140 children in her group. Probably the reason that children learn to make the *b, p, m, w, d, t, n, g, k, ng,* and *y* sounds so early is that feeding exercises the tongue muscles required to make these sounds.

The *z* and *s* sounds are listed twice because after the age of five, when dentition causes a spacing between the teeth, they become distorted in a lisp. This lisp disappears when normal dentition is reestablished.

Although serious deviation from normal speech development is not too frequent among first graders, Davis (1938) indicates that quite commonly children have difficulty with *zh, sh, l, th, z, s, r,* and *wh.* Van Riper and Butler (1955, p. 64) point out that most articulatory errors made by children involve *r, s, l, k, sh, th, ch,* and *f* and that the average child does not

TABLE 7-1 *Ages When Children Normally Have Mastered the Consonant Sounds*

AGES	CONSONANTS
3.5	b, p, m, w, h
4.5	d, t, n, g, k, ng, y
5.5	f, v, z, s
6.5	sh, zh, l, th*
8.0	z, s, r, wh,
	ch, j

*Th as in thin or then.

attain complete mastery of *s, l, r,* and *th* or their blends until the age of eight years (Van Riper, 1964). For example, it is not uncommon to hear a first or second grader speak in this manner:

> This is the boat that my gwandfathe' sent me fo' my bufday. . . . The postman bwought it just befo' we went to the lake on Satu'day. It will weally sail! One time when I wasn't watching it, it sailed wight unde' the wope to the deep pa't of the lake and my fathe' had to swim out fast and get it. It wides waves too. The moto' boats on the lake made some waves, but my boat didn't tu'n ova.[1]

The sounding errors in the above are chiefly: *r, th,* and *l.* Many children show even more serious deficiencies in language structure. They cannot formulate sentences or turn ideas into words. Undoubtedly many pupils who are deficient in reading actually are deficient in general language ability. Warfel (1957) suggests that the initial step in reading instruction should relate what is in the ear and on the tongue to what is to be put into the eye. Warfel (1958) believes that good reading initially must be accompanied by vocal sounds. He adds that only after much experience is the child able to change marks into meaning without putting them first in the ear and on the tongue. Davis (1938) adds that the earliest reading materials should contain a minimum of late-developing sounds and a minimum of words in which a single spelling combination indicates a number of different sounds. Van Riper (1964) notes that the speech pathologist shudders when he scans primers, because they are filled with late maturing sounds. " 'Look' and 'see' and 'say' and 'run, Sally, run' probably fix and perpetuate consonant errors which otherwise would be outgrown."

The Phoneme

Basically two kinds of sound are produced by the human speech mechanism. Phones are sounds of any kind that have not become a part of the language. Young children always produce a far greater number of sounds than they later use in the production of speech. Phonemes are speech sounds that are a part of the language. Thus, all phonemes are phones, but not all phones are phonemes.

Language consists of phonemes, morphemes, words, and utterances. The phoneme has one prime purpose in language. It individualizes human utterances. The phoneme is the smallest unit of language which can differentiate one utterance from another (Gleason, 1955, p. 9). For example, the sentences "Tom, will you wash these carrots?" and "Tom, will you wash those carrots?" are completely alike except for one phoneme. A single letter representing a simple sound changes completely the meaning the following sentences: "A stitch in time saves none" or "There's no business like shoe business."

[1] Mary Peebles Hinman, "The Teacher and the Specialist," *NEA Journal* 49 (November 1960): 24–25.

Phonemes, of which there are about forty-six in English, are thus not single sounds; they are rather a collection of sounds; they are a class of closely related sounds constituting the smallest unit of speech that will distinguish one utterance from another (Smith, 1971, p. 31). They are perhaps better described as a network of differences between sounds (Hockett, 1958, p. 24). A *grapheme* (the counterpart of the phoneme) is a class of closely related graphs constituting the smallest unit of writing that will distinguish one word from another.

Language thus is a continuum of sound classified into a limited number of permitted single sounds called phonemes that join in a limited number of permitted combinations (Jolly, 1972).

Morphology and Syntax

A morpheme is the smallest linguistic unit in our language that has meaning. It has lexical meaning if it has a meaning of its own (for example, prefixes and suffixes), and it has relational meaning if it has a grammatical meaning. For example, in the sentence, "She insists on it," the *in* in insists has lexical meaning. It has meaning wherever it occurs; the *s* at the end of the word has no meaning of itself. It has meaning only to the extent that it makes the verb a third person singular. It is said to have relational meaning. The *s* may take on a relational meaning also when it changes a noun from the singular to the plural or when it denotes the possessive case.

Words are the smallest linguistic units that have meaning and that can stand alone in a sentence. The study of how words are constructed is called morphology. An utterance is a series of words that are spoken at one time. The manner in which words are grouped into utterances is called syntax. And syntax and morphology compose the grammar of a language. Figure 7-1 illustrates the relationships existing between the various factors.

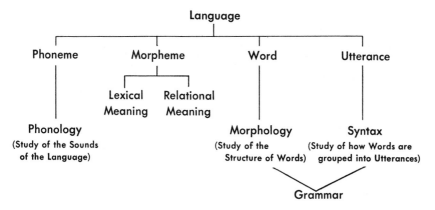

FIGURE 7–1 *The Components of Language*

Grammar has only one basic function: to make our utterances clearer. It is an aid to the expression and interpretation of meaning. Morphology, for example, allows us to introduce minute changes into the word to bring out a special meaning. The various uses of *s* given above are examples of this. Syntax permits us to group words to suggest certain nuances of meaning. For example, the same words might be grouped in this way to suggest various meanings: "The weak girl is playing a game of tennis," or "The girl is playing a weak game of tennis"; "The boy sat in a chair with a broken arm," or "The boy with a broken arm sat in a chair"; "The lion in the cage roared at the man," or "The lion roared at the man in the cage." The formal distinction between *runs* as a verb and *runs* as a_ noun (He runs home. The runs on the bank were many.) is syntactic in nature (Ives, 1964). The reader must first recognize the distinction in arrangement before he can perceive the distinction in meaning. An adjective can be given a noun meaning by syntax: "The *best* is not good enough for him." To read the word "lead," the reader must know whether it is a noun or a verb (Reed, 1965).

In addition to phonemes, morphemes, and words there are certain characteristics about the utterance that add to and develop meaning. The loudness of the voice changes or certain words are stressed more than others. We give a heavy, medium, light, or weak stress. The pitch is either low, normal, high, or extra high. High pitch is often associated with heavier stress. In speaking, utterances are combined by what are termed "plus junctures"; they are ended by "terminal junctures." (Lloyd, 1962). The plus junctures separate words; the terminal junctures are usually accompanied by falls or rises in pitch, and differentiate one phrase unit from another or one type of sentence from another. The declarative sentence has a slight drop in pitch at the end. Phrasing depends on the placement of the junctures.

Words do not give meaning to sentences; rather, words receive their meaning from the sentence or the verbal and syntactic context of which they are a part. The pupil who has become a word reader has fallen into the error of not "reading" the phrase unit that gives meaning to the word. The word must be looked upon merely as *one* element in a series of elements that constitute a sentence. The sentence circumscribes the word, giving it the distinct meaning intended by the speaker or writer. The word "run" means many things dependent upon its usage in the sentence. Its meaning depends also upon the structure of the sentence.

Lloyd (1962) notes that reading instruction should begin with familiar materials, materials that represent the child's speech. In this way the child learns that what he says can be written and read. The implications for beginning with experience charts in teaching reading are obvious.

The broader implications of a linguistic approach to reading seem to be (Lefevre, 1962):

1. Children should learn to read the language they already speak.
2. Efficient reading means an awareness of the spoken language structures represented by the graphic language.

Perhaps we have too long ignored the meaning-bearing language patterns. We may not have paid enough attention to the child's need to perceive language structures as wholes for *total comprehension* (Lefevre, 1962). Teachers of reading need to become more familiar with the structure of the language.

What are the implications of all this for reading? If the pupil cannot sound the individual phoneme, he probably will not be a good oral reader. He will have difficulty with phonics. He also may have difficulty in transmitting meaning.

The child's proficiency in reading, and certainly his word identification and recognition skill, is dependent upon his ability to articulate, enunciate, and pronounce the sounds met in his language.

Furthermore, genuine reading proficiency may mean the ability to read language structure. The best reader may be one mentally aware of the stresses, elongations of words, changes of pitch and intonation, and rhythms of the sentences that he reads. If he reads what was spoken the way the writer would like it to have been said, true communication of meaning may be possible.

NEURAL ADEQUACY AND READING

The brain controls the rest of the body by sending commands, as it were, through a network of eighty-six major nerves that expand into thousands of smaller nerves. The nerves spread from the brain through the brain stem down the spinal cord. The nerves may be likened to miles of telephone wire; the brain, to a central switchboard. The impulses travel through the neural network, transmitting sensory data and messages.

Obviously, brain activity is much more complex than a telephone switchboard connection. In the neurons, through a combination of glucose and oxygen, an electrical charge builds up. At a certain level of buildup it discharges. And, this electrical discharge is the nerve impulse that moves from neuron to neuron. It is a combination of these impulses or tiny bursts of electrical energy that we record on electroencephalographs and that result in thoughts and actions. The transmission of the impulse from one neuron to another is chemically controlled. It is not the impulse itself but a resulting chemical, acetycholine, that stimulates a muscle and makes it move.

The mysteries of brain activity are many. The reticular formation in the brain stem seems to make it possible for us to pay attention or to ignore the multitude of stimuli that bombard us. The thalamus plays a role in the perception of pain. Rage and fear are produced when the amygdala is stimulated. Destruction of the amygdala leads to extreme nymphomania in the female cat and to satyrism in the male. Electrical stimulation at the proper spot can cause a cat to purr contentedly when hurt or to become panicky at the sight of a mouse. The usually fierce rhesus monkey will permit itself to be petted when stimulated at the caudate nucleus.

Projection and Association Areas

Recent experiments with electrical stimulations of the brain have given us much information concerning the projection areas of the brain. Figure 7-2 shows the auditory, visual, motor, somesthetic, and olfactory areas. Two fissures, the central and the Sylvian fissure, separate the brain into lobes. That part lying in front of the central and Sylvian fissure is known as the frontal lobe. The sense organs are connected with their special projection areas in the cortex, and the essential sensory processes occur there. An injury to the visual projection area, for example, may cause blindness.

The functions of the brain, however, are not restricted to the projection areas. More than three-fourths of the brain consists of association areas. The associations between the various sensory and motor areas are the result of learning.

When the child touches a burning match, a sharp signal of pain is received in the projection area. He avoids a burning match later, not because of the pain, but because he associates the pain with the sight of fire. To be meaningful, the experience of the present must be related to the experiences of the past. This occurs in the association areas. There the

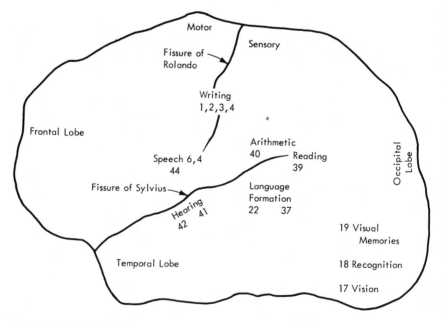

FIGURE 7-2 *The Brain*

Thomas H. Eames,   "Visual Handicaps to Reading," *Journal of Education* 141, February 1959, p. 35.

sensory and motor areas are united into the countless hookups and the "memory" of the past is preserved.

Gray (1948, p. 34) notes that the brain must have memory in order to relate the information of the moment with that of the past and to recognize its significance. This means millions of functional correlations, countless hookups of sensory centers with one another and with motor centers, repeated exchanges of data for analysis, comparison, and synthesis. These elaborative functions of the cortex are performed by the association areas.

The impulses that travel through the neural network may be blocked by injuries along the neural path or by damage to the brain itself. Eames (1962) notes that interferences with the frontal-occipital fasciculus affects auditory memory and creates difficulties in the learning of phonics. Other interferences in the association areas affect eye movement and eye span.

The visual projection area is surrounded by an association area known as the parastriate cortex. A second association area, known as the peristriate cortex, surrounds the parastriate cortex. If the parastriate cortex is injured, the person cannot recognize or identify what he sees. If the peristriate cortex is injured, the person may be able to recognize what he sees, but he cannot recall the appearance of objects when they are not in view (Eames, 1962).

The nerve impulse travels from the retina along the optic nerve to visual area 17 in the occipital lobe. This area is concerned with seeing without recognition. In areas 18 and 19 recognition and visual memory occur. There the words are recognized as words. In area 39, the angular gyrus, the meaning of the word is comprehended. Eames (1959, p. 4) notes that this part of the brain deals with the *interpretation of symbols* (letters, words, syllables) and with the *recognition and visual memory* for word forms. He adds that a lesion here will interfere with the ability to read. In the part of the brain lying between the hearing and reading areas, roughly areas 22 and 37, the association of sounds and visual symbols occurs. Thus, since reading is commonly an association of a visual symbol with an auditory symbol, this part is of major importance in reading and is called the language-formation area. Injury here results in the inability to name one's concepts.

Neural Adequacy and Reading Proficiency

The term, "learning disabilities," may be applied to a variety of difficulties encountered in the learning process, but for our purposes it will be defined as "a condition or syndrome characterized by specific difficulty in learning to read, spell, and write."

This specific learning disability or syndrome has been given many names: primary reading disability, specific reading disability, congenital reading disability, (acquired during development in the uterus or during birth), Strauss Syndrome, constitutional reading disability, developmental dyslexia, congenital word blindness, specific language disability, strephosymbolia or simply dyslexia.

It has at times been equated with visuo-motor perceptive disorders, minimal brain dysfunction (MBD), or aphasia.

The disability of which we speak was a handicap to such famous people as Thomas Edison, Harvey Cushing, brain surgeon: Woodrow Wilson, William James, Albert Einstein, George Patton, Auguste Rodin, artist; David Lloyd George, British Prime Minister; Paul Ehrlich, German bacteriologist; Hans Christian Andersen, Albert Lawrence Lowell, Harvard President; and Nelson Rockefeller.

A lot of mystery surrounds the concept of dyslexia and the explanations for the syndrome have become extremely far-fetched. James Strachey (1930) postulated that in the child's unconscious, reading may have the significance of taking knowledge out of the mother's body; thus, he suggested that fear of robbing the mother is an important reason for reading failure.

W. Pringle Morgan (1896) originated the term, "congenital word blindness" to identify the syndrome. He concluded that the symptoms were congenital and due to defective development of the left angular gyrus in the brain.

James Hinshelwood, in 1917, published a book entitled *Congenital Word Blindness*. He stressed brain pathology or neural lesions as causing the disability. Hinshelwood (1917, pp. 40–63) used the term "congenital word-blindness" to indicate a reading disability due to localized brain defect though not necessarily associated with lack of intelligence. He suggested that abnormality in specific portions of the cortex of the left parietal lobe (in right-handed persons) might cause severe problems in learning to read. He proposed that such conditions required that a new center for visual memory be established in the opposite hemisphere, and suggested that the best way to deal with the problem was:

1. To develop a visual memory for the letters of the alphabet.
2. To develop an auditory memory for words by having the child spell aloud the word letter by letter.
3. To develop a visual memory for words.

Samuel T. Orton (1928) disagreed with Hinshelwood, rejected the brain lesion hypothesis, and suggested that the major problem was one of *developmental lag* or delayed maturation. According to his view, the dyslexic child had failed to establish unilateral brain superiority with definite dominance on one side. This, according to Orton, accounted for reversals, poor directionality, mirror reading, etc.

Later explanations of reading disability, in addition to the neurological deficit and developmental lag models, have adduced a language deficit model and an ecological deficit model. For some children, at least, learning disability represents a deviance or faulty interaction between a child's available *learning modalities* and his educational *eco-system:* teachers, teaching materials, methods, etc.

In other explanatory systems, reading difficulty is attributed to some malfunction preventing the student from benefiting from experience (neural lesion), to the absence of some function which needs to be added (lack of phonic skills), to something that is present but must be removed (dislike for reading), or mismatches between student and task (mode of instruction). The etiology of dyslexia is still very debatable and so at least three etiological positions have emerged: the *internalist* places the origin of dyslexia within the learner (the Neurological Deficit or Development Lag Models); the *externalist* interprets dyslexia as an environmentally-controlled phenomenon (the Ecological Deficit Model); the *interactionist* considers roots both in the environment and the learner (the Language Deficit Model).

Dechant (1970, 1975) proposes a functional-structural model and groups all severe reading disabilities into four types:

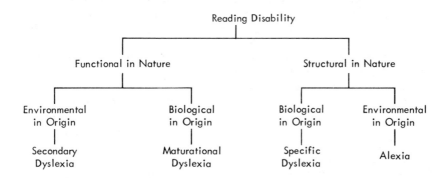

In its generic sense, dyslexia, a term first coined by Rudolf Berlin of Stuttgart, Germany in 1887, is simply a difficulty with words and the letters that compose a word, making it impossible for the pupil to read. It is a severe reading disability. However, there seem to be different levels of intensity of this more generic condition and indeed the etiology seems different. It is thus that we speak of secondary dyslexia, maturational dyslexia, specific dyslexia, and alexia. Each of these identifies a type of dyslexia, a type identified with a describable etiology and pathophysiology.

It is impossible to distinguish between the two forms of wordblindness or disability on the basis of symptoms alone. Jensen (1943) uses the term "reading disability" to designate cases manifesting organic injury and the term "reading inability" to designate cases manifesting functional difficulties. If the disturbance is of functional origin, perhaps only reading is affected; if the disturbance is structural (delayed maturation or neural damage), the pupil's perceptual functioning is generally affected and difficulties will show up in areas other than reading.

There is great diversity of thought and indeed of experimentation on the question of whether reading disability is structurally or functionally caused or for that matter perhaps jointly.

Schilder (1944) concluded that severe reading disability can and must be interpreted from a neurological point of view.

Hallgren (1950) found that reading disabilities showed a familial history of reading disability. He concluded that a primary disability in reading is inherited as a dominant characteristic. He believed that secondary disabilities could be explained on the basis of poor intelligence, environmental conditions, or emotional disorders.

Vernon (1957, p. 81) argued that there is inadequate evidence for Hallgren's conclusion that reading disability is linked to a single congenital disability. She suggests that reading disability may be a sign of deficient cortical maturation and that there may be a congenital disposition toward the occurrence of certain related defects such as reading disability, speech defects, motor incoordination, and ambidextrality.

Gesell (1941) suggests that in many instances the symptoms of minimal injury are so benign that they escape attention and that the type which expresses itself in speech difficulties, poorly defined unilateral dominance, and in delayed integration may later result in serious difficulty in the acquisition of reading.

Johnson (1955) reports that 21 percent of thirty-four clinical reading disability cases had had accidents resulting in brain injury. Preston and Schneyer (1956) report on nine severely retarded readers. Five of these were nonreaders, ranging in age from eight to fifteen. Seven showed evidence of significant reversal tendencies. Neurological examination indicated that three had damage to the nervous system, four had difficult births, three had head injuries in childhood, and two had suffered high fever in childhood. Neurologists suggested that it was possible that in all cases brain injury might have induced the reading retardation.

Although, as can be seen here, there has been considerable interest in the possibility that hereditary brain defects and brain damage are basic causes of reading disability, not all psychologists agree that these are the most general causes. Blau (1946, pp. 149–166), for example, argues against hereditary and neurological explanations. He emphasizes personality and emotional disturbances and considers reading disability as a symptom of a basic personality maladjustment. He believes that a child may unconsciously discharge hostile and rebellious feelings against reading content.

Structural defects may either be the result of brain injury or they may have been biologically determined. The brain may suffer injury, or it may not develop adequately. The latter condition is known as aplasia. Microcephaly, mongoloidism, epilepsy, and mental retardation are symptoms of inadequate development.

Injuries to the brain are numerous. Cerebral tumors, infections, and changes accompanying old age may damage brain tissues. Tumors crowd brain tissues and restrict the metabolism of the nerve cells. Encephalitis and paresis are infections that damage brain tissue. Pick's disease, Alzheimer's disease, and arteriosclerosis are degenerative diseases that result in impaired functioning.

Finally, the brain may be damaged by certain metabolic disorders and toxins. Disordered chemistry may have serious effects on brain functioning. Enzyme, vitamin, and hormone deficiencies may lead to metabolic disturbances. Pellagra, for example, is caused by a vitamin deficiency. Cretinism is the result of an endocrine disturbance. Toxic conditions resulting from excessive intake of lead, alcohol, carbon monoxide, or opium and high fever and lack of oxygen also may damage brain tissue. A lack of oxygen, for even a few seconds, may lead to irreparable damage of brain cells. Increasing or decreasing significantly the sugar content of the blood may result in coma.

Cerebral Dominance

A condition thought to be dependent on the development of the brain is cerebral or lateral dominance. Cerebral dominance implies that one cerebral hemisphere is more important in behavior or functionally more efficient than the other. Lateral dominance refers to the consistent use of and preference for the muscles of one side of the body. The left hemisphere commonly is the language hemisphere and for most individuals, since most of us are right-handed, it also is the dominant hemisphere.[2]

Broca was the first to ascribe speech dominance to the cerebral hemisphere contralateral to the preferred hand (McNeil and Hamre, 1974).

Lenneberg (1967, pp. 152–153) reports that when the left hemisphere is diseased from childhood, removal of the hemisphere results in little or no language impairment because the other hemisphere assumed language function. However, removal of the left hemisphere in an adult results in permanent aphasia; not so when the right hemisphere is removed (Basser, 1962).

It has generally been hypothesized as a result of these findings that both cerebral hemispheres possess equal potential for language until at least four or five years of age (Lenneberg, 1967, pp. 153–154). It is noteworthy that lateralization of cerebral functions is unique to man (Pribram, 1971, pp. 362–365).

In the human, right and left cerebral hemispheres are connected by the corpus callosum, the largest associative fiber tract system in the brain. When the corpus callosum is cut, each hemisphere seems to function autonomously. Lenneberg (1967, p. 67) notes that congenital failure of the corpus callosum to develop does not impede language. Pribram (1971, pp. 362–365) points out that the human cerebral hemispheres are maximally connected anatomically and maximally separated functionally in terms of the specialized duties each performs.

There are exceptions to the general rule. Some persons are left-handed (right dominance), some are ambidextrous with neither hemisphere being dominant (lack of dominance), and in others the dominance

[2]Speech musculature is served by both hemispheres simultaneously. It is a bilateral function, permitting recovery of articulation following unilateral injury or excision (Ketchum, 1964). The young child can tolerate damage to the language hemisphere because the function can be transferred to the other hemisphere. In older children such damage will lead to aphasic disorders.

changes from activity to activity. The latter is termed mixed laterality. In other instances, there is a case of crossed dominance—right-handed, left-eyed or vice versa. Do these conditions hinder reading proficiency?

Orton (1928) suggested that in learning to read, the pupil develops memory traces or "engrams" for words both in the dominant (left for the average individual) and the nondominant (right) hemisphere, but that those in the nondominant hemisphere normally are mirror images of the former and thus are suppressed.[3] He adds that if cerebral dominance is well developed by the time reading begins, reading proficiency is not affected. If, however, no special dominance is developed or if the engrams or memory traces in the right hemisphere (left dominance) become active, reading difficulties occur, and the child will read once with a left and then with a right orientation.

In cases of lack of dominance (as in the ambidextrous person), the engrams of each hemisphere are equally dominant, and the reader may become confused and indecisive in his reading. He sometimes reads in a left-to-right direction and at other times reverses the direction. Letters and words are reversed because the pupil sometimes uses the mirror images developed in the nondominant hemisphere.

Although Orton did not concern himself with the left-handed individual[4] similar difficulties may arise. The left-handed person has a natural tendency to move from right to left, and it is presumed that it is most natural for him to move his eyes also from right to left in attacking words. And if he follows this natural tendency in reading, he will see little difference between the printed words and their mirror images. This results in reversals of words and word forms.

There is indeed substantial evidence that left-handedness, a symptom of right-cerebral dominance, frequently is associated with poorer reading and indeed with various other undesirable traits such as mental deficiency. In examination of both children and adults, Burt (1937), Fitt and O'Halloran (1934), Karlin and Strazzula (1952), Blau (1946), and Milne and Milne (1948), have all found strong correlations between left-handedness and various undesirable traits such as low I.Q. or unqualified mental deficiency and, frequently, even psychopathy, as well as explicit speech and reading disabilities.

Studies of reading disability cases have provided some further evidence for a relationship between poor reading and cross laterality and lack of dominance, and poor readers, especially those showing up in reading clinics, generally show a greater frequency of undeveloped dominance.

[3]Injury to the nondominant hemisphere usually does not lead to reading difficulties. Lindsley (1940) found that the percentage of alpha waves out of phase between the cerebral hemispheres is greater among the ambidextrous than among those consistently right sided, thus substantiating Orton's theory of hemispheric conflict.

[4]In an eight-year study of handedness involving some 92,000 pupils in grades one through six, Enstrom (1962) found that the percentage for boys was 12.5; for girls, 9.7. These percentages, higher than those reported in previous studies, were generally constant from grade to grade and suggest that fewer teachers are changing the handedness of the pupil.

Harris (1956, p. 254) for example, reports a high proportion of reading disability cases develop preference for one hand later than the age of nine. In a later study (1957) he suggests that if tests are sufficiently discriminative, genuine relationships between reading disability and laterality are found.

Silver and Hagin (1966), in an intensive study of eighteen subjects over a period of years, concluded that the persistence of anomalies of laterality, even when maturation in perceptual areas has occurred, suggests that for some children "reading disability may be a basic biologic defect resulting from the failures to establish clear-cut cerebral dominance."

Alexander and Money (1967) believe that defective direction sense and defective space-form perception may explain some cases of reading retardation, but the presence of these defects alone is not sufficient to cause retardation. The defect may be explained in some children by a maturation lag or developmental defect in direction sense and in space-form perception (Money, Alexander, Walker, 1965). The authors developed the *Road Map Test,* which is an outline map of several city blocks, to measure direction sense. The pupil is required to follow a route and to report whether he turns to the left or to the right at each corner. It was found that right-left spatial orientation normally becomes established between eleven and fourteen, but dyslexic boys of age eleven through fourteen made significantly more errors than did the standardization group.

Testing 429 second-graders, Ginsburg and Hartwick (1971) found that left-right confusion was significantly associated with all types of reading errors, but mixed eye-hand dominance was not so related.

Muehl (1963) found that left lateral subjects made more left and right recognition errors than consistent right lateral subjects, suggesting that left-laterality might be associated with unique patterns of visual or perceptual behavior.

Unfortunately, it is not at all clear that reversals, confusion in orientation and reading disability are related to lack of or left cerebral dominance. Ketchum (1964) states that Orton's views are no longer tenable. He suggests that difficulties in directional stability may arise from inefficiencies within the nonverbal hemisphere itself.

Dominance is not an either-or proposition; rather it is a matter of degree. To some degree everyone is two-handed, the embryo is completely symmetrical, and the development of a dominant hand is a gradual process with the dominance of one hand over the other, increasing with age. And a different member may be preferred for a different function.

At one time it was thought that the preferred use of one eye over the other was an indication of the dominance of one cerebral hemisphere. More recent knowledge of eyedness has furnished little evidence for this belief. The nerves from each eye are connected to both hemispheres of the brain. In each eye the right half of the visual field in the retina is related to the right cerebral hemisphere, and the left half is related to the left hemisphere. The assumption that eye dominance is related to hand dominance resulted in part from a misunderstanding of the data. For example, studies indicate that not more than 5 to 10 percent of the population is left-handed, whereas about 30 percent is left-eyed. These data make Orton's theory suspect.

Let us look at left-handedness. Studies generally have indicated that handedness is a hereditary and familial trait with right-handedness behaving as does a Mendelian dominant trait and left-handedness as a recessive trait (Brain, 1945). However, not all children are left-handed even when both parents are left-handed.

Speaking to this point, Blau (1946, pp. 182–183) believes that there are personal, dynamic explanations for left-handedness other than that it is related to brain dominance or to heredity. He (p. 86) points out that left-dominance is more prevalent among males than females. He suggests that it is acquired through imitation of left-handed parents and/or older children; through a temporary physical injury to the right hand that compels the child to use his left hand; and through emotional negativism. In this last case left-handedness may be an expression of hostility, resentment or aggression.

Harris (1956, pp. 255–256) has concluded that for the teacher the significant question is not the child's specific pattern of lateral dominance but whether or not he shows directional confusion. He says that if the transition is completed before reading instruction is begun, a left-handed child ordinarily may be converted to right-handedness with no serious effect upon his ability to learn to read. However, if the change-over is attempted just before or during the early stages of reading instruction, the child is likely to experience directional confusion and, consequently, to exhibit reversal symptoms in reading and in writing, spelling, and numbers, as well.

However, Lauterbach (1933), studying thirty-seven left-handed adults with speech defects, found that 50 percent had been forced to write with the right hand. He says that it is not the transfer itself that causes the speech defect. It is, instead, the method used coupled with a particular type of child personality. In instances of paralysis or amputation, transfer from one hand to another occurs without the development of speech disorders. Mintz (1946), after citing studies that suggest correlations between unstable cerebral dominance and stuttering, psychosis, psychopathy, drug addiction, and feeble-mindedness, also suggests that the basic cause of the relationship of the change of handedness to reading-personality problems may be the harsh measures taken by certain parents or teachers to make children right-handed.

Stephens et al. (1967) found no relationship between crossed eye-hand preferences and reading readiness; Balow (1962, 1964) reported that hand preference and eye preference, either singly or in interaction, or knowledge of right or left were not significantly associated with readiness or with reading achievement; Belmont and Brick (1965) reported that retarded readers were not differentiated from normal readers by mixed dominance; and Tinker (1965) concluded from her study that laterality is not a factor in reading disability.

The research data are far from being definitive. Cohen and Glass (1968) found significant relationships between knowledge of left and right and hand dominance and reading ability in the first grade, but not so in the fourth grade. Those first-grade pupils who knew the difference between left and right and who had a dominant hand tended to be the better readers. Crossed dominance was found not to be related to reading ability. The data indicated that it might be better to be left-handed than to be mixed. The authors suggest that in the first grade it may be worthwhile to develop techniques for firmly establishing hand dominance and directional certainty.

Gardner (1973) notes that although a *causal* relationship between incomplete lateralization and dyslexia has yet to be confirmed, a correlation between a developmental lag in the attainment of dominance and reading problems is well documented. He adds that Bernard Sklar, working at UCLA's Brain Research Institute, used a computer to analyze the electroencephalogram (EEG) data of a group of normals and a group of dyslexics. Computer analysis showed that the EEGs of the two groups differed in three ways. The dyslexics showed less synchronization between the two hemispheres of their brains, more synchronization within each hemisphere, and generally more theta waves. Sklar believes the first two findings support the theory that dyslexia is related to incomplete cerebral dominance.

Summarizing the data we might make the following observations:

1. Both cerebral hemispheres have equal potential for language until four or five years of age.
2. The left hemisphere is the language hemisphere for most individuals, most of whom are right handed.
3. Some, however, are left-handed (right dominance), some are ambidextrous (lack of dominance), and for some dominance changes from activity to activity. And, there are those who are right-handed, left-eyed and vice versa (crossed dominance).
4. Orton felt that right dominance or lack of dominance hinders development in reading.
5. Data favorable to Orton's position:
    a. Many studies show a relationship between left-handedness and reading disability.
    b. Harris, (1956, 1957): Reading disability cases, especially in clinics, develop hand preference later than the age of nine.
    c. Silver & Hagin (1966), Ginsberg and Hartwick (1971), and Muehl (1963) all found a positive relationship.
    d. Alexander and Money (1967): Defective direction sense seems related to reading disability. Dyslexic boys of age eleven through fourteen made more direction sense errors than a standardization group.
6. Views contrary to Orton are held by many people:
    a. Ketchum (1946): Difficulties in directional stability may also arise from inefficiencies within the non-verbal hemisphere.
    b. Dominance is not an either-or proposition, but depends on the function in question.
    c. There is little evidence that crossed dominance is related to reading disability.

    d. Blau (1946): Left-handedness can just as easily be explained by environmental and/or emotional factors as by brain dominance and/or heredity.

    e. Harris (1956): The significant element is directional confusion rather than dominance.

    f. Lauterbach (1933), Mintz (1946): The *method* of conversion from left to right handedness rather than dominance may be the causal factor.

    g. Stephens et al., (1967); Balow (1962, 1964), Belmont and Brick (1965), and Tinker (1965) all had negative findings.

Some new interesting data have accrued from research on brain asymmetry. We have already noted the dual asymmetry of the brain. The left hemisphere tends to be the locus of speech, language activities and analytic capacities, and the right hemisphere is involved in high-order integrative visuo-spatial nonverbal functioning (Kershner and Kershner, 1973), specifically spatial, relational, synthetic, holistic, and Gestalt-type abilities (Rosenthal, 1973).

Anatomical differences between the temporal speech region on the left side and the corresponding region of the right hemisphere have been observed (Geschwind, 1970). Kershner and Kershner note that recent studies have found a marked hemispheric asymmetry in both amplitude and stability of the visually evoked potential, with the evoked response greater in the right hemisphere than in the left (Beck and Dustman, 1970), and that electrocortical responses to speech stimuli have been shown to be larger in the left hemisphere than in the right (Morrell and Salamy, 1971).

The asymmetric model has been used to explain laterality differences in the development of visual-perceptual abilities. Studies (Kimura, 1966) indicate that the perception of nonverbal material is indeed superior when the stimuli are presented in the left visual half field and that of verbal material when the stimuli are presented in the right visual half field.

Kershner and Kershner note that dual neurological asymmetry has been found to be absent in retarded children, suggesting that this development was necessary for the development of abstract intelligence (Rhodes, Dustman, and Beck, 1969). J. Levy-Agresti (1968) has found evidence for different perceptual, cognitive, and affective capacities in the two hemispheres, suggesting that brain asymmetry provides man with two different methods of processing sensory information.

Furthermore, it appears that *both* cerebral hemispheres are dominant for qualitatively different kinds of information and that each perceives and processes some identical information in different ways. All the evidence suggests that the left and right sides of the brain are differentially specialized in function (Ornstein, 1972). It is probable that if something interferes with the development of hemispheric asymmetry or if there is a neurological disturbance localized in one hemisphere, problems in academic tasks could be expected to follow. Sperry (1970) reports that interaction between the two hemispheres is required for high-level complex thinking and success in advanced academic tasks. Therefore, hemispheric cross-integration deficiencies must be added as another possible cause of learning difficulties.

The relationship of dual cerebral asymmetry to sidedness preferences and left-right spatial awareness is not known. It may be that body laterality, lateral awareness, and brain asymmetry are completely independent, but the prospect of a functional interdependency among them is clear from preliminary data (Kershner, 1971).

REVERSALS AND READING

The topic of reversals is closely related to the topic of dominance. Reversals (or strephosymbolia, a term originated by Orton) may be defined (Furness, 1956, p. 38) as the tendency to reverse letters, parts of words or even whole words. This inversion tendency may be observed occasionally in the very young child who has difficulty in putting on his garments the right way; or in a child who fails to remember right and left distinctions.

The Causes of Reversals

The child's perceptual and cognitive behavior reflect the developmental mode in which the child finds himself. Thus, perceptual activities develop with age. *Initially* the child perceives only a vague impression of the object. At this stage figures do not stand out clearly against background. One detail often becomes the signal for recognition of the whole. Such a pupil will confuse letters like *b* and *d,* or *l* and *i.* He obviously has not learned to distinguish the salient features of these letters, or of words. He will readily confuse similar-appearing words.

At this stage of a child's development, it is common for children to experience *reversals* but it is also common to explain them developmentally. Strephosymbolia or reversals are errors of temporal integration. The concern is: How do they come about?

Orton suggested that reversals are indicative of defective neurological organization or of the inadequate development of cerebral dominance. Orton inferred that in the case of defective dominance the child on one occasion would attack the written word with a left and, at another time, with a right orientation. The implication was that reversals result from defective dominance (Orton, 1928).

Spache took a quite different position on the meaning of reversals. He believed that they are an indication of the unfamiliarity of the individual with the particular symbols he is trying to learn (Spache, 1953).

After an intensive study Krise (1949) decided that reversals result from a lack of familiarity with the relationship that exists between symbols and their background. He implies tht some persons find it more difficult than others to differentiate between certain similar symbols. In a later study of twenty adult subjects Krise (1952) concluded that everyone exhibits some reversal tendencies. He found a correlation of .62 between reversal tendencies and inability to perceive space relations. This seems to support the thesis that reversals may be due to difficulties in perceiving space relations or, more specifically, figure-ground relations.

Actually, Fildes (1923) made this suggestion as long ago as 1923. She concluded that the tendency of younger children toward mirror-writing was only part of their general tendency to reproduce forms of any kind without apparent heed to the position that they occupy in space. Anderson and Anderson (1951) report that a rotation of the entire figure in the *Thematic Apperception Test* indicates disturbance in spatial orientation and add that this is not uncommon in young children, in some left-handed subjects, and in children with reading disabilities. Neisser (1968) notes that reversals are very frequent in young children but decrease rapidly with age.

Stott (1973) suggests that reversals of errors of temporal integration are caused when the pupil advances from the decoding of individual graphemes to the standard combinations. Any slight uncertainty about the phonemic value of a letter may permit a following letter, about which there is no uncertainty, to be decoded ahead of it, thus producing a reversal. This happens especially when a consonant follows a vowel (at) since consonants tend to be better known. It happens with impulsive children who psychologically speaking are unable to inhibit a hypothesis for action long enough to enable its consequences to be mentally rehearsed. The central processes of the behavioral system get out of sequence.

Studies of groups of children reveal little relation between dominance and reversals, but in individual clinical cases left-handedness, left-eyedness, mixed dominance, lack of dominance, or behavioral habits developing from one of these factors may be involved in reversals. Other causes of reversals advanced by various writers are: lack of maturation, visual defects, a habit of perceiving objects from right to left, and improper teaching methods which involve the exclusive use of the whole-word method and overemphasizing the final sounds of words by concentrating on word families. In interpreting the data it may be necessary to take the position that both good and poor readers encounter problems but the good readers somehow have overcome their difficulties better than the poor readers.

The *second stage* in perceptual development is identified as the *analytic stage* (Werner, 1948). The child responds to the first dominant stimulus and thus is unable to use the most salient features which distinguish words from one another. The pupil cannot delay or inhibit his first response. Such a child may know the letter-sound discriminations in isolation, but his cognitive style does not permit him to consider alternatives. He impulsively selects the first solution that comes to mind. He needs to learn to scan the word, looking for salient features. These often are larger chunks than a single letter. They more commonly are phonograms.

It is readily apparent that perceptual immaturity is not only a major factor in causing reversals but also in causing early reading difficulty. Reversing is clearly associated with inadequate perceptual development; it also is indicative of the child's stage of cognitive development. The way the child perceives and thinks is governed by his ability to look (Cohen and Schwartz, 1975).

The Relation of Reversals to Reading Ability

There have been numerous studies of the possible relationship of reversals to poor reading achievement. Even though the causes of reversals are not firmly identified, we recognize that reversals do occur. We are concerned as to how, if at all, they influence reading.

Wolfe (1939), studying eighteen boys averaging nine years of age and with two years' retardation in reading and a matched group of eighteen normal readers, found more reversals of letters, words, and letters within words among the retarded readers. They could read mirrored words better than could the normal readers.

The Types of Reversals

Let us examine some of the different types of reversals. The term *static reversal* refers to the reversal of letters showing right-left symmetry (*p* and *q*, *b* and *d*) (Furness, 1956). Children tend to have more difficulty with the lowercase letters than with capitals.

In another type of reversal, the *kinetic reversal,* the sequence of letters is reversed and a new word is formed, as for example, *was* for *saw.* Other types of reversals involve various transpositions of letters. There are numerous kinds of transposition (initial letter to an internal position, terminal letter to an initial position, internal letter to a different internal position, etc.).

Also the parts of phrases and compound words may be reversed as when "in the house" becomes "house in the," or "barnyard" becomes "yardbarn."

Reversals and the Teaching of Reading

The child must learn to proceed from left to right not only in reading a line, but also in reading a word. Yet a child's early experiences in perception required no such directional sequences. The teacher must emphasize the order and direction of letters in words. Writing the word serves to call the pupil's attention to this order.

A child should early learn to identify his right and left hand, to experience objects on the right and objects on the left so that gradually the concepts of "leftness" and "rightness" will acquire meaning. Reading is a left-to-right activity. This is a new concept for young children. They have not been taught to observe directions in their everyday perceptions. A dog looks like a dog whether the eye movement is from left to right or from right to left. Unfortunately, in reading a word this is not so. The letters, *s-a-w,* read from left to right say *saw,* but read from right to left say *was.* Thus, one of the first requirements in learning to read is the learning of new habits of perception. The child must perceive from left to right.

During the early school years reversals have been considered to be normal phenomena. Unfortunately, this assumption may have hindered progress in working with the difficulties. Reversals certainly become a serious problem in reading when they continue beyond the second or third grade. After those years children who reverse generally do not make normal progress in reading. (For a discussion of how to eliminate reversals in reading, see: Dechant, 1970, pp. 190–193.)

SUMMARY

In this chapter we have examined those reading problems that accompany certain physical deviations, speech defects, brain defects and injuries, and incomplete dominance.

Physical conditions that lower vitality, such as glandular dysfunction, vitamin deficiencies, and nutritional and digestive problems generally are associated with a reduction in efficiency.

We have examined the phonological system of language and language structure, and have offered some ideas on the importance of accurate reproduction of both the individual phoneme and the word.

Neurological lesions or cerebral imbalance may impair both reading and speech and may influence handedness. There is a high incidence of brain injury among clinical reading disability cases. And left, lack of, or mixed cerebral dominance seems to have some relation to reading disability. Mixed laterality frequently seems to be related to retarded speech and retarded linguistic development. The left-handed child and the ambidextrous child find it less natural to proceed from left to right and consequently may find it harder to understand the orientation of words.

Reversals that continue beyond the second grade are associated with poor reading achievement. Regardless of their interpretation—as symptoms of incomplete, left, or crossed dominance, or as spatial disorganizations and figure-ground disturbances—they are nevertheless symptoms of underlying difficulties.

There is also much evidence that certain children seem to be congenitally predisposed to a group of correlated defects. Reading disability is usually found in combination with one or more additional problems such as speech defects, motor incoordination, left-handedness, crossed-dominance, or ambidexterity.

QUESTIONS FOR DISCUSSION

1. List and discuss types of physiological defects commonly found related to reading failure.
2. What is meant by functional disorder? Structural? Which type should be most closely related to reading problems?
3. What if any relationships exist between speech disorders and brain localization? Reading and brain localization? Handedness and reading problems?
4. What is meant by word-blindness?

5. What relationships appear to exist between brain damage and reading retardation?
6. What relationships appear to exist between dominance and reading?
7. What is cerebral dominance and what is its importance?
8. Of what concern is left-handedness to the reading teacher?
9. Discuss the origin of reversals.
10. Discuss:
    a. The phonological system of a language is a network of differences between sounds.
    b. Speech defects tend to be positively associated with faulty word recognition, with poorer comprehension, and with poorer reading achievement.

BIBLIOGRAPHY

ALEXANDER, DUANE and MONEY, JOHN. "Reading Disability and the Problem of Direction Sense." *The Reading Teacher* 20 (1967): 404–9.

ANDERSON, HAROLD H. and ANDERSON, GLADYS L. *An Introduction to Projective Techniques.* Englewood Cliffs, N.J.: Prentice-Hall, 1951.

BALOW, I. H. "Lateral Dominance Characteristics and Reading Achievement in the First Grade." *Journal of Psychology* 55 (1962): 323–28.

BALOW, I. H. and BALOW, B. "Lateral Dominance and Reading Achievement in the Second Grade." *American Educational Research Journal* 1 (1964): 139–43.

BASSER, L. "Hemiplegia of Early Onset and the Faculty of Speech with Special Reference to the Effects of Hemispherectomy." *Brain* 85 (1962): 427–60.

BECK, E. and DUSTMAN, R. "Hemispheric Asymmetry in the Evoked Potentials." Paper presented to the American Psychological Association, Miami Beach, September 1970.

BELMONT, LILLIAN and BRICK, H. G. "Lateral Dominance, Lateral Awareness, and Reading Disability." *Child Development* 36 (1965): 57–71.

BERRY, MILDRED F., and EISENSON, JON. *Speech Disorders: Principles and Practices of Therapy.* New York: Appleton-Century-Crofts, 1956.

BLAU, ABRAM. *The Master Hand.* New York: American Orthopsychiatric Association, 1946.

BRAIN, W. RUSSELL. "Speech and Handedness." *The Lancet* 249 (1945): 837–42.

BURT, CYRIL. *The Backward Child.* London: University of London Press, 1937.

CAVANAUGH, LYMAN A. "Reading Behavior With Regard for Endocrine Imbalances." *Implementing the Process of Reading,* Thirteenth Yearbook of the Claremont College Reading Conference. Claremont College Reading Conference, Claremont, 1948, pp. 95–102.

COHEN, ALICE and GLASS, GERALD G. "Lateral Dominance and Reading Ability." *The Reading Teacher* 21 (January, 1968): 343–48.

COHEN, ALICE S. and SCHWARTZ, ELAINE. "Interpreting Errors in Word Recognition." *The Reading Teacher* 28 (1975): 534–37.

DAVIS, IRENE P. "The Speech Aspects of Reading Readiness." *The National Elementary Principal* 17 (1938): 282–88.

DECHANT, EMERALD. *Improving the Teaching of Reading.* Englewood Cliffs, N.J.: Prentice-Hall, 1970.

EAMES, THOMAS H. "The Blood Picture in Reading Failures." *Journal of Educational Psychology* 44 (1953): 372–75.

EAMES, THOMAS H. "Physical Factors in Reading." *The Reading Teacher* 15 (1962): 427–32.

FILDES, LUCY G. "Experiments on the Problem of Mirror-Writing." *British Journal of Psychology* 14 (1923): 57–67.

FITT, ARTHUR B. and O'HALLORAN, K. H. "The Relation Between Handedness and Some Physical and Mental Factors." *Journal of Educational Psychology* 25 (1934): 286–96.

FURNESS, EDNA LUE. "Perspective on Reversal Tendencies." *Elementary English* 33 (1956): 38–41.

GARDNER, HOWARD, "Developmental Dyslexia." *Psychology Today,* 7 (1973): 62–67.

GESCHWIND, N., "The Organization of Language and the Brain," *Science* 170 (1970): 940–44.

GESELL, ARNOLD, and AMATRUDA, C. S. *Development Diagnosis: Normal and Abnormal Child Development.* New York: Paul B. Hoeber, 1941.

GINSBURG, G. P. and HARTWICK, ANN. "Directional Confusion as a Sign of Dyslexia." *Perceptual and Motor Skills* 32 (1971): 535–43.

GLEASON, H. A., Jr. *An Introduction to Descriptive Linguistics.* New York: Holt, Rinehart & Winston, 1955.

GRAY, GEORGE W. "The Great Ravelled Knot." *Scientific American* 179 (1948): 26–39.

HALLGREN, BERTIL. "Specific Dyslexia (Congenital Word Blindness)." *Acta Psychiatrica Et Neurologica,* Supplement No. 65, Copenhagen, 1950.

HARRIS, A. J. *How To Increase Reading Ability,* 3rd edition. New York: Longmans, Green and Company, 1956.

HARRIS, A. J. "Lateral Dominance, Directional Confusion, and Reading Disability." *Journal of Psychology* 44 (October 1957) 283–94.

HILDRETH, GERTRUDE. *Teaching Reading.* New York: Holt, Rinehart & Winston, Inc., 1958.

HINMAN, MARY PEEBLES. "The Teacher and the Specialist." *NEA Journal* 49 (1960): 24–25.

HINSHELWOOD, JAMES. *Congenital Word-Blindness.* London: J. K. Lewis and Company, Ltd., 1917.

HOCKETT, CHARLES F. *A Course in Modern Linguistics,* New York: Macmillan, 1958.

IVES, SUMNER. "Some Notes on Syntax and Meaning." *The Reading Teacher* 18 (1964): 179–83, 222.

JENSEN, M. B. "Reading Deficiency as Related to Cerebral Injury and to Neurotic Behavior." *Journal of Applied Psychology* 27 (1943): 535–45.

JOHNSON, MARJORIE S. "A Study of Diagnostic and Remedial Procedures in a Reading Clinic Laboratory School." *Journal of Educational Research* 48 (1955): 565–78.

JOLLY, ALLISON. *The Evolution of Primate Behavior.* New York: Macmillan, 1972.

KARLIN, ISAAC W. and STRAZZULA, MILLICENT. "Speech and Language Problems of Mentally Deficient Children." *Journal of Speech Disorders* 17 (1952): 286–94.

KERSHNER, J. "Children's Acquisition of Visuo-Spatial Dimensionality: A Conservation Study." *Developmental Psychology* 5 (1971): 454–62.

KERSHNER, JOHN R. and KERSHNER, BARBARA A. "Dual Brain Asymmetry: Another Cause of Learning Disorders." *Academic Therapy* 8 (1973): 391–93.

KETCHUM, E. GILLET. "Neurological and Psychological Trends in Reading Diagnosis." *The Reading Teacher* 17 (1964): 589–93.

KIMURA, D. "Dual Functional Asymmetry of the Brain in Visual Perception." *Neuropsychologia* 4 (1966): 275–85.

KRISE, MORLEY. "Reversals in Reading: A Problem in Space Perception?" *Elementary School Journal* 49 (1949): 278–84.

KRISE, MORLEY. An Experimental Investigation of Theories of Reversals in Reading." *Journal of Educational Psychology* 43 (1952): 408–22.

LAUTERBACH, C. E. "Shall the Left-Handed Child be Transferred?" *Journal of Genetic Psychology* 43 (1933): 454–62.

LEFEVRE, CARL A. "Reading our language Patterns: A Linguistic View— Contributions to a Theory of Reading." *Challenge and Experiment in Reading,* International Reading Association Conference Proceedings 7 (1962): 66–70.

LENNEBERG, E. *Biological Foundations of Language.* New York: Wiley, 1967.

LEVY-AGRESTI, J. "Ipsilateral Projection Systems and Minor Hemisphere Function in Man after Neocommissuratomy." *Anatomical Record* 160 (1968): 384.

LLOYD, DONALD. "Reading American English as a Native Language Process." *Challenge and Experiment in Reading,* International Reading Association Conference Proceedings 7 (1962): 247–51.

MATEER, FLORENCE. "A First Study of Pituitary Dysfunction in Cases of Reading Difficulty." *Psychological Bulletin* 32 (1935): 736.

MCNEIL, MALCOM R. and HAMRE, C. E. "A Review of Measures of Lateralized Cerebral Hemispheric Functions." *Journal of Learning Disabilities* 7 (1974): 51–59.

MILNE, LORUS J. and MILNE, MARGERY J. "Right Hand, Left Hand." *Scientific American* 179 (1948): 46–49.

MINTZ, ALEXANDER. "Reading Reversals and Lateral Preferences in a Group of Intellectually Subnormal Boys." *Journal of Educational Psychology* 37 (1946): 487–501.

MONEY, J.; ALEXANDER, D.; and WALKER, H. T. JR. *A Standardized Road-Map Test to Direction Sense.* Baltimore: Johns Hopkins Press, 1965.

MORGAN, W. P. "A Cast of Congenital Wordblindness." *British Medical Journal* 2 (1896): 1378.

MORRELL, L. and SALAMY, J. "Hemispheric Asymmetry of Electrocortical Responses to Speech Stimuli." *Science* 174 (1971): 164–66.

MUEHL, S. "Relation Between Word Recognition Errors and Hand-Eye Preference in Preschool Children." *Journal of Educational Psychology* 54 (1963): 316–321.

NEISSER, U. "The Processes of Vision." *Scientific American,* (1968): 204–14.

ORNSTEIN, ROBERT E. *The Psychology of Consciousness.* San Francisco: W. H. Freeman Company, 1972.

ORTON, SAMUEL T. "An Impediment to Learning to Read: A Neurological Explanation of the Reading Disability." *School and Society* 28 (1928): 286–90.

POOLE, I. "Genetic Development of Articulation of Consonant Sounds in Speech." *Elementary English Review* 11 (1934): 159–61.

PRESTON, RALPH C. and SCHNEYER, J. WESLEY. "The Neurological Background of Nine Severely Retarded Readers." *Journal of Educational Research* 49 (1956): 455–59.

PRIBRAM, K. *Languages of the Brain.* Englewood Cliffs, N.J.: Prentice-Hall, 1971.

REED, DAVID W. "A Theory of Language, Speech and Writing." *Elementary English* 42 (1965): 845–51.

RHODES, L.; DUSTMAN, R.; and BECK, E. "The Visual Evoked Response: A Comparison of Bright and Dull Children." *Electroencephalography and Clinical Neurophysiology* 27 (1969): 364–72.

ROSENTHAL, JOSEPH H. "Recent Advances in the Neurophysiology of Some Specific Cognitive Functions." *Academic Therapy* 8 (1973): 423–28.

SCHIFFMAN, GILBERT B. "An Interdisciplinary Approach to the Identification and Remediation of Severe Reading Disabilities." *Junior College and Adult Reading Programs,* National Reading Conference, Milwaukee, 1967, pp. 14–26.

SCHILDER, PAUL. "Congenital Alexia and Its Relation to Optic Perception." *Journal of Genetic Psychology* 65 (1944): 67–88.

SCRIMSHAW, N.S. "Early Malnutrition and Central Nervous System Function." In S. Chess and A. Thomas, eds., *Annual Progress in Child Psychiatry and Child Development.* New York: Bruner/Mazel, 1970.

SILVER, ARCHIE A. and HAGIN, ROSA A. "Maturation of Perceptual Functions in Children with Specific Reading Disability." *The Reading Teacher* 19 (1966): 253–59.

SMITH, FRANK. *Understanding Reading: A Psycholinguistic Analysis of Reading and Learning to Read.* New York: Holt, Rinehart and Winston, 1971.

SPACHE, GEORGE D. "Factors Which Produce Defective Reading." *Corrective Reading in Classroom and Clinic,* Supplementary Educational Monographs, No. 79. Chicago: University of Chicago Press, 1953, pp. 49–57.

SPERRY, R. "Perception in the Absence of the Neocortical Commissures." *Perception and Its Disorders* (Research Publication of the Association for Research in Nervous and Mental Disease) 47 (1970): 123–138.

STEPHENS, W. E.; CUNNINGHAM, E. S.; and STIGLER, B. J. "Reading Readiness and Eye Hand Preference Patterns in First Grade Children." *Exceptional Children* 33 (1967): 481–88.

STOTT, D. H. "Some Less Obvious Cognitive Aspects of Learning to Read." *The Reading Teacher* 26 (1973): 374–83.

STRACHEY, J. "Some Unconscious Factors in Reading." *International Journal of Psychoanalysis* 11 (1930): 322–32.

TINKER, KAREN J. "The Role of Laterality in Reading Disability." In J. A. Figurel, ed., *Reading and Inquiry,* Proceedings of the International Reading Association, 1965, pp. 300–303.

VAN RIPER, CHARLES and BUTLER, KATHARINE G. *Speech in the Elementary Classroom.* New York: Harper and Row, 1955.

VAN RIPER, CHARLES. "The Speech Pathologist Looks at Reading." *The Reading Teacher* 17 (1964): 505–10.

VERNON, M. D. *Backwardness in Reading.* Cambridge: Cambridge University Press, 1957.

WARFEL, HARRY R. "Prolegomena to Reading Instruction." *Journal of Developmental Reading* 1 (1958): 35–45.

WARFEL, HARRY R. and LLOYD, D. J. "The Structural Approach to Reading." *School and Society* 85 (1957): 199–201.

WERNER H. *Comparative Psychology of Mental Development.* New York: International Universities Press, 1948.

WOLFE, LILLIAN S. "An Experimental Study of Reversals in Reading." *American Journal of Psychology* 52 (1939): 533–61.

8

Interest and Personality Factors in the Reading Process

The reading teacher employs his knowledge of motivated learning to direct children first toward learning to read and later toward reading to learn. Interests are closely related to motivation: they develop from attempts to satisfy basic motives. Lack of interest is an important cause of poor reading. To plan appropriate educational experiences, the teacher must also understand the nature of personality development and the personality patterns that are related to success or failure in reading.

In the preceding chapters we examined the perceptual nature, the learning principles, and some of the psychological and physiological bases of reading and reading readiness. We will now consider additional factors that have a bearing on reading and achievement.

Here we will examine motivation, interests, and personality factors. We wish to know why children read and why they choose the specific materials that they do read.

Children generally come to school wanting to learn to read. The reading teacher must foster this interest and expand it. He must locate those children who are not motivated to read. He must know how to further the interest of the child who wants to read. He also must be concerned with the type of reading materials that will encourage extensive reading and that will raise the child's general level of reading interests and tastes.

The teacher of reading also needs to understand the facts, principles, and symptoms of social and emotional development of the child. He needs to be able to interpret pupil behavior. He must know how a child's social and emotional reactions influence his reading and how reading failure or success influences his emotional and social development. Let us turn our attention first to motivation and interest.

THE FRAMEWORK OF MOTIVATION

As was seen in Chapter 4, human motives may be grouped into three general categories—physiological motives, psychological motives, and habit motives.

Physiological Motives

The physiological motives are sometimes spoken of as the primary motives or drives. They are the motives, including hunger, thirst, and the sex drive, that have provided for the very survival of man.

Cannon (1939) suggests that the organism strives to maintain a balance within the bodily tissues: the temperature of the body, the acidity and the sugar concentration of the blood, and the water and salt balance of the body can deviate only slightly without threat to the life of the organism. Cannon called this internal self-regulatory system "homeostasis." Whenever the body deviates from these "steady states," the organism is "motivated" to action.

We know, of course, that much of an infant's behavior is controlled by his visceral hungers. A child cries when he is hungry or thirsty. Even an adult is subject to physiological motivation. Under certain circumstances the need for air, water, or food may dominate behavior. Physical defects such as bad vision, poor hearing, endocrine disturbances, malnutrition, or illness of any kind may prevent a child from becoming interested in the educational tasks that we provide for him. Generally a normal child will not be lackadaisical, indifferent, and unconcerned; but we cannot expect a child who is faced with elemental threats to his survival to be interested in classroom learning.

Data gained from experiments demonstrate the responsiveness of animals to physiological needs. Removal of the parathyroid gland is followed by a sharp reduction in the calcium content of the blood. After such an operation a rat almost immediately seeks solutions containing large amounts of calcium. Experimenters have remarked that the animal's behavior seems to be governed by changes in his taste organs directing him to a food required for his survival. Similarly, loss of the pancreas is followed by avoidance of sugar, loss of the thyroid by building larger nests, and loss of the adrenal by seeking salt (Richter and Eckert, 1939; Wilkins and Richter, 1940).

Psychological Motives

Although much of man's basic animal behavior is governed by his physiological motives, fortunately behavior does not depend on physiological motives alone. Even though some psychologists suggest that all motives are reducible to organic needs and that tension reduction serves as an adequate explanation of human motivation, we can best gain an understanding of human behavior by examining the so-called psychological motives. We know that children continue playing after their physiological need for exercise is adequately satisfied. Man does not always work to eat, as drive reduction theory might suggest; perhaps more often he eats to work. A chief characteristic of the dynamic development of man is his inability to resign himself to rest and equilibrium. Even in the animal world physiological drive reduction seems inadequate to explain all behavior. Harlow (1953) reports that rhesus monkeys learn even though they are fed prior to the experiment and are munching food during both right and wrong responses. He concludes that learning efficiency is much more closely related to tensions in the brain than in the belly.

As teachers we are likely to be far more interested in the psychological than in the physiological aspects of motivation. We are concerned with the conscious direction of a person's activity. Psychologists stress man's desire for self-actualization and realization of his potentialities (Goldstein, 1939, pp. 196–207). Man wishes to use his abilities and his organs. If he can see, he is motivated to look. And if he can read, he is motivated to read. Man finds pleasure in the efficient use of his mind and hands.

Often an external object seems to exert a positive attraction. The child sometimes eats ice cream, not because he is hungry, but because of the peculiar qualities possessed by the ice cream. Thus objects sometimes appear to have valences of their own. They attract the individual. The task itself appeals: it challenges the individual; it upsets his mental equilibrium; it creates an anxiety that prompts him to give it his attention. Harlow (1953) is convinced that the key to human learning is motivation aroused by external stimuli. This has important implications for reading instruction. Certainly high interest value is as important as constant repetition and drill.

As we examine the topic of motivation, we come to see the importance of psychological motives. Self-esteem, self-realization, curiosity, security, and a need to be adequate, successful, and to belong are the motives that most commonly energize human behavior. These needs and drives sometimes are referred to as secondary or learned motives, and it is assumed that they are extensions of the primary or unlearned motives.

Habit Motives

It is well recognized that habits are formed through the repetition of some act that satisfies a motivating condition. However, once well formed, habits no longer need draw on other motives for energy. They acquire their own ability to energize. A child learns to read because he is motivated by basic, personal needs. But gradually, as he becomes skilled in reading, reading acquires a motivating force of its own. Allport (1937, p. 201) points out that a skill learned for some extraneous reason can turn into an interest and become self-propelling, even though the original reason for acquiring it has been lost.

INTEREST IN READING

As teachers, we are concerned with two somewhat distinct relationships of interest to reading—*interest in reading* and *reading interests*. First, let us examine interest in reading. Reading interests will be examined later in the chapter.

Interests are learned. They arise from the interaction of our basic needs and the means that we discover for satisfying them. Interest in reading parallels learning how to read. As William James suggested, "Only what we partly know already inspires us with a desire to know more" (1890, p. 111).

Attitudes and Interests

Attitudes and interests are closely related. Attitudes represent general predispositions, and specific interests operate within this broader sphere. Sometimes interests are defined as positive attitudes toward objects or classes of objects to which we are attracted (Eysenck, 1953, p. 213). Ryans (1942, p. 312) says interests are learned responses which predispose the organism to certain lines of activity and which facilitate attention. Getzels (1956, p. 7) defines an interest as a disposition which impels an individual to seek out particular objects, activities, understanding, skills, or goals for attention.

Cummins and Fagin (1954) suggest that interest is an emotional involvement of like or dislike which is associated with attention to some object. Interest is the set of attending; the tendency to give selective attention to something.

Influence of Interest

Lack of interest in reading may be an important cause of poor reading. There often seems to be a "substantial and marked relationship" between ability and interest (Nemoitin, 1932). High interest in a subject tends to be associated with high ability in that subject, and low interest with low ability.

If the child is to learn to read, his interest somehow must be captured. He must need to learn to read. And further, his interest must be retained. He must continue to need to read.

As teachers, then, we are concerned with two phases of interest. First, the interest of the child somehow must be captured if he is to learn to read, and second we must help the child to make reading an habitual activity.

Wheat (1955, pp. 57–58) points out that as a person learns to read, reading enters his mental make-up as a permanent mode of behavior. He now uses reading as a means of enjoyment, studying, and thinking. He will arrange his work and play in order to provide time for reading. He will use reading to discover new interests. Reading is now a dominating interest that is within.

Indeed, it is at this point that reading acquires a motivational force of its own.

We now recognize that to increase reading skill, promote the reading habit, and produce a generation of book-lovers, there is no other factor so powerful as interest (Norvell, 1946, p. 536). With the advent of radio, movies, and television, teachers have become greatly concerned lest these reduce the amount that children will read. Almost universally, however, studies have shown a constant increase in the number of books that are being sold and in the number that are being checked out from libraries.

DETERMINANTS OF READING INTEREST

Many writers have emphasized the importance of the reader's interests in promoting ability to read and encouraging and directing reading. Interests determine not only the area within which the child will make his reading choices, but more important they determine how much he will read or even whether he will become a "reader" at all. Of course, we must assume that a child can read at a level somewhat appropriate to his mental age before a discussion of reading interests is apropos. However, acquiring an ability to read is pointless unless that ability is used. Our first aim should be to produce children and adults who want to read and who do read (Southgate, 1973). As Strickland has said, a reader ". . . is not a person who can read; he is a person who does read" (1957, p. 240).

Our prime concern is that pupils do read (Weiss, 1967). The kindergarten teacher, especially, is more interested in fostering interest in reading than in developing specific reading skills, but even the primary teacher should not be so busy teaching reading skills that she neglects to develop readers (Chambers, 1966). Although children come to school with an attitude favorable to reading, this attitude is not necessarily self-perpetuating. As children learn how to read, they must be directed to materials that appeal to their basic needs. By observing what a child reads, we may see what his special interests are. We then can provide him with reading materials appropriate not only to his intelligence and age but also to those broader interests that stem from his basic needs.

The reader's capabilities play a very significant role in the development of his interests. The boy who is skilled in crafts may be an avid reader of books dealing with scouting or camping but find most historical novels or biography boring. His capabilities affect both his interest and interests.

Cultural factors, too, play an important role in determining our interests. We are directed toward certain interests through our membership in a particular culture, by specific religious affiliation, and by living in a certain country or specific area within a country. To a great extent society decides what interests are appropriate to our age and sex. Society does not expect the girl of sixteen to engage in the doll play of the six-year-old. And sixteen-year-old girls do not enhance their self-esteem by being the neighborhood tomboys.

The schools likewise channel our interests toward certain ends. In general our schools emphasize middle-class attitudes, ideals, and standards of behavior. The pressures to do well in school, to seek social approval, and to obey adult authority are more peculiar to middle-class homes than to homes of either the upper or the lower socioeconomic classes.

Social influences also have been shown to be important determinants of reading choice. Wightman (1915) long ago found that teachers exert a strong influence on children's preferences. The pupils generally preferred books that the teacher was enthusiastic about. He concluded that a teacher's enthusiasm was a vital determinant of reading preferences.

Socio-Economic Factors

The exact nature of the role of socioeconomic status in determining whether a child will become a "reader" and his choice of reading matter is not clear. There is some indication that the proportion of time spent in book reading is not highly related to socioeconomic status but that the specific type of reading done may be highly related (Havighurst, 1949). Link and Hopf (1958) report that the more years of formal education an individual has, the more books he tends to read. A positive, but not a significant, correlation exists between the number of books read and personal income or socioeconomic status.

Intelligence as a Factor

Intelligence plays a major part in determining what students will read. Generally, the areas of interest of more-intelligent students are on a slightly higher level than are those of less-intelligent students. Students with high IQ's read books that are more difficult and more adult. Mental age rather than the intelligence quotient appears to be the major factor and it seems to direct interest toward specific areas of content rather than toward reading as distinguished from other activities. Boys who score high on intelligence or aptitude tests (IQ 130 or more) read mystery stories, biographies, history, historical fiction, comics, scientific materials, sports, humor, and westerns; girls of above-average intelligence read historical fiction, modern novels, biographies, mystery stories, teen-age books, sports, animal stories, science, history, and books treating social problems (Barbe, 1952).

Walberg (1968), in a study of the reading habits of students "who elect to take physics in high school," found that almost a quarter indicated that they had not read much nonfiction. These students seem to have more interest in science fiction than in literature. Girls expressed more interest in historical novels, mystery stories, literary classics, biographies, and autobiographies. Boys more often enjoyed technical and professional books. Both boys and girls ranked mystery stories as first in interest, and roughly half indicated that they did not enjoy technical-professional books.

Sex Differences

Generally, it is found that girls are more interested in reading than are boys. Some writers suggest that the books used in the classroom are more in accord with girls' than with boys' interests.

Norvell made extensive studies of the reading interests of children in grades three through six (1958) and seven through twelve (1950). He found that changes were more rapid during the elementary than during the junior or senior high school grades. He says that whereas during the primary and elementary school years increased maturity seems as important as sex in determining reading choice, during the high school years the most powerful determinant is the sex of the reader. Unfortunately, from grades seven through twelve about two-thirds of the literature selections commonly used in the classroom are better liked by girls than by boys. We do not know how this affects general reading development. It seems likely that it contributes to the tendency for fewer boys than girls to be interested in reading.

On the basis of his study of children in grades four to twelve, Thorndike (1941, p. 36) felt that the sex of the reader is "conspicuously more important" than are age or intelligence in determining what children will read.

Norvell (1946, p. 532) found that in grades seven through twelve both sexes react favorably to adventure; humorous poems, stories, and essays . . .; poems and stories of patriotism; stories of mystery, of games, and of animals. Boys prefer strenuous adventure, including war, to stories of wild animals, to science, and to speeches. Girls prefer romantic love to sentiment in general, and to poems and stories of home and family life.

Chiu (1973) found that fourth grade boys preferred adventure, fantasy, humor, and poetry.

In general, we may conclude that girls read more than boys, but that among children below the third grade sexual differences in choice of reading interest are negligible. Gradually, however, the differences in interest between boys and girls diverge and this divergence is particularly prominent after the age of nine. From this point on boys tend to become increasingly interested in sports and adventure and girls in stories of a sentimental nature.

Chasen (1974) suggests that sexes behave differently because they are treated differently. Tibbetts (1974) adds that they may have different interests because they have been trained to have such differences. She feels that social pressure and training may be the most significant determinant of sex differences. Children are taught to prefer certain types of materials.

Age and Interests

Some writers have suggested that interests are an expression of the child's stage of development. In adolescence, for example, the child has a strong need for success, and the characters of his books must be successful, be they athletes or romantic lovers.

A recent study (Beta Upsilon Chapter, 1974) reports the following:

1. *Seven-year-olds*
   Boys: content, plot, humor, and illustrations. Animal stories were of special interest.
   Girls: plot, good characters, content, humor. Animal stories were especially popular as were make-believe.
2. *Eight-year-olds*
   Boys: content (animals, science, history) and humor.
   Girls: humor, content (animals), plot, good characters, exciting style, make-believe.
3. *Nine-year-olds*
   Boys: content (animals, transportation, science, sports), humor, plot
   Girls: exciting, good characters, plot, animal stories, mysteries, stories about people.
4. *Ten-year-olds*
   Boys: exciting, content (animals, mystery, science)
   Girls: exciting, plot, characters, content (animals, mysteries, people), humor.
5. *Eleven-year-olds*
   Boys: content (mystery, animals, transportation, history, sports, science), excitement.
   Girls: content (mystery, animals, people, house-home, romance, make-believe), excitement, characters, plot.
6. *Twelve-year-olds*
   Boys: content (animals, science, transportation, sports), exciting plot, good character.
   Girls: content (animals, mystery, people), plot, humor.

Conclusions drawn from the study were:

1. Children at all age levels most often mentioned content; girls mentioned plot and character more than boys except at age twelve. Girls showed greater interest in people and make-believe; boys more in science, sports, and transportation.
2. Excitement was the most often mentioned stylistic trait, followed by humor and information.
3. Animals were the favored content, with a slacking off of interest at eleven and twelve.
4. Interest in mystery grew with age.
5. Reading interests start to vary with sex at about age eleven.

Carlsen (1954) proposes that interests result from an emerging self-concept. It appears that books can help to build the self-concept: by strengthening the child's feeling of importance and confidence; by letting him see himself and his feelings and emotions as part of the normal pattern of all human life; and by helping him identify, accept, and prepare for the role that he is to assume in society as an adult.

Tyler has made a unique suggestion about how interests develop. After a longitudinal study (1951, 1955) of children's interests, she concluded that generally the younger child's attitude is favorable toward everything and his later interests are selected through his acquisition of dislikes.

Nature of the Materials

Bettelheim (1961, pp. 386–88) notes that if teachers want to promote an interest in reading, they must let children read materials that are realistic. He points out that it is difficult to find children's stories that describe differences between parents or between parent and child; stories in which mother is not always willing to go for walks or to play with the child; stories in which children do not love the newborn baby; and yet, these are reality. The pupil reads *"run, run"* in the book, but must sit quietly at his desk. Thus, the reading program is built around pleasant experiences and may create unrealistic images of life and encourage reading that is pointless to the child.

In summary, children generally prefer fictional materials to informational materials and prose to poetry. Their preferences for reading content show great variations and are influenced most by their age, sex, and intelligence. Girls read more than boys and before the age of eight or nine prefer the same content as boys. Interest in reading reaches a peak during the junior high years and then declines sharply.

Primary children like fairy tales, animal stories, nature stories, humorous tales, adventure stories, comics, and how-to-do-it books. Boys show special interest in animal stories; girls like stories with child characters.

Children in the *intermediate grades* are interested in adventure stories, animal stories, fantasies, in stories about family life, famous people, and children; they are interested in sports, humor, and in stories dealing with machines, personal problems, physical science, and social studies (Wolfson, 1960). Boys generally are most interested in real-life adventure; girls prefer fantasy stories and those dealing with school, home, and personal problems. Comics become especially popular during this period.

In the *junior high* years boys prefer comic books, animal stories, western stories, adventure, fiction, humor, and biography; girls prefer fiction, comic books, animal stories, biography, and western stories.

On the *high school* level girls prefer romance, society, and fashion, but also read adventure, science, and mystery stories; boys like sports, adventure, mystery, action, exploration, travel, science, mechanics, and politics. Humorous books and books on hobby pursuits also are popular during this period.

Emans and Patyk (1967) note that interests are influenced by (1) the nature of the topic and (2) the motive of the reader; usually the more closely the topic and the reader's motives are interrelated, the more intense will be the interest of the reader. Waples (1940) and Getzels (1956) list various motives for reading: informative, identificational, aesthetic, and recreational. Emans and Patyk (1967) found that high school students read chiefly for recreation. Boys ranked seeking information considerably higher than did girls. Students above the median in intelligence ranked reading for aesthetics higher than those below the median. The poor reader tended to seek identification in his reading.

DEVELOPING INTERESTS AND TASTES

Before we can do much to improve a child's reading interests and tastes, we should know what his present interests and tastes are. We need more than a general knowledge of the interests of children. We can never be certain that any one child has the same interests as does the "average" child. Various methods have been developed for finding out what interests an individual child may have. Interest blanks or inventories are found in most major professional books of reading.

Developing Reading Interests

The teacher must be aware of the fundamental interests of children. Interests are the result of experience and are consequently susceptible to nurture.

Few deny the importance of a lifetime interest in reading. Norvell noted that the reading habit is the most important academic aim of the school (1958).

This interest in reading is not self-perpetuating. The seventh grader probably reads more than he ever did before; by the time he is through high school his reading has decreased tremendously. Few high school graduates habitually read books. An impressive proportion of young people recall that they virtually stopped reading (or at least stopped enjoying reading) in high school (Broening, 1963).

It is often said that "Appreciation should be caught, not taught," but, as Duffy (1967) notes, the evidence seems to indicate that children cannot catch it by themselves. They need help, especially from teachers.

Children develop interests through learning, conscious or unconscious emulation, and identification. The child readily identifies with parents or individuals who take their place. He generally accepts their values and develops their interests. Getzels (1956) notes that the most important objects of identification are the mother or mother-surrogate and the father or father-surrogate. If reading is important to these figures, reading will ordinarily also be important to the child.

The teacher, as a parent-substitute, also serves as an object of identification. The child incorporates the expectations, values, and interests of the teacher, and of course, if the teacher has a genuine interest in reading himself, the child will interiorize this interest. One cannot so much teach interests as offer appropriate models for identification (Getzels, 1956, p. 9).

The development of interests has been described as a lure and ladder procedure (Committee of the Upper Grades Study Council, 1943). A pupil must be lured to new interest through the ladder of suitable materials. There is a great deal of similarity between methods for promoting reading interests and methods for promoting an interest in learning to read. The parent helps by providing an environment that stimulates the child to read. Magazines, books, story telling, and story reading are important. Reading projects in cooperation with school and community libraries may help to advance reading as a leisure-time interest. Bookmobiles may increase the availability of good books. A television program may provide a basis for interests that both lead to further reading and broaden present interests, increase vocabularies, and generally help children to understand the world about them. The greatest use for television perhaps is still for "enriching the intake of ideas" (Durrell, 1962).

Adults do not directly teach the child his interests so much as they provide opportunities for the pursuit of interests. Identification with parents and teachers may be an important determinant of the child's interests. In general, however, the adults' responsibility is to open all possible doors to appropriate reading material and try to provide situations that stir the child to action.

The root of the reading difficulties of a given pupil often is the mental attitude of the pupil. He may not like school and he may like reading less. In such a case, there may be no genuine disability. The pupil is disinterested and therefore has not developed competency.

Motivation flows from interest. Without interest there is usually no will to do, no drive to learn. Without motivation, the pupil simply will not develop into a mature reader.

The solution to the reluctant reader's problem begins then with a change of attitude. This pupil will not be an adequate reader until he wants to read. How do you get him to read? We refer the reader to Emerald Dechant, *Improving the Teaching of Reading,* Prentice-Hall, Inc., 1970, pp. 95–97 and to Harold H. Roeder and Nancy Lee, "Twenty-five Teacher-Tested Ways to Encourage Voluntary Reading." *The Reading Teacher* 27 (1973): 48–50. Both of these sources provide numerous illustrations of how to promote interest in reading.

The teacher cannot ignore the interests of children, nor can he always feed the pupil only what he likes. He must stimulate the child to acquire tastes and to increase the variety of his interest. Harris (1956, p. 491) makes the observation that children do not develop discrimination by being allowed contact only with superior reading matter. Taste develops through comparison and contrast.

Developing Reading Tastes

Developing reading tastes is a step beyond developing an interest in reading. We frequently hear that children do not read, that the quality of what they read is exceedingly inferior, and that schools are failing to promote a persisting interest in reading.

The teacher can remedy this situation. *First:* He must use his understanding of the pupil to help the pupil choose books that will lead him to a higher level of appreciation. It is not enough to know that the book does not positively "harm" the child. The teacher must encourage the pupil to read books that make a positive contribution to his cultural, social, and ethical development. *Second:* He must be well acquainted with the books that he recommends to the pupil. When he suggests a book to a child, he must have the conviction that the content and the style will motivate him to read it. *Third:* He must know the specific interests of each child. If he is to help the pupil to develop reading tastes, he must consider the pupil's interest patterns, his voluntary reading, the availability of materials, and the time that he has for leisure reading. He must also know the level of the pupil's reading abilities. He cannot nurture pupil interest with books too difficult to be read easily.

Painter (1965) adds that the key to the building of lifetime reading habits lies with an interested teacher who will help students in basic reading skills, who has read so extensively that he is able to guide young people to books congruent with their interests, who can present poetry effectively, who helps with materials and background to build an understanding of literature, and who uses various methods of teaching literature.

As taste improves, interest in reading is likely to be still further stimulated. And the more proficient a child becomes in reading the better are his chances for developing more refined tastes. Through intelligent direction progression can be from narrower to broader interests, from lower levels of taste to higher levels. But basic to all progress in reading is this: the child must learn to read and he must find reading enjoyable.

SUMMARY

Stott (1973) notes that the overriding causes of reading failure are the use of incorrect strategies: lack of attention, withdrawal from the learning task, and *nonuse* of cognitive and perceptual powers. Failure to match letters is due usually to inattention, but may give the appearance of a perceptual handicap. Similarly, the largest variable in cognitive functioning is not the quality or level of cognitive thought, but rather whether mentation occurs or not. If a child has no interest in discerning similarities or regularities, the precise level of his mental capacity to form associations and to make generalizations is irrelevant. A child learning to read faces certain motivational hazards, and were it not for his culture which leaves him no alternative, he would rather leave well enough alone. Sometimes he does in fact respond by avoidance.

Motivational and cognitive variables are substantially interdependent, with the prime mover being motivation. Because a child's cognitive development depends to a great degree on the *use* of his mental faculties, the unmotivated child ends up with poor conceptual equipment. Thus cognitive inefficiency may be merely a *lack* of cognition.

PERSONAL AND SOCIAL DEVELOPMENT
OF THE LEARNER

Educators have long debated what the goals of the school program are or should be. On one thing all are agreed. The student is the focal point of this program. In essence, educators believe that good education generally (and reading instruction particularly) should enhance the personal and social adjustment of the student.

Educators frequently overlook the child's wholeness. They have dealt separately with his intelligence, his physique, his emotions, and his social skills. Each expert sees the child in light of his own biases and his own discipline. Each fragments the child and each is a piece worker. Someone has suggested that if a child were to appear in the midst of a group of educational psychologists he would be a stranger to them. We sometimes forget that all aspects of the child's development are interrelated and that the child usually advances on an even front in all areas. And yet, it is easier to discuss the pupil's development by dissecting him as it were. Let us then continue to examine those factors about all pupils' development that have a bearing on their achievement in reading.

By the age of six the average child has already become a rather well-structured individual. He has learned to walk, can control his bowels and bladder, can dress and undress, and can feed himself. He ties his shoes, bathes, and brushes his teeth. He lives an orderly life, eating three times a day and sleeping a desirable number of hours.

He has become a member of his family. He identifies with his brothers and sisters and with his father and mother.

He is curious. He wants to know. He has developed his senses and communicates in sentences. He discriminates, generalizes, and makes judgments. He generally accepts society's rules and can discriminate between right and wrong.

He wants things for himself, is egocentric, and has unbounded faith in rules. "It's not fair" are common words for the six-year-old. He tags along with the "gang" and by seven or eight would rather be with them than his family, but is still somewhat of an outsider looking in.

In the middle years of childhood the development started at an earlier age is continued. Social interest is developing. White (1961) notes that three- and four-year-old children prefer to be with one or two companions. They do not like big crowds. By age seven children align themselves into groups, but these flounder without adult guidance. At nine the first unsupervised activities occur and it is common for one child to praise the accomplishments of another. Prior to that there are many criticisms of others and few compliments. Eleven- and twelve-year-old children are able to see others as they see themselves. They have some idea of why the other person does whatever he is doing. Friendship takes on new meaning. It is not mere interest in what another can do for the giver of friendship. Friendship is sought for its own sake. The person is concerned with doing something for the well-being of another.

Sex roles become rather clearly differentiated by age nine. The boy would not be caught crying (and so he develops an ulcer later in life). He will not be a sissy or a crybaby, nor will his father let him be. The girl has no such inhibitions. She is dainty and sweet but cries freely.

Preadolescence

The preadolescent, who is from nine to thirteen years of age, is another person altogether and because of this is perhaps the most difficult to understand. He is neither child nor adolescent. Generally no visible sex change has as yet taken place. The voice is shrill and penetrating. The "other" sex is still something that he cannot deal with if left alone for any length of time.

The preadolescent is difficult to live with. He does not want to be loved and he does not appreciate what he gets. He is extremely restless, especially physically. He is easily bored and does not know what to do to occupy his time. He enjoys the wild fantastic story and is fascinated by gory detail. He is easily offended and is constantly accusing the adult of not understanding him or of mistreating him. The concept of gratitude seems to be stricken from the inventory of his emotions. The worst meal at the neighbors' is described more glowingly than the best-planned feast his mother arranged for his birthday (Redl, 1944).

The preadolescent does not want to submit to parent-accepted manners. He often reverts to infantile habits, antics, or irritating behavior. A cleavage develops between *you* and *us,* between the parents and the child. The preadolescent consequently develops a deep need for the peer clique or gang. He would rather side with his pal than with his parent, despite deep love for the parent. Peer codes and values take precedence over adult values.

Adolescence

The teacher of reading in the high school should understand the nature of the period of transition known as adolescence—the needs and development tasks of the adolescent, the influence that the peer group exerts over his behavior, the effects that body and biological changes have on his behavior, and the problems that he encounters. The teacher should also take a close look at his own attitude toward adolescents. A principal is said to have commented thus: "My most difficult problem is due not to the pubescence of the pupil, but to the menopause of the teacher."

PERSONAL ADJUSTMENT
AND READING ACHIEVEMENT

Let us with the above background now take a closer look at some of the dynamics of development and how these relate to achievement in reading.

Even though developmental sequences are fairly uniform, the behavior differences among children are numerous. Some are egocentric and preoccupied with themselves. They are shy and timid and recoil from social interaction. Others plunge into social interaction with reckless abandon. They are alert and sensitive and reach out for the experiences around them. Some like to fight; others will never fight. Some lie and steal; some daydream or work too much. Some pay attention; others ignore everyone around them. Some are easily discouraged; others constantly show off in class. Some are unhappy, moody and quick tempered; others are quiet and contented just to be left alone. Some are cool and indifferent to reading, avoid it completely, and may actually learn to hate it. Others love to read and can't wait to tell another what they have read.

How can the teacher deal with these children? What has he learned from the normal development of children that can help him to plan for the proper personal development of the pupil? How can he deal with the anxious child, with the daydreamer, and with the exuberant one? How can he individualize the reading program so that it will meet each child's needs? How can he satisfy the child's basic psychological needs? How can he satisfy the child's need for accomplishment, for success, for self-realization?

There are no easy answers to these questions. Children vary in their behavior for many reasons, and to adjust the school program to meet the needs of each is practically an impossible task.

Emotions are an important aspect of human development. Without emotional behavior, life would be dull and personalities would be flat and uninteresting. Few individuals would achieve, for none could feel the joy of success or long for the esteem of others.

Sometimes, however, emotional development is maladjustive. Thus, studies show that the incidence of maladjustment among poor readers is greater than among good readers. It is not always easy to establish whether personality maladjustment is the cause, the effect, or a concomitant circumstance. Frequently it is impossible to tell whether emotional maladjustment or social maladjustment causes reading failure, or whether reading failure causes maladjustment. Some studies have failed to find a positive correlation between reading failure and personality maladjustment. Not all emotionally disturbed students are poor readers, nor are all poor readers emotionally disturbed.

Everyone needs security, success, and social acceptance. Failure of any kind threatens both one's self-esteem and the esteem he receives from others. Failure in reading may pose a large and continuing block to the child's normal emotional development. The child who cannot read is deprived of a means for widening his interests, for satisfying his needs for new experiences, for filling his leisure time, and for promoting his emotional and social adjustment. Thus reading failure blocks the child from adequate communication with an important portion of his world.

Psychologists recognize that we are attracted to the persons and the situations that serve to satisfy our motives. When we say that something is rewarding we mean that it is satisfying to one or more of our basic motives.

For him to find it rewarding the reading situation must prove satisfying to the child. And only if it is rewarding will he identify himself positively with it. Not only does inadequate achievement in reading lead to negative identification with reading itself, but it makes other aspects of the school, including persons identified with it, unattractive.

Because, in our culture, reading is an essential developmental task, failure in reading prevents adequate adjustment. There is no satisfactory substitute for success in reading. A reading disability is a disability in almost every area of learning.

The human individual is a unified organism. His various needs and drives are not independent subdivisions but are interrelating aspects of his total personality. As we study the human personality we see that the individual's conception of himself is the unifying force. How he views himself will determine how he views his world and to a large extent how his world views him. White points out that without the self-concept we can find no point of anchorage for an interpretation of the pattern of tendencies that is characteristic of each individual. The self-concept functions as an integrating force and each person's self-concept is different from that of any other person (White, 1956).

The Self-Concept

We all strive for self-esteem. We acquire and nurture it through success in dealing with our environment. It is closely related to our need for the esteem of others but it goes beyond that. Silverberg (1952, p. 29) notes that self-esteem has two sources: an inner source, the degree of effectiveness of one's own aggression; and an external source, the opinions of others about oneself. Both are important, but the former is the steadier and more dependable one.

The self-image, or self-concept, of the learner is so obviously a significant determinant of learning that sometimes it does not receive the attention that it deserves. A major contributor to almost every disabled reader difficulty is an inadequate self-image. Kinch (1963, p. 481) defines the self-concept as "that organization of qualities that the individual attributes to himself." Self-esteem is the degree of similarity between the self you are and the self you would like to be. Kinch believes that the individual's self-concept guides or influences the behavior of the individual. He proposes that the actual responses of others to the individual are important in determining how the individual will perceive himself and that this perception will influence his self-concept which, in turn, will guide his behavior.

Brookover and others (1964) studied the significance of the self-concept on achievement. They defined self-concept in a learning situation as one's own conception of one's ability to learn. They found, using seventh-grade pupils, a significant relationship between self-concept and performance in the academic role (GPA), even when IQ was held constant.

Snyder (1974) notes the value of feelings of self-worth upon achievement. Earlier studies reported by Snyder indicate self-perceptions may be as good or better a predictor of later reading achievement as are intelligence scores.

Williams and Cole (1968) found significant, positive relationship between the self-concept of sixth-grade students and their reading and mathematical achievement.

Because of their necessary dependence and their domination by others, particularly their parents, many children come to school with very little self-confidence. The school must help these children acquire feelings of success and achievement. Unfortunately, our academic program tends to emphasize intelligence and intellectual pursuits, and the child who is lacking in these areas has a particularly difficult problem in achieving self respect.

Esteem of Others

The child's personality is developed also through his interactions with others. He needs social acceptance, but full social acceptance seldom is extended to those considered "stupid", "slow learners", or "remedial cases."

The psychologist recognizes that each experience affects the entire organism. Poor reading ability not only contributes directly to a sense of inadequacy but it threatens social acceptance. It makes the child an object of bad publicity as it were. Such a child suffers social humiliation and hurt. He is bound to feel ashamed. He is likely to become shy and withdrawn. Reading failure frequently is interpreted as a sign of stupidity, both by other students and by the poor reader himself. Failure tends to breed more failure, just as success tends to lead to more success. In such circumstances the reading failure seems likely to precipitate emotional maladjustment. This may be reason enough for the personal problems that frequently accompany serious reading problems.

And in numerous ways parents create problems for their children. If a child is somewhat retarded mentally, parents may easily stifle any possible interest in reading and promote maladjustment by a too-ambitious program. They may compound his problem by comparing him with his more fortunate brothers or sisters or, by convincing him that his slowness is all the teacher's fault, they may block the teacher from helping him.

As Gray and Reese have pointed out, if a child is already confused by reading, an anxious, nagging parent may be the last straw (1957, p. 221). When we consider the special pressures placed on a child who fails, a causal relationship between reading failure and personal maladjustment not only is possible; it seems likely. In today's school, reading success is so vital to personal esteem and social acceptance, that failure almost invariably forces the child to behavioral deviations of one form or another. Obviously, the teacher must make every attempt to help each child achieve social acceptance. Although some children will need little special help from the teacher, others will require close attention.

It is not difficult to see why the poor reader, rejected by others and lacking the self-confidence that comes with success, should be tense, antagonistic, self-conscious, nervous, inattentive, defensive, discouraged, irritable, fearful, frustrated, defiant, indifferent, restless, and hypercritical. Unable to achieve recognition through success in reading, he may stutter, be truant, join gangs, and engage in destructive activity. He may show evidence of a psychological tic, of psychosomatic conditions, or of enuresis; he may bite his nails and suck his thumb.

Siegel (1954) found that disability in reading frequently is accompanied by personality maladjustments, but he also cautions us that there is no "typical" personality pattern which is characteristic of reading failure.

Bettelheim (1961, p. 392) notes that the poor student who fears failure, even if he does his best, frequently will protect himself by *deciding not to learn*. He convinces himself that he wants to fail rather than that he can't succeed. He begins to feel that he could do rather well if he wished. Bettelheim adds that this is an insidious process. The more the pupil falls behind academically, the more his pretense of adequacy is threatened and the more pronounced becomes his deviant behavior. The fourth grader might defy the teacher; by the eighth grade he defies police and society.

Schiffman (1967) believes that many retarded readers, especially on the secondary level, have such a negative level of aspiration and such a low self-estimation that they can't succeed. This lack of achievement motivation is often encouraged by parents and teachers. In a study of 84 functional junior high slow learners, Schiffman found that 78 percent had average intelligence scores on either the Verbal or Performance scales of the WISC and 39 percent had average scores on both, but teachers felt that only 7 percent and the pupils themselves and their parents felt that only 14 percent had average ability.

MALADJUSTMENT AND READING ACHIEVEMENT

Children learn to behave in ways that they consider appropriate to themselves. What is considered appropriate often depends upon the expectations of the significant people about them (Brookover, 1959; Brookover et al., 1964). It is in his interaction with significant others that the pupil develops an image of himself as a learner. In the classroom, the child often learns only that which he believes significant others in his life expect him to learn. If others think him to be a poor reader or a poor learner, he tends to be one.

Research tends to indicate that most children come to school with rather well-adjusted personalities. Personal maladjustment seems more frequently to be an effect of rather than a cause of reading failure. However, in some cases, personal maladjustment seems to precipitate problems with reading. Educational malfunctions, most commonly those of reading, frequently signify emotional problems.

Harris (1954) suggests that painful emotional events during early efforts at reading may turn the young learner against reading (Tulchin,

1935). The young reader may also at times transfer feelings of resistance from his mother to the teacher, or from his eating to his reading. A pupil may seek gang approval by not learning to read. Finally, he may exert so much energy in repressing hostile impulses that he has little left for intellectual effort.

There are numerous other factors of an emotional nature that may hinder success in learning generally. Difficulties in adjusting to a new environment make it impossible for the child to expend the energies needed for learning. Poor parent-child relationships, sibling rivalry, unfair comparisons with a neighborhood prodigy, lack of encouragement from the home (Robinson, 1946), and negative attitudes of parents to learning in general may lead to failure.

The child may be afraid that he is "no good" and thus is sure that he cannot learn to read. Reading makes such a child feel "bad inside." Another child may be afraid of making mistakes. He doesn't want to be wrong because at home he has learned that it is "bad" to be wrong. A third child may look upon success in reading as a sign of growing up, and this is the last thing he wants to do.

Children literally punish themselves by not learning to read (Blanchard, 1936). They feel a deep sense of guilt and atone for it by receiving the reprimands that accompany failure. Others use failure as a way of punishing the adult. They demonstrate their independence by refusing to read. Their attitude is: "I'll show you."

A study of fifty White and fifty Black junior high boys revealed that inadequate readers had verbal deficits (that aspect of verbally retained knowledge obtained through formal education), came from low socioeconomic homes, and were either aggressive (excitable, impulsive, unrestrained, and demanding); negative (did not acquiesce to authority); or passive (obedient, calm, phlegmatic, low psychic energy) (Bell, Lewis, and Anderson, 1972). The retarded reader in this study did not benefit appropriately from formal education. He showed tendencies toward pugnacity and destructiveness and had difficulty in inhibiting his aggression. Low socioeconomic status was found to be a better predictor of reading retardation among Black children than among White children. The retarded reader avoided responsibility by acting or appearing to be helpless and by putting significant others (parents and teachers) into his service.

Graham (1951) hypothesized that the similarity of the profiles of unsuccessful readers and adult hysterics indicates that reading may serve as a symbol for repressed resistance to oppressive or hostile emotional climates encountered by the child. He also found that the scattergrams of ninety-six unsuccessful readers obtained from the *Wechsler-Bellevue* and the *Wechsler Intelligence Scale for Children* (WISC) approximated those of adolescent psychopaths (Graham, 1952). His group consisted of pupils between the ages of eight and seventeen who had an IQ of 90 or higher. He found that the unsuccessful reader tends to do better on performance than on verbal scales, but this pattern does not hold in all cases. On arithmetic, digit span, information, digit symbol, and vocabulary the poor readers were below the mean. He hypothesizes that perhaps both the psychopath and the unsuccessful reader may be unconsciously resisting the emotional climate of the school.

Eisenberg (1966) notes that no single pattern of psychopathology is characteristic of the retarded reader. Among the more common patterns are anxiety states which preclude attention to academic tasks, passive-aggressive syndromes, and low self-esteem. Eisenberg adds that reading difficulty is in itself a potent source of emotional distress. Ineptness in reading penalizes the retarded reader in all subjects and leads to his misidentification as a dullard. However begun, the psychiatric disturbances and the reading disability often are mutually reinforcing and psychiatric treatment may be necessary before response to remedial techniques can be expected.

Not all poor readers are emotionally maladjusted and not all emotionally maladjusted children are poor readers. Children are attracted to things that satisfy their basic needs of security, success, self-esteem, and social acceptance. To the extent that reading failure blocks the satisfaction of these needs, it may be said to cause emotional disturbances. And to the extent that emotional disturbances block adequate learning, they interfere with normal reading development. On the other hand, it is quite conceivable that for some children reading results in satisfactions that may improve emotional adjustment and in turn result in more reading and in improved reading.

Reading failure poses an important problem to any child. Even though reading failure may sometimes be attributed to attempted adjustment to emotional problems, persistant reading failure, whatever its cause, is certain to block the child from performing a basic developmental task. Thus reading failure serves to increase his emotional maladjustment. Emotional maladjustment, in turn, makes reading achievement more difficult because it interferes with all types of learning.

The teacher must be slow in attributing reading difficulties of even one child to emotional and/or social problems. Poor readers do not have an identifiable personality. Poor readers may be adjusted or maladjusted; they may run the gamut of personal deviation. There is no one-to-one relationship between type of adjustment difficulty and type of reading retardation.

The direction of the relationship between reading and personality is difficult to establish from group studies. Whether reading failure causes maladjustment or maladjustment causes reading failure must be established for each specific case. Berkowitz and Rothman (1955) point out emotional maladjustment can cause academic retardation, and academic retardation can contribute considerably to a child's emotional problems.

The relationship between reading disability and emotional and social maladjustment frequently is circular in nature. Early reading failure leads to maladjustment and personal maladjustment in turn prevents further growth in reading. It is quite conceivable that in certain cases reading failure and personal maladjustment have their own distinct cause. As Challman (1939) has suggested, however, even when the child is both emotionally maladjusted and a disabled reader, it is quite possible that one complex of factors caused the emotional maladjustment whereas a different set of factors caused the reading disability.

Generally, if the reading failure is emotional in nature, the child will have difficulties in other academic areas also. If the emotional problem was caused by failure in reading, the emotional difficulty is reduced when the child learns to read. Personal development and the learning of reading are so intertwined that the weakness of one may sap the strength and prevent the growth of the other.

In summary:

1. Emotions are reactions to environmental stimuli that also motivate behavior.
2. Some types of emotion facilitate learning and some hinder or prevent learning.
3. The relationship between maladjustment and learning to read might be any of the following:
   a. Maladjustment causes reading failure.
   b. Reading failure causes maladjustment.
   c. Maladjustment and reading failure have a common cause.
   d. Maladjustment and reading failure have each their own distinct cause.
   e. The relationship often is circular: maladjustment causes reading failure and the reading failure in turn increases the maladjustment or reading failure causes the maladjustment which in turn increases reading failure.

TYPES OF TREATMENT

Because of the intimate relationship between emotional adjustment and reading, therapy and remedial reading frequently are combined in dealing with reading disability cases.

In a detailed study of 500 disabled readers Klasen (1972) found that 65 percent of the children showed anxiety, 92 percent showed some element of psychopathology, 63 percent were handled successfully by reading therapy alone, and 28 percent needed psychotherapy.

Various forms of therapy (art therapy, language therapy, drug therapy, play therapy, psychodrama, group interview therapy, sociodrama, and individual interview therapy) have been found to help the child to overcome emotional difficulties and to achieve in reading. For severely emotionally disturbed children who are also reading disability cases, therapy combined with the remedial reading program appears to be highly successful. The greater the intensity of the emotional problem, the greater tends to be the need for both therapy and individual instruction (Burfield, 1949). Therapy may remove pressures and tensions and clear the way for attentive concentration on the reading material. In some cases it may remove a fear of reading and allow the child to develop attitudes favorable to reading. Thus the child may be led from a negative to a positive identification with reading.

Obviously, many of the special intensive treatments that have been tried with seriously retarded children can not be used in the typical classroom. Some of them are far too time-consuming and others require clinical training beyond that possessed by most teachers. They have been mentioned here as illustrations of what can be done and has been done in the way of remediation. However, from a knowledge of these special methods the classroom teacher may encounter ideas or find certain techniques that he can adapt for children in his classroom who are encountering reading problems.

Although therapy designed to alleviate underlying emotional disturbances will not be a cure-all for reading problems, the evidence certainly suggests that when a pupil is not accessible to reading instruction because of emotional disturbance, he should be treated by someone who is expert in psychotherapy.

SUMMARY

The development of a habit of reading for all normal children may well be one of the most important objectives of the school. Our educational goal is children who *will* read rather than merely children who *can* read.

To become a "reader" the child must first find in reading a satisfaction for his needs for self-esteem, the esteem of others, security, and new experiences. We know that reading proficiency builds reading interest and, in turn, reading interest fosters reading proficiency. One must understand to be interested, and when one is interested he strives to understand.

In guiding the child's interests in reading we must lure him to want to read and we must offer him a ladder of materials that lead him to become a more competent and discriminating reader.

The teacher must also understand how the child's personal development affects his reading achievements. He may need to intervene in the child's life style through counseling and psychotherapy to help him achieve at an optimum level.

It is not uncommon to find that secondary emotional and behavioral disorders often mask the true nature of a reading handicap and often become the stated reason for referral. This fact alone may explain why the ratio of boys to girls referred to reading centers is approximately four to one.

Finally, it is almost impossible to have serious difficulties in reading without experiencing some adjustment difficulties or without a strong emotional overlay. A major portion of dyslexia often involves the student's self-image and self-concept.

QUESTIONS FOR DISCUSSION

1. What is meant by *motivation?* How is it related to an effective learning situation?
2. Suggest reasons for the presence of physiological motives in man. Psychological motives. Habit motives.
3. What advantages may psychological motives have over physiological motives for energizing and directing classroom learnings?
4. How are attitudes and interests alike? How are they different? How are interests related to abilities?
5. Discuss the correlates of interests.
6. How may a child's reading affect and be affected by his personality?
7. Discuss the cause-and-effect relationship between emotional symptoms and reading difficulty.
8. Identify, discuss, and evaluate some of the types of treatment that have been suggested for children with emotional problems.
9. Discuss some ways in which the self-concept may (a) affect the learning of reading and (b) be affected by the learning of reading.

BIBLIOGRAPHY

ALLPORT, GORDON W. *Personality: A Psychological Interpretation.* New York: Holt and Company, 1937.

BARBE, WALTER B. "A Study of the Reading of Gifted High-School Students." *Educational Administration and Supervision* 38 (1952): 148–54.

BELL, D. BRUCE; LEWIS, FRANKLIN D.; and ANDERSON, ROBERT F. "Some Personality and Motivational Factors in Reading Achievement." *Journal of Educational Research* 65 (1972): 229–33.

BERKOWITZ, PEARL, and ROTHMAN, ESTHER. "Remedial Reading for the Disturbed Child." *The Clearing House* 30 (1955): 165–68.

BETA UPSILON CHAPTER, PI LAMBDA THETA. "Children's Reading Interests Classified by Age Level." *The Reading Teacher* 27 (1974): 694-700.

BETTELHEIM, BRUNO. "The Decision to Fail." *The School Review* 69 (1961): 377–412.

BLANCHARD, PHYLLIS. "Reading Disabilities in Relation to Difficulties of Personality and Emotional Development." *Mental Hygiene* 20 (1936): 384–413.

BROENING, ANGELA M. "Development of Taste in Literature in the Senior High School." *English Journal* 52 (1963): 273–87.

BROOKOVER, W. B. "A Social Psychological Conception of Classroom Learning." *School and Society* 87 (1959): 84–87.

BROOKOVER, W. B.; SHAILER, T.; and PATERSON, A. "Self-Concept of Ability and School Achievement." *Sociology of Education* 37 (1964): 271–78.

BURFIELD, LEONE M. "Emotional Problems of Poor Readers Among College Students." *Clinical Studies in Reading,* Vol. I. Supplementary Educational Monographs, No. 68. Chicago: University of Chicago Press, 1949, pp. 123–29.

CANNON, WALTER B. *The Wisdom of the Body.* New York: Norton, 1939.

CARLSEN, G. R. "Behind Reading Interests." *The English Journal* 43 (1954): 7–12.

CHALLMAN, ROBERT. "Personality Maladjustments and Remedial Reading." *Journal of Exceptional Children* 6 (1939): 7–11, 35.

CHAMBERS, D. "Let Them Read." *The Reading Teacher* 20 (1966): 254–57.

CHASEN, BARBARA. "Sex-Role Stereotyping and Prekindergarten Teachers." *Elementary School Journal* 74 (1974): 220–35.

CHIU, LIAN-HWANG. "Reading Preferences of Fourth Grade Children Related to Sex and Reading Ability." *Journal on Educational Research* 66 (1973): 369–73.

Committee of the Upper Grades Study Council. "Developing the Reading Interests of Children." *Elementary English Review* 20 (1943): 279–86.

CUMMINS, W. D. and FAGIN, BARRY. *Principles of Educational Psychology.* New York: Ronald Press, 1954.

DURRELL, DONALD D. "Challenge and Experiment in Teaching Reading." *Challenge and Experiment in Reading.* International Reading Association Conference Proceedings, Vol. 7 (1962): 13–22.

EISENBERG, LEON. "Epidemiology of Reading Retardation." In *The Disabled Reader* by John Money. Baltimore: John Hopkins Press, 1966, pp. 3–19.

EMANS, ROBERT and PATYK, JOHN. "Why Do High School Students Read?" *Journal of Reading* 10 (1967): 300–304.

EYSENCK, H. J. *The Structure of Human Personality,* London: Methuen & Co. Ltd., 1953.

GETZELS, JACOB W. "The Nature of Reading Interests: Psychological Aspects." *Developing Permanent Interest in Reading,* Supplementary Educational Monographs, No 84. Chicago: University of Chicago Press, 1956, pp. 5–9.

GRAHAM, E. E. "An Exploration of a Theory of Emotional Bases for Reading Failure." *Unpublished Doctoral Thesis,* University of Denver, 1951.

GRAHAM, E. E. "Wechsler-Bellevue and WISC Scattergrams of Unsuccessful Readers." *Journal of Consulting Psychology* 16 (1952): 268–71.

GRAY, LILLIAN and REESE, DORA. *Teaching Children to Read.* New York: Ronald Press, 1957.

GOLDSTEIN, KURT. *The Organism.* New York: American Book Company, 1939.

HARLOW, H. F. "Mice, Monkeys, Men, and Motives." *Psychological Review* 60 (1953): 23–32.

HARRIS, ALBERT J. *How to Increase Reading Ability,* 3rd edition. New York: Longmans, Green and Company, 1956.

HARRIS, A. J. "Unsolved Problems in Reading: A Symposium II." *Elementary English* 31 (1954): 416–30.

HAVIGHURST, ROBERT J. "Relations Between Leisure Activities and the Socio-Economic Status of Children." *Growing Points in Educational Research,* Official Report, American Educational Research Association, 1949, pp. 201–208.

JAMES, WILLIAM. *Principles of Psychology,* Vol. 2. New York: Holt and Company, 1890.

KINCH, JOHN W. "A Formalized Theory of the Self Concept." *American Journal of Sociology* 68 (1963): 481–86.

KLASEN, EDITH. *The Syndrome of Specific Dyslexia.* Baltimore: University Park Press, 1972.

LINK, HENRY C. and HOPF, HARRY A. *People and Books.* New York: Book Manufacturers' Institute, 1946. Abridged in Hunnicutt, C. W., and Iverson, William J. *Research in the Three R's.* New York: Harper and Brothers, 1958, pp. 6–9.

NEMOITIN, BERNARD O. "Relation Between Interest and Achievement." *Journal of Applied Psychology* 16 (1932): 59–73.

NORVELL, GEORGE W. "Some Results of a Twelve-Year Study of Children's Reading Interests." *English Journal* 35 (1946): 531–36.

NORVELL, GEORGE W. *The Reading Interests of Young People.* Boston: Heath, 1950.

NORVELL, GEORGE W. *What Boys and Girls Like to Read.* Morristown, N.J.: Silver Burdett Company, 1958.

PAINTER, HELEN W. "The Teacher's Role in the Development of Lifetime Reading Habits of Secondary School Students." *Journal of Reading* 8 (1965): 240–44.

REDL, FRITZ. "Pre-Adolescents—What Makes Them Tick?" *Child Study* 21 (1944): 44–48, 58–59.

RICHTER, CURT P. and ECKERT, JOHN F. "Mineral Appetite of Parathyroidectomized Rats." *American Journal of the Medical Sciences* 198 (1939): 9–16.

ROBINSON, HELEN M. *Why Pupils Fail in Reading.* Chicago: University of Chicago Press, 1946.

RYANS, DAVID G. "Motivation in Learning," *Psychology of Learning.* Forty-first Yearbook of the National Society for the Study of Education, Part II. Chicago: University of Chicago Press, 1942.

SCHIFFMAN, GILBERT B. "An Interdisciplinary Approach to the Identification and Remediation of Severe Reading Disabilities." *Junior College and Adult Reading Programs.* Milwaukee: National Reading Conference, 1967, pp. 14–26.

SIEGEL, MAX. "The Personality Structure of Children with Reading Disabilities as Compared with Children Presenting Other Clinical Problems." *The Nervous Child* 10 (1954): 409–14.

SILVERBERG, W. V. *Childhood Experience and Personal Destiny.* New York: Springer Publishing Company, 1952.

SNYDER, DORIS C. "Said the Mirror, 'It is Good.' " *The Reading Teacher* 28 (1974): 273–76.

SOUTHGATE, VERA. "The Language Arts in Informal British Primary Schools." *The Reading Teacher* 26 (1973): 367–73.

STRICKLAND, RUTH G. "Children, Reading, and Creativity." *Elementary English* 34 (1957): 234–41.

THORNDIKE, ROBERT L. *Children's Reading Interests.* New York: Bureau of Publications, Teachers College, Columbia University, 1941.

TIBBETTS, SYLVIA-LEE. "Sex Differences in Children's Reading Preferences." *The Reading Teacher* 28 (1974): 279–81.

TULCHIN, SIMON H. "Emotional Factors in Reading Disabilities in School Children." *Journal of Educational Psychology* 26 (1935): 443–54.

TYLER, LEONA E. "The Relationship of Interests to Abilities and Reputation Among First-Grade Children." *Educational and Psychological Measurement* 2 (1951): 255–64.

TYLER, LEONA E. "The Development of Vocational Interests: I. The Organization of Likes and Dislikes in Ten-Year-Old Children." *Journal of Genetic Psychology* 86 (1955): 33–44.

WALBERG, HERBERT J. "Reading and Study Habits of High School Physics Students." *Journal of Reading* 11 (1968): 327–32, 383–89.

WEISS, M. JERRY. "More Than One Way to Develop Lifetime Readers." *Junior College and Adult Reading Programs.* Milwaukee: National Reading Conference, 1967, pp. 254–58.

WHEAT, H. G. *Foundations of School Learning.* New York: A. Knopf, 1955.

WHITE, ROBERT W. *The Abnormal Personality.* New York: Ronald Press, 1956.

WIGHTMAN, H. J. "A Study of Reading Appreciation." *American School Board Journal* 50 (1915): 42.

WILKINS, LAWSON and RICHTER, CURT P. "A Great Craving for Salt by a Child with Cortico-Adrenal Insufficiency." *Journal of American Medical Association* 114 (1940): 866–68.

WILLIAMS, R. L. and COLE, S. "Self-Concept and School Adjustment." *Personnel and Guidance Journal* 48 (1968): 478–81.

WOLFSON, BERNICE J. "What Do Children Say Their Reading Interests Are?" *The Reading Teacher* 14 (1960): 81–82.

9

Basic Reading Skills: Identification and Association

To a large extent at least, the development of reading ability is the acquisition of a series of skills. The first of these are the word-recognition skills.

In this and in the succeeding chapter, we detour somewhat from the pattern set in the previous chapters. In Chapters 2 through 8, as we examined the perceptual nature of the reading process, the nature of learning, and the determinants of readiness and achievement, we focused on the nature of the reader. In Chapters 9 and 10 our focus will be upon the nature of the skills that are required for effective reading.

For even a low level of reading development numerous basic skills must be acquired. And the development of the more advanced reading skills depends upon the successful acquisition of these basic skills. Thus skill development proceeds both vertically and horizontally. New and more complex skills are built upon the foundation of earlier and simpler skills while at the same time the basic foundation skills are perfected and enlarged. Growth in skills is gradual but it must be continuous. As new learnings are added, old learnings are practiced and strengthened. How the basic reading skills are developed is a tremendously large topic. Our long-range goal is to develop those basic skills that make reading a means for learning and for enjoyment.

ORAL READING

Before we examine specifically the basic readings skills, let's consider some of the general relationships between silent and oral reading.

Recently there has been renewed emphasis on oral reading as an essential portion of a reading program. There are definite reasons for this. Studies have indicated that the young people of today are not as proficient in oral reading as those of forty years ago. Just as complaints that pupils today generally are less proficient than those of former years in attacking new words led to an added emphasis on phonics, so the recognition of deficiencies in oral-reading skills has led to renewed efforts in that area. A second reason for the added emphasis on oral reading is our awareness of its importance as an avenue to learning.

Oral reading can have many purposes (Ammon, 1974). Pupils benefit educationally by reading aloud prose, poetry, or drama. There are many benefits in choral reading—oral reading by a group. It leads to better appreciation of literature and to improved pronunciation, phrasing, interpretation, rhythm, and flexibility.

Oral reading also has diagnostic values. It is helpful in testing for fluency and accuracy in reading. Since reading usually requires the association of a printed form with an oral equivalent, especially at the learning to read level, it would seem only logical that oral reading would be used to emphasize this relationship.

But most important perhaps is that oral reading teaches the pupil that writing is a record of the oral language, an incomplete record to be sure (Botel, 1964). The intonation pattern cannot be fully represented by writing. The tone of voice (the paralanguage) and the gestured bodily movements (the kinesics) are only crudely represented by underlined words, exclamation points, or word choice (sauntered, gesticulated). The pupil right from the beginning should read aloud the whole sentence. This develops an awareness of the intonation pattern and is probably the best preventer of word-by-word reading.

Most writers suggest that there are basic differences between oral and silent reading. And the non-oral method of teaching reading, as advocated by McDade, assumed that oral and silent reading are distinct processes. McDade (1937) recommended that the child refrain entirely from saying the word to himself and suggested that the oral and the printed symbol should never be presented at the same time. In the non-oral method vocalization is avoided. Silent reading is considered to be a "see and comprehend process" rather than a "see, say, and comprehend" process. Buswell (1947), too, saw value in the non-oral method of teaching reading. He noted that silent reading should be a process of association between perceptual stimulation and meaning "without a mediating subvocalization." And, as we noted in Chapter 2, the psycholinguists maintain that the fluent reader decodes directly from the graphic symbol to meaning.

Oral reading requires all the sensory and perceptual skills required in silent reading, such as visual discrimination, rhythmic progression along a line of print, and the ability to take to the word those experiences that the writer, by his peculiar choice and arrangement of words, hoped to call to the reader's attention.

Oral reading also requires skills beyond those needed in silent reading. Habits of oral reading usually are quite different from those in silent reading. In oral reading there are generally more fixations, more regressions, and longer pauses. Oral reading generally is slower than silent reading. In oral reading, reading rate is limited by pronunciation; in silent reading, it is limited only by the ability to grasp meaning. Oral reading calls for interpreting to others; silent reading, only to oneself. Oral reading demands skills in voice, tempo, and gesture and in sensing the mood and feeling intended by the author.

In oral reading, we are concerned with the eye-voice span.[1] This is the space (measured in words) between the word being vocalized and the word being fixed by the eye (the eye fixation). Good readers tend to have a much wider span and more moment-to-moment variations in span than do poor readers. Thus, the good reader's voice can proceed smoothly even though his eyes may stop for a time on difficult words with his eye-voice span dropping to near zero. But the poor reader's voice flow will show hesitation as he meets difficult words because he has little or no eye-voice span.

It is, of course, possible to consider oral and silent reading to be overt and implicit expressions of the same basic mental processes. It seems likely that speech traces are a part of all, or nearly all, silent reading. Gray and Reese (1957, p. 240) point out that tiny throat vibrations are present in even the best silent reading.

Actually implicit speech seems to accompany thinking as well as reading. When one thinks, the muscles of the tongue or upper-lip vibrate as if he were saying the words. Jacobson (1932) found evidence that the muscles controlling the eyes, for example, contract during imagination as though the subject were looking at the object. And when the subject imagines that he is performing a muscular act, contractions occur in the muscle fibers which would be used in the actual performance of the act. It seems also that deaf mutes accompany their reading with finger and hand movements. Although persons who are unable to speak frequently do learn to read, it is much more difficult for them to do so.

Edfeldt (1960), studying the electromyographic records[2] of university students and adults, found that all engaged in silent speech while reading. Good readers engaged in less silent speech than poor readers, and the more difficult the material, the more silent speech occurred. This, of course, does not mean that reading without silent speech is impossible. It simply means that in these experiments silent speech was always present. It would seem that recommendations to the effect that training to remove silent speech be discontinued are somewhat premature. Reading may begin with almost total dependence upon speech; it perhaps can be freed from this dependence. The fluent reader is not so stimulus bound.

There is little doubt that a certain amount of vocal behavior and lip and tongue movement accompany many thought processes. Experiments show that students preparing for an examination actually become hoarse

---

[1] Quantz (1897, pp. 46–47) was the first to measure eye-voice span and found that, on the average, this was 5.4 words. His method was to have the subject read aloud and as he was reading, a card was slipped over the page. The number of words the subject could then add was his eye-voice span.

[2] In this process surface and needle electrodes pick up electrical potentials from the contracting muscles.

after four hours of intensive study. Hebb (1958, pp. 59–60) suggests that some verbal behavior may play a vital role in problem solving. Intensive thought is much more than a simple intracranial process. Hebb (1958) adds, however, that sentence construction shows that thought and speech are not entirely the same process. Thought processes run well ahead of our articulations. Van Riper and Butler (1955, p. 100) note that just as there is an eye-voice span in oral reading, so also there is a scanning process preceding utterance. The mind is continually looking ahead of the mouth, scanning memory drums for the words which will be needed.

Although the evidence suggests a close relationship between thought and language and between implicit speech and reading, it certainly does not mean that to proceed from graphic symbol to meaning always means going through the auditory-vocal counterparts of the printed symbol. We do know, however, that a beginning reader often uses a technique that may be of very little use to him once he becomes a fluent reader. These data suggest that although vocalization may not be essential to reading, it may well aid beginning reading. However, after silent reading attains the maximum speed of oral reading, vocalization tends to block further increases in rate.

McKee (1948, p. 606) sees some disadvantages in the non-oral methods. He suggests that a non-oral approach would lead the pupil to disregard voice intonations and would deprive him of the use of much of the achievement in language that he has acquired as a listener. This would tend to divorce printed from spoken language.

It has already been suggested that oral reading could be used as a diagnostic device in giving clues to a child's eye movements and speech defects. The teacher can observe the student's mispronunciations, repetitions, omissions, additions, and reversals. These reflect many of the mistakes he makes in his silent reading. Oral reading also provides practice in pronouncing words and in grammatical usage. Through it the child's speaking vocabulary may be developed, and poise and voice control may be fostered. The teacher, of course, wishes to discover deficiencies and improve the oral reading itself as well as to find clues to silent-reading errors.

Deficiencies in oral-reading skills are shown (Bond and Tinker, 1957, p. 343) by an inappropriate eye-voice span, improper phrasing, improper rate and timing, and emotional tenseness. Actually an eye-voice span may be too wide as well as too narrow. Improper phrasing results in word-by-word reading or in a clustering of words that do not fit into thought units. An improper rate may be either too slow or too fast.

Oral reading certainly is not a basic reading skill in the same way that word recognition, comprehension, and rate are. Instead, oral and silent reading are two approaches to reading, and children must become proficient in both. Both require skill in word recognition, comprehension, and rate. Thus oral reading requires all the skills of silent reading and some special ones of its own. Seen in this light, oral reading may itself be termed a special reading skill.

READING AS AN ASSOCIATIVE PROCESS

Meaning is an absolute prerequisite in reading. Even so, it is only one aspect of the reading process. Reading cannot occur unless the pupil can identify and recognize the printed symbol. The pupil cannot read unless he can associate the appropriate meaning with the appropriate symbol.

This section consequently concerns itself with two elements: (1) the identification of the printed symbol, and (2) the association of meaning with the symbol.

First, let us examine how the child learns to associate meaning with the appropriate symbol. Logically, identification of the symbol comes before the association of meaning with it. However, the latter phase is more easily discussed and is much less controversial than is reading method.

Before we do this let us make a few observations. Association of meaning with a symbol and "reading" are quite different from the identification of a symbol. The ability to cognize symbolic units, to identify or recognize words, is not predictable by the IQ. The IQ best predicts the pupil's ability to take meaning to the symbolic unit, to cognize semantic units, or to excel in verbal comprehension (Guilford, 1960).

"What is the basic word identification skill?" Many answers to this question reflect a confusion of this question with the following: "What is the basic reading skill?" The answer to the latter question is a twofold answer, involving both the identification of the symbol and the association of meaning with it; the answer to the first question merely concerns itself with the discrimination of one word from another word.

Is the acquisition of meaning a basic reading skill? Association of meaning with a symbol is one of the basic reading skills. The acquisition of meaning is not. The definition of reading suggests this distinction. Reading is the process of giving the significance intended by the writer to graphic symbols by *relating* them to our previous fund of experience. This definition stresses the importance of relating meaning as obtained through experience with the symbol. The teaching or development of meaning, then, is a distinct process. It is prerequisite for reading, but is not reading.

Meaning can be associated with the printed word only by associating the word with an experience, whether real or vicarious, or by associating it with another symbol (spoken word) that has meaning for the child. For most children this is a natural process. Teachers do not really provide the child with a method in making the association but only with the opportunity to do so (Langman, 1960, p. 7).

Learning almost universally involves an association of the unknown with the known. It is well at this point to reacquaint yourself with classical conditioning, for as we examine how a child learns to speak and to read, we see a striking similarity between these processes and the classical conditioning experiments. Certainly, both presuppose an association process. Reading is the linking of written or printed symbols with experience, just as the salivary response was the result of associating the tone with the food.

Generally, the child already has developed most of the meanings that he encounters in his early reading experiences. He also has associated these meanings or experiences with an aural-oral symbol. Teaching this child to read then means that the teacher must get him to identify the visual symbol and to associate with it the meaning that he already has associated with a spoken symbol. The child must associate the spoken and written word a sufficient number of times so that he comes to react to the written word with the same meaning that he previously took to the spoken word.

Rarely in English (especially in beginning reading) is meaning associated with the written symbol prior to associating it with the spoken symbol. The English language has an alphabet that represents sounds which in turn symbolize meanings. Chinese is an ideographic language in which the written symbols convey meaning directly.

Thus, in learning to read, the spoken word is the familiar stimulus; the written word is the novel stimulus. Gradually, with repeated associations between the written and the spoken word, the child brings to the written word the same meanings that he previously attached to the spoken word. Through association, meaning becomes attached to the written word.

Association of the spoken and the written word seems necessary in learning to read. In Chapter 3 we identified two basic facts: (1) reading is a *sensory* process; and (2) reading is a *perceptual* process. Here we have stressed that reading also is an *associative* process. Whether learning to read always or ever involves conditioning is another consideration.

In 1928 Hollingworth used the term redintegration to refer to a situation in which a portion of a complex stimulus gave rise to the total response which originally was made only to the stimulus as a whole. In the beginning the dog in Pavlov's conditioning experiment responded to the meat, later he responded also to the more complex stimulus of the meat and the bell. Finally his response was evoked by only a part of the complex stimulus, the bell. In similar manner the principle of redintegration applies to reading. A child learns to bring to the printed word the same response pattern that was previously evoked by the spoken and the written word together. And even more significant, the written word comes to evoke all the affective and emotional concomitants of the experience suggested by the spoken word.

Some children may experience much difficulty in associating meaning with the written word. Many of these difficulties stem from failure to properly identify the word. Some may not see the word distinctly and correctly. Some may even fail to look at the word. The tracing or writing method of teaching the word is effective precisely because it forces the child to pay close attention to the word and thus to make a proper association.

Children also learn to identify a word by rather intangible properties of the word. Thus, they identify the word by a certain splotch on the paper on which the word is printed. They look at the word *house* and perceptually read *horse*.

The following incident illustrates the statement above. A certain major had a dog that reacted with joy and excitement whenever his master was ready to go out for a walk. One day the major, pretending to go out, put on his hat, got his cane, and made ready for his walk. To his surprise the dog just sat in his corner. After investigation it was found that the major had not checked, as he usually did, whether the drawer containing his valuables was locked.

The rattling of the drawer was the stimulus that to the dog meant that the master was ready to venture out of the house. For some children the stimulus for the printed word may be just as inconsequential and just as erroneous. We constantly must check on the validity of the child's perceptions. Only if his perception is valid, can the child make the proper association between meaning and the word.

Other errors in association of meaning with the word result from inadequacies in meaning. The child simply has not had the experiences necessary to develop meaning.

Finally, the association process itself may break down. Generally, the child needs more than one association between stimulus and meaning. The child needs to see the word in many and varied situations. Varied practice extends and refines meaning; repetitive practice makes the association habitual. Practice must be varied so that the child's perceptions and meanings for a word come closer to the meaning intended by the writer and practice must be repetitive so as to increase proficiency in meaningful response.

METHODS OF TEACHING WORD RECOGNITION

Now let us examine how the child learns to identify the printed word, how he discriminates it from every other word, and how he recognizes it upon seeing it again in a different context. *Identification* is the initial acquaintance with a word, *recognition* is a subsequent acquaintance. The child then recognizes the word form as one that he previously identified and that he now knows. Smith (1971, p. 4) speaks of mediated and immediate word identification. Identification and recognition are not the same process and the means of identifying a word may be completely different from those of recognition.

The history of the teaching of reading[3] is replete with the various methods used to help the child to identify and recognize the printed symbol. These methods have been labelled the synthetic, analytic, or analytic-synthetic methods.

[3]See: Robert Schreiner and Linda R. Tanner, "What History Says About Teaching Reading," *The Reading Teacher* 29 (1976): 468–73.

Synthetic Methods

Methods that begin with word elements, with letters (Alphabet Method), with sounds (Synthetic Phonic Method), or with syllables (Syllable Method) are called synthetic methods. They are so called because the letters, sounds, and syllables must be combined (synthesized) to form words. Writers have used other terms to identify the same categorizations.

The Alphabet Method. Probably the earliest formal attempt to teach the reading of our language was a synthetic method—the alphabetic approach. Each new word was spelled out. Even the Greeks and the Romans appear to have used this method. The *New England Primer* in 1690 and the *Webster American Spelling Book* in 1793 were based on the ABC method. The child first learned to recognize the letters and gradually proceeded toward the word.

Although the letter may be the crucial unit in writing and spelling, its validity as a unit for reading is not easily established. Certainly the chief weakness in the alphabetic method is that the sounds of the names of the letters do not always indicate the sounds to be used in pronouncing the words.

Recent studies show that the pupil who has learned to associate a name with a letter has already learned a basic reading skill. He has learned how to discriminate one visual form from another (an A is different from a B), and he has associated a sound and consequently a name and meaning with that symbol.

The Synthetic Phonic Method. The second synthetic method to be used by teachers was the phonic method. It was originated by Ickelsamer in 1534 and was introduced to America in 1782 by Noah Webster. The alphabet method starts with the name of the letter; the phonic method, on the other hand, starts with the phonetic sound of the letter.

Unfortunately, sounds as well as letters lack meaning and most of the various letters in the English language may be used to suggest many different sounds. We see a portion of the problem involved when we consider the "ou" sound in the following words: sour, pour, would, tour, sought, couple.

The Syllable Method. The third synthetic method is the syllable method. Here syllables are combined to form words. It is used, for example, in African languages like the Sudanese Dinka. Since structural analysis is based on syllable analysis, a syllable approach is an essential aspect of today's reading program. Groff (1971) has adduced much interesting evidence suggesting that the phonogram is the natural unit for the beginner and that it is the most useful unit in learning how to decode words.

Gleitman and Rozin (1973a, 1973b) advocate the use of the syllable as a unit for initial acquisition of reading. Goodman (1973) rejects the approach, suggesting that the syllable is subject to the complex relationship between morphology and dialect. He notes that the syllable method does not consider reading as a psycholinguistic process.

Analytic Methods

Historically, the analytic methods of teaching reading are three: the word method, the phrase method, and the sentence method. They are called analytic methods because they begin with the word, phrase, or sentence, and these larger units then are broken down into their basic elements.

The Word Method. The word method is the most common analytic method in use today. It was introduced in Europe in 1648 by Comenius in his book, *The Orbis Pictus,* and was proposed in the United States in 1828 by Samuel Worcester (Slover, 1957, p. 86; Smith, 1934).

It frequently is termed the sight or configuration method, but often in error. Various sense avenues may be used in teaching the word method. There is a method of teaching reading that begins with the total word, but whose emphasis is on sound, or phonics. It is termed analytical phonics. Another word method emphasizes the kinesthetic sense avenues and is termed the Kinesthetic Method. This method is most frequently associated with the name of Fernald (1943). It has been very successful with remedial readers. However, it generally has not been used as a regular part of the developmental reading program.

Vandever and Neville (1973) found that first grade poor decoders learned more words when visual and auditory cues were stressed than when tracing cues were emphasized.

Spearman (1923) points out that touch discrimination is a valuable technique, especially in the preschool and kindergarten years, but notes that it degenerates after age seven because of the increasing thickness of the skin.

The child comes to school possessing an abundance of kinesthetic meanings for sensations. He already has learned how to learn with this medium. He has felt and touched objects. The object is hot or cold, soft or hard, round or straight.

Perhaps the primitivity of the kinesthetic sense has not been sufficiently utilized in leading the child from the known to the unknown. For example, we do not associate the auditory sound of the word with the kinesthetic meaning that the child already possesses for the word. It may well be that *all* children may profit from making associations between the various sense organs. They may profit from writing, hearing, and seeing the word.

The Sentence Method. The sentence method of teaching reading was emphasized especially in the early 1900s by Huey (1912). Huey suggested that the sentence, not the word or letter, was the true unit in language. He inferred that therefore it also was the true unit in reading.

Lefevre (1961, pp. 247–248) suggests an analytical method of teaching reading emphasizing language patterns. He emphasizes that meaning comes only through the grasping of the language structures exemplified in a sentence. Meaning thus depends on the intonation, the word and sentence order, the grammatical inflections, and certain key function words. Only by reading structures can full meaning be attained. Or to put it in another way, unless the reader translates correctly the printed text into the intonation pattern of the writer, he may not be getting the meaning intended (Lefevre, 1961, p. 250).

Perhaps Huey was speaking of something quite different than method of word attack. It may well be the sentence which is the basic unit of meaning, but the word, the letter, or the sound may be the basic unit of identification and recognition. We are more concerned at present with recognition than with comprehension, with identification rather than with reading. Meaningful reading seems to occur only when the reader comprehends the total sentence unit. However, few would suggest that the pupil should learn to *identify* sentences as units. The word seems to be the largest linguistic unit that readily lends itself to identification. Thus, the sentence method and the linguistic method may be the way we should read; they may have less significance for identification.

The psycholinguistic model, proposed in Chapter 2 with specific input from the cognitive model, the information processing model, and the linguistic models especially as described by Lefevre, Smith, and Goodman, suggests that the good reader is one who can read the deep structures of the language, who can make optimal use of both semantic and syntactic cues. The fluent reader operates at the deep structure level, predicts as he reads, and samples the surface structure as he tests out his predictions. He uses the semantic and syntactic cues to identify words, but even he must resort to other means. The beginning reader and poor reader are more likely to focus on discriminating one symbol from another.

Beginning With the Whole Word

Much debate has centered about the question: "Should reading teaching begin with an analytic approach or the whole word or with a synthetic approach or a part of a word?" Most reading programs today begin by introducing the child to whole words.

Is there justification for beginning reading in this way? If so, what is the justification?

In the discussion that follows we are not attempting to refute the validity of the word method nor to suggest that it is the only valid method. We merely raise the question whether the validity of this method rests on the assumptions often advanced, and we shall try to state the reasons why beginning with the whole word seems best in most circumstances. Let us evaluate the arguments commonly advanced for beginning the teaching of reading with the whole word.

In 1885 Cattell and in 1898 Erdmann and Dodge demonstrated that in a given unit of time only three or four unrelated letters could be recognized, but that in the same unit of time it was possible to recognize two unrelated words containing as many as twelve letters (Anderson and Dearborn, 1952, pp. 212–213). In 1885, Cattell, using a tachistoscopic technique, found that in 10 ms. of exposure time (.01 seconds) a child could comprehend equally well three or four unrelated letters, two unrelated words (up to 12 letters) or a short sentence of four words. Obviously, in recognizing entire words the reader was not reacting to the individual letter in the word.

These and other experiments like them and Gestalt psychology gave rise to the principle that the child characteristically reacts to the *whole* word rather than to its elements. As a consequence, the word became the unit of teaching in reading.

However, such an interpretation is not at all necessary. Studies have shown that even when every other letter has been deleted in a word or words, it frequently is possible to reconstruct the whole word. It is quite possible that the subjects in Cattell's experiment, for example, had learned to infer letters and hence the word, even though they did not actually recognize all the letters or even the total configuration of the word.

Furthermore, in the experiments mentioned above the subjects already knew how to read. They were recognizing rather than identifying the words. Unfortunately, the appropriate method of recognizing a word may not be the appropriate method for teaching word identification. Even though the mature reader may react to the *total* word in recognition and meaningful interpretation, it does not follow that he does so in learning to identify the word (Ausubel, 1967). The unit of meaning and of recognition may not be the unit of identification. Or to put it in another way, words may be the basic meaning units but are not necessarily the basic units of visual identification or even of recognition.

The mature reader sees the word as a Gestalt or as a whole. The word's configuration or physiognomy stands out from the letters that compose the word, giving it individuality. The word's form becomes the figure and stands out from the ground and from the letters. The mature reader perceives the figure. He sees the characteristic features of the word.

The beginning reader has not attained such perceptual refinement. He may quite frequently see the letter as a distinct Gestalt or form, and indeed there is no difference between the perception of a letter and a word. The letter is as much a Gestalt as is the word. The simple fact is that mature readers are capable of perceiving more complex Gestalten than are beginning readers, but even they have to analyze some words into their parts.

The second major support for the whole-word method also came from Gestalt psychology. This theory teaches that the perceiver generally reacts not only to the whole but to the *meaningful* whole in perceiving reality. The person sees a house not as a bundle of parts, but as a distinct and organized unit. Reading teachers immediately inferred that in learning to read the child perceives the smallest linguistic unit that has meaning and that can stand alone as a part of an utterance. This unit is the word.

The correctness of this interpretation seems to depend upon the meaning of the word "meaningful." Although meaning is associated with the word, this is not what is meant by "meaningful" in Gestalt psychology. Meaning in this theory refers to the organization or structure rather than to the object or event to which the word refers. It is systematic meaning rather than referential meaning (Brown, 1958, p. 71).

Gestalt psychologists look upon perception and learning primarily as the structuring of experience. The learner must perceive the relationship between the parts and from this develops insight. Their experiments were concerned with the learning of meaningful and meaningless materials. Material is said to be meaningful if the person has had some experience with it, if he has organized it, if he has identified its structure, or if previous learning transfers to it. Meaningful materials, in this sense, are already learned materials.

Unfortunately, in learning to read there is no such previous experience. The word form or its configuration is not any more meaningful than is a single letter. The learner does not "see" the meaningfulness of its structure. The word form becomes meaningful to the learner (here we are *not* dealing with referential meaning or with the task of associating meaning with the word) if he can see the interrelationship of its parts.

The word, *fitting,* is meaningful only if the pupil understands why it is pronounced *"fiting"* but written *fit-ting.* Each letter of the word receives its pronunciation or "meaningfulness" from the other parts of the word and the total word represents a different systematization or organization than the sum of its parts. Thus, the sound value of letters is established only through their appearance in the context of a word. Experience has shown that the spelling of the long *e* sound in words like wreath and reef often is confused because of the phonetic similarity of the final phonemes *f* and *th;* the long *e* sound in seek and beak is rarely misspelled because of the great phonetic dissimilarity between the initital *s* and *b* sounds (Wepman, 1960).

The systematic meaningfulness of which Gestalt psychologists speak can only come through an understanding of the interrelationship of the parts. Only in this way can the pupil transfer his knowledge about a given word to others.

In the Gestalt use of the term *meaningful,* the combination *tac,* has just as much meaning to the child as has the word *cat.* True, after he has associated the word *cat* with a real or vicarious experience, the child will more readily learn it than he will learn *tac.* He is more interested in it, or to put it in another way, the word has greater ego reference for him or has meaning for him since he probably has seen and played with cats, but the form itself may still not be meaningful in the Gestalt use of the term.

Katona (1940) gives an example of systematic meaning. He asked one group of subjects to learn the sequence, 5-8-12-15-19-22-26-29, from memory. A week later he asked them to reproduce the series. No one was able to do so. Another group learned the organization of the sequence of numbers, namely, that their differences were 3-4-3-4-3-4 respectively. Katona used the following technique (see Fig. 9-1) to illustrate the organization:

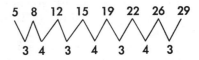

The latter group learned and retained the series because learning was "meaningful."

This connotation of meaning is quite different from the concept of referential meaning in reading. To say that a word is "meaningful" is not the same as saying that it has "meaning."

A *third* argument centers about the most desirable mode of learning. Much time and effort have been spent in establishing a difference between "whole methods" and "part methods" of learning. This difference may not be entirely real. The "perceptual whole" is a relative term. It is not the same for all children in all circumstances. Furthermore, there is no evidence to indicate how much the so-called whole unit entails. The whole may be an entire novel, a chapter, a poem, a paragraph, a sentence, or a letter. Just as a word is both a "whole" and a "part," so also a letter is both a "whole" and a "part."

It is rather arbitrary to say that for every child the perceptual whole is the word. Surely, what constitutes the whole is dependent on the ability, experience, purposes, maturation, perceptual skill, and learning habits of the learner; hence, his general readiness for learning. It also depends on the nature of the materials being learned. Thus, at times it is wise to teach the principle or generalization. Other principles can only be developed inductively.

The psychology of individual differences would suggest that each child characteristically reacts to the "perceptual whole," but that for one child it may be the total word, for another, it may be a part of the word. In general, the whole child reacts, but he is not necessarily stimulated holistically.

Perception is holistic only if the form itself is quite simple and uncomplicated. If the "whole" is meaningless to the perceiver, the details then tend to dominate individual perception. What constitutes a "whole" is different from individual to individual, and is determined by the meaningfulness of that unit to the individual.

Interesting also are the results of eye-movement studies. These studies indicate that children rarely see one word per fixation. In the first grade not more than one-half of a word is usually seen. This means that the child must look at the parts of words, retain them in memory, and combine them mentally to form the total word.

To say that the whole-word method is the correct method of teaching word identification because children characteristically perceive wholes rather than parts is to ignore the basic relativity of the perceptual whole. This statement overlooks the fact that the smallest unit of meaningfulness in perception must necessarily be a whole.

It would seem that the three arguments commonly advanced for beginning with the whole word are of doubtful validity. Does this mean that the whole-word method is invalid? Although it is very difficult to prove that for any given child analytical methods harmonize more closely with the child's normal mode of learning than do synthetic methods, there are other valid reasons for beginning with the total word:

1. Any method of reading must keep meaning in the limelight. Reading is never complete without the apprehension of meaning. Reading is the process of securing meaning and it would seem that from the beginning the child should be dealing with meaningful language units. Thus the child from the beginning should be introduced to the smallest linguistic unit that can stand alone and that has meaning. This is the word. He should learn that he is responding to a symbol with which he can associate meaning—not necessarily systematic meaning but referential meaning. Words have meanings; the sounds of the individual letters in a word do not.

   Starting with the word *and* meaning makes learning to read an interesting and rewarding process from the beginning. These side effects perhaps have greater significance for successful learning and for the development of habitual reading than the method that is used.

2. The pupil has had numerous experiences with words, listening to them and speaking them.

3. There is a one-to-one relationship between the spoken word and the printed word symbol, even though the spelling irregularities are many.

4. There are, finally, many words that cannot be learned letter by letter or sound by sound. These words often defy phonic analysis and must be learned as *sight words*.[4]

   A somewhat broader view suggests that sight words are the stock of word images in the brain which enable the successful reader to recognize printed words at high speed. They are one's recognition vocabulary. In this sense any word becomes a sight word as soon as the reader has easy recognition of it.

Emphasizing Parts of Words From the Beginning

Through the years the whole-word method has come to mean the sight method or the configuration method. This is not necessarily correct. The child must *see* the word if he wants to learn it, but the question still remains: What does he see? Does he see the total configuration or outline of the word, or does he react to the parts of the word? Of even greater importance, should he be taught to look for more than the word's general configuration?

For beginning reading the configuration method has been generally effective. However, the pupil also must become self-directive in learning.

[4]See: Patrick Groff, "The Topsy-turvy World of Sight Words," *The Reading Teacher* 27 (1974): 572–78.

He must become an independent reader. He needs skill in analyzing those words that are not in his recognition vocabulary. In evaluating reading methods it seems legitimate to ask: Which method best develops the child's skill in attacking new words? Which method makes him self-directive in identifying new words?

Bruner (1957) notes that in perception the person often goes beyond what the senses provide. We already have alluded to the ability of readers to recognize words when certain letters are deleted or to recognize numbers when numbers in a sequence are missing as in 1, 3, 9, and 3, 9,—. As soon as the person sees that the numbers are multiples of three, it becomes obvious that the missing number is twenty-seven. Studies also have shown that in the sentence, "George———was our first president," the word Washington is readily read into the sequence. The above examples of redundancy are like those observed in grammar (Osgood, 1957, p. 87). Thus, the singular subject calls for a verb ending in s (Jack sits); a time element calls for an appropriate tense (*Today,* I *am* king); a dependent clause calls for an independent clause (If you see him, call me); and the order of words itself is set (The boy sat on the log—the log sat on the boy). Changing the order usually alters the meaning.

The question of what the person learns in the above situation is not immediately answerable. Bruner (1957), believes that the *perceiver learns certain formal schemata that are used to order the probabilistic relationships between the data.*

In support of his assumption Bruner refers to a study by William Hull. Hull found that in learning to spell, the good speller learned a general "coding system" which permitted him to reconstruct the sequence of letters. The good and poor spellers both learned, but *what* they learned was substantially different. Bruner notes that the poor speller learned words by rote; the good speller learned a system, based on the transitional probabilities that characterize letter sequences in English (Bruner, p. 48).

Bruner adds that when the perceiver goes beyond what the senses give, he places the present in a more generic coding system. He "reads off" from the coding system additional information either on the basis of learned contingent probabilities or learned principles of relating material. Bruner adds that what has been called transfer of training is merely the application of learned coding systems to new events.

The letters in the language are used in a way that permits us to reconstruct them from what we know about the surrounding letters. The letters follow one another in a predictable order. Some sequences never occur in English; others occur frequently. The letter q is only followed by u. The chances are rather good that the letter p completes the word *com act.* The probability of occurrence of the p is greater than that of any other letter. Listeners, even though they have not heard a letter or word, infer it from the context.

The three-year-old is using the context or the transitional probabilities that characterize the English language when he uses regular endings such as selled, runned, or mans for the irregular *sold, ran,* or *men,* and so does the first grader who reads come as $k\bar{o}m$. Because he was dealing with an irregularity, he got into error. Thus, the letter sequence is not an exact indication of the pronunciation of a word. The pupil must learn that sometimes there are other alternatives, but the system of transitional probabilities or sequence is a valuable cue in perhaps 85 percent of the cases.

What implications do the data that Bruner presents have for reading method? They *seem* to suggest that the child must develop a coding system that will permit him to simplify the task of having to learn to read thousands of words.

The configuration method is a valuable technique, but it alone cannot guarantee mastery of the multiple words needed for independent reading. In fact, as we shall see later, the configuration method *per se* offers little opportunity for transfer of learning from one reading situation to another. The pupil, it seems, gains much from learning a system based on the probabilities that characterize the spoken-written or sound-print relationships of the English language. This seems possible in our present teaching of reading only through analysis of words, through learning a *system* of phonic and structural analysis.

Unquestionably, both the beginning reader and the mature reader frequently identify a word through its general shape and configuration. They see the word as a unified symbol rather than as a collection of related letters.

Experience has shown that the configuration method initially works with "most" children. The child learns the shape or configuration of the word, and his perception of the word is strengthened by the picture that accompanies the word, by using the word in a meaningful context, and by practicing it on flash cards, card games, tachistoscopes, and in spelling lessons.

Teachers of reading should take advantage of a word's general configuration. The length of the word, the number and variety of letters that it contains, and the ascending and descending letters are important clues to the identification of the word. For some children, the configuration method may be the only usable method. They cannot analyze the word into its parts, or have such poor auditory-discriminatory skills that they cannot deal with phonics.

There are other young children and poor readers who do not perceive clearly either the total configuration of the word or the details of the letters. The word tends to be a jumble of lines. Nothing stands out. In Gestalt terms, the figure and the ground are fused and the page looks like an undifferentiated mass. Such children have not acquired an understanding of the importance of particular details in letter shapes, and of their relationship to one another within the total word. Retarded readers, unable to analyze words, sometimes treat words as solid wholes defying analysis; or they may perceive the general structure of words only in a vague and inaccurate way without attending to the details. Vernon (1957, p. 15) also notes that children may see letters as unanalyzable wholes whose structure cannot be differentiated.

The conclusion seems clear. There is no one method that works with all children. The configuration method is a useful method, especially in introducing the pupil to reading. However, the configuration method is not necessarily the only way, nor even the best way of developing independence and self-direction in reading.

Marchbanks and Levin (1965), in a study of fifty kindergarten children and fifty first-grade children who had been taught by "the whole-word sentence method," found that the specific letters were much more important in determining recognition than was the overall shape of the word. The initial letter was the most salient cue, next came the final letter, and finally the middle letter. The least used cue was the word shape.

Timko (1970), like Marchbanks and Levin, found that the first letter was the most-oft used cue and that word shape was a weak cue. These findings were supported by Williams, Blumberg, and Williams (1970).

Children pay particular attention to the parts of words when they are required to discriminate between similar-appearing words. When the total word is not identifiable they attend to special elements and observe individual letters. Four and five year old children and poor readers generally tend to identify words by certain key letters, letter arrangements, or other outstanding characteristics, and for this reason confuse them with other words having the same letter or characteristics.

The poor reader can perceive shapes, but perhaps he has a greater tendency to be attracted by specific details than has the normal reader.

There are other young children and poor readers who frequently do not perceive clearly either the total configuration of the word or the details of the letters. The word tends to be a jumble of lines, and unless it contains some striking characteristic the child has difficulty in perceiving it. Vernon (1957, p. 29) suggests that they have not acquired an understanding of the importance of particular details in letter shapes and of their relationships to one another within the total word. And even if they can perceive these details, they fail to remember their significance. Such children often are taught to use tricks to identify the word, but these tricks betray them. For example, the word *purple* is identified by the one ascending and the two descending letters. The configuration looks like this:

Unfortunately, the word *people* has the same visual configuration and the ascending and descending letters fall in the same place (Terman and Walcutt, 1958, p. 65).

Adults, who have become proficient in reading, need less and less visual stimulation to identify and interpret a word. The rapid reader is noted for his ability to use minimal visual and perceptual clues. A single letter may be an adequate cue, and the mature reader is quite conscious, even when reading rapidly, of a misspelling of a word such as *percieve*.

Unfortunately, we still find *some* teachers who put all their cards in the configuration basket. They teach reading as though the average child could and should learn each new word as a distinct form or configuration.

The child cannot be taught the thousands of words that compose his language as individual units. In fact, some symbols such as ÷ must be thus learned. However, such an approach would make the English language ideographic, and it would turn the learning of reading into a conditioning process, thus unnecessarily complicating the process for the child.

The memory load that is created by having to learn hundreds of new and ever less discriminable words surely is excessive for some children, and may partially contribute to the negative reading attitudes that one sees so frequently among third and fourth graders.

As the differences between configurations become ever finer, with letters curving left and right (b-d) and upward and downward (n-u) (Elwell, 1961, p. 129), the child may become confused, lose confidence, and turn against reading. He will have difficulty progressing because the problems of visual discrimination increase proportionately as the rate of the introduction of new words increases (Heilman, 1961, p. 116). Terman and Walcutt (1958, pp. 50–51) note that asking all children to recognize all words as configurations also ignores the very basic fact that printed words are symbols of sounds and are made of letters which are symbols of sounds.

The child needs to develop a system for attacking words that allows him to use and apply what he has learned to other words. The configuration of a word is a pattern or Gestalt, but it has relatively little value in the identification of other words. The basic pattern or Gestalt in language seems to be the phoneme-phonogram interrelationship. The basic identification skill is the "seeing" of the sound in the printed word; the association of the phonogram with the phoneme. When the pupil learns a Gestalt for a word that is based on the perception of these interrelationships, he learns a code that is applicable to other words.

McKee (1966, p. 101) feels that the pupil should use only two aids in unlocking strange words: (1) the context and (2) the sounds that letters or groups of letters stand for in a word—hence phonics—and the pupil should always use them together, never either one alone. Today, we add that he needs to use both the semantic and the syntactic context. Ausubel (1967) notes that word recognition is more a matter of rational problem-solving than of random guessing. It is the process of lawfully decoding the unknown written word through the application of one's knowledge of grapheme-phoneme correspondences.

The basic contribution of phonics instruction may be that it requires the child to visually study the word (Mason, 1962). Phonics instruction forces the child to look at the parts of a word and thus may lead to a somewhat different Gestalt than is seen if the word were perceived strictly as a unit. The artist sees a picture as a Gestalt, but his Gestalt is substantially more detailed and refined than that of the casual observer. Through phonics the pupil may learn to more adequately scrutinize the configuration and thus may develop the habit of being unsatisfied with a general, overall view of a word.

The sound of the word should be used to get to the meaning. If the child has been taught that what can be said also can be written, it seems most natural for him to want to work out the pronunciation of the printed word and then to associate with it the meaning that he previously associated with the spoken word. Reading in this sense is "the responding to visual forms with vocal or subvocal ones. The 'thoughtful' or 'meaningful' reactions that accompany or follow this process are responses to the vocalized or subvocalized forms and the underyling neurophysiology." (Soffietti, 1955).

Writers (Squire, 1962, Tabachnick, 1962) have suggested that present reading programs spend too little time on the basic sounds and the basic sentence structure of the language. But these same people, while emphasizing the relationship between reading and linguistics and between the letters of the alphabet and the sounds of the language, intimate that this does not mean that the child should learn to associate sound with a *single* letter. This, they suggest, is the basic fault of synthetic phonic methods.

Smith (1971) suggests that letter and word identification are alike in that both involve the discrimination and categorization of a visual configuration. He adds that there are traditionally three types of word recognition: whole-word identification, letter-by-letter identification, and letter cluster identification.

The whole word view suggests that readers do not stop to identify individual letters or even groups of letters. We already noted that the reader can in a single tachistoscopic exposure recognize either four or five random letters or four or five words. This suggests that the word is as easily identified as a letter and obviously must be recognizable *as a whole* rather than as a sequence of letters. It is also obvious that words are recognizable when the component letters are not clearly discriminable. How then can word identification depend on individual letter identification?

After citing the above evidence for the whole-word point of view, Smith (1971, p. 125) asks: "If words are recognized 'as wholes,' how are the wholes recognized? What does the reader look for—what exactly does the reader know if he knows what a word looks like?"

The letter-by-letter approach also has some strong points in its favor. As already noted, the reader appears to be sensitive to individual letters in the identification of words. We cited the example of the misspelling of *perceive*. We also noted the fact that readers are very sensitive to the predictability of letter sequences. Again, the real question is not whether knowledge of letters can be used to identify words (Smith, 1971, p. 127); rather, it is whether the reader normally and necessarily identifies words by letter-by-letter analysis and how the letters themselves are identified. Similar observations can be made about the letter cluster approach.

Smith (1971, pp. 127–128) suggests then an alternative to the above approaches is what he terms the feature-analytic alternative. He does believe that words are identified as wholes and that this identification involves the same internal mechanisms as the identification of letters.

Smith rejects the whole word configuration approach or the template-matching model and speaks of a feature analysis method. What are the distinctive features of words? What feature (element or elements) of a stimulus configuration is so distinctive that it constitutes a significant difference or that enables a perceiver to eliminate some of the alternative categories to which a configuration might be allocated (Smith, 1971, p. 132)? Smith suggests that we come to know these distinctive features from the visual information available to the eye and from our knowledge of the way words are constructed.

The feature-analytic position (Smith, 1971, p. 137) does not intimate that every part of a word is analyzed simultaneously. It does not pass judgment on whether features are discriminated and analyzed in groups (parallel processing) or one at a time (serial processing). It does explain that words may be identified by their shapes because it defines shapes in terms of features. And, it stresses that featural information from all parts of the word may be taken into account in identifying a word.

Smith (1971, p. 160) notes that phonics provides clues to the sound of written words or to letter-sound correspondences. It is a strategy for mediated word identification. Smith's analysis, which we have reported above, refers essentially to the process of immediate word identification, to fluent reading more than beginning reading. Phonics tells us where a significant difference or similarity lies.

The child that is learning to read must discover the distinctive features of written material, the significant differences by which alternative letters and words can be differentiated (Smith, 1971, p. 226). He thus must first be shown what the alternatives are. He needs to see examples and contrasts. Phonics can be a very useful aid in this regard.

Smith's analysis, though terminologically somewhat different, closely parallels our own description.

Newer Approaches in Reading

We have witnessed in the last fifteen years the proliferation of methods, theories, approaches, and programs. Apart from configuration and phonic approaches, and basal, individualized, kinesthetic, and special remedial approaches, there have been presented to educators models of various types that have sought to alter the stimulus situation in reading or that have sought to provide a more penetrating analysis of the reading process.

We have divided these newer approaches into (1) those that emphasize method, that which the teacher does—hence the stimulus aspects—and (2) those that emphasize the pupil's capacities, potentials, and behavior, or the organism—especially the mediational aspects. Let us begin with stimulus approaches.

Stimulus Approaches. The relationship between the sounds of the English language and the way these are represented is not entirely consistent. Many approaches have been made to this problem. One approach is to change the word form. The printed symbols themselves are modified so as to make the relationship more consistent. Approaches which do this we have labelled stimulus approaches, because they emphasize the stimulus variables. The emphasis in these approaches is simply this. Change the nature of the stimulus in a given way, such as by changing the alphabet, and it will lead to easier and improved learning.

Illustrations of such methods, which the author has discussed at length in *Improving The Teaching of Reading,* pp 225–32, are: the Initial Teaching Alphabet (ITA), Diacritical Marking System, Words in Color, the linguistic approaches, programmed learning models, the language-experience approach, and the Textfilm Reading Program.

Mediational Approaches. The mediational approaches emphasize the neurological, physiological, and chemical changes that accompany reading. They note that learning and indeed reading occur in the cranium. Some children do not learn to read because internal events have gone awry. Specialists in remedial reading are aware that faulty teaching methods per se are not always the cause of reading failure. The conditions limiting learning often appear to be not in the method but in the learner.

Some today lean toward a biological-neurological explanation of reading disability. Reading difficulties thus often are said to have been caused by damage to or dysfunction of certain localized areas of the brain or of other physiological mechanisms.

Delacato[5] (1959, 1963) has revived Orton's mixed dominance theory with some changes and has built a reading program on it. He believes that neurological development and organization of the human organism are the key to language and reading development and to language and reading difficulties. It is suggested that the basic difference between man and the animal world is that man has achieved cortical dominance, rather than cellular quantity. When the dominant hemisphere experiences certain trauma, loss of language skills results.

INTRODUCING THE PUPIL TO LINGUISTIC PHONICS

We have intimated that an eclectic or combination approach is probably best and that the teaching of reading might best begin with the total word, but that for genuine independence in reading the parts of words should be emphasized from the beginning. The pupil must become self-directive in the process of identifying new words. The linguistic phonics program can offer much in this regard, and for this reason we single it out for special treatment here.

The focus in this section is on the identification process. It explores the skills needed by the reader if he is to identify graphic symbols with ease and accuracy. It must be clearly understood, however, that reading is complete only when meaning is associated with the printed symbols.

Some would define reading as "the act of turning the stimulus of the

---

[5]For a discussion of Delacato's method, see *Improving the Teaching of Reading,* pp. 232–34.

graphic shapes on a surface back into speech" and Bloomfield differentiated between the *act of reading* (recognition of grapheme-phoneme correspondences) and the *goal of reading* (comprehension). Reading, however, always involves comprehension. Reading is not simply the recognition of the symbol-sound correspondences to the point where the reader responds to the marks with appropriate speech.

This section emphasizes the development of an understanding of the correspondences between the English spelling system and the English sound system, in other words, the grapheme-phoneme correspondence. It is based on the assumption that if the student is ever to become a mature reader, he must be adept in the use of the graphic, or written, code of language.

Phonetic instruction (and consequently phonetic analysis) is not reading; it is only *one* of the skills required for successful reading. It is not even the only method of word attack. Other ways of identifying and recognizing a word are: through the use of picture cues, the use of the configuration of the word, the use of context cues, semantic and syntactic cues, and structural analysis. Weber (1967) found that children use all types of cues (phonic, grammatical, and meaning) to recognize words, but he also noted that toward the end of first grade children become more reliant upon phonic cues. The high-achieving children used phonic cues to a greater degree then did the nonachievers.

Word attack skills are needed to attain one of the basic goals of teaching reading. It is hoped that the reader eventually will commit the word so well to memory that he can respond to it spontaneously without having "to figure it out." Each word should then become a sight word that is instantly recognized.

Terminology

Before getting into the specifics of lingusitic phonics instruction, let us clarify a few items.

1. *Phonics* is the study of the speech equivalents of printed symbols and the use of this knowledge in identifying and pronouncing printed words (Harris, 1956, p. 324). It is learning which involves the association of the appearance of a letter or letter combinations with a given sound (Harris, 1956, p. 330). Lamb (1975) notes that phonics refers to a group of techniques used by the reader to recode or decode, using primarily his knowledge of the phonology, morphology, and syntax of his language and the graphemic options available to him in the language. Phonics is the study of sound-letter relationships in reading and spelling. It represents the various teaching practices that aim to develop the pupil's ability to sound out a word by matching individual letters by which a word is spelled with the specific sounds which these letters say. Phonic analysis is the actual process of sounding out letters or letter combinations to arrive at the pronunciation of the word.

2. *Phonetics* is the study of the sounds used in speech, including their pronunciations, the symbolization of the sounds, and the action of the larynx, tongue, and lips in sound production. Phonetics does not concern itself with the ways words are spelled by the traditional alphabet. It seeks to develop

phonetic alphabets which represent graphically the actual pronunciations of linguistic forms. Dictionaries contain phonetic transliterations. It furthermore deals with the variant pronunciations in different regions of a country and with the perception of speech sounds by the hearing mechanism. *Applied* phonetics includes (1) correction of defective speech; (2) teaching of "standard" speech in a given region; (3) devising symbols to represent speech sounds (Betts, 1973).

3. *Phonemics* is the study of the speech sounds that are used in a language. It is thus a study of phonemes. Phonemic analysis deals only with those sounds that are significant in the language (the phonemes) and ignores the nonsignificant differences (the allophones). The *p* sound in *pet, spot, suppose,* and *top* is slightly different in each instance, but the difference is considered to be nonsignificant. The phonemes are the smallest sound units in a language. Phonemes combine to form morphemes which are the smallest units of language that can bear meaning. The written phoneme is a grapheme, and the writing of graphemes in proper order to form morphemes is orthography or spelling.

4. *The Alphabet* is a set of graphic shapes that represent the phonemes of the language.

5. *Word Analysis* is an inclusive term which subsumes all methods of attacking words. Phonics is one form of word analysis.

6. *Phonic or Phonetic Method*—There are various methods of teaching reading. The phonic method is often considered to be a synthetic method because it begins with the word element or the sound of the letter and gradually advances to the total word. This designation is actually in error. There are some "phonic methods" that are termed "whole word phonics" which begin with the total word.

7. *A linguist* is a scientist who studies a language in terms of its basic structure, including sound patterns, stress, intonation, and syntactic structure.

8. *Linguistic Phonics*—We have entitled this section "Introducing the Pupil to Linguistic Phonics," because we recommend that the letter be sounded only in the context of the total word. This approach sometimes is referred to as the phonemic-word approach because the structure of the language is studied through symbol-sound relationships in whole words.

It is our view that comparing and contrasting basic spelling patterns with the appropriate or correlative sound patterns lead to independence in attacking new words. Thus, the individual letter is never sounded; it is only named. The sounds represented by *b, c, d* exist only in the context of a word or syllable. The *o* combination with *y*, as in boy, has a distinct sound; its sound depends on the pattern in which it occurs. Blending, which is a common problem in phonics, ought not to be a problem in a linguistic approach.

Whenever the word *phonics* is used alone in this section, it is meant to signify whole-word phonics as opposed to synthetic phonics.

The Phonetic Consistency of Our Language

Teaching of reading has paid relatively little attention to the phonic consistency of the English language. And yet, Hanna and Moore (1953) found English to be 86.9 percent phonetic. We do not mean that English is less phonetic than other languages. It is not correct to say that one language is more phonetic than another. All languages, in that they involve the use of phonemes or speech sounds, are phonetic. One language may have a more consistent spelling system and thus is more alphabetic than another. Thus, Hanna and Moore (1953) report that single consonants are represented by regular spellings about 90 percent of the time.

It is not difficult to find examples of the problems that one would encounter if one assumed that the English language provided a completely consistent spelling system for the sounds of the language. Systems like *ITA* and *Words in Color* are attempts to provide this consistency and to deal with the inconsistencies.

Every so often in the literature somebody pokes fun at anyone who talks of phonic consistency. George Bernard Shaw asserted, years ago, that the word *fish* might just as well be spelled *ghoti*. There is no doubt that the *f* sound is sometimes spelled *gh* (enough); the short *i* sound, as *o* (women); and the *sh* sound, as *ti* (nation). But, as Lefevre (1964, p. 182) notes, not a one of these three phonemes is regularly represented by these graphemes. The *gh* is never used initially. *Ti*, representing (sh), occurs in regular spelling only medially, namely in the initial part of a suffix such as *tion* or *tiate*. The *o*, as (short i), occurs precisely once in English, in the word *women*. The correspondence between written and spoken English is weak if one attempts to relate individual letters and sounds, but if the graphemic unit is a letter pattern, words, or word groups, a high degree of correspondence is found (Keislar, 1964).

It has been found that training on regular sound-to-spelling correspondences was less than optimal for transfer. Levin (1966) suggests that it seems reasonable early in one's schooling to simultaneously learn more than one associated sound to letters and letter groups. The indication is that this will lead to greater flexibility in trying out sounds when the child meets new instances. The study showed that dual associations were more difficult to acquire, but that once acquired they facilitated the child's learning to read new words. It is our contention therefore:

One. That pupils learn to associate letter and sound patterns. The relationship emphasized by the linguistic approach is not letter-to-sound, but rather letter patterns to sound patterns.

The first task is to break the alphabetic code and to grade words according to their phonetic difficulty, not their semantic difficulty (Barnhart, 1967). The pupil should be taught to associate specific letters in words with specific sounds without conscious analysis of a word into its individual sounds by presenting the whole word in lists and contexts (Barnhart, 1967). There should be no analysis of individual sounds as occurs in phonics. Reading should not be confused with the infant's acquisition of speech sounds.

Sullivan, Okada, and Niedermeyer (1971) note that when they contrasted the single-letter approach in teaching of word attack with letter combinations (vc or vcc) taught as single grapheme-phoneme units, of the forty-eight first graders, those of high ability learned best through the letter combination approach; those of low ability learned best through a single letter approach.

Two. That the pupil be taught from the beginning that nearly every generalization has exceptions and that if the word does not make sense in the sentence that he try another approach. We need to teach him flexibility.

Three. That the exceptions be taught immediately from the beginning as *sight* words and that they be clearly labelled as exceptions. The pupil might benefit from this introduction of variation; however, this does not mean that he should be exposed to the total range of variation.

The reading program should be flexible enough to include words which are irregular if these words are needed to make the language more meaningful. It should provide contextual settings for words that permit them to be learned in a more natural linguistic environment (Botel, 1967).

One of the chief objections to phonic and/or linguistic programs has been the limitation that it has put on initial reading materials. Such controlled materials are often viewed as uninteresting and quite meaningless. Edwards (1966, p. 356), however, notes that the beginning reader is intrigued by the magic of the decoding process. Nevertheless, the child's reading vocabulary probably does not need to be controlled to the extent that it now is. The child's early language training in the home is not structured for him. He hears thousands of words and learns to understand and to speak them. His training is sequential only as he makes it so. No one formally teaches him the word.

However, there seems to be value in some control. *We suggest control in his phonic vocabulary* (not in the number of words necessarily but in the rate of introduction of phoneme-phonogram pattern relationships) *so that he will more quickly master the principles that undergird language structure. This control seems sensible only when formally teaching skills of phonic analysis. Introducing the pupil to the phonetic consistencies will make him more conscious of the sounds in words, and having learned the principles that guide their relative consistency, he will be able to attack hundreds of words that he has not previously seen in print.*

When a word is met in the child's reading that is alphabetic, it should be taught as such. Thus, if the pupil reads *cat* and he has experienced the *k* sound of *c*, the short *a* sound, and *t,* it should be pointed out to him that the spelling is quite regular. There is no great virtue in teaching this word as a sight word. If in reading he comes across such a word as *come*, it should be taught immediately as a sight word. If the word is actually regular (came) but he has not yet been formally introduced to such words or to the principles governing the sounding of such a word, the word might simply be pronounced and teaching of the appropriate word analysis skills might be deferred until later. There is no reason to insist that the child should learn it as a sight word, or as a configuration, if, by application of the principle of pacing, the pupil will soon know it and understand it as a phonetically consistent word.

Four. That the best way of breaking the language code may not yet have been developed, but it seems easier to break the code when the child is introduced to words in which the letters behave consistently. Burns (1973) suggests the use of a single-sound-symbol alphabet to teach beginning reading. The alphabet must demonstrate an isomorphic correspondence between phonemes and graphemes and the construction of the phoneme-grapheme relationship should be according to the frequency of occurrence in American English.

Five. That rather than establish a new system in which there is a separate symbol for each sound, such as *I T A* or even such a distinctive cueing device as *Words in Color,* it is better to teach the present system, emphasizing the consistency of sound-symbol patterns most often encountered (Stone, 1966).

Six. That the pupil develop the habit of "reading through" words by proceeding from left to right (Hildreth, 1958, p. 335). The order of the letters in a word symbolizes the time-order in which the sounds are made, but it seems far safer to teach the pupil to sound the whole word.

Linguistic Systems of Teaching Reading

Since we have termed our approach linguistic phonics, it may be advantageous to summarize various linguistic systems of teaching reading. There is really no one linguistic method; all methods of teaching reading are linguistic methods in that they teach the comprehension of linguistic material (Ives, 1964). Linguists emphasize that reading is primarily a language process and that the major task facing the child is the mastery of the graphic system that reflects the spoken language system. The linguist maintains that he has more to offer than a retreat back to synthetic phonics.

Bloomfield & Barnhart (1961) presented a linguistic approach in *Let's Read: A Linguistic Approach.* The central thesis of the Bloomfield-Barnhart method is that there is an inseparable relationship between the words as printed and the sounds for which the letters are conventional signs, and that converting letters to meaning requires from the beginning a concentration upon letter and sound to bring about as rapidly as possible an automatic association between them (Pooley, 1961). Barnhart (Bloomfield and Barnhart, 1961, p. 9) points out that Bloomfield's system is a linguistic system of teaching reading which separates the problem of the study of word-form from the study of word-meaning. He notes that children come to school knowing how to speak the English language, but they do not know how to read the form of words.

Bloomfield makes the following points:

1. In spite of its many imperfections, the system of writing used in the English language is basically alphabetic, and reading is merely the act of responding vocally to the printed letter as it functions with other letters. The alphabetic nature of our writing is most obvious when we put together a combination of

letters to make a word. The linguistic emphasis thus is not so much on the representation of a single phoneme, but rather of a pattern of phonemes. The emphasis is on the relationship between patterns of phonemes and patterns of graphemes, especially between spoken words and written words. The linguist admits that the correspondence between written and spoken English often is weak if one relates individual letters and sounds, but notes that the correspondence between letter patterns and word groups is high (Gibson et al., 1962, 1963, 1964): The letter is not sounded alone; it is sounded only in the context of other letters of the word.

2. In order to read alphabetic writing the reader must have developed an ingrained habit of producing the phonemes of the language when he sees the written marks which conventionally represent these phenomes (Bloomfield and Barnhart, 1961).

3. English writing is alphabetic, but only imperfectly so. The child should not be introduced to the exceptions until he has mastered the regularities of the language. The child's early reading experiences should be dealing with letters and sounds as they function in monosyllabic regular words. Hildreth (1958, p. 348) notes that it is easier to learn the relationships among sound elements within words by studying monosyllabic words. When all words are three-letter words the pupil cannot use the length of the word to identify it, and quite frequently he cannot use the configuration: *bat, hat.* Both words obviously have the same configuration. The words should contain only short vowels. Long vowel sounds, diphthongs, consonant blends, speech consonants, and words containing silent letters should be introduced only after the pupil has mastered some of the phonetic consistencies of the language. The goal of this approach to reading instruction is to familiarize children with the phonetic consistencies of the language as a basis for generalizations to new words. In beginning reading materials, every letter should represent only one single phoneme. The pupil must learn the equation: *printed letter = speech sound to be spoken.*

   The first material should contain no words with silent letters (*k*nit), none with double letters (be*ll*), and none with combinations of letters having a special value (*ea* as in bean). Letters such as *x* or *q* should also be delayed until later.

4. Bloomfield decries the fact that synthetic phonic methods isolate speech sounds. Synthetic phonics proceeds as though the child were being taught to speak. Phonemes do not occur by themselves and should not be taught in isolation.

5. The child should first be taught the names of the letters. Presenting the letters in color increases interest and emphasizes shape. Writing of the letters should be delayed until after reading has begun.

Lefevre (1962, 1964, pp. 247–78), having a different emphasis than Bloomfield, adapted lingusitic ideas to meaningful reading. He suggests an analytical method of teaching reading emphasizing language patterns. He emphasized that meaning comes only through the grasping of the language structure exemplified in a sentence. Meaning thus depends on the intonation, the word and sentence order, the grammatical inflections, and certain key function words. Intonation, or the pauses and stresses in oral language, is represented by (1) capital letters, periods, semi-colons, and question marks, (2) by the order of the words, (3) by grammatical inflections signaling tense, number, and possession, and (4) by such function words as *the, when, nevertheless,* or *because.* Only by reading structures can full meaning be attained. Or, to put it another way, unless the reader translates correctly the printed text into the intonation pattern of the writer, he may not be getting the meaning intended.

Bloomfield felt that initial teaching of reading for meaning is incorrect and that meaning will come quite naturally as the alphabetic code or principle is discovered. Lefevre is critical of Bloomfield's approach, criticizing him for confining himself largely to phonemic analysis and for neglecting intonation and syntax.

Lefevre makes the following observations:

1. If the reader is to comprehend printed matter, he must perceive entire language structures as wholes—as unitary meaning-bearing patterns (1964, p. XI). Reading comprehension requires "recognition and interpretation of the graphic counterparts of entire spoken utterances as unitary meaning-bearing patterns" (Lefevre, 1956).

2. Lefevre decries the emphasis on letters and words as the significant units of language (1964, p. XVII). He notes that in English the most significant structures are intonation patterns, grammatical and syntactical word groups, clauses, and sentences. Words are relatively minor elements in meaning-bearing patterns. The pupil needs to be taught to read by language patterns that carry meaning. Word-order provides one of the most reliable clues to the total meaning-bearing pattern. Intonation is another. The child should be taught first to read and write the language patterns he brings to school.

3. Writing and print are mnemonic devices whose chief function is to effect recall of entire language patterns, especially sentence-level utterances (1964, p. 4).

4. Misapprehension of the relationships between spoken and printed language or sentence patterns is a decisive element in reading failures (1964, pp. 4–5). The crippled reader's worst fault is literal word calling or word-by-word reading with virtually no sentence sense (1964, p. 23). The poor reader registers only random elements (words)—many can't even do this and that is why we need phonics—but miss language structures altogether.

5. Children taught to read with chief emphasis on larger patterns than words develop their own generalizations of spelling-sound relationships (phonics). If they do not, special instructions may need to be devised to help them (1964, p. 6). Although attention to word analysis and spelling may be necessary, isolated words must be brought back into the larger patterns and structures that function linguistically and carry meaning; this is true reading (1964, p. 174).

6. Reading readiness is the child's understanding that the language he hears and speaks can be represented graphically in writing and print, and that the writing and print he sees can say something to him" (1964, p. 39).

Soffiétti's system (1955), that of Daniels and Diack (1954, 1959, 1960) in the *Royal Road Readers,* and Fries' system (1963) are basically linguistic systems. Daniels and Diack call their system "the phonic word method." They teach letter meanings functionally in words and do not isolate speech sounds. Soffiétti emphasizes, contrary to Bloomfield, the importance of meaning, structure, and form clues, but he nevertheless stresses the importance of beginning with words in which each letter has only one phonetic value.

Fries, in *Linguistics and Reading* (1963, pp. 120–24, 146, 194–208), offers the following suggestions for the teaching of reading:

1. Learning to read is a process of transfer from the auditory signs for language signals (sounds) to the new visual signs (letters) for the same signals. In speech, contrastive bundles of sound features represent the language signals; in reading, contrastive patterns of spelling represent these same signals.

2. Writing represents the time sequence of auditory patterns (sounds follow one another in time) by means of a sequence of direction in space.

3. The first set of recognition responses to be developed by the pupil are those for the letters of our alphabet, which must be identified as contrasting shapes. Identifying and distinguishing the graphic shapes does not necessarily mean attaching conventional names to these distinctive shapes. The names, however, are very useful in checking the identification response.

4. There must be no attempt to connect the letters themselves with sounds. Reading is not the matching of words, letter by letter, with words, sound by sound. Furthermore, the pronunciation of a word is not a fusion or blending of the sounds represented by the individual letters.

   The pupil must develop the automatic habit of responding to the contrastive features of spelling-patterns as identifying the word-patterns they represent. For example, even in the three letter word . . . *man,* it is not the single letter A that indicates t ie vowel sound /ae/. It is the spelling-pattern *m a n* in contrast with the sp lling-pattern *m a n e* or that of *m e a n* that signals the different vowel pho iemes that make these three different words.

5. This spelling-pattern approach, learning to respond to the contrastive features that separate and identify whole word-patterns, is a word-method. The basic difference between this spelling pattern approach and the usual 'word-method' lies in the kind of identifying characteristics used to recognize the words.

6. a. The sound-patterns of the words used and the particular meanings selected must include only those within the actual *linguistic* experience of the pupil.

   b. The grammatical signals must also include only those within the pupil's linguistic experience.

   c. The simple contrasts used should always be of items within a whole pattern, never of items less than a word.

   d. At the beginning the teacher pronounces each new word and each pair of contrastive words as it is introduced and makes sure that the pupil, from that pronunciation, identifies the words as ones he knows.

   e. Only complete words are pronounced. The pronunciation for the "word" is thus attached to the total spelling-pattern that represents that word. The spelling-pattern *c a t* represents the word /kaet/ as pronounced. . . . The understanding of the difference that any particular letter makes in the spelling-pattern is built up out of the experience of pronouncing a variety of word pairs with minimum differences in their spelling patterns.

CAT—AT
CAT—RAT
CAT—PAT

7. If the reader is to learn to read well, that is, if the graphic devices are to function fully for him, there must be some way by which he can learn to supply the meanings contributed to speech by the patterns of intonation and stress. The mature readers, as they read, carry along and build up such a cumulative comprehension of so much of the total meanings of a discourse that their automatic recognition-responses fill in the appropriate intonation and stress patterns. The very least that teachers should accept at the beginning, is the 'saying' of a sentence, after it has been "mechanically read," as the child would "talk" it to a companion. In other words, the second stage of the development of reading ability is complete only when the responses to the spelling-patterns have become so automatic that the contrastive features of these bundles of the graphic shapes themselves sink below the threshold of attention leaving only consciousness of the body of meaning as it develops, and when the cumulative understanding of this body of meaning enables the reader to supply the appropriate patterns of intonation and stress that are only partially represented in the graphic materials.

It seems that before the pupil can do what Lefevre wants him to do, the pupil must be able to do what Bloomfield and Fries are most interested in. They are emphasizing the importance of being able to identify the word; they thus have a lot to offer in word identification. Lefevre is more concerned with the total reading act and thus has much to offer in word comprehension. But since context is often invaluable in identifying a word, Lefevre's ideas have meaning also when the pupil cannot identify the word, for unless the word makes sense in the sentence, both in meaning sense and structurally, word identification was faulty.

SUMMARY

In this chapter we have discussed the two basic reading skills: word identification, and the association of meaning with a printed symbol. We have pointed out that a good reading program must give due consideration to both identification and meaning. Neither one by itself is adequate.

We have emphasized the importance of both analysis and synthesis in reading and have suggested that neither the configuration nor the phonic method meets the needs of every pupil nor perhaps *all* the needs of even one pupil.

What does good teaching include? In reading, good teaching seems to mean that the teacher devises techniques of instruction which help the pupil to construct a generic code or a coding system that has wider applicability in reading than would the rote identification of individual words. The code has wider application than in the situation in which it was learned. The child learns to "read off" from this generic code information that permits him to attack other words. Such learning maximizes the transfer of learning. The child, in a sense, is taught to be a better guesser by knowing the language system and the phonogram-phoneme interrelationships.

However, there are differences as to the route to ultimate progress in reading. Should the earliest emphasis be on meaning or on word discrimination? We have tried to show that this is a pseudo-question, that both are essential from the beginning. There must be a delicate balance between the two, lest the child be dragged too far afield in either.

The child, in this approach to reading, must be viewed as a learner capable of discrimination and generalization who can, with guidance, learn a generalized coding system which he can use in identifying numerous words not previously seen by him.

Perhaps a few generalizations are apropos in closing this chapter.

1. Most children learn to read regardless of the method. Many different methods can and do eventually lead to reading proficiency. One type of program does not seem to be clearly superior to all others or best for all children.
2. There are methods or specific teaching approaches that make a world of difference for the individual child.
3. The method that works best for a given child depends on the individual child. Not all children profit to the same extent from a given method. What is good for slow learners may not work with gifted learners.
4. No one program seems to provide for all the child's reading requirements.
5. The best method for *most* children has both an analytical *and* a synthetic emphasis. There are few pure-configuration methods, and few programs ignore phonics completely.
6. Some teachers do not make use of the best that is available, but if the teacher is a good teacher, other factors often pale into insignificance. Differences in program effectiveness often can be attributed to teacher effectiveness.
7. A given method may well produce excellent results under one set of conditions, but may result in failure under a different set of circumstances.

QUESTIONS FOR DISCUSSION

---

1. What are the values of oral reading? What place does oral reading have in basic instruction in reading?
2. What are the advantages and disadvantages of vocalizing during reading?
3. Discuss: "The quickest way to the meaning of a word is through its sound."
4. Discuss the validity of the word method in the light of newer research and new interpretations of previous research.
5. Discuss Bruner's thesis that the good reader must develop some sort of coding system which permits the pupil to achieve independence in attacking words.
6. Discuss: Children react to the perceptual whole but this may be the total word or only a specific characteristic of that word such as an ascending letter.

7. Discuss:
   a. The unit of meaning and of recognition may not be the unit of identification.
   b. The basic pattern or Gestalt in language is the phoneme-phonogram interrelationship rather than the size or shape of the word.
   c. The perceptual whole is a relative term, dependent for its formation upon the ability, experience, purposes, maturation, perceptual skill, and learning habits of the learner.
   d. The good "identifier" of words learns a coding system based on the transitional probabilities that characterize letter sequences in English and that characterize the sound-print relationships of the language.
   e. Pupils generally achieve significantly higher on a word recognition test when taught by a phonic method than when taught by a look-and-say method.

BIBLIOGRAPHY

AMMON, RICHARD. "Reading Aloud: For What Purpose?" *The Reading Teacher* 27 (1974): 342–46.

ANDERSON, I. H. and DEARBORN, W. F. *The Psychology of Teaching Reading.* New York: Ronald Press, 1952.

AUSUBEL, DAVID. "Cognitive Structure: Learning to Read." *Education* 87 (1967): 544–48.

BARNHART, CLARENCE L. "A Reaction to Sister Mary Edward Dolan's Linguistics in Teaching Reading." *Reading Research Quarterly* 2 (1967): 117–22.

BETTS, EMMETT ALBERT. "Confusion of Terms." *The Reading Teacher* 26 (1973): 454–55.

BLOOMFIELD, LEONARD and BARNHART, CLARENCE L. *Let's Read: A Linguistic Approach.* Detroit: Wayne State University Press, 1961.

BOND, GUY L. and TINKER, MILES A. *Reading Difficulties: Their Diagnosis and Correction.* New York: Appleton-Century-Crofts, 1957.

BOTEL, MORTON. "What Linguistics Says to the Teacher of Reading and Spelling." *The Reading Teacher* 18 (1964): 188–93.

BOTEL, MORTON. "Strategies for Teaching Sound-Letter Relationships." *Vistas in Reading.* Newark, Del.: International Reading Association, 1967, pp. 156–59.

BROWN, ROGER. *Words and Things.* Glencoe, Illinois: The Free Press, 1958.

BRUNER, J. S. "Going Beyond the Information Given." *Contemporary Approaches to Cognition,* Cambridge: Harvard University Press, 1957, pp. 41–49.

BURNS, ALAN R. "Overcoming Difficulties in Learning to Read." *Elementary English* 50 (1973): 911–20.

BUSWELL, G. T. "Perceptual Research and Methods of Learning." *The Scientific Monthly* 64 (1947): 521–26.

DANIELS, J. C. and DIACK, H. *Royal Road Readers.* London: Chatto and Windus, 1954.

DANIELS, J. C. and DIACK, H. "The Phonic Word Method." *Reading Teacher* 13 (1959): 14–21.

DANIELS, J. C. and DIACK, HUNTER. *Progress in Reading in the Infant School.* Institute of Education, University of Nottingham, 1960.

DELACATO, CARL H. *The Treatment and Prevention of Reading Problems.* Springfield, Ill.: Charles C Thomas, 1959.

DELACATO, CARL H. *Diagnosis and Treatment of Speech and Reading Problems.* Springfield, Ill.: Charles C Thomas, 1963.

EDFELDT, AKE W. *Silent Speech and Silent Reading.* Almquist and Wiksell, Stockholm, 1959, Chicago: University of Chicago Press, 1960.

EDWARDS, THOMAS J. "Teaching Reading: A Critique." In John Money, ed., *The Disabled Reader.* Johns Hopkins Press, Baltimore, 1966, pp. 349–62.

ELWELL, C. E. "Phonics Indeed—But When?" In J. Allen Figurel, ed., *Changing Concepts of Reading Instruction,* International Reading Association Conference Proceedings, Vol. 6. New York: Scholastic Magazines, 1961, pp. 127–30.

FERNALD, G. M. *Remedial Techniques in Basic School Subjects.* New York: McGraw-Hill, 1943.

FRIES, CHARLES C. *Linguistics and Reading.* New York: Holt, Rinehart & Winston, New York, 1963.

GLEITMAN, LILA R. and ROZIN, PAUL. "Teaching Reading by Use of Syllabary." *Reading Research Quarterly* 8 (1973a): 447–83.

GLEITMAN, LILA R. and ROZIN, PAUL. "Phoenician Go Home? (A Response to Goodman)." *Reading Research Quarterly* 8 (1973b): 494–501.

GOODMAN, KENNETH S. "The 13th Easy Way to Make Learning to Read Difficult: A Reaction to Gleitman and Rozin." *Reading Research Quarterly* 8 (1973): 484–93.

GRAY, LILLIAN and REESE, DORA. *Teaching Children to Read.* New York: Ronald Press, 1957.

GROFF, PATRICK. *The Syllable.* Portland, Ore.: Northwest Regional Educational Laboratory, 1971.

GUILFORD, J. P. "Frontiers in Thinking That Teachers Should Know About." *The Reading Teacher* 13 (1960): 176–82.

HANNA, R. R. and MOORE, T. JR. "Spelling—From Spoken Word to Written Symbol." *Elementary School Journal* 53 (1953): 329–37.

HARRIS, ALBERT J. *How to Increase Reading Ability,* New York: David McKay Co., 1956.

HEBB, D. O. *A Textbook of Psychology.* Philadelphia: W. B. Saunders Co., 1958.

HEILMAN, ARTHUR W. *Principles and Practices of Teaching Reading.* Columbus: Charles E. Merril Books, 1961.

HILDRETH, GERTRUDE. *Teaching Reading.* New York: Holt, Rinehart and Winston, 1958.

HUEY, EDMUND B. *The Psychology and Pedagogy of Reading.* New York: Macmillan, 1912.

IVES, SUMNER. "Some Notes on Syntax and Meaning." *The Reading Teacher* 18 (1964): 179–83, 222.

JACOBSON, EDMUND. "Electrophysiology of Mental Activities." *American Journal of Psychology* 44 (1932): 677–94.

KATONA, G. *Organizing and Memorizing: Studies in the Psychology of Learning and Teaching.* New York: Columbia University Press, 1940.

KEISLAR, EVAN. "Conference on Perceptual and Linguistic Aspects of Reading." *The Reading Teacher* 18 (1964): 43–49.

LAMB, POSE. "How Important is Instruction in Phonics?" *The Reading Teacher* 29 (1975): 15–19.

LANGMAN, MURIEL POTTER. "The Reading Process: A Descriptive, Interdisciplinary Approach." *Genetic Psychology Monographs* 62 (1960): 1–40.

LEFEVRE, CARL A. "A Comprehensive Linguistic Approach to Reading." *Elementary English* 43 (1956): 561–69.

LEFEVRE, CARL A. "Language Patterns and Their Graphic Counterparts: A Linguistic View of Reading." In J. Allen Figurel, ed., *Changing Concepts of Reading Instruction,* International Reading Association Conference Proceedings, Vol. 6, New York: Scholastic Magazines, 1961, pp. 245–49.

LEFEVRE, CARL A. "Reading Our Language Patterns: A Linguistic View— Contributions to a Theory of Reading," *Challenge and Experiment in Reading,* International Reading Association Conference Proceedings, Vol. 7 (1962): 66–70.

LEFEVRE, CARL A. *Linguistics and the Teaching of Reading.* New York: McGraw-Hill, 1964.

LEVIN, HARRY. "Reading Research: What, Why, and For Whom." *Elementary English* 43 (1966): 138–47.

MARCHBANKS, G. and LEVIN, H. "Cues by Which Children Recognize Words." *Journal of Educational Psychology* 56 (1965): 57–61.

MASON, GEORGE E. "The Role of Phonics in the First Grade Program." *Challenge and Experiment in Reading,* International Reading Association Conference Proceedings, Vol. 7 (1962): 27–29.

MCDADE, JAMES E. "A Hypothesis for Non-Oral Reading: Argument, Experiment, and Results." *Journal of Educational Research* 30 (1937): 489–503.

MCKEE, PAUL. *The Teaching of Reading in the Elementary School.* Boston: Houghton Mifflin, 1948.

MCKEE, PAUL. *Reading: A Program for the Elementary School.* Boston: Houghton Mifflin, 1966.

NEWBURG, JUDSON, E. *Linguistics and the School Curriculum.* Chicago: Science Research Associates.

OSGOOD, CHARLES E. "A Behavioristic Analysis of Perception and Language as Cognitive Phenomena." *Contemporary Approaches to Cognition.* Cambridge: Harvard University Press, 1957, pp. 75–118.

POOLEY, ROBERT C. "Introduction." In Leonard Bloomfield and Clarence L. Barnhart, *Let's Read.* Detroit: Wayne State University Press, 1961, p. 6.

QUANTZ, J. O. "Problems in the Psychology of Reading." *Psychological Review Monograph Supplements* 2 (1897): 1–51.

SLOVER, VERA. "Reading: Then and Now." *The Education Forum* 21 (1957): 413–20.

SMITH, FRANK. *Understanding Reading.* New York: Holt, Rinehart and Winston, 1971.

SMITH, NILA B. *American Reading Instruction.* New York: Silver Burdett and Company, 1934.

SOFFIETTI, JAMES P. "Why Children Fail to Read: A Linguistic Analysis." *The Harvard Educational Review* 25 (1955): 63–84.

SPEARMAN, C. *The Nature of Intelligence and the Principles of Cognition.* New York: Macmillan, 1923.

SQUIRE, JAMES R. "New Directions in Language Learning." *Elementary English* 39 (1962): 535–44.

STONE, DAVID R. "A Sound-Symbol Frequency Count." *The Reading Teacher* 19 (1966): 498–504.

SULLIVAN, HOWARD J.; OKADA, MASAHITO; and NIEDERMEYER, FRED C. "Learning and Transfer Under Two Methods of Word-Attack Instruction." *American Educational Research Journal* 8 (1971): 227–39.

TABACHNICK, B. ROBERT. "A Linguist Looks at Reading: Leonard Bloomfield and the Phonemic Criterion." *Elementary English* 39 (1962): 545–48, 561.

TERMAN, SIBYL and WALCUTT, C. C. *Reading: Chaos and Cure.* New York: McGraw-Hill, 1958.

TIMKO, HENRY G. "Configuration as a Cue in the Word Recognition of Beginning Readers." *Journal of Experimental Education* 39 (1970): 68–69.

VANDEVER, THOMAS R. and NEVILLE, DONALD D. "The Effectiveness of Tracing for Good and Poor Decoders." *Journal of Reading Behavior* 5 (1972–73): 119–25.

VAN RIPER, C. and BUTLER, KATHARINE G. *Speech in the Elementary Classroom.* New York: Harper and Row, 1955.

VERNON, MAGDALEY DOROTHEA. *Backwardness in Reading.* London: Cambridge University Press, 1957.

WEPMAN, JOSEPH M. "Auditory Discrimination, Speech, and Reading." *The Elementary School Journal* 60 (1960): 325–33.

WILLIAMS, JOANNA P.; BLUMBERG, ELLEN L.; and WILLIAMS, DAVID W. "Cues Used in Visual Word Recognition." *Journal of Educational Psychology* 61 (1970): 310–15.

10

Basic Reading Skills: Comprehension Skills

Word recognition is but one of the basic reading skills. Comprehension is at least as important. Meaning is the sine qua non of reading. Recognition of the word is not the ultimate goal in reading. Without comprehension reading is mere verbalism.

The goal of all reading is the comprehension of meaning. The initial step in this process is the association of an experience with a given symbol. This is absolutely necessary, but it is the most elemental form of comprehension. Complete meaning is not conveyed by a single word. The good reader learns to interpret words in their contextual setting. He comprehends words as parts of sentences, sentences as parts of paragraphs, and paragraphs as parts of stories.

Effective reading includes not only a literal comprehension of an author's word, but also an interpretation of his mood, tone, feeling, and attitude. The reader must also comprehend the implied meanings and prejudices of the writer. He must recognize summary statements, make inferences and applications, and see the broader implications of a passage. He must familiarize himself with the time and place in which the words were written. He must use the periods, commas, quotation marks, and questions as aids to interpretation.

Schell (1972) speaks of three levels of comprehension:

1. *Literal comprehension:* getting the primary, direct, literal meaning of a word, idea, or sentence in context.
2. *Interpretation:* getting deeper meanings—anticipating meanings, drawing inferences, making generalizations, reasoning from cause to effect, detecting significance, making comparisons, identifying purpose.
3. *Critical reading:* evaluating the quality, accuracy, or truthfulness of what is read.

Lanier and Davis (1972), in summarizing comprehension skills, categorize them as literal skills (recall and recognition of facts), interpretative skills (inferring, drawing conclusions, generalizing, deriving meaning from figurative language, predicting, anticipating, and summarizing), critical skills (judging, detecting propaganda, analyzing, checking validity, checking the author's biases and purposes), and creative skills (applying information, responding emotionally).

Too often comprehension simply involves the student in the retrieval of the trivial factual data of a story (Guszak, 1967). Comprehension questions are often directed at literal comprehension rather than at broad understandings. The student quickly learns to parrot back an endless recollection of trivia. The purpose of this chapter then is to help teachers to instruct the student to look for intricate relationships, implications, subtle meanings, conjectures, evaluations, and inferences; in other words, to move from literal comprehension to interpretation, to critical reading, and to creative reading.

We expect the student to be a comprehender, and yet perhaps one student in four on the high school level cannot adequately understand his reading assignments or the textbooks on which his assignments are based. Let us look more closely, then, at what comprehension is all about.

THE NATURE OF COMPREHENSION

Comprehension is difficult to define. In fact, no one has as yet been able to identify the components of reading comprehension (Traxler, 1952, p. 92). Comprehension includes the correct association of meanings with word symbols, the evaluation of meanings which are suggested in context, the selection of the correct meaning, the organization of ideas as they are read, the retention of these ideas, and their use in some present or future activity (Yoakam, 1951, p. 32). It includes the ability to reason one's way through smaller idea segments and to grasp the meaning of a larger unitary idea (Edwards, 1957, p. 38).

To comprehend, a pupil needs also an understanding of language patterns. He must be able to recognize the structural elements composing a sentence and he must perceive the syntactic interrelationships of these elements. In other words, he must understand syntax (Allen, 1964; Jenkinson, 1971). Briggs (1969) noted that reading programs too often focus on the semantic elements and ignore the contributions that syntactical skill can make to comprehension. Readers frequently do not perceive the "deep structure" of a sentence.

Written English presents special difficulties in this regard. It is less redundant than oral English (Martin, 1969), often containing logical and subordinate connectives, thus increasing sentence complexity (Jenkinson, 1966).

Structure words, or markers or empty words (because, why, out, where), next to intonation and sentence order, are the most significant clues to language patterns. The adversative connectives (but, although) are particularly difficult to understand (Katz, 1968; Robertson, 1968).

Davis (1956, p. 542) notes that underlying comprehension are two general mental abilities: ability to remember word meanings and ability to reason with verbal concepts. He adds that neither of these general abilities lends itself to specific teaching; they are probably part of the pupil's native endowment.

This observation implies that certain limitations are imposed on training in comprehension. Skills can be developed only within the potentials that already exist. Sommerfeld (1954) suggests that the basic problem of reading is not that of getting the material to the brain, but of assimilating it after it gets there.

There are a number of reasons for our concern with reading comprehension. For one thing, we know that it is highly related to academic grades. We should expect this to be true because intelligence and vocabulary skills are basic determinants of school achievement. They also correlate highly with comprehension.

However, comprehension and reading performance are related in still other ways. Fairbanks (1937) found that poor readers made an average of 5.8 oral errors per 100 words, but that good readers made only 2.1 errors per 100. More relevant is the fact that in 51 percent of the cases the errors of the poor readers tended to change the meaning, but the errors of the good readers never did. The good readers also corrected their own errors more often than did the poor readers. This indicates that the basic problem of the poor reader is lack of comprehension.

DEVELOPING COMPREHENSION SKILLS

Comprehension involves a complex of abilities. The good comprehender possesses the ability to:

1. Associate experiences and meaning with the graphic symbol.
2. React to the sensory images (visual, auditory, kinesthetic, taste, smell) suggested by words.
3. Interpret verbal connotations and denotations.
4. Understand words in context and to select the meaning that fits the context.
5. Give meaning to units of increasing size: the phrase, clause, sentence, paragraph, and whole selection.
6. Detect and understand the main ideas.
7. Recognize significant details.
8. Interpret the organization.
9. Answer questions about a printed passage.
10. Follow directions.
11. Perceive relationships: part-whole; cause-effect; general-specific; place, sequence, size, and time.
12. Interpret figurative expressions.
13. Make inferences and draw conclusions, supply implied details, and evaluate what is read.
14. Identify and evaluate character traits, reactions, and motives.
15. Anticipate outcomes.
16. Recognize and understand the writer's purpose.
17. Recognize literary and semantic devices and identify the tone, mood, and intent or purpose of the writer.

18. Determine whether the text affirms, denies, or fails to express an opinion about a supposed fact or condition.
19. Identify the antecedents of such words as *who, some,* or *they.*
20. Retain ideas.
21. Apply ideas and integrate them with one's past experience.

Of major import for interpretative reading is a *purpose* for reading. The purposeful reader is an interested reader. If the student is to understand what he is reading, he must know why he is reading. He must know whether to read for information, to solve a problem, to follow directions, to be entertained, to obtain details, to draw a conclusion, to verify a statement, to summarize, or to criticize.

As already mentioned, learning to comprehend involves a complex of skills. Let us begin with a few words about the significance of word meaning.

Word Meaning

Studies generally indicate that vocabulary is highly related to comprehension. Vineyard and Massey (1957) found that even when intelligence is held constant there still is a sufficiently high relationship between comprehension and vocabulary proficiency to justify attempts to improve comprehension through vocabulary training. To comprehend, the student must have a knowledge of word meanings and be able to select the correct meaning from the context (Davis, 1944).

Fortunately, it appears that children have a far greater knowledge of the meaning of words than we usually credit to them. First graders generally have a speaking vocabulary of over 2500 words (Smith, 1926) and possibly a recognition vocabulary of over 20,000 words (Robinson, 1961; Shibles, 1959). Certainly, no teacher ever taught a child even most of the words that he knows.

Association of meaning with a symbol cannot occur unless the person has had some experience, whether real or vicarious, with that something represented by the symbol. The word *thermostat,* for example, has no meaning to the student who has never had either a first-hand or a vicarious experience with a thermostat.

Few students have had sufficient experience to appreciate all the connotations of a word. Even if students do have a broader understanding of a word, they are usually content to settle for the first meaning that comes to mind. Poor readers especially tend to do so.

Many students have not learned that words can have more than one meaning. For example, the word *run* can mean to move swiftly; to go back and forth (the boat runs between Georgia and New York); to run in an election; to win a race (the horse ran first); to run into debt; to run (trace) a story back to its source; to run (smuggle) contraband; and to run a store. These are only a few examples. In addition, we speak of a run of fish, a run of bad trouble, a run on the bank, a running brook, the ordinary run of people, and a cattle run.

Multiple meanings and pronunciations are not the only ambiguities of language that hinder communication and that make the apprehension of meaning difficult. Two words may have the same meaning: two words, although pronounced alike, may have different spellings and meanings; and words may have generic or specific meanings. Numerous idiomatic expressions also add to the reader's predicament.

Growth in meaning and vocabulary has many levels. The student must develop precision in meaning; he must become acquainted with multiple meanings; he must learn specific and generic meanings; he must interpret idiomatic expressions; and for successful speech and writing he must be able to call to mind the word needed and then apply it correctly.

The grasping of meaning is obviously important for learning. Educational psychologists have found that students prefer to deal with materials that have meaning. They apply data that bear meaning more easily, and they remember these data for longer periods of time.

Before discussing specific techniques for teaching meanings, let us summarize a few principles that should guide the teacher in the development of meaning. The following seem especially pertinent:

1. Words by themselves are not valid units of meaning. The meanings connoted by a word have been arbitrarily assigned to the symbol.

2. Most words have more than one meaning. Generally, the more frequently a word is used, the more meanings it tends to have.

3. The specific meaning elicited by a word is a function of the context in which the word occurs. It is a function of the environment of the word. This is not only the verbal or semantic context but also the cultural, syntactic, and structural context.

4. The number of meanings actually elicited by a word depends on the number and quality of experiences that the reader has associated with the word. Each new level of meaning requires a corresponding broadening of experience with objective reality.

5. The quality of meaning is greatly influenced by the quantity and quality of previously acquired meanings and concepts. Thus the teacher must build upon the student's previous background of experience.

6. The student has numerous means at his disposal for developing word meanings. He may use the semantic and syntactic context. The word may be explained to him by giving a synonym, by classifying the word, and by pointing out differences and similarities. Or, the meaning of the word may be illustrated through activities, picture clues, structural analysis, and the dictionary.

The teacher's major task in the development of meaning is to select the materials and experiences that will help the student to become more discriminative and learn to generalize. Unfortunately, there is no clear-cut evidence that suggests what materials to use in the teaching of specific concepts. This leaves much to guesswork and taxes the teacher's ingenuity.

The major question then is this: How can the teacher help the student to develop meaning? Generally, the approaches to the teaching of meaning are twofold: (1) the direct experience approach, such as through visiting a farm or acting out an activity, or (2) the vicarious experience approach, such as through looking at pictures, storytelling, or reading explanatory material. The vicarious experience approach in the classroom comes to mean (a) direct vocabulary instructions, (b) incidental instruction of vocabulary, and (c) wide or extensive reading.

The following techniques are frequently used in developing vocabulary skills during the elementary years:

1. Offering direct experience with the concrete object.
2. Labeling.
3. Learning to read pictures.
4. Conversing and storytelling.
5. Participating in description, riddle, rhyme, and puzzle games.
6. Making use of audiovisual aids.
7. Making use of dramatization, marionette and puppet shows, pageants, and operettas.
8. Constructing and using picture dictionaries.
9. Giving both oral and written directions.
10. Fitting objects and words into categories.

Each of these techniques can be applied on upper-grade levels. For example, "learning to read pictures" may be "interpreting charts, graphs, and maps" on the fourth- and fifth-grade level. "Labeling" may consist of labeling instruments in a science laboratory.

Studies (Severson, 1963; Vanderlinde, 1964) tend to indicate that vocabulary study is beneficial but that students of average or above-average ability profit more than those of below-average ability. Students also tend to learn words better if they have an immediate need to use them. A combination of methods in teaching seems to be better than the use of any one method alone. Some common methods include dictionary work, word study in context, use of context clues, attention to multiple meanings and figurative language, study of the history and etymology of words, application of new words in oral and written language, and wide reading (Karlin, 1967).

Let us now look at some of these more advanced meaning skills. Perhaps the first of these is the need for increased competency in the use of the context to arrive at the appropriate meaning.

Study and Analysis of the Context. The pupil's first reading experiences encourage him to use the verbal context in which the word occurs to decipher the meaning of the sentence. Reading teachers have always suggested that the pupil should look at the word, that he should not guess, and that he should see whether the word makes sense in the sentence. The teacher should encourage the pupil to *anticipate* and to *predict* meaning. The student needs to think along with the author. If students learn to anticipate probable meaning, they have also learned a most useful means of word identification (Leary, 1951). Deighton (1959, pp. 2–3) identifies four general principles of context operation: (1) Context reveals the meaning of unfamiliar words only infrequently; (2) context generally reveals only one of the meanings of an unfamiliar word; (3) context seldom clarifies the whole of any meaning; and (4) vocabulary growth through context revelation is a gradual matter. Deighton goes on to note that what the context reveals to a given reader will depend on the reader's previous experiences.

Despite these limitations, the testimonials to the importance of context clues are many. Context is considered one of the most important aids to word identification and to interpretation. Emans (1968) notes that context clues help students to (1) identify words they previously identified but forgot, (2) check the accuracy of words tentatively identified by the use of other clues, (3) gain rapid recognition of words by permitting them to anticipate what a word might be, and (4) identify words that are not identifiable in any other way.

Skill in using the context needs constant refinement, and indeed it becomes increasingly more valuable as the student advances through school. Some students, however, rely too much on the context. Their reading makes sense, but sometimes it is not the meaning intended by the writer. Their counterparts are those readers who are so preoccupied with details that they read a word into the sentence that makes little or no sense.

Steiner, Wiener and Cromer (1971) found that poor readers fail to extract contextual cues essential for identification, and they fail to utilize such cues in identification even when they are presented with them. "They seem to be identifying words as if the words were unrelated items unaffected by syntactical or contextual relationships."

Artley (1943), McCullough (1943), Deighton (1959), Ames (1965), and Emans (1968) have identified various types of contextual aids or context clues useful in interpreting what one is reading:

1. Typographical aids, such as quotation marks, italics, boldface type, parentheses, and footnotes or glossary references.
2. Structural aids, such as appositive phrases or clauses, nonrestrictive phrases or clauses, or interpolated phrases or clauses, indications of comparison and contrast.
3. Verbal context or substitute words, such as linked synonyms or antonyms, summarizing words, definitions, examples, modifiers, restatements, description, direct explanation.
4. Word elements, such as roots, prefixes, and suffixes.
5. Figures of speech, such as simile or metaphor.
6. Pictorial representations or illustrations; that is, accompanying pictures, diagrams, charts, graphs, and maps.
7. Inference, such as where cause-effect relationships lead the reader to a new meaning.
8. Background of experience, where preexisting knowledge sheds direct light upon a new word or expression.
9. Subjective clues, such as tone, mood, setting, and intent.
10. Presentation clues, such as the position of words, the sequence of a sentence

or paragraph, the general organization of a selection, or clues derived from a pattern of paragraph organization involving a main idea and supporting details.

Dulin (1969), in a study using 315 tenth graders, found that the clues that made the acquisition of meaning the easiest were ranked as follows: language experience, cause-effect relationships, contrast, direct description, and linked synonyms and/or appositives. Contrast functioned better with nouns, and direct description functioned better with adjectives. Verb meanings were more easily generated by cause-effect relationships, language experience, and contrast; adverb meanings were more easily generated by language-experience and cause-effect relationships.

In summary, the student gradually needs to expand both the number and the quality of the meanings that he attaches to a single word. Many words, even in the "simplest" of books, have more than one meaning. Frequently, only by understanding the verbal context can the student select the meaning intended by the writer.

At the junior high and high school levels the student's comprehension of what he reads is also aided significantly by the ability to identify the writer's style. Shaw (1958, p. 239) points out that a writer's rhetorical and grammatical contrivances characterize his writing. He notes that much like the ice-cream cone which is both container and confection, the contrivances of the writer both support ideas and are digestible themselves. The writer has so many peculiar characteristics that upon rereading some of his work the reader finds that he has better conception of what the writer is trying to say. The mood of the writer colors the meaning of what is written and frequently can be identified only by reading between the lines.

The reader operates in the context of a special writer, but to get the most out of what he reads he should also become familiar with the rhetorical devices used in a poem, a play, a short story, an essay, a novel, or a bibliography (Shaw, 1958). The title, topical headings, topic sentences, graphs, and summarizing sentences are additional clues to meaning. For example, the title at the head of an article helps the reader anticipate what is to come.

Finally, the *structure* of the phrase, sentence, and paragraph serves as a clue to the fuller meaning of what is written. Rhetorical terms of coherence such as the correlative conjunctions (both–and; not only–but also; either–or) mark pairing of ideas. Subordinating conjunctions signal cause-effect relationships (because, since, so that), conditions (if, unless, although), contrast (whereas, while), and time relationships (as, before, when, after) (Shaw, 1958, p. 243).

Stoodt (1972) found a significant relationship between reading comprehension and comprehension of conjunctions. The most difficult conjunctions were *when, so, but, or, where, while, how, that, if;* the easiest were *and, how, for,* and *as.* Being able to identify the relationships that conjunctions signal has a positive effect on reading comprehension. In such a sentence as "Ed was talkative when Bill remained taciturn" (McCullough,

1958), the sentence structure provides the parallelism and the contrast necessary for understanding the word *taciturn*.

But the reader must also be taught that meaning or context clues are seldom adequate alone because they provide only one aid to word recognition. In some instances context may even lead to confusion or error. In general, the reader should be taught to combine the sense of the sentence with phonic or other word-recognition clues. Deducing an unrecognized word from the context should not be chance guessing; it should be more in the nature of inferential reasoning.

Synonyms and Antonyms. The student reaps much benefit from exercises with the synonyms of words. Initially these exercises are oral. The teacher asks: "What word has the same meaning as *azure?*" An exercise is more effective when the student uses the word in a sentence and then substitutes his own synonym.

Synonyms are actually a part of the context. They are defined as one of two or more words or expressions of the same language that have the same or nearly the same meaning. Thus, a synonym for *azure* may simply be *blue,* more correctly the blue color of a clear sky. A synonym may thus be a simple word, or perhaps a phrase or definition. For example:

1. Mary and Bill are sister and brother. They are *siblings.*
2. A *stalactite,* an iciclelike formation hanging from the roof of a cave, is created when limewater drips from the cave ceiling.
3. The first *cartologist* was making maps long before the discovery of America.
4. A *speleologist* is a scientist who studies and explores caves.

Antonyms are words opposite in meaning to certain other words. The student perhaps best learns meanings for some words by contrasting them with their opposites. The teacher may ask the student to select the antonym for a given word from a list of three or four words: *tart*—sweet, sour, sharp, caustic.

Qualifying Words. The meaning of a sentence is sometimes dependent upon key qualifying words. Such words are *all, always, almost, many, more, less, few, only, none, nearly, likely, probably, in all probability, true, false, some, usually, frequently, never, sometimes, little, much, great,* and *small.* The ability to interpret these words is especially helpful in taking objective tests.

Overworked Words and Phrases. Overworked words and phrases are those that have lost much of their meaning. Some common words in this category are *divine, grand, great, keen, awful, nice, lovely, perfect, swell, terrible, thing, lot, fit,* and *wonderful.*

Such similes and metaphors as *shaking like a leaf, white as snow, eat like a horse, raining cats and dogs, strength of a giant, heart was broken, money to burn, slow as molasses in January,* or *worked like a beaver* are probably overworked.

Homonyms. *Homonyms* are words that sound alike but have different spellings and meanings. They frequently lead to recognition and meaning difficulties. To illustrate their difference, the teacher must use them in various contexts: Thus, the difference between *blue* and *blew* is brought out in the following sentences:

1. The wind blew down the house.
2. Mary wore a blue dress.

Following is a sample of some common homonyms:

doe-dough	night-knight	slay-sleigh	whole-hole
fair-fare	no-know	sole-soul	wood-would
feet-feat	one-won	some-sum	wring-ring
fir-fur	or-ore	sore-soar	write-right
flee-flea	owe-oh	staid-stayed	wrote-rote
flew-flue	pain-pane	stare-stair	you-yew-ewe

For a more complete listing, see: Emerald Dechant, *Improving Reading in the Secondary School,* Prentice-Hall, 1973, p. 214.

Labov (1966) notes that dialect can increase the number of homonyms in the spoken language, leading to confusion in interpretation of the written language and the need to put extraordinary reliance on context. The omission of the /r/ in *guard* makes homonyms of *guard* and *god;* omission of the /l/ in toll makes homonyms of *toll* and *toe.* The poor academic performance of black youth can often be traced to such confusions. On the secondary level especially, the teacher needs to give particular attention to word endings and letter sound omissions.

High Imagery Words. Perhaps we have not paid enough attention to the sense appeal of words. Words make the reader touch, see, hear, taste, and smell. Some sample words are:

Touch (Feeling)	Sight	Sound	Taste	Smell
cold	green	mellow	sweet	fresh
warm	rippled	bang	sour	pungent
hot	spotted	crash	bitter	stuffy
rough	glistening	thud	salty	fragrant
bumpy	ruffle	bellow	smoky	choking
sandy	pale	thumping	ripe	clean
soft	grassy	thrashing-	tender	stifling
sticky	whirling	around	tasty	aroma
wet	weather-	stampeding	well-	burning
limp	beaten	splash	seasoned	

Wolpert (1972) found that high imagery words were learned significantly more easily than low imagery words and imagery value had a substantially greater effect on learning than did word length or shape.

Roots, Prefixes, and Suffixes. Apart from using the context to work out the meaning of unfamiliar words, being able to break a word into its root, prefix, and suffix is another valuable skill in developing meaning for a word.

Word analysis of this type generally results in an assigning of fixed values to each part of a word (prefix, root, suffix), and ends up with a literal meaning for the parts. Unfortunately even the simplest part of a word (*de*) can have multiple meanings. Sometimes the part has lost all its original meaning, with the meaning somehow absorbed by the word, as in *precept*. The *pre* in *precept* has no meaning. Sometimes what looks like a prefix is not a prefix, as in *pre*carious or *pre*datory. The *pre* does not function as a prefix in these words. Clearly, many parts of words do not have fixed, invariant values, but this should not deter the reader from engaging in structural analysis. It simply means that he should be more cautious in equating the literal meaning with the meaning that operates in a given sentence.

In teaching the student the structural skill here indicated, the teacher must follow definite steps. He must show the student that most two- and three-syllable words are composed of a root, prefix, and/or suffix. He next develops meaning for the words *root, prefix,* and *suffix.*

The root is the main part of a word. It is the reservoir of meaning. The prefix is that something that is put before the main part of a word or at the beginning of a word. The word *prefix* is composed of a root and a prefix. It comes from the Latin root *figere,* meaning "to put or fix," and the Latin prefix *prae* meaning "before or at the beginning of."

The teacher should demonstrate to the student that prefixes change the meaning of a word, much as an adjective changes the meaning of a noun. In the sentence "The test was very difficult," the word *difficult* is an adjective, and it changes the meaning of the word *test.* The test could have been described as *easy.* Prefixes work in a similar way. *Circumnavigate* is composed of the prefix *circum* and the root *navigare. Navigare* is a Latin word meaning "to sail." The prefix *circum* means "around," and the entire word, *circumnavigate,* means "to sail around." The prefix *circum* thus changes the meaning of the root by indicating that in this instance *navigate* is not just sailing but is actually a particular type of sailing.

The suffix is another part of many two- or three-syllable words. It comes at the end of the word. It comes from the Latin word *sub* and *figere,* meaning "to add on." The suffix frequently indicates what part of speech the word is. Thus, *ly* in *badly* is a suffix and usually indicates that the word is an adverb. The *ion* in *condition* is a suffix and usually indicates that the word is a noun. This might be termed the grammatical function of the suffix. The suffix also has a meaning function. The suffix *able* means "capable of," as in the word *durable.* Suffixes also serve as an important structural clue and are therefore helpful in the word-recognition program.

Five combinations of root, prefix, and suffix are immediately indicated:

1. Root by itself as in *stand*
2. Prefix + root as in *prefix*
3. Root + suffix as in *badly*
4. Prefix + root + suffix as in *insisting*
5. Root + root as in *cowboy.*

Studies have shown that a few Latin and Greek roots are very helpful in deciphering the meanings of thousands of words. Webster's *New International Dictionary* lists 112 words that begin with the root *anthrop*—man (National Association of Secondary-School Principals, 1950). Numerous other words have this root in the middle of the word: *philanthrophy, misanthrope*. Approximately twenty prefixes account for something like 85 percent of the prefixes used in words. There also are some key suffixes.

Stauffer (1942) reports that 24 percent of the words in the *Thorndike Teacher's Word Book* have prefixes and that fifteen prefixes account for 82 percent of all the prefixes in the 20,000 words. A list of those fifteen prefixes appears below (p. 455):

ab (from)	dis (apart)	pre (before)
ad (to)	en (in)	pro (in front of)
be (by)	ex (out)	re (back)
com (with)	in (into)	sub (under)
de (from)	in (not)	un (not)

Brown and Wright (1957) found that 14,000 words in the desk dictionary and some 100,000 words from the unabridged dictionary contain one or more of the elements found in fourteen master words. The master words contain two Greek roots, twelve Latin roots, and twenty prefixes. The list of fourteen words appears below:

Master-words	Prefix	Common meaning	Root	Common meaning
Precept	pre-	(before)	capere	(take, seize)
Detain	de-	(away, from)	tenere	(hold, have)
Intermittent	inter-	(between)	mittere	(send)
Offer	ob-	(against)	ferre	(bear, carry)
Insist	in-	(into)	stare	(stand)
Monograph	mono-	(alone, one)	graphein	(write)
Epilogue	epi-	(upon)	legein	(say, study of)
Aspect	ad-	(to, towards)	specere	(see)
Uncomplicated	un-	(not)	plicare	(fold)
	com-	(together with)		
Nonextended	non-	(not)	tendere	(stretch)
	ex-	(out of)		
Reproduction	re-	(back, again)	ducere	(lead)
	pro-	(forward)		
Indisposed	in-	(not)	ponere	(put, place)
	dis-	(apart from)		
Oversufficient	over-	(above)	facere	(make, do)
	sub-	(under)		
Mistranscribe	mis-	(wrong)	scribere	(write)
	trans-	(across, beyond)		

For a more complete listing of prefixes, roots, and suffixes see: Emerald Dechant. *Reading Improvement in the Secondary School*, Prentice-Hall, Inc., 1973, pp. 215–38.

Compound Words. The student must also learn that sometimes root and root are combined to form compound words. Some of these keep the basic meaning of each root; others have a completely new meaning.

Figurative and Idiomatic Expression. We have already indicated that numerous idiomatic expressions also add to the reader's predicament. We speak (Durrell, 1956, p. 245) of facing the music, leaving no stone unturned, or breaking the ice with someone. We say that someone's hands are tied or that he is cutting the ground from under someone. We speak of a Jack-of-all-trades, of a devil-may-care attitude, and of someone being penny-wise and pound-foolish. We speak of George Washington as the Father of our country, we are as cozy as a bug in a rug, the wind whistles and the rain patters, and someone jumps up as if he had been shot or runs out the door like a shot. A bill is thrown into the legislative hopper, a candidate sweeps the field, the United States is a melting pot, and someone almost dies laughing (National Association of Secondary School Principals, 1950). Embler (1959) lists numerous idiomatic expressions: to be down-and-out, to be looked down upon, to be at the bottom of the heap, high living, ladder to success, social climber, too keyed up, to settle down, down to earth, going to the root of the matter, big wheel, great guy, soft drink, hot-headed, cold-headed, be in hot water, frozen with fear, square meal, dead pan, kiss of death, to be out of line, open minded, and heavy heart. Other examples might include the following: young at heart, don't cry over spilt milk, cost a pretty penny, burn the candle at both ends, blow off steam, birds of a feather flock together, between you and me and the lamppost, to play with fire, rose between two thorns, bed of roses, beat about the bush, get down to brass tacks, have an ax to grind, cast one's bread on the waters, cook someone's goose, talk through one's hat, sit on the fence, put through the mill, something rotten in Denmark, read between the lines, raining cats and dogs, take with a grain of salt, take the bull by the horns, snake in the grass, and smell a rat.

Vander Meulen (1973) provides among others the following examples: High stakes, ace in the hole, blue chip, par for the course, to wolf one's food, to weasel out of a situation, eating high on the hog, rough row to hoe, railroad a bill, blow off steam, in-fighting, campaign kickoff, landlubber, on a steady keel.

Groesbeck (1961, p. 75), in an analysis of four third-grade readers, *Looking Ahead* and *Climbing Higher* by Houghton Mifflin Company and *Finding New Neighbors* and *Friends Far and Near* by Ginn & Company, found that these contained 424 figurative expressions. Two fourth-grade readers (*High Roads* by Houghton Mifflin Company and *Roads to Everywhere* by Ginn & Company) contained 815 figurative expressions. The fifth-grade readers contained an even greater number.

Obviously, the elementary pupil has a real need to master figurative reading skills. Unfortunately, most children interpret expressions literally. They seem to be unconscious of both the figurative use of language and of their own inaccuracies in interpretation (Groesbeck, 1961).

Figurative language differs from the literal or standard construction; figures of speech are the various types of departures from the literal form (see Table 10-1).

TABLE 10-1 *Figures of Speech*

FIGURES OF RESEMBLANCE	FIGURES OF CONTRAST AND SATIRE	OTHERS
Allegory	Antithesis	
Onomatopaeia	Epigram	Hyperbole
Personification	Irony	Euphemism
Metaphor	Apostrophe	Synecdoche
Simile		
Metonomy		

An *allegory* is the prolonged metaphor, e.g., *Pilgrim's Progress.*

Onomatopoeia is the use of words whose sounds suggest the meaning.

A *metaphor* is simply an analogy or an expression of comparison: unlike the simile, the metaphor does not use *as* or *like* (You're a clumsy ox).

Personification is the endowment of an inanimate object or abstract idea with personal attributes.

A *simile* compares two objects or actions and usually joins them with *as* or *like*, for example: My car goes like the wind.

Antithesis is the contrasting of ideas.

An *epigram* is a short, terse, satirical, or witty statement.

Metonomy is the use of one word for the other, the first word being suggestive of the other, for example: The woman keeps a good table.

A *hyperbole* is an exaggeration; *euphemism* is the substitution of an inoffensive expression for one that is unpleasant; *apostrophe* is the addressing of the living as dead or the absent as present; and *synecdoche* is the use of the part for the whole.

Developing Skill in Using Punctuation Marks as Clues to Meaning. Punctuation is frequently looked upon merely as a discipline in writing rather than as a help in reading (Cook, 1959). Yet, the writer punctuates not for himself but for his reader. Punctuation is not only a set of rules to be learned but also a way to facilitate the grasp of meaning.

Punctuation (Furness, 1960) replaces the intonation pattern in speech—the pauses, pitch, and stress. Intonation in speech is used to convey surprise, anger, or satire; it also indicates whether the utterance makes a statement, gives a command, or asks a question. In written language the comma and the semicolon indicate a pause. The comma is also used to set off a nonrestrictive clause, to note a series, and to set off an appositive. The period is used to end a statement; the question mark, to end a question; and the exclamation point, to end a command. The question mark indicates that in speech there would be a sharp rise in voice and then a drop back to the normal level. The colon indicates that something additional is about to follow:

Here is an example of how punctuation can affect meaning:

1. The school, kitchen, cafeteria, and auditorium are off bounds during regular school hours.

2. The school kitchen, cafeteria, and auditorium are off bounds during regular school hours.

The comma after the word *school* in sentence 1 falsifies the intended meaning.

Study of the Dictionary, Text Glossaries, and Word Lists. Glossaries become important as soon as students engage in any type of content-area reading. The teacher discusses the new words that will be met in the day's lesson. He identifies the word through its visual form, pronunciation, accent, and meaning. The discussion is completed when the word is met in its contextual setting. In this way teacher and student develop their own glossary.

Although the student has learned to use the context and other clues to decipher the meaning of words, he must sometimes go to the dictionary. In the junior high and high school, the dictionary becomes a very useful tool. To be able to use it correctly, the student should do the following:

1. Develop alphabetization skills.
2. Understand the use of guide words and be able to locate entry words quickly.
3. Understand dictionary symbols—the breve, macron, circumflex, tilde, etc., and understand each item included in an entry. To do this the student needs to be able to deal with such abbreviations as *cap* (capitalized), *cf* (compare, see), *esp* (especially), *exc* (except), *fr* (from), *i.e* (that is), *illus* (illustration), *mod* (modern), *opp* (opposite), *orig* (originally).
4. Use the dictionary to work out the pronunciation of words to help him in his spelling, and to identify accents, derivations, and parts of speech.
5. Use the dictionary to learn the various meanings of words and to select the definition that applies to a word as it is used in a sentence.

Study of Word Origins and Change. Numerous other vocabulary exercises help to enlarge the vocabulary and broaden meanings. The most common are: a study of word origins; study of the new terms recently added to the language; exploration of the encyclopedia; and the study of word lists..

A recent article by Warren (1960) has outlined a program for leading the pupil beyond the simple fact that words mean something. It is a program designed to familiarize the pupil with the nature, origin, and growth of words.

Warren recommends that we *begin with the origin of surnames.* For example, names like Baker, Butler, Binder, Bishop, Cook, Guard, Hunter, King, Miner, Miller, Rider, Smith, Taylor, Teller, and Weaver identify occupations.

Other surnames represent objects: for example, Ball, Bell; some surnames identify certain characteristics of an object or person: thus, Belle, Breit, Fair, Good; some identify colors: Black, Braun, Brown, Gray, Green, Roth, Schwartz (Schwartzkopf), and White; and finally, some are animal names: thus, Beaver, Bee, Bird, and Crow.

The teacher also may find it useful to familiarize the student with the history and origins of the names of streets, parks, rivers, countries, and states. Each of them has a history.

The *second step* in studying word origins may be an analysis of the foreign origin of many words. The Dutch, the French, the Germans, and the Italians have given us many words. Let us list just a few: Italian (soprano, piccolo, piano, contralto); French (carburetor, chauffeur, coupe, beau, chateau, trousseau, chamois, machine, boudoir, bouquet, barrage, croquet, sachet, ballet); and German (kindergarten, waltz, sauerkraut, wiener). Words of Latin and Greek origin are so numerous that a list is not necessary.

A *third phase* of the study of origins is an analysis of how words disappear, change, or appear. Language is man's tool and he has always used it for his convenience. He has discarded certain words, added others, and frequently has associated new meanings with old words.

The last twenty-five years have witnessed a lot of language activity. Numerous new words have been coined (Horn, 1958; Warren, 1960). Here are just a few:

ack-ack	amtrac	audiophile	babushka
bamboo curtain	bazooka	discophile	intercom
junkie	calypso	megaton	me-too-ism
Molotov cocktail	deltiology	oscar	pedal pushers
rev	genocide	prefab	rabbit ears
snow (television)	spelunker	satellite	schmoe

Warren (1960) notes that the pupil needs to look upon good English as up-to-date English. The dictionary thus is not the ultimate authority. It lists acceptable and unacceptable words (illit., arch., and obs.) People decide what is correct.

Study of Technical Vocabularies. The student should become familiar with the technical vocabularies of the content areas. Only by knowing them can he read with meaning in those areas.

Phrase Meaning

Phrase reading is not synonymous with word meaning. A phrase is more than the sum of the individual words that it contains. The meaning of phrases like *to spin a yarn, to throw away one's money,* or *to pitch a tent* cannot be deciphered from individual words. In the preceding section we gave numerous examples of similar idiomatic and figurative phraseology.

In developing the student's phrase-reading skill, an exercise like the following is useful:

Phrase	*Synonym*
1. big wheel	
2. great guy	
3. open-minded	
4. pig-headed	
5. cold-hearted	

Phrase reading becomes especially difficult when one has to deal with idiomatic expressions and with proverbs. Examine the following proverbs:

1. Many hands *make light work.*
2. A rolling stone *gathers no moss.*
3. Smooth seas *make poor sailors.*
4. If you would enjoy the fire, you must *put up with the smoke.*

Sentence Meaning

Effective reading implies an understanding and an interpretation of language patterns. The full meaning of a sentence depends on the punctuation, the word order, and the grammatical inflections signaling tense, number, and possession and on such key words as *because* or *nevertheless.* Until the reader correctly translates the printed text into the intonation pattern of the writer, he may not be getting the meaning intended.

The following exercises help the student to decode simple sentences and to formalize the teaching of language patterns:[1]

1. Below are some word-for-word translations of French sentences. Beneath each translation rewrite the English sentences in the correct patterns.
   a. *Je lui ai donné le chien noir.* (I her gave the dog black)
   b. *Elle lui a parlé de la porte cassée.* (She to him spoke about the door broken)
2. Put the following groups of words into English sentence patterns.
   c. the out cat fat red went
   d. of gone some the were cookies

Before using such exercises the student must first become familiar with the basic sentence patterns. Figure 10-1 illustrates the four different types: subject–verb, subject–predicate–object, subject–linking verb–adjective, and subject–linking verb–noun.[2]

Reading materials usually do not come in single word or phrase units. The meaning of a sentence is not obtained by piling up, as it were, the meanings of individual words. The student must learn to master the skills of relating the various words that form a logical sequence in a sentence. Unfortunately, the dynamics of converting single word meanings into the total thought of a sentence or paragraph has not been sufficiently investigated.

Sentences are parts of paragraphs and not only receive their full meaning from the context in which they occur but give meaning to the sentences that surround them. Thus, some sentences are introductory or lead-in sentences; some are transitional sentences; and some are concluding sentences.

---

[1]*Listen and Read,* M. N. Educational Development Laboratories, p. 26.

[2]Ibid., p. 27.

Pattern 1.

	Subject—Verb	Examples—Pattern 1	
	which can also be expressed	N	V
	Noun—Verb	Birds	fly

Pattern 2.

	Subject—Predicate—Object	Examples—Pattern 2		
	or	S	V	O
Noun (one)—Transitive Verb—Noun (two)		Mary	hit	Jack

Pattern 3.

	Subject—Linking Verb—Adjective	Examples—Pattern 3		
	or	S	LV	A
	Noun—Linking Verb—Describer	Games	are	interesting

Pattern 4.

	Subject—Linking Verb—Noun	Examples—Pattern 4		
		S	LV	N
		Jane	is	(my) sister

FIGURE 10–1 *Basic Sentence Patterns*

Paragraph Meaning

Paragraphs are basically a series of sentences that give one basic idea. All the sentences are written in such a way that they relate to one another. Exercises may require students to:

1. Locate the topic sentence of a paragraph.
2. Write a topic sentence for the paragraph.
3. Write a title for the paragraph.
4. Outline paragraphs.

Reading for the Main Idea

The ability to identify the main idea is necessary for interpretation and understanding of what is written. It is based on an accurate comprehension of the word, the phrase, and the sentence. All the other interpretative reading skills are secondary. Students who do not get the main idea cannot identify the theme of a paragraph, do not understand the implied meanings, and usually cannot organize or summarize what they have read.

To help the student find the main idea, the student may be required to:

1. Read a selection and select the best title, from several listed for the selection.
2. Read a selection and give it a title, in the pupil's own words.

3. Read the summary of a chapter and tell what the chapter covered.
4. Have students select a headline that best describes the narration of an incident in a newspaper.

Other means are the following: Look for comparisons that the author is making, study his use of vocabulary, look for analogies, study the figurative language, read between the lines, and study the topic sentence.

Robinson (1961) suggests that the student be taught to identify the main idea of a sentence by being required to underline key words. He then moves to identifying the key sentence in a paragraph. This is the topic sentence. Some paragraphs, however, do not have a single sentence that summarizes the main idea. Thus the third step consists of teaching the student to make an inference from a series of sentences as to what the basic idea is. Eventually the student needs to learn that a main idea may be spread over two or three paragraphs.

Reading for Details

After the student has had some success in reading for and stating the main idea, he is ready to read for details. Reading for details becomes especially important in science, geography, arithmetic, home economics, and history.

Learning to follow directions through reading is essentially reading for details. In directions every little step is significant. The student must give full attention and must look for a definite sequence of data (Dawson and Bamman, 1959, p. 182). This process is particularly important in doing arithmetic and in carrying out experiments.

The *Specific Skill Series* by Barnell Loft, Ltd., provides numerous exercises in reading for details. It contains books entitled *Following Directions, Locating the Answer, Getting the Facts*. The upper level of these books is sixth grade, but they may well be used on the junior high level.

The following activities promote reading for detail:

1. Have students read a paragraph into which have been inserted some irrelevant sentences and let them identify these sentences.
2. After the students have read a paragraph, let them choose from a prepared group of sentences those that agree or disagree with the paragraph.
3. Analyze a written paragraph into its main and supporting ideas by making a formal outline of it.

Reading for Organization

The good reader also comprehends the organization of what is being read. He thinks with the reading material, outlining it as he goes along. He sees the relationship between the main and the subordinate ideas and arranges these in some logical order. He uses materials from many sources and is able to draw conclusions.

Bruner (1966) notes the importance of structure for learning. It makes it easier to understand by simplifying information, by generating new propositions, and by increasing the manipulability of a body of knowledge. Without structure, knowledge is more readily forgotten. Bruner (1962) notes that the key to retrieval (or recall of the information) is organization. Organization of information reduces the aggregate complexity of material by embedding it into a person's cognitive structure.

Oakan, Wiener, and Cromer (1971) found that comprehension results from an ability to identify or decode words plus the ability to organize these words into meaningful units such as phrases, clauses, etc. The poor reader has a deficit in his patterns of linguistic organization. Good identification is not a sufficient condition for good comprehension. This study supports the work of Lefevre. The poor reader is a poor reader because he cannot put organization into what he reads.

This study also confirmed that good readers have a higher level of comprehension for the good-visual input material than for the good-auditory-input material.

Elkind and Weiss (1967), in studying the responses of children five to eight when presented with structured and unstructured arrangements, found that all children explored the structured arrays systematically and this tendency increased with age.

Reading in the content areas especially depends upon proficiency in organization skill. Textbooks have a characteristic paragraph organization. The topic sentence sets the theme of the paragraph. A sequence of details follows. The paragraph is concluded by a summarizing sentence.

Numerous activities help the student to learn how to organize what he is reading. For example:

1. Have the student group a series of details about a main idea.
2. Have the student develop an outline for a story, with headings and subheadings.
3. Have the student arrange records, directions, or ideas in a sequential order.
4. Have the student assemble various bits of information and group them into an informative story.

Niles (1965) suggests the following patterns of organization: enumerative sequence, time sequence, cause-effect, and comparison-contrast. Other authors speak of organization by size and distance, according to sequence of events, from general to specific ideas, or from specific to general. Birkley (1970) speaks of the thesis-proof pattern (begins with a thesis and is followed by a series of proofs), the opinion-reason pattern (this is most common in editorials), the problem-solution pattern, the information pattern, and the narrative pattern. Niles adds that efficient study is a matter of perceiving these organizational patterns as one reads and responds to what one has read.

The student should be taught to watch for time sequences in paragraphs (indicated by such words as *next, while, when, later*), to look for organization according to position or degree, to look for categorization (hoofed mammals, winged mammals, toothless mammals, sea mammals), and to look for comparisons, contrasts, and cause-and-effect organizations.

Paragraphs may thus be described as narration and description paragraphs, comparison and contrast paragraphs, cause and effect paragraphs, definition paragraphs, example paragraphs, reasons paragraphs, and classification paragraphs.

The organizing of what is read is also an important part of effective learning or integrative reading. There are various approaches to this task. Summarizing, outlining, note making, and combinations of these have been recommended. The specific approach used is not so important as that the student perceive the interrelationship of the various elements.

Summarizing. Summaries help to preserve the essential facts and the main ideas in capsule form. They are especially necessary when the student is not using his own book.

Summaries are particularly useful when reading literature, essays, or social science materials; they are not so useful in chemistry, physics, or biology. A summary or synopsis is all that may be necessary in reading the former. As for the latter, a summary is usually longer than the original.

Outlining. Outlining is just another way of organizing information. It is closely related to summarizing. When the reader owns the book, he sometimes outlines by underlining and by using letters and numbers to designate main and subordinate points.

The outline, like any other summarization, has certain limitations. It does not contain the original material. It cannot contain everything that was said or written. But, in the beginning at least, it may be better for the student to write too much rather than not enough. An outline that is too skimpy is not very useful. It must contain enough material so that the student will see the relationships between the facts, ideas, or statements made. The perceiving of relationships is true organization.

Teaching the student to outline may be done in many ways:

1. Have students organize a series of objects into specific categories.
2. Have students select the two or three main ideas in a series of paragraphs.
3. Have them group details about each of several main ideas.
4. Teach outline form.
5. Have students check their outlines against teacher-prepared outlines of the same material.

Underlining. Another form of organizing information is underlining. Many students use underlining of key words and phrases in a book to organize what they have read. Unfortunately, the technique used is frequently not good. The student reads and underlines words and phrases in a hit-and-miss fashion. He finds out too late that his underlining was not planned. In short, it does not show the organization of what was read. When the student returns to the underlining later, he finds that he can no longer decipher the reasons for underlining. Underlining thus may become a poor substitute for the thinking and organizing that accompanies good reading.

Proper underlining requires the student:

1. To survey the chapter.
2. To read the chapter.
3. To mentally familiarize himself with the organization of the chapter.
4. To underline main ideas and supporting details after having read each paragraph.
5. To underline only those words and phrases that actually indicate the organization of the paragraph.

Some writers disparage underlining; however, one might ask: Why spend time taking notes on something that one can have in its entirety? Underlining prevents the learner from taking too few notes. It also permits him, during review, to again read the entire paragraph if, in the meantime, he has lost the trend of thought.

Note Making. Effective note making is a high-level study or integrative reading skill.[3] It requires attention, concentration, skillful reading and listening, and the putting into practice of one's organizing abilities.

The making of good notes whether in reading or in listening requires the student to learn to write notes and to pay attention at the same time. The making of notes is certainly more than a secretarial job. Digestion and learning should be taking place. However, all notes do not need to be in the student's own words. Usually there is nothing wrong with the teacher's words, if the student understands them. Comprehension is the prime consideration. The student should learn to listen and read for meaning rather than for mere words.

The student needs to be taught to focus on the main idea and on those points that support the main idea. The student's notes should be a clue to the organization of the original material.

There are three basic forms of note making:

1. *The Paragraph*—This is probably most easily developed, but it frequently is not the best organized. Each paragraph represents a new idea.
2. *The Sentence*—This is better than the paragraph form in that it attempts to organize the material by stating a series of sentences. It thus may also be easier to use in review.
3. *The Outline*—This provides the best opportunity for organization.

Kollaritsch (1969) suggests an outline method of note-making that involves relatively little writing. Instead of detailed description, the method consists of (1) stating the section heading of a chapter, noting the page on which it is found; (2) noting what each paragraph in the chapter is

[3] See Robert A. Palmatier, "Comparison of Four Note-Taking Procedures." *Journal of Reading* 14 (1971): 235–40; and Don Butcofsky. "Any Learning Skills Taught in High School?" *Journal of Reading* 15 (1971): 195–98.

about, and what kinds of things the student needs to remember from the paragraph without writing out the details (e.g., definition of *parapsychology*); (3) reviewing immediately after reading and indicating by a check if he can recall what each written heading elicits without referring to the text. The same procedure is used for review.

READING FOR EVALUATION (CRITICAL READING)

Critical reading involves literal comprehension, but it also demands that the reader evaluate—pass personal judgment on the quality, value, accuracy, and truthfulness of what is read (Smith, 1965). It involves the evaluation of the validity, accuracy and intellectual worthwhileness of printed materials (Eller, 1966). It means that the reader must be able to recognize the author's intent and point of view, to distinguish fact from opinion, and to make judgments and inferences (Olson, 1966).

Larter and Taylor (1969), in a study of 197 students in grades ten to twelve in Winnipeg, found that IQ and academic achievement were the best predictors of an individual's ability to think critically. The critical thinkers were aggressive, daring, incisive; they were interested in power, influence, and renown; their fathers were well educated and had a prestigious position; they were alert and poised.

The student must constantly read to evaluate. The good comprehender is a critical reader. He checks the truth, logic, reliability, and accuracy of what is written. He looks for contradictory material. He relates the material to his experience. He distinguishes fact from fiction, is concerned with the timeliness of the material, and tries to understand the author's motives.

The critical reader is as much interested in why something is said as in what is said. He is sensitive to how words are used and is slightly suspicious of the author's biases. He pays particular attention to words with several meanings. He checks the copyright data, the author's reputation, and the publisher's past performance. He looks for errors of reasoning, of analogy, of overgeneralization, of oversimplification, and of distortion. He looks for one-sided presentations, prejudices, biases, faulty inferences, and propaganda. He avoids jumping to quick conclusions.

The critical reader examines the arguments and the language. He needs to be able to follow inductive and deductive argument, to spot generalizations, to be sensitive to analogies and such simple devices as guilt through association. He needs to know the functions of language: to inform (the informative), to vent or excite feelings (the expressive), to move people to do things (the incitive). The teacher can and must lessen the difficulties of critical reading, among which are the following (Olson, 1966): the use of a single textbook, the halo effect that is attached to the printed word, the desire on the part of school people to avoid controversial subjects, the emphasis on conformity, and the natural involvement of personal prejudices and emotions.

Huelsmann (1951) mentions three ways of teaching critical reading:

the direct approach, the incidental approach, and the functional approach.[4] Kottmeyer (1944) experimented with a direct approach. Newspapers, magazines, editorials, and cartoons were read critically. Students were given definitions of propaganda techniques and sought to discover their presence in the materials read. The functional approach is one in which class materials are taught with the definite purpose of promoting critical skills. The least effective is an incidental approach. It refers to the training in critical reading that may come as a mere by-product of social studies learning.

Russell (1965) recommends group discussions as a way of getting at assumptions or preconceptions. Artley (1965) suggests that the essential process is one of raising questions or of setting up situations based on reading that require an evaluative response and then, by a process of guidance, helping the student to think his way through to an answer. A simple technique is to stop the student before he comes to the writer's conclusion and to let him state all the possible solutions.

Harvison (1967) points out that teachers will have to depend upon their own creativity and initiative in teaching critical reading. Activities are as many and as varied as the teacher's imagination permits. In the intermediate grades and in the junior-senior high school years the student may be encouraged to read many texts to find answers, with the emphasis being on problem solving, inductive thinking, and frequent verbal expression among students.

The critical reader reads all materials in a questioning way. He constantly asks: Why? He is constantly concerned lest the writer's prejudices, biases, or assumptions may be coloring his presentation and consequently lead to an acceptance of a wrong point of view.

The critical reader reads beyond the materials. He is not satisfied with the simple statements. He uses his previous experiences and previous learning to understand fully what he is reading.

The critical reader thinks with the writer. He formulates the question clearly, checks the authenticity of the materials, evaluates the author's credentials, looks for errors in reasoning, and develops a sensitivity to the rightness or wrongness of what is presented.

The critical reader suspends judgment until the writer has finished his argument. As he proceeds with the material he asks himself: Is the author consistent? Is he logical? Are his motives noble? Are his facts true? Are his conclusions correct?

Critical reading is slow, sentence by sentence, and thought by thought reading. It requires the reader to analyze carefully the writer's words, his purpose, and his implications.

Let us look at these:

Words. Many words can be used by writers to arouse unfavorable feelings toward a person or an idea. For example, the words *fascist,*

---

[4] For a discussion of techniques for teaching critical reading see: Catherine S. Boyan, "Critical Reading: What is it? Where is it?" *The Reading Teacher,* 25 (March, 1972) 517–522.

communist, or *socialist* usually arouse antagonism and distrust. In so circles, to be labelled *black, Jew,* or *Catholic* may leave similar impressions. The words *conservative, capitalist, warmonger, isolationist, progressive educator, selfish, conformist, world-minded, idealist, overzealous,* and *liberal* similarly mean many things to many people.

Purpose. What is the writer's purpose? Does he wish to inform or to entertain, to teach or to move emotionally? Is his motive open or hidden? The reader should constantly ask: Who would benefit if I agreed with the speaker or writer? What kind of evidence does he bring forth?

Implications. It is obvious that the reader must prepare himself so that he can detect generalities, fallacious reasoning, and unwarranted clichés. As citizens, as buyers of somebody's products, or as students in a classroom, individuals are constantly subject to writings that attempt to make them think in a given way. They are asked to give allegiance to one thing and to turn against something else.

Some common techniques used by speakers and writers to sway public opinion are the following:

1. False or glittering generalization.
2. Bias or prejudice.
3. Unwarranted inference or cliché.
4. Confusion of fact and opinion.
5. Distortion of truth.
6. Begging the question.
7. False analogy.
8. Error in inductive or deductive reasoning.
9. Ignoring alternatives.
10. Oversimplification.
11. Changing the meaning of terms.
12. Misleading headline.
13. Failure to cite sources for one's information.
14. Using prominent names to bolster one's point of view (testimonial).
15. Assuming all relationships are casual.
16. Use of bandwagon appeals.
17. Use of questionable sampling.
18. Appeal to emotion rather than to intellect.
19. Relating only one side.
20. *Argumentum ad hominem*—Getting the reader to accept a conclusion by ridiculing the opposition, by snubbing it, or by ridiculing the person who holds the argument rather than by attacking the argument. Name-calling is such a technique.
21. Use of straw men, straw issues, outright lies, digs, and snide remarks.
22. Transfer techniques (I'm Jimmy Jackson, I drink Mayberry).

READING FOR LEARNING

Complete reading is said to involve four steps: recognition, understanding, reaction, and integration. Ideally, the reading a student does will influence and direct some future activity. In a very real sense, then, whenever the student integrates what he is reading, he is studying. This may be the ultimate in comprehension. Gray (1957) points out that integration is "the heart of the learning act in reading." The reading act is complete only when that which is read becomes assimilated.

Integrative reading is commonly identified with study-type reading. Herber (1969) defines study skills as work skills that produce useful knowledge for a learner; they are reading skills especially adapted to execute particular tasks. They help us to develop ideas, to remember ideas, and to use ideas. Russell (1961) defines study skills as including skill in locating, selecting, using, and evaluating information, ability to adjust method and rate of reading to the purpose for reading and to the nature of the material and skill in retaining what is read.

Study habit inventories typically measure four study variables: morale or self-confidence, scholarly drive (motivation) and values, study mechanics, and planning for study. To teach study skills effectively, we must know which study skills are needed. Many specific plans and concrete suggestions for improving study skills have been devised by those directing special classes in this area. Let us examine some of these and hope to find applications to all grade levels. There seems to be general agreement that the following skills are basic to effective study:

1. Ability to identify and state the specific purposes for the reading.
2. Ability to locate information.
3. Ability to select the correct and needed information.
4. Ability to comprehend what is read.
5. Ability to organize the information.
6. Ability to utilize the information.
7. Ability to remember the information.
8. Ability to adjust the method and rate of reading to the purposes and the nature of the materials.

Berg and Rentel (1966) note the general lack of agreement as to what study techniques to teach and state that at least some evidence shows that both failing and successful students use about the same study skills, but they nevertheless conclude on the basis of their evaluation of studies in this area that instruction in study skills does produce significantly higher study skill levels than were obtained through trial-and-error methods.

Let us look at a method of integrative reading, such as that proposed by Robinson (1961, pp. 13–14). It involves five steps: survey, question, read, recite, and review (SQ3R). The SQ3R method is especially designed for history, social science, science, and prose materials.

How good is the SQ3R method? Donald (1967) found that the use of the SQ3R method on the junior high level resulted in a significant difference in factual type of knowledge of content material. The method seemed to develop better powers of organization, association, and critical thinking.

Various modifications of the SQ3R method are available today. Pauk (1963) developed a reading technique for prose, poetry, and drama called the EVOKER system—explore, vocabulary, oral reading, key ideas, evaluations, and recapitulation. Later Pauk (1969) developed the OK4R method—overview, key ideas, read, recall, reflect, and review. Johnson (1964) developed the Three-Level Outlining Method. It requires the student to outline and to locate information.

Survey

Surveying is the first step in the SQ3R method and is the process of becoming familiar with the broad outlines, the chapter title, the main headings, the topic sentences, and the summary.

The good student gets an overall picture of what he is reading or studying. The reason is obvious. The driver consults a road map before venturing on a trip. The race driver drives the course many times before the actual race. The diner surveys a menu. In rapid fashion he notices the dinners, sandwiches, appetizers, and drinks, and the prices do not escape him. The baseball player checks the infield for chuckholes, and the general surveys the terrain before initiating his attack. Each of these persons wants to know what lies ahead so he may proceed with the proper technique. The student must know what type of article he is reading before he can choose his techniques well.

In surveying a book, the title tells in general what the book is about; the preface gives a more detailed statement. In it the writer tells why he wrote the book and what he seeks to accomplish.

The table of contents gives a more detailed outline of the book. It gives clues to the writer's organization.

The chapter titles, headings, and summaries should come next. The headings are especially important. They are the clues to the chapter organization. In general, the chapter title tells the main idea. The major headings give the broad outlines of the chapter and show how the writer supports the main idea. Under each major heading may be one or more side headings.

The topic sentence in each paragraph is especially important. It summarizes the paragraph. It contains the main idea of the paragraph and usually is the first sentence in a paragraph. Sometimes, however, it occurs at the end of the paragraph or in the middle of the paragraph, or it may even not be stated.

Surveying thus allows the reader to "warm up" to the reading task ahead. It gives an overall view of the material. It is a preview. Elementary teachers have always prepared the pupil for the reading task. They have made certain that the child had the necessary experience for understanding and that he had a purpose for reading. This is what surveying accomplishes for the more mature student.

Smith and Hesse (1969), in a study of 340 eleventh-grade students in Madison, Wisconsin, found that listening to a cognitive organizer or preview had a positive effect on the attitudes of poor readers and on their ability to identify the main idea. It did not have the same effect on good readers. It seemed that the good readers had reasonably well-developed styles of organizing themselves cognitively to comprehend what they read, and in fact, an organization different from the one that they might naturally develop might even hinder comprehension.

Skimming is frequently used in previewing. Skimming gives a quick glimpse at the organization. It is a sort of threshing process in which the wheat is separated from the chaff. The reader is after certain information or perhaps wishes to decide whether or not to read the selection more intensively.

Question

The second step in integrative reading is the question. Sometimes the writer poses questions at the beginning or at the end of the chapter. The teacher may suggest questions as a part of the assignment. The student should become able to make his own questions. In doing this, he may turn the main headings or italicized words into questions. The teacher has many questions at his disposal. His questions may call for memorization, evaluation, recall, recognition, comparison, summarization, discussion, analysis, decision making, outlining, illustration, refutation, and inductive or deductive thinking (Gray and Reese, 1957, p. 253).

Melnik (1965) notes that questions establish a basis for identifying and clarifying the purpose for reading. Taba and others suggest that the teacher's questions circumscribe the mental operations that students can perform and determine what points they can explore and what modes of thought they can learn (Taba et al., 1964). Frederick (1968), however, found that the introduction of vocabulary terms and questions prior to reading did not result in better learning or retention on the part of students. Rothkopf (1970) suggests that the set of questions that students *expect* largely determines what they learn. He feels it is the inspection activities that determine learning rather than immediate feedback of knowledge of results and that questions asked after the reading are more important for understanding and retention than those asked before.

Nevertheless, it would appear that questions provide a certain "readiness" for reading and guide the student's reading by creating a set to respond in a particular manner. They are motivational stimuli, permitting the selection of relevant information and the rejection of incidental information.

Melnik lists two main functions of questions. As a diagnostic tool, the unstructured question permits the teacher to observe the variety of individual responses: how the student approaches the reading passage; his tendency to relate ideas or perhaps to focus on isolated details; his ability to organize; his tendency to let emotions and prejudices influence his comprehension. As an instructional tool, the question helps the student to identify the author's pattern of thought or to clarify meaning. Questions are most effective in enhancing delayed and immediate recall for the largest number of meaning values. The question technique tends to surpass both careful reading without questions and rereading of the same material (Berg and Rentel, 1966).

Formulating questions encourages the reader to seek answers as he reads. Many writers believe that students should write down these questions as a basis for review. Additional questions may be added during the actual reading.

Here are a few suggestions about asking questions:

1. The student should ask questions both before and after he reads. He must turn the chapter title, headings, unfamiliar terms, etc., into questions.
2. He should ask questions during reading.
3. He should try to answer his questions before actually beginning reading.

Read

The third step of an effective study procedure is *purposeful reading.* Let us examine some of the objectives of purposeful reading. The reader should do the following:

1. Have a definite reason for his reading.
2. Define clearly the problem that he wishes to solve.
3. Focus his attention on the main points.
4. Try to group the supporting details with the main idea.
5. Keep in mind the nature of the assignment.
6. Pay special attention to illustrations of all kinds, graphs, maps, charts.
7. Be a flexible reader, adjusting his rate to the purpose of the reading and the nature of the material.
8. Try to remember that he is seeking to answer questions.

Study-type reading frequently is intensive reading. It is careful, rather slow reading with emphasis upon remembering details. (Spache and Berg, 1955, p. 29). Intensive reading requires that upon reaching the end of the chapter the reader recognize the main idea. He should know where the author was heading and how he got there. He tends to form an outline of what he has read. He sees the major and supporting points.

Nevertheless, not all reading in a textbook needs to be, nor even should be, intensive reading. Gates (1956) calls for greater stress on a flexible approach to reading. Reading should vary in speed—from very slow, to moderate, to very fast—from detailed study to skimming and scanning. The student should become able to shift from reading to recall and vice versa. If he has learned to adapt his reading to the nature of the specific problem being met, his purposes and the nature of the paragraph or chapter will determine the type of reading that he will use. Even in comprehension there must be flexibility. Certain parts of a textbook chapter, perhaps most of it, must be read intensively, but frequently much can profitably be skimmed. The flexible reader reads rapidly or even skips those parts that are trivial, familiar, or unrelated to his goals and purposes.

Recite

The fourth step of Robinson's SQ3R study method, *recite,* is literally a self-examination. Here the student attempts to answer the questions that he has posed without referring to his notes or other aids. Only when he fails should he consult his notes or refer to the book. One study method has been labelled a "self-recitation method" because of the great importance of recitation in learning. Recitation directs our attention to specific questions, thereby aiding concentration. Concentration is a by-product of having a goal that challenges the person's whole mind (Perry and Whitlock, 1952).

Generally it is recommended that the recitation should occur as soon as possible after the reading. Weigand and Blake (1955, p. 39) emphasize two other aspects of effective recitation and study: (a) whenever possible substitute understanding for rote memorization and *recite in your own words,* and (b) if you *must* memorize (formulas, poetry, etc.) overlearn at once, that is, repeat the piece of material several times after you have proved to yourself that you know it.

Self-recitation makes a number of contributions to effective learning. The student is immediately aware of how well he read, how accurately he accomplished his purposes, and whether he can express his newfound knowledge in his own words. If he can verbalize his knowledge to his own satisfaction, he can generally explain or recite to another. Recitation is the heart of effective study; it is the seeking of answers to self-imposed questions and putting new learnings into one's own words.

Self-recitation also can be justified by what we know about transfer of training. Transfer has special significance when tasks are similar. Self-recitation tends to be similar to the use of the learnings the child later makes in examinations, in other learning tasks, and meeting life situations. Studies show that the closer the learning situation is to the test situation or the life situation, the greater are the chances that the training will be used.

Review

The fifth and final step of Robinson's method is *review.* Study is not complete until it includes a plan for retention. If learning is to be of any use in later situations, the student must remember what he has learned. Actually, remembering itself is defined in various ways. We say that one remembers data if he can recall them, relearn them more quickly, recognize them, use them in test situations, or use them to learn something else more easily. Perhaps the most important criterion of retention is the transfer that is made from the school situation to the life situation, to future acquisition of knowledge, and to future behavior.

Review becomes a relatively simple process if the reading has been done correctly. If the student developed an outline, wrote out questions for himself, developed the textbook into an outline, or made a summary, he might use any one of these as the basis for a good review.

Review, whether through notes or through rereading, should be an exercise in critical reading and thinking. Basically there are two methods of review: symbolical review and review by reimpression. Reimpression is the type of review that occurs when the person rereads. Symbolical review is done through recall, self-recitation, class discussion, tests, summaries, and lecture notes. This type of review encourages thinking, assimilation, integration, and organization. It is review with a purpose and with an eye on application. It is a critical reexamination with a goal of integrating the content and acquiring useful generalizations. Unless we do something to slow it, forgetting proceeds at a rapid pace immediately after learning. Thus review should come as soon as possible. And, generally, we need more than one review. The first reviews should follow each other rather closely with the interval of time between reviews gradually increasing. Lyon (1914, p. 161) suggested that when associations have once been formed they should be recalled before the original associations have lost their "color" and cannot be recalled in the same "shape," time, and order. The student is advised to review his "lecture notes" shortly after taking them, and if possible, again the evening of the same day. When the associations originally made have vanished, a considerable portion of the material is irretrievably lost.

Location Skills

The good student is one who has learned "to find the facts." He knows how to locate information. This means a familiarity with library aids and with such library resources as the Dewey classification system and card catalog, the various indexes, encyclopedias, and almanacs, but it also means the ability to find the desired material within a book, a chapter, a paragraph, or a sentence. It means that he knows how to use a table of contents, an appendix, and the footnotes. There is a high degree of relationship between a student's ability to locate and use reference materials and the grades that he gets in school.

READING MAPS, GRAPHS, TABLES, AND CHARTS

Sometimes the writer cannot accurately put into words what he wants to say. Writers thus frequently use pictures, maps, graphs, tables, and charts to explain more fully than is possible through words. Unfortunately, the student gets from these materials what is intended only if he can read the symbols, terms, and colors that the writer incorporates into these illustrations. Research (Weintraub, 1967) indicates that children can be taught to read maps, charts, and graphs, perhaps as early as first grade. The more capable first-grade children can learn to handle simple graphs. Children can interpret pictorial graphs more easily; next in order of difficulty come circle or pie graphs, two-dimensional graphs, and line graphs. Vertical bar graphs seem to be easier to read than horizontal bar graphs. Finally, the type of graph used depends on the materials and the context in which it is used.

Reading Maps

Map reading requires numerous skills. The student needs to identify natural features such as rivers and lakes; land shapes such as continents and islands; and man-made features such as railroads and highways. He needs to know the meaning of gulf, bay, earth, distance, scale, latitude, longitude, sphere, hemisphere, pole, and equator. He needs to be able to read map symbols.

He needs to read physical and political maps of the United States, of North America, and of the world. He needs to read maps depicting crops, rainfall, population, vegetation, wind belts, and ocean routes. He must learn to read maps of cities. And he should be able to read topographic and polar maps.

At the earliest level the pupil will learn simple concepts of direction (north, south, east, west), of distance, and of scale. He next advances to a recognition of large land and water forms on the globe, and he may learn to identify water, land, forests, and mountains by their color designation. Gradually, his learning becomes more specific. He will learn to locate continents, seas, oceans, and countries on a map.

In the upper elementary grades and on the junior high level the student usually learns to use map symbols, scales, and legends. He learns to find and use the equator, longitude, and latitude, and he can understand the causes of night and day and of the seasons. He translates latitude into miles and longitude into time. He becomes familiar with the poles, the Arctic and Antarctic Circles, the Tropic of Capricorn and the Tropic of Cancer. He understands meridians and parallels. He develops skill in location, in direction (upstream, downstream, etc.), and in identification of natural features (continents, countries, islands, peninsulas, oceans, rivers, lakes, gulfs, mountains, plains, deserts) and cultural features (cities, capitals, railroads, industries, crops).

He learns that in the tropics it is warm all year; that between the tropics and the Arctic-Antarctic Circles the temperature varies from season to season; that near the poles it is cold all year.

Rushdoony (1963) found that third graders can be taught the map reading skills usually taught in grades four and five, and he recommends that readiness for such teaching be developed in grades one and two.

Teaching the student to read maps includes the following steps:

1. Studying the title of the map.
2. Studying each symbol (the legend).
3. Noting direction on the map.
4. Analyzing and applying the map scale.
5. Relating the area under study to a more general or larger area (Kansas in relation to the United States).

Reading Graphs[5]

Another important skill is the ability to read graphs. There are four kinds of graphs. The *pictorial* graph in which the units are expressed in picture form is the easiest to read. It uses pictures to show relationships between realities. The *bar* graph compares the size of quantities. It expresses amounts. For example, one may want to compare the heights of various buildings or dams in the United States; the number of ticket sales made by the boys and girls in a class; or the number of deaths that are attributable to various causes, such as drowning, car accidents, and airplane accidents. In each instance, the bar graph shows how much more or less one type is than another. A bar graph may be either vertical or horizontal.

The *line* graph shows changes between quantities. It indicates what has happened over a period of time. It indicates whether there has been an increase or a decrease, for example, in the amount of rain each month of the year, in the price of foods, in daily temperature.

The *circle* graph shows the relation of parts to a whole. It may be used, for example, to indicate the percentage of As, Bs, Cs, and Ds in a certain class; how much of the family budget goes to food, clothing, shelter, savings, car, miscellaneous; or the percentage of the school budget that is allotted for salaries, maintenance, and the general operation of the school plant.

To read graphs of one kind or another the student should learn to observe the following steps:

1. Read the title of the graph—this tells what the graph is about.
2. Discover what is being compared—persons, places, or things.
3. Be able to interpret the legend and the meaning of the vertical axis and the horizontal axis.
4. Identify the scale of measure that has been used. What does each figure represent?
5. Discover what conclusions can be drawn from the graph.

Reading Tables

A table is a simple listing of facts and information. In reading a table the student should first look at the title. He should then look at the headings of the various columns with their major headings and subhead-

[5]See Dechant, E. *Improving Reading in the Secondary School,* Prentice-Hall, Inc., 1973, pp. 279–93.

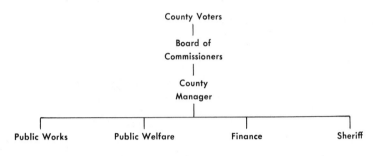

COUNTY MANAGER PLAN

FIGURE 10–2

ings, if there are any. Finally, he must read the details. These are usually written in the left-hand column.

Reading Charts

Possibly the most common type of chart is the *flow chart,* which shows the flow of organization. The student needs to be able to read it in social studies. Figure 10-2 illustrates one such chart.

SUMMARY

In this chapter we examined such skills as the ability to comprehend words, phrases, sentences, and paragraphs; the ability to read the context; and the ability to read for main ideas, for details, and for organization. We also examined critical reading, reading for learning, and the reading of maps, graphs, tables, and charts.

We must lead the students from literal comprehension through inferential comprehension to evaluation and appreciation. Appreciation involves all the other cognitive dimensions of reading.

QUESTIONS FOR DISCUSSION

---

1. What comprehension skills seem not amenable to training? Which seem most amenable to training?
2. What principles in addition to those mentioned in this chapter should guide the teacher in the development of word meanings?
3. What types of organization do paragraphs normally fall into? Either write or locate materials that illustrate various organizations and that might be used at junior high or high school level.
4. What is critical reading? How might newspapers be used to develop critical-reading skills?

5. Discuss Robinson's SQ3R Method.
6. Discuss the special problems of map reading.
7. Discuss four kinds of graphs and the problems they present in interpretation.
8. Discuss:
   a. The specific meaning elicited by a word is a function of the context in which it occurs.
   b. Drill and training in comprehension increase comprehension achievement rather than comprehension potential.
   c. Comprehension depends upon such variables as vocabulary, intelligence, perception, interpretation of language (getting meaning from context), and speech.
   d. Organizing of what is read as by summarizing or outlining is positively related to comprehension.
   e. The closer the reading skills stressed in a reading program are to the skills used in a specific content area, the more transfer occurs and the more the student tends to learn when reading in that area.

BIBLIOGRAPHY

ALLEN, ROBERT L. "Better Reading Through the Recognition of Grammatical Relations." *Reading Teacher* 18 (1964): 194–98.

AMES, W. S. "A Study of the Process by Which Readers Determine Word Meaning Through the Use of Verbal Context." Unpublished doctoral dissertation, University of Missouri, 1965.

ARTLEY, A. S. "Teaching Word-Meaning through Context." *Elementary English Review* 20 (1943): 68–74.

ARTLEY, A. S. "Implementing a Critical Reading Program on the Primary Level." *Reading and Inquiry,* International Reading Association Proceedings, Vol. 10 (1965): 111.

BERG, PAUL C. and RENTEL, VICTOR M. "Improving Study Skills." *Journal of Reading* 9 (1966): 343–48.

BIRKLEY, MARILYN. "Effecting Reading Improvement in the Classroom through Teacher Self-Improvement Programs." *Journal of Reading* 14 (1970): 94–100.

BRIGGS, F. A. "Grammatical Sense as a Factor in Reading Comprehension." In G. B. Schick, ed., *The Psychology of Reading Behavior.* Milwaukee: National Reading Conference, 1969, pp. 145–49.

BROWN, JAMES I. and WRIGHT, EUGENE S. *Manual of Instruction for Use with the Minnesota Efficient Reading Series of Tachistoslides.* Meadville, Pennsylvania: Keystone View Company, 1957.

BRUNER, J. S. "The Act of Discovery." *On Knowing.* Cambridge: Harvard University Press, 1962, pp. 81–96.

BRUNER, J. S. *Toward a Theory of Instruction.* Cambridge: Harvard University Press, 1966, p. 41.

COOK, LUELLA B. "Language Factors Involved in Interpretation." *The Reading Teacher* 12 (1959): 152–57.

DAVIS, FREDERICK B. "Fundamental Factors of Comprehension in Reading." *Psychometrika* 9 (1944): 185–97.

DAVIS, FREDERICK B. "The Teaching of Comprehension in Reading in the Secondary School." *Education* 76 (1956): 541–44.

DAWSON, MILDRED A. and BAMMAN, HENRY A. *Fundamentals of Basic Reading Instruction.* New York: David McKay Co., 1959.

DEIGHTON, L. *Vocabulary Development in the Classroom.* New York: Teachers' College Press, Columbia University, 1959.

DONALD, SISTER M. "The SQ3R Method in Grade Seven." *Journal of Reading* 11 (1967): 33–35, 43.

DULIN, KENNETH LAMARR. "New Research on Context Clues." *Journal of Reading* 13 (1969): 33–38.

DURRELL, DONALD D. *Improving Reading Instruction.* New York: Harcourt, Brace & World, 1956.

EDWARDS, THOMAS J. "Oral Reading in the Total Reading Process." *The Elementary School Journal* 58 (1957): 36–41.

ELKIND, DAVID and WEISS, JUTTA. "Studies in Perceptual Development, III: Perceptual Exploration." *Child Development* 38 (1967): 553–56.

ELLER, WILLIAM and WOLF, JUDITH G. "Developing Critical Reading Abilities." *Journal of Reading* (December 1966).

EMANS, ROBERT. "Context Clues." *Reading in the Total Curriculum.* International Reading Association Proceedings (1968) p. 13.

EMBLER, WELLER. "Metaphor in Everyday Speech." *Etc. A Review of General Semantics* 16 (1959): 323–42.

FAIRBANKS, GRANT. "The Relation Between Eye Movements and Voice in the Oral Reading of Good and Poor Silent Readers." *Psychological Monographs* 48 (1937): 78–107.

FREDERICK, E. C. "A Study of the Effects of Certain Readiness Activities on Concept Learning." Unpublished doctoral dissertation. Syracuse University, 1968.

FURNESS, EDNA LUE. "Pupils, Pedagogues, and Punctuation." *Elementary English* 37 (1960): 184–89.

GATES, ARTHUR I. "Developing Higher Levels of Reading Instruction." *Better Readers for Our Times,* International Reading Association, Conference Proceedings. New York: Scholastic Magazines, 1956, pp. 95–98.

GRAY, LILLIAN and REESE, DORA. *Teaching Children to Read.* New York: Ronald Press, 1957.

GRAY, W. S. "Is Your Rreading Program a Good One?" University of Kansas Conference of Reading, International Reading Association, October 12, 1957.

GROESBECK, HULDA GWENDOLYN. "The Comprehension of Figurative Language by Elementary Children: A Study in Transfer." Unpublished Doctoral Dissertation, University of Oklahoma, Norman, Oklahoma, 1961.

GUSZAK, FRANK J. "Teacher Questioning and Reading." *The Reading Teacher* 21 (1967): 227–34, 252.

HARRIS, ALBERT J. *How to Increase Reading Ability*, 3rd Edition. New York: Longmans, Green and Company, 1956.

HARVISON, ALAN R. "Critical Reading for Elementary Pupils." *The Reading Teacher* 21 (1967): 244–47, 252.

HERBER, HAROLD L. "Study Skills: Reading to Develop, Remember and Use Ideas." *Reading in the Content Areas*. Syracuse, N.Y.: Syracuse University, 1969, pp. 13–21.

HORN, T. D. "What's New in Words These Days?" *Education* 79 (1958): 203–5.

HUELSMANN, CHARLES B., JR. "Promoting Growth in Ability to Interpret When Reading Critically: In Grades Seven to Ten." *Promoting Growth Toward Maturity in Interpreting What is Read*. Supplementary Educational Monographs, No. 74. Chicago: University of Chicago Press, 1951, pp. 149–53.

JENKINSON, M. D. "Comprehension and Some Linguistic Fallacies." In G. B. Schick, ed., *New Frontiers in College-Adult Reading*. Milwaukee: National Reading Conference, 1966, pp. 180–87.

JENKINSON, M. D. "Information Gaps in Research in Reading Comprehension." In. G. B. Schick, ed., *Reading: Process and Pedagogy*. Milwaukee: National Reading Conference, 1971, pp. 179–92.

JOHNSON, HARRY W. "Another Study Method." *Journal of Developmental Reading* 7 (1964): 269–82.

KARLIN, ROBERT. "Research Results and Classroom Practices." *The Reading Teacher* 21 (1967): 211–26.

KATZ, E. W. "Understanding Connectives." *Journal of Verbal Learning and Verbal Behavior* 7 (1968): 501–9.

KOLLARITSCH, JANE. "Organizing Reading for Detailed Learning in a Limited Time." *Journal of Reading* 13 (1969): 29–32.

KOTTMEYER, WILLIAM. "Classroom Activities in Critical Reading." *School Review* 52 (1944): 557–64.

LABOV, WILLIAM. *Some Sources of Reading Problems for Negro Speakers of Non-Standard English*. National Cash Register Company, 4936 Fairmont Avenue, Bethesda, Md. 20014, 1966.

LANIER, RUBY JEANNE and DAVIS, ANITA PRICE. "Developing Comprehension Through Teacher-Made Questions." *The Reading Teacher* 26 (1972): 153–57.

LARTER, S. J. and TAYLOR, P. A. "A Study of Aspects of Critical Thinking." *The Manitoba Journal of Education* 5 (1969): 35–53.

LEARY, BERNICE E. "Developing Word Perception Skills in Middle and Upper Grades." *Current Problems of Reading Instruction*. Seventh Annual Conference on Reading. Pittsburgh: University of Pittsburgh Press, 1951, pp. 22–27.

LYON, DARWIN OLIVER. "The Relation of Length of Material to Time Taken for Learning and The Optimum Distribution of Time, Part III." *Journal of Educational Psychology* 5 (1914): 155–63.

MARTIN, R. G. "Decoding and the Quest for Meaning." *Journal of Reading Behavior* 1 (1969): 22–29.

MCCULLOUGH, C. M. "Context Aids in Reading." *The Reading Teacher* 11 (1958): 225–29.

MCCULLOUGH, CONSTANCE M. "Learning to Use Context Clues." *Elementary English* 20 (1943): 140–43.

MELNIK, AMELIA. "The Formulation of Questions as an Instructional-Diagnostic Tool." *Reading and Inquiry.* International Reading Association, Vol. 10 (1965).

National Association of Secondary-School Principals, "Teaching Essential Reading Skills," *Improving Reading Instruction in the Secondary School,* II, 34 (February 1950): 39–130.

NILES, O. S. "Organization Perceived." *Developing Study Skills in the Schools,* Perspectives in Reading No. 4, pp. 57–76. International Reading Association, 1965.

OAKAN, ROBERT; WIENER, MORTON; and CROMER, WARD. "Identification, Organization, and Reading Comprehension for Good and Poor Readers." *Journal of Educational Psychology* 62 (1971): 71–78.

OLSON, ARTHUR V. "Teaching Critical Reading Skills," *Reading Improvement* 4 (1966): 1–4, 19.

PAUK, WALTER. "On Scholarship: Advice to High School Students." *The Reading Teacher* 7 (1963): 73–78.

PAUK, WALTER. "Techniques for Textbook Study." *Reading Improvement* 6 (1969): 7–10.

PERRY, WILLIAM G. JR. and WHITLOCK, CHARLES P. "The Right to Read Rapidly." *Atlantic Monthly* 190 (1952): 88–96.

ROBERTSON, JEAN E. "Pupil Understanding of Connectives." *Reading Research Quarterly* 3 (1968): 387–417.

ROBINSON, ALAN. "A Cluster of Skills: Especially for Junior High School." *The Reading Teacher* 15 (1961): 25–28.

ROBINSON, FRANCIS P. *Effective Study,* revised edition. New York: Harper & Row, 1961.

ROTHKOPF, ERNEST Z. "The Concept of Mathemagenic Activities." *Review of Educational Research* 40 (1970).

RUSHDOONY, HAIG A. "Achievement in Map Reading: An Experimental Study." *Elementary School Journal* (November, 1963).

RUSSELL, DAVID H. *Children Learn to Read.* New York: Ginn and Company, 1961, p. 359.

RUSSELL, D. H. "Research on the Process of Thinking with Some Implications to Reading." *Elementary English* 42 (1965): 375.

SCHELL, LEO M. "Promising Possibilities for Improving Comprehension." *Journal of Reading* 15 (1972): 415–24.

SEVERSON, EILEEN. "The Teaching of Reading-Study Skills in Biology." *American Biology Teacher* 25 (1963): 203–4.

SHAW, PHILIP. "Rhetorical Guides to Reading Comprehension." *The Reading Teacher* 11 (1958): 239–43.

SHIBLES, BURLEIGH. "How Many Words Does a First Grade Child Know?" *Elementary English* 37 (1959): 42–47.

SMITH, MADORAH E. "An Investigation of the Development of the Sentence and the Extent of Vocabulary in Young Children." *University of Iowa Studies in Child-Welfare* 3 (1926): 1–92.

SMITH, NILA B. "Reading for Depth." *Reading and Inquiry.* International Reading Association Proceedings, 10 (1965): 118.

SMITH, RICHARD J. and HESSE, KARL D. "The Effects of Prereading Assistance on the Comprehension of Good and Poor Readers." *Research in the Teaching of English* 3 (1969): 166–77.

SOMMERFELD, ROY E. "An Evaluation of the Tachistoscope in Reading Improvement Programs." *What Colleges are Doing in Reading Improvement Programs.* Fort Worth, Texas: Texas Christian University Press, 1954, pp. 7–25.

SPACHE, G. D. and BERG, P. C. *Better Reading for College Students.* New York: Macmillan, 1955.

STAUFFER, RUSSEL G. "A Study of Prefixes in the Thorndike List to Establish a List of Prefixes That Should Be Taught in the Elementary School." *Journal of Educational Research* 35 (1942): 453–58.

STEINER, ROLLIN; WIENER, MORTON; and CROMER, WAR. "Comprehension Training and Identification for Poor and Good Readers." *Journal of Educational Psychology* 62 (1971): 506–13.

STOODT, BARBARA D. "The Relationship Between Understanding Grammatical Conjunctions and Reading Comprehension." *Elementary English* 49 (1972): 502–4.

TABA, HILDA, et. al. *Thinking in Elementary School Children.* Cooperative Research Project, No. 1574, p. 53. San Francisco: San Francisco State College, 1964.

TRAXLER, ARTHUR E. "The Right to Read Rapidly." *The Atlantic Monthly* 190 (1952): 88–96.

VANDERLINDE, L. "Does the Study of Quantitative Vocabulary Improve Problem Solving?" *Elementary School Journal* 65 (1964): 143–52.

VANDER MEULEN, KENNETH. "Reading in the Secondary School: 'Carbon Dating' Figures of Speech." *Reading Horizons* 14 (1973): 27–32.

VINEYARD, EDWIN E. and MASSEY, HAROLD W. "The Interrelationship of Certain Linguistic Skills and Their Relationship with Scholastic Achievement When Intelligence is Ruled Constant." *Journal of Educational Psychology* 48 (1957): 279–86.

WARREN, JAMES E., JR. "The Heart of Language." *Education* 80 (1960): 259–63.

WEINTRAUB, SAMUEL. "Reading Graphs, Charts, and Diagrams." *The Reading Teacher* 20 (1967): 345–49.

WEIGAND, GEORGE, and BLAKE, WALTER S., JR. *College Orientation.* Englewood Cliffs, N.J.: Prentice-Hall, 1955.

WOLPERT, EDWARD M. "Length, Imagery Values and Word Recognition." *The Reading Teacher* 26 (1972): 180–86.

YOAKAM, GERALD A. "The Development of Comprehension in the Middle Grades." *Current Problems of Reading Instruction,* Seventh Annual Conference of Reading. Pittsburgh: University of Pittsburgh Press, 1951, pp. 28–35.

11

Rate of Comprehension, Readability and Legibility

Effective reading emphasizes economy, which includes comprehension and rate. These two skills are so intertwined that we speak of them as rate of comprehension. Furthermore, the rate of comprehension that the pupil will attain is dependent upon both the readability and the legibility of the materials that he uses.

RATE OF COMPREHENSION

In a previous article we (Dechant, 1961) pointed out that rate of reading has frequently been described as rate of comprehension. Perhaps it is better described as speed in grasping the meanings intended by the writer. To read is to comprehend, but one may comprehend at a slow rate or at a relatively more rapid rate.

Although comprehension thus remains of importance, and rate has no meaning apart from comprehension, rate of reading is worth considering. No one actually reads faster than he comprehends, but many read much more slowly than comprehension would permit. Generally the limiting factor to rate improvement is the mind rather than the vision.

Katz and Wicklund (1971) note that the differences in reading speed between good and poor readers could possibly show in (1) the visual read-in phase when visual information or part of word is received and encoded; (2) in the phonemic transformation or representation which is generated by the visual input; or (3) in the memory search when the phonemic representation interacts with memory to produce meaning. Their study indicated that the differences in reading speed do not stem from either phase one or phase two. Calfee and Jameson's study (1971) confirmed this finding. They found that central memory load limits reading speed, not scanning and decoding. They concluded that central cognitive processes involving the storage or maintenance of information play a critical role in the performance of skilled readers. The rate at which chunks of words are read depended on the amount of time required to complete the memory search process.

Relationship Between Rate and Comprehension

The correlations between rate of reading and comprehension, especially on the secondary and the college level, are positive but quite low (circa .30) (Lanigan, 1947; Shores and Husbands, 1950; Thurstone, 1944).

Carlson (1949) found that individuals with high intelligence tend to comprehend better when reading rapidly than when reading slowly; those with average or low intelligence comprehend better when reading slowly than when reading rapidly. This tendency was even more clear when the purposes for reading were made more exacting and the difficulty of the material was increased.

These relationships between rate and comprehension are important to the teacher because he must decide when to stress rate improvement and when to emphasize comprehension skills. A reader who is low in both comprehension and rate will generally not benefit from an emphasis on speed. He needs training in basic comprehension skills. One who reads rapidly but with low comprehension likewise needs comprehension training. One who reads all materials slowly but with good comprehension, however, may well profit from training in speed. Perhaps this is because rapid reading requires his full attention, whereas when he plods along, his attention wanders. On the other hand, the slow learner's rate is limited by his comprehending or thinking rate.

In mathematics and science the correlations between comprehension and rate of reading tend to be low and negative. In general, the faster the student reads in these areas, the less he tends to understand.

In summary, the degree of correlation between rate and comprehension depends on the age of the reader, the intelligence of the reader, the kinds of materials employed, the methods used in measuring the two characteristics, and the purpose for the reading.

The Value of Speed Reading

Despite some of the ambivalent research and the uncertainty of the conclusions that one can deduce therefrom, rapidity in reading seems to have an economy value in its own right and should be investigated as a separate skill. Harris (1956) suggests that the rate training should be included in developmental reading programs and should begin at or above the sixth grade. Most readers cease improving in rate, if no attempts are made to increase it, by about the sixth grade. Ordinarily they read from two hundred to three hundred words per minute at that time.

There are fast readers, average readers, and slow readers, and on an average it seems more desirable to be a fast reader than a slow reader. Pauk (1963), however, believes that speed reading has little if any positive effect on success with college assignments. He notes that he has never encountered a single case in which academic failure was the result of a student's inability to read fast enough. Rather, it was a lack of understanding of what was read. He adds that he has dealt with cases where speed reading was responsible for academic difficulties.

Flexibility in Reading

We must constantly ask: What is speed for? What purpose does it serve? A lot of speeding has no reasonable justification (Mathews, 1966). Mortimer J. Adler notes: "In the case of good books, the point is not to see how many of them you can get through, but rather how many can get through you."

Thus slow reading is not necessarily poor reading. It affords the reader an opportunity to evaluate, to linger, to enjoy the beauty of the description (much as the traveler who stops to see points of scenic interest), and to read between the lines. At times, slowness is beauty. To read slowly, to think critically, and to feel deeply may be true enrichment.

Rate of reading obviously is not the ultimate goal in reading. The ultimate aim is comprehension according to one's abilities and needs. This means that the good reader is a flexible reader.[i] Just as cars have in them the power to go slowly or to go rapidly as the occasion demands, so also the good reader can slow down or speed up as the nature of the material and his own needs change. He can shift gears in reading.

Flexibility appears to point to a critical difference between good and poor readers. The good reader sets comprehension as his goal and adjusts his rate rather automatically. The poor reader mechanically plods from word to word, and such comprehension as he obtains seems to be a by-product of the process rather than the central goal of his reading.

Research (Harris, 1968) unfortunately indicates that most readers are rigid rather than flexible in rate of reading. Most readers tend to maintain a characteristic approach and use a relatively invariant rate with all types of material. This relatively invariant rate of reading may be constitutional or learned, or it may simply be the result of lack of appropriate training (Maxwell and Mueller, 1967).

Efficiency in reading means simply this: with some purposes and some materials one should read slowly; with others, one should read more rapidly. This means that the reader should read as rapidly as possible, always meeting the comprehension specifications that he has set for himself or that the task has set for him (Shores, 1968).

Braam (1963), in a study with high school seniors, demonstrated that flexibility could be taught in a six-week summer session. The mean difference between highest rate and lowest rate was only 19 words per minute before training; after training it was 159 words. Steinacher (1971), on the other hand, suggests that instruction in reading flexibility is weakly supported and thus may not be justified.

---

[i] The *Reading Versatility Test,* by Arthur S. McDonald, measures flexibility of reading. It is designed for pupils in the fifth through ninth grades; see also, Rankin, Earl F. *The Measurement of Reading Flexibility: Problems and Perceptive.* International Reading Association, Newark, 1974.

Improving Rate of Reading

Rate of comprehension can undoubtedly be improved. Students who have undertaken some form of rate improvement training do increase their speed and will generally read faster than those who have not had such training. Labmeier and Vockell (1963), for example, found significant improvement in rate and comprehension of ninety-four ninth-grade girls who had a reading development course.

Rate of reading, because the emphasis should be on flexibility, should always be dependent on the purposes, intelligence, and experience and knowledge of the reader and upon the difficulty level of the material. The rate is always dependent on the reader's motivation and his psychological and physical state, his mastery of the basic reading skills, and the format of the materials. More specifically, factors that affect speed and comprehension are the following (Shores, 1968): size of type, type style, blackness and sharpness of print, quality and tone of the paper, size of the page, organization of the material, amount of white space, kind and placement of illustrations, headings and subheadings, clarity of the writing, the field of knowledge from which the writing is drawn, the complexity of the ideas, the author's style, the kind of writing (poetry, narrative, or descriptive), the reader's personality, the way the reader feels (sleepy, alert, calm, nervous), the reader's mental ability, reading skill, and his likes and dislikes, the environment in which reading occurs, the reader's background of experience, his purpose, and his interest in the field or area in which he is reading, and his familiarity with the peculiarities of style and phraseology of the author.

The reader gets into trouble in reading and must proceed more slowly when the writer's style is too difficult; when the ideas are too abstract; when he is trying to learn and to remember what he is reading; when he is following directions such as the carrying out of an experiment; when he is reading poetry; when he is reading critically—trying to evaluate what he reads; and when he reads such specialized materials as science.

It is interesting to note that when the good reader reduces his speed, he does so for a purpose. It does not create a gap between his reading rate and his thinking rate. He reduces his speed because the materials require him to think more slowly. The good reader seeks to increase his understanding without sacrificing speed unnecessarily, or he may want to increase his speed without sacrificing his understanding. In short, he is a flexible reader. The flexible reader gears his reading rate to his thinking rate.

Rate improvement cannot be built on inadequate word-identification and word-recognition skills. It cannot be built on an experimental background that keeps the reader from understanding what he is reading. It cannot be built upon immaturity in intellectual development.

Advocates of rate improvement programs claim that such programs may also lead to more accurate perception, more accurate and more rapid visual discrimination, wider span of apprehension and of perception, better attention and concentration, shorter reaction time, fewer regressions, decrease in the number and duration of fixations, reduction of vocalization, better comprehension, and general improvement in perceptual skills.

There are certain technical terms that are used in the experimental research on reading rate. Let's define some of these before proceeding to the research itself. Among these are visual field, visual span, and recognition span.

The *visual field* generally consists of a lateral arc of approximately 180 degrees. The visual field includes both peripheral and foveal (spot of clearest) vision and depth of vision.

The *visual span,* or the *perceptual span,* or the span of apprehension, is the amount (usually in terms of the number of digits or letters) that can be *seen* by the eye in a single fixation. This is measured by a tachistoscopic exposure and usually is more than what would be seen during a single fixation in normal reading. Poor readers frequently have a wider visual span than good readers because they do not organize what they see.

The *recognition span* is the amount that a reader sees and organizes during a single fixation pause. It is the number of words that are recognized or understood at a single fixation and it is computed by dividing the number of words in a selection by the number of fixation pauses made by the reader.

A wide span of recognition contributes to a wide eye-voice span in oral reading and to a wide eye-memory (organization) span in silent reading. Taylor (1957, p. 505) points out that a narrow span of recognition contributes to narrow eye-voice span and forces the child to pronounce each word as it is recognized in order to obtain meaning from the text. He cannot keep his eyes several words ahead of his voice, to carry the context in his mind.

Let us now turn our attention to rate improvement studies. Numerous studies have indicated that tachistoscopic training broadens the visual span. Weber (1942) reported that tachistoscopic training broadens the visual span or perceptual span, both horizontally and vertically. Fink (1956) suggested that such rate gains as do occur through tachistoscopic training in digit perception are due to the elimination of regressive eye movements.

Paterson and Tinker (1947) suggested that peripheral vision has an important role in reading and determines the width of the recognition span. They pointed out that the proficient reader tends to make maximum use of cues in peripheral vision at least in reading easy material.

Studies by Renshaw (1945), Cosper and Kephart (1955), and Robinson (1934), suggested that training on mechanical devices frequently is accompanied by improvement in reading rate. Sutherland (1946), besides finding a relationship between visual span and rate of visual perception as well as visual span and reading rate, indicated that both rate of perception and reading rate can be increased through improvement of the perceptual span.

Smith and Tate (1953) reported substantial rate gains for a small group of students at the University of Kansas. All subjects participated in at least twenty-five fifty-minute sessions using both rate controllers and tachistoscopes. A part of the findings showed that gains as measured by tests were less than gains as measured by controller settings.

The above are only a few of the many reports of gains in reading rate with machine-centered programs. The basic questions are the following: Are mechanical devices essential for rate improvement? Is machine-training the best way to obtain increased speed?

Gates (1953, p. 26) felt that tachistoscopic training is unnatural. He suggested that the reader actually can do more to improve his reading rate by sliding a piece of cardboard down a page than by using mechanical devices. He indicated that in evaluating any device used to develop rate we should consider the extent to which it introduces artificial factors, distorts the natural process, or lacks proper flexibility and adaptability to the reader's needs.

Vernon (1956, p. 88) suggested that devices which force the reader's eyes to move at an even speed whatever the nature of the material read, or his purpose in reading it, might in the long run destroy the flexibility necessary for intelligent reading.

There is evidence also that the ordinary reader's tachistoscopic (visual) span is already much larger than the recognition span he commonly uses. Robinson (1934), studying fifty-one college students, found that their average reading (recognition) span was only 41 percent as large as their tachistoscopic span.

Studies generally have found that a wide divergence exists between visual span as measured on the tachistoscope and reading rate and that an increase in visual span fails to produce significant gains in reading rate. It may be that the reader uses a different span during motivated training than during normal reading. As stated earlier in the chapter, the mind, not the vision, generally seems to be the limiting factor. The evidence suggests that the more meaningful the material is to the individual, the wider will be his recognition span.

What then, is the real function of tachistoscopic training? Do mechanical devices actually have little to do with eye movement and merely motivate the mind to work closer to its capacity and at a faster rate (Gray and Reese, 1957, p. 257)? Does an increase in mental activity also account for the fact that improvement in rate of reading (or rate of thinking?) may result in better comprehension and in a better retention of what is read? There seems to be evidence for this. Thurstone (1944, p. 130) concluded that fast and slow readers are differentiated on the basis of "central processes." He points out that reading is primarily a perceptual function. The reader learns to make quick associations with rapidly changing visual stimuli. Thurstone implies that rate of association could well be the critical factor in distinguishing the rapid reader from the slow reader. Buswell (1951), studying seventy-seven college seniors, found some evidence that those who excelled in rate of thinking tended to be high in rate of comprehension.

Taylor (1957) observed that improvements in rate of reading can result from an increase in the lateral amount of print that can be perceived and organized rapidly. He noted (p. 503) that the primary value of short exposure training is to contribute to an increase in the size of the span of recognition, to increase the accuracy and precision of perception, and to develop the reader's ability to organize perceived material more rapidly.

Certainly the mechanical devices have motivational value. Jones (1951, p. 313) points out that the inventors of these machines may have overlooked the psychological effect of the purring of a little motor on the machine-conscious younger students, especially boys.

Studies also generally indicate that rate gains have an adequate degree of permanency. Cole (1957); Reed (1956); Cosper and Kephart (1955); Mullins and Mowry (1954); and Weber (1939) have reported follow-up studies that indicated permanency in rate gains. In reviewing five such studies, Spache found that 51 to 84 percent of the improvement in rate was reported to be retained six to twelve months after training (Spache, 1958).

Gadgetry for Rate Improvement

Let us take a look at the vast array of gadgetry available today that is intended to help the student develop rate skills. These gadgets might be grouped into tachistoscopes, accelerating devices, and other reading-related instruments.

Tachistoscopes. Tachistoscopes expose numbers, letters, words, phrases, or other images for short periods of time, usually ranging from 1/100 to 1½ seconds. Most training on these machines is at the higher speeds.

The tachistoscope, whether individual or group, primarily develops the person's perceptual intake skills. By forcing the student to cope with intake speeds of 1/10 of a second or less, the tachistoscope requires the student to see more rapidly, more accurately, and more orderly; to pay more attention to what was seen; and to organize what he has seen. He also has to develop better directional attack.

Since the tachistoscopic span is greater than the span in normal reading, researchers have asked: What are the effects of tachistoscopic training, and is there any value in increasing the tachistoscopic span?

A tachistoscopic exposure is followed by a period of "nonreading" in which the person can assimilate and integrate what he saw; in reading, there is continuous perceptual activity, the images overlap each other, and there is relatively little time to assimilate and interpret. Obviously, increasing the tachistoscopic span further seems to be of little value in reading. The training should be directed toward developing the intake aspect of perception and toward improving the seeing skills as a basis for better reading rather than toward developing reading skills per se (EDL Newsletter, No. 19).

"Seeing" can be improved, and tachistoscopic training is one of the better ways of doing this. It has been used in the armed services, in remedial reading, in orthoptics, in teaching spelling and arithmetic, in art and business education, and even in physical education. In each instance the emphasis has been on the development of general accuracy in seeing and remembering. This is of value in all learning situations in which the student must come to understanding through the use of vision (Taylor and Frackenpohl, 1960a, p. 6).

There are many by-products of tachistoscopic training. The student learns self-discipline, better habits of work, and better eye-hand coordination and improves his focusing ability. Tachistoscopic training has greatest value in the elementary years when the pupil is learning to "see." Since much of the material is designed to develop accuracy of seeing and the retention of the particular placement of certain elements (for example, the pupil needs to see and remember 24571 in definite order), it may have value in a word-attack program.

Accelerating Devices. The accelerating devices provide rate training for the competent readers. The *Controlled Reader,* for example, presents materials in a left-to-right direction at a predetermined rate. A moving slot travels across the screen in a left-to-right direction, covering and uncovering the materials as it moves along (Taylor and Frackenpohl, 1960b).

Such devices lead to a reduction in fixations and regressions, better attention and concentration, more rapid thinking, and improved organization of what is read.

Once the student has attained a speed of 450 to 500 words, the words may be more satisfactorily uncovered a line at a time.

Accelerating devices are most useful in the upper elementary years and in junior high school.

Much group training with accelerators is at far-point. This is undesirable for students with myopic vision and for those who have difficulties with fusion because they are required to improve rate while handicapped visually. At far-point the person can also "read" more words than in normal reading. It is possible that this explains the relatively little transfer that occurs from machine programs to normal book reading.

Reading-related Machines. The reading teacher might also have use for one of the following machines in his reading program.

Aud-X. (Educational Developmental Laboratories). As students listen to interesting stories, they watch the screen to learn new words. Each time the narrator pronounces one of the several words being taught in a lesson, it appears on the screen in exact synchronization with its pronunciation. In follow-up word study lessons, students discover the graphic and sound qualities of words through the unique sight-sound synchronization afforded by the Aud-X. Though the students may be part of a small group during Aud-X sessions, each one listens, looks, and responds in an individual manner. Through its autoinstructional capability, the Aud-X makes an important contribution to truly individualized learning.

Delacato Stereo-Reading Service. (Mast Development Co.). This service with stereo reader is designed for remedial use with students who suffer from laterality confusions. It develops binocular reading. The Zweig-Bruno Stereo-Tracing Exercises, to be used with the Stereo-Reader, are effective in the correction of letter reversals, letter substitutions, in-word reversals, and poor hand-eye coordination.

Language Master Machine. (Hoover Brothers, Kansas City, Missouri). This machine comes with cards designed to teach vocabulary, sounds of English, phonics, etc.

Leavell Language Development Service. (Mast Development Co.). This service with instrument develops eye control and hand-eye coordination. It is useful with mirror writers and children who reverse.

Skimming and Scanning

The only machine available today that is designed to develop the skimming skill is the *EDL Skimmer*. This machine is equipped with a bead of light that travels down the center fold of the book at the rate of one-half minute per page, or about eight hundred to one thousand words per minute. This informs the reader how rapidly he should proceed and keeps him perceptually alert. The device is useful also in developing scanning skills.

Skimming is selective reading. In skimming the reader chooses what he wants to read. He selects those sentences, clauses, and phrases that best serve his purposes. He gets a general impression of the selection and decides on the basis of his examination whether to read the selection more intensively. He takes a quick glance at the table of contents, the index, the chapter titles, the paragraph headings, the topic sentences, and the summary. These provide valuable clues to the main idea.

In scanning, the reader runs his eyes down the page with the purpose of finding an answer to a specific question.

We scan a crowd to find a certain person; we scan a bowl of candy for the right piece; and we scan a box of tools for pliers. In reading, we scan to find an answer to a particular question, to locate a specific date or number, or to locate a reference, a name, a city, or a quotation.

Skimming and scanning are not accelerated reading. In them the reader switches from looking to reading to looking and so on. In fact, there may be less reading than looking, and when the person reads he reads in the usual way (Grayum, 1952).

Schale (1965) discusses three techniques, all involving skimming, for increasing rate of reading by learning to read vertically: the vertical skimming method, the square span method, and the narrow column method. In the vertical skimming method, the reader may glide his eyes over the irrelevant content until he lands on what he is looking for (exclusive skimming); he may survey material, identifying main ideas and inferring less important details (inclusive skimming); or he may, using nondirected skimming, move his eyes down the page in a narrow span. The square span method and the narrow column method both involve moving the eye over a small span—either the eye focuses on the center of a page or all the words are placed in narrow columns. Less skimming is involved in the latter two approaches.

Research tends to indicate that reading rates above eight hundred words per minute are in the nature of skimming and scanning. The reader characteristically omits part of the content and reads with considerably less comprehension (Taylor and Frackenpohl, 1961). Skimming usually takes the form of preview, overview, or review (Taylor, 1962). Skimming for preview purposes has already been described. In skimming for overview purposes the reader gets a general impression of the content. He reads more of the material than when doing preview skimming. He looks for the writer's organization, thinks along with the writer, and notes the transitions. Skimming for review is a useful technique in preparing for tests or to increase retention generally.

When the student should be taught to skim is difficult to say, Taylor and Frackenpohl (1961, pp. 9–12) have identified the *type* of student who is ready for selective reading. The student must be a flexible reader. He needs visual coordination. He must have developed a proper directional attack, and he must be able to organize a series of data. He must be able to identify words rapidly, must retain them, and must relate them to each other. He must develop attention and concentration, while maintaining his composure. He must be relaxed and willing to settle for less than complete comprehension.

To skim, the student must develop a new perceptual skill. In selective reading "looking" is as important as is reading. The person must look back and forth and down the page in a "floating" manner as it were (Taylor and Frackenpohl, 1961, p. 11). He learns to take in words, ideas, and organization at a subliminal level.

Evaluation of Machine Programs. No one would suggest that reading instruments make a total program. On the other hand, few would deny that they have a legitimate role in a balanced reading program. In evaluating their effectiveness one must always be cautious in generalizing from one instrument to all others. Each has its own strength and weakness and must be separately evaluated.

Certain principles, however, guide all evaluations. It is not enough to simply look for rate gains. The reader's relative efficiency is more than rate; it is also a function of the fixations and regressions:

$$(RE) = \frac{Rate}{Fixations + Regressions}$$

An increase in rate is significant only when it is accompanied by a reduction in fixations and regressions.

Mechanical devices are motivating. They may even increase comprehension achievement; however, they cannot increase comprehension potential. They merely help the mind to operate on a level approximating its potential.

Persons working with mechanical devices repeatedly have noticed among students an increase in interest in reading and in a desire to improve their reading skills. For some of these a successful experience in a machine program may develop a new attitude toward reading generally which may lead to improved performance in a number of areas including rate of comprehension.

It thus frequently is impossible to attribute rate improvements to machines alone. Increased motivation and increased teacher effectiveness may be as significant. No one would suggest that because no gains were made the machine was necessarily useless. Nor could one infer that because gains were made in a machine program that these were the sole result of the machine. The effectiveness of any mechanical device depends on the user.

How good then are these gadgets? Tinker (1967) makes the following observations:

1. Reading speed can be improved, but it is not at all certain that the gains are lasting.[2]
2. Improved rate is not automatically transferred to other types of material.
3. There is evidence to indicate that pacers and accelerating devices are more effective developers of reading rate than are tachistoscopes. Tinker adds, "The tachistoscope is without value for increasing speed of reading."
4. The improvement through mechanical devices is no greater than that resulting from motivated reading alone. However, Maxwell and Mueller (1967), in a study involving forty college students, found that those students who were given specific techniques for improving their speed showed significantly greater gains than either the control group or the group that was simply "motivated" to increase rate.
5. Pacing devices often are emphasized more than the processes of perception, apprehension, and assimilation, with a resultant decrease in flexibility.
6. There is perhaps too much of an emphasis upon "oculomotor mechanics."

We would add the following generalizations:

1. The visual span or the perception span can be increased both vertically and horizontally.
2. Gains in rate tend to have an adequate degree of permanency.
3. Mechanical devices may destroy some flexibility in reading.
4. The tachistoscopic span (visual span) is already much larger than the recognition span of the average reader.
5. The mind, not vision, is generally the limiting element in reading. Fast and slow readers are differentiated on the basis of the central processes. Read-

[2]We believe the research indicates that at least some of the gains are lasting.

ing is primarily a perceptual function. Those who excel in rate of thinking tend to be high in rate of comprehension.

6. The more significant the material is to the individual, the wider will be his recognition span.

7. The machine and the purr of the motor have a psychological and motivational effect on students, especially boys. They do not stretch the visual span but rather spur the mind (Dearborn, 1938, p. 6).

8. Rather than speed training, with some students it might be better to improve the poor vocabulary and the word-recognition and word-analysis skills of the learner. Weaknesses in basic reading skills should be diagnosed and corrected before any consideration is given to rate of reading.

9. If, in fact, the good reader reacts to ever decreasing or minimal cues, then mechanical training may at times be successful simply because it teaches the student to read with fewer cues, to guess better what he sees peripherally, and to be more confident in dealing with indistinct portions of words.

10. Perhaps those traits that lead a student to seek reading improvement are the same traits that cluster to produce higher grades.

11. Marvel (1959), working with high school sophomores, found that motivational factors, verbal set or mind set, without tachistoscopic training were most significant in improving both rate and permanency of rate.

12. The best use of mechanical devices may be with average and better-than-average readers having specific problems in rate of reading.

13. The amount of transfer of rate gains from machine-oriented programs to more typical reading is quite variable and unpredictable.

14. Morton (1964) found that readers shortened reading time or increased speed by using greater contextual constraint. Fast readers tend to use contextual clues more efficiently. In effect, they see fewer words when reading. If this is so, then instruction in key-word or key-phrase reading should be encouraged (Rose, 1969).

15. Research also shows that it is desirable to say the word subvocally while reading. The fade-out of the visually acquired stimulus seems rapid if it is not recoded in acoustic form (Rose, 1969). An acoustic factor seems to be involved in immediate memory and recall. And, if this is so, it seems that instruction in fast reading should not do away with inner speech. Amble (1967), reviewing the research on reading by phrases, concludes that perceptual span, reading comprehension, and reading rate can all be increased by phrase-reading training. He adds that reading by phrases is a unique reading skill, that it can be developed through training, and that it is a durable skill.

Implications of Rate Improvement Programs

There are still other concerns that constantly perplex the practitioner. For example: What is optimal reading speed on specific materials and how can it be determined? Which rate skills should receive most reinforcement? What are the side effects of speed programs? In some programs the student is taught rhythmic phraseology. Yet, the good reader is a flexible reader. Normal reading is continuous, textual and nonrhythmic reading.

Finally, what is the student learning in rate improvement programs using tachistoscopic or other mechanical devices? Fletcher (1959) found that when three equivalent forms were used in testing the student's performance, at the end of the first, second, and last tachistoscopic training session, most of the gains occurred between the first and second session. The technique of rapid performance on a tachistoscope seems to be acquired rather quickly.

There seems to be little justification for emphasis on speed of reading in the primary school years. The intermediate pupil and the high school student, on the other hand, must be taught to adjust their reading speed to the materials and purposes for reading. They must be taught, either through book or machine programs, facility and speed in perceiving words and relating them to their meaning. They must be taught to read in thought units. They must be helped to overcome such faulty habits as moving the lips, pointing to words, or moving the head while reading.

The student must be encouraged to move his eyes as rapidly across the line of print as is possible. Too frequently, the student can read faster, but he has developed the habit of moving slowly. To overcome this habit the student should time himself on passages of a particular length. In the beginning the passages should be simple and interesting. If the print is in narrow columns, as in newspapers, the student should be encouraged to make only one fixation per line, forcing himself to move the eyes down the page.

The student is constantly tempted to regress so that he can read more accurately. Normally this may be good procedure, but it does not lead to increased speed. The student must fight against this. He can be helped to overcome excessive caution by cutting a slot out of a piece of paper and moving the paper down the page. This forces him to move ahead and keeps him from looking back or too far ahead. Another device consists simply of a sheet of paper which he may move down the page, covering a line at a time.

The student must learn that there is no best rate of reading. The good reader uses a flexible approach in reading. He uses a greater variety of approaches when reading, even though he may have learned this skill on his own (Smith, 1965). His reading varies in speed from very slow to moderate to very fast; from detailed analysis of what he reads to skimming and scanning; from rapid reading, skimming, and recreational reading to intensive reading. Even his comprehension tends to be flexible. Some materials need to be understood thoroughly; others, only generally. Certain parts of a textbook must be read intensively; others may be skimmed. The flexible reader may read very rapidly or even skip those parts that are trivial, are already known, or are related to his goals and purposes.

The flexible reader knows what he wants from the material. He has asked himself: Need I understand only the main idea, the supporting facts, or a combination of these? Am I reading for pleasure or for information? What is my purpose?

The flexible reader has also developed a flexible attitude toward reading. He adjusts his speed to the purpose for which he is reading and to the difficulty of the reading matter. He realizes that different reading situations call for different ways of reading. He reads differently when reading newspapers, magazines, advertisements, encyclopedias, textbooks, novels, how-to-do-it books, and editorials.

READABILITY

Our focus here is on readability and legibility—those characteristics of the reading materials that are important determinants of both comprehension and rate. If the major aim of reading is the comprehension of meaning, the teacher must be interested in the measurement of the comprehensibility of materials. He wants some means for quantifying his statements about the difficulty of material. It is not enough to say that reading material is difficult or easy. He must have reference points or a scale with which to judge printed materials (Chall, 1957, p. 153).

Although writers frequently use the term readability to refer to a composite of understandability and legibility, in this section the term readability generally will refer to the perceptual problems of understandability or comprehensibility. The sensory problems will be reserved for the latter portion of the chapter and will be discussed under the topic of legibility.

Teachers have a basic interest in the nature of readability. A knowledge of readability is important to the teacher so that he will be able to provide reading material that will meet the needs and capacities of each child in the classroom. The teacher must constantly ask: Should *this* pupil read *this* material? Is it appropriate to his abilities, is it *readable for him?*

The Nature of Readability

Readability is not an easily defined concept. It involves an interaction between reader and book. Because communication between writer and reader seldom is perfect, readability rarely can be absolute. It usually is a matter of degree. The teacher thus must make some practical decisions as to the degree of understanding that is necessary before a book may be considered readable by a child at a certain grade level. In short, he must determine how much the reader must get from the printed material before it becomes readable for him.

The concept of readability generally refers to the success that the average individual has with a book. Dale and Chall (1949) point out that readability refers to those elements within printed material that affect the success that a group of readers have with it.

Unfortunately, the teacher cannot be completely satisfied with this concept. A book that is readable for one child may not be readable for another child even if he has the same general level of reading ability. The teacher cannot make prescriptions for the average individual. He must make decisions for a specific child. For example, *Gulliver's Travels* might be readable as an interesting tale at a much lower grade level than would be appropriate if we expected it to be understood as a political satire. What is readable thus depends not so much on the material to be read as on the background, abilities, and interests of the person doing the reading.

Variations in Readability

A developmental reading program designed to start each student at an appropriate level and to lead him to progress at his own rate must be concerned with the difficulty level of the books that are being used. We recognize, of course, that there will be variations of from five to nine grades in the reading abilities of the children in a single class. This is one of the key reasons that the trend has been away from the use of single texts and toward the use of a variety of books and other materials chosen to meet the individual needs of various members of a class. However, any book considered for use as a basic text should be readable by all those who are to use it.

Research (Burkey, 1954; Dunlap, 1951; Faison, 1951; Jones, 1954; Mallinson et al., 1950b; 1950a, 1952; Smith, 1954; Walchak, 1954; Wyatt and Ridgway, 1958) has shown that textbooks as well as other types of books are not always suited to the students for whom they are intended.

Simmons and Cox (1972) report that 74 percent of their seventh grade students were reading at a level too low to adequately comprehend their English text; on the eighth grade level, 59 percent; on the ninth grade level, 60 percent.

Johnson and Vardian (1973), in their analysis of sixty-eight social studies textbooks designed for grades one through six, found that most of the books were readable only by the above-average readers. Of the thirty-one textbooks recommended for grades four, five, and six, seventy-two of the ninety-three reading levels were above the designated grade level. Of the thirty-seven books for grades one, two, and three, forty-one of the seventy-four reading levels were at least one grade level above that recommended by the publisher.

Cline found that of 279 freshmen students in a mid-Missouri community college 50 percent could not read eleven of their seventeen textbooks. The readability of seven of the seventeen textbooks was above the reading ability of 75 percent of the students. The average reading ability of the students sampled was computed at 12.6.

Perhaps the fact that textbooks are frequently too difficult is not as significant as is the fact that in a developmental program the teacher must cope with *two* problems: the reading ability of each pupil and the readability of each book used. He dare not complacently use a "fifth-grade reader" for all fifth graders because not all fifth-grade readers are actually fifth grade in difficulty level, and not all fifth-grade children have fifth-grade reading skill.

Studies suggest that, typically, textbooks may be more "readable" in the upper- than in the lower-elementary grades. However, Chall (1958, p. 132) points out that some formulas may lead to higher estimates of difficulty at the primary level than are warranted because they are not specifically designed for that level. For example, the Flesch formula does not discriminate below the fifth grade and the Lorge formula does not do so below the third grade.

Measuring Readability

In using the term readability we are assuming that it is possible to equate the reader and the reading material. We know that it is desirable to do so. We assume that there are identifiable and measurable factors that make reading materials too difficult or too easy to meet the needs and abilities of a given child.

One approach to the study of the readability of books is to ask teachers or librarians to rate books according to difficulty (Russell and Merrill, 1951). This has been tried and has been found to be inadequate. Teachers and librarians have not been found to be proficient in designating the grade-level for which a given book is written. Jongsma (1972) found a great variation in estimates of readability level by librarians, sometimes from three to nine grade levels. It is doubtful that teachers have a greater degree of accuracy in picking the right book for the individual youngster.

Another approach was made by Vogel and Washburne (1928). They surveyed 37,000 children and developed the Winnetka Graded Book List. This list contained 700 books that children from the second to the eleventh grade claimed to have read and enjoyed. The grade placement of each book was found by determining the average reading ability of the children who read and enjoyed the book.

Teachers frequently use a similar technique. In helping children choose books, they select books somewhat below the pupil's estimated level of reading ability. They obtain a rough estimate of the appropriateness of a book by having the child read orally. They choose two or three selections of 100 words each from the book for the pupil to read, noting the errors as the child reads orally. If he misses more than five words out of a hundred or has less than 85 to 95 percent comprehension, the child is directed to another book.

A third approach is to develop and apply a readability formula to the book. Generally, the authors of these formulas have attempted to identify the factors that make materials difficult to read, even though it may be an impossible task to assess all the factors which affect readability. The factors most agreed upon are vocabulary, or some aspect of word difficulty, usually frequency (Klare, 1968), some aspect of sentence difficulty, usually length, and the number of prepositional phrases. Miller and Hintzman (1975) found that overall sentence length was a valuable estimator of the syntactic complexity as measured by the Syntactic Complexity Formula. Of these, the two linguistic features which have the highest predictability seem to be word difficulty and sentence length (Klare,

1963). Hunt (1966), however, found that clause length may be a better index of language maturity than sentence level or number of subordinate clauses. He notes that when writers build up long clauses, the reader must break them down.

Readability Formulas

We are interested in readability formulas for a number of reasons. We recognize that reading is a chief tool for learning. We know that there is a relationship between the readability of instructional materials and frustrations shown by pupils in reading situations. Teachers have found vast discrepancies between grade scores achieved on standardized tests and the ability to read instructional materials (Betts, 1949). We have seen that not all books with the same grade-level designation are equally readable; we have felt, for one thing, the need to control the vocabulary load of books, especially in the elementary grades. We have become aware that books that are readable are read and that improved readability leads to better retention, better recall, and to more economical reading speed (Klare et al., 1955, 1957).

Lively and Pressey (1923) made what may have been the earliest attempt to secure an objective estimate of the vocabulary difficulties of textbooks. Betts (1949), however, points out that the graded McGuffey readers, in about 1840, aroused professional interest in readability. Since 1923, more than thirty different formulas have been devised to measure the readability of printed materials. The best known of the early studies of readability is that developed by Vogel and Washburne (1928). As we already noted, they surveyed 37,000 children and published the Winnetka Graded Book List. Vogel and Washburne also developed a readability formula by analyzing 150 of these books. They identified ten factors which, in their opinion, determined the relative difficulty of reading materials. However, in a revision of the formula in 1938 (Washburne and Morphett, 1938) they retained but three of the factors: (1) Number of different words in a sample of 1,000 words; (2) Number of words (including duplicates) per 1,000 that were not in Thorndike's most common 1,500 words; and (3) Number of simple sentences in 75 sample sentences. Although some formulas have used this same general approach, others have emphasized different factors. For example, the Lorge formula (Lorge, 1944) is based on (1) average sentence length; (2) the number of prepositional phrases; and (3) vocabulary. The Yoakam formula (Yoakam, 1951) estimates vocabulary difficulty only. The Dale-Chall formula (1948b) considers both average sentence length and vocabulary. Flesch's 1943 formula (1948) was based on average sentence length, the relative number of words with prefixes, suffixes, and inflectional endings, and the number of personal references.[3] Spache (1953), noting that none of the three leading formulas (Flesch, Lorge, and Dale-Chall) is applicable

---

[3] Personal references are names of persons, personal pronouns, and nouns such as mother, uncle, friend, people, lady, and child.

for pupils reading below fourth-grade level, has proposed a formula for primary reading materials. His formula emphasizes vocabulary difficulty and sentence length. He suggests that for the primary grades sentence length may be a more significant determinant of readability than it is in the upper grades.

Betts (1949) suggests that the major determinants of readability are the average number of words per sentence, the number of simple sentences, the number of prepositional phrases, the percentage of different words, the number of uncommon words, the number of words beginning with certain letters, the number of polysyllabic words, and the number of adjectives, adverbs, personal pronouns, and other words having a personal reference. He concludes that easy-to-read material generally has the following charactersitics: personal references, a high percentage of common words, and short sentences. On the other hand, difficult material contains many uncommon words, different words, polysyllabic words, prepositional phrases, and complex and lengthy sentences.

Dale and Tyler (1934) found that among adults of limited ability the following four factors were closely associated with comprehension difficulties: the number of different technical terms, the number of those non-technical terms known to but 10 per cent of sixth-grade pupils, the number of prepositional phrases, and, oddly enough, the number of words beginning with "i." Sochor (1954) has suggested that the difficulty of materials depends largely on the number and unusualness of the facts that are presented, the vocabulary or terminology that is used to present them, and the context or language setting in which they are presented.

Peterson (1954, pp. 4–5), after reviewing the research on readability, suggests that the following factors deserve further study.

1. Density, or quantity of facts presented in a limited space.
2. Degree of directness with which ideas are presented.
3. Interest appeal.
4. Difficulties of ideas caused by remoteness of ideas from reader's experience and by lack of explanation.
5. Abstractness of treatment.
6. Use of verbal or pictorial illustrations.
7. Patterns of organization.

Bernstein (1955) found that the more interesting story is read with greater comprehension. There is also some evidence that comprehension is best when the reading material is well-organized. Robinson (1961, pp. 14–16) found that comprehension was better when a paragraph contained topic headings, questions, enumerations, and summaries.

Wilson (1944) reports that intermediate-grade children comprehend better when explanatory material is included in a reading selection. Longer versions of the same articles lead to better comprehension even though the same statements that are in the shorter versions are retained. The children seem to find the longer versions more interesting and they are able to discuss the content more logically.

The teachers, librarians, and publishers who took part in the Gray and Leary (1935) study deemed style, format, organization, and the reader's interest in the content most significant determinants of readability. Halbert (1944) reports that when the text is illustrated by pictures (improved format), children comprehend better.

As we examine the readability formulas and the factors on which they are based, it appears that readability generally is a function of the following factors:

1. Word length.
2. Percentage of different words.
3. Sentence length.
4. Personal references.[4]
5. Number of syllables.
6. Number of pronouns.
7. Number of affixes.
8. Number of prepositional phrases.
9. Number of difficult words according to word lists.
10. The use of simple or complex sentences.
11. Density and unusualness of the facts.
12. Number of pictorial illustrations.
13. Interest and purpose.
14. Concept load—abstractness of words.
15. Organization of the material and format.
16. Interrelationship of the ideas.

The goal in developing readability formulas is to get the highest degree of prediction while having to deal with the smallest number of factors. Thus, although the abstractness of the words, the organization and format of the materials, the interest and purposes of the reader, and the experience background of the reader influence the readability of materials, these elements have not been incorporated into readability formulas.

Estes and Vaughan (1973) support the idea that interest is as potent a factor in comprehension as is difficulty of the material.

Vocabulary seems to be the most significant determinant of reading comprehension. Materials are more easily understood when there are few different words than when there are many. They are more difficult when they contain words that call for concepts that are strange and rare. Hittelman (1973), however, points out that using word difficulty as a

---

[4] Flesch (1948) uses this in his formula. He found a correlation of .27 between the number of "personal sentences" and comprehension. And Engelman (1936) reported that children (particularly girls) definitely preferred conversational to expositional types of narrative.

means of judging the readability of a passage is questionable. Researchers who used word lists or formulas for controlling vocabulary difficulty in revised passages report no significant differences in the performance of the subjects between their original and altered versions.

There also is a complicating factor in attempting to determine vocabulary difficulty. The ordinary meaning of a word may be easily understood, yet in certain usages the word calls for unusual, and thus difficult, meanings. For example, dog, cow, run, and fall have common meanings but also frequently demand uncommon interpretations.

Readability formulas certainly have not explored the full implications of diversities within the vocabulary. That it is an important consideration is readily apparent. For example, Bachmann (1944) studied the various meanings of relatively common words found in two books chosen from the Juvenile Department of a city library. She concluded that the word *made* was used to designate twenty-five relatively distinct concepts and that *close* was used for twenty separate meanings. Among words used for ten or more meanings were: bear, time, end, way, give, command and light.

Sentence structure is another factor frequently related to the comprehensibility of the material. Furthermore, sentence length and the number of simple sentences as compared with the number of complex sentences must be considered. The number of phrases and clauses seems to be related positively to the ideational loading of the sentences, and thus is related to difficulty of reading material. Easy materials generally contain short, simple sentences or clauses with few prepositional phrases. However Blue (1964), investigating whether a passage could be made more readable by simplifying vocabulary and shortening sentences, found no difference between students' ability to understand the so-called easier passaage and the original passage.

Glazer (1974) notes that recent research has shown that almost all language elements correlate with difficulty of printed materials. The Botel, Dawkins, Granowsky Syntactic Complexity Formula assesses the effect of each syntactic element of language. Glazer's study suggests that sentence length can be considered a good indication of difficulty because most sentences that are long in fact are syntactically complex (include noun modifiers, dependent clauses, nominalized verbs, deletions in coordinate clauses, appositives, etc.). Kaiser et al. (1975), noting that until the advent of the Syntactic Complexity Formula, the only syntactic measure incorporated into reading formulas had been sentence length, report that even when the sentence length is held constant, there is still a great deal of variability between passages of primary reading materials in terms of syntactic complexity.

There are indications that the more verbs and nouns in the sentence, the harder materials are to comprehend. Chall (1958, p. 47) also points out that personal pronouns, proper names, and colorful words are related positively to ease of comprehension, but they add little to the overall prediction of reading difficulty obtainable through other measures.

Evaluation of Readability Formulas

Readability formulas are difficult to evaluate. Tibbetts (1973), notes that perhaps we are expecting readability formulas to do too much. Manzo (1970) notes that readability formulas do not consider purpose of the reader and interest and there is no measure of idea load and esthetic differences.

It is even more difficult to compare readability formulas because they have different bases and generally are intended for use only with specific materials. Formulas that have been used most widely are those of Flesch (1948), Dale-Chall (1948a), Lorge (1944), Yoakam (1951), and Spache (1953, 1974).[5] Formulas have been proposed by many others, including Gray-Leary (1935), Wheeler-Smith (1954), Washburne-Morphett (1938), and Dale-Tyler (1934).

The Flesch formula appears to be used primarily with adult, the Dale-Chall and Yoakam formulas with middle- and upper-grade, and the Spache and Wheeler formulas with primary materials. The Wilkinson and Lewerenz formulas also are used with primary-level materials, but are quite time-consuming in application. Hildreth (1958, p. 374) suggested that the Washburne-Vogel formula remained the formula most valid for rating reading materials of elementary-school level. A simplification of the Revised Lorge Readability Formula is reported in the *Journal of Educational Research* 61 (1968): 398–400.

Williams (1972) provides a table for rapid determination of the Revised Dale-Chall Readability Scores. Other formulas mentioned today are the Gunnings Fog Index, McLaughlin's Smog Formulas, and the Syntactic Complexity Formula. (Botel, Dawkins, Granowsky, 1972.)

Granowsky and Botel (1974) note that sentence length as measured by the number of words used does not provide a reliable indication of the grammatical make-up and the complexity of a sentence. The Syntactic Complexity Formula is an attempt to deal with this inadequacy.

Although readability formulas generally emphasize similar factors, they alone cannot give a complete measurement of readability. Lorge (1949) cautions that they tell us nothing about the kind of ideas expressed or the interrelationships among them. Dale and Chall (1949) say that the readability formulas do not directly measure conceptual difficulty, organization, or abstractness of subject matter, though these factors are known to affect comprehensibility.

Readability formulas are not a panacea for meeting comprehension problems. They frequently yield different results and fail to measure many elements considered important for readability. However, they are useful in giving a relative estimate of the difficulty of books, in determining the sequence to be followed in recommending books to a child, and in detecting the difficult words and sentences in the book (Chall, 1954).

---

[5] See Lou E. Burmeister, "A Chart for the New Spache Formula," *The Reading Teacher* 29 (1976): 384–85.

Each teacher should become familiar with the formula that is designed for reading materials on the level that he is teaching. He will be better prepared to put the right book in the right hands at the right time. The pupil profits greatly. If he understands what he reads, he will be more interested, will read more rapidly, will retain it better, and will be less frustrated.

Developed by Wilson Taylor (1954) in 1953 the cloze procedure is the most recent trend in measuring readability (Kingston and Weaver, 1967; Weintraub, 1968). This technique comes from the Gestalt concept of closure and involves the deletion of every *n*th word in a selection and the evaluation of the success a reader has in supplying the deleted words. It is assumed that the individual's score is an index of his ability to comprehend reading matter. Bormuth (1965, 1966, 1967a, 1967b) feels that the cloze tests are reliable and valid predictors of the comprehension difficulties of a passage and furthermore that they have an advantage in that they permit computerization.

Bickley, Ellington, and Bickley (1970) concluded from their analysis that the cloze procedure appeared to be a valid measure of specific reading comprehension. Hafner (1964) used the cloze procedure to identify the student who tends to use information not near the blank. He noted that the poor reader "apparently does not take advantage of the structure of the material." It is suggested that the student who does not use the information to complete the blank may be deficient in ability to reason.

Louthan (1965) found that when articles and possessive or other pronouns were deleted from a passage that subjects received better comprehension scores. The explanation is offered that deleting such noun determiners forces the reader to be unusually aware of the noun. Perhaps the attention of poor readers should be focused on the meaning-bearing words—nouns, verbs, and specific modifiers (Hafner, 1966). It is possible of course that missing words can frequently be identified without an understanding of the passage. Thus cloze tests may be measures of language redundancy rather than of comprehension (Weaver and Kingston, 1963). Teachers can improve the readability of materials by adding illustrative and explanatory materials in lectures, discussion, and written materials (Hafner, 1966).

Other studies have shown a high correlation (.73, .69, .72) between word deletion tests and test of intelligence. Hafner (1964) reported that poorer readers in college as measured by cloze procedures were less rapid workers on the cloze task, were less able to use contextural clues to meaning, were less intelligent and less knowledgeable, and were less able to reason well than the better readers.

The style of the author is another determiner of performance on cloze tests (Bormuth and McDonald, 1965). It might be profitable for the literature teacher to vary approaches to different authors and various works of literature.

Because cloze tests with deleted content words (nouns, verbs, and adjectives) were found to be significantly more difficult than the cloze tests with every *n*th word deleted (Hittelman, 1971), Hittelman (1973) concluded that the cloze procedure may measure only an entity within the surface features of the reading passage and these measurements are only partly representative of those factors which determine readability.

Chall (1958, pp. 156–158) drew the following generalizations from the research: (1) A variety of factors contribute to reading difficulty. (2) Thus far, only stylistic elements have been amenable to quantitative measurement: namely, vocabulary load, sentence structure, idea density, and human interest. (3) Of the four types of stylistic elements, vocabulary load (diversity and difficulty) is most significantly related to difficulty. (4) Almost every study reports a significant relationship between sentence structure and comprehension difficulty. However, once a vocabulary measure is included in a prediction formula, sentence structure does not add very much to the prediction. (5) Readability formulas measure idea intensity only indirectly through the percentage of prepositional phrases and, less often, through the percentage of different content words. Prepositional phrases add little to the overall prediction of difficulty, once vocabulary and sentence structure are included in a formula. (6) Human interest has been measured by the number of personal pronouns, persons' names, and nouns denoting gender and by the number of personal sentences—dialogue and sentences addressed to the reader. These measures add little to a readability formula, once vocabulary difficulty and sentence structure are used.

Hittelman (1973) suggests that readability is a moment at which the reader's emotional, cognitive, and linguistic backgrounds (the reader's characteristics) interact with the topic, with the purposes for reading, and with the author's choice of semantic and syntactic structures. Readability, so perceived, is not an absolute entity inherent within a passage and measured by a scale or index, but it is rather a relative concept.

The effect on readability of the reader's purpose has been amply demonstrated. Concerns about concept load and concept difficulty (which is closely related to the experiential background of the reader), cognitive capacity, cognitive orientation, and interest have been frequently voiced. Semantic elements have been investigated more aggressively in the last ten years. Amster (1967) found that an unknown word is easier to know in a "good" contextual setting. However, very little research has been done on the effect of word connotations and idiomatic expressions on the readability of passages.

It has generally been found that the closer the patterns of language structure in written materials approximate the child's oral patterns, the easier the material is to read (Ruddell, 1965; Tatham, 1970). Ruddell used cloze procedures with fourth graders. Smith (1971) found a correspondence between the reader's level of syntactic maturity and the syntactic level of the material. Stoodt (1972) reported a significant relationship between reading comprehension and the comprehension of conjunctions and Robinson and Hittelman (1973) found that irrelevant or extraneous details and examples confuse the reader.

LEGIBILITY

Although comprehension is of primary importance, efficiency in reading is worthy of attention. The mature reader not only is a comprehending reader; he comprehends at a satisfactory rate. Legibility of materials is a major determinant of reading efficiency and ease.

Legibility refers to the physical appearance of the printed materials. It involves such factors as line length, type size, style of type face, space between lines and between letters, margins, and physical format. Closely related to legibility are certain visibility factors. Among these are color of print, color and finish of the paper, and the contrast between the print and the paper. In a sense the visibility factors form the "setting" for the legibility factors. Legibility and visibility are determinants of the ease and speed with which the sensory phase of the reading act may be accomplished. Thus they reflect the relative suitability of printed materials for reading.

Some Vocabulary Terms

The reports of studies on legibility and visibility contain a number of special vocabulary terms employed in typography. To understand the reports we need to know the meaning of some of these terms. The printer has certain special units of measurement. His unit for measuring type height is the *point* which is approximately one seventy-second of an inch. Though faces (styles) of type vary in boldness and design, the type size is measured in points based on the height of the letter from the top of the highest ascender to the bottom of the lowest descender.

The *pica*, which is equivalent to 12 typographical points (or one-sixth of an inch) is used as a measurement for line width. The term *pica* is used also to designate twelve-point type.

The *spacing of type* may refer to space between letters, words, or lines. *Leading* refers to the space that may be placed between lines of print. One-point leading would be one seventy-second of an inch. Spaces between lines normally appear larger than their actual leading measurements would indicate because the type line itself is high enough to accommodate ascenders and descenders even though they may be infrequent.

Space between letters is dependent on several factors: type size, line length, the syllabification of the words to be set in type, and the means used for setting the type. Hand-set type uses spacers of blank type termed *em quad* (a square of the point size of the type) or smaller spacers such as *en quad* (same height as em quad but half as wide). These spacers, and other still narrower ones, permit equated spacing between words and letters within a line of print. Automatically-set type utilizes wedge-shaped spacebands to adjust the spacing.

Experimental Procedure

Before we consider the factors governing the legibility of printed materials, let us examine some of the experimental procedures used for studying legibility and the closely related problems of visibility and illumination. In any experiment a major task is to hold constant all factors except the one being studied. Thus if one wishes to determine the relative legibility of various type sizes, other aspects of legibility and visibility such as distance between lines (leading), length of line, style and boldness of type, and color and finish of the paper, usually will be kept the same. And, of course, the difficulty (readability) of the materials being compared must be held constant.

One experimental procedure is the distance method. The assumption in using this procedure is that the relative legibility of different printed materials may be determined by the distance at which they can be read. Another procedure is to use reading rate as the criterion. When this method is used those materials which can be read at the most rapid rate are considered most legible. A third approach uses rate of blinking as the criterion of legibility.

Another approach is to use accuracy of reading as the gauge of legibility. The fewer the number of errors made, the more legible the materials are judged to be. The tachistoscope presenting two or three words or four to eight letters during a very short exposure, perhaps one-hundredth of a second, has been used to study legibility. Still another procedure is to photograph eye movements. The assumption here is that, with the more legible materials, the reader will make fewer fixations and regressions and shorter pauses.

Evaluations of Experimental Procedure

Each procedure has had its advocates. Unfortunately, different results often are obtained by using different experimental methods. For example typewritten materials rank high in legibility when the distance method is used but rank low when studied by the method of comparative rate of reading.

While this has something to do with the particular problems of the typewriter mechanism and the equidistant letter-spacing peculiar to it, to an extent it illustrates a difference between legibility and visibility and points to a weakness in the distance method for studying legibility. Larger type or type of the same size but with additional leading and linear spacing between the letters may be visible at greater distances and yet is not necessarily more legible at ordinary reading distances. Paterson and Tinker (1940) point out that when using about a three-inch line, type sizes ranging from eight to twelve point were about equally legible although the twelve-point type certainly would be much more visible.

Obviously in choosing materials for our students to read, we are concerned with legibility under typical classroom conditions. Thus the tests of legibility using reading rate for actual classroom-type materials, relative absence of fatigue, and accuracy of reading, seem to be closer to classroom conditions than do methods using a distance technique or a tachistoscope. We are particularly concerned that the materials chosen continue to be legible after prolonged reading and are not merely "see-able" under the short intensive effort that may be typical of some laboratory procedures.

With these points in mind let us examine some of the evidence concerning legibility factors.

Kinds of Type

Considerable interest has been shown in the legibility of various type faces. Probably the teacher's major interest will be in readability of materials. However, he should have enough knowledge of the determinants of legibility so that he makes his choice of readable materials from those that also rank high in legibility. And perhaps the furthest he can expect to go in his concern for legibility is to be aware that the type should be of an appropriate size and that each letter should be clear, definitely distinguishable from each other letter, and not too different in form from that with which the child is likely to be most familiar. In short, he will wish to choose plain rather than fancy type—type that is easy to read rather than stylized or "arty."

However, some of the studies of legibility of type are worth considering. Tinker (1952) reports that italic type results in about a three per cent reduction in speed when compared with roman print. Paterson and Tinker (1940, p. 16ff) report that typewritten type reduces speed by about five per cent when compared with ordinary book type and that capital letters (upper case) require about twelve per cent more time to read than do lower case letters. They also found that students prefer to read lower case rather than upper case letters and prefer a lightface to a boldface type.

Type Size

One of the determinants of legibility is type size. Paterson and Tinker (1940, p. 148) conclude that most adult readers prefer an eleven-point type, with ten-, twelve-, nine-, and eight-point types next in order of preference. Russell (1949, p. 76), however, notes that, whereas adults do prefer ten- to twelve-point type, children read best with fourteen- to eighteen-point type.

In general it has been observed that as the size of type is either increased or decreased from the optimum, more eye fixations per line are required, the fixation pause becomes longer, and there are more regressions. It may be that the disruption in eye movements accompanying the smaller type is primarily a result of reduced visibility. On the other hand the larger type may be less readable because a lesser number of characters can be seen at normal reading distance during each fixation.

Studies (McNamara et al., 1953; Tinker, 1959) indicate that speed of reading is not a valid criterion for determining the effect of type sizes on reading ease below the fourth-grade level. Speed is not an important characteristic of reading at this stage. The pupil is concerned more with the recognition and interpretation of what he reads. Marks (1966) found that type size and face did alter reading competency; color, double spacing, and underlining did not. The best evidence indicates that the type size should be between fourteen and eighteen points in grade one, between twelve and fourteen points in grades two and three, and between ten and twelve points in the upper grades (Tinker, 1959). Too large or too small type results in more fixations, more regressions, and a smaller perception span (Tinker, 1955).

Spacing

As noted earlier, there are several aspects of spacing that are related to legibility—spacing between letters, words, lines (leading), and paragraphs. Probably the most commonly studied is leading.

Leading increased above the zero point improves legibility and promotes speed of reading. However, optimum leading depends on the type size used and the length of the line. It also depends somewhat on the style of the type (the length of the ascenders and descenders and the height differences between upper and lower case letters vary with type style). Additional leading between paragraphs generally is considered an aid to legibility. It helps break visual monotony and points up the introduction of new ideas. The recommended spacing between paragraphs is that it be from two to four points greater than the lines within the paragraph (Hymes, 1958, p. 79). Generally a two-point leading is used with adult materials. Most preprimers use approximately a twelve point leading. Tinker (1959) recommends a four to six point leading in grade one, a three to four point leading in grade two, and a two to three point leading in grades three and four.

The addition of spacing between letters in a word normally will not improve legibility. However, titles or other material composed of upper case letters, and material set in large-sized lower case letters, are made more legible by adding some space. Generally, the space between words should be about the same as the apparent space between the lines.

Length of Line

Tinker and Paterson (1949), experimenting with twenty college students, found that very short or very long lines of print resulted in longer fixation pauses and less words read per fixation. There were fewer regressions with short lines than with long lines. The long lines made it more difficult to make the proper return sweep. On the other hand short lines necessitate more return sweeps and lead to "choppy" reading partly because the eye is unable to make effective use of peripheral vision.

Experimenting with ten-point type with two-point leading, Paterson and Tinker (1940, p. 148) report that line lengths of from 2½ inches to 5

1/16 inches were equally good. Tinker and Paterson (1946) also state that for eight-point type, an eighteen-pica line with one- or two-point leading is optimal. In a study (Tinker and Paterson, 1949) using nine-point type they found that for college students the optimal line length was from fourteen to thirty picas with one to four points leading.

Hymes (1958, p. 87) says that line length must depend on size of type and that a line should contain about forty characters.

In Table 11-1 we have summarized Tinker's (1959) recommendations for primary reading materials.

Adult readers generally prefer lines from about seventeen to twenty-eight picas in length.

Illumination

Authorities differ somewhat in the levels of illumination that they suggest. Russell (1949, pp. 75–76) says that for efficient work in ordinary reading lighting of from 15 to 20 foot-candles[6] is required, whereas Luckiesh and Moss (1937, p. 345) recommend 20 to 50 foot-candles for ordinary reading and 50 to 100 foot-candles for difficult reading.

Tinker (1939a, p. 13), in a summary of numerous studies, points out that there is a rapid rise in acuity up to about 5 foot-candles. From 5 foot-candles on, the rise in acuity becomes slower and reaches a maximum at about 20 foot-candles. The improvement in visual acuity from about 15 foot-candles to higher intensities is scarcely noticeable.

Rose and Rostas (1946) found that for college students increased illumination does not necessarily lead to better comprehension or to a more rapid rate of reading. They concluded that so long as there is sufficient light to distinguish print (2 or 3 foot-candles), illumination seems to be one of the least important determinants of reading efficiency. They add, however, that even though they do not affect reading effi-

TABLE 11-1 *Recommended Type Sizes, Leading, and Line Widths for the Primary Grades and Above*

	GRADE 1	GRADE 2 AND GRADE 3	GRADE 4 AND ABOVE
Size of Type	14-18 point	12-14 points	10-12 points
Leading	4-6 point	3-4 points	2 points
Line Width	19-20 picas	19-22 picas	19-24 picas

[6]One foot-candle is the amount of illumination produced by a one-inch-thick candle measured at a distance of one foot. The amount (intensity) of light on a surface depends upon candle power and the distance from source of light to the receiving surface. It varies inversely with the square of the distance from source to surface. If candle power is 100 and distance is 10 feet the intensity is 1 foot-candle. That is, 100 (candle power) divided by 10 × 10 (square of distance) equals 1 foot-candle.

A hundred-watt bulb usually gives an illumination of about 100 foot-candles one foot away; 25 foot-candles, two feet away; and approximately 11 foot-candles three feet away.

ciency, such low intensities as 2 to 3 foot-candles should not be used because they lead to poor postural habits. Tinker (1939b, p. 571) suggests that with ten-point type an intensity of from 10 to 15 foot-candles is sufficient for ordinary reading conditions, with the critical level of illumination being about 3 foot-candles. Speed of reading is not increased and clearness of seeing (fatigue) after two hours reading is not significantly changed when the intensity is raised about 3.1 foot-candles.

Contrast

Illumination is merely a means to an end. The letters receive as much light as does the paper. They are made visible because of the difference in the amount of light that they reflect to the reader. Thus black letters reflect only about one-fortieth as much light as does the white paper (Luckiesh and Moss, 1937, p. 306). Various studies (Taylor, 1934; Tinker and Paterson, 1931) have shown that black print on a light background is a good combination for ease of readability. Generally a white paper with a slight tint of gray or cream is recommended (Russell, 1949, p. 76). Tinker (1958) points out that the brightness contrast between the ink and the paper, rather than the specific colors of the ink and paper, determine the legibility of printed material.

Interacting Effects

As was mentioned earlier, one difficulty in determining the relative effect of certain factors on legibility is that one factor may depend upon another. For example, optimum spacing depends on size of type and length of line and optimum illumination depends on glossiness of paper and color of type. An experiment by Tinker has illustrated the dependence of one factor on another. He (1948) reports that neither eight-point type, italic type, nor as little as 3 foot-candles of illumination reduced speed of reading significantly but that when all three were combined, speed was reduced by about ten percent.

SUMMARY

This chapter has dealt with three related but somewhat distinct topics: *rate of comprehension, readability,* and the *legibility* of printed materials.

The term *readability* has been used in reference to those textual factors that either aid or hinder the understandability of reading materials. We have considered also the presentational or *legibility* factors that either promote or hinder reading. Sometimes these are referred to as elements in the "hygiene of reading."

The visibility factors form a "setting" for legibility. And to an extent legibility and visibility form a setting for readability. Legibility and visibility allow the sensory process to operate efficiently and thus form a basis for the perceptual process of comprehensibility or readability.

As we know, children generally come to school with a favorable attitude toward reading. They desire to learn to read. Because they are willing, they are easily stimulated. But this attitude is not enough to assure a persisting interest in reading. The best materials must be readable and legible if they are to prove satisfying to the reader.

QUESTIONS FOR DISCUSSION

---

1. What relationships commonly are found between *rate* and *comprehension?*
2. What methods are used to improve reading rate? What problems arise?
3. What conclusions can you form concerning the place of mechanical devices in reading programs or various grade levels?
4. Enumerate key factors that are positively related to speed of reading.
5. Give the pros and cons of machine and book-centered programs.
6. Differentiate between *skimming* and *scanning.*
7. Discuss:
   a. The mind, not vision, is generally the limiting factor in reading.
   b. The good reader reacts to ever-decreasing cues.
8. Relate readability of materials to comprehension and rate of comprehension.
9. Describe the cloze procedure and discuss its purposes.
10. What are the determinants of readability? of legibility? Which determinants are of most importance? Which are and which are not measurable?

BIBLIOGRAPHY

AMBLE, BRUCE R. "Reading by Phrases." *California Journal of Educational Research* 18 (1967): 116–24.

AMSTER, HARRIETT. "Two Processes of Concept Formation: Associative and Deductive." *Reading and Concept Attainment.* Newark, Del.: International Reading Association, (1967), pp. 15–33.

ANDREWS, JOE W. "An Approach to Speed Reading." *English Journal* 41 (1952): 352–56.

BACHMANN, HELEN MARIE. "A Semantic Study of the Books of Two Authors

Dealing with Classical Antiquity." *The Graduate School Abstracts of Theses* 40 (1944): 16–27. University of Pittsburgh, Bulletin No. 3.

BERNSTEIN, MARGERY R. "Relationship between Interest and Reading Comprehension." *Journal of Educational Research* 49 (1955): 283–88.

BETTS, EMMETT A. "Readability: Its Application to the Elementary School." *Journal of Educational Research* 42 (1949): 438–59.

BICKLEY, A. C.; ELLINGTON, BILLIE J.; and BICKLEY, RACHEL T. "The Cloze Procedure: A Conspectus." *Journal of Reading Behavior* 2 (1970): 232–49.

BLUE, LARRY L. "A Study of the Influence of Certain Factors in Science Materials on the Reading Comprehension of Seventh Grade Pupils." Unpublished doctoral dissertation, Indiana University, 1964.

BORMUTH, JOHN R. "Validities of Grammatical and Semantic Classification of Cloze Test Scores." In J. A. Figurel, ed., *Reading and Inquiry,* Proceedings of the International Reading Association Convention, 1965, pp. 283–86.

BORMUTH, JOHN R. "Readability: A New Approach." *Reading Research Quarterly* 1 (1966): 79–132.

BORMUTH, JOHN R. "Comparable Cloze and Multiple-Choice Comprehension Test Scores." *Journal of Reading* 10 (1967a): 291–99.

BORMUTH, JOHN R. "Designs of Readability Research." In J. A. Figurel, ed., *Vistas in Reading,* Proceedings of the International Reading Association Convention, 1967, pp. 485–89.

BORMUTH, J. R. and MACDONALD, O. L. "Cloze Test as a Measure of Ability to Detect Literary Style." *Reading and Inquiry,* International Reading Association Conference Proceedings, Vol. 10 (1965): 287–90.

BOTEL, MORTON and GRANOWSKY, ALVIN. "A Formula for Measuring Syntactic Complexity: A Directional Effort." *Elementary English* 49 (1972): 513–16.

BRAAM, LEONARD. "Developing and Measuring Flexibility in Reading." *The Reading Teacher* 16 (1963): 247–54.

BURKEY, JACOB E. "The Readability Levels of Recently Published Elementary Science Textbooks." Unpublished doctoral thesis, University of Pittsburgh, 1954; *Dissertation Abstracts,* 145 (1954): 1328.

BUSWELL, GUY T. "The Relationship Between Rate of Thinking and Rate of Reading." *School Review* 59 (1951): 339–46.

CALFEE, ROBERT C. and JAMESON, PENNY. "Visual Search and Reading." *Journal of Educational Psychology* 62 (1971): 501–5.

CARLSON, THORSTEN R. "The Relationship Between Speed and Accuracy of Comprehension." *Journal of Educational Research* 42 (1949): 500–12.

CHALL, JEANNE S. "The Measurement of Readability," *Readability: Finding Readable Material for Children,* Tenth Annual Conference on Reading, University of Pittsburgh, 1954, pp. 26–37.

CHALL, JEANNE S. "Locating, Introducing and Using Easy-to-Read, High-Interest Reading Matter." *Reading in Action,* International Reading Association, Conference Proceedings. New York: Scholastic Magazines, 1957, pp. 54–57.

CHALL, JEANNE S. *Readability: An Appraisal of Research and Application.* Bureau of Educational Research Monographs, Ohio State University, No. 34, 1958.

CLINE, TERRY A. "A Comparison of the Readability of Community College Textbooks with the Readability of Students Who Use Them." Mountain States Community College Consortium, Boulder.

COLE, GEORGE K., JR. "Adult Reading Clinic." *Library Journal* 82 (1957): 497–500.

COSPER, RUSSELL and KEPHART, NEWELL C. "Retention of Reading Skills." *Journal of Educational Research* 49 (1955): 211–16.

DALE, EDGAR and CHALL, JEANNE S. "A Formula for Predicting Readability." *Educational Research Bulletin,* Ohio State University 27 (1948): 11–20.

DALE, EDGAR and CHALL, JEANNE S. "The Concept of Readability." *Elementary English* 26 (1949a): 19–26.

DALE, EDGAR and CHALL, JEANNE S. "Techniques for Selecting and Writing Readable Materials." *Elementary English* 26 (1949b): 250–58.

DALE, EDGAR and TYLER, RALPH W. "A Study of the Factors Influencing the Difficulty of Reading Materials for Adults of Limited Reading Ability." *The Library Quarterly* 4 (1934): 384–412.

DEARBORN, WALTER F. "Motivation Versus 'Control' in Remedial Reading." *Education* 59 (1938): 1–6.

DECHANT, EMERALD. "Rate of Comprehension: Needed Research." In J. Allen Figurel, ed., *Changing Concepts of Reading Instruction,* International Reading Association Conference Proceedings, Vol. 6. New York: Scholastic Magazines, 1961, pp. 223–25.

DUNLAP, CAROLYN C. "Readability of Newspaper Items and of Basic Reading Material." *Elementary School Journal* 5 (1951): 499–501.

EDL, *Report on Reading Instrument Usage,* EDL Newsletter No. 19. Huntington, N.Y.: Educational Developmental Laboratories.

ESTES, THOMAS H. and VAUGHAN, JOSEPH L., JR. "Reading Interest and Comprehension: Implications." *The Reading Teacher* 27 (1973): 149–53.

FAISON, EDMUND, W. J. "Readability of Children's Textbooks." *Journal of Educational Psychology* 42 (1951): 43–51.

FINK, AUGUST A. "The Effects of Tachistoscopic Training in Digit Perception on Eye Movements in Reading." Unpublished doctoral dissertation, Columbia University, 1956; *Dissertation Abstracts* 162 (1956): 1289.

FLESCH, RUDOLF. "A New Readability Yardstick." *Journal of Applied Psychology* 32 (1948): 221–33.

FLETCHER, J. EUGENE. "Rapid Reading Perception, and the Tachistoscope." *College of Educational Record,* University of Washington, 25 (1959): 52–55.

GATES, ARTHUR I. "Teaching Reading." *What Research Says to the Teacher.* Washington, D.C.: Department of Classroom Teachers, and American Educational Research Association for the National Education Association, 1953.

GLAZER, SUSAN MANDEL. "Is Sentence Length a Valid Measure of Difficulty in Reading Formulas?" *The Reading Teacher* 27 (1974): 464–68.

GRANOWSKY, ALVIN and BOTEL, MORTON. "Background for a New Syntactic Complexity Formula." *The Reading Teacher* 28 (1974): 31–35.

GRAY, WILLIAM S. and LEARY, B. E. *What Makes a Book Readable.* Chicago: University of Chicago Press, 1935.

GRAY, LILLIAN and REESE, DORA. *Teaching Children to Read.* New York: Ronald Press, 1957.

GRAYUM, HELEN S. *An Analytic Description of Skimming: Its Purposes and Place as an Ability in Reading.* Studies in Education, Indiana University, 1952.

HAFNER, LAWRENCE E. "Relationships of Various Measures to the Cloze." *New Concepts in College-Adult Reading.* Milwaukee: National Reading Conference, 1964, pp. 135–45.

HAFNER, LAWRENCE E. "Cloze Procedure." *Journal of Reading* 9 (1966): 415–21.

HALBERT, MARIE GOODWIN. "The Teaching Value of Illustrated Books." *American School Board Journal* 108 (1944): 43–44.

HARRIS, ALBERT J. *How to Increase Reading Ability,* 3rd edition. New York: Longmans, Green and Company, 1956.

HARRIS, ALBERT J. "Research on Some Aspects of Comprehension: Rate, Flexibility and Study Skills." *Journal of Reading* 1 (1968): 205–10, 258–60.

HILDRETH, GERTRUDE. *Teaching Reading.* New York: Holt, Rinehart and Winston, 1958.

HITTELMAN, DANIEL R. "The Readability of Subject Matter Material Rewritten on the Basis of Students' Oral Reading Miscues." Unpublished Doctoral Dissertation, Hofstra University, 1971.

HITTELMAN, DANIEL R. "Seeking a Psycholinguistic Definition of Readability." *The Reading Teacher* 26 (1973): 783–89.

HORN, ERNEST. *Methods of Instruction in the Social Studies.* New York: Charles Scribner's Sons, 1937.

HUNT, KELLOGG W. "Recent Measures in Syntactic Development." *Elementary English* 43 (1966): 732–39.

HYMES, DAVID. *Production in Advertising and the Graphic Arts.* New York: Holt, Rinehart and Winston, 1958.

JOHNSON, ROGER E. and VARDIAN, EILEEN B. "Reading, Readability and Social Studies." *The Reading Teacher* 26 (1973): 483–88.

JONES, HAROLD. "Readability and the Results of Applying a Readability Formula to Health Textbooks." *Readability: Finding Readable Material for Children,* Tenth Annual Conference on Reading, University of Pittsburgh, 1954, pp. 56–66.

JONES, NELLIE F. "A 'Motorized' Reading Project." *The English Journal* 40 (1951): 313–19.

JONGSMA, EUGENE A. "The Difficulty of Children's Books: Librarians' Judgment Versus Formula Estimates." *Elementary English* 49 (1972): 20–26.

KAISER, ROBERT A.; NEILS, C. F.; and FLORIANI, B. P. "Syntactic Complexity of Primary Grade Reading Materials: A Preliminary Look." *The Reading Teacher* 29 (1975): 262–66.

KATZ, LEONARD and WICKLUND, DAVID A. "Word Scanning Rate for Good and Poor Readers." *Journal of Educational Psychology* 62 (1971): 138–40.

KINGSTON, ALBERT J. and WEAVER, WENDELL W. "Recent Developments in Readability Appraisal." *Journal of Reading* 11 (1967): 44–47.

KLARE, GEORGE R.; MABRY, JAMES E.; and GUSTAFSON, LEVARL M. "The Relationship of Style Difficulty to Immediate Retention and to Acceptability of Technical Material." *Journal of Educational Psychology* 46 (1955): 287–95.

KLARE, GEORGE R.; SHUFORD, E. H.; and NICKOLS, WILLIAM H. "The Relationship of Style Difficulty, Practice, and Ability to Efficiency of Reading and to Retention." *Journal of Applied Psychology* 4 (1957): 222–26.

KLARE, G. R. *The Measurement of Readability.* Ames, Iowa: Iowa State University Press, 1963.

KLARE, GEORGE R. "The Role of Word Frequency in Readability." *Elementary English* 45 (1968): 12–22.

LABMEIER, ANGELA M. and VOCKELL, EDWARD L. "A Reading Development Course." *Reading Horizons* 13 (1973): 64–71.

LANIGAN, MARY A. "The Effectiveness of the Otis, the A.C.E. and the Minnesota

Speed of Reading Tests for Predicting Success in College." *Journal of Educational Research* 41 (1947): 289–96.

LIVELY, BERTHA A., and PRESSEY, S. L. "A Method for Measuring the 'Vocabulary Burden' of Textbooks." *Educational Administration and Supervision* 9 (1923): 389–98.

LORGE, IRVING. "Predicting Readability." *Teachers College Record* 45 (1944): 404–19.

LORGE, IRVING. "Readability Formulae: An Evaluation." *Elementary English* 26 (1949): 86–95.

LOUTHAN, V. "Some Systematic Grammatical Deletions and Their Effects on Reading Comprehension." *English Journal* 54 (1965): 295–99.

LUCKIESH, MATTHEW and MOSS, FRANK K. *The Science of Seeing.* New York: Van Nostrand, 1937.

MALLINSON, GEORGE G.; STURM, HAROLD E.; and MALLINSON, LOIS M. "The Reading Difficulty of Textbooks in Junior High School Science." *School Review* 58 (1950): 536–40.

MALLINSON, GEORGE G.; STURM, HAROLD E.; and MALLINSON, LOIS M. "The Reading Difficulty of Textbooks for High School Physics." *Science Education* 36 (1952): 19–23.

MALLINSON, GEORGE G.; STURM, HAROLD E.; and PATTON, ROBERT E. "The Reading Difficulty of Textbooks in Elementary Science." *Elementary School Journal* 50 (1950): 460–63.

MANZO, ANTHONY V. "Readability: A Postscript." *Elementary English* 47 (1970): 962.

MARKS, MERLE B. "Improve Reading Through Better Format." *Journal of Educational Research* 60 (1966): 147–51.

MARVEL, JOHN. "Acquisition and Retention of Reading Performance on Two Response Dimensions as Related to Set and Tachistoscopic Training." *Journal of Educational Research* 52 (1959): 232–37.

MATHEWS, JOHN W. "Some Sour Notes on Speed Reading," *Journal of Reading* 9 (1966): 179–181, 185.

MAXWELL, MARTHA J. and MUELLER, ARTHUR C. "Relative Effectiveness of Techniques and Placebo Conditions in Changing Reading Rates." *Journal of Reading* 11 (1967): 184–91.

MCNAMARA, WALTER J.; PATERSON, DONALD G.; and TINKER, MILES A. "The Influence of Size of Type on Speed of Reading in the Primary Grades." *Sight Saving Review* 23 (1953): 28–33.

MILLER, JOHN W. and HINTZMAN, CHARLES A. "Syntactic Complexity of Newberry Award Winning Books." *The Reading Teacher* 28 (1975): 750–56.

MILLS, LLOYD. "The Functions of the Eyes in the Acquisition of an Education." *Journal of the American Medical Association* 93 (1929): 841–45.

MORTON, JOHN. "The Effects of Context Upon Speed Reading, Eye Movement and Eye-Voice Span." *Quarterly Journal of Experimental Psychology* 16 (1964): 340–54.

MULLINS, CECIL J., and MOWRY, H. W. "How Long Does Reading Improvement Last?" *Personnel Journal* 32 (1954): 416–17.

PATERSON, DONALD G. and TINKER, MILES A. *How to Make Type Readable.* New York: Harper and Brothers, 1940.

PATERSON, DONALD G. and TINKER, MILES A. "The Effect of Typography Upon the Perceptual Span in Reading." *American Journal of Psychology* 60 (1947): 388–96.

PAUK, WALTER. "On Scholarship: Advice to High School Students." *The Reading Teacher* (November, 1963): 73–78.

PETERSON, ELEANOR M. *Aspects of Readability in the Social Studies*. New York: Bureau of Publications, Teachers College, Columbia University, 1954.

REED, JAMES C. "Some Effects of Short Term Training in Reading Under Conditions of Controlled Motivation." *Journal of Educational Psychology* 47 (1956): 257–64.

RENSHAW, SAMUEL. "The Visual Perception and Reproduction of Forms by Tachistoscopic Methods." *Journal of Psychology* 20 (1945): 217–32.

ROBINSON, FRANCIS P. *Effective Study*, Revised edition. New York: Harper and Brothers, 1961.

ROBINSON, FRANCIS P. "The Tachistoscope as a Measure of Reading Perception." *American Journal of Psychology* 46 (1934): 132–35.

ROBINSON, FRANCIS P. "An Aid for Improving Reading Rate." *Journal of Educational Research* 27 (1934): 453–55.

ROBINSON, H. ALAN and HITTELMAN, DANIEL R. *Readability of High School Text Before and After Revision*. Washington, D.C.: United States Office of Education, 1973.

ROSE, FLORENCE C. and ROSTAS, STEVEN M. "The Effect of Illumination on Reading Rate and Comprehension of College Students." *Journal of Educational Psychology* 37 (1946): 279–92.

ROSE, LYNDON. "The Reading Process and Some Research Implications," *Journal of Reading* 13 (1969): 25–28.

RUDDELL, R. B. "The Effect of Oral and Written Patterns of Language Structure on Reading Comprehension." *The Reading Teacher* 18 (1965): 270–75.

RUSSELL, DAVID H. *Children Learn to Read*. Boston: Ginn and Company, 1949.

RUSSELL, DAVID H. and MERRILL, ANNE F. "Children's Librarians Rate the Difficulty of Well Known Juvenile Books." *Elementary English* 28 (1951): 263–68.

SHORES, J. HARLAN and HUSBANDS, KENNETH L. "Are Fast Readers the Best Readers?" *Elementary English* 27 (1950): 52–57.

SHORES, J. HARLAN. "Dimensions of Reading Speed and Comprehension." *Elementary English* 45 (1968): 23–28, 43.

SIMMONS, JOHN S. and COX, JUANITA. "New Grammar Texts for Secondary Schools: How Do They Read?" *Journal of Reading* 15 (1972): 280–85.

SMITH, HENRY P. and TATE, THEODORE R. "Improvements in Reading Rate and Comprehension of Subjects Training with the Tachistoscope." *Journal of Educational Psychology* 44 (1953): 176–84.

SMITH, HELEN K. "The Development of Effective, Flexible Readers." *Proceedings of the Annual Reading Conference*. Chicago: University of Chicago Press, 1965, pp. 159–68.

SMITH, RUTH I. "Readability of Social Studies Books and Materials." *Readability: Finding Readable Material for Children*, Tenth Annual Conference on Reading, University of Pittsburgh, 1954, pp. 18–25.

SMITH, WILLIAM. "The Effect of Transformed Syntactical Structures on Reading." *Language, Reading and the Communication Process*. Newark, Del.: International Reading Association, 1971.

SOCHOR, ELONA E. "Readiness and the Development of Reading Ability at All School Levels." *Education* 74 (1954): 555–60.

SPACHE, GEORGE. "A New Readability Formula for Primary-Grade Reading Materials." *Elementary School Journal* 53 (1953): 410–13.

SPACHE, GEORGE D. "A Rationale for Mechanical Methods of Improving Reading." *Significant Elements in College and Adult Reading Improvement,* Seventh Yearbook of the National Reading Conference, Texas Christian University Press, Fort Worth, 1958, pp. 115–32.

SPACHE, GEORGE D. "The Spache Readability Formula." *Good Reading for Poor Readers.* Champaign, Ill.: Garrard Publishing Company, 1974.

STEINACHER, RICHARD. "Reading Flexibility: Dilemma and Solution." *Journal of Reading* 15 (1971): 143–50.

STOODT, BARBARA D. "The Relationship Between Understanding Grammatical Conjunctions and Reading Comprehension." *Elementary English* 49 (1972): 502–4.

SUTHERLAND, JEAN. "The Relationship Between Perceptual Span and Rate of Reading." *Journal of Educational Psychology* 37 (1946): 373–80.

TATHAM, SUSAN M. "Reading Comprehension of Materials Written With Select Oral Language Patterns: A Study at Grades Two and Four." *Reading Research Quarterly* 5 (1970): 402–26.

TAYLOR, CORNELIA D. "The Relative Legibility of Black and White Print." *Journal of Educational Psychology* 25 (1934): 561–78.

TAYLOR, EARL A. "The Spans: Perception, Apprehension, and Recognition." *American Journal of Opthalmology* 44 (1957): 501–7.

TAYLOR, STANFORD E. *Speed Reading vs. Improved Reading Efficiency.* Huntington, N.Y.: Educational Developmental Laboratories, 1962.

TAYLOR, STANFORD E. and FRACKENPOHL, HELEN. *Teacher's Guide: Tach-X Flash-X.* Huntington, N.Y.: Educational Developmental Laboratories, 1960a.

TAYLOR, STANFORD E., and FRACKENPOHL, HELEN. *Teacher's Guide: Controlled Reader,* Huntington, N.Y.: Educational Developmental Laboratories, 1960b.

TAYLOR, STANFORD E. and FRACKENPOHL, HELEN, *EDL Skimmer,* Huntington, N.Y.: Educational Developmental Laboratories, 1961.

TAYLOR, W. L. "Application of Cloze and Entropy Measures to the Study of Contextual Constraint in Samples of Continuous Prose." Unpublished doctoral dissertation, University of Illinois, 1954.

THURSTONE, L. L. *A Factorial Study of Perception.* Chicago: University of Chicago Press, 1944.

TIBBETTS, SYLVIA LEE. "How Much Should We Expect Readability Formulas to Do?" *Elementary English* 50 (1973): 75–76.

TINKER, MILES A. "Motor Efficiency of the Eye as a Factor in Reading." *Journal of Educational Psychology* 29 (1938): 167–74.

TINKER, MILES A. "Illumination Standards for Effective and Comfortable Vision." *Journal of Consulting Psychology* 3 (1939a): 11–20.

TINKER, MILES A. "The Effect of Illumination Intensities Upon Speed of Perception and Upon Fatigue in Reading." *Journal of Educational Psychology,* 30 (1939b): 561–71.

TINKER, MILES A. "Cumulative Effect of Marginal Conditions Upon Rate of Perception in Reading." *Journal of Applied Psychology* 32 (1948): 537–40.

TINKER, MILES A. "The Effect of Intensity of Illumination Upon Speed of Reading Six-Point Italic Print." *American Journal of Psychology* 65 (1952): 600–602.

TINKER, MILES A. "The Effect of Typographical Variations Upon Eye Movement in Reading." *Journal of Educational Research* 49 (1955): 171–84.

TINKER, MILES A. "Recent Studies of Eye Movements in Reading." *Psychological Bulletin* 55 (1958): 215–31.

TINKER, MILES A. "Print for Children's Textbooks." *Education* 80 (1959): 37–40.

TINKER, MILES A. "Devices to Improve Speed of Reading." *The Reading Teacher* 20 (1967): 605–9.

TINKER, MILES A. and PATERSON, DONALD G. "Studies of the Typographical Factors Influencing Speed of Reading: VII. Variations in Color of Print and Background. *Journal of Applied Psychology* 15 (1931): 471–79.

TINKER, MILES A. and PATERSON, DONALD G. "Effect of Line Width and Leading on Readability of Newspaper Type." *Journalism Quarterly* 23 (1946): 307–9.

TINKER, MILES A. and PATERSON, DONALD G. "Speed of Reading Nine Point Type in Relation to Line Width and Leading." *Journal of Applied Psychology* 33 (1949): 81–82.

VERNON, M. D. "The Improvement of Reading." *British Journal of Educational Psychology* 26 (1956): 85–93.

VOGEL, MABEL, and WASHBURNE, CARLETON. "An Objective Method of Determining Grade Placement of Children's Reading Material. *The Elementary School Journal* 28 (1928): 373–81.

WALCHAK, FRANK A. "Trends in the Readability of School Readers." *Readability: Finding Reading Material for Children.* Tenth Annual Conference on Reading, University of Pittsburgh, 1954, pp. 138–48.

WASHBURNE, CARLETON, and MORPHETT, MABEL VOGEL. "Grade Placement of Children's Books." *Elementary School Journal* 38 (1938): 355–64.

WEAVER, W. W. and KINGSTON, A. J. "A Factor Analysis of the Cloze Procedure and Other Measure of Reading and Language Ability." *Journal of Communication* 13 (1963): 252–61.

WEBER, C. O. "The Acquisition and Retention of Reading Skills by College Freshmen." *Journal of Educational Psychology* 30 (1939): 453–60.

WEBER, C. O. "Effects of Practice on the Perceptual Span for Letters." *Journal of General Psychology* 26 (1942): 347–51.

WEINTRAUB, SAMUEL. "The Cloze Procedure." *The Reading Teacher* 21 (1968): 567–71, 607.

WESTOVER, F. L. *Controlled Eye Movements Versus Practice Exercises in Reading.* Contributions to Education, No. 917, Bureau of Publications, Teachers College, Columbia University, 1946.

WHEELER, LESTER R. and SMITH, EDWIN H. "A Practical Readability Formula for the Classroom Teacher in the Primary Grades." *Elementary English* 31 (1954): 397–99.

WILLIAMS, ROBERT T. "A Table for Rapid Determination of Revised Dale-Chall Readability Scores." *The Reading Teacher* 26 (1972): 158–65.

WILSON, MARY CAROLINE. "The Effect of Amplifying Material Upon Comprehension." *Journal of Experimental Education* 13 (1944): 5–8.

WYATT, NITA M. and RIDGWAY, ROBERT W. "A Study of the Readability of Selected Social Studies Materials." *Bulletin of Education,* University of Kansas 12 (1958): 100–105.

YOAKAM, GERALD A. "Determining the Readability of Instructional Materials." *Current Problems of Reading Instruction,* Seventh Annual Conference on Reading, University of Pittsburgh, 1951, pp. 47–53.

12

Reading
in the Content Areas

In each content area[1] reading for learning requires certain specific skills. The teacher must know the unique reading demands of social studies, science, mathematics, and the language arts. Special problems are posed by the vocabulary, symbolism, and concepts of each area.

Although reading in each of the content areas requires certain specific skills, this by no means reduces the importance of the general reading skills. However, it does mean that as the child advances through the school grades, it becomes increasingly difficult for him to be weak in reading and strong in the content subjects. We should expect this to be true.

Good readers generally are more fortunate than poor readers in a number of ways. They have found reading interesting, they have good vocabularies, and, generally, they are of higher intelligence. These traits, as well as their better basic reading skills, should help them to become good readers in each content area. There is considerable evidence that this actually happens.

For example, Swenson (1942) has pointed out that there are far more similarities than differences between general reading abilities and ability to read scientific materials. And she has concluded that if a group of pupils is found to be high in ability to read scientific materials, it is almost certain that the group average will be high also in vocabulary, rate, and comprehension skills when they read either scientific or general materials.

Writers have sought to identify those general reading abilities that are needed in all content-area reading. These include the ability to interpret facts and data, to apprehend the main idea, to organize ideas, to draw conclusions, to appreciate the literary devices of the writer, to evaluate ideas for relevancy and authenticity, to interpret graphs and charts, to

[1]See Leo Fay, *Reading in the Content Fields: Annotated Bibliography,* International Reading Association, 1969.

follow directions, and to remember and use the ideas. In addition, students should be able to survey materials, choose appropriate reading techniques, and acquire a flexible reading rate.

The acid test of a reading program is the transferability of the learnings it provides to content areas. The goal has to be the infusion of reading skills instruction into every subject area where reading is a prime medium for learning (Early, 1969). Research shows that general reading ability alone is often not enough to assure reading improvement in content courses; the student must be equipped with special skills to meet his needs. And, he must be taught these skills.

The assumption in the recent literature has been that certain reading-study skills are nontransferable—that certain skills are peculiar to specific subject areas and are inappropriate to others. We have assumed that transfer occurs within subject areas but not from subject to subject. Even though Herber (1969) challenges this assumption, the evidence is such that it still seems wiser to distinguish between general reading skills that do transfer and those skills that do not.

At one time reading was considered to be a general ability applicable to any reading material, reading instruction occurred only in the reading class, often the first four elementary grades, and ability to read was measured by a general reading test. Today we realize that reading consists of many skills, reading comprehension in a given subject area can be broken down into many subskills and abilities, and the student might read exceptionally well in a given content area, but extremely poorly in another.

Content-area reading presents many problems. For example: Vocabulary in the content fields is usually more difficult; new terms are introduced faster and with fewer repetitions; more facts are presented to the reader; and greater retention and application are expected (Gray & Reese, 1957, p. 375).

Each reader's background of vocabulary and experience will vary from one content area to another. Consequently, in a given content area equally intelligent readers may greatly differ in readiness for reading. And each area possesses its own problems. Specialized vocabulary, maps, tables, graphs, abbreviations, indexes, diagrams, and footnotes are but a few of the new problems that the reader must deal with as he learns to read effectively in the content areas.

Studies have indicated that these specific demands of the content fields require special reading skills. Malter (1948) found that children in grades four to eight had difficulty with diagrammatic materials. Hansen (1943), comparing sixth-grade children who were superior in solving verbal arithmetic problems with sixth-grade children who were inferior in this skill, found that general language ability and the ability to read graphs, charts, and tables were most closely related to the ability to solve arithmetic problems.

In the content areas the emphasis is on *purposive* reading. The specific purpose for reading should determine both the degree of comprehension that is required and the rate at which the reading is done. A recognized purpose promotes concentration and attitudes favorable toward reading. "One of the bases for forming favorable attitudes toward reading is a perception of its inherent value" (Glock, 1958, p. 170).

The content-area teacher helps the child to develop his reading and study skills by formulating questions that require the application of specific comprehension skills. Sometimes it is desirable that the child get only the general import of a selection; at other times he needs to get its literal meaning. Sometimes he must make inferences and applications, see implications and connotations, or understand the specific meaning of a word in context (Lorge, 1957). Through appropriate questions, the skillful teacher encourages the child to form summary statements, examine the authority of the writer, and bring to light misconceptions or gaps in knowledge that should be remedied.

Teachers need to relate the teaching of reading to the teaching of a sensitive and accurate response to written materials. They need to differentiate between reading and the teaching of reading, between literature and the reading of literature.

KNOWLEDGE OF VOCABULARY AND CONCEPTS

Although an earlier chapter was devoted to vocabulary development, it may be apropos to outline vocabulary study in the content areas. The teacher cannot simply be satisfied with a student answer such as "I know what it means, but I can't really tell you." The student needs to develop exact meanings, and he must be able to translate these meanings into exact words.

That vocabulary development is particularly significant in content-area reading is hardly debatable. Words are "advance organizers" and provide cues to the structure of the materials. Ausübel (1960) noted that the learning and retention of unfamiliar, but nevertheless meaningful, verbal material can be facilitated by the advance introduction of relevant subsuming concepts. These concepts and the words that represent them help the learner to mobilize the most relevant existing concepts that the learner already possesses (past learning) and provide anchorage for the learning material (help him to organize).

The vocabulary is a distinct problem in each of the content areas. Thus, Stauffer (1966), comparing the vocabulary appearing in primary arithmetic, science, and health texts with the vocabulary of basal readers for grades one through three, found that 1331 words in arithmetic, 900 words in health, and 809 words in science did not appear in basal readers.

The following techniques are generally useful in developing vocabulary skills:

1. Arouse interest in word study by an experiment or a curiosity-arousing question.
2. Help students to become collectors of words—have them develop their own dictionary.
3. Require students to use the word.

4. Create opportunities for frequent contact with or review of the words.
5. Teach the skill of deriving meaning from the context.
6. Encourage frequent use of the dictionary.

COMPREHENSION IN A SPECIFIC CONTENT AREA

In the preceding chapters we have discussed numerous reading skills. We have emphasized the importance of grasping the main idea, of surveying materials, of choosing appropriate reading rates, of interpreting graphs, maps, charts, tables, and diagrams, of reading for a purpose, of organizing what one reads, of drawing inferences, and of retaining and applying what has been learned.

In the content areas, these and all the other reading skills are needed for successful comprehension. In addition, in the individual content areas each of these reading skills must be applied in a specific way.

Let us take a look at some of the major content areas, and let us attempt to identify some of the causes of reading difficulties.

Literature [2]

The goals in the teaching of literature are somewhat different from those of the other content areas. As our immediate goal we wish to have the child find that the reading act is rewarding so that for him reading becomes an end in itself rather than a means to an end. As an ultimate goal we wish to lead the child to enjoy literature. We hope that he will come to adopt reading as an important portion of his recreational program.

However, for greatest enjoyment, certain special skills, attitudes, and appreciations must first be learned. Thus in teaching literature, we teach it as a content area. We must teach the child the skills and approaches that will lead him to read for enlightenment and entertainment.

Gainsberg (1953) has suggested that the child must be taught to read literature *critically*[3] and that critical reading is *creative* reading. The reading of literature calls for an emotional involvement not generally demanded by other types of content-area reading. The effective reader is alert to shades of meaning and the interrelationships of details; he employs an active rather than a passive approach; he evaluates and questions as he reads; and his focus is less on what the author *says* than on what the author *means* by what he says.

The emotional and reading maturity of the reader will influence the depth of his understanding and appreciation of what he reads. Betts

[2]See J. W. McKay, "Developing Reading Skills Through Literature," *Reaching Children and Young People Through Literature*, Helen W. Painter, *ed.* International Reading Association, 1971, pp. 50–57.

[3]See Bernice D. Ellinger and Sister Mary Julia MacDougall, "Reading Literature Critically." *Critical Reading*, ed. by Martha L. King et al., J. B. Lippincott Company, 1967, pp. 301–12.

(1957, p. 494) says that ". . . the development, extension, and refinement of concepts is an important prerequisite to reading and a crucial outcome from reading." And it is well to remember that the appreciation of literature is much the same as the appreciation of all art forms—the more one knows of the techniques of any art, the more he will appreciate the art. Knapton and Evans (1967, p. 6) feel that "the best thing a work of literature . . . can do is to provide *the experience of itself as a work of art.*" Murphy (1968, p. 21) suggests that the reader of literature experiences the sense of order and order is the source of aesthetic literature. Shuman (1973) notes that literature develops an understanding of self and of the world about him.

Reading literature requires special appreciation of the mood and style of the author.[4] It requires the reader to respond to form, to connotative meanings, to rhyme, and to emotional overtones. It requires interpretative reading and emotional involvement. It requires the reader to deal with such literary forms as the sonnet, the essay, and the metaphor. The reader needs to read with his mind and with his emotions. He must find in literature splotches of the ever-flowing stream of human behavior and emotions. He must analyze the characters, appreciate the style, and digest the sequence of development (Tremonti and Algero, 1967). Reading literature requires literal understanding, analysis, appreciation, symbolic interpretation, and recognition of the relevance of literature to life (Petitt, 1967). Students need to go beyond mere passive acceptance of literal comprehension; they must do something with what they read (Simmons, 1965). They need to get involved. Reading includes not only word perception and comprehension but also reaction and assimilation. Literature is the basis for good reading instruction when it serves as a vehicle for critical insight and aesthetic revelation (Simmons, 1965).

Literature allows for identification between reader and character or with a particular group, assists in the solution of personal problems, reinforces views already held, teaches appreciation of beauty, and permits escape. Literature has effects that are personal and often original. The same passage may produce different effects at different times on the same student and different effects on different students.

Fiction is a biography of conflict in human motives (Maloney, 1959, pp. 211–13). It traces the conflict from its inception to its conclusion. Since motives are "within" the individual, the writer must "psychoanalyze" the fictional character, report what the character is saying to himself, use soliloquies or asides in which the character tells the audience what his motives are, or portray the character's motives through his appearance, speech, or action. The successful reader of literature must understand

---

[4]See Helene W. Hartley, "Teaching the Reading of Literature in the Elementary School," *Challenge and Experiment in Reading*, International Reading Association Conference Proceedings, 7 (1962), 43–45; J. W. McKay, "Developing Reading Skills through Literature," *Reading Children and Young People through Literature*, International Reading Association, 1971, pp. 50–57; Saul Bachner, "Teaching Reading and Literature to the Disadvantaged: Part II Theory: The Curriculum," *Journal of Reading* 18 (1974): 50–55.

these literary contrivances of the author and read between the lines for a comprehension of the basic meaning.

Each literary form has its own mode of expression. In *poetry* the writer communicates through words and concepts and also through tone, mood, repetition, rhythm, and rhyme. Poetry is literary work in metrical form. It is the art of rhythmical composition (Shapiro, 1969).

Poetry presents all kinds of grammatical and structural difficulties. The syntax is irregular; it is sometimes difficult to identify the verb; the juxtaposition of words for auditory and aesthetic effects is peculiar; and the writing is littered with irregular constructions. It is absolutely necessary to understand metaphors.

In reading *drama* it is necessary to understand the action and the setting. The latter is largely supplied by stage directions which break up the dialogue, making it more difficult to follow the sequence of events. The student must also learn to visualize various actions going on at the same time.

In *essays* the mood may take a formal, pedantic, humorous, satiric, philosophical, inspirational, persuasive, or political form. The *short story* presents its own literary contrivances. It is characterized by uniformity of tone and plot and by dramatic intensity.

To appreciate novels, short stories (Hynes, 1970), poems, and plays, the student must learn to analyze the elements of plot, characterization, style, and theme.

Plot. The student must learn to ask himself a series of questions. Did I like the ending? How would I have changed it? Did the writer use surprise, suspense, or mystery to keep me interested? What was the conflict or the major motive of the story? What are the time and place settings? Is it fanciful or realistic literature?

An exercise similar to the following teaches the student to appreciate plot:

Read the following sentences and select the word that best characterizes the plot:

1. We stood on the bridge not knowing whether to go forward, backward, or just remain where we were. In front of us and behind, the flood waters were rushing across the highway. Broken tree limbs, barrels, and household goods were floating by.

   This series of sentences indicates that the plot is based upon

   a. Surprise
   b. Suspense
   c. Adventure
   d. Intrigue

2. How wonderful it would be if the world were really at peace. There wouldn't be this constant distrust among all of us. People could intermingle freely. The fear of atomic destruction would disappear.

   This series of sentences indicates that the plot is

   a. Fanciful
   b. Realistic

Characterization. The student should ask: What character did I like best? Which one would I like to be? Were the characters true to life?

The student learns characterization skills by analyzing statements and answering certain questions about them. For example:

1. The man just sat. His eyes stared into empty space. No smile or grin ever adorned his face. When he spoke, it was about the wickedness of man and the burning fires of hell.

   This series of sentences describes a person who is probably

   a. Discontented with life
   b. Satisfied with life
   c. Successful in life
   d. Proud of living

2. The wrinkled old man with curved back was ambling toward the park. Behind him in droves came the pit-pat of little feet. Little ones and not-so-little ones were laughing and jumping trying to get his attention.

   This series of sentences describes an old man who

   a. Is discontented with life
   b. Enjoys the little things of life
   c. Has few friends
   d. Is considered an old fogy

Or, the teacher may require the student to underline one of three words that best characterizes the person described in key sentences. For example:

1. Jim grabbed Johnny by the shoulder and threw him against the wall. "That's for ratting on me."

   Jim is generous, unethical, brave.

2. Mary's eyes shot darts of fire at anyone who in the slightest way disagreed with her.

   Mary is rude, generous, opinionated.

Style. The student should ask: What was the writer's style? What is his distinctive manner of presentation? What figures of speech did he use? What was the general mood or tone of the writing?

Exercises such as the following may teach the student to read for style.

1. We were awakened by the sound of a man trying to break open the door. Quietly my father peered out of the window but there was only darkness. The noise continued. My father got his revolver from the closet and loaded it, and we advanced toward the door with trepidation.

   This series of sentences describes a set of circumstances characterized by

   a. Annoyance
   b. Dismay
   c. Fright
   d. Anger

2. Lori wiggled and crawled and splashed in the pool. It was her first outing for the summer, and what an occasion it was!

This series of sentences describes a little girl who is

a. Comfortable
b. Contented
c. Joyful
d. Successful

3. All afternoon Marie thought of what would happen when her father came home. She had just broken her father's pipe. Then the moment arrived. Dad was just pulling up his ashtray and said, "Honey, where is my pipe?"

This series of sentences describes a girl who is

a. Ashamed
b. Embarrassed
c. Guilty
d. Shy

Theme. The student should ask: What was the moral of the story? Which character best exemplified the morals and ideals of the writer? How do the morals and ideals portrayed fit with the reader's morals?

Social Studies

Reading in the social studies involves a special skill, and it is one that the student is obliged to use innumerable times.[5] The student must learn a new verbal vocabulary. He must be able to deal with detailed information in historical sequence and with cause-and-effect relationships. He must be able to organize materials, locate facts, interpret abstract ideas, and understand concepts of time, space, and chronological order. He must also learn to handle new symbols: maps, charts, diagrams, and graphs (Smith, 1964). And, he must be a *critical* reader.

Simmons (1965) equates critical reading with critical thinking and uses the description of Pingry (1951) to state the various aspects of critical thinking: (1) collecting data, organizing data, and formulating hypotheses from data; (2) use of correct principles of logic and understanding the nature of proof; (3) criticism of thinking; (4) understanding of the psychology of propaganda and advertising techniques; (5) problem solving.

Simmons then identifies the characteristics of critical reading. He notes that it is a skill involving cumulative comprehension (a student must understand, reorganize, and find the main idea of a selection, and in that order before critical reaction to it is possible); it includes the understanding of that which is explicit in the selection read and the use of higher

[5]For additional discussion see Paul A. Witty, "The Role of Reading in the Social Studies," *Elementary English,* 39 (1962): 562–69; also Helen Huus, "Antidote for Apathy —Acquiring Reading Skills for Social Studies." *Challenge and Experiment in Reading,* International Reading Association Conference Proceedings, 7 (1962): 81–88.

mental processes (certainly in the secondary school students must develop the ability to use and understand association, generalization, symbolic revelation, and the like); it can be contrasted with literal reading (critical reading goes beyond the passive acceptance of ideas and information stated in print); and it is the habit of examining printed statements and attacking problems in the light of related objective evidence.

Effective reading in the social studies presents three principal difficulties that require the development of specialized background and skills:

1. The vocabulary may be highly specialized and the reading material is likely to be heavily loaded with complex concepts.
2. The diagrammatic materials require considerable interpretive skill for their effective use.
3. The content frequently is emotionally loaded and controversial. A critical evaluation rather than blind acceptance is required.

In teaching the student to read social studies content one must begin with social studies materials. The teacher must know what specific skills to teach and how they should be taught.

Let us dwell on the *how:*

1. Call attention to the new words, duplicate them for the student, have the student consult the dictionary definition, use them in the appropriate context, give attention to root words and shades of meaning, use Latin derivatives and prefixes to increase vocabulary, pay special attention to words of foreign origin, and require students to use them in meaningful sentences (Christ, 1960).
2. Use films, charts, pictures, recordings, dramatizations, cartoons, models, exhibits, etc., to illustrate new concepts.
3. Teach students to comprehend social studies materials.
   a. Common words in social studies often take on technical meanings: gold rush, cold war, diet, raw materials, etc.
   b. Social studies textbooks are full of abstract terms: latitude, longitude, democracy, etc.
4. Require students to read for special purposes: to answer a question, to identify the cause, to locate a certain fact, to verify an opinion, to compare different points of view, and to adjust speed of reading to purpose and type of content.
   a. Teach the value of skimming in preparation of assignments.
   b. Encourage students to experiment with different rates for different materials and purposes.
   c. Require intensive SQ3R reading of textbook.
   d. Have those who experience difficulty understanding or retaining the material take notes or make an outline.
5. Teach students how to locate materials. Teach library usage, use of *Readers' Guide,* card catalog, and sources of social studies materials.
6. Provide numerous activities that stimulate critical thinking and analysis and that teach students to infer, to evaluate, and to integrate what they read.
   a. Discuss steps to follow in problem solving.

b. Teach students how to develop their own point of view.
c. Use the discussion method and require students to state their own opinions and how they arrive at them.
d. Use debate-type presentation of beliefs and supporting factual evidence to teach students how to collect and evaluate facts and how to relate facts to points in an outline (Christ, 1960).

7. Make assignments specific enough so the student will know how to read (Strang et al., 1961, p. 149). For example, the teacher may require the student to identify the author's point of view.

8. Test and constantly evaluate the student's proficiency in reading social studies materials (Strang et al., 1961, p. 147).
   a. Prepare a self-evaluation checklist, use class evaluation of oral and written reports, and evaluate the adequacy of outlines and summaries.
   b. Organize interrogation periods in which student leaders ask questions about material read and evaluate responses (Christ, 1960).

9. Teach students to perceive the organization of materials.
   a. Have them identify main idea-detail structure of writing.
   b. Have them find and understand the purpose of cue words, such as *furthermore, nevertheless, moreover, since, because.*
   c. Have students differentiate between chronological organization and fictional approach where events lead to a climax.
   d. Have them use the SQ3R approach.

Mathematics

Reading in mathematics requires the student to comprehend a new set of symbols.[6] He must react to numerical symbols that synthesize verbal symbols. He must be able to read *and* to compute. He must know both the individual and combined meanings of verbal symbols and mathematical signs. He must read deductively. He must translate formulas into significant relationships, and generally, he must read slowly.

Fay (1950), in a study in which he controlled chronological and mental age, found no differences in arithmetic achievement between good and poor readers. Lessenger (1925) analyzed errors on the Stanford Achievement Test to determine loss in arithmetic as a result of faulty reading. He found that among sixty-seven poor readers, the average loss was 10.1 months of arithmetic age. After one year of instruction in specific reading skills, the loss was all but eliminated. Russell (1960) also reported that the correlation between problem solving and general reading ability was relatively low. Hansen (1944) found that poor achievers were, on the average, faster readers. Balow (1964), after an analysis of this research, noted that whenever reading skill was important in problem-solving ability, each increase in reading ability might well be accompanied by an increase in problem-solving achievement. It might also require a minimum level of reading ability to do well in problem solving at any given grade level. Lyda and Duncan (1967) and Corle and Coulter (1964)

[6]*Academic Therapy* (Fall 1970) is entirely devoted to the teaching of and reading in mathematics. See also Calhoun C. Collier, and Lois A. Redmond, "Are You Teaching Kids to Read Mathematics?" *The Reading Teacher* 27 (1974): 804–808.

indicate that a pupil's success in mathematics is directly related to his ability to read. From his own study, involving fourteen hundred sixth graders, Balow concluded that general reading ability had an effect on problem-solving ability; that much of the degree of relationship between reading and problem-solving ability was the result of the high correlation of each of these factors with IQ; that computation ability did have a significant effect on problem-solving ability; and that one should consider children's reading ability as well as computation ability when teaching problem-solving skills.

In mathematics, comprehension is not limited to the understanding of a story. It is not even limited to the understanding of one experiment. One concept is built on another in mathematics and can have meaning only on the basis of the understood meaning of the former. In no other area is it more true than in mathematics that new learning depends upon previous learning.

Reading in mathematics also requires other rather diverse skills. Smith (1964) identified the following writing patterns in mathematical textbooks: classification, explanation of a technical process, instructions for an experiment, detailed statement of facts, descriptive problem solving, abbreviations and equations, mathematical problems, and various combinations of each of these. Such patterns point up the diverse reading task a student must be prepared to handle.

The student should early be introduced to the procedures involved in reading mathematics. Bond and Wagner (1950, p. 317) point out that the student must know what the problem calls for, what facts are needed for the solution, what steps are appropriate in leading to a solution, and what is the probable answer.

Coulter (1972) notes that arithmetic texts have a distinct style and format, emphasizing logical sequence of arithmetic skills and principles and non-story-type written exercises. Mathematic material is concise, abstract, and presents complex relationships. Moulder (1969) adds that mathematical materials have more ideas per line and per page than other writing. In mathematics every word is critical. Capoferi (1973) notes that the reader of mathematical materials must possess a verbal symbol vocabulary, a numerical symbol vocabulary, a literal symbol vocabulary, and an operational symbol vocabulary.

Aaron (1965) notes that the mathematics teacher must develop the mathematical vocabulary, teach the student to select appropriate rates for reading various materials, provide training in reading word problems, equations, charts, graphs, and tables, and develop skill in dealing with mathematical symbols and abbreviations.

Mathematics texts are full of technical terms: *addend, factor, exponent, isosceles, reciprocal.* Some of these terms are peculiar to mathematics; others are common words used with a different meaning: *axis, chord, cone, set.*

Because what the reader takes to the printed page determines in large measure what he gets from the page, the teacher of mathematics needs to provide students with the understandings and the prelearning necessary to read the mathematics textbook. He must be sure that the student has the necessary background to understand mathematical concepts. He needs to ascertain the student's readiness for the materials: Can he read the mathematical symbols? Can he read the graphs, tables, and diagrams which help to develop concepts?

In learning to read in mathematics, the student should do the following:

1. Read the problem quickly to get an overview.
2. Read for main ideas or the specific question asked.
3. Learn technical mathematical terms.
4. Read for organization, listing perhaps in one column the points given and in the second the points needed.
5. Translate the verbal symbols into mathematical symbols and formulas.
6. Read for relationships and translate these into an equation.
7. Analyze carefully all mathematical symbols and formulas.
8. Analyze carefully all graphs, figures, illustrations, etc.
9. Follow a definite procedure:
   a. Learn the meaning of all words.
   b. Find what the problem asks for.
   c. Decide what facts are needed to find a solution to the problem.
   d. Decide what mathematical process is required (addition, subtraction, etc.).
   e. Identify the order for solving the problem.
10. Make a drawing of the problem. A problem such as the following can be easily represented by a drawing:
    Harry has fifteen pictures. If he can paste three pictures on each page of his scrapbook, how many pages will be filled?
11. Study the contrast between the way words are used in mathematics and the way they are used in other areas.
12. Learn the proper symbols and abbreviations: ft. = foot; $7^3 = 343$.
13. Proceed slowly and be willing to reread.
14. Learn to follow directions.

Does direct instruction in reading help in mathematics? Call and Wiggin (1966) devised an experiment to answer this question. They concluded that teaching specialized mathematical reading-study skills had a definite effect on the ability to solve mathematical word problems. The experimental group did better even when reading abilities and mathematical aptitude were controlled. Their procedures are described in sufficient detail to permit replication.

Science

Reading in science requires the ability to follow a sequence of events.[7] It requires an orderly, systematic approach, including the ability to classify, categorize, and memorize (Tremonti and Algero, 1967).

[7]See Don H. Parker, "Developing Reading in a Science Program," *Challenge and Experiment in Reading*, International Reading Association Conference Proceedings, 7 (1962): 88–90.

Technical vocabulary must be mastered, formulas must be learned, and theory must be understood.

Directions become very important. The success of an experiment depends on the student's ability to follow directions. Reading in science, as in mathematics, is usually careful, analytical, and slow. It puts a premium on inductive reasoning and on detail. Every formula, chart, and graph is important. It demands a problem-solving approach similar to the steps of the scientific method. The student must learn to follow the scientist as he states the problem, enumerates the facts, formulates his hunch or hypothesis, investigates the facts to test the hypothesis, works toward his conclusion, and makes his verification. He must observe the facts, keep them in mind, relate them to each other, and determine whether or not they support a theory.

Difficulties encountered in problem solving (Davis, 1973) are due to: (1) Inability to read analytically in order to select details, locate and remember information, organize what is read, separate essential data from nonessential data, distinguish between what is known and what is unknown. (2) Failure to understand what is read because of lack of experience. (3) Lack of knowledge of quantitative relationships implied. (4) Lack of a basic understanding of the differences among and between the fundamental operations. (5) Inability to determine the reasonableness of the answer. (6) Inability to translate verbal statements into mathematical sentences. (7) Failure to see the relationship between reality and the situation in verbal problems.

Science reading is even more difficult because (Mallinson, 1960):

1. There is a tremendous growth of new vocabulary and an accelerated obsolescence of other vocabulary each year.
2. Science teaching suffers from lack of sequence, with great overlap between grade levels, and thus is not conducive to developing a sequence in reading skills from grade level to grade level.
3. Scientific ideas are becoming increasingly complex, and it is difficult to utilize a one-syllable word for a ten-syllable science concept.
4. Writers of science materials do not agree on what the readability level of books should be.
5. Many of the terms are mathematical.
6. Many common words are used in a special sense (force, body).
7. Statements are concise (laws, definitions, formulas).
8. Students must learn to deal with equations, formulas, scales, cross-section and longitudinal models, and flow charts.

The teaching method used may direct the student's reading approach. Boeck (1951), pp. 249–53) compared the learning of students taught by the "inductive-deductive" and by the "deductive-descriptive" method in nine high-school chemistry classes. The essential difference in the two methods as studied by Boeck was in the laboratory approach. The inductive-deductive method used the laboratory to gather data for solving previously identified problems. The results then were used to formulate a general principle. Learning progressed from the particular to the general. In the deductive-descriptive method, the laboratory work followed exercises in a published manual. The general principle to be illustrated was first discussed in class and the laboratory experiment then provided an illustration of the principle. Under the inductive-deductive method the student had an important part in planning the experiment and in forming generalizations after the experiment was completed.

Boeck concluded that the methods led to equal attainment in general outcomes, but that the inductive-deductive method was significantly superior in attaining knowledge of and ability in the use of the methods of science with an accompanying scientific attitude.

The low-ability student in science has the following added difficulties (Moore, 1962):

1. The textbooks in science, which often are too difficult even for the average or above-average reader, are especially handicapping to the slow learner.
2. Textbooks written for the slow learner do not match the junior high-school reader's interest and maturity.
3. Since appropriate texts are not available, and since the extension of the reader's vocabulary is secondary to the acquisition of science concepts, the teacher may have to prepare materials. The following guidelines might be helpful:
   a. Use simple, concrete, and familiar vocabulary.
   b. Use fewer different words.
   c. Use only one difficult word for every two hundred running words.
   d. Use short sentences.
   e. Provide repetition of ideas.
   f. Provide more cues in the way of details, more illustrative material.
   g. Use a readability formula to check the readability level of the materials.

Vocational Subjects
(Ferrerio, 1958; Levine, 1960)

There are few books that help the trade instructor with the problem of teaching students to read, and yet vocational students do need training in reading in trade subject areas. In general we would recommend that the language arts—listening, speaking, writing, and reading—all be intertwined in the study of a lesson. Only after a study and reading of the job sheet should the teacher move the student back to the text.

The student in vocational courses should be able to do the following:

1. Read job and instruction sheets.
2. Deal with the new vocabulary: *splice, junction, tap, tee, pigtail*, Western Union, *modulator, tailstock, keratin, lunula, pledget, sebum, bias wave, reverse roll, mortise, cat whisker, headstock, offset, inside caliper.*
3. Understand the directions, but also *act* them out—apply his knowledge.
4. Understand prints, charts, graphs.
5. Read the selection orally.
6. Understand the concepts shared.

7. Associate symbol with concrete referend.
8. Visualize the steps read about.

For a discussion of the teacher's role in the vocational classroom see: Johnston, Joyce D. "The Reading Teacher in the Vocational Classroom" *Journal of Reading* 18 (1974): 27–29.

THE TEACHER AND THE CONTENT AREAS

Most educators have accepted the position that reading in the content areas demands careful guidance. This may be provided through superivsed study, differential assignments, and the cultivation of the special reading skills required in the various content fields.

Fay (1952, pp. 39–40), in his nine point list, suggests, among other things, that the teacher plan with students the organization of the topics to be studied . . . that he organize instruction about broad topics or problems; that he give assignments that set purpose, that indicate specific methods of study, and that provide each student with material that he can read.

SUMMARY

Effective reading in the content areas demands all the general reading skills the student has been taught throughout the primary grades. However, each content-area course has its special vocabulary and concepts and requires its special reading skills.

The content-area teacher must assume full responsibility for teaching the special vocabulary, concepts, and reading skills required by his subject. To teach content effectively, he must teach reading effectively.

QUESTIONS FOR DISCUSSION

---

1. Apart from variations in the ability to read, what are the most important differences between good and poor readers?
2. Identify and discuss some of the specific skills needed for effective reading in general science, citizenship, world history, geography, and mathematics.
3. How may a teacher ensure that the child will acquire the skills he needs for content-area reading?
4. What special skills and attitudes are needed for critical reading?
5. How may critical reading be taught?
6. Show how the scientific method is used for solving problems outside the field of science.

7. What skills acquired during reading in the language arts are likely to make for better reading in the other content fields? And what skills acquired in other content fields contribute toward better reading in the language arts?
8. How do the goals of reading in the language arts differ from those of reading in other content fields?

BIBLIOGRAPHY

AARON, I. E. "Reading in Mathematics," *Journal of Reading* 8 (1965): 391–5, 401.

AUSÜBEL, D. "The Use of Advance Organizers in the Learning and Retention of Meaningful Verbal Material." *Journal of Educational Psychology* 51 (1960): 267–72.

BALOW, IRVING H. "Reading and Computation Ability as Determinants of Problem Solving." *The Arithmetic Teacher* 11 (1964): 18–22.

BETTS, EMMETT ALBERT. *Foundations of Reading Instruction.* New York: American Book Company, 1957.

BOECK, CLARENCE H. "The Inductive-Deductive Compared to the Deductive-Descriptive Approach to Laboratory Instruction in High School Chemistry." *Journal of Experimental Education* 19 (1951): 247–53.

BOND, G. L. and WAGNER, E. B. *Teaching the Child to Read,* revised edition. New York: Macmillan, 1950.

CALL, R. J. and WIGGIN, N. A. "Reading and Mathematics." *The Mathematics Teacher* 59 (1966): 149–57.

CAPOFERI, ALFRED. "The Mathematics Teacher Looks at Reading." *Mathematics in Michigan* 12 (1973): 4–11.

CHRIST, ALEX. "Reading Skills and Methods of Teaching Them," *Kansas Studies in Education* 10 (1960): 12.

CORLE, C. G. and COULTER, M. L. *The Reading Skills Program: A Research Project in Reading and Arithmetic.* University Park, Pennsylvania: The Pennsylvania School Study Council, 1964.

COULTER, MYRON L. "Reading in Mathematics: Classroom Implications." In James Laffey, ed., *Reading in the Content Areas.* Newark, Del.: International Reading Association, 1972.

DAVIS, ELAINE C. "Practice in Problem Solving." *Instructor* (April 1973): 82, 84–88.

EARLY, MARGARET J. "What Does Research in Reading Reveal About Successful Reading Programs?" *What We Know About High School Reading,* National Council of Teachers of English, 1969, pp. 40–53.

FAY, LEO C. "The Relationship Between Specific Reading Skills and Selected Areas of Sixth-Grade Achievement." *Journal of Educational Research* 43 (1950): 544–47.

FAY, LEO C. "Adjusting Learning Activities and Reading Materials to Individual Differences: In Grades Seven to Nine." *Improving Reading in All Curriculum Areas,* Supplementary Educational Monographs, No. 76. Chicago: University of Chicago Press, 1952, pp. 36–40.

FERRERIO, A. J. "Use of the Industrial Arts in the Remedial Reading Program." *High Points* 40 (1958): 58–61.

GAINSBERG, JOSEPH C. "Critical Reading is Creative Reading and Needs Creative Teaching." *The Reading Teacher* 6 (1953): 19–26.

GLOCK, MARVIN D. "Developing Clear Recognition of Pupil Purposes for Reading." *The Reading Teacher* 11 (1958): 165–70.

HANSEN, CARL W. "Factors Associated with Superior and Inferior Achievement in Problem Solving in Sixth-Grade Achievement." Unpublished doctoral dissertation, University of Minnesota, 1943.

HANSEN, CARL W. "Factors Associated with Successful Achievement in Problem Solving in Sixth Grade Arithmetic." *Journal of Educational Research* 38 (1944): 111–18.

HERBER, HAROLD L. "Study Skills: Reading to Develop, Remember, and Use Ideas." *Reading in the Content Area*. Syracuse, N.Y.: Syracuse University, 1969, pp. 13–21.

HYNES, SISTER NANCY. "Learning to Read Short Stories." *Journal of Reading* 13 (1970): 429–32.

KNAPTON, JAMES and EVANS, BERTRAND. *Teaching a Literature-Centered English Program*. New York: Random House, 1967.

LESSENGER, W. E. "Reading Difficulties in Arithmetical Computations." *Journal of Educational Research* 11 (1925): 287–91.

LEVINE, ISIDORE N. "Solving Reading Problems in Vocational Subjects." *High Points* 43 (1960): 10–27.

LORGE, IRVING. "Reading, Thinking, and Learning." *Reading in Action*, International Reading Association, Conference Proceedings. New York: Scholastic Magazines, 1957, pp. 15–18.

LYDA, W. J. and DUNCAN, F. M. "Quantitative Vocabulary and Problem Solving." *Arithmetic Teacher* (April, 1967): 289–91.

MALLINSON, GEORGE G. "Methods and Materials for Teaching Reading in Science." Reprinted from *Sequential Development of Reading Abilities*, Helen M. Robinson, editor, Supplementary Educational Monographs, No. 90. Chicago: University of Chicago Press, 1960, pp. 145–49.

MALTER, MORTON S. "Children's Ability to Read Diagrammatic Materials." *Elementary School Journal* 49 (1948): 98–102.

MALONEY, MARTIN. "The Writer's Itch (III): How to Write Obvious Lies." *Etc.: A Review of General Semantics* 17 (1959–1960): 209–16.

MOORE, ARNOLD J. "Science Instructional Materials for the Low-Ability Junior High-School Student." *School Science and Mathematics* 62 (1962): 556–63.

MOULDER, RICHARD H. "Reading in a Mathematics Class." In H. Alan Robinson and Ellen Lamar Thomas, eds.; *Fusing Reading Skills and Content*. Newark, Del.: International Reading Association, 1969.

MURPHY, GERALDINE. *The Study of Literature in High School*. Waltham, Mass.: Blaisdell Publishing Co., 1968.

PETITT, DOROTHY. "Reading Literature: An Act of Creation." *Vistas in Reading*. Newark, Del.: International Reading Association, 1967, pp. 176–81.

PINGRY, ROBERT E. "Critical Thinking—What Is It?" *The Mathematics Teacher* (November 1951): 466–67.

RUSSELL, DAVID H. "Arithmetic Power Through Reading." *Instruction in Arithme-*

tic, Twenty-fifth Yearbook, Chap. 9, pp. 211–12. Washington, D.C.: National Council of Teachers of Mathematics, 1960.

SHUMAN, R. BAIRD. "Values and the Teaching of Literature." *The Clearing House* 48 (1973): 232–38.

SHAPIRO, PHYLLIS P. "The Language of Poetry." *Elementary School Journal* 70 (1969): 130–34.

SIMMONS, JOHN S. "Reasoning Through Reading." *Journal of Reading* 8 (1965): 311–14.

SIMMONS, JOHN S. "Teaching Levels of Literal Understanding." *English Journal* 54 (1965): 101–2, 107, 129.

SMITH, NILA B. "Patterns of Writing in Different Subject Areas," Part I. *Journal of Reading* 8 (1964): 31–37; Part II, *Journal of Reading* 8 (1964): 97–102.

STAUFFER, R. G. "A Vocabulary Study Comparing Reading, Arithmetic, Health, and Science Tests." *The Reading Teacher* 20 (1966): 141–47.

STRANG, RUTH; MCCULLOUGH, CONSTANCE M.; and TRAXLER, ARTHUR E. *The Improvement of Reading.* New York: McGraw-Hill, 1961.

SWENSON, ESTHER J. "A Study of the Relationships Among Various Types of Reading Scores on General and Science Material." *Journal of Educational Research* 36 (1942): 81–90.

TREMONTI, JOSEPH B. and ALGERO, CELESTINE. "Reading and Study Habits in Content Areas." *Reading Improvement* 4 (1967): 54–57.

13

Providing for Individual Differences

Reading and the entire process of growth and development are interdependent. Differences among children of the same age in physical, social, emotional, and attitudinal development guarantee that we cannot successfully use a patent-medicine approach to teaching children to read. When we add to the problems generated by these divergences the tremendous problems stemming from differences in intellectual development, we see why the teaching of reading at all grade levels is so extremely complex and why we must make individual diagnoses and prescriptions for each child.

In this chapter we shall try to identify the bases of a reading program that interprets in practice the principles arising from a recognition that reading is both a *growth process* and a *developmental task*. This requires two steps: (1) We must identify the psychological principles underlying a developmental program; and (2) we must interpret and integrate these principles into educational applications.

Development, of course, is a function of both nature and nurture. The child is a product of these two interacting forces. Because of the vast differences among children in both nature and nurture, no two children at any time are identical in any given characteristic.

Development in reading closely parallels human development in general. It involves the child's *total growth*. A child's reading development is a product of his biology and his culture.

If we could divorce reading from other fundamental aspects of growth, we might hope to produce a standardized product (Olson, 1956). But this is not possible. For example, the range in achievement levels by the second grade is commonly about four grades. By the sixth grade this range may have increased to as much as seven grades (Bond and Tinker, 1957, p. 37). Sheldon (1956) reports that the reading levels of seventh-graders vary from the second to the eleventh grade.

Witty (1938) already noted that all high school teachers face the responsibility of adapting assignments to, of utilizing to a maximum, and of further developing the reading abilities of students who differ as much as six or eight grades in reading competence.

An analysis by a national advisory committee on dyslexia, entitled *Reading Disorders in the United States,* August 1969, published by the Department of Health, Education, and Welfare, gives the following statistics: (1) The National Center for Health Statistics reports in a study of seven thousand children between the ages of six and eleven that 25 percent of the eleven-year-olds read at levels two or more years below their grade level; (2) the norms on the *Metropolitan Achievement Test* indicate that the number of children who have not advanced beyond the primary level is 15 percent by the end of the fifth grade even among those who have never repeated a grade; and (3) a study in 1968 in Montgomery County, Maryland, a prosperous area with a well-supported school system, indicated that 13.3 percent of the children were underachievers in reading.

In the city of New York, 4,000 seventh graders were retained in 1958 because they were reading at or below fourth-grade level (Simmons, 1963, p. 5). Foster (1955) reports that in the Phoenix, Arizona, high schools, out of 1,106 entering freshmen tested, 21.4 percent had a reading ability of fifth grade or lower and 34 percent could not read at the seventh-grade level.

Furthermore, even among those who are reading at their level of ability, there are too many whose reading ability is not adequate for reading the textbook and the reference materials used on their grade level. It is said that at least three million young people in grades seven to twelve in America today are being given American literature, English literature, and World literature textbooks that they cannot read (Aukerman, 1965).

This tremendous range of achievement calls for a reading program that provides all children at all levels with the special reading skills they need. Obviously, a single-standard basal reading program fails to adjust to the wide variety of individual differences in reading development and reading needs. It is delimited by grade levels, although development is not and needs cannot be thus limited. Reading development is a life-long process. It is not completed with the ending of elementary school nor even with the ending of formal education.

Educators have come to accept that reading instruction and learning to read are lifelong, sequential, and developmental processes, extending from kindergarten through high school, college, and adult life. We expect gradual refinement of all skills (Summers, 1965). We look for both horizontal and vertical growth in word knowledge, comprehension, study skills, rate skills, content-area reading skills, and overall reading habits and interests. We have come to accept that direct teaching of reading skills must proceed in an unbroken line from first grade through twelfth, buttressed by the application of skills in every subject where reading is a significant means of learning (Early, 1964).

We now realize that not even the brightest youngster in the best of schools can learn all he needs to know about reading by the end of six or eight years of schooling (Davis, 1960). The reasons for this are readily apparent. First of all, as Einstein noted, "reading is the most complex task that man has ever devised for himself." Reading involves the interpreting of printed symbols and the making of discriminative reactions to the ideas expressed by them. Second, it is the experience of teacher after teacher that reading processes can be taught and learned only in the context of the ideas and the content of the reading materials themselves (Davis, 1960). Third, with the tremendous variety of knowledge that is being discovered and accumulated each day, we are literally "burning up" reading skills faster than we can develop them (Squire, 1965). It is rather preposterous to assume that by the time the pupil reaches sixth grade he has developed all the skills needed to assimilate the vast amount of knowledge taught at the high school level. Fourth, and perhaps of greatest significance, many students come to the secondary school with a definite lag in the development of their reading skills.

And yet, there exists today a noticeable void in the teaching of reading, after the elementary years. Squire (1965), surveying 158 high schools, found that in the tenth grade less than 5 percent of the instructional time was devoted to the teaching of reading and in the twelfth grade it was less than 3 percent. There is still far too little provision for developmental reading programs in the junior and senior high schools. We are still not helping enough students meet the more complex demands of the curriculum that they are being asked to master. Society requires adolescents to read so they may come to know and to learn, but we are not doing our best in helping them to master the developmental tasks necessary for such learning.

It is not enough for the subject-matter teacher to complain, "But he can't read." What is usually meant by such a statement is that the student cannot read *this* or *that* textbook with adequate understanding. The word *read* should always be used as a transitive verb. The student is not just reading; he is reading in a given area. As a little boy said, "You can't read readin', you gotta read sumpin' " (Jones, 1966).

One of the major characteristics of reading education in the late 1970s and 1980s may well be the witnessing of an organized extension of the developmental reading program into the secondary grades. More and more junior high and high school teachers are looking upon themselves not only as teachers of history or science but also as teachers of reading.

It is a safe estimate (see Figure 13-1) that at the ninth-grade level, in a classroom where IQs range from 85 to 145 and where the average age is 14, there will be roughly eight grade levels represented in that class. There will be some student who is capable of functioning mentally like the average youngster of 11.9, and there will be another who will function like the average youngster of 20 (college sophomore). About two-thirds of the group will have mental ages ranging from 11.9 to 16.1.

It is a well-known fact that the more effective the instruction on the elementary level, the greater will be the range of differences on the high school level. Thus, a chief reason for some of our problems on the high school level is the very fine education that many elementary school children are receiving.

The high school teacher is faced with the task of individualizing

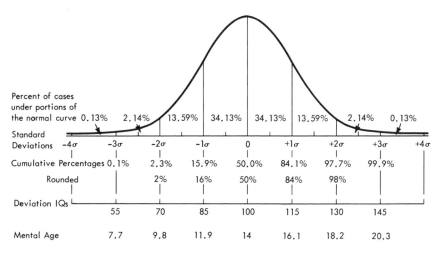

FIGURE 13–1

education for these youngsters without the benefit of multiple-level texts, often in covercrowded classrooms, in a school setting that does not have an organized reading program or a specific time set aside for the teaching of reading, with a student who often does not want to improve his reading, and more importantly without adequate preparation in reading. Crowded classrooms and inadequate materials are no less causes of educational inadequacies than is teacher ineffectiveness, and yet teachers and teaching methods have to bear the brunt of public attack.

Reading Programs, which must also come in for some criticism, are about "as different as the colors in Joseph's coat" (Mills, 1963). It would be desirable if we could say: "This is the way to organize the reading program," or "Here is the blueprint for an ideal program," but we are not that fortunate nor that omniscient. Nevertheless, there must be a *master* plan (Bradley, 1957, pp. 28–29). Without it, the special programs for developmental teaching are liable to be nothing more than a conglomerate of bits and pieces.

Today there are various innovative practices such as performance contracts by private industries, use of tutors, teacher aides, or other para-professionals, individualized instruction, programmed materials, and use of multimedia approaches and computers, but a good reading program cannot be lifted from a book or purchased from a commercial source (Otto and Smith, 1970, p. 33). It must be developed locally by a fully committed staff. Flashy hardware, shelves of material, and indeed specialized personnel do not make a good reading program. It is the product of the coordinated efforts of many people working over a long period of time (Otto and Smith, 1970, p. 119).

The problem is especially serious on the junior high-school level. After surveying and evaluating high school reading programs, Courtney

(1966) noted that 50 percent or less have reading programs and that most of these are essentially remedial or feebly developmental, usually voluntary, and unfortunately too often without strong administrative fiat, and yet there seems to be little doubt that the junior and senior high have need for both developmental and remedial programs. In this chapter our concern will be the developmental program. It reaches all students at each level of accomplishment. Its basic assumption is that reading improvement is a lifelong process. Let us now take a closer look at what constitutes a developmental program.

THE DEVELOPMENTAL PROGRAM

Otto and Smith (1970, pp. 28–29) have schematically described the developmental program. We concur with them that there is a single overall reading program consisting of several specialized forms of instruction.

Teachers need a clear understanding of the word *developmental*. Too often, developmental comes to mean a program essentially different from the remedial program. We do not like the term *remedial reading program*. Remediation along with diagnosis is an integral phase of the developmental program. Diagnosis and remediation must accompany all effective teaching. The developmental program is responsible for systematic reading instruction at all school levels. It includes developmental, corrective (Johnson, 1967), and remedial instruction. We use the term *corrective instruction of reading* to refer to situations in which remedial activities are carried on in the regular classroom. When the remediation occurs outside the regular classroom, we term it *remedial teaching*. It seems clear that in an ideal situation or some sort of educational utopia, where there would be no retardation, the concept of and need for remedial teaching might disappear.

Corrective instruction usually occurs in the regular classroom. If a special teacher is available, the student might be assigned to him several times a week for forty-five to sixty minutes.

Corrective instruction stresses sequential development in word attack and comprehension skills but uses special techniques and materials and concentrates on a particular reading deficiency. The corrective program is in addition to regular reading instruction.

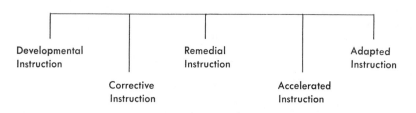

FIGURE 13-2 *The Developmental Program*

Remedial teaching, because of its expensiveness, is necessarily limited. It is a slow process, on a one-to-one basis or at most on the basis of one teacher to three to eight students. Because of the expenses involved, even when a special remedial teacher is available, it is probable that instruction will be individualized rather than strictly individual (Otto and McMenemy, 1966).

The school thus needs to limit the number of students that will find themselves in a remedial classroom. Some poor readers, and in this group belong slow learners reading up to their ability, reluctant readers, and disadvantaged readers, for the most part should be kept in the regular classroom. Some retarded readers need corrective reading but can still stay in the regular classroom. Only the severely retarded readers need to be taken out for full-time special instruction.

Remedial teaching or corrective teaching is not justified if it is not different from a regular reading instruction. The instruction needs to be on a broader basis. *The corrective or remedial teacher needs to be completely familiar with the skills to be taught at all levels. He must be able to telescope, as it were, the total reading program into a relatively brief period of instruction. He must appreciate and understand the continuity of the total reading program.*

Accelerated instruction provides for the needs of the bright and well-motivated learner. *Adapted* instruction is an adaption of pace and expectations to the limitations of the slow learner.

The ultimate aim of the reading program is achievement by each learner up to the limit of his abilities.

The focus of the reading program is upon each individual learner, not upon groups of learners or upon grade-level performance (Bradley, 1957, pp. 28–29). It is not what the group does that is important, nor even whether an individual measures up to grade level. The chief concern is that the individual learner do as well as he can.

General Principles of a Developmental Program

Various writers have attempted to identify basic principles that may guide teachers and supervisors as they strive to make the developmental program workable and effective. Here is a selection of principles on which there seems to be general agreement:

1. The developmental program coordinates reading with the pupil's other communicative experiences.
2. The developmental program is a continuous program extending through the elementary and secondary grades and college. It provides instruction and guidance in basic reading skills, both silent and oral, in content-area reading, in study skills, and in recreational-reading.
3. The developmental program is a flexible program that is adjusted at each level of advancement to the wide variations in pupil characteristics, abilities, and reading needs. Readiness for reading as a concept is applied at all age and grade levels.
4. The developmental program has a stimulating classroom setting in which

attitudes and interests favorable to the development of habitual reading are developed effectively.

5. The developmental program provides plentiful reading materials, basal readers, experience charts, films, film readers, etc. that cover a wide range of difficulty and interest.

6. The developmental program provides for continuous measurement and evaluation of the effectiveness of the program as a whole and of its more specific aspects.

7. The developmental program provides for continuous identification and immediate remediation of deficiencies and difficulties encountered by any pupil.

8. The developmental program includes differentiated instruction to meet the needs of each child, but it does not ignore the commonality of needs, interests, and abilities among children.

9. The developmental program looks upon reading as a perceptual process rather than as a subject. Reading is taught on all levels in all subject areas by all teachers.

10. The developmental program emphasizes reading for understanding, thinking and learning and aims to develop critical skills and flexibility in comprehension and rate in accordance with the pupil's abilities and purposes and the difficulty levels of the materials.

11. The developmental program allows each pupil to progress at his own success rate for his maximum capacity.

12. The developmental program seeks to develop reading maturity. A mature reader reads all kinds of materials. He perceives words quickly and accurately and reacts with correct meaning. He reads both for information and recreation. He gets personal satisfaction from reading. He is a skillful, self-reliant reader who enriches his understandings and satisfactions throughout his life by reading.

13. The developmental program, based on sequential instruction in the basic skills and upon the need for differentiated instruction, gives appropriate emphasis to the sight and phonic methods, to group and individualized instruction.

Specific Principles of any Reading Program

In this section we have tried to identify those principles that have a direct and practical effect or bearing on the development of a reading program in a given setting.

1. As we already mentioned, the most significant prerequisites seem to be administrative conviction, direction, and provision. The administrator alone possesses the prestige and persuasion to carry through a sound reading program (Courtney, 1966). He must encourage and insure that the reading philosophy is implemented in logical and innovative ways (Sanders, 1971). He needs to provide the impetus for defining the reading program's philosophy and must be the facilitator of that philosophy by extending it to the entire school. On the other hand, the administrator cannot turn on the reading program by a mere flick of a switch. The administrator does not accord reading the respect it deserves when he assumes that anyone can

teach reading and assigns reading classes to whatever teacher has a free period.

2. It must be clear why the program exists, and its purpose, goals, and objectives must be closely identified and stated behaviorally. There is only one goal of the reading program, and that is that each student read up to his ability level. The objectives must be explicitly defined in terms of student needs. The program must help each student to read as well as his abilities permit; his progress should not be gauged to the grade level in which he is.

3. The program should reflect the cooperation and involvement of the entire staff. Only in this way will teachers come to accept that "every teacher is a reading teacher." In the more successful programs a reading committee, composed of representatives of all areas of the curriculum, usually functions in the determination of the definition of reading, the philosophy of the program, and its implementation.

4. The program must be tailor-made for the school in which it is housed.

5. It should be clear whether the program will be a separate entity or perhaps on the junior-high, high school level have subdepartmental status within the English or counseling departments.

6. The staff needs to exhibit competency in reading. The staff must be well trained. They must be able to teach reading skills in a logical, structured fashion.

7. Facilities, materials, and equipment must be adequate. They should vary in type, in interest, and in range of ability.

8. There should be careful and continuous appraisal of each student's reading proficiency together with diagnosis of special difficulties as well as continuous appraisal of the effectiveness of the program as a whole. The diagnosis determines the level at which instruction is to begin and the specific reading needs of each student. Goal setting and diagnosis go hand in hand. The *Teacher Informal Reading Package* (Lichtman, 1970) can be used to do this.

9. An effective program touches every student and utilizes the talents of every teacher (McDonald, 1971). The content-area teachers must assume major responsibility for teaching the reading/study skills needed in the content areas. But this is not enough. Special reading teachers must work with the content teacher by developing units of instruction, by team teaching in subject areas, and by diagnosing students' disabilities in the content areas. In addition there must be an ongoing evaluation and in-service education and a well-staffed clinic to which students with special problems can be referred.

10. The procedures for reinforcing the objectives and skills must be clearly identified.

11. The program should emphasize reading as a lifelong, mature habit, and the aim should be to produce a mature reader.

12. The program needs to have the support of the parents.

13. While we generally look unfavorably at in-service programs that encroach on teachers' time, in-service teachers can help classroom teachers in many ways (Olson, 1967). They can distribute journal articles on reading instruction, discuss and evaluate standardized test results, have teachers investigate new and effective reading programs, or get teachers to try out new materials and practices. The classroom teacher needs *practical* help (Olson, 1967). He benefits most when the idea is demonstrated in the classroom, when he is shown how to use materials, and when he himself is given the time to formulate a plan for implementation of new ideas.

Systematic Instruction in the Basic Skills

It has been our experience that even when a program seems to grow out of sound developmental principles, there still is concern as to *what to teach* and *how to teach* whatever needs to be taught. It is not enough to know how to teach; one must also know *what* to teach. What are the specific skills that the student must learn?

Because of the nature of the reading process and the individuality of youngsters, it seems illogical to suggest that certain learnings are peculiar to third grade, seventh grade or to senior high school. *Skill development does not come in capsule form.* One cannot dish out to seventh graders the seventh-grade capsule and to twelfth graders the twelfth-grade capsule.

It is also for these reasons that all teachers should be familiar with the *total* reading program. Each teacher needs to appreciate its continuity. He needs to know at what level the student is working, what he has learned, and what he probably needs to learn. Introduction of reading skills is useless unless the student's subsequent reading experiences serve to maintain those skills.

The student must gradually pass from learning to read to reading for learning. There are differences here among students as in almost any other area of human accomplishment. There are differences among students in *rate* of learning, but also in *capacity* of learning. Some students will never master all the skills. This again reinforces the need for individualization of each student's reading program. The teacher must start each student at the point of success that he has attained and must permit him to advance as far as he can as rapidly as he can.

In general, reading skills can be divided into the following seven broad areas:

1. Perceptual skills
2. Literal-comprehension skills
3. Word-recognition skills
4. Interpretative and appreciative skills
5. Reading-study skills
6. Rate-of-comprehension skills
7. Oral-reading skills

These skills encompass all those that the mature reader acquires in the course of his successful progress through the developmental program. It is only when he fails to do so that we need to provide corrective and remedial instruction, which is the concern of Chapter 14.

Today it is fashionable to assert that most reading failures are the result of faulty approaches in beginning reading. Chall (1964) notes that with regard to where the problem lies, whether in the initial reading approach or in the deficiencies of the child, there probably is an interaction effect between the two. "Severe reading disability seems to require both—a predisposition in the child and an initial approach that ignores it."

GROUPING

Historical Notes

Originally the major adjustment made for individual differences in achievement was to fail the weak and accelerate the gifted students. Historically, the next approach was some form of homogeneous grouping. Homogeneous grouping attempts to bring together those children who are most similar in age, ability, industry, previous experience, or other factors that affect learning. Age-groups were used initially, but children of the same age did not achieve alike. In the 1880s educators were already complaining about the lockstep in reading education. The complaint was that *all* students of similar age were forced to advance along a common front at the same rate of speed. Each student had the same book, was asked to learn the same material, and was judged by the same academic standards.

With the increased emphasis on individual differences in the 1920s and with the publication of the twenty-fourth yearbook of the National Society for the Study of Education, *Adapting the School to Individual Differences,* came a new classroom organization. It was termed *ability grouping* and for some time was thought to be the answer to the problem. In this approach pupils of the same ability used the same basic reader, and it was assumed that their individual needs were being met.

Unfortunately, pupils were commonly divided into three groups, average, above average, and below average. The pupil was rarely able to move from one level to another.

Frequently, *reading ability* is used as the basis for forming instructional groups. Here classes or subgroups within a class are organized on the basis of how well the child reads.

Dolch (1954) identifies three kinds of grouping that are commonly used in the elementary school. In one the teacher works with the entire class but may use different materials for those of higher and lower reading ability. Generally, the emphasis is on free reading and individualized assignments rather than use of a single text. The entire class, however, is working on the same general topic and joins in the discussions. Another procedure is to divide the class into fast and slow learners. The basic readers are the same, but the slow group progresses at a slower pace. Unfortunately, it is impossible to make a fourth-grade textbook into third-grade difficulty by proceeding more slowly. Schools have tried to overcome this problem by using different readers for the slow and for the fast groups. A third approach extends the number of groups to three or more. Unfortunately, whatever approach is used there are numerous unsolved problems.

The major problem pervading all attempts to group homogeneously is that children in the same grade have many differences in addition to their differences in reading ability. Our search must be for grouping methods that emphasize the similarities among children but make adjustments for their differences. Although most data concerning the effects of grouping come from studies of fixed or rigid ability grouping, some of these studies are worth examining.

Strang, McCullough, and Traxler (1955, p. 19) point out that the most common arguments for homogeneous grouping state that:

1. it makes it easier for the teacher to provide the experiences and materials of instruction which each level needs;
2. it does not waste the time of the superior readers nor bore them; and
3. it does not undermine the self-esteem of the poor readers by throwing them into constant comparison with the superior readers.

Arguments against homogeneous grouping declare that:

1. poor readers need the stimulation of better readers;
2. better readers need to learn to understand and to be of service to others;
3. being in a "low" group may give students a feeling of inferiority.

Homogeneity is nonexistent when we consider the interpersonal and the intrapersonal differences among students (Bamman, 1964). There is obviously no economy in trying to teach students what they are not ready to learn or for that matter in making students who have already learned a skill mark time until all others in the class will have learned the same skill (Walker, 1965). The teacher therefore needs to make curricular changes and class organizational changes to provide for these differences. We have seen the emergence of dual track systems, such as college preparatory and vocational; sometimes acceleration is practiced. In many schools various forms of intraclass grouping occur (Hoover and Hoover, 1968).

Mills (1963) notes that corrective and remedial programs often take the form of:

1. Semihomogeneous grouping in the regular classroom.
2. Provision for special instruction in small groups.
3. Team teaching, involving instruction in basic skills as well as reading in content areas.
4. In-service training for regular classroom teachers.
5. The reading laboratory.

The following additional suggestions might prove helpful in planning within-classroom modifications:

1. Use team teaching, permitting the grouping of students into very small units when needed. Disadvantaged students might be assigned to small classrooms or subgrouped for specific teaching.
2. Reduce the teacher-student ratio.
3. Use "reserve teachers" or "supplemental teachers" to work with groups of eight to twelve for one hour each day to help the lowest reading groups.
4. Assign "master teachers" on the basis of one master teacher to six to ten less-experienced teachers to help them and to work with small groups.

5. Use "remedial reading teachers" to give demonstrations for classroom teachers and to secure needed materials for teaching reading.
6. Use parents in the classroom as aides to help students listen to tapes and to use the library and to help the teacher with record keeping.

A program that includes paraprofessionals might use them in one of the following ways (Rauch, 1971):

1. Have them listen to a student read.
2. Have them assist students in selecting books.
3. Have them help the slow learner in carrying out directions as he does an assignment.
4. Have them correct workbook or other specific assignments.
5. Have them supervise seatwork or makeup assignments.
6. Have them supervise committee activities.
7. Have them help students who missed instruction through illness, etc.
8. Have them direct remedial drill work.
9. Have them operate audiovisual equipment.
10. Have them distribute and collect materials.

Reading method always functions in the context of a specific type of classroom organization, but "a plan of organization is not a method of teaching. It is a facilitator of method, perhaps, but no more" (Karlin, 1967). Either the classroom is organized on a group basis with some attempt at individualization, or individualized instruction is emphasized and groups are formed as needed.

Historically classrooms have been organized into groups, and the emphasis has been upon the development of a group organization that would permit the greatest amount of individual growth. Unfortunately, the search for a happy balance between grouping and individualization is still in progress.

Four characteristics typically affect the differences between and within individuals: normality, variation, covariation, and velocity (Powell, 1967). Most traits show the characteristic of normality, or normal distribution. Variation refers to the deviations among the members of any species. Normal distribution of traits necessarily implies variation.

Grouping is an attempt to reduce variation, but because of intraindividual differences as well as interindividual variation, homogeneous grouping results in only about a 20 percent reduction of the variation (Anastasi, 1958). Variations in student ability thus remain about 80 percent as great in so-called homogeneous groupings as in the heterogeneous or unselected classroom.

Traits and abilities also covary. A student's word perception skills normally develop in close relationship to his comprehension skills. It is when selected reading skills do not covary in the usual way that difficulties occur and that a differential diagnosis becomes necessary (Powell, 1967).

Students also grow, develop, mature, and learn at an *individual* rate or velocity.

The chief concern in reading has unfortunately been how one child differs from another. Perhaps we should focus on the way an individual reader differs within himself. We need to be concerned whether the learner is reading up to his expectancy level or up to his capacity. Many important instructional decisions can and must be based on an analysis of this differential (Powell, 1967).

Individualized Reading[1]

In an attempt to overcome some of the inadequacies of ability grouping, there arose in the early 1960s an interest in individualized reading.

This approach suggested that the student *seeks* for what he is physiologically and psychologically ready and that he shows his readiness through the spontaneous *selection* of the materials that he wants to read (Olson, 1959; Miel, 1958; Veatch, 1959).

Self-selection is considered to be a necessary aspect of individualized reading. Teachers have always encouraged youngsters to explore reading materials apart from those used in the classroom. Perhaps, in individualized reading, the pupil is encouraged to take a more active part in the selection of the materials.

The advantages claimed for individualized reading are many. Perhaps the most significant is the attitudinal change in the learner (Calder, 1967). Students seem to be more interested in reading. They read more at home. They show more interest in improvement and develop more favorable attitudes toward school in general. They often show improvement in work habits, self-motivation, and self-confidence. They seem to engage in more independent thinking and show better self-management.

In individualized reading, the purposes for reading are primarily individual and only secondarily group. The group serves as a sounding board for the individual to test the accuracy of the ideas acquired and to permit him the luxury of sharing the knowledge and insight that he has acquired.

The teacher thus works with the individual, detecting his needs and providing for these needs as the student's work reveals them. He keeps an accurate record of the student's accomplishments and inadequacies and helps him to pace his activities in accordance with his interests, aptitudes, and previous achievements. The teacher is not the prime director of the learning process and indeed never has been. Teaching may be a group process, but learning has always been an individual process.

Individualized reading does not seem suitable for students who cannot work independently or who cannot select or pace themselves wisely, and it is not economical when instruction can be provided more simply and in less time in a group situation than in a one-to-one teacher-

[1]See Emmett Albert Betts, "What is Individualized Reading?" *The Reading Teacher* 26 (1973): 678–79.

student conference. And skills are not learned simply by reading. The poor reader does not become a good reader by selecting and reading materials that he enjoys. Practice of itself is not enough.

The Need for Eclecticism in Classroom Organization

Since total homogeneous groups are never possible, it seems that when formed, groupings should be related to the specific learning task. Groups are occasioned (Strang et al., 1955, p. 112; Blanchard, 1952; and Gowan, 1955) when students show a commonality of achievement, interest, or need. Students may be grouped to help each other in a learning activity (tutorial or research grouping). Such groups may be labelled *team groups*. Students may be grouped when they show the need for the same skill development. The teacher may form intraclass groups for the purpose of reinforcement, reteaching, or independent work (Hamm and Jacobson, 1968).

Another approach, "Homorthic grouping," (Shannon, 1957) has been suggested. Here children are divided into two groups; those who want to learn and those who require additional motivation. Canfield (1957) adds that groups may also be formed on the basis of friendship patterns (sociometric techniques may be used to group on this basis). Also the varying work habits of the children may be used as a basis for grouping. Flexibility is perhaps the most significant attribute of effective grouping.

Flexible grouping seems to have more advantages and less disadvantages than other approaches. A flexible group is formed from time to time to satisfy a particular need such as for practice of word recognition skills, and the group is dissolved when the need has been satisfied. No rigid lines are formed differentiating the good from the poor reader. The child may advance from one group to another, and he may belong to more than one group at a time.

Under flexible grouping there is no need to limit the number of groups to two or three. The number of groups formed depends on such factors as the size of the class, the range of abilities and needs of the groups, the length of the reading period, the social maturity of the class, and the teacher's skill (Betts, 1949).

Groups should be changed (Hawkins, 1967) when students give evidence of growth or when their reading needs can be better met in another group. More specifically, a learner may be moved from one group to another because of excessive absence, because he does not understand words, because he has not learned certain basic skills, because the book is too difficult, or because he is falling too far behind others in the group. He may move because he has shown rapid improvements in an area or because he might profit from the exposure to a faster moving group. At times, the teacher may simply want to know what a trial in a new group can do.

Obviously, class organization is only one phase of the total reading program. To group heterogeneously, homogeneously, or individually is not the total answer.

The good educational program has always had some aspect of the individualized program, and the individualized program does not eliminate all group aspects. If indeed we do believe in the individuality of the learner, then it is difficult to ignore either approach, for one student may learn better in group situations, another in independent study. And even the same student may learn better when shifting from one approach to another as the occasion and his own needs demand.

Total individualization of instruction thus may *not* be individualizing the reading program. For some students it may be an inappropriate organization. Individualization really means that the teacher accommodates the situation to the learner and not the learner to the situation. He does not force him entirely either into a group structure or into an individualized, one-to-one, student-teacher structure. We now realize that some types of learning may best be obtained through individualized instruction; others, through group instruction. Groups of five may be best for discussion purposes; groups of two or three may be best for practice exercises (Murphy, 1961); and the teacher may be best for testing the student's comprehension of what he read individually.

Thus, the teacher's role is ultimately determined by the situation in which he finds himself. Sometimes he must become quite directive and sometimes he functions best in a permissive, laissez-faire role. He moves between the two extremes, neither advocating a just-let-them-read point of view nor limiting all the student's reading to the textbook. He avoids both the turn-them-loose, permissive approach and the stick-strictly-to-the-textbook approach (Betts, 1961).

The instructional procedures must be altered to accommodate individuals within the group. "Taking the student where he is" does not simply mean selecting materials on his grade level. Emphasis must be placed on his specific needs.

Individualized reading and grouping are not incompatible. A teacher-student conference is a group. Sometimes the teacher will have three, five, or as many as eight youngsters about him. All the group may need help in the same reading skills, may want to discuss the same story, or may want to real aloud to each other. Students may be grouped on an interest basis, on a need basis, or for social reasons. It is even possible to subgroup within ability groupings and to individualize instruction in each of them. Some students learn better with a friend. A study by Bradley (1957) indicates that children worked better in pairs than under the direction of a teacher or when working alone.

When students work on a unit acitivity, they may work in groups. Education cannot become so individual that socialization is ignored. The student is by nature individual; with learning he becomes a social animal. There are even occasions when the entire class can and should work together.

Mobile groups based on constantly changing objectives and the needs of the learners imply a constant awareness of the individuality of the learner. The groups should be based on the achievement of students in a particular skill rather than on their overall achievement. It is possible that the best and the poorest reader will be in the same group. Both may need help in a specific reading skill such as vocabulary, speed, or comprehension. Flexible groups thus are ever changing and make the attainment of immediate objectives that are consistent with immediate needs possible (Knight).

Recent studies have not resolved the issues of organization. Vite (1961), in analyzing seven controlled studies, found that four favored individualized reading and three favored grouping. Sister M. Marita (1966), evaluating three types of grouping, including individualized grouping, found no clear superiority of one over the other and concluded that the whole-class pattern in a child-centered context might be as useful as any others. McDonald and others (1966) found that first-grade children taught individually did not have greater reading achievement than others who were taught in groups. Lambert (1965), in a study involving over 600 pupils in grades one and six, reported significant gains in reading and study skills for pupils who were grouped regularly, but not so for those grouped on a pupil team basis; in the second year, the team groups showed greater gains. Williams (1966) reported no significant differences in achievement between comparative groups of pupils who attended graded and nongraded primary schools. Newport (1967), evaluating the Joplin interclass ability grouping plan—where fourth through sixth-grade pupils are grouped homogeneously without regard to grade level, reported on nine studies of the plan and concluded that the results of most studies have not favored the plan, but interclass grouping seemed as effective as ability grouping within the self-contained classroom. In general, parental, teacher, and pupil acceptance of the plan was good, but pupils in the low group expressed dissatisfaction and would rather be transferred to higher groups (Kierstead, 1963). Justman (1968) found that reducing the range of ability in fourth grade was not associated with increased achievement in reading.

Borg and Prpich (1966), in a two-year study comparing the performance of slow-learning tenth-grade students assigned to ability-grouped English classes with students of comparable ability and past achievement who were members of regular heterogeneous English classes, found:

1. No significant differences in English achievement for both replications of the study. Ability-grouped students made significantly greater gains on the *STEP Essay Test* during the year.
2. No significant differences in study methods or attitudes.
3. No significant differences on the *STEP Listening Test*.
4. Some evidence that the ability-grouping treatment was associated with better self-concept, better class participation, and more positive attitudes.

Borg (1966) and Heathers (1968) found that bright students get brighter and slow students get slower in homogeneous groups. Thompson (1974) in a study of matched pairs in two high schools found that heterogeneously grouped students showed significantly greater achievement gain in eleventh grade American history than did homogeneously grouped students. However, 32 of 120 subjects performed better in homogeneous groups, leading Thompson to conclude that students perhaps ought to have a choice as to what type of grouping they prefer.

Despite these findings, the easiest study to find is one expounding the strengths of either the basal or individualized approach. Each has its defenders and its antagonists. Unfortunately, many studies either do not control teacher competence, pupil abilities, and teacher-pupil motivations, or they compare a poor "basal" program with a good individualized approach or a poor individualized approach with a good basal program.

The Developmental Reading Program has little quarrel with attempts to individualize the reading program. It does insist that principles of student development should guide the methods and procedures used. With this in mind, let us make a few observations:

1. At times it is desirable to teach a class as a whole. In Russian schools (Durr and Hickman, 1974) reading is taught as a total class activity.

2. Grouping may reduce or narrow, but it will not completely eliminate the range of differences or the ranges of achievement in a group.

3. Teachers often seem to prefer homogeneous grouping.

4. Grouping on the basis of one criterion does not necessarily make individuals more alike on other measures, nor is the particular trait chosen for the grouping necessarily the dominant determinant of his behavior in the group. Thus, a good reader may not act as a good reader in certain groups because other personal characteristics keep him from performing up to his potential. Grouping of children into slow and fast sections seems to leave the slow learner with feelings of inadequacy, failure, and frustration. Flexible grouping may tend to prevent the stigma of failure. The pupil sees that the grouping is temporary and is to help him overcome a specific weakness. He is not set apart permanently from his peers. Even the slow pupil may come to understand that slowness in one area does not mean slowness in all areas. A study by Luchins and Luchins (1948) in a New York elementary school illustrates this. Grouping in this school was on the basis of IQ and previous achievement. Interviews with 190 children in the fourth, fifth, and sixth grade revealed that a high percentage (above 75 percent) of the pupils in the bright, average, and dull classes preferred to be in the "bright" class. More than 80 percent of the children reported that they believed their parents would want them to be in the accelerated group. An interesting finding was that 94 percent of the bright students said that they would not change to another group even if the teacher were better and kinder. Only 18 percent of the average students said that they would not change to another group under similar circumstances; and only 23 percent of the dull students said that they would not change.

5. Combinations of group and individual instruction seem to be indicated at present.

6. No organizational plan of itself insures reading success. Even the most

careful grouping does not eliminate the need for teaching reading to several different levels at the same time (Dolch, 1954).

7. The reading program should make provision for the progressive development of skills.

8. The effectiveness of the program depends on the number and quality of reading materials.

9. The search for a happy balance between grouping and individualization is still in progress. It is our feeling that heterogeneous grouping with mobile flexible subgrouping, rather than homogeneous grouping, has the most to offer in the regular classroom. Flexible subgrouping seems especially helpful in dealing with the problems of the student who needs corrective reading instruction. It permits the organization of clusters or subgroups of students with common reading needs.

Organizing for Corrective and Remedial Reading

Corrective Reading in the Classroom. As we have stated previously, corrective reading instruction should be reserved for the regular classroom. A few cautions are in order. Corrective instruction cannot be so organized as to embarrass the child and should certainly not be substituted for such pleasurable activities as recess or physical education. Neither should it give the appearance of simply being squeezed into the school day.

Because of the nature of the pupil needing corrective or remedial reading, drill sessions should necessarily be short. This means that on the lower elementary levels pupils may move from one group to another at fifteen or even ten minute intervals, if there are three groups.

The classroom teacher needs to spend some time with the entire class at the beginning of the class to introduce a new unit or topic or to give special assignments and directions. He may want to teach the entire class if he finds that all or most of the pupils are deficient in a particular skill, such as the rules of punctuation. He probably needs to spend some time with the entire group at the end of the class to summarize and to make homework assignments. Between the beginning few moments and the end of the class the teacher frequently will find it necessary to group the youngsters according to their similarity of needs. Table 13-1 shows an organization of the reading period that makes group instruction possible and permits greater individualization through the process of subgrouping.

The organization suggested in the table permits the teacher to have simultaneously three groups, each at a different level of reading performance, each using its own set of materials, and each advancing at its own success level. Dividing the class into three groups according to reading levels or needs permits the teacher to use basal readers more closely approximating the individual pupil's achievement level. At another time, one group may be working on word recognition, another on comprehension, and a third on rate improvement, even though the youngsters

TABLE 13-1 *The Reading Hour*

9:00–9:10	Common activities
9:10–9:55	Subgrouping within the classroom
9:55–10:00	Common subgrouping activities

Group I 9:10–9:25 Directed reading	Group II 9:10–9:25 Free reading	Group III 9:10–9:25 Reading group with teacher
(Practice on what has been taught)	(Application of what has been taught)	(Actual teaching)
1. Workbooks 2. Mimeographed seatwork 3. Questions on the board to answer 4. Use of programmed materials 5. Use of listening stations	1. Games 2. Free reading of library books—recreational reading	1. Basal reading instruction 2. Specific skill instruction
9:25–9:40 Free reading	9:25–9:40 Reading with teacher	9:25–9:40 Directed reading
9:40–9:55 Reading with teacher	9:40–9:55 Directed reading	9:40–9:55 Free reading

composing a given group might be reading on different levels. Thus a child readig on third-grade level might be working with one reading on a fourth-grade level. Both of them may need help with diphthongs, consonants, or speech consonants.

If the situation prevails where all children on the same reading level are grouped together for reading instruction as in the Joplin plan, there still may be need of flexible subgrouping on a learning-activity basis in the classroom. There still might be three groups: those receiving actual instruction, those practicing what has been taught, and those applying what has been taught. Children also may be subgrouped on an interest basis. In the ungraded primary, the pupils move from level to level on the basis of their achievement.

Even with a reduction of the teacher-pupil ratio and with subgrouping, there is no easy solution to children's reading problems. The teacher may need outside help. One pattern of organization for corrective instruction may include the use of additional teachers or aides. The use of team teaching or of reserve or supplemental teachers to work with small groups has been found beneficial. Some schools assign a master teacher to work directly with the teacher during the regular reading period. The remedial reading teacher may help the classroom teacher by giving classroom demonstrations in the use of specific methods or materials. It may be possible to use parents or aides to help children listen to tapes, do workbook exercises, listen to children's oral reading, or make comprehension checks. The teacher may initiate team learning, in which pupils subgroup as a team and work together in the learning of new concepts, in applying skills, or in reviewing. Tutoring, a situation in which one pupil works with one or more pupils who need help, has been used by many teachers.

Staggered scheduling is another organizational device useful in planning developmental and corrective reading instruction. In the developmental setting staggered scheduling is sometimes labelled divided-day, split-day, extended-day, or staggered-day organization. It provides a reading period in the morning with one-half of the class, which arrives early, and another period in the afternoon with the other half of the class, that stays late. Warner's study (1967) indicates that this form of organization is advantageous to both teacher and pupil and results in superior reading achievement.

In the corrective setting, those youngsters who are to be kept in the regular classroom but who need special help in reading may be asked to report to school an hour early or leave an hour late. Lunch periods could be staggered for similar effect.

Remedial Reading. Pupils who are seriously retarded may have to be taken out of the regular classroom and put into a special room where a remedial reading teacher or a special teacher will work with them. Sometimes there is no classroom space available, and the school may have to use mobile equipment. In another school the remedial teacher may function out of the reading materials center.

Regardless of where the remedial room is, it should probably have two glass-partitioned offices: one for the remedial teacher and one for testing purposes. The glass partition permits the teacher to observe the testing from his own office. The room should also contain an audiovisual center, small group practice rooms, individual practice cubicles, desks, chairs, bookshelves, and office furniture. The reading room should make provision for a testing room and for individual practice cubicles.

Organizing for *remedial* instruction requires that pupils be dismissed from the regular classroom at scheduled times during the regular school day so that they can go to the remedial classroom for special instruction. The pupil reports to the remedial class for perhaps one lesson per day and then returns to his own classroom. It is important that we get the pupil back to the regular classroom as soon as possible. We recommend, therefore, that every nine weeks the following question should be asked and answered about every pupil: "Is he ready to be excused from the remedial class?"

Remedial instruction may be given during a regular study period or during a subject-matter class which requires reading for efficient performance. Sometimes the pupil is given remedial instruction before school begins or after school ends. In some schools remedial instruction is provided during the homeroom or the activity period. In other schools remedial instruction becomes a part of the English class.

The remedial room should be equipped with audiovisual materials of various types, filmstrip projector, tachistoscopes, accelerating devices, record players, children's records, tape recorder, listening stations, flashcards, and art supplies. It should contain books of all types, supplementary readers, programmed reading materials, multilevel reading laboratories, testing and diagnostic materials, magazines, games, and all kinds of word recognition and comprehension development materials.

THE SLOW LEARNER

The remainder of this chapter concerns itself with the specific needs of the slow learner, the gifted learner, and the disadvantaged learner. A sound developmental program is concerned with children of all levels of ability—the average, the slow, the gifted, and the disadvantaged. Considerable information has been gathered about the special needs and potentialities of children in each of these general categories. Let's begin with the slow learner.

Generally, children with IQs of 50 to 89 are classified as slow learners. Of the slow-learning children, those with IQs from 50 to 70 commonly are referred to as mentally retarded. However, even the mentally retarded children are considered educable and will be in our regular schools although frequently in special classes.

The slow learner may or may not be retarded in terms of his ability level, but he is almost always retarded as to grade level. He generally has an IQ between 70 and 90, and thus *his major deficiency may be in the area of intellectual development*. This pupil begins to read at age seven or later, will read slowly and haltingly, and achieves below grade level in areas other than reading, such as spelling or arithmetic. He generally does not need a remedial program. Pushing him may only hurt him. He may interpret it as dissatisfaction with his wholehearted efforts. By the time he reaches ninth grade, he may be reading three or four grade levels below his actual grade placement.

Certainly major adjustments must be made for the slow learner. He requires a longer readiness program than does the average child. To begin reading instruction before the child has a mental age of six or more is to waste the time of both teacher and pupil and results in pupil discouragement. The extended readiness program of the slow-learner demands a variety of concrete experiences. It must progress slowly, with an emphasis on pupil activity. Films and filmstrips are important sources of materials. The program for the slow learner should emphasize social interaction, story telling, arts and crafts, dramatizing, music, and recreational activities. The education of the slow learner requires a large amount of repetition. Reading charts built from the direct experiences of the children are especially useful. Muller (1952) points out that these charts will be read and re-read with pride and satisfaction by mentally retarded pupils at chronological ages considerably beyond those at which they can be used with normal children. In the early stages of their learning, listening will need to be stressed more than reading.

In the slow learner's reading program, we generally spend considerable time on phonetic and structural analysis and, frequently, we encourage lip movements, vocalization, and pointing at the word. We emphasize word knowledge and mastery of simple comprehension skills.

The slow learner appears to have little need for rapid reading skills. He will not read many different materials. He has a difficult time reading for practical purposes. Groelle (1949) suggests that the reading of the slow learner, especially when he is about ready to leave school, should be functional in nature. He needs to learn the working vocabulary required in his future job and how to read and fill out application blanks; he needs to be able to read telephone books, city directories, road maps, street guides, menus, recipes, directions, radio and theater programs, advertisements, catalogues, want-ads, and newspapers; and he should become thoroughly familiar with the dictionary and book tables of contents and indices.

The classroom teacher can help the slow learner by making adjustments in the *content* of the developmental program and in the rate at which he progresses through it, and by applying one or a combination of the following techniques in his content-area teaching.

1. By providing a friendly, accepting, and encouraging relationship. Teacher attitudes substantially affect the performance of the slow learner. The teacher must believe in the improvableness of the learner.
2. By creating a learning environment where simple reading is important. Each learning experience should grow out of a need. Teach him to read road signs, city directories, a letter from a friend, want ads, newspapers, an application blank, a menu. The slow learner needs to learn the working vocabulary required to function effectively as an American citizen (Groelle, 1949).
3. By pacing the learning according to the student's ability.
   a. Introduce only a few materials at any given time.
   b. Review daily.
   c. Introduce materials in varied contexts.
   d. Simplify materials, explanations, and techniques.
   e. Use short periods of instruction.
   The basic vocabulary needs to be carefully controlled. Build many reading situations which require him to use his limited vocabulary over and over again. These students need aural-oral experience with words. The use of workbooks is especially recommended.
4. By coordinating all the language arts. Let the student do oral reading. Sometimes he needs to hear himself say the word to understand what he is reading. A multisensory approach makes learning a concrete process for him.
5. By not underestimating the slow learner's ability to learn. Don't simply let him do busy work.
6. By having the student see his progress in each lesson through individual and objective evidence. Nothing succeeds like observed and tangible success.
   a. Have him keep a card file of words that he has learned to spell or read.
   b. Have him construct a picture dictionary, perhaps of shop tools. The teacher needs to provide opportunities for the student to "shine" in some area.
   c. Have him graph his progress each day.
7. By providing drill on new words.
   a. Let the student write, pronounce, and read the word.
   b. Use all the sense avenues.

8. By providing ample opportunity for review, repetition, and overlearning. The slow learner has difficulty with both immediate and delayed memory. The slow learner profits greatly from repetition. He needs this to retain the information and to reinforce learning. He may get the gist of a story only in spurts. Each rereading adds more to his understanding. The teacher needs to spend a great deal of time in developing new concepts. The slow learner has a great need for a systematic and developmental reading program. He needs step-by-step instruction. He must be permitted to use his knowledge in various contexts.

9. By individualizing instruction. The teacher needs to give as much individual help as possible.

10. By not putting him into a remedial program simply because he is reading below grade level. Far too many slow learners fill Title I classes.

11. By using concrete illustrations to develop concepts and generalizations. The slow learner has difficulty with abstract reasoning. He is slow to perceive relationships, to make inferences, to draw conclusions, or to generalize. He needs to be helped to reason through discussion periods, dramatization, etc.

12. By providing short-range goals. Projects should not be too long, and rewards should be frequent.

13. By emphasizing the visual and auditory characteristics of words. Word analysis is very helpful. The teacher may encourage lip movements, vocalization, and pointing to a word. The teacher needs to emphasize phonogram-phoneme relationships.

14. By breaking complex learning tasks into small steps. The use of programmed materials and teaching machines is especially recommended for slow learners. They divide the task into small steps and use frequent repetition and other supportive cues to make the correct response dominant.

15. By employing a variety of teaching techniques.

16. By emphasizing far more the quality of the student's learning experiences than their quantity. Going too fast produces nothing but confusion. The slow learner appears to have little need for rapid reading skills. The student needs repetitive practice but also varied practice.

17. By seeing to it that all directions are definite, specific, and detailed.

18. By familiarizing himself with methods of teaching specifically designed for the slow learner.

19. By familiarizing himself with and by using materials designed for the slow learner.

THE GIFTED LEARNER

From the days of Aristotle and Plato to the present time, writers have recognized that the gifted child should and would, if properly guided, grow up to become a leader in his society. Obviously, such leadership is needed in political life, in education, in religion, in science, and in business. In recent years the need for a more conscious, deliberate, and intelligent direction of human affairs has become most glaringly evident. As our need for leadership becomes greater, education's responsibility for identifying and developing the gifted child increases.

The very strength of an educational system designed to offer maximum educational advantages to children of all levels of ability frequently results in a weakness in our education of the gifted. It is extremely difficult to help the gifted achieve maximum growth under a system that must frequently be geared to the needs of the average.

Too often in a discussion of reading, the needs of the gifted learner are overlooked. Whereas most gifted students are probably reading substantially above grade level, there are many whose reading achievement is substantially below their ability level. In fact, many of them are seriously retarded. Many of them are deficient in study approaches to chapter-length materials or demonstrate inflexibility in reading rate. Helping these students to achieve appropriate educational growth requires that the teacher know how to identify the gifted, know their characteristics as learners, and know how to make educational adjustments to meet their needs.

Identification of the Gifted Learner

To identify the gifted learner, we must reach some agreement as to what we mean by *gifted*. In the case of the slow learner, our criterion was low IQ. However the IQ as the criterion of giftedness is not completely satisfactory for at least two reasons: (1) although low IQ generally guarantees low accomplishment, high IQ does not guarantee high accomplishment; (2) although the gifted learner generally learns anything quite easily, frequently gifted children are highly successful in one area and less successful in others. Thus Witty (1956) would consider a child gifted if his performance is consistently remarkable in *any* valuable line of human activity.

Generally, however, standardized intelligence test results have been used as criteria both to identify the gifted and to define giftedness even though tests are never completely reliable or valid and some types of gifted children do not express their full capabilities on intelligence tests. Even when we use high IQ as our criterion, we still must decide the specific range of IQ levels that is to mark giftedness. Generally, the educational program for the gifted is extended to those with an IQ of 130 and above, although some programs use a higher cut-off point (Barbe, 1954).

In defining giftedness the trend has been to combine intelligence with other criteria. Havighurst et al. (1952, p. 1) suggested that we speak of four areas of talent: intellectual talent—a child with high intelligence or high IQ; artistic talent—talent in music, drawing, or dramatics, and so on; social leadership; and creative intelligence or ability to find new ways of doing things and solving problems.

Characteristics of the Gifted Learner

Even the most dedicated user of intelligence test results recognizes that children of the same general level of intelligence frequently differ greatly in specific strengths and weaknesses among the various areas sampled by the test. And such children may differ even more in traits that the intelligence test is not designed to appraise. This variability in characteristics is most marked among the gifted.

As a group, children with superior IQ's are less neurotic, less selfish, more self-sufficient, more mature socially, more self-confident, taller, heavier, and healthier than average children. Their major strength, however, is their academic prowess. They tend to learn through association rather than through rote memory. They perceive relationships and like to deal with abstractions. They are curious, creative, and imaginative. They tend to work individually but they enjoy preparing and giving oral and written reports and organizing and cataloguing materials and information, and sharing their experiences with their classmates. They tend to write both prose and poetry creatively and effectively. Frequently what they choose to read and learn is on an adult level and they are attracted to school subjects that require abstraction. Also, their social consciousness and responses indicate a higher degree of maturity than do those of average children.

The Need for Guidance of the Gifted

The tremendous potential of the gifted students for academic achievement and social leadership carries with it a high challenge and responsibility for educational guidance. This calls for creative teaching. The following points summarize some of the problems that will emerge in teaching the gifted learner.

1. Gifted learners are likely to become irritated by the repetition that slow learners need to reinforce their learning (Strang, 1954).
2. The student usually prefers to read to learn.
3. Materials are often too simple.
4. The student should be exposed early to critical reading, rate improvement, use of the dictionary, and content-area reading. He needs guidance in appreciation, in detecting mood and tone, and in recognizing literary devices. He needs to question and evaluate the authority of the source material. He must learn to identify the author's purpose, to understand inferences, to anticipate outcomes, and to analyze the author's style (Bland, 1956).
5. In teaching the gifted learner, the teacher should emphasize such things as abstracting principles and significant interrelationships, synthesizing facts and drawing conclusions, tracing themes and analyzing their importance to the selection as a whole, and criticizing on the basis of all the various forces involved (Murphy, 1954, p. 418).
6. The intellectual qualities of the gifted often render superfluous traditional patterns of classroom instruction. The student needs problem-centered teaching and student-teacher planning.
7. The teacher must know when to guide, when to direct, and when to get out of the way.
8. The teacher must help the student to develop intrinsic rather than extrinsic motivations.
9. The gifted are not impressed by light scheduling, close supervision, rigid administration, authoritative teaching, and traditional forms of evaluation.

10. The student needs to be provided broad exposure to and immersion in content (Plowman, 1967). He needs to be taught to see interdisciplinary relationships and to reorganize knowledge. He needs active encounters with academic knowledge.
11. Basic changes in the curriculum rather than simply "patchwork adjustments" are necessary.

Barbe (1954) points out that when the material is too easy the gifted child may withdraw from the group, become a clown to gain attention, or even pretend not to know answers. We cannot permit the gifted child to develop his skills through personal initiative alone. He is likely to find that he need make little effort and consequently his educational development falls far short of what his intellectual endowment should promise. The end result, often, is that the gifted child's educational development frequently is retarded by as much as one to three years below his mental age level. Wheeler and Wheeler (1949, pp. 230–231) note that the most seriously retarded readers in our schools and colleges are the mentally superior students.

Educational Adjustments for the Gifted Learner

Various procedures have been suggested for adjusting instruction to the needs of the gifted child:

1. Honors courses.
2. Seminars especially on the high school level. These are often for non-credit (Mosso, 1945).
3. Special course work.
4. Noncurricular groupings. These bring students together in drama, crafts, language, music, etc.
5. Regular classroom grouping.
6. Credit by examination.
7. Telescoped curriculum. This provides a two-year program in one year.
8. Early admissions, especially on the high school and college levels.
9. Extra courses for credit.
10. Sectioning. Students of all levels of ability are together in the morning but in the afternoon the more able participate in a special program.
11. Acceleration.
12. Enrichment in the regular classroom. The best form of adjustment may still be a diversification of instruction by a competent teacher.

THE DISADVANTAGED LEARNER

The disadvantaged learners are the ill housed, ill fed, ill clothed, and ill educated. They are white, black, Indian, Chicano, Puerto Rican. The disadvantaged learner is of no single race or color. Poverty and failure to achieve the goals established by the mainstream of society (Black, 1965) are shared by people of all colors and national origins. The culturally deprived student is a learner who simply lacks enough of the opportunities and advantages available to most American youth. The disadvantaged families are not deprived because they are black or Puerto Rican, but because they have been deprived of adequate employment and income.

We need to differentiate between the student who is retarded because of a verbally impoverished environment and the student who is retarded because of deficient brain matter. It is also obvious that we need to present different stimuli, and we need to present them in a different way for the learner who is deficient because of lack of previous learnings.

What characterizes the disadvantaged child? (Black, 1965; Riessman, 1962):

1. He lacks a proper self-image. He feels alienated from the larger social structure.
2. He expects little from life and has little academic drive. He has a weak sense of the future.
3. He tends to be afflicted with more health and physical difficulties.
4. He is deficient in language development, has a limited vocabulary, and even though he uses short sentences, these are sprinkled with grammatical errors. Sentence structure is faulty.
5. He has mastered the public language (this uses simple declaratory sentences) but cannot deal with the formal language. His language contains few clauses or structural complexities. He does not use the school language.
6. He has more perceptual difficulties. He recognizes fewer objects than most children. He is deficient in auditory attention and interpretation skills and experiences great difficulty in blending sounds. He learns less from what he hears than does the middle class child. Cohen (1967) believes most disadvantaged children tend to be visual rather than auditory or phonic readers, but emphasizes that a linguistic-phonic program should be built into the beginning reading program.
7. He tends to perform poorly on tests and his achievement in school is low. He is slow at cognitive tasks. He is unaware of the ground rules for success in school. He is not willing to sit still while having to read, "Look, Jane! Look!," to get in a line in a hurry, or to do meaningless homework (Cohen, 1967).
8. His reading achievement tends to be substantially below his ability level.
9. He learns more readily through a physical and concrete approach.
10. If he is a boy, he values masculinity and views intellectual activities as unmasculine.
11. His attention span is short, and he is not motivated by long-range goals.
12. His experiential background is meagre. He does not have the experience to make words meaningful.
13. He approaches learning in an inductive rather than a deductive manner. He reasons from parts to wholes and from particulars to generals. His culture does not help him to deduce conclusions from given premises and so he may do well in computational mathematics, but poorly in thought problems (Cheyney, 1967, p. 47).

The need for concerted effort to improve the language and reading skills of the disadvantaged child is apparent. The following techniques might prove helpful (Mackintosh, 1965; Olson, 1967; Rauch, 1967; Whipple and Black, 1966):

1. Make every effort to obtain a true estimate of the pupil's potential. The *Wechsler Intelligence Scale for Children,* the *Stanford-Binet Intelligence Scale,* the *I.P.A.T. Culture Fair Intelligence Test,* or a similar test should be used to obtain an IQ or mental age score. Do not use tests which only hammer home the point that the pupil is stupid.

2. Teach disadvantaged children to "learn how to learn."

3. Build on oral language as a prerequisite to dealing with printed language. This child will not know a word like steeple, although a dozen steeples may be visible from the classroom window. Develop experiential and oral meanings for words. The *Peabody Lanugage Development Kit* (American Guidance Service, Inc., Minneapolis) and the *Ginn Language Kit A* provide a systematic program of language experiences on the first grade level.

4. Develop speaking-reading-writing relationships through the use of experience stories, audiovisual devices, and concrete illustrations. Many visual stimuli should be presented together with the verbal stimuli. Make tapes of the pupil's oral reading.

5. Teach reading as a life-related process. When saying: "We wash our hands," have the children do it and write the sentences on the blackboard for them to read. Experientially-deprived children perhaps more so than any other group learn by doing. In the middle and upper grades the pupil needs to develop an awareness that reading is important. Too often, the fact that he cannot read causes him little concern.

6. Make frequent use of experiences charts. Permit children to verbalize and to communicate orally. Reading assignments should be brief and concrete.

7. Display books strategically and attractively for personal and group examination. Show a filmstrip about a book; read from a book. Make available materials that present his own ethnic group in a good light. Instead of trying to get him to adopt a new culture, help him to improve within the framework of his own culture.

8. Only gradually introduce books as readers, moving back and forth from charts to books as the situation demands.

9. Give special attention to readiness for reading and for learning. Be reasonably certain that pupils have a chance of understanding the materials.

10. Do not limit the approach in reading to any one method or one approach.

11. Teach phonics and structural analysis as means of figuring out the pronunciation of words. Few disadvantaged children know either the alphabet of letters or the alphabet of sounds. Emphasize visual and auditory discrimination, but especially auditory discrimination.
    Disadvantaged children profit from a great deal of auditory and visual perception activities. The *Michigan Successive Discrimination Listening Program* and the *Frostig Program for the Development of Visual Perception* stress such activities. A new program with similar emphasis is *Readiness for Learning: A Program for Visual and Auditory Perceptual-Motor Training* by J. B. Lippincott. It is designed for kindergarten-first grade level.

12. Provide an atmosphere of trust where the pupil can learn self-assurance and self-direction, raise his aspirational level, and develop pride in himself. For example, choral reading may be used to great advantage. This permits the pupil to respond and yet it does not single him out if he makes an error.

Programmed materials give him all the time he wants or needs without pressuring him for an answer. They permit him to check on his own answer without subjecting him to embarrassment because the teacher or another pupil saw his error or deficiency. The teacher must proceed on the assumption that the pupil can improve.

13. Make use of materials that are specifically designed for culturally-deprived children. The Detroit city schools have been using multicultural readers. Some recommend the use of the Montessori approach. *The Progressive Choice Reading Program* is designed specifically for the disadvantaged child. Another program on junior high–senior high school level for disadvantaged children is *Reading in High Gear* by Science Research Associates. The *Miami Linguistic Readers*, D. C. Heath and Company, form a two-year beginning reading program for bilingual and culturally disadvantaged pupils. A brochure, *A Reading List for Disadvantaged Youth,* is available through the American Library Association. Another source of books is Allan C. Ornstein, "101 Books for Teaching the Disadvantaged," *Journal of Reading,* 10 (May, 1967), 546–51. *Dandy Dog's Early Learning Program,* American Book Company, is a combination book-record program useful with slow learners and nonEnglish speaking children.

14. Greatly expand the amount of time that is devoted to reading instruction. On the upper-grade levels put special emphasis on study skills.

15. Structure the reading program in such a way that the pupil thinks of reading as the process of bringing meaning to the page (Kincaid, 1967). Don't ask the child, "What does this word mean?" His answer will probably be wrong. Rather, ask him: "What does this word make you think of?" Such a question preserves his self-concept and allows the teacher to develop new or additional meanings.

16. Take an attitude of "positive expectancy" (Strang, 1967) toward the pupil, focusing on his assets rather than his weaknesses. As Niemeyer, President of Bank Street College, notes: "A major reason for low achievement among children in poor neighborhoods is the low expectation as to their learning capacity held by teachers."

The disadvantaged learner often manifests considerable ingenuity in expression, but teachers do not appreciate the language through which it is voiced. Mark Twain once remarked: "Nothing so needs reforming as other people's habits." This is about the way teachers proceed in dealing with the speech problems of the disadvantaged.

It may well be that many reading failures among minority children are explained by the teacher's ignorance of nonstandard English rules. It cannot be emphasized enough that the use of nonstandard English is not caused by cognitive defects (Welty, 1971). Labov et al., (1968) have analyzed the idiosyncrasies of black English and noted its *r-lessness.* This makes homonyms of such words as guard-God, court-caught, carrot-Cat, Paris-pass. The *l* is also consistently dropped, producing homonyms out of such words as toll-toe, help-hep, fault-fought. Frequently, such double consonant sounds as /st/, /ft/, /nt/, /nd/, /ld/, /zd/, and /md/ are reduced to one: rift-rif, mend-men, wind-win. Labov suggests that these language idiosyncrasies may cause difficulty for black children in recognizing many words in their standard spelling. Stewart (1969) notes, however, that if the differences are regular and consistent enough, the black child may develop his own sound-spelling correspondences which will permit him to deal effectively with word-identification problems. Recent analyses certainly indicate that black English is a highly structured system that is not inferior to any other system in a linguistic sense. This does not mean that standard speech should not be taught, but it raises questions[2] as to how to introduce reading to these children. Some readers are now available through the Education Study Center, Washington, D.C., where the same story is written both ways: one in black English and one in standard speech.

Because differences in grammar are often considered more significant than differences in pronunciation, oral language training should probably focus on them. There is also a need to develop listening skills (Welty, 1971).

McDavid (1964) notes that a reading program is effective in proportion to its use of the language habits that the student has acquired in speaking. The disadvantaged youth is disadvantaged precisely because he brings to school language habits that are not used in the reading program, are not recognized as legitimate by the school, and all too often are either overtly or covertly punished by the school. This learner suffers as long as the school is not willing to use the language that he brings to school (Stewart, 1969).

Teachers need to realize that differences in language do not mean inferiority (Johnson, 1971). And yet, this is exactly what is conveyed when there is a pedagogical attack on the student's language in school. Book after book describes the minority youngster as nonverbal, but he is nonverbal only in the classroom. The black child, through his word games and bantering, amply demonstrates his verbal ability. Instead of being nonverbal, he is actually verbally different.

It is an error to assume that the minority pupil has lazy lips and a lazy tongue or that his language is sloppy and he is a verbal cripple. He shows amazing consistency in his language production. Black students always pronounce the final voiceless /th/ as /f/ in words like mouth, bath, both, south; they do not generally pronounce the final /b/, /d/, /g/, /k/, /p/, and /t/.

Johnson (1971), after making the above observations, concludes that instead of teaching standard English to black youth as a replacement dialect, we should teach it as an alternate dialect; we should teach it as an additional linguistic tool to be used in appropriate situations.

The disadvantaged learner is essentially inexperienced in language. He knows too few words and too few meanings. The teacher must accept his manner of expression but also must guide the learner toward using complete sentences. This learner's language, while quite adequate away from school, is not adequate for success in school. Engaging the learner in conversation, fostering language development through role playing and dramatic representation, and reading aloud to him each day are all good procedures to use in developing language competency.

[2]See Joanne L. Vacca, "Bidialectism—Choose Your Side." *The Reading Teacher* 28 (1975): 643–46.

SUMMARY

This chapter has concerned itself with the nature of the developmental program, with the specific problems of grouping, and the special needs of the slow learner, the gifted learner, and the disadvantaged learner.

QUESTIONS FOR DISCUSSION

---

1. Why is it impossible to divorce reading achievement from other aspects of development?
2. What administrative implications do the following two principles have:
   a. reading instruction begins at the level that the student has attained and
   b. reading instruction should permit each student to advance at his own success rate?
3. Why is it incorrect to speak of a "Remedial Reading Program"?
4. Distinguish between homogeneous grouping and ability grouping.
5. Why should one try to group homogeneously when, if teaching is adequate, the individuals almost certainly will be further apart at the end of a learning period than they were at the beginning?
6. Explain why equality of opportunity doesn't mean equal education.
7. What are some of the advantages and disadvantages of flexible subgrouping?
8. Discuss some of the special plans that have been proposed for adjusting for individual differences.
9. Distinguish between the slow learner and the retarded learner.
10. Compare the reading habits of the gifted and the slow learner.
11. What are some of the advantages and disadvantages of acceleration?
12. What adjustments can be made in the reading program for the gifted learner? Which do you consider to be most desirable?

BIBLIOGRAPHY

ANASTASI, ANNE. *Differential Psychology.* New York: Macmillan, 1958, p. 320.

AUKERMAN, ROBERT. "Readability of Secondary School Literature Textbooks: A First Report." *English Journal* 54 (1965) 533–40.

BAMMAN, HENRY A. "Organizing the Remedial Program in the Secondary School," *Journal of Reading* 8 (1964): 103–8.

BARBE, WALTER B. "Differentiated Guidance for the Gifted." *Education* 74 (1954): 306–11.

BETTS, EMMETT A. "Adjusting Instruction to Individual Needs." *Reading in the Elementary School.* Forty-eighth Yearbook of the National Society for the Study of Education, Part II. Chicago: University of Chicago Press, 1949, pp. 266–83.

BETTS, EMMETT ALBERT. "Issues in Teaching Reading." *Controversial Issues in Reading,* 1 (1961): 33–41. Tenth Annual Reading Conference, Lehigh University.

BLACK, MILLARD H. "Characteristics of the Culturally Disadvantaged Child." *The Reading Teacher* 18 (1965): 465–70.

BLANCHARD, MARJORIE. "Adjusting Learning Activities and Reading Materials to Individual Differences: In Grades Four to Six." *Improving Reading in All Curriculum Areas,* Supplementary Educational Monographs, No. 76. Chicago: University of Chicago Press, 1952, pp. 32–36.

BLAND, PHYLLIS. "Helping Bright Students Who Read Poorly." *The Reading Teacher* 9 (1956): 209–14.

BOND, GUY L. "Teaching Selections in Reading." *The Road to Better Reading.* Albany, New York: Bureau of Secondary Curriculum Development, The State Education Department, 1953, pp. 30–37.

BOND, GUY L. and TINKER, MILES A. *Reading Difficulties: Their Diagnosis and Correction.* New York: Appleton-Century-Crofts, 1957.

BORG, W. R. *Ability Grouping in the Public Schools.* Madison, Wisconsin: Dembar Educational Research Services, 1966.

BORG, WALTER R. and PRPICH, TONY. "Grouping of Slow Learning High School Pupils." *Journal of Secondary Education* 41 (1966): 231–38.

BRADLEY, MARY A. "The Construction and Evaluation of Exercises for Providing Meaningful Practice in Second Grade Reading." Unpublished doctoral dissertation, Boston University, School of Education, 1957.

CALDER, CLARENCE R., JR. "Self-directed Reading Materials." *The Reading Teacher* 21 (1967): 248–52.

CANFIELD, JAMES K. "Flexibility in Grouping for Reading." *The Reading Teacher* 11 (1957): 91–94.

CHALL, JEANNE. "How They Learn and Why They Fail." *Improvement of Reading Through Classroom Practice.* International Reading Association Conference Proceedings, Newark, 1964, pp. 147–48.

CHEYNEY, A. B. *Teaching Culturally Disadvantaged in the Elementary School.* Columbus, Ohio: Charles E. Merrill, 1967.

COHEN, S. ALLEN. "Some Conclusions About Teaching Reading to Disadvantaged Children." *The Reading Teacher* 20 (1967): 433–35.

COURTNEY, BROTHER LEONARD. "Characteristics of a Good High School Reading Program." North Central Association Annual Meeting, March 29, 1966.

DAVIS, STANLEY E. "High School and College Instructors Can't Teach Reading? Nonsense." *North Central Association Quarterly* 34 (1960): 295–99.

DOLCH, E. W. "Groups in Reading." *Elementary English* 31 (1954): 477–84.

DURR, WILLIAM K. and HICKMAN, ROBERTA. "Reading Instruction in Soviet Schools: Methods and Materials." *The Reading Teacher* 28 (1974): 134–40.

EARLY, MARGARET J. "The Meaning of Reading Instruction in Secondary Schools." *Journal of Reading* 8 (1964): 25–29.

FOSTER, GUY L. "Freshman Problem: 44% Couldn't Read Their Texts." *The Clearing House* 29 (1955): 414–17.

GOWAN, MAY SEAGOE. "Why Homogeneous Grouping." *California Journal of Secondary Education* 30 (1955): 22–28.

GROELLE, MARVIN C. "Techniques and Adjustments for Slow Learners with Special Reference to Reading." *Classroom Techniques in Improving Reading*, Supplementary Educational Monographs, No. 69. Chicago: University of Chicago Press, 1949, pp. 182–86.

HAMM, RUSSELL L., and JACOBSON, VICTORIA. "In-Class Grouping in Reading at the Secondary Level." *Reading Improvement* 5 (1968): 36–38.

HAVIGHURST, ROBERT J.; ROGERS, VIRGIL M.; and WITTY, PAUL A. *Are the Community and the School Failing the Unusual Child?* Chicago: The University of Chicago Round-Table, No. 735, April 27, 1952.

HAWKINS, MICHAEL. "Changes in Reading Groups." *The Reading Teacher* 21 (1967): 48–51.

HEATHERS, G. "Grouping." *Encyclopedia of Educational Research*. London: Macmillan, 1968.

HOOVER, KENNETH H. and HOOVER, HELENE M. "A Plan for Grouping in the Secondary Classroom." *Education* 88 (1968): 208–12.

JOHNSON, KENNETH R. "Teacher's Attitude Toward the Nonstandard Negro Dialect—Let's Change It," *Elementary English* 48 (1971): 176–84.

JONES, DAISY M. "Teaching Reading Skills in the Content Areas." Claremont Reading Conference Yearbook. Calif.: Claremont Graduate School, 1966, pp. 159–69.

JUSTMAN, JOSEPH. "Reading and Class Homogeneity." *The Reading Teacher* 21 (1968): 314–16, 334.

KARLIN, ROBERT. "Research Results and Classroom Practices." *The Reading Teacher* 21 (1967): 221–26.

KIERSTEAD, R. "A Comparison and Evaluation of Two Methods of Organization for the Teaching of Reading." *Journal of Educational Research* 56 (1963): 317–21.

KINCAID, GERALD L. "A Title I Short Course for Reading Teachers." *The Reading Teacher* 20 (1967): 307–12.

KNIGHT, ELVA E. "Mobility Grouping." *Reading Bulletin 224*. Chicago: Lyons and Carnahan, Educational Service Department.

LABOV, W. et al. *A Study of the Nonstandard English of Negro and Puerto Rican Speakers in New York City*, Columbia University Cooperative Research Project: Phonological and Grammatical Analysis, 1 (1968) *Use of Language in the Speech Community*, 2 (1968).

LAMBERT, P. et al. "A Comparison of Pupil Achievement in Team and Self-Contained Organizations." *Journal of Experimental Education* 33 (1965): 217–24.

LICHTMAN, MARILYN. *Teacher Informal Reading Package*. Washington, D.C.: Catholic University of America, June 1970.

LUCHINS, ABRAHAM S. and LUCHINS, EDITH H. "Children's Attitudes Toward Homogeneous Groupings." *Journal of Genetic Psychology* 72 (1948): 3–9.

MACKINTOSH, HELEN K.; GORE, LILLIAN; and LEWIS, GERTRUDE M. *Educating Disadvantaged Children in the Primary Grades*. U.S. Department of Health, Education, and Welfare. U.S. Office of Education, 1965.

MARITA, SISTER M. "Beginning Reading Achievement in Three Classroom Organizational Patterns." *The Reading Teacher* 20 (1966): 12–17.

MCDAVID, RAVEN. "Dialectology and the Teaching of Reading." *The Reading Teacher* 18 (1964): 206–13.

MCDONALD, THOMAS F. "An All-School Secondary Reading Program." *Journal of Reading* 14 (1971): 553–58.

MCDONALD, J.; HARRIS, T.; and MANN, J. "Individualized Versus Group Instruction in First Grade Reading." *The Reading Teacher*, 1966, 19, 643–46.

MIEL, ALICE, (Ed.). *Individualizing Reading Practices*. New York: Teachers College, Columbia University, Bureau of Publications, 1958.

MILLS, DONNA M. "Corrective and Remedial Reading Instruction in the Secondary School." *Reading as an Intellectual Activity*, 8 (1963): 56–59.

MOSSO, ASENATH M. "A Seminar for Superior High School Seniors." *School Review* 53 (1945): 464–70.

MULLER, FRANCES A. "Distinctive Problems Presented by Poor Readers: The Slow Learner." *Improving Reading in All Curriculum Areas*, Supplementary Monographs, No. 76. Chicago: University of Chicago Press, 1952, pp. 104–8.

MURPHY, GERALDINE J. "The Education of Gifted Children: Suggestions for a Philosophy and a Curriculum." *The School Review* 62 (1954): 414–19.

MURPHY, HELEN A. "Mutual Aid in Learning in the Primary Grades." In J. Allen Figurel, ed., *Changing Concepts of Reading Instruction*, International Reading Association Conference Proceedings, vol. 6, pp. 81–84. New York: Scholastic Magazines, 1961.

NEWPORT, JOHN F. "The Joplin Plan: The Score." *The Reading Teacher* 21 (1967): 158–62.

OLSON, ARTHUR V. "Organizing the Secondary Reading Program." *Reading Improvement* 3 (1966): 33–38.

OLSON, ARTHUR V. "Teaching Culturally Disadvantaged Children." *Education* 87 (1967): 423–25.

OLSON, WILLARD C. "Child Growth and Development." *Reading*. Washington, D.C.: Association for Childhood Education International, 1956, pp. 2–5.

OLSON, WILLARD C. *Child Development*, 2nd Edition. Boston: Heath and Company, 1959.

OTTO, WAYNE and MCMENEMY, RICHARD. A. *Corrective and Remedial Teaching of Reading*. Boston: Houghton Mifflin, 1966.

OTTO, WAYNE and SMITH, RICHARD J. *Administering the School Reading Program*. Boston: Houghton, Mifflin Company, 1970.

POWELL, WILLIAM R. "The Nature of Individual Differences." *Organizing for Individual Differences*, Perspectives 9. International Reading Association, 1967, pp. 1–17.

PLOWMAN, PAUL D. "Encouraging the Development of the Talented—In Academic Areas." *Education* 88 (1967): 35–42.

RAUCH, SIDNEY J. "Ten Guidelines for Teaching the Disadvantaged." *Journal of Reading* 10 (1967): 536–41.

RAUCH, SIDNEY J. "Using Paraprofessionals as Reading Aids." *Reading Methods and Teacher Improvement*. Newark, Del.: International Reading Association, 1971, pp. 184–95.

RIESSMAN, FRANK. *The Culturally Deprived Child.* New York: Harper and Row, 1962.

SANDERS, PETER L. "Impetus, Participant, Facilitator—A Definition of the Administrator's Role." *Journal of Reading* 14 (1971): 547–52.

SHANNON, J. R. "Homorthic Grouping—A New Proposal." *The Clearing House* 32 (1957): 133–34.

SHELDON, WILLIAM D. "The Nature and Scope of Reading Programs Adapted to Today's Needs: In the Upper Grades and Junior High School." *Better Readers for Our Times,* International Reading Association, Conference Proceedings. New York: Scholastic Magazines, 1956, pp. 30–33.

SIMMONS, JOHN S. "The Scope of the Reading Program of Secondary Schools." *The Reading Teacher* 17 (September 1963): 31–35.

SQUIRE, JAMES. "Reading in the American High Schools Today." *Reading and Inquiry.* Newark, Del.: International Reading Association, 1965, pp. 468–72.

STEWART, W. A. "On the Use of Negro Dialect in the Teaching of Reading." In Joan C. Baratz and Roger W. Shuy, eds., *Teaching Black Children to Read.* Washington, D.C.: Center for Applied Statistics, 1969, pp. 156–219.

STRANG, RUTH. "Basic Issues and Problems in Reading Instruction for Capable Students." *Promoting Maximal Reading Growth Among Able Learners,* Supplementary Educational Monographs, No. 81. Chicago: University of Chicago Press, 1954, pp. 6–10.

STRANG, RUTH. "Teaching Reading to the Culturally Disadvantaged in Secondary Schools." *Journal of Reading* 10 (1967): 527–35.

STRANG, RUTH; McCULLOUGH, CONSTANCE M.; and TRAXLER, ARTHUR E. *Problems in the Improvement of Reading.* New York: McGraw-Hill, 1955.

SUMMERS, EDWARD G. "A Suggested Integrated Reading Outline for Teacher Education Courses in Secondary Reading." *Journal of Reading* 9 (1965): 93–105.

THOMPSON, GERALD WAYNE. "The Effects of Ability Grouping Upon Achievement in Eleventh Grade American History." *Journal of Experimental Education* 42 (1974): 76–79.

VEATCH, JEANNETTE. *Individualizing Your Reading Program: Self-Selection in Action.* New York: G. P. Putnam's Sons, 1959.

VITE, IRENE W. "Individualized Reading—The Scoreboard on Control Studies." *Education* 81 (1961): 285–90.

VITE, IRENE W. "Grouping Practices in Individualized Reading." *Elementary English* 38 (1961): 91–98.

WALKER, JERRY L. "Conducting an Individualized Reading Program in High School." *Journal of Reading* 8 (1965): 291–95.

WARNER, DOLORES. "The Divided-Day Plan for Reading Organization." *The Reading Teacher* 20 (1967): 397–99.

WELTY, STELLA L. "Reading and Black English." *Language, Reading and the Communication Process.* Newark, Del.: International Reading Association, 1971, pp. 71–93.

WHEELER, LESTER R. and WHEELER, VIOLA D. "The Relationship Between Reading Ability and Intelligence Among University Freshmen." *Journal of Educational Psychology* 40 (1949): 230–38.

WHIPPLE, GERTRUDE and BLACK, MILLARD H. *Reading for Children Without—Our*

Disadvantaged Youth. Newark, Del.: International Reading Association, 1966.

WILLIAMS, WILMAJEAN. "Academic Achievement in a Graded School and in a Non-Graded School." *The Elementary School Journal* 67 (1966): 135–39.

WITTY, PAUL. *Reading in High School and College,* Forty-Seventh Yearbook, National Society for the Study of Education, Part II, pp. 18–19. Chicago: University of Chicago Press, 1938.

WITTY, PAUL. "Reading and the Gifted Child." *The Reading Teacher* 9 (1956): 195–96.

14

Diagnosis
and Remediation

We know that, in learning to read, all children do not progress at the same rate. Even among those of adequate ability, some meet problems that delay or block their learning. We must strive constantly to discover these deterrents to learning and plan individualized work to further each child's development. An effective developmental reading program is built on a foundation of early diagnosis of inadequacies, careful evaluation of needs and abilities, and the utilization of professionally designed materials and methods.

Before we get into the more technical aspects of diagnosis and remediation, let us make a few general observations about the prevention of reading disabilities.

Many educators today are concerned that we may be overemphasizing remediation and ignoring prevention. Their fears are not entirely groundless. In too many instances the best teachers are removed from regular classroom teaching and put into the role of special or remedial reading teacher. This may lead to poorer instruction in the classroom and increased numbers of children with reading problems. It may well be that we are thus producing retarded readers at a rate much faster than we will ever be able to remediate.

Although we have done a better job of remediation than of prevention, it is far better to prevent than to remediate; it is far better that we deal with the problem in the classroom rather than wait until the pupil acquires a reading disability.

Prevention is not an easy task. No one has found the appropriate preventions, or we would not have the number of reading disabilities that we do have. Perhaps we have not looked for ways of preventing reading disability but merely have been satisfied with cures.

Reading failures can be prevented only if every lesson is a diagnostic and, in a sense, a remedial lesson. Perhaps even then many failures cannot be prevented, but the teacher must operate on the assumption that failures can be prevented, and it is only through accurate and continuous diagnosis of the child's needs and difficulties, of his assets and strengths, that the teacher can modify instruction to meet these needs. Continuous diagnosis is a must in the reading classroom; prevention is its end-product. Diagnosis identifies minor difficulties before they become disabilities and thus occasions adjustments in instruction that might remove these difficulties.

It is not uncommon for the teacher to observe within the classroom children who fit the following descriptions. Jane has completed the readiness program but still cannot identify rhyming words. Dick has missed a significant amount of reading instruction because he was ill. June has an abnormal amount of difficulty with similar-appearing words such as *them* and *then*. Pat, in reading orally, gets the meaning but cannot say some of the words. Jim has difficulty remembering such high frequency words as *in* or *the*.

Others are developing habits of word-by-word reading, of vocalizing, of backtracking, of daydreaming while reading, of rereading, of plodding along at a snail's pace, of word blocking, of following words with their finger, or of moving the head from side to side rather than moving their eyes across the page.

Serious problems? No, but these innocuous difficulties tend to snowball. Most remedial cases are probably instances of "an accumulation of unmet reading needs." Reading deficiency begins with simple inadequacies. Despite the good work of the classroom teacher, some pupils lose increasingly more ground with each year of school attendance. Retardation is cumulative.

To detect and diagnose the incipient reading problems, then, is a prime responsibility of the teacher. Prevention of reading difficulties should begin before the child begins formal reading instruction and continue throughout his entire school career. Prevention is best brought about by diagnosis of and constant alertness to any incipient or existing difficulty.

The child with a reading disability must have the benefits of recognition (Ellingson, 1968). His problem needs to be identified early, or he will grow up with the disability intact. Beyond a certain point he no longer may be interested in or be able to benefit from educational recognition (Ellingson, 1968).

It does not make sense to delay remedial instruction until, say, the third grade. We cannot permit children to become imprisoned in faulty learning habits. At the first instance the teacher notices that the child is not progressing satisfactorily, diagnostic study and appropriate remedial education are indicated.

Schiffman (1964), in a survey of 10,000 children, found that pupils with reading problems who were identified and received remedial education in the second grade had ten times as great a chance for successful outcome of the remedial treatment as those identified only at the ninth-grade level.

DEFINITION OF DIAGNOSIS

Diagnosis is defined in *Webster's New Collegiate Dictionary* as the art or act of recognizing disease from its symptoms. Brueckner (1935, p. 2) notes that educational diagnosis refers to the techniques by which one discovers and evaluates the strengths and weaknesses of an individual. The diagnostician gathers data and then on the basis of the analysis and interpretation of these data suggests developmental or remedial measures.

Tiegs (p. 5) adds that educational diagnosis facilitates the optimum development of every pupil and determines (1) which of his factors of intelligence are strong and which are weak, (2) whether he learns better through language or non-language materials, (3) what his unattained objectives are, and (4) the nature of his desires, fears, and frustrations.

Diagnosis is an identification of weakness or strength from an observation of symptoms. It is an inference from performance. It must include assessment of both level of performance (reading retardation) and manner of performance (inability to integrate visual stimuli). It is concerned with determining the nature of the problem, identifying the constellation of factors that produced it, and finding a point of attack.

PRINCIPLES OF DIAGNOSIS

As one scans the literature on diagnosis, a few general principles emerge:

1. Diagnosis begins with each pupil's unique instructional needs:
   a. What can he do?
   b. What are his difficulties?
   c. What are the causes of his difficulties?
   d. What can be done to remedy his difficulties?
2. Diagnosis is a continuous process.
3. Diagnosis should be directed toward formulating methods of remediation. Educational diagnosis is productive only if it is translated into specific educational strategies.
4. Diagnosis and remediation are no longer the special privileges of the slow or retarded learner—they are extended to the gifted and the average as well.
5. Diagnosis may be concerned merely with the symptomatology, but genuine diagnosis looks toward the causes of the symptoms. The diagnostic viewpoint is that behavior is caused. The teacher thus needs to understand the causes of inadequate performance rather than to blame the pupil for it. The child should not be labelled dumb or lazy, even though each may be a cause once in a while.
6. The causes of pupil inadequacy are usually multiple rather than single or unitary.
7. The teacher needs more than simply skill in diagnosing the causes of the child's difficulty. He needs ability to modify instruction to meet the need identified by diagnosis.
8. Decisions based on diagnosis should flow from a pattern of test scores and a variety of other data.
9. The analysis of reading difficulties is primarily an *educational-analysis* task; it is best done by an experienced teacher who knows the essential elements of reading instruction (Durrell, 1956, 354–55).

STEPS IN DIAGNOSIS

Diagnosis leads to an ever more detailed study of the problem. It begins in reading with simple observation and possibly a survey test and ends up with a hypothesis for remediation. It involves the identification and description of the problem, the discovery of the causes, and projection of remediation required. More specifically, the steps of the diagnostic procedure may be the following:[1]

1. The Overall Screening Process—Compare expected functioning level as determined by IQ and other tests and personal data with actual functioning level as determined by the reading survey test or by other less formal procedures. This is the level of *survey diagnosis* and consists chiefly of classroom screening.

2. Diagnostic Testing—Describe the condition more specifically, checking on such specifics as knowledge of vocabulary, inability to associate sound with the beginning consonant, inability to phrase correctly, or reversal problems. Informal observations of the pupil's reading and diagnostic testing will help to identify the difficulties. This is the level of *specific diagnosis* and is identified with individual diagnosis.

3. Detailed Investigation of Causality—Make an analysis of the disability, looking for the correlates of disability. If the test results in Step 2 show a weakness in phonic skills, the pupil's auditory discrimination might be

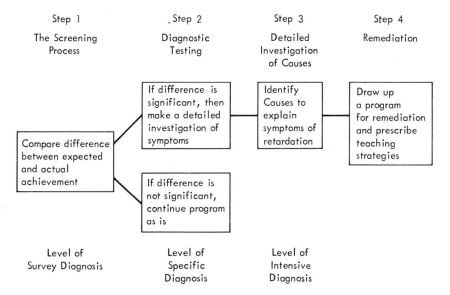

FIGURE 14–1 *Sequential Steps in Diagnosis*

[1] Barbara Bateman, "Learning Disabilities—Yesterday, Today, and Tomorrow," *Exceptional Children*, 31 (1965): 167–76.

checked. This is the level of *intensive diagnosis* and is associated with identifying the underlying causes of the reading disability.

4. Remediation—Finally, draw up a program of remediation. Diagnosis is complete only when remediation occurs. The diagnostic-remedial process is a single process.

Step 1: The Screening Process

Let us assume that we have a typical elementary school that has about 500 children and in which the administration and staff want to begin a special reading program for those children who are more or less retarded in reading. The immediate aim will be to reduce the number of pupils for this special education to something below 500.

Screening separates those persons who *are* most likely to need special attention from those who *are not* likely to need it. It is commonly applied to large groups of pupils by classroom teachers. This first step tends to be comprehensive in *breadth;* the later steps in diagnosis are more comprehensive in *depth.* Screening procedures should be simple, fairly quick, inexpensive, valid, reliable, and productive.

For many children we do not need a detailed diagnosis. A more general diagnosis is sufficient. It is enough in most instances that we acquire sufficient knowledge about the 500 children or the 30 children in a given classroom so that instruction might be adjusted to the group. This overall screening process should identify the overall reading proficiency of the group or class, help to adjust instruction to individual differences within the group, and locate those pupils who are in need of further analysis of their disability.

There needs to be adequate provision for remediation of most reading disability cases in the regular classroom. One factor that operates against remediation in the regular classroom is the high pupil-teacher ratio. It is difficult to provide individual remediation when there are 30 children, all clamoring for the teacher's time and attention.

The Nature of Retardation. Perhaps the first prerequisite for anyone associated with the reading program, and indeed the educational program, is to have a clear conception of the meaning of retardation. There is a difference between slow learners, reluctant readers, experientially-deprived readers, and retarded readers. Table 14-1 delineates some of these differences.

Retardation generally is defined in relation to level of general development, with perhaps the greater emphasis being on mental development. Retardation is associated with slower progress than is expected. A retarded reader is one whose reading capacity is considerably greater than his reading achievement. Wilson (1967) suggests that on the high school level the retarded or problem reader is one who cannot read his textbooks effectively. He is a reader who benefits little from regular classroom instruction in the various content areas. Bryant (1963) notes that disability is always dependent upon the material and methods used in

TABLE 14–1 *Characteristics of Various Poor Readers*

SLOW LEARNER	RELUCTANT READER	DISADVANTAGED READER	RETARDED READER
ability level below 90 IQ ↓ generally reads on ability level ↓ generally reads below grade level ↓ ↓ instruction needs to be adapted to his limited ability—the pace of instruction and teacher expectations must be realistic	can read but will not ↓ the root of the reading difficulties is the mental attitude of the pupil ↓ solution to the reading problem begins with a change of attitude	potential often far exceeds performance ↓ generally can learn and wants to learn ↓ lacks adequate oral language because of inadequate experience ↓ does not look upon reading as life-related ↓ often feels alienated from the larger social structure ↓ often deficient in auditory attention ↓ needs to learn how to learn	is usually of average or above average intelligence, although a retarded reader could also be a slow learner ↓ does not read on ability level ↓ may or may not be reading below grade level ↓ may show blocks to learning, especially emotional or neurological, which keep him from learning to read.

instruction. A child may not be able to learn by one method, but he may not be "disabled" if a different method is used.

A reader is also more or less retarded. The retarded reader of fifty years ago was more likely to be a pupil who could not read. Today, he often is a pupil who is not reading as well as he might. Durrell (1940, p. 279), notes that a retardation of six months at the first-grade level is more serious than is a retardation of six months at the sixth-grade level. Harris (1961a, p. 299) does not consider a first-grade child retarded unless his reading age is at least six months below his mental age. For a child to be considered a retarded reader, the difference between performance and potential ought to be at least nine months for children in grades four and five and about a year in grades six and above.

Reading Potential. The first diagnostic step involves an analysis of (1) reading potential or reading expectancy level and (2) reading achievement. This presents the teacher with a knowledge of what the child's present level of achievement is and to what level he might progress.

Without knowing a student's potential, education is target practice in the dark. No one can know where he is going if he does not know where he is at.

Various ways of assessing reading potential have been tried. The tests most frequently used to assess reading potential are intelligence or scholastic aptitude tests. These tests often provide IQ or mental age scores.

Since the idea is to obtain intelligence or scholastic aptitude test scores on all 500 children in our sample school, or perhaps on a class of 30, it is recommended that the first test be a group paper and pencil test. Tests useful for this purpose are:

1. *California Test of Mental Maturity,* California Test Bureau, Monterey, Calif.
2. *Kuhlmann-Anderson IQ Test,* Personnel Press, Inc., Princeton, N.J.
3. *Kuhlmann-Finch IQ Test,* American Guidance Service, Inc., Minneapolis.
4. *Lorge-Thorndike Intelligence Tests,* Houghton Mifflin Company, Boston.
5. *Otis-Lennon Mental Ability Test,* Harcourt, Brace & World, Inc., Chicago.

Most primary tests use pictures and thus can generally be used with retarded readers. Tests for fourth grade and above usually require reading. Some of these, however, provide nonverbal scores, and these scores can give clues for diagnosis. When the verbal score is substantially lower than the nonverbal score, the teacher might suspect that the pupil's performance on the verbal sections is limited by the lack of reading ability. The test is thus an unfair test for him. It often places the poor reader in the dull-normal category, thus underestimating his real ability.

Probably every child whose IQ score falls below 90 or below the twenty-fifth percentile on a test requiring reading should be given another intelligence or scholastic aptitude test. Another IQ test should also be given when the pupil's reading level score as determined by a reading achievement test is significantly below his grade level. This means that perhaps 25 percent or 125 pupils of the original group of 500 need retesting. It may mean that from six to eight pupils in a given classroom need to be retested. Their abilities need to be measured by a test that does not require reading to get the correct answer. Here is a list of tests that are specifically designed to deal with this problem. Some of them may be administered to a group of children and others must be given individually. Some of the latter require special training for their administration.

GROUP

IPAT Culture Fair Intelligence Tests, Institute for Personality and Ability Testing, Champaign, Ill.

INDIVIDUAL

1. *Chicago Non-Verbal Examination,* Psychological Corporation, New York.
2. *Columbia Mental Maturity Scale,* Harcourt, Brace & World, Inc., Chicago.
3. *Full Range Picture Vocabulary Test,* Psychological Test Specialists, Missoula, Mont.
4. *Peabody Picture Vocabulary Test,* American Guidance Service, Inc., Minneapolis.
5. *Quick Test,* Psychological Test Specialists, Missoula, Mont.

6. *Slosson Intelligence Test for Children and Adults,* Slosson Educational Publications, East Aurora, N.Y.
7. *Stanford-Binet Intelligence Scales,* Houghton Mifflin Company, Boston.
8. *Wechsler Intelligence Scale for Children,* Psychological Corporation, New York.

The IQ score should not be used as an absolute measure. A mechanical formula cannot decide for us when a pupil *is* a retarded reader, and it cannot tell us when the child is no longer a disabled reader (McLeod, 1968). Nevertheless, the IQ, though perhaps too simple an estimate of the pupil's present academic potential, is the best that we have. It is indicative of the minimum that we might expect from the pupil; it is certainly not indicative of the maximum of which he is capable. Reading potential or readiness for reading instruction on the kindergarten–first-grade level also may be assessed through readiness tests.

There is a third way of estimating the pupil's potential. The pupil's listening ability is a good indicator of the level on which the pupil could be reading. Reading might be defined as listening through print. The following tests provide a measure of the pupil's listening comprehension.

1. *Stroud-Hieronymus Primary Reading Profiles,* Houghton Mifflin Company, grades 1 and 2.
2. *Botel Reading Inventory,* Follett Publishing Company, grades 1–12.
3. *Sequential Tests of Educational Progress: Listening,* Cooperative Test Division, Educational Testing Services, grades 4–14.
4. *Brown-Carlson Listening Comprehension Test,* Harcourt, Brace and World, grades nine–adult.
5. *Durrell Listening-Reading Series,* Harcourt, Brace and World, grades 7 to 9.

Reading Achievement. Having discovered the approximate potential of the 500 youngsters, or the 30 in the individual classroom, it is next necessary to get an estimate of their reading achievement. A reading survey test should be administered to each of the pupils.

The survey test is concerned with general achievement and typically is the first reading achievement test that the teacher will use. Usually it emphasizes vocabulary knowledge, comprehension of sentences or paragraphs, and perhaps speed of comprehension. It gives a general picture by identifying broad areas in which the pupil excels or is weak. It may tell, for example, that a certain child is reading at a level typical of children one or more grades above or below his present grade level. It indicates the general level of pupil progress and provides data for determining a pupil's proper grade placement and the reading materials that he should be expected to use with understanding. Some common survey tests are the following:

1. *California Reading Test,* California Test Bureau, Monterey, Calif., grades 1–14.
2. *Gates-MacGinitie Reading Test,* Teachers College Press, Columbia University, grades K–12.

3. *Iowa Silent Reading Tests,* Harcourt, Brace & World, New York, grades 4–14.
4. *Metropolitan Achievement Test, Reading,* Harcourt, Brace & World, New York, grades 2–9.

After having obtained the intelligence test score and the survey reading test scores, it is possible to identify the number of students whose reading scores are significantly below their intelligence or scholastic aptitude test score.

To determine degree of retardation, proceed as follows. Group the reading and scholastic aptitude scores into two columns.

STUDENT	READING SCORE (GRADE LEVEL)	IQ SCORE
1	11.6	122
2	6.1	113

Then compare each student's reading performance with his mental age. The purpose of this procedure is to determine whether the reading score (reading age score) is substantially below the mental age score. You may also want to check whether it is below his listening comprehension score. To carry out this manipulation, it is necessary to know the student's age and IQ. Begin by converting the reading grade score into a reading age score. This is done by adding 5 to the grade score. In our sample below, the test itself furnished the reading age score. Then find the mental age. This may be done (as shown) by multiplying the age by the IQ, being careful to put a decimal point at the proper place in the IQ score.

Student	Grade-Level Reading Score	Reading Age Score (RA)	Chronological Age	IQ Score	Mental Age	Difference Between MA and RA
1	11.6	16.9	14.0	122	17.0 (14 × 1.22)	— .1
2	6.1	11.3	14.2	113	16.0 (14.2 × 1.13)	—4.7

In the two samples given, student 1 is retarded only .1 of a year; student 2 is retarded 4.7 years. Student 2 ought to be performing like the average youngster of sixteen (high school sophomore or junior level), but he is performing on the sixth-grade level.

Student 2 obviously calls for more thorough analysis. It is with this type of student that we need to follow through with steps 2, 3, and 4 of diagnosis.

By completing Step 1, we should have greatly reduced the number of students who need special attention. We should have differentiated students who are genuinely retarded (e.g., student 2) from those who simply need adapted instruction.

There are numerous other criteria besides mental age by which to gauge a pupil's achievement. Bruininks, Glaman, and Clark (1973) list the following formulas (see Table 14-2).

The formulas generally do not yield identical levels of expected achievement for the same children, especially at the extreme ends of the intellectual continuum. It is for this reason that the formulas must all be used with caution. A number of observations seem pertinent:

1. The wide differences between various estimates of the percentages of retarded readers may be the result of a difference of definition of retardation, differences in analysis, characteristics of the samples, instructional history, etc. (Bruininks et al., 1973).

2. As we noted earlier, surveys of school populations involving several grade levels should vary the criterion of disparity between predicted and actual achievement (Bruininks et al., 1973). This simply means that at upper grade levels the difference between expected and actual achievement must be larger to be termed significant.

TABLE 14-2 *Commonly used achievement expectancy formulas*

	FORMULAS
1. Mental Grade	$AE^a = MA - 5$ years
2. Bond and Tinker	$AE^a = \left(\dfrac{IQ}{100} \times \text{years-in-school} \right) + 1.0$
3. Monroe	$AE^a = \left(\dfrac{\text{Arithmetic Age} + CA + MA}{3} - 6 \right) + 1.0$
4. Horn (age: 6-0 to 8-5)	$AE^a = \left(\dfrac{MA + CA}{2} - 6 \right) + 1.0$
(age: 8-6 to 9-11)	$AE^a = \left(\dfrac{3MA + 2CA}{5} - 6 \right) + 1.0$
(age: 10-0 to 11-11)	$AE^a = \left(\dfrac{2MA + CA}{3} - 6 \right) + 1.0$
(age: 12-0+)	$AE^a = \left(\dfrac{3MA + CA}{4} - 6 \right) + 1.0$
5. Myklebust	$AE^a = \left(\dfrac{MA + \text{Grade Age}}{2} \right)$

[a]Achievement expectancy

3. Test data do not make judgments; they are only aids to judgment. Interpretation without an understanding of errors of measurement is almost certainly going to be erroneous.

4. Using the nonverbal IQ score rather than the verbal IQ score identifies a much larger percentage of children having learning difficulties. The mental age formula identifies the largest percentage; the Bond and Tinker formula, the lowest.

5. Rodenborn (1974), after noting that the various expectancy formulas provide wide differences when predicting reading achievement of children with intelligence levels greatly above or below normal or in evaluating the effectiveness of reading programs, adds that expectancy levels derived from expectancy formulas in estimating reading potential are merely estimates and something less than precise indicators.

Dore-Boyce, Misner, and McGuire (1975) found that the mental age formula was the best predictor of reading expectancy at the fourth and fifth grade level.

The screening which occurs in Step 1 serves to provide differential early programming for some children who may not be progressing adequately. Hill (1970) suggest there are four early screening models: illness, immaturity, coping, and environmental match-mismatch. Coping refers to a crisis which has caused a disruption of expected growth (perhaps too early introduction to reading). The match-mismatch model refers to discrepancies between what a child does and what he is expected to do (mismatch of the middle-class teacher and the disadvantaged child). Most diagnoses in the early stages are based on the discrepancy model (Myers and Hammill, 1969).

Step 2: Diagnostic Testing

Diagnostic testing continues the diagnostic process begun in Step 1 and is the beginning of detailed diagnosis. It is directed toward defining the actual nature of the individual's reading difficulties and toward identifying the conditions causing them. It is a detailed investigation of the symptoms of reading disability, leading to a clinical diagnosis. Here the teacher is not satisfied to know that the pupil is reading on a second-grade level when in fact he might be able to read on a fourth-grade level. The teacher wants to know the specific reasons for the over-all low performance: Is it the inability to attack words? Is it the limited vocabulary? Is it the failure to use context? Is it the lack of ability in auditory blending? Is it an orientational difficulty? Or is it a combination of factors?

Smith and Carrigan (1959, p. 91) note that diagnosis must be based on a careful investigation of the symptoms, on psychological test behavior, and often on intensive clinical case studies. They note that such dead-end diagnosis as "he isn't trying" or "he needs more disciplining" must be replaced with a clinical diagnosis.

Step 2 thus is a specific, an individual, and a clinical diagnosis. It is a detailed analysis of the reading problems of pupils identified in Step 1 as retarded readers. Let's assume that about 20 percent of the pupils studied in Step 1 are actually retarded in reading. It is now necessary to determine what their specific difficulties are and where, whether in the regular classroom or in the remedial room, their difficulties might best be taken care of.

In many schools, the classroom teacher is still the person primarily responsible for the diagnosis and remediation of reading problems. In others, the teacher is assisted by a remedial teacher or a reading specialist. This special reading teacher might then direct the diagnostic process or actually do the diagnosing himself.

Step 2 should include, if possible, the following in addition to the data acquired in Step 1:

1. A complete physical examination.
2. An analysis of WISC subtest data on each pupil with special consideration of their relationship to the pupil's retardation. Studies generally indicate that poor readers score low on arithmetic, coding, information, digit span, and similarities.
3. Administration and interpretation of a Reading Inventory and/or an oral reading test.
4. Administration and interpretation of a Reading Diagnostic Test.
5. A determination of the student's preferred mode of learning using one or a combination of the instruments listed later in this section.
6. Evaluation of the student's hearing, vision, and eye movements.
7. An evaluation of the child's self-concept using the *Piers-Harris Children's Self-Concept Scale, grades 3–12,* Counselor Recordings and Tests, Box 6184, Acklen Station, Nashville, 37212.

Before these data are compiled, the pupil's classroom teacher should complete the Personal Data Sheet and Personal and Reading Symptomatology Checklist.

Personal Data Sheet and Personal and Reading Symptomatology Check List. The first report on each pupil who was revealed in Step 1 to be reading significantly below his ability should summarize personal data on the pupil. This report might be used as the referral form from the classroom teacher to the special teacher if this becomes necessary. It might also be sent to the pupil's new teacher when the pupil moves from one grade to another. In this way, the new teacher would have some knowledge of the pupil's needs and could then adjust his instruction to the pupil.

The personal data sheet includes such data as pupil's name, age, grade level, address, his previous grades, his attendance record, statements about his health, standardized test results, a compilation of the anecdotal reports by other teachers, and most of all the reason for the referral. The reason may be that the pupil is not reading up to ability level. The statement might simply read: "The test results indicate that he is reading about one grade level below his ability"; "He has a mental age of

Student's Name _____ Date of Birth _____

Mo.   Day   Year

Parent's Name _____ Age _____ Grade _____

Address _____ Phone _____

Academic Progress
   Report last year's grade(s)

Attendance Record
   Number of days absent for each grade: 9 _____ 10 _____ 11 _____ 12 _____

Health
   (List physical infirmities, accidents, and severe illnesses as listed in school record.)

Standardized Tests

   (Include all test results available—intelligence tests, achievement tests, etc.)

Date Given	Name of Test	Score by	
		Grade Level	Percentile

Reason for Referral

Anecdotal Reports or Comments of Former Teachers (Report on back of this page)

Signed _____

Position _____

Date of report _____ 19 _____

FIGURE 14-2 *Personal Data Sheet*

ten, but is reading like the average eight year old"; or, "His reading level is substantially below his listening comprehension level."

Whether the pupil is referred or kept in the regular classroom, it is imperative that the teacher know at least in a general sense what the problem is. The remaining instruments discussed in this chapter delve more deeply into the pupil's more specific problems and symptoms.

A form similar to Figure 14-2 might be used to compile the basic information of a pupil. Fig 14-3 identifies personal and reading behaviors associated with reading disability.

FIGURE 14–3

PERSONAL AND READING SYMPTOMATOLOGY CHECKLIST

Please complete the checklist below, simply checking *"Yes"*, *"No"*, or *"Don't Know"* for each of the items.

NAME OF STUDENT _____

SEX _____ AGE: _____

　　　　　　　　　　　　　　　　Years　　　　　　　　Months

NAME OF EVALUATOR: _____

PERSONAL SYMPTOMATOLOGY*

	(Yes)	(No)	(Don't Know)
1. BACKGROUND OF PERSONAL EXPERIENCE			
1.1　Has a foreign language background	✓		
1.2　Is from a low-level socio-economic home	✓		
1.3　Comes from a broken home	✓		
1.4　There is a familial history of reading disability	✓		
1.5　Either he or members of the family are left-handed or ambidextrous	✓		
1.6　Was a premature child or survived some complication of pregnancy	✓		
1.7　Has suffered some type of neurological injury	✓		
1.8　Was introduced to formal teaching of reading before age six	✓		
2. GENERAL MENTAL AND COGNITIVE DEVELOPMENT			
2.1　Verbal IQ is significantly below the performance IQ	✓		
2.2　Can give the amount of attention needed to learn		✓	
2.3　Has a short attention span	✓		
2.4　Perseverates excessively	✓		
2.5　Can easily shift attention		✓	
2.6　Attends equally to all stimuli	✓		
2.7　Is unable to withhold attention from some stimuli	✓		
2.8　Produces immature drawings of human forms	✓		
2.9　Shows frequent reversals of concepts: go for stop, east for west, etc.	✓		
2.10　Has a poor memory for sequences	✓		
2.11　Thinks on a concrete level rather than in abstract terms	✓		
2.12　Has difficulty remembering what he read	✓		
2.13　Has greater difficulty in *recalling* infor-			

*The check indicates whether a "Yes" or "No" answer to the question is associated with reading disability.

	(Yes)	(No)	(Don't Know)

mation than in *recognizing* a bit of information ✓

2.14 Can count to twenty or recite the alphabet but cannot tell what number comes after 8 or what letter comes after *C* ✓

2.15 His usable vocabulary is small ✓

3. MANUAL/MOTOR DEXTERITY

3.1 Has poor manual dexterity ✓

3.2 Has poor motor and/or visuo-motor patterning or coordination ✓

4. PERCEPTION SKILLS: AUDITORY AND VISUAL DISCRIMINATION

4.1 Has a hearing loss of 15 or more decibels ✓ (Yes)

4.2 Has at least 20/60 visual acuity ✓ (No)

4.3 Can distinguish between shapes and letters ✓ (No)

4.4 Is weak in visual memory ✓ (Yes)

4.5 Auditory discrimination is poor ✓ (Yes)

4.6 Has intrasensory transcoding difficulties ✓ (Yes)

4.7 Has a very short eye memory span ✓ (Yes)

4.8 Can sequence correctly, especially auditorily ✓ (No)

4.9 Can copy shapes and sequences ✓ (No)

4.10 Has an inner ear disturbance causing a permanent motion sickness and resulting in the scrambling of incoming visual signals ✓ (Yes)

5. WRITING AND SPELLING

5.1 His writing is clumsy, jerky, arrhythmic; the characters are poorly formed, irregular, malaligned ✓

5.2 Spelling of words is peculiar and odd ✓

5.3 He spells by "ear" ✓

6. LANGUAGE AND SPEECH

6.1 His language is sprinkled with grammatical errors ✓

6.2 He exhibits various speech difficulties: articulation errors, enunciation difficulties, pronunciation errors, etc. ✓

6.3 He stutters, lisps, or stammers ✓

6.4 His speech is cluttered or stumbling, characterized by explosive speech ✓

6.5 Has little sentence sense or feel for the structure of the language ✓

6.6 Has a narrow eye-voice span ✓

		(Yes)	(No)	(Don't Know)
7. SPATIAL RELATIONSHIPS				
7.1	Shows disturbances of body image	✓		
7.2	Has difficulty in putting on his garments the right way	✓		
7.3	Has difficulty with figure/ground discriminations	✓		
7.4	Can place objects in space		✓	
7.5	Shows poor spatial orientation to graphemes or the temporal order of phonemes	✓		
7.6	Can see the relationship of the part to the whole		✓	
7.7	Has a poor sense of direction	✓		
7.8	Has inadequately developed dominance, is either ambidextrous, left-handed, or shows mixed dominance	✓		
7.9	Knows the difference between right & left		✓	
7.10	His EEGs show less synchronization between the two hemispheres and more synchronization within each hemisphere	✓		
7.11	Has hemispheric cross–integration difficulties or lacks brain asymmetry making it difficult to engage in high level complex or abstract thinking	✓		
7.12	Has deficient cortical maturation resulting in reading disability, speech defects, motor incoordination, ambidextrality or poorly defined unilateral dominance	✓		
8. PERSONAL/MOTIVATIONAL/SOCIAL				
8.1	Has a low frustration tolerance	✓		
8.2	Has a low self-image	✓		
8.3	Is hyperactive, easily distracted, excitable, and impulsive	✓		
8.4	Is motivated to use his cognitive and perceptual powers		✓	
8.5	Is aggressive and demanding	✓		
8.6	His concentration is poor	✓		

READING SYMPTOMATOLOGY

		(Yes)	(No)	(Don't Know)
1. WORD RECOGNITION SKILLS				
1.1	Exhibits wild guessing at words	✓		
1.2	Can deal with individual letters and the sounds they represent—is able to associate the phoneme with the grapheme or to deal with phoneme/grapheme correspondences		✓	
1.3	Sees words on the printed page as an undifferentiated design	✓		
1.4	Can distinguish between letters		✓	
1.5	Can name letters		✓	

		(Yes)	(No)	(Don't Know)
1.6	Can name words		✓	
1.7	Has much difficulty remembering and recalling familiar words. Needs to ask again and again for help with the same word	✓		
1.8	Sees the letter or word as an entity. Experiences the global identification of a word as a whole		✓	
1.9	His reading is full of errors: reversals, vowel and consonant errors, omissions, additions, substitutions, and frequent repetitions	✓		
1.10	Can blend satisfactorily		✓	
1.11	Can spell the word b-a-n-a-n-a but can't pronounce it	✓		
1.12	Easily confuses similar appearing words	✓		
1.13	Has much difficulty learning sight words	✓		
1.14	Can synthesize the word out of its component parts		✓	
1.15	Makes frequent mismatches between phoneme and grapheme	✓		

2. COMPREHENSION SKILLS

		(Yes)	(No)	(Don't Know)
2.1	Can match words with pictures		✓	
2.2	Can associate experiences, perceptions, and meaning with symbols—is able to deal with letters and words as symbols		✓	
2.3	Can name his concepts (height for tallness)		✓	
2.4	Can infer meanings from context clues		✓	
2.5	Is able to use the syntactic cues to identify words and to read with comprehension		✓	
2.6	Identifies words as if the words were unrelated items unaffected by syntactical or contextual relationships	✓		
2.7	The miscues he makes in reading fit the syntactic structure into which they are substituted		✓	
2.8	He notices that he made a misreading		✓	
2.9	Is content to settle on the first meaning that comes into his mind	✓		
2.10	Is able to read materials on his grade level		✓	
2.11	Achieves much better in non-reading than in reading or language subjects	✓		
2.12	Can read in phrase units		✓	
2.13	Can identify main ideas		✓	
2.14	Can recall facts and details		✓	
2.15	Can organize words into meaningful units such as phrases, clauses, etc.		✓	
2.16	Is able to organize what he reads		✓	
2.17	Is able to follow directions in reading		✓	
2.18	Focuses most of his processing capacity on the visual aspect or the surface structure	✓		

(Personal and Reading Symptomatology Checklist *cont.*)

		(Yes)	(No)	(Don't Know)
2.19	Can use redundancy clues to work out the meaning of a sentence		✓	

3. AUDITORY SKILLS

		(Yes)	(No)	(Don't Know)
3.1	He is deficient in auditory attention and interpretation skills	✓		
3.2	Can move from sound to printed symbol		✓	
3.3	Is poor in phonic skills	✓		
3.4	Can detect differences between sounds		✓	
3.5	Learns more easily through listening than through reading	✓		
3.6	Hears speech as undifferentiated noise	✓		
3.7	His rendition of a word is often unrelated to the desired response (dog becomes chay)	✓		
3.8	Can distinguish such sounds as /f/, /v/, /s/, /z/, /sh/, /zh/, /th/,/t/, /d/, /b/, /k/, /g/		✓	
3.9	Can handle the late developing sounds: /z/, /s/, /r/, /wh/, /ch/, /j/		✓	
3.10	Can interpret sentences modified by intonation		✓	

4. REVERSALS

		(Yes)	(No)	(Don't Know)
4.1	Reverses letters (b-d, p-b, p-d, p-q, u-n, o-e, e-c, q-b, etc)	✓		
4.2	Reverses entire words	✓		
4.3	Transposes letters or syllables in words: animal becomes aminal	✓		
4.4	Can read upside down with ease	✓		
4.5	Can read mirror images of words with ease	✓		

5. RATE AND FLUENCY

		(Yes)	(No)	(Don't Know)
5.1	His reading is arrhythmical	✓		
5.2	Vocalizes excessively	✓		
5.3	Rate of comprehension is significantly below the norm	✓		

6. EYE MOVEMENT

		(Yes)	(No)	(Don't Know)
6.1	Frequently loses his place	✓		
6.2	Moves easily from the end of one line to the beginning of another		✓	
6.3	Sequences saccadic eye movements too rapidly, thus skipping material	✓		

7. MODALITY OF LEARNING

		(Yes)	(No)	(Don't Know)
7.1	Learns easier when he sees information in print		✓	

(Personal and Reading Symptomatology Checklist *cont.*)

	(Yes)	(No)	(Don't Know)
7.2 Learns easier when he hears information	✓		
7.3 Learns easier when he can write or use his hands	✓		

8. OTHER

	(Yes)	(No)	(Don't Know)
8.1 Reading performance is exceedingly variable	✓		
8.2 Has difficulty in arithmetic	✓		

Formal or Informal Inventory[2]

A teacher's prime task (or the special teacher's as the case might be) with the retarded may be to identify the pupil's frustration, instructional, and independent reading level. To do this, he may administer additional individual intelligence tests, such as the *Wechsler Intelligence Scale for Children* (WISC) or the *Revised Stanford-Binet Scale* and additional achievement tests, but he certainly makes use of informal and formal reading inventories.

Interpretation of WISC Test Data. The WISC consists of subtests that have proven useful in diagnosis. Neville (1967) found that poor readers score low on the Arithmetic, Coding, and Information subtests, and score relatively higher on the Picture Arrangement and Picture Completion. Reid and Schoer (1966) also reported readers scored significantly lower on the Arithmetic subtest of the *WISC* but showed relative high performance on the Picture Completion subtest. The retarded readers likewise scored lower on the Digit Span and Similarities subtests. Ekwall (1966) found that 43 retarded readers in grades four, five, and six scored significantly low on Information, Arithmetic, and Digit Span and significantly high on Picture Completion, Block Design, Picture Arrangement, Object Assembly, and Coding. Sawyer (1965) reports that the Wechsler subscales did discriminate between severely disabled and mildly disabled readers.

Informal Inventories. The classroom teacher has probably already used informal procedures in gauging the reader's achievement as well as his frustration, instructional, or independent level. He frequently determines the level of the child's performance through an informal analysis of the pupil's oral reading.

Betts (1957) considers a child to be reading on a frustration level if he reads with less than 75 percent comprehension and less than 90 percent of accuracy. He reads on an instructional level if he reads with 75 percent comprehension and 95 percent accuracy in word recognition. He reads on an independent level if he reads with 90 percent comprehension and with 99 percent accuracy in word recognition. Elder (1963) reports

[2]See John Pikulski, "A Critical Review: Informal Reading Inventories," *The Reading Teacher* 28 (1974): 141–51.

that children can use materials for instructional purposes in which they know 88–89 percent of the words.

Generally, the teacher will select a passage for the pupil to read orally. The teacher ought to have picked out the passages, made a readability check on each, and have some questions prepared to measure pupil competency before he uses a given book to make an informal check on a pupil's reading. The reading by the pupil tells something of the pupil's background of experience, of his vocabulary knowledge, of his reading habits (slowness in reading, lip movements, or finger pointing), of his comprehension, and of his specific difficulties.

As the child reads, the teacher looks for pupil interest in materials, pupil concentration or apathy, the speed with which he completes his work, the willingness to read orally, and the ability to follow directions. The first sign indicative of poor reading is often the pupil's attitude toward reading. A pupil who does not read well generally is not willing to read aloud. He would rather hear others.

The teacher notes whether the child's oral reading indicates deficiencies in sight reading, in vocabulary, in structural or phonetic analysis, in comprehension, in eye-voice span, in phrasing, or in inflection. He checks whether in his silent reading the pupil follows instructions, reads for meaning, and uses the context to determine the meaning of the story. He is interested in whether the learner hears and sees likenesses and differences in letters and words. He evaluates the pupil's expressive and receptive abilities in the oral language area.

Inventories help the teacher to determine changes in instructional, frustration, and independent reading level and to detect improvements or continuing inadequacies in dealing with individual reading skills. They provide a good measure of the child's true growth.

Powell (1971) notes that the student does not really have an instructional level; he has only a performance level. He sees instructional modifications as being a teacher task. Perhaps we are talking of a situation where there is enough of a match and yet enough of a challenge in the materials (hence, a mismatch to a degree) so that the student has something to learn and, conversely, where he can be taught or instructed. The student's performance level is not at 100 percent efficiency or does not meet certain criteria, but the student's experience with similar materials is such that he can use it to advance in learning. We need experience to learn.

The question certainly arises as to how effective are the teacher's informal diagnostic procedures. Hitchcock and Alfred (1955, p. 422) found that teachers' observations can be reliable and valid, and they suggest standards for guiding teacher observation. They report that a teacher of English, using eight criteria, attempted to judge the reading ability of 101 eight-grade pupils. The teacher's ratings were then compared with standardized test results and correlations of .74 to .83 were obtained. It was concluded that carefully-made teacher estimates may be nearly as reliable as standardized test results.

Henig (1949) found that teachers' forecast of the success of first-grade pupils in reading had about the same validity as a readiness test. In his study the teachers had observed the pupils for three weeks before making an evaluation. Kottmeyer (1947) reported that a group of 142 teachers predicted the reading readiness of 3,156 children with 71.4 percent accuracy. Kottmeyer found that the most experienced teachers made the most accurate predictions. And, in general, teacher prediction was more accurate than scores on the Metropolitan and Detroit Readiness tests. These findings have been supported by those of Haring and Ridgway (1967).

Formal Inventories. Many classroom teachers use formal or standardized inventories to gauge a child's reading level. These are usually compilations of graded reading selections with questions prepared in advance to test the reader's comprehension.

Frequently, the formal inventory is administered by the special or remedial reading teacher to pupils identified as retarded readers. He is especially interested in a more detailed diagnosis of the pupil's reading deficiencies. He is not satisfied with an overall estimate of the pupil's reading ability, but wants to know specific strengths and weaknesses.

Three standardized inventories are the *Botel Reading Inventory;* the *Classroom Reading Inventory;* and the *Standard Reading Inventory.*[3] The *Botel Reading Inventory,* designed for grades 1–12 and published by Follett Publishing Company, is useful only when the reading level is below fourth grade.

Standardized tests often overestimate the child's reading ability and thus greater reliance needs to be placed upon the results of formal and informal reading inventories. Betts (1957, pp. 450–51) felt tests place children at their frustration level; Harris (1961a, p. 180) thinks that they identify the instructional level rather than the independent level. Sipay (1964) found that standardized tests overestimate the pupil's instructional level of fourth graders by about one grade level and underestimate the frustration by about one grade level, leading him to conclude that it is impossible to generalize as to whether standardized tests indicate the frustration or instructional level. *The Classroon Reading Inventory,* by Nicholas Silvaroli and published by Wm. C. Brown Company, 135 South Locust Street, Dubuque, Iowa, is designed specifically for teachers who have not had prior experience with individual diagnostic reading measures. It is useful in grades two through eight.

Inventories have an advantage in that they provide some clues as to why a pupil pronounced the word in a peculiar way, why he reversed letters, or why he skipped a word. They make it possible to evaluate reading behavior in depth and to study the behavior of the learner in an actual reading situation (Kuhn, 1966). In diagnosing, we are especially interested in the causes of errors. Our interest does not cease with a yes or no answer; we want to know why and how the child got his answer.

---

[3] The *Standard Reading Inventory* by Robert A. McCracken is available through Pioneer Printing Company, Bellingham, Washington. It is usable on preprimer through seventh-grade level.

Recently, there has been a lot of emphasis on *process analysis*. This is a form of analytical analysis focusing on the sequence of steps or structure that the individual learner uses to produce the responses he gives (Brown and Botel, 1972). It is designed to generate instructional procedures which will assist the individual in acquiring the responses needed for good reading. Process analysis requires (1) a description of the action; (2) halting the action at appropriate points; and (3) analyzing each aspect (Brown and Botel, 1972, p. 40). From such analysis should emerge a knowledge of under what conditions and within what context an error occurs.

In using inventories we generally are trying to determine what books a child can read independently and how difficult an assigned reading can be and still be used as instructional material. Although, unfortunately, grade-level designations furnished by the publishers of many books are far from accurate, the experienced teacher can select a suitable set of books and other materials for use in informal determinations of children's reading abilities. The informal reading inventory analysis is more clinical in nature than test interpretation, but studies (Kuhn, 1966; McGee, 1966) show that teachers are quite accurate in predicting children's readiness for reading. However, Emans (1965) did not find that the experienced teachers in his study were particularly apt in determining the reading deficiencies of children without the benefit of diagnostic testing.

Oral Reading Tests.   Oral reading tests are helpful both in measuring pupil reading achievement (especially in oral reading) and in making diagnostic evaluations. They possess many of the same advantages as the reading inventories in that they permit the teacher to detect the errors made by the pupil and to identify the reasons why the error was made. Some common oral reading tests are the following:

1. *Gilmore Oral Reading Test,* Harcourt, Brace & World, New York, grades 1–8.
2. *Gray Standardized Oral Reading Paragraphs,* The Bobbs-Merrill Co., Inc., Indianapolis, grades 1–8.
3. *Leavell Analytical Oral Reading Test,* American Guidance Service, Inc., 720 Washington Avenue S.E., Minneapolis, Minn., grades 1–10.
4. *Slosson Oral Reading Test,* Slosson Educational Publications, East Aurora, N.Y., grades 1–12.
5. *New Gray Oral Reading Test,* The Bobbs-Merrill Co., Inc., Indianapolis, grades 1–16 and adult.

Oral reading tests are very useful in the diagnosis of reading difficulties. There is strong evidence to suggest that the oral reading errors of a pupil tend to be carried over to silent reading. The oral reading test thus reveals pupil strengths and weaknesses and suggests the kinds and types of reading experiences which should be provided. Analysis of pupil errors should help to identify areas where most of the mistakes occur and toward which remedial teaching ought to be directed.

Diagnostic Reading Tests. The diagnostic reading test, like some of the instruments already described, seeks to discover specific strengths and weaknesses. It is especially useful in planning remedial procedures. It is no doubt possible to make a successful diagnosis without using any objective test measures, just as it is possible for a physician to diagnose a disease correctly without x-ray analysis. However, for the most part diagnostic tests prove helpful.

The survey test, the type given in Step 1, tells us, for example, that a boy or girl who is in fifth grade is reading at a level typical for third graders. The diagnostic test, on the other hand, identifies the pupil's specific deficiencies, his inability to work out unfamiliar words, his inability to blend sounds, or his tendency to reverse. It helps to locate those areas of deficiencies that need to be investigated further. It also may indicate which instructional adjustments are needed. It provides the basis for planning remedial teaching of such specifics as word analysis or phonic skills.

Unfortunately, there is no unanimity of purpose among the diagnostic tests. They attempt to measure such diverse areas as potential reading level, silent and oral reading performance, or independent, instructional, or frustration reading levels, and they claim to be able to identify inhibitory factors in reading, areas of skill deficiency, or inadequacies in word identification (Winkley, 1971). At present, no instrument assesses even all the word-recognition skills, much less the total spectrum of reading performance. Diagnostic tests do not diagnose; *they can help the diagnostician* to identify strengths and weaknesses in reading performance.

The following diagnostic tests have demonstrated their usefulness:

1. *Diagnostic Reading Tests,* Committee on Diagnostic Reading Tests, Mountain Home, N.C., grades 1–13.
2. *Scholastic Diagnostic Reading Test,* Scholastic Testing Service, Bensenville, Ill., grades 4–9.
3. *Silent Reading Diagnostic Tests* (Bond, Clymer, Holt), Lyons and Carnahan, Chicago, grades 3–8.
4. *Doren Diagnostic Reading Test,* American Guidance Service, Inc., Circle Pines, Minn., grades 1–9.
5. *Gates-McKillop Reading Diagnostic Tests,* Bureau of Publications, Columbia University, New York, grades 1–8.

INSTRUMENTS USEFUL IN IDENTIFYING MODE OF LEARNING

The teacher may want to give tests such as the following to evaluate even more closely a pupil's problem:

AUDITORY DISCRIMINATION TEST (Wepman), Language Research Associates, Chicago, ages 5 and up.

AUDITORY SKILLS TEST BATTERY, Goldman-Fristoe-Woodcock, ages 3 and older. American Guidance Service, Inc., Circle Pines, Minn. 55014.

BASIC CONCEPT INVENTORY, Follett Educational Corporation, ages 3 to 10.

BENTON VISUAL RETENTION TEST, Psychological Corporation, ages 8 and up.

CALIFORNIA PHONICS SURVEY, California Test Bureau, Monterey, California, grades 7 to college.

DENNIS VISUAL PERCEPTION SCALE, Western Psychological Services, grades 1–6.

DENVER DEVELOPMENTAL SCREENING TEST, Ladoca Project and Publishing Foundation, age 2 weeks to 6 years.

DEVELOPMENT TEST OF VISUAL MOTOR INTEGRATION, Follett Educational Corporation, ages 2 to 15.

FORM REPRODUCTION, Educational Testing Service, preschool and early primary.

ILLINOIS TEST OF PSYCHOLINGUISTIC ABILITIES, Institute for Research on Exceptional Children, University of Illinois, Urbana, ages 2 to 10.

LEAVELL HAND-EYE COORDINATION TEST, Keystone View Company, Meadville, Pa.

MARIANNE FROSTIG DEVELOPMENTAL TEST OF VISUAL PERCEPTION, Follett Educational Corporation, ages 3 to 8.

MCCULLOUGH WORD ANALYSIS TEST, Ginn and Company, Boston, grades 5 and up.

MCKEE INVENTORY OF PHONETIC SKILLS, Houghton Mifflin Company, Boston.

MICHIGAN VOCABULARY PROFILE TEST, Harcourt, Brace & World, Inc., New York, grades 9–16.

MILLS LEARNING METHODS TEST, Mills Center, Fort Lauderdale, Fla., grades K through 3.

MODALITY ASSESSMENT PROFILE by Richard L. Carner, University of Miami Reading Center, Coral Gables, Fla.

OLIPHANT AUDITORY DISCRIMINATION MEMORY TEST, Educators Publishing Service, grades 2 and up.

PERCEPTUAL FORMS TEST, Winter Haven Lions Research Corp., Winter Haven, Fla., ages 5 to 8.

PHONICS KNOWLEDGE SURVEY, Columbia University, New York.

PHONICS MASTERY TEST, Follett Publishing Company, Chicago.

PRIMARY VISUAL MOTOR TEST, Grune and Stratton, ages 4 to 8.

PURDUE PERCEPTUAL-MOTOR SURVEY, Charles E. Merrill Publishing Co., ages 6–10.

READING VERSATILITY TEST, Educational Developmental Laboratories, Huntington, New York, grades 6–16 and adult.

ROAD MAP TEST OF DIRECTION SENSE, Johns Hopkins Press, Baltimore, ages 7–18.

ROBBINS SPEECH SOUND DISCRIMINATION AND VERBAL IMAGERY TYPE TESTS, Expression Company, Magnolia, Mass.

ROSNER PERCEPTUAL SURVEY, University of Pittsburgh Learning Center, ages 6 to 10.

ROSWELL-CHALL AUDITORY BLENDING TEST, Essay Press, P.O. Box 5, Planetarium Station, New York, N.Y., grades 1 to 4.

SCREENING TEST FOR IDENTIFYING CHILDREN WITH SPECIFIC LANGUAGE DISABILITY, Educators Publishing Service, Cambridge, Mass., grades 1 to 4.

SOUTHERN CALIFORNIA FIGURE-GROUND VISUAL PERCEPTION TEST, Western Psychological Services, ages 4 to 10.

SOUTHERN CALIFORNIA KINESTHESIA AND TACTILE PERCEPTION TESTS, Western Psychological Services, ages 4 to 8.

SOUTHERN CALIFORNIA MOTOR ACCURACY TEST, Western Psychological Services, ages 4 to 7.

SOUTHERN CALIFORNIA PERCEPTUAL-MOTOR TEST, Western Psychological Services, ages 4 to 8.

SPATIAL ORIENTATION MEMORY TEST, Research Associates, Inc., grades 5 to 8.

SPECIFIC LANGUAGE DISABILITY TEST, Educators Publishing Service, Cambridge, Mass., grades 6–8.

TEST OF AUDITORY DISCRIMINATION, American Guidance Service, Inc., Circle Pines, Minn., 56014.

TEST OF LISTENING ACCURACY, Brigham Young University Press, ages 5 to 9.

TINKER SPEED OF READING TEST, University of Minnesota Press, Minneapolis, grades 7–16 and adult.

WATSON-GLASSER CRITICAL THINKING APPRAISAL, Harcourt, Brace & World, Inc., New York, grades 9–16.

The Symptomatology of Reading Disability. What is the significance of Step 2? It is an intensive study of the symptoms of reading disability. At this level we are still concerned primarily with identifying the areas of difficulty—with an intensive study of the symptoms. We are dealing with symptomatology. We study symptoms to identify levels of retardation.

Many reading disabilities become disabilities because teachers are not familiar with some of the symptoms of disability. The result is that some reading needs are not met, leading to disability cases. It is obvious that a clear identification of the symptoms of reading disability is needed.

Symptoms are observable characteristics which help the teacher to make some educated guesses about the pupil's reading problems. Symptoms rarely appear singly. There usually is a pattern of symptoms, a syndrome that characterizes the individual reading disability case. The teacher needs to know the pattern, must attempt to understand it, and must have the educational know-how to deal with the syndrome. The diagnostic responsibility of the classroom teacher or the reading specialist is to identify the pattern of symptoms, relate it to the appropriate skill area or areas, and plan a program to correct the deficiency. The interpretation of the syndrome pattern is much more significant than are the data themselves.

The Developmental Reading Program

Let us again look at pupils found to be retarded. Our concern is to decide the type of help the pupil needs and where he can best receive help. Perhaps at this time we should take a look at various phases of the total reading program. Authorities in the field speak of the developmental reading program, the corrective reading program, and the remedial reading program.

The developmental program emphasizes reading instruction that is designed to develop systematically the skills and abilities considered essential at each level of reading advancement. It thus encompasses also the corrective and remedial program. Perhaps we should then speak of developmental, corrective, and remedial instruction. Developmental instruction is the type of instruction that is given to the majority of children in the regular classroom.

Corrective instruction consists of remedial activities usually carried on by the regular classroom teacher within the framework of regular classroom instruction. Corrective instruction is provided when the entire class or a small group of pupils is deficient in a particular skill. Corrective reading deals with the problems of the partial disability case, that type of pupil who can identify words and comprehend what he reads, but only after great difficulty. The pupil may not have been ready for initial reading experiences, instruction may have consistently been above or below his level of ability, or classroom stimulation may have been inadequate.

Remedial instruction consists of remedial activities taking place outside of the framework of regular class instruction and is usually conducted by a special teacher of reading. Remedial instruction should thus be restricted to a small clinical group with severe symptoms of reading retardation—those having difficulty mastering even the simplest mechanics of reading. Such pupils are often identified as word blind, alexiac, or dyslexic learners. They have difficulty in remembering whole word patterns, do not learn easily by the sight method, and show orientational difficulties. The total reading program might schematically be portrayed as in Figure 14-4.

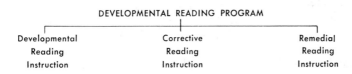

DEVELOPMENTAL READING PROGRAM

Developmental	Corrective	Remedial
Reading	Reading	Reading
Instruction	Instruction	Instruction

FIGURE 14–4

If the student has a reading problem and if he is not a slow learner, a reluctant reader, or a disadvantaged reader, he needs corrective or remedial instruction and should be able to be classified as either a general retardation or a specific retardation case or as a remedial disability case. It is on the basis of the symptoms that reading disability cases are divided into corrective and remedial readers.

This is another way of saying that there are six basic types of retardation or combinations of the same. Some of these call for corrective instruction and some call for remedial instruction. Figure 14-5 summarizes the various types.

It should be understood that the classification scheme outlined above is necessarily a tentative grouping that may have some implications for differential treatment. Independence of categories is seldom achieved (Brown and Botel, 1972). And, it should be cautioned that labeling often

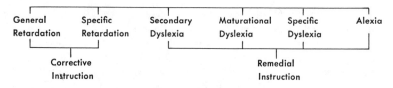

FIGURE 14–5 *Types or levels of Retardation*

merely hides our ignorance. A label may be an excuse for not teaching (Lovitt, 1967, p. 234).

Cohen (1973) notes that labeling does not change the teacher's responsibility. He still must produce a certain sort of behavior. Cohen adds that "knowing the history of the development of a behavior adds nothing to the management of that behavior . . . etiology is the educational therapist's cop-out" (1973, p. 255).

As one studies various forms of dyslexia, especially specific dyslexia and alexia, one should remember that direct central nervous system manipulations are beyond the domain of the educator (Bateman, 1974). The teacher cannot overemphasize the deviant or pathological in the child; he must constantly analyze the inadequacies in the environment. Too often, learning disabilities may be merely teaching disabilities. As we shall see later, the most effective techniques and materials often are those derived from an analysis of the task to be taught, not of the child who is to learn (Bateman, 1974).

Overline and Quayle (1971), after noting that learning disability has been explained by neurological deficit models, development lag models, and language deficit models, suggest an ecological approach to learning disability. To them learning disability represents a deviance or faulty interaction between a child's available learning modalities and his educational eco-system: teachers, peers, teaching materials, methods, educational tasks, etc.

Dyslexia in this section is used in its generic sense (Adams, 1969). It in general symbolizes and is synonymous with severe reading disability. An adjective before the word (specific dyslexia) identifies the type of dyslexia, a type hopefully identified with a describable etiology and pathophysiology. The reader is referred back to Chapter 7, p. 157, where the concept of reading disability is introduced.

It is extremely difficult to differentiate between a disabled reader and a disabled learner (Artley and Hardin, 1976). Some would restrict the use of the term, learning disability, to a learning difficulty resulting from some type of cerebral injury or dysfunction. Thus, if the problem is constitutional in origin, that is, the result of brain injury or some type of cerebral dysfunction, they consider it an instance of learning disability even though it is manifested in reading. In our categorization given below (see Figure 14-6), types four, five, and six would thus be learning disabilities. The causes of reading might be considered to lie on a continuum with educational-mental-social-emotional problems at one end and with cerebral dysfunction at the other.

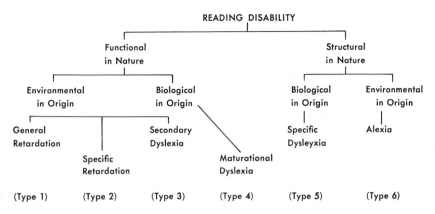

FIGURE 14–6

CHARACTERISTICS OF THE CORRECTIVE READER

Type 1: Case of General Retardation

1. The reading level is substantially lower than the mental age, but no other specific problem exists. He is a case of partial disability.
2. He is a student who learns only after undue and laborious effort; he is like the underweight child whose eating habits are not conducive to gaining weight but who, if he follows the proper diet, will gain. He learns after inhibiting factors have been removed.
3. He may not have been ready for initial reading experiences and thus fell further behind as his schooling continued.
4. Instruction and reading materials generally have been above the student's level of ability and above his level of achievement in word-recognition and comprehension skills.
5. He perhaps was absent from school at critical periods.
6. He perhaps was not stimulated to learn because instruction was below his ability level.
7. The reading profile of the generally retarded student is relatively uniform.
8. He needs more experience in reading, including systematic instruction at his level of ability. Usually a visual auditory technique or method is adequate. He does not need a VAKT method of teaching, such as the Fernald or the Gillingham method. There is a need for major adjustment in materials and instruction and for a reading program that motivates the student to learn.

Type 2: Case of Specific Retardation

There is a definite weakness in a given area. This is usually a skill weakness. This is a case of reading retardation not complicated by neurological difficulties.

1. Learning capacity is adequate, but deficiencies in regard to certain specifics in word analysis or comprehension indicate that he has not profited from regular classwork as well as he might. He has missed or has not profited from basic instruction in a given area.

2. Although each learner presents a distinct pattern of acquisition and remediation, there will usually be others in the class with similar problems.

3. His reading performance may be high overall in relation to his ability, but diagnostic testing will reveal a low subscore on a test.

4. There is usually a need for training in the area of weakness rather than a need for total remediation in the basic skills.

5. The student should be kept in the regular classroom in which reading is taught to subgroups of three to five.

CHARACTERISTICS OF THE REMEDIAL READER

Type 3: Secondary Dyslexia

Secondary dyslexia is often termed a secondary reading disability.[4] It is by far the most common form of disability seen in remedial readers. This syndrome is characterized by the following:

1. The learner's problems are more severe than those of the corrective reader and include inability to use contextual clues, poor comprehension, wild guessing at words, inability to deal with individual letter sounds or to move from sound to symbol (Rutherford, 1971), reversal tendency, and difficulty in structural analysis.

2. There usually is no single identifiable cause of the disability. Multiple causality is indicated, with the reading disability closely related to intellectual, emotional, environmental, psychological, or educational factors. It is probable that some factor is the precipitating cause; other factors are contributing causes.

3. The major cause is not attributable to dysfunction or delayed development of the brain. The capacity to read is intact. The causative factors are exogenous, that is, the disability is not innate or the result of a deficit in structure or functioning of the brain. There is usually no familial history of reading disability. This learner reads poorly, but he has a normal reading potential. His reading differs from the normal in quantity but not in quality.

4. Dyslexics are found among all races and countries even where there is great regularity between the sounds and symbols of the language (Critchley, 1964). The child who cannot remember sounds and symbols is not aided by their regularity (Money, 1962b).

5. A therapeutic diagnosis is adequate. This concerns itself with the conditions that are now present in the learner in order to give direction to a program of reeducation. The diagnostician is concerned with the reading strengths and limitations of the learner and any characteristics within the environment that need to be corrected before remedial instruction can be successful or

---

[4]See Janet W. Lerner, "A Thorn by Any Other Name: Dyslexia or Reading Disability," *Elementary English*, 48 (1971): 75–80.

with conditions that need to be adjusted to before he can be expected to make maximum progress.

Etiology deals with cause-effect relationships, preferably demonstrable through the establishment of experimental variables. If an entity of dyslexia were genuinely identifiable, then it is logical to expect that it is amenable to understanding, subject to prediction and control. Three etiological positions emerge: the *internalist* places the origin of dyslexia within the learner; the *externalist* interprets dyslexia as an environmentally-controlled phenomenon; the *interactionist* considers roots both in the environment and the learner (Brown and Botel, 1972). Secondary dyslexia is an environmentally-controlled phenomenon.

6. This learner should be taught in small groups in a remedial setting.

Type 4: Maturational Dyslexia

Maturational dyslexia indicates the presence of some brain pathology, the causative factors are *endogenous* but it is not aphasic in nature. There is no structural defect, deficiency, or loss. It is more like aplasia in that the neural tissues have failed to develop. There is an absence of function rather than a loss of function. The condition flows from cerebral immaturity or a maturational lag or slowness in certain specialized aspects of neurological development. There is delayed or irregular neurological development. The potential is there, but it has not yet been realized. He is a late bloomer. He is not yet matured, but he is capable of maturing.

The characteristics that identify this reader are very much like those of type five, specific dyslexia.

Generalized language disturbances frequently run in families and are associated with disturbances in body image, poor motor and visuo-motor patterning, inadequate figure-ground discriminations and hyperactivity. Clumsiness in manipulation of small muscle groups (such as in writing) is rather common. The execution in writing is jerky and arrhythmic. The jerkiness in writing is accompanied by jerky, stumbling, and explosive speech (cluttering). The writing looks as the speech sounds. Drawings of the human form are immature and distorted. The limbs are out of proportion, incorrectly placed, or perhaps omitted. Finally, because of inadequate figure-ground discrimination, children with general language disabilities hear speech as an undifferentiated noise and see words on the printed page as an undifferentiated design. On more advanced levels (ten–fourteen years) these children will usually have difficulty in organizing what they read or study. In explaining the language-disturbance syndrome, the underlying cause is often delayed or disorganized maturation of the neural system.

Satz and Friel (1974) summarize their position, based on their earlier studies (Satz and Ross, 1973) which suggests that developmental dyslexia reflects a lag in maturation of the brain which delays differentially those skills which are in primary ascendancy at different chronological ages. This theory is congruent with the thinking of Piaget and Bruner that the child goes through consecutive stages of thought during development, each of which incorporates the processes of the preceding stage into a more complex and hierarchically integrated form of adaptation. Using the developmental lag model, Satz and Friel found that the reading achievement levels of children at the end of grade 1 can be validly predicted from an assessment of the developmental and neuropsychological performance at the beginning of kindergarten.

Delacato's description of reading disability, with its emphasis on neurological maturity, neurological organization, and hemispheric dominance, fits here.

The key fact here is that the maturational-lag view allows for plasticity and the potential for future growth. The emphasis thus is on the constitutional origin of the syndrome, perhaps even genetically determined. It is presumed that there is an inherent biological basis for the development lag.

There frequently is a familial history of reading disability and generalized language disturbances. Orton, from his first paper in 1925, repeatedly gave family histories showing the existence of language disabilities and confused dominance among the relatives.

Bertil Hallgren (1950) of Sweden, in a study of 276 cases, found reading problems in one or more relatives in 88 percent of the cases. Edith Norrie (1960) in Denmark, and Hallgren studied twins—their combined total of pairs investigated was 45—of whom 12 pairs were monozygotic and 33 were dizygotic. Concordance was 100 percent in the former group and 30 percent in the latter. Hallgren concluded that developmental dyslexia follows a monohybrid autosomal dominant mode of inheritance. Knud Hermann (1959) in his book, *Reading Disability,* notes "It is highly probable that the specific pathogenic factor must be sought in heredity, whereby a predisposition to the under-development of this function is transmitted in certain families by means of a dominant inheritance" (p. 179).

Norman Geschwind (1971) demonstrated that an area behind the primary auditory cortex in the upper surface of the temporal lobe (Wernicke's area) is larger on the left side in 65 percent of brains, but larger on the right side in 11 percent. This is an anatomical difference, not a lesion, and it appears to be genetically determined. It could be that, in the remaining 24 percent where no appreciable difference exists, an anatomical basis for language disability may be found.

Type 5: Specific Dyslexia

Specific dyxlexia is difficult to describe because there is no single clinical feature that can be accepted as pathognomic (Critchley, 1964). There is no invariable common core of symptoms. It is a massive unreadiness for reading (Money, 1962a). It is a defect in the visual interpretation of verbal symbols (Willson, 1968), and in the association of sounds with symbols. It is a failure to learn to read even though the child has had appropriate instruction, comes from a culturally adequate home, is properly motivated, has adequate sensory equipment, has normal intelligence, and shows no gross neurological defect or brain pathology (Eisenberg,

1966, p. 19). Retardation nevertheless is based on some organic incapacity (Quadfassel and Goodglass, 1968). The neurological signs are minimal. The condition is often described as inborn or genetically rather than environmentally determined (Rutherford, 1971), and in this respect the condition is similar to maturational dyslexia, but there is a *structural* variation that makes it difficult to learn to read. There is a loss of function rather than simply an absence of function.

The student is deficient in even the most fundamental basic reading skills. It is almost as though he had never been in school. Remedial instruction often seems to have little effect, and where it is effective, it may well be that the learner is a type 4 rather than a genuine case of specific dyslexia.

The specific dyslexic reader, on the basis of symptoms, can usually be identified as one of three types (Boder, 1968):

1. *Auditory Dyslexics:* They may show deficits in symbol-sound integration, cannot develop phonic skills, or cannot auditorize. They have difficulty differentiating between the sounds that they hear. Their ability to visualize may be quite normal. They are visual learners and may best be taught initially through a whole-word configuration or sight method. They remember the shapes of the letters but cannot associate the proper phoneme with the proper shape. They are phonics weak but "Gestalt" strong.

2. *Visual Dyslexics:* They cannot develop gestalts for letters or words, and they show little ability in distinguishing between shapes and patterns. They are weak in visual imagery, have poor visual memory, and have poor visual discrimination skill. They are "phonics strong" but spatially "Gestalt weak." Initial remedial teaching might begin with tactile-kinesthetic techniques (the Fernald method) if the learners have not yet acquired visual recognition for letters. Remedial phonics, such as the Orton-Gillingham approach, might be used if letter recognition has occurred.

3. *Auditory-Visual Dyslexics:* This group represents a combination of groups one and two. The pupil cannot read by sight or by ear. Jastak (1965) speaks of "intrasensory transcoding difficulties." He notes that learning to transcode messages by intersensory cooperation is a difficult and complex task for many children. Visual and auditory stimuli are received in the reception areas in the brain, but the meanings are not correctly decoded and encoded.

The basic difficulty, however, is one of three: (1) deficiency in visual identification of symbols; (2) inability to associate sound with graphic symbols—he cannot deal with the phoneme-grapheme correspondences; or (3) inability to associate meaning with symbols.

Let us look at each of these.

Deficiency in Visual Identification. This deficiency reveals itself in many ways and can be described in many ways. The learner has a letter or a word-naming difficulty (anomia). Boder (1970) refers to these readers as the dyseidetic group. He cannot deal with letters or words as symbols, with resultant diminished ability to integrate the meaningfulness of written materials (Rabinovich and Ingram 1962). He has great difficulty with visual recognition and recall of familiar words.

The following observations relating to deficiencies in visual identification are common when one deals with a severe disability:

a. The student does not experience the "flash," global identification of a word as a whole, and cannot synthesize the word out of its component letter units. He does not see the word as an entity.

b. The letter standing alone has no language identity. *S* may be described as traffic sign.

c. Spelling of words may be peculiar and odd. This is because the student ignores many details in words.

d. His reading is arrhythmical and replete with word-recognition errors. He demonstrates more vowel, consonant, reversal, omission, addition, substitution, perseveration, and repetition errors.

e. He will ask again and again for help with the same word.

f. The student cannot pronounce unfamiliar words. He has a tendency to guess wildly at words. He pays attention to specific letters and guesses wildly at the rest (*horse* becomes *house*). His rendition of a word is often phonetically unrelated to the desired response (*dog* becomes *chay*).

g. He has difficulty blending sounds so as to constitute a word. He can spell b-a-n-a-n-a but cannot pronounce it.

h. He confuses similar-appearing words: e.g., *bed-fed*.

i. He frequently loses his place in reading and does not move easily from the end of one line to the beginning of another line.

j. He vocalizes excessively while reading silently.

k. The reading behavior of the dyslexic is extremely variable. On a given day he may reverse; the following day no reversal problem occurs.

Deficiency in Associating Phoneme and Grapheme. The basic deficiency here is one of inability to relate symbols. Sometimes this happens because the auditory symbols fail to achieve identity. Boder (1970) refers to this group as the dysphonetic group who because of their limitation in phonic skills read in a global fashion. Thus, the pupil reads "funny" for laugh.

There are numerous examples of the phoneme-to-grapheme mixup in the English language: The phoneme /f/, for example, can be written as *f* (scarf), *ff* (chaff), *gh* (laugh), and *ph* (graph). Another term for the mixup is *irregular orthography*, and it is the mismatching of phoneme and grapheme that is the heart of the problem for many dyslexic children. Dyslexia is nothing more than an oral/written disorder. (Bannatyne, 1971). Rosenthal (1973) asks: Wouldn't it be fascinating if indeed the youngsters of Boder Group I (dysphonetic), who are "phonics-weak" and "Gestalt-strong," would tend to read with their right brains and rest their left brains, thus causing an increase in alpha on the left? And if those in Boder Group II (diseidetic), who are "spatially-Gestalt-weak" and "phonics-strong," would tend to read with their left brains and turn off their right brains, thus causing an increase in alpha on the right?

Deficiency in Associating Meaning with Symbols. The student will also have meaning and comprehension problems. He frequently exhibits an associative learning disability, making it impossible for him to associate experiences and meanings with symbols.

Rutherford (1971) notes that the inability to generalize from word to concept seems to be one of the three most limiting features of dyslexia. The others are inability to translate from sound to symbol and faulty memory for sequences. The symbolic abilities are impaired with the result that even though the learner has conceptual strengths he cannot come up with proper symbolic designations (height for tallness or summer for hot weather). He cannot translate perceptions into symbols (Zintz, 1972, p. 328). Comprehension is poor, and rate of comprehension is significantly below the norm.

Additional identifying characteristics or correlates of dyslexia are the following:

1. The dyslexic reader is usually a boy, although girls are also dyslexic. Delacato suggests that boys have bigger heads, and so the incidence of difficult birth is greater among boys. This does not mean that the disability is inherited. It simply means that predisposing conditions are present in certain families. It may be that reading disability is related to the body structure of the woman which in some instances causes difficulty of birth (Kolson & Kaluger, 1963).

2. His IQ is usually in the normal range, but the verbal IQ tends to be significantly below the performance IQ. Belmont and Birch (1966) found that retarded readers are generally inadequate in language functioning rather than in perceptual and manipulative skills.

3. There is more persistent and frequent left-right confusion.
   a. There is a reversal of concepts (*floor* for *ceiling, go* for *stop, east* for *west*). The dyslexic frequently makes kinetic reversals. He reads entire words backward (*saw-was*); he reverses letters (*flim* for *film*); and he confuses sounds (*graduate* for *gratitude*). He may perform as well if the book is held upside down.
   b. He often comes from a family in which there is left-handedness or language disorders or both.
   c. He shows evidence of delayed or incomplete establishment of one-sided motor preferences. He tends to be left-handed or ambidextrous, or he shows mixed dominance. These orientational problems may not be present in the older dyslexic.

4. Penmanship is characterized by poorly formed and irregular characters, untidiness, malalignment, omissions, linkages that are too short or too long, and fusion of letters. Drawing and copying are poor. Poor manual dexterity is fairly common.

5. He often has speech difficulties and poor auditory discrimination. Stuttering, lisping, stammering, and cluttering often are quite noticeable.

6. He is more likely to have been premature or to have survived some complication of pregnancy.

7. He is hyperactive, distractive, distractable, and impulsive, shows poor motor coordination, especially visual-motor, has a short attention span, perseverates excessively, and has a low frustration tolerance (Orlow, 1974; Hartman, 1974). And, there is some evidence that retarded readers, because of too great attention to the stimulus characteristics, are unable to shift attention, an ability required for successful reading.

Sawyer (1974) noting that problem solving requires the ability selectively to direct one's attention to relevant information, points out some learners may be disabled because they have constricted attention abilities. They either attend equally to all stimuli or find it difficult to withhold attention from some stimuli (Santostefano, Rutledge, and Randall, 1965). Good learners exhibit flexible attention abilities, being able to attend to some stimuli while ignoring others. The constricted cognitive style is perhaps seen in the reader who sounds out every word or who cannot infer the main idea or grasp cause-effect relationships. The Purdue Perceptual-Motor Survey is a diagnostic remediation instrument useful in assessing the perceptual motor abilities of children.[5]

8. He has difficulty in spatial relationships and in figure-ground perception. There is an inappropriate spatial orientation of graphemes or temporal order of phonemes and poorly developed body image (Brown & Botel, 1972).

Type 6: Alexia

Alexia is the *loss* of the ability to read as a result of damage, injury, or lesion to the association and connection areas in and around the angular gyrus of the dominant cerebral hemisphere. For most of us this is the left hemisphere. There is clear brain pathology which prevents the learner from becoming a reader, or which takes away the reading ability that once existed. He may see black marks on paper, but he does not recognize that they represent words. The past history of such an individual often reveals normal speech development initially. There may be no family history of reading difficulty. Instructional techniques alone cannot come directly to grips with the reading problem. This is a reader who is neurologically unable to read. The reading disability is actually a symptom of an earlier lesion to the nervous system (Quadfassel and Goodglass, 1968). The symptoms of reading disability are much like those that are seen in type 5.

Aphasia shows up as (1) receptive oligophasia or a disturbance in auditory perception of sound; (2) as expressive or motor oligophasia or a disturbance in recognizing and forming phonemic patterns and translating them into speech; (3) as central oligophasia or a disturbance of symbolization; (4) as agraphia; or (5) as alexia.

In Area 39, the angular gyrus, in the left parietal lobe for right-handed persons, the meaning of the word is comprehended, symbols are interpreted; it is the locus of the recognition and visual memory for word forms. Area 22 and 37 are the loci of the association of sounds and visual symbols. Injury here results in the inability to name one's concepts. In Areas 18 and 19, recognition and visual memory occur. We refer the reader to Chapter 7 where the location of these areas is identified.

The dyslexia that results from right-sided lesions is not the same as that caused by left-sided ones (Hécaen, 1967). In the latter, the problems relate chiefly to graphic code comprehension or transcription malfunc-

---

[5]E. G. Roach, and N. D. Kephart, *The Purdue Perceptual-Motor Survey.* (Columbus, Ohio: Charles E. Merrill Books, Inc., 1966).

tioning; in the former, the reading difficulties are mainly related to perceptual problems in the spatial arrangements of letters, words, and sentences. Spatial dyslexia occurs with occipital as well as parietal lesions (Rosenthal, 1973).

The aphasic or brain-injured child (Nelson, 1961) is hyperactive. He flits from one activity to another without apparent purpose or meaning. His behavior is compulsive, and the condition may be associated with difficulties in perception, memory, attention, and social control. Frequently, he is destructive.

A mild brain damage, frequently undetected, is associated with difficulties in reading (alexia), writing, and arithmetic. The child finds abstract thinking difficult and has poor coordination and concentration. His speech is rapid and mumbled and hence unintelligible. He can count to twenty or recite the alphabet but cannot tell what number comes after eight or what letter comes after *c*. He reverses the letters in writing, omits letters, and spells as though English were a completely phonetic language. The writing is cramped and angular. The letters vary in size and slant.

The hyperactive[6] child or the "driven child" has a short attention span, is impulsive, has impaired perception, conceptualization, and language, and exhibits low frustration level.

The brain-injured child frequently has not developed dominance. He switches from one hand to the other and confuses left with right. He perseverates, repeating activities again and again.

Harris (1961b) notes that in reading disability cases exhibiting neurological defects, the whole-part relationship is inadequate. Parts (letters) are seen as discrete units rather than as parts of a whole, and wholes (words) are seen as undifferentiated wholes. He also points out that frequently there is a figure-ground disturbance. The figure (word) does not have clear boundaries. The problem seems to become more acute when the figure is discontinuous or when the contrast with the ground is minimal. Harris raises the question whether word perception might be improved if the letters were continuous or if they were in a different color, perhaps red.

Hinshelwood (1917, p. 53) points out that any condition that reduces the number of cortical cells within the angular area (area 39) and supramarginal (area 40) gyri of the left side of the cortex or that interferes with the supply of the blood to that area lowers the functional activity of that part of the brain and will be accompanied by a diminished retention of the visual images of letters and words. He (1917, p. 102) believes that treatment for structural wordblindness consists of developing (1) a visual memory for the letters of the alphabet; (2) an auditory memory for words by having the child spell aloud the word letter by letter; and (3) a visual memory for words.

---

[6]For a discussion of the hyperkinetic child see: Claire A. Glennon, and Doris E. Nason, "Managing The Behavior of the Hyperkinetic Child: What Research Says." *The Reading Teacher* 27 (1974): 815–24.

The following instruments are useful in testing for brain damage:[7]

AYRES SPACE TEST, Western Psychological Services, ages 3 and up.

BENDER-GESTALT TEST, Western Psychological Services, ages 4 and up.

ELIZUR TEST OF PSYCHO-ORGANICITY, Western Psychological Services, age 6 to adult.

GOODENOUGH-HARRIS DRAWING TEST, Harcourt, Brace, Jovanovich, ages 3 to 15.

MEMORY FOR DESIGNS TEST, Psychological Test Specialties, ages 8½ and up.

MINNESOTA PERCEPTO-DIAGNOSTIC TEST, Clinical Psychology Publishing Co., ages 5 and up.

ORGANIC INTEGRITY TEST, Psychodiagnostic Test Co., ages 5 and up.

SLOSSON DRAWING COORDINATION TEST FOR CHILDREN AND ADULTS, Slosson Educational Publications, ages 1½ and up.

THE FIVE TASK TEST, Western Psychological Services, ages 8 and up.

Figure 14-7 summarizes what has been said about each of the four types of servere reading disability with respect to familial history of reading disability and its endogenous or exogenous causality.

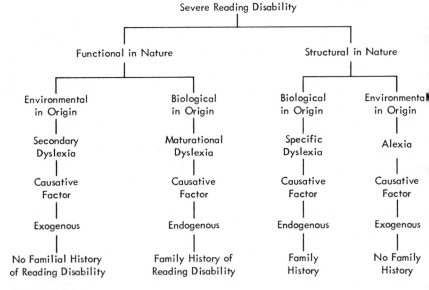

FIGURE 14-7

Step 3: A Detailed Investigation of Causality

Step 3 of diagnostic procedure is a thorough analysis of the reading disability leading to an identification of the causal factors involved. It is the level of intensive diagnosis, a detailed study of the correlates of disability.

[7]For fuller descriptions of these instruments see: Nancy A. Mavrogenes, Earl F. Hanson, and Carol K. Winkley, "A Guide to Tests of Factors That Inhibit Learning to Read," *The Reading Teacher* 29 (1976): 343–58.

TABLE 14–3 *Two Common Symptoms of Reading Disability*

SYMPTOM	POSSIBLE CAUSE	POSSIBLE REMEDY
1. Inability to remember a letter visually or makes frequent substitutions of words.	a. Poor vision.	a. Check and remediate visual defect. Have pupil engage in exercises teaching discrimination of letters.
	b. Inability to tie letters together and remember them (c-a-t). Poor visual memory span.	b. Provide tracing exercises to develop a "feel" for the word; stress training in visual discrimination of words.
	c. Reverses letters and so can't discriminate and remember them (b-d).	c. Check if he also reverses nonsense syllables. Have pupil engage in exercises designed to change the pattern.
	d. Inattention, not wanting to learn.	d. Use language-experience approach.
2. Inability to discriminate word sounds. For example, the teacher might say, "Now listen for the sound pig . . . big, dig, pig, pick." The child cannot deal with this problem.	a. Poor hearing—poor auditory acuity.	a. Check hearing and consult doctor.
	b. Speech defects: "Father becomes fodder," "Shishter for sister," "Kool for school."	b. Provide training in articulation.
	c. Poor auditory discrimination.	c. Seat child near teacher; check for high tone deafness and watch for sounds $f, v, s, z, sh, zh, th, t, d, p, b, k,$ and $g;$ provide exercises in auditory discrimination.

Chapters 5 to 8 looked at some of the major causes of reading disability. We discussed such areas as inadequate experiential background, inadequate language background, inadequate maturation, inadequacies in intellectual-social-emotional development, lack of motivation, instructional inadequacies, visual and auditory inadequacy, and deficiencies in other physical-physiological areas.

An important question is surely: "So what? You know the causes of reading disability, but what can you do about it?" The special or remedial reading teacher is by definition an expert in tying together symptom and cause. The classroom teacher can become quite expert in doing the same thing.

It requires considerable skill and care to transfer the diagnostic data into an accurate prescription that can serve as the basis for remediation. In making the transfer we must recognize certain dangers. Sometimes the learner's symptoms may lead us to take faulty steps toward his remediation. What may appear to be the cause of his difficulty may be quite unrelated to it or may even be a result or symptom of his problems. But skill and experience in the translation of diagnostic data and an earnest desire to help each student attain the highest goals that his capabilities permit should serve as a firm foundation for remediation.

The two symptoms in Table 14-3 are common symptoms of reading disability. but what is their cause? We have suggested four possible ones for symptom 1 (there are others) and three for symptom 2 and have suggested remediation in each instance. This is the type of skill needed by the classroom teacher.

An important phase of diagnosis is the checking of one's own hypothesis about causality. For example, in Step 2 on the basis of symptomatology you may have decided that you are dealing with a case of secondary dyslexia. In Step 3 you have analyzed possible causes to explain the symptoms. Do your conclusions match with the causal structure in the categorization of causes of reading disability given in Figure 14-8?

As one completes this third step, the chances are that the following has been done:

1. A case history has been compiled.
2. The pupil's capacity has been analyzed including, if possible, the results of hearing tests, visual screening tests, eye-movement data, hand and eye preference tests.
3. The level of oral and silent reading achievement has been determined.
4. The reading problem has been identified.
5. The factors that interfere with reading have been isolated.
6. The data have been collated and interpreted.

The written report of the diagnosis should include recommendations as to *how* the child should be taught and should suggest materials that may be used in teaching. It should outline specific weaknesses in word analysis and in comprehension. There might be statements about the child's spontaneity or lack of it in correcting his own errors; statements about the ease or lack of it with which the pupil develops insight into

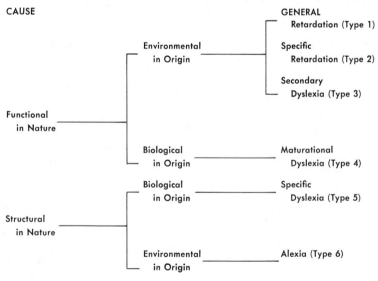

FIGURE 14–8 *Causes of Reading Disability*

phonic generalizations; statements about the pupil's awareness or lack of awareness of phonetic differences in words; or statements about the reasons why the pupil substitutes words of similar meaning.

The teacher needs to become expert in reading the causes of reading disability. Smith and Carrigan note (1959) that clinicians are like a small group standing beside a river full of drowning people. The victims are being swept seaward. The clinicians can pull out a few, but the rest are lost. Few clinicians are willing to go upstream to find out how the victims got into the river in the first place.

The teacher needs to know how the disabled reader gets into the river in the first place. To do this, he needs to be able to read the causes of reading disability. It is not enough to known the symptoms. The symptom has to be hooked up with the proper cause. Only in this way is remediation of reading disability possible.

Step 4: Remediation

Step 4 of diagnostic procedure is actually the development of a plan for remediation. Identification of symptoms and causes is simply not enough.

Diagnosis is meant to lead to remediation; it must serve as a blueprint from which remediation is structured. From a study of the diagnostic data, the teacher evolves a plan by and through which it is hoped the learner will improve in reading. The principles which we will discuss later in this section should help the teacher to formulate such a plan. They are basic procedures and principles that should guide all remedial instruction, irrespective of the type of reading disability. Unfortunately, too often there is little or no correspondence between diagnosis and prognosis for the individual or for the precise specification of remediation procedures. Too often diagnosis serves only to emphasize the point that there is a problem which requires contact with the remedial service (Brown & Botel, 1972).

This section thus deals with four questions: What decisions or what knowledge does the teacher of reading need before he can plan an effective remedial program? What principles should guide remedial instruction? What are the skills that must be developed in all remedial programs? And how can a corrective or remedial program be organized? Let us consider the first of these.

Decisions Required of the Teacher. Somehow, either on his own or with specially skilled help if it is available, the teacher must identify the child's problems and then plan and carry through the best possible corrective measures. This requires certain decisions based on particular information.

1. The teacher must decide whether the pupil actually is a retarded reader rather than a child of low ability. If he is a retarded reader, he must identify the nature of his retardation.

2. He must decide what type of teaching is needed. Teacher objectives must be translated into pupil tasks.

3. He must determine whether the needed remedial work can best be done in the classroom or in separate facilities and, if in the classroom, whether individually or in a subgroup.

4. He must make an estimate of the proper length of the instructional period. The length will depend upon the skill being taught and on the physical well-being and social-emotional maturity of the child.

5. He must determine the most efficient methods and materials that can be used. He needs to determine what the difficulty level of the materials should be and whether the materials are interesting to the pupil. Bond and Tinker (1967, p. 454) emphasize ". . . there should be no compromise with difficulty even to get material of high interest."

6. He must be alert to and decide how to make adjustments for the child's special interests, for any emotional or physical defects, or conditions in the child's home and community environment that may block his reading growth.

7. He must be alert to and decide how to deal with the environmental factors, institutional factors, that might be keeping the pupil from progressing in reading.

8. He must decide how to interpret to the pupil the progress he might make.

9. He must plan independent work activities for the pupil.

Principles of Remediation. Remedial teachers have developed certain principles that should guide all remedial or corrective instruction. A general observation might be that the principles underlying remedial or corrective reading instruction are basically the same that govern developmental reading instruction (O'Bruba, 1974). Of these principles, the following seem most significant.

1. Develop a plan of remediation, put it on paper, and refer to it frequently as remediation progresses. Incidental teaching is simply inadequate with the retarded reader. Write flexibility into the plan. There needs to be flexibility in materials, methods, and attitudes.

2. Discover the child's area and level of confidence (Dolch, 1953). Start where the pupil knows something. Nothing succeeds quite like success (Julitta, 1956). One of the most therapeutic experiences for reading disability cases is success. Thus remedial instruction should begin at the level at which the pupil can be successful, probably about one grade level below the pupil's ability. It must begin where the pupil is, not where the curriculum guide suggests that sixth-grade learners on the average are. It should begin with short assignments, inspire confidence, and restore status to the child in the eyes of his peers, his parents, and teachers.

   In dealing with corrective or remedial cases it is necessary to remember that:

   a. The pupil is generally anxious and fearful of discussing his problem with an adult.

   b. His anxiety and guilt are especially high when he has experienced disapproval of his parents. Reich (1962) notes that over every remedial reading case hovers an anxious parent: a parent who is overprotective, disappointed, and often feels guilty himself.

c. The pupil's "don't care" attitude toward reading frequently is a "do care very much" attitude. It is a safety valve that permits the pupil to save face. Both teacher and parent should permit the pupil to have this apparent attitude without developing a feeling of guilt on the part of the pupil.

3. The corrective or remedial methods are hardly distinct from developmental methods. One cannot "reteach" a pupil who never learned. One cannot remedy what was always lacking. Children receiving remedial education are distinct from normal readers in that they did not learn as a result of the educational procedures that were effective with most children. All the principles that apply to effective developmental instruction also apply to what is termed remedial teaching. The good teacher, whatever his title may be, starts at the child's present reading level, builds self-confidence in reading, and uses a variety of reading methods. Perhaps the remedial teacher is somewhat more permissive, delves more precisely into the causes of the reading problem, uses a greater variety of materials and motivational devices, and individualizes the program to a greater degree. The methods and principles of remedial teaching and developmental teaching are distinguishable, if at all, by the emphasis on individualization. Remedial reading is not a magic hocus-pocus of special methods, but a more intense and personal application of the techniques used with all others. Consequently, it is the nature of the child rather than the nature of the teaching that distinguishes the two procedures. Remedial measures are not curealls. They do not correct and eliminate all reading difficulties.

4. Develop those skills and abilities which are most necessary for immediate successful reading. Educational growth is rarely a unitary process. The child may "catch-on" quickly to one skill or in some areas of knowledge but lag in others. Thus, diagnosis and remediation must continually accompany all effective teaching.

5. Remediation should be based on and accompanied by continuous diagnosis. This identifies areas that need unteaching and helps to identify the pupil who is ready for regular classroom instruction.

6. No one symptom, error, or mistake of itself implies an ailment or a general deficiency. Even the best reader will err at times.

7. Perfect results on a test do not mean complete mastery. An average score of second-grade level, on any test, does not mean that all the pupil's reading skills are on a second-grade level. It is not uncommon to find children getting the correct answer through the use of an incorrect method. By incorrect method is meant any method that will hinder future progress (such as guessing).

8. The child's symptoms, if not correctly interpreted, may lead the teacher to provide the improper remediation. The so-called cause, upon careful analysis, frequently is found to be an effect of poor reading. The teacher thus expects, from the expert, some psychological insight into why a given method is recommended. Too often, the expert comes up with a diagnosis such as "He is a dyslexic reader," without any recommendations as to the type of program to follow. The expert's diagnosis must be translated into "what to do" in the classroom. It is the going from the diagnostic hypothesis to the remedial method that is the difficult task.

9. The pattern of symptoms is usually more significant than the individual symptom.

10. Cures do not necessarily mean that the correct method of cure has been found. The intangibles of teacher-pupil motivations and teacher effectiveness generally play an important role. The good teacher may have good results regardless of method used. The poor teacher may experience only failure.

11. No remedial method has universal application. Methods of instruction should be selected which are in harmony with the best mode of learning for a given child.

12. The teacher's personality and his ability to enlist each child's active cooperation are often more important than the specific method used. Learning occurs in a relationship. Rapport is a subtle thing. The pupil needs to develop a desire to learn.

   In dealing with remedial cases, psychotherapeutic principles should be incorporated into the process. The teacher should:
   a. Develop a constructive relationship with the pupil (rapport). Drop the role of an authoritative teacher. Become an interested teacher.
   b. Be a genuine person.
   c. Give total and unequivocal acceptance of the pupil despite his frequent failures in school.
   d. Have complete faith in the pupil's improvableness and ability to read. It is a fact that if the significant adults in a pupil's life believe that he can succeed, his chances for success are appreciably improved.
   e. Develop a feeling of empathy, not sympathy. Objectivity must be maintained. If sympathy develops, the pupil feels that he has to please his teacher and that he cannot make mistakes. This often leads to tension (Klausner, 1967; Roswell, 1964).
   f. Have a structured, well-defined program. The remedial program is more structured than the psychotherapeutic session.
   g. Arouse interest by judicious choice of materials. If the corrective or remedial teacher provides a relationship in which he is (a) genuine, internally consistent; (b) acceptant, prizing the learner as a person of worth; (c) empathically understanding of the learner's private world of feelings and attitudes, then certain changes are likely to occur in the learner. Some of these changes are: the learner becomes (a) more realistic in his self-perceptions; (b) more confident and self-directing; (c) more positively valued by himself; (d) less likely to repress elements of his experience; (e) more mature, and adaptive in his behavior; (f) less upset by stress and quicker to recover from it; (g) more like the healthy, integrated, well-functioning person in his personality structure; and (h) a better learner (Rogers, 1961).

13. No two reading disability cases probably stem from the same source, have exactly the same pattern, or need the same instruction.

14. Select materials that the pupil can handle and in which he is interested. To do this, the teacher needs to know the pupil's instructional level. It is very important to remember that reading skills don't operate in a vacuum. The teacher needs proper materials, perhaps packets and kits, however, "packets and kits are fine for practice, tackling the dummy, but practice isn't to be confused with playing the game, of football or reading." It is often not what materials that are used with retarded readers that is most significant, but rather what the teacher does with the materials.

15. Instill in the pupil a feeling of responsibility for his own progress. It is important that the student does not gain a false sense of security and that he realize that remediation is a result of his personal effort; it cannot be donated by the teacher (Bamman, 1964). Not only must the teacher give, but the student must be able and willing to take and to utilize the help given (Mills, 1963). Progress charts should be developed. The units of improvement need to be small enough so that progress can be recorded at frequent intervals.

16. Some remedial approaches, if used flexibly, appear applicable to reading disability cases almost irrespective of cause.

17. Remedial sessions must be adapted to the pupil. Half-hour sessions are probably suitable for third and fourth graders: eighth graders might be able to handle hour-long sessions.

18. When we speak of remedial reading or reading disability, we often imply that there is a basic deficiency in the learner that impedes progress. It may be helpful to remind ourselves that the basic deficiency may be poor teaching.

Improvement in reading is not necessarily brought about by spending more money, by bringing in consultants, by buying more gadgets and mechanical devices, or by resorting to newer approaches. Outstanding instructional programs in reading will be achieved "only through outstanding instruction," (Heilman, 1967). This means, as Heilman notes, that our teaching practices ought to be in accord with what we know about pupil-learning and what we know about reading and its relation to all school learning.

Individualization of instruction is the chief identifying mark of good teaching and is totally dependent upon pupil diagnosis. The wise teacher identifies individual differences and teaches each pupil accordingly. The aim of remediation is to direct a pupil into that set of learning experiences most appropriate for him. The teacher thus must be extraordinarily sensitive to the needs of the learner.

But what if the diagnosis is incorrect? This would obviously result in wrong remediation; the greater the error in diagnosis, the greater might be the harm. We all realize that even the best diagnosis often is not totally reliable. The diagnostic information is fallible, but this does not make it worthless. It does mean that the degree of differentiation in remediation that should be attempted is directly proportional to the accuracy of the diagnosis. It would seem wise, then, to begin remediation by using those principles, methods, and procedures that are developmentally sound. Only gradually and with great care should the remediation depart from these.

The diagnostic-remediation process may be viewed as a matter of obtaining and transmitting information. Diagnosis brings forth information about the pupil. We have suggested in this chapter a positive and direct way of doing this by observation, questionnaire, inventory, and test. Another approach is to begin the remediation process with the problem as the pupil presents it and to help the pupil rather immediately in solving it. This latter approach consists of observing the pupil, working with him, and studying, analyzing, and remediating during actual instruction and practice in reading. This approach calls for the use of few tests.

One teacher might want to narrow the point where remediation might be applied. He is confident that he can and actually has identified the significant areas of difficulty. A second teacher believes that it is not possible to predict what areas will be significant in the case before him. He prefers to risk some loss of time in order to avoid the risk of overlooking a significant area. The first teacher would thus at once plunge into a reading diagnosis. The second teacher would fear that such a direct attack might actually cause the pupil to fail to mention the real reason of why he hates reading.

Each teacher is gambling. It would appear that if the teacher strongly believes, because of his experience and knowledge, that the significant area is to be found in a limited area, he should study that area with maximum precision (Cronbach, 1955). It would appear that experienced teachers would be safer in doing this than inexperienced teachers.

Remedial Methods

This chapter would not be complete without a résumé of remedial methods and remedial methodology. We have already indicated that there is no one best method for teaching reading and there is no one best remedial or corrective method. There may be a best method for a given learner. There may be a best method for a special segment of the learner population. There may even be a best method for a given teacher because he is most comfortable with it. The teacher of reading thus has to look at many methods. Because he doesn't know whose brand of reading method is the best buy, he has to consider a variety of possibilities, each of which might have some merit and validity in a specific teaching situation.

It is not possible to survey all remedial methods, but the following are some key ones.

Monroe Method. Numerous writers have advocated phonetic methods both for remedial work and as a general portion of the developmental program. Monroe (1932, pp. 111–136) in 1932 evolved a synthetic phonetic approach using considerable repetition and drill. The basic emphasis was the development of auditory discrimination. Pictures are mounted on cards and the child is taught to identify initial consonants and consonants followed by a vowel. After a few of these phonetic elements are known, blending is begun. Gradually, the child is initiated into the reading of specially written stories. Tracing is used in this method as the need arises, but the child uses a pencil rather than the forefinger for tracing. Monroe found her method to be highly successful with serious reading disability cases and with children who have great difficulty in making visual associations.

Fernald Method (Fernald, 1966). The steps in the Fernald method vary from word tracing to word analysis and are determined somewhat by the ability and progress of the child. At the lower ranges of achievement, the child selects a word that he wishes to learn. The teacher writes the word on paper in large script or print. The child may even dictate a sentence such as "I like my mother." The teacher records this on paper. There is little or no control of the vocabulary. The child then traces each word with the forefinger, saying each part of the word as he does the tracing. The process continues until the child can write the word without the benefit of the copy. The child's fingers must make contact with the paper as he traces. Words thus learned are later typewritten and then included in stories for the child to read. As new words are learned, they are collected by the pupil in an alphabetical file. As the child advances, tracing may cease entirely, but pronouncing the word while writing it is always an essential feature.

The kinesthetic method develops through four stages:

1. Tracing, calling and writing the word.
   a. The teacher writes the word for the pupil in large print, perhaps on the chalkboard.
   b. The pupil traces the word, pronouncing the word in syllables as he traces.
   c. The pupil tries to write the word, repeating steps one and two if he is unable to do so.
2. Writing without tracing. Gradually the pupil attempts to write new words without having to trace them.
3. Recognizing the word. The pupil gradually comes to recognize the word on sight. He learns the printed word by saying it to himself before writing.
4. Word analysis. The pupil is taught to break the word into smaller parts. He now recognizes words by their similarity to words that he already knows.

Niensted (1968) adapted the Fernald method to group use with high school juniors. The method involves teacher-prepared duplicated manuscripts to be traced by the students as the graphemes are pronounced, followed by an underlining of the syllables and a reading of the passage, using meaningful phrasing.

The kinesthetic method is time-consuming, but it has many advantages. It teaches left-to-right orientation, and the sound of the word is associated with the visual stimulus. The child seems to acquire phonic skills without having formal training, and he develops skills in syllabication. The method is designed especially for clinical use and requires almost constant direction from the teacher.

The Hegge, Kirk, and Kirk Grapho-Vocal Method (1955) requires the pupil to sound out and write each word. The pupil pronounces the word entirely phonetically (synthetic phonics) and later writes the word from dictation. The steps thus are:

1. Sound the words letter by letter.
2. Blend the sounds together.
3. Pronounce the words.
4. Write the words.

Fernald's method is a VAKT (visual, auditory, kinesthetic, and tactile) method. There are similar methods labelled only VAK. In these, the pupil does not do any tracing of the word.

Cooper (1971) found that there were no distinct differences in modality preference between good and poor first graders, but that modality preference was more important for poor readers than for good readers. More surprising was the finding that poor readers tended not to learn best through the kinesthetic modality, whereas good readers did.

The Unified Phonics Method. The Unified Phonics Method by Spalding and Spalding[8] is a phonics method which teaches reading through a spelling-writing approach and through a study of some seventy phonograms in the English language. These are single letters or letter combinations which represent forty-five basic sounds. The authors recommend their program as a beginning reading program and suggest that through the use of this program remedial reading will not be needed later. The steps in teaching are the following (pp. 40–42):

1. Teach the phonograms by having pupils say in unison the one or more sounds of each of the phonograms.
2. The pupil writes each phonogram. The letters are not named.
3. Any phonogram of two or more letters is called by its sound. Thus *eigh* is *a*.
4. Have children write words from the Ayres list.
5. Teach the basic laws of spelling.
6. Reading is begun only when the pupils have learned enough words to comprehend instantly the meaning of a sentence.

The Color Phonics System. The Color Phonics System[9] presents the letters in color in such a way that once the principle of coding has been mastered, the pupil can immediately identify the sound. The method is designed to be used with the dyslexic reader. It is not to be used with the color blind or with the brain injured suffering from color agnosia. The system is based, among others, on the following assumptions:

1. The most successful techniques for teaching dyslexics are founded on a phonetic basis.
2. Each letter should be taught separately or in given combinations which can be arranged and rearranged again and again in various orders. Bannatyne (1966) believes that the fundamental neuropsychological deficit of the dyslexic child is the inability to sequence correctly, especially auditorily. The pupil must vocalize constantly, sounding out the successive phonemes which make up a word.
3. The dyslexic child has difficulty mastering the irregular orthography of the

---

[8]Romalda Bishop Spalding and Walter T. Spalding, *The Writing Road to Reading* (New York: Whiteside, Inc., William Morrow & Co., Inc., 1962).

[9]Color Phonics System (Cambridge, Mass.: Educators Publishing Service, 301 Vassar Street).

English language, but replacing the irregular phonetic structure of the language with a regular one requires the child to transfer to the traditional orthography at a later date. As the dyslexic child finds it extremely difficult to memorize a set of sound-symbol associations, an additional set of symbols for the same sounds is scarcely likely to solve his problems (Bannatyne, 1966, p. 196). Color coding permits the child to identify the sound in a direct way.

4. The pupil must overlearn sound-symbol associations through a variety of stimuli and sensory pathways.

Bannatyne (1966) believes that the Color Phonics System can be used in conjunction with the Fernald Method, the Gillingham Method, or Daniel's and Diack's systems as developed through the Royal Road Readers. For teaching with this system the following points are emphasized by Bannatyne:

1. If the child suffers from severe dyslexia, the teacher usually begins with the phonetically regular words and short sentences, and initially short vowels. Consonants are introduced later.

2. The vowels are printed in red. The pupil learns that there must never be a word or syllable without a red letter (the letter *y* has a red band because it can be used as a vowel).

3. At all times, words are broken up into syllables whenever the individual letters are used. One technique which helps the child with breaking a word into syllables, memorizing colors, and spelling generally is the use of rhymes and rhyming.

4. A problem frequently encountered is that of blending phonemes. Frequently, the inability to blend is a direct result of faulty teaching, inasmuch as the pupil has learned to voice unvoiced consonants by adding unwanted vowels. The word *lit* cannot be blended if the *l* is pronounced *luh*. More often than not, this inability to synthesize sounds into meaningful speech is an aspect of the primary inability of the dyslexic to sequence auditory material in the absence of auditory sounds. Clear vocalization and auditory sequencing of words are the most important requisite for successful remediation.

5. There are only two methods for facilitating blending. The first is to tell the child to form his mouth in preparation for saying the initial consonant of a syllable but then to say the following vowel instead. This technique is useful when the initial consonants are unvoiced ones anyway. The second technique consists of demonstrating a single syllable in two parts, namely, the initial consonant and the remainder of the syllable as a whole. Thus cat is taught not as *c a t*, but as *c at*. At the same time, the word, *cat*, as a *gestalt*, is presented in both its written and spoken forms, and these are simultaneously analyzed into their component letters and phonemes.

6. The child is introduced to the twenty or so spelling rules one by one. He is given plenty of practice in applying the rules. In the long run, it is easier for a dyslexic, with his weak verbal memory, to remember a few set principles than thousands of those arbitrary letter-sound sequences called (printed) words.

7. Gradually, the black vowels replace the colored ones.

The Progressive Choice Reading Method. The Progressive Choice Reading Method[10] is an outgrowth of studies by Myron Woolman. Two programs based on Woolman's ideas are available today. The first of these, entitled *Lift Off to Reading*[11] is useful with educable and trainable mental retardates, culturally disadvantaged, the emotionally disturbed, bilinguals, and dyslexics. *Reading in High Gear*[12] is designed for older, underachieving, culturally disadvantaged readers at the adolescent level. Woolman emphasizes elements in words. He begins with a "target word" by discussing its meaning. The learner then must differentiate the linear and curvilinear components which compose the letters of the target word. These components are then combined into individual letters and discrimination of the letters is stressed. The pupil next writes the letter by tracing the letter, finally writing the letter without tracing. The third step consists of learning the sound that is most commonly associated with the letter. Woolman teaches the *g*, for example, as *guh,* noting that this is a necessary crutch in the beginning and that the pupil quickly gets rid of it when he has mastered a "feeling" for the consonant. The pupil must utter the sound when he sees the printed form of the letter and he must write the letter when he hears it pronounced for him. Fourthly, the reader must learn to combine various vowels and consonants into single sounds. Finally, the pupil must read and write the "target words."

Gillingham Method. The Gillingham method[13] is a multisensory approach emphasizing the linguistic and graphic regularities of English words. It is termed an alphaphonetic method and begins by teaching the child a few short vowels and consonants that have only one sound. It does not use letters that, if reversed, become new letters. Thus initially it steers clear of letters like *b* and *d*. It is a combination method, using the auditory, visual, and kinesthetic sense avenues. It is a synthetic phonics system rather than an analytical phonics approach. The teaching processes that result in the association of the visual, auditory, and kinesthetic processes are called linkages. The method consists of eight such linkages.

1. The name of the letter is associated with the printed symbol; then the sound of the letter is associated with the symbol.
2. The teacher makes the letter and explains its form. The pupil traces it, copies it, and writes it from memory. The teacher directs the pupil to move in the right direction and to begin in the right place when making the letters.
3. The phonogram is shown to the pupil and he names it. The child learns to associate the letter with its "look" and its "feel." He learns to form the symbol without looking at the paper as he writes.

[10]M. Woolman, *The Progressive Choice Reading Program* (Washington, D.C.: Institute of Educational Research, Inc., 1962).

[11]M. Woolman, *Lift Off to Reading* (Chicago: Science Research Associates, 1966).

[12]M. Woolman, *Reading in High Gear* (Chicago: Science Research Associates, 1965).

[13]Anna Gillingham and Bessie W. Stillman, *Remedial Training for Children With Specific Disability in Reading, Spelling, and Penmanship* (Cambridge: Educators Publishing Service, 1966). Available also are: *Phonetic Drill Cards, Phonetic Word Cards, Syllable Concept, Little Stories*, and *Introduction of Diphthongs.*

4. The teacher says the phoneme, and the child writes it.
5. The child is shown the letter and asked to sound it. The teacher moves the child's hand to form the letter, and the child sounds it.
6. The teacher gives the name of the phonogram, and the pupil gives the sound.
7. The teacher makes the sound, and the pupil gives the name of the letter.
8. The teacher makes the sound, and the pupil writes the phonogram. Sometimes the pupil writes without looking at the paper and also names the letter.

Using the multisensory approach, the Gillingham method introduces the linguistic and graphically regular words first. Only gradually the pupil is introduced to exceptions.

A commonly accepted principle in remedial teaching is that remedial approaches, if used flexibly, are applicable to reading disability cases almost irrespective of cause.

The normal sequence for the teaching of reading might be the following:

1. Picture reading (associating meaning with a picture). Studies tend to indicate that learners remember the most from their reading when deep involvement is required and the cues supplied by instruction (such as pictures) are kept at a minimum (Robeck and Wilson, 1974).
2. Associating the sound with the whole word. *Include words with a high semantic content.* The most difficult words are words like *but, if, the, their,* because they lack strong semantic associations (Gardner, 1973).
3. Learning the names of the letters.
4. Writing or printing the letter.
5. Associating the sound with the beginning consonant and medial vowel letter.

If this procedure does not work with a given learner, the teacher has two basic options: (1) He can use a fully developed method, such as Gillingham's alphaphonetic method, or (2) he can develop a system of his own incorporating a combination of tested techniques.

Varying educational strategies, as we have just surveyed, have been used to help nonreaders. The success of these efforts has essentially been quite modest, especially with dyslexic readers. There is thus today no clearcut remedy to the remediation of these difficulties.

We hypothesize that dyslexic readers can improve significantly in both their attitudes toward reading and in actual reading performance if they receive the benefits of the following treatments. These relate to reading method, the attitude of the teacher, and the application of learning theory in teaching.

Teaching Method: Word Recognition Skills. One of the recommended teaching approaches is to introduce the teaching of reading to the child by teaching him to associate *letter and sound patterns*, a pattern of graphemes with a pattern of phonemes. Sound is associated only with the total word. The letter is not sounded alone. It is sounded only in the context of other letters or the word.

This approach emphasizes the need for the pupil to be able to identify the contrastive patterns of spelling which represents the sounds. And, it suggests that the pupil learns this most easily when dealing with monosyllabic words in which each letter represents only one single phoneme.

The pupil must learn the identifying characteristics as they are incorporated into the alphabetic spelling pattern (the word is thus identified as being different or variant from every other word). He must learn to discover the critical difference between two words or two letters.

The understanding of the difference that any particular letter makes in the spelling pattern is built up out of the experience of pronouncing and reading a variety of word pairs with minimum differences in their spelling patterns; cat—rat—fat. Phonic methods or the letter cluster approach are useful only in that they teach the pupil where a significant difference lies.

There are many materials, including some that the writer has prepared, which are suitable for this purpose.

This linguistic method can be used by all teachers with all students provided the following conditions exist:

1. The pupil has adequately developed auditory discrimination or phonematic hearing skills:
    a. He can notice similarities or differences between a pair of words spoken to him.
    b. The pupil can hear phonemes spoken to him at one-second intervals in the serial order they occur in a word.
    c. The pupil can blend sounds. In the Calfee-Venezky model, letters are identified specifically but sounds are processed only in the environment of the total word (Geyer, 1971). Others have the child listen to each separate sound /m/ — /ā/ — /l/, and the child is expected to come up with /māl/. Linguists argue that the sounds cannot be produced in isolation without creating a new phonology.
    d. The pupil can tell whether a particular phoneme occurs at the beginning, middle, or final position of a word spoken to him.
2. The pupil can discriminate between letters. (The pupil must be able to identify letters as contrastive shapes. He must be able to develop a visual memory of the letter).
3. The pupil knows the names of the letters of the alphabet.
4. The pupil can write the letter when named.

If the above conditions are not present, besides teaching steps 1 through 4, the teacher will need to use the following tested techniques:

1. Focus on the simplest, most basic perceptual-associational element within a total word or gestalt (*m*ap-*n*ap).
2. Write or trace the letter, form it in clay, or write in wet sand, etc. Monroe has pupils use a pencil to trace the letter. Fernald has pupils trace each letter

with the forefinger. The pupil must learn to segregate the letter segments and to identify them.

3. Associate sound with this element. This element may be a letter or syllable. Monroe put pictures on a card and the pupil learned first to hear the consonant sound. Others show the letter and associate the sound with it.

4. If the pupil begins with separate letters that represent distinct sounds, he must *learn to blend.*
   a. Have the student form his mouth in preparation for saying the initial consonant but then say the following vowel instead: b-y
   b. Have the student learn cat, not /c-a-t/, but /c-at/. The beginning consonant is joined to the ending phonogram and the vowel is joined to the consonant that follows.
   c. Scott (1973) notes that blending might better be described as an instance of sequential decoding. He feels that this process is best taught by using the Half Moon Cards of the *Programmed Reading Kit,* Scott Foresman, 1970.

5. Use all senses. Hear, say, see, and write the word. A good example of this multisensory approach is the Gillingham method. Fernald's method is a VAKT method (the T implies tracing of the word). Blau and Blau (1968) suggest use of AKT in which the visual modality is blocked. The eyes are blindfolded, with the learner saying the letters as he traces them.

6. Use a spelling-writing approach. Sooner or later the learner must be able to write the letter or the word from memory. After the learner has developed a visual memory for the letter, Hinshelwood has him develop an auditory memory for words by spelling aloud the word letter by letter.

7. Teach the phonograms by having students say the sounds in unison, have them write them, etc. (In the Unified Phonics Method, phonograms include all the letters, such as b, c, d plus such phonograms as *eigh, igh, ug, ed*).

8. Use color to regularize the phoneme-grapheme correspondences, as in *Words in Color* and in the *Color Phonics System.*

9. Gradually move from the letter and sound to the total words, which is the smallest linguistic unit that can represent meaning.

10. Have the child say the word (or sentence), after he has read it mechanically, as he would "talk it" to a companion.

11. Use the oral neurological-impress method (Heckelman, 1966). This is a system of unison reading whereby the student and the teacher read aloud simultaneously at a rapid rate. This approach is especially effective with those who are phonics-bound, who have had intensive phonics training but still are not reading fluently.

Comprehension Skills. It is not enough to simply develop the pupil's word-recognition skills. The comprehension skills also need development. Reading is a two-fold process: word identification *and* comprehension.

Development of comprehension skills begins on two levels:

a. Association of *semantic* meaning with a symbol or symbols. This should not be a major difficulty for the dyslexic readers of which we are speaking.
b. Association of *syntactic* meaning with words. This is what is commonly referred to as sentence sense. The dyslexic is deficient in sentence sense. This is often demonstrated orally in word calling.

The materials for the program consist of two types: the child's own language productions and the textbooks that he is expected to use in the coming school year.

Using the Language-Experience approach, children are asked to talk, write, and read about their own experiences in their own idiom. This assures proper *motivation* for children who like to read what they have written, and it will also *prevent a mismatch* between the student's oral language and the written language of his instructional material. This approach thus deals with the problems of the Reluctant Reader and the Disadvantaged Reader. It has an in-built motivational element and the writing reflects the background of the reader. The language-experience approach assures that the reading materials will be already within the linguistic experience of the pupil and will be within his control.

A common exercise has children write about their personal reactions to an external stimulus such as a photograph, a short article, etc. The pupil may be asked to dictate a letter to a friend or write a menu.

Textbooks are used to assure that what is being learned in the program will *transfer* to what will be expected of him when he re-enters the classroom.

The acid test of a reading program is the transferability of the learnings it provides to content areas. Research shows that general reading ability alone is often not enough to assure reading improvement in the content areas. The pupil must be taught special skills. This is even more so in the case of the dyslexic.

An identification must be made of resource materials that meet the pupil's peculiar needs in word recognition and comprehension.

Cloze Procedure. The cloze procedure has been used quite effectively for diagnostic purposes (as a test of reading comprehension) as well as an instructional tool. The latter use is the point of emphasis here.

The *cloze procedure* is an effective way to zero in on the use of contextual cues (both semantic and syntactic) as aids in word recognition and comprehension.

In the cloze procedure the reader must generate words for the blank spaces which meet the syntactic and semantic constraints of the sentence (Ammon, 1975). In the sentence, "The boy threw the _____", sentence structure says only nouns can be used to complete it. The noun could be baseball, football, etc. Semantic and syntactic context suggests that relatively few nouns are possible. Adding a *b* in the blank space, a phonic cue, restricts the choices even more.

Cloze passages have every nth word deleted (usually every fifth word). However, a variation is to delete preselected words, such as every nth noun or verb. This technique is useful also in teaching such things as mastery of structural and functional words (prepositions, conjunctions).

Another variation is to delete a portion of a word. This technique is particularly helpful in teaching phonic skills. Deleting every nth word focuses the learner's attention on the relationships within the passage. It forces the pupil to deal with such situations as "Bill went _____ the hill."

The student will have to use the context to come up with the right word, perhaps *up, down,* etc.

Gove (1975) notes that deleting parts of words (initial consonants should usually be provided) should teach the pupil how to use graphic cues as a bridge between grammatic cues to obtain meaning. The strength of the cloze technique as an instructional tool is that it teaches the pupil to use syntactic and semantic information to comprehend print.

It appears that adverbs, adjectives, and prepositions are hardest for children to produce. Modifier deletions may distort the meaning of the passage (Heitzman and Bloomer, 1967).

The steps to be used are (Lopardo, 1975):

1. A language sample is dictated by the child.
2. The sample is typed as dictated without changes.
3. The child reads the language sample.
4. A cloze passage is prepared *with the particular goal of the reading lesson in mind.*
5. The child and teacher compare the cloze passage with the original.
6. Teacher discusses with the child the *goal* of the cloze passage.

Combining the language experience textbook approach with cloze procedure seems to be the best way to deal with the problems of the dyslexic reader, the culturally deprived child, and even the reluctant learner.

Teacher Attitude. Study after study has shown that the method of teaching may not be as significant for learning as is the teacher. Unfortunately, we have not been able to identify what it is about a teacher that makes the difference. We suspect that part of the answer lies in the attitudes that the teacher brings to the learning situation. Teacher attitudes substantially affect the performance of the retarded reader. We thus believe that the eco-system is an important variable.

The remedial teacher must be particularly conversant with the use of mental health concepts in the classroom and the effect that mental health has upon achievement in the classroom. We have discussed these earlier under the heading, "Principles of Remediation".

Learning Principles. The good teacher is one who also has some understanding of basic principles of learning. A common plea is that teachers learn more about the learning process. Outstanding educational programs can be built only on practices which are in accord with what we know about pupil learning. The following concepts, in particular, are guidelines to be followed by teachers of dyslexic children:

1. The approach recommended is a behavioral modification approach, concentrating on the acquisition of those behaviors which are related to success in learning to read. We stress systematic, environmental manipulation and require the teacher:
   a. to set terminal goals
   b. to analyze the goals into reasonable task components

     c. to reward the child each step of the way

     d. to provide individual instruction

     The teacher is involved in the gradual shaping of behavior toward a goal through successive approximation.

2. Learning can occur only if the teacher gains the child's attention. The teacher must make psychic contact with the learner, get him to participate, and get him to respond.

3. Review, repetition, and overlearning are of crucial importance to poor readers. Retarded readers generally become better in word recognition the more frequently they see the word.

4. The learner cannot learn without doing, but he won't do anything without being rewarded. The best rewards in the remedial setting are often pleasant pupil-teacher relationships, permissiveness on the part of the teacher, and feelings of success. However, with the dyslexic the reward may need to be more concrete.

The reader may want to refer back to the end of Chapter 4 where the learning principles as they apply to reading are summarized in detail.

Evaluating Remedial Instruction. The reading teacher, whether in or out of the regular classroom, must constantly evaluate his instruction. He needs to determine the effectiveness of various procedures in terms of the gains in reading achievement. Over the course of years many quite different procedures have been suggested for evaluating remedial teaching, but too few data are available concerning their relative effectiveness. And for that matter, some writers actually challenge the effectiveness of special methods of remediation. Young (1938), for example, suggests that the personality of the teacher and his ability to enlist each child's active cooperation are more important than the specific method used. On the other hand, numerous studies on remedial and diagnostic methods indicate that reading difficulties can be either entirely or at least largely eliminated.

Balow (1965) found that remedial instruction was effective in dealing with the problems of the disabled reader, but he also notes that severe reading disability is not corrected by short term intensive treatment, but that it should be considered a relatively chronic illness needing long term treatment rather than the short course typically organized in current programs. Buerger (1968) also reports that children who received remedial instruction demonstrated significant reading gains, but they did not make greater long term educational progress than other children who did not receive remedial instruction.

Rankin and Tracy (1965, 1967) and Tracy and Rankin (1967) list three methods of measuring and evaluating individual differences in reading improvement.[14]

1. *Crude gain.* In this situation comparable tests are given before (the pretest) and after (the posttest) a remedial program. The score at the start of the

[14]Another good survey of various evaluative procedures is by George H. Maginnis. "Evaluating Remedial Reading Gains." *Journal of Reading* 13 (1970): 523–28.

program is subtracted from the score at the end of the program, and the difference is considered as improvement. Children will naturally show improvement if a difficult test is given in the beginning and if an easier test is administered after the completion of the program.

2. *Percentage gain.* In this approach the gain between the pre- and posttest is expressed as a percentage of the initial score. The formula then is:

$$\text{per cent of gain} = \frac{\text{pretest—posttest}}{\text{posttest}}$$

3. Residual gain. This is the difference between the actual posttest score and the score that was predictable from the pretest score. For a discussion of this third procedure the reader may want to consult the articles by Rankin and Tracy in the *Journal of Reading,* March, 1965, and March, 1967.

Carpenter, Gray, and Galloway (1974) report that in their study residual gain appeared to be no more effective than the crude gain technique in measuring progress at the elementary level.

Ekwall (1972) suggests three methods for measuring pupil progress: (1) compare pretest and posttest results; (2) use a control group; (3) use the ratio of learning criterion which is a measurement of children's learning rates (amount learned per year) prior to entering a special program versus their learning rate during the program.

Many faulty conclusions apparently have been drawn from reading research because residual gain was not considered. As Sommerfield (1957) points out, there is a natural tendency for those people who score at the extremes of a distribution on the first test to score closer to the mean of the distribution on the second test. The scores tend to regress toward the mean.

Although the research worker can use control groups or make statistical corrections to eliminate regression effects, this frequently is not done.

Dolch (1956, p. 80) has cautioned that research can come up with the wrong answer unless it is carefully planned and watched. He recommends vigilance in these areas:

1. Compare equal teachers working equally hard.
2. Compare pupils of equal ability and equal home influences.
3. Compare equal school time and emphasis.
4. Watch carefully size of class.
5. Beware of misleading averages.
6. Watch for unmeasured results.

In discussing these points, Dolch emphasizes that the teacher using the method frequently is far more important than the method used. Numerous variables enter into any experiment. Sommerfield (1957, p. 56) indicates that the reported results of experimental reading programs may be influenced by the subjects involved, the techniques and materials used, the conditions under which the study was done, the tests that were employed, the statistical devices used, and perhaps the bias or misinterpretations of the investigator.

Studies often do not make allowance for the differences in both skill and motivation among teachers. Control groups are taught by the "regular" teachers; experimental groups are taught by teachers who have a special interest in the project and can give more time to their students. Studies do not control for the Hawthorne effect[15] which is the learning that results simply because the program is new and presents for students and teachers alike an opportunity for recognition. Brownell (1966) notes that the critical determinant of achievement is teaching competency rather than the system of instruction. He also notes that results frequently are evaluated by means of test scores, but this is not necessarily what is educationally significant. The measurable is not necessarily the significant, and the significant is not necessarily measurable. There are no published tests available that measure how well students read to gain information in specific courses. In this area general reading tests are of limited value. In many instances achievement at the moment is evaluated; the transfer value of what has been learned is rarely evaluated. There may also be differences in motivation between the pupils in a control group using the regular methods and the experimental group using a new method.

There also is a difference between educational significance and statistical significance. Sometimes a difference of one tenth of a year is significant at the .05 level of confidence, but it may have no practical significance.

Weiner (1961) notes that to evaluate changes in reading behavior we must consider all relevant functions: perceptual, integrative, and motivational. We need to evaluate processes rather than simply end-products, measurable and nonmeasurable changes, and changes in self-concept and attitudes as a result of remedial programs. We need to find ways of analyzing the process that produced the outcome and of determining cause-and-effect relationships. Hardy (1968) found that early referral for help was related to superior achievement in a remedial program. When assessing process, we encounter such difficult-to-evaluate variables as student-teacher interaction, attitudes, interests, and enthusiasm. Weiner notes that evidence of improvement is greater accuracy in responses to printed material, greater dependability, greater retention of and confidence in one's responses, and greater speed.

In advancing a clinical concept of assessment Weiner (1961) stresses the qualitative aspects of assessment and suggests that gains must be measured from the point of actual departure and not from an arbitrary zero point on a grade-level scale. Pupils in need of remedial services start not from scratch, but from behind scratch.

---

[15]Willard J. Congreve, "Implementing and Evaluating the Use of Innovations," *Innovation and Change in Reading Instruction,* 67th Yearbook of the National Society for the Study of Education (Chicago: University of Chicago Press, 1968), pp. 291–319.

SUMMARY

In this chapter we have examined some general principles of diagnosis and remediation and have proposed certain practical techniques. In diagnosis we must strive for accurate measurement. Numerous tests —intelligence, readiness, survey, and diagnostic—are at the teacher's disposal. But, for effective diagnosis, the teacher must rely on his own observations of the child and his reading skills and deficiencies.

We have seen that diagnosis is a continuous process designed to encourage the growth of all learners. The teacher must understand and be able to identify the numerous possible causes of retardation. Without this knowledge he cannot apply the appropriate remedial techniques nor, if the situation demands, can he be certain to make the appropriate referral to the specialist. And the reading teacher needs to familiarize himself with a variety of remedial methods. No one method is effective in all cases.

Finally, it is important that we recognize remediation to be an integral part of a developmental reading program. Diagnostic and remedial techniques are not reserved for "retarded" readers. Children of any level of ability, even those making normal or above-normal progress, may benefit from the identification and treatment of specific areas of weakness.

QUESTIONS FOR DISCUSSION

1. Discuss prevention of reading disability as an important principle in the teaching of reading.
2. What constitutes a comprehensive individual diagnosis?
3. What are the criteria for estimating a child's independent reading level?
4. Compare the advantages and disadvantages of the informal and formal reading inventory.
5. Which diagnostic test would you recommend for grade levels four through six?
6. Identify basic symptoms of reading disability and suggest possible causes for each. How would you go about identifying the specific cause?
7. Suggest four possible classroom organizations that make allowance for corrective instruction.

8. List the factors to be considered when evaluating the effectiveness of remedial instruction.
9. What is the purpose of Betts' three levels of reading proficiency?
10. How may reading retardation be defined? How can it be identified?

BIBLIOGRAPHY

ADAMS, RICHARD B. "Dyslexia: A Discussion of its Definition." *Journal of Learning Disabilities* 2 (1969): 616–26.

AMMON, RICHARD. "Generating Expectancies to Enhance Comprehension." *The Reading Teacher* 29 (1975): 245–49.

ARTLEY, A. STERL and HARDIN, VERALEE B. "A Current Dilemma: Reading Disability or Learning Disability." *The Reading Teacher* 29 (1976): 361–66.

AUSTIN, MARY C. "Identifying Readers Who Need Corrective Instruction." *Corrective Reading in Classroom and Clinic,* Supplementary Educational Monographs, No. 79. Chicago: University of Chicago Press, 1953, pp. 19–25.

BALOW, BRUCE. "The Long-Term Effect of Remedial Reading Instruction." *The Reading Teacher* 18 (1965): 581–86.

BALYEAT, RALPH and NORMAN, DOUGLAS. "LEA-Cloze-Comprehension Test." *The Reading Teacher* 28 (1975): 555–60.

BAMMAN, HENRY A. "Organizing the Remedial Program in the Secondary School." *Journal of Reading* 8 (1964): 103–8.

BANNATYNE, ALEX D. "The Color Phonics System." In John Money, ed., *The Disabled Readers.* Baltimore: Johns Hopkins Press, 1966, pp. 193–214.

BANNATYNE, ALEX. "Spelling and Sound Blending." *Academic Therapy* 7 (1971): 73–77.

BATEMAN, BARBARA D. "Educational Implications of Minimal Brain Damage." *The Reading Teacher* 27 (1974): 662–68.

BELMONT, LILLIAN and BIRCH, HERBERT G. "The Intellectual Profile of Retarded Readers." *Perceptual and Motor Skills* 22 (1966): 787–816.

BETTS, EMMETT A. "Reading Disability Correlates." *Education* 56 (1935): 18–24.

BETTS, EMMETT A. *Foundations of Reading Instruction.* New York: American Book Company, New York, 1957.

BLAU, HAROLD and BLAU, HARRIET. "A Theory of Learning to Read." *The Reading Teacher* 22 (1968): 126–29, 144.

BODER, ELENA. "Development Dyslexia: A Diagnostic Screening Procedure Based on Three Characteristic Patterns of Reading and Spelling." *Claremont Reading Conference,* 1968, pp. 173–87.

BODER, ELENA. "Developmental Dyslexia." *Journal of School Health* 40 (1970): 289–90.

BOND, GUY L., and TINKER, MILES A. *Reading Difficulties: Their Diagnosis and Correction.* New York: Appleton-Century-Crofts, 1967.

BROWN, VIRGINIA L. and BOTEL, MORTON. *Dyslexia: Definition or Treatment.* ERIC Clearinghouse on Reading, Indiana University, 1972.

BROWNELL, W. A. "The Evaluation of Learning Under Dissimilar Systems of Instruction." *California Journal of Educational Research* 17 (1966): 80–90.

BRUECKNER, LEO J. "Introduction." *Educational Diagnosis.* Thirty-fourth Yearbook of the National Society for the Study of Education. Bloomington: Public School Publishing Company, 1935, pp. 1–14.

BRUININKS, ROBERT H; GLAMAN, GERTRUDE M.; and CLARK, CHARLOTTE R. "Issues in Determining Prevalence of Reading Retardation." *The Reading Teacher* 27 (1973): 177–85.

BRYANT, N. DALE. "Learning Disabilities in Reading." *Reading as Intellectual Activity.* International Reading Association Conference Proceedings. New York: Scholastic Magazines, 1963, pp. 142–46.

BUERGER, THEODORE A. "A Follow-Up of Remedial Reading Instruction." *The Reading Teacher* 21 (1968): 329–34.

CARPENTER, TERYLE W.; GRAY, GORDON W.; and GALLOWAY, ELIZABETH B. "A Comparison of Individual Reading Gain." *The Reading Teacher* 27 (1974): 368–69.

CHALL, JEANNE. "How They Learn and Why They Fail." *Improvement of Reading Through Classroom Practice,* International Reading Association Conference Proceedings. Newark, Del.: 1964, pp. 147–48.

COHEN, S. ALLEN. "Minimal Brain Dysfunction and Practical Matters Such as Teaching Kids to Read." In *Minimal Brain Dysfunction,* Annuals of the New York Academy of Science, Vol. 205, New York, 1973, pp. 251–61.

COOPER, J. DAVID. "A Study of the Learning Modalities of Good and Poor First Grade Readers." *Reading Methods and Teacher Improvement,* Newark, Del: International Reading Association, 1971, pp. 87–97.

CRITCHLEY, MACDONALD. *Developmental Dyslexia,* London: William Heinemann Medical Books, Ltd., White Friars Press, 1964.

CRONBACH, LEE J. "The Counselor's Problems from the Perspective of Communication Theory." *New Perspectives in Counseling,* University of Minnesota Press, 1955.

CROSBY, R.M.N. and LISTON, ROBERT A. *The Waysiders.* New York: Delacorte Press, 1968, p. 38.

DECHANT, EMERALD. *Diagnosis and Remediation of Reading Disability.* West Nyack, New York: Parker Publishing Company, 1968.

DOLCH, E. W. "Poor Readers are 'Made'." *Education* 67 (1947): 436–41.

DOLCH, E. W. "Success in Remedial Reading." *Elementary English* 30 (1953): 133–37.

DOLCH, E. W. "School Research in Reading." *Elementary English,* 33 (1956): 76–80.

DORE-BOYCE, KATHLEEN; MISNER, MARILYN S.; and MCGUIRE, LORRAINE D. "Comparing Reading Expectancy Formulas." *The Reading Teacher* 29 (1975): 8–14.

DURREL, DONALD D. *The Improvement of Basic Reading Abilities.* Yonkers, New York: World Book Company, 1940.

DURRELL, DONALD D. *Improving Reading Instruction.* Yonkers, New York: World Book Company, 1956.

EISENBERG, LEON. "Epidemiology of Reading Retardation." In John Money, ed., *The Disabled Reader,* Baltimore: Johns Hopkins Press, 1966.

ELDER, R. "Behavioral Criteria and Pupil Achievement." *Michigan Educational Journal* 40 (1963): 502–36.

EKWALL, E. E. "The Use of WISC Subtest Profiles in the Diagnosis of Reading Difficulties." Unpublished Doctoral Dissertation, University of Arizona, 1966.

EKWALL, ELDON E. "Measuring Gains in Remedial Reading." *The Reading Teacher* 26 (1972): 138–41.

ELLINGSON, C. C. "The Obsolescent Child." *Journal of Learning Disabilities* 1 (1968): 34–37.

EMANS, ROBERT. "Teacher Evaluations of Reading Skills and Individualized Reading." *Elementary English* 42 (1965): 258–60.

FERNALD, GRACE M. *Remedial Techniques in Basic School Subjects.* New York: McGraw-Hill, 1966.

GARDNER, HOWARD. "Developmental Dyslexia." *Psychology Today* 7 (1973): 62–67.

GESCHWIND, N. "The Organization of Language and the Brain." *Science* 170 (1971): 940–44.

GEYER, JOHN J. "Comprehensive and Partial Models Related to the Reading Process." In F. B. Davis, ed., *The Literature of Research in Reading With Emphasis on Models.* Rutgers Graduate School of Education, 1971.

GOVE, MARY K. "Using the Cloze Procedure in a First Grade Classroom." *The Reading Teacher* 29 (1975): 36–38.

HALLGREN B. *Specific Dyslexia ("Congenital Word-Blindness").* Acta Psychiat. Scand. Supplement 65, 1950.

HARDY, MADELINE I. "Disabled Readers: What Happens to Them After Elementary School?" *Canadian Education and Research Digest* 8 (1968): 338–46.

HARING, N. and RIDGWAY, R. "Early Identification of Children With Learning Disabilities." *Exceptional Children* 33 (1967): 387–95.

HARRIS, ALBERT J. *How to Increase Reading Ability*, 3rd edition. New York: David McKay Company, 1961a.

HARRIS, ALBERT J. "Perceptual Difficulties in Reading Disability." *Changing Concepts of Reading Instruction,* International Reading Association Conference Proceedings. New York: Scholastic Magazines, 1961b, pp. 282–90.

HARTMAN, NANCY C. "Response: Low Tolerance for Frustration: Target Group for Reading Disabilities." *The Reading Teacher* 27 (1974): 675.

HÉCAEN, HENRY. "Studies of Parietal Lobes." In Frederic L. Darley and Clark H. Millikan, eds. *Brain Mechanisms Underlying Speech and Language.* New York: Grune and Stratton, 1967.

HECKELMAN, R. G. "Using the Neurological-Impress Remedial-Reading Technique." *Academic Therapy Quarterly* 1 (1966): 235–39.

HEGGE, T.; KIRK, SAMUEL; and KIRK, WINIFRED. *Remedial Reading Drills.* Ann Arbor, Michigan: George Wahr, Publisher, 1955.

HEILMAN, ARTHUR W. "Moving Faster Toward Outstanding Instructional Programs." *Vistas in Reading,* Proceedings of the Eleventh Annual Convention. Newark, Del.: International Reading Association, 1967, pp. 273–76.

HEITZMAN, ANDREW J. and BLOOMER, RICHARD H. "The Effect of Non-Overt Reinforced Cloze Procedure upon Reading Comprehension." *Journal of Reading* 11 (1967): 213–23.

HENIG, MAX S. "Predictive Value of a Reading-Readiness Test and of Teachers' Forecasts." *Elementary School Journal* 50 (1949): 41–46.

HERMANN, K. *Reading Disability.* Springfield, Ill.: Charles C Thomas, 1959.

HILL, J. "Models of Screening." Paper presented at the annual meeting of the American Educational Research Association, March 4, 1970, Minneapolis, Minn.

HINSHELWOOD, JAMES. *Congenital Word-Blindness.* London: H. K. Lewis and Company, Ltd., 1917.

HITCHCOCK, ARTHUR A. and ALFRED, CLEO. "Can Teachers Make Accurate Estimates of Reading Ability?" *The Clearing House* 29 (1955): 422–424.

JASTAK, J. D. and S. R. JASTAK. *The Wide Range Achievement Test Manual.* Wilmington, Del.: Guidance Associates, 1965.

JOHNSON, MARJORIE S. and KRESS, ROY A., eds. *Corrective Reading in the Elementary Classroom.* Newark, Del.: International Reading Association, 1967.

JULITTA, SISTER MARY, O. S. F. "Classroom Methods in Correcting Reading Deficiencies in Elementary School." *Better Readers for Our Times,* International Reading Association, Conference Proceedings. New York: Scholastic Magazines, 1956, pp. 134–38.

KLAUSNER, DOROTHY C. "Screening and Development of the Remedial Reading Teacher." *Journal of Reading* 10 (1967): 552–59.

KOLSON, CLIFFORD J. and KALUGER, GEORGE. *Clinical Aspects of Remedial Reading.* Springfield, Ill.: Charles C Thomas, 1963, p. 27.

KOTTMEYER, WILLIAM. "Readiness for Reading." *Elementary English* 24 (1947): 355–66.

KUHN, VIRGINICE M. SR. "A Comparative Study of Teacher Judgment and the Metropolitan Reading Readiness Test in Predicting Success in First Grade Reading." *Research Abstracts* 8 (1966) Cardinal Stritch College, Milwaukee.

LOPARDO, GENEVIEVE S. "LEA-Cloze Reading Material for the Disabled Reader." *The Reading Teacher* 29 (1975): 42–44.

LOVITT, T. C. "Assessment of Children with Learning Disabilities." *Exceptional Children* 34 (1967): 233–39.

MCGEE, ROBERT T. and MCCLINTIC, JEAN M. "Early Instruction in Readiness: Who Speaks for the Children?" *The Reading Teacher* 20 (1966): 122–24.

MCLEOD, JOHN. "Reading Expectancy from Disabled Learners." *Journal of Learning Disabilities* 1 (1968): 7–15.

MEREDITH, PATRICK. *Dyslexia and the Individual: A Study of Reading Difficulty in "Word Blind" Children.* London: Elm Tree Books, Ltd., 1972.

MILLS, DONNA M. "Corrective and Remedial Reading Instruction in the Secondary School." *Reading as an Intellectual Activity* 8 (1963): 56–59, International Reading Association. Newark, Del.

MONEY, JOHN, ed. *Reading Disability.* Baltimore: Johns Hopkins Press, 1962a.

MONEY, JOHN. "Dyslexia: A Postconference Review." In J. Money, ed., *Reading Disability: Progress and Research Needs in Dyslexia.* Baltimore: Johns Hopkins Press, 1962b, pp. 9–33.

MONROE, MARION. *Children Who Cannot Read.* Chicago: University of Chicago Press, 1932.

MYERS, PATRICIA and HAMMILL, D. *Methods for Learning Disorders.* New York: Wiley, 1969.

NELSON, C. DONALD. "Subtle Brain Damage: Its Influences on Learning and Language." *The Elementary School Journal* 61 (1961): 317–21.

NEVILLE, DONALD. "Learning Characteristics of Poor Readers as Revealed by Results of Individually Administered Intelligence Tests." *Vistas in Reading,* Proceedings of the Eleventh Annual Convention, Newark, Del.: International Reading Association, 1967, pp. 554–59.

NIENSTED, SERENA. "A Group Use of the Fernald Technique." *Journal of Reading* 11 (1968): 435–37, 440.

NILA, SISTER MARY, O.S.F., "Foundations of a Successful Reading Program." *Education* 73 (1953) 543–55.

NORRIE, E. "Word Blindness in Denmark: Its Neurological and Educational Aspects." *Independent School Bulletin* 3 (1960): 8–12.

O'BRUBA, WILLIAM S. "Basic Principles for Teaching Remedial Reading in the Classroom." *Reading Improvement* 11 (1974): 9–10.

ORLOW, MARIA. "Low Tolerance for Frustration: Target Group for Reading Disabilities." *The Reading Teacher* 27 (1974): 669–74.

OTTO, WAYNE and MCMENEMY, RICHARD A. *Corrective and Remedial Teaching of Reading.* Boston: Houghton Mifflin, 1966.

OVERLINE, HARRY M. and QUAYLE, K. SUZANNE. "Learning Disabilities from an Ecological Perspective." *Education* 92 (1971): 28–33.

POWELL, WILLIAM R. "The Validity of the Instructional Reading Level." *Diagnostic Viewpoints in Reading,* Newark, Del.: International Reading Association, 1971, pp. 121–33.

QUADFASSEL, F. A. and GOODGLASS, H. "Specific Reading Disability and Other Specific Disabilities." *Journal of Learning Disabilities* 1 (1968): 590–600.

RABINOVICH, R. D., and WINIFRED, INGRAM. "Neuropsychiatric Considerations in Reading Retardation." *The Reading Teacher* 15 (1962): 433–38.

RANKIN, EARL F., JR. and TRACY, ROBERT J. "Residual Gain as a Measure of Individual Differences in Reading Improvement." *Journal of Reading* 8 (1965): 224–33.

REICH, RIVA, R. "More Than Remedial Reading." *Elementary English* 39 (1962): 216.

REID, WILLIAM R. and SCHOER, LOWELL A. "Reading Achievement, Social Class and Subtest Pattern on the WISC." *Journal of Educational Research* 59 (1966): 469–72.

ROGERS, CARL R. "The Place of the Person in the New World of the Behavioral Sciences." *Personnel and Guidance Journal* 39 (1961): 442–51.

ROBECK, MILDRED COEN and WILSON, JOHN A. R. *Psychology of Reading.* New York: Wiley, 1974.

RODENBORN, LEO V. "Determining, Using Expectancy Formulas." *The Reading Teacher* 28 (1974): 286–91.

ROSENTHAL, JOSEPH H. "Recent Advances in the Neurophysiology of Some Specific Cognitive Functions." *Academic Therapy* 8 (1973): 423–28.

ROSWELL, FLORENCE. "Psychotherapeutic Principles Applied to Remedial Reading." *Improvement of Reading Through Classroom Practice,* International Reading Association Conference Proceedings. Newark, Del.: 1964, pp. 145–47.

RUTHERFORD, WILLIAM L. "What is Your DQ (Dyslexia Quotient)." *The Reading Teacher* 25 (1971): 262–66.

SANTOSTEFANO, S.; RUTLEDGE, L.; and RANDALL, D. "Cognitive Styles and Reading Disabilities." *Psychology in Schools* 2 (1965): 57–63.

SATZ, PAUL and FRIEL, JANETTE. "Some Predictive Antecedents of Specific Reading Disability: A Preliminary Two-Year Follow-Up." *Journal of Learning Disability* 7 (1974): 48–55.

SATZ, P. and ROSS, J. eds. *The Disabled Learner: Early Detection and Intervention.* Rotterdam, The Netherlands: Rotterdam University Press, 1973.

SAWYER, DIANE J. "The Diagnostic Mystique—A Point of View." *The Reading Teacher* 27 (1974): 555–61.

SAWYER, RITA I. "Does the Wechsler Intelligence Scale for Children Discriminate Between Mildly Disabled and Severely Disabled Readers?" *The Elementary School Journal* 66 (1965): 97–103.

SCHIFFMAN, GILBERT. "Early Identification of Reading Disabilities: The Responsibility of the Public School." *Bulletin of the Orton Society* 14 (1964): 42–44.

SIPAY, E. A. "A Comparison of Standardized Reading Scores and Functional Reading Levels." *The Reading Teacher* 17 (1964): 265–68.

SMITH, D. E. P. and CARRIGAN, PATRICIA M. *The Nature of Reading Disability.* New York: Harcourt, Brace and Company, 1959.

SOMMERFIELD, ROY E. "Some Recent Research in College Reading." *Techniques and Procedures in College and Adult Reading Programs,* Sixth Yearbook of the Southwest Reading Conference. Fort Worth, Texas: Texas Christian University Press, 1957, p. 24.

STOTT, D. H. "Some Less Obvious Cognitive Aspects of Learning to Read." *The Reading Teacher* 26 (1973): 374–83.

TIEGS, ERNEST W. "Educational Diagnosis." *Educational Bulletin* No. 18, California Test Bureau, a Division of McGraw-Hill Book Company.

TRACY, ROBERT J. and RANKIN, EARL F., JR. "Methods of Computing and Evaluating Residual Gain Scores in the Reading Program." *Journal of Reading* 10 (1967): 363–71.

WARNER, DOLORES. "The Divided-Day Plan for Reading Organization." *The Reading Teacher* 20 (1967): 397–99.

WEINER, BLUMA B. "Dimensions of Assessment." *Exceptional Children* 28 (1961): 483–86.

WHEELER, LESTER R. "Distinctive Problems Presented by Poor Readers: The Retarded Reader." *Improving Reading in All Curriculum Areas.* Supplementary Educational Monographs, No. 76. Chicago: University of Chicago Press, 1952, pp. 109–14.

WILLSON, MARGARET F. "Clinical Teaching and Dyslexia." *The Reading Teacher* 21 (1968): 730–733.

WILSON, ROBERT M. "Diagnosing High-School Students' Reading Problems." *Junior College and Adult Reading,* National Reading Conference, 1967a, pp. 263–67.

WILSON, ROBERT M. *Diagnostic and Remedial Reading.* Columbus, Ohio: Charles E. Merrill Books, 1967b.

WINKLEY, CAROL K. "What Do Diagnostic Reading Tests Really Diagnose?" *Diagnostic Viewpoints in Reading,* Newark, Del.: International Reading Association, 1971, 64–80.

YOUNG, ROBERT A. "Case Studies in Reading Disability." *American Journal of Orthopsychiatry* 8 (1938): 230–54.

ZINTZ, MILES V. *Corrective Reading.* Dubuque, Iowa: Wm. C. Brown Company, 1972.

Index

Ability grouping, 341
Abstract thinking, 44
Accelerators, 283
Acuity:
  auditory, 137
  visual, 129
Age, mental, 93
Alexia, 402
Alphabet method, 209
Amplitude, 137
Analytic method, 210
Aniseikonia, 132
Antonyms, 245
Aphasia, 402
Articulation, 151
Astigmatism, 131
Attitudes (and reading), 179
Audiometer, 139
Auditory acuity, 137
Auditory blending, 137
Auditory deficiency:
  causes of, 138
  symptoms of, 138
Auditory discrimination, 103, 137
  definition of, 105
Aud-X, 283

Basic Reading skills:
  comprehension, 237, 240
  rate, 276
  word recognition, 24, 202, 208, 340, 418
Belonging, law of, 61
Binocular vision, 131
Bloomfield, L., 20, 227
Brain functioning and reading, 356
  association areas, 156
  asymmetry, 166
  damage of, 402
  dominance, 161
  instruments to measure brain damage,
    403
  projection areas, 156

Cerebral dominance, 161
Classical Conditioning, 62

Cloze procedure, 420
Cognition, 34, 52, 68, 69, 212
Color Phonics System, 414
Communication:
  change, 17
  noise, 17
  theory, 17
Compounds, 248
Comprehension, 10, 237
  definition of, 238
  developing, 239, 419
  levels of, 237
  rate of, 276
Concept formation, 39
  abstract thinking in, 44
Conditioning:
  classical, 62
  operant, 15, 64
Congenital Wordblindness, 158
Content areas:
  literature, 317
  mathematics, 323
  reading in, 314
  science, 325
  vocational subjects, 327
Context analysis, 242
Contiguity, law of, 63
Corrective reader, 395
Corrective reading, 336, 349, 393
Critical reading, 259
Crossed dominance, 162

Deafness:
  intensity, 138
  tone, 138
Decoding, 10
Deep structure, 12, 23
Details, reading for, 255
Developmental program, 336, 392
  principles of, 337
Developmental task, 87
Diagnosis, 368
  definition of, 369
  principles of, 370
  steps in, 371

433

Dictionary cues, 251
Differentiation, 73
Disadvantaged learner, 357
Dominance:
    cerebral, 161
    crossed, 161
Dyslexia, 157, 394, 396
    causes, 89
    maturational, 397
    secondary, 396
    specific, 398

Ecological validity, 72
Effect, law of, 60
Emotional disorders:
    and reading failure, 193
    treatment of, 196
Encoding, 10
Esophoria, 132
Exercise, law of, 55
Exophoria, 132
Expectancy formulas, 377
Experience (and reading), 37, 71, 101
Eye-memory span, 128
Eye-movements, 122
    developmental aspects, 126
    measurement of, 129
Eye-voice span, 128
Eyes:
    binocular defects, 131
    defects and reading deficiency, 133
    movements of, 122
    refractive defects, 130

Farsightedness, 131
Fernald Kinesthetic Method, 210, 412, 419
Field, definition of, 72
Field theories of learning, 52, 68
Figurative expressions, 249
Fixations, 123
Flexible grouping, 345
Flexibility in reading, 278
Foot-candle, 303
Formal reading inventory, 386, 388
Fries, C. C., 20, 229, 230

Gestalt Psychology, 34, 52, 68, 69, 212
Gifted learner, 354
Gillingham method, 416
Grammar, 154
Grapheme, 153, 400
Graphs, reading of, 269
Grouping, 341
    flexible, 345
    homogeneous, 341
    homorthic, 345
    individual, 344
Guthrie, Edwin R., 62

Hearing, 136
    defects of, 138
    definition of, 137
    high frequency losses, 105
    loss, 137
    tests of, 139
Heterophoria, 131

Hinshelwood, James, 158
Homogeneous grouping, 341
Homonyms, 245
Hull, Clark L., 66
Hyperopia, 131
Hyperphoria, 132

Illumination, 303
Individual differences, 332
Individualized reading, 344
Informal inventory, 386
Insightful learning, 75
Intelligence:
    definition of, 91
    quotient, 93
    tests, 374
Interest:
    definition of, 176
    determinants of, 180
    developing, 185
    and reading, 178

James, William, 2, 11, 35
Javal, Emile, 122

Kinesthetic method, 210, 412, 419
Kinetic reversal, 169

Lalling, 150
Language (and reading), 149
    and reading readiness, 109, 149
    structures (deep and surface), 12, 23
Laws:
    of belonging, 61
    of contiguity, 63
    of effect, 60
    of exercise, 55
    of readiness, 54
Learner:
    disadvantaged, 357
    gifted, 354
    slow, 352
Learning:
    definition of, 51
    field theories of, 52, 68
    motivation and, 56
    principles of, 50
    reading for, 262
    S-R theories of, 50
Lefevre, C. A., 20, 228
Left-handedness, 162
Legibility, 299
Letter, name knowledge, 104
Lewin, Kurt, 77
Linguistic methods, 229
Listening (and reading), 140
Literature, reading of, 317

Main idea (reading for), 254
Maladjustment:
    and reading achievement, 193
    types of treatment, 196
Maps (reading of), 268
Mathematics (reading in), 323
Maturation (and reading), 95
Meaning (determinants of), 36

Mechanical devices:
  accelerators, 283
  evaluation of, 279
  tachistoscopes, 282
Methods of teaching reading, 208, 221
  alphabet, 209
  analytic, 210
  linguistic, 227, 229
  newer methods, 221
  phonic, 209
  remedial, 412, 419
  sentence, 210
  syllable, 209
  synthetic, 209
  word, 210
Modality, tests of, 390
Models (theoretical) of reading, 14
  cognitive, 16
  information processing model, 17
  linguistic, 20
  psychological, 15
  psychometric, 15
  synthesis of, 22
  taxonomic, 15
  transformational grammar, 21
Monroe Method, 412
Morphology, 153
Motivation (and reading), 176
Motives, 175
  habit, 178
  psychological, 177
  physiological, 177
Myopia, 130

Nearsightedness, 130
Neural adequacy, 157
Noise (in communication), 17
Note making, 258

Operant conditioning, 16, 64
Oral reading, 202
Organization (reading of), 255
Orton, Samuel T., 158, 162, 165, 167, 222
Outlining, 257

Paragraph (reading of), 254
Perception:
  definition of, 34
  personal nature of, 35
  and reading, 72, 82
  terminology, 34
  theories of, 34, 69
Perception span, 124
Perceptual veridicality, 38
Personal data sheet, 379
Personality (and reading), 188
Phi-phenomenon, 33
Phonematic hearing, 105
Phoneme, 152, 400
Phonemics, 224
Phonetics, 223
Phonics, 223, 224
Phrase reading, 252
Piaget, Jean, 39
Pica, 299
Prefixes, 246

Progressive Choice Reading Method, 416
Psycholinguistics, 12, 22, 23, 26
Punctuation, 250

Rate (in reading):
  and comprehension, 276
  and flexibility, 278
  gagetry, 282
  improving, 279
  value of, 277
Readability:
  evaluation of, 296
  formulas of, 292
  measuring of, 291
Reading:
  as associative process, 206
  checklist, 380
  comprehension, 10, 237
  in content areas, 314
  critical, 259
  correlates of, 88, 148
  cue systems in, 13
  definition of, 8, 32, 72
  for details, 255
  disability, 89, 157, 394, 396, 404
  at early age, 110
  and eye defects, 133
  graphs, 269
  as information gathering, 11, 78
  interest in, 176
  legibility and, 299
  models of, 14
  oral, 202
  paragraph, 254
  perceptual nature of, 32
  and personality, 188
  phrases, 252
  physiological correlates of, 148
  physiology of, 18
  rate, 276
  readability, 289
  readiness, 87
  research in, 1
  sensory bases of, 121
  sign system in, 9
  tastes, 186
  thought units, 124
  veridicality, 38
Reading eye camera, 129
Reading readiness, 87, 110
  and auditory discrimination, 103
  correlates of, 88
  and experience, 37, 71, 101
  and intelligence, 91
  and language development, 109, 149
  and maturation, 95
  and neural development, 155
  psychological bases of, 87
  and physical conditions, 148
  and sex of the reader, 97
  and vision, 121
  and visual discrimination, 107
Recoding, 10
Recognition span, 124
Redundancy, 18, 25
Refractive errors, 130

Regression, 124
Remedial instruction, 336, 351, 393, 408
  evaluation of, 422
  methods of, 412
  principles of, 408
Remedial reader, 396
Retardation (definition of), 372
Return sweep, 126
Reversals, 167
Robinson Study Method, 262
Roots, 246

Scanning, 284
Science (reading in), 324
Screening tests (vision), 135
Secondary reinforcement, 60
Self-concept, 191
Senses (and reading), 121
  hearing, 136
  listening, 140
  vision, 122
Sentence meaning, 253
Sentence method, 210
Sex (and readiness), 97
Skimming, 284
Skinner, B. F., 15, 64
Slow learner, 352
Snellen Formula, 130
Social development (and reading), 188
Social studies (reading in), 321
Socio-economic status (and reading), 101
Spacing, 299, 302
Speed reading, 276, 279
S-R Learning theory, 50
Strabismus, 131
Strephosymbolia, 167
Study reading, 263
Suffixes, 246
Summarizing, 257
Surface structure, 12, 23
Syllable method, 209
Synonym, 245
Syntax, 13, 26, 153
Synthetic methods, 209
Synthetic phonic method, 209

Tables (reading of), 269
Tachistoscopes, 282
Tastes (development of reading), 186
Tests:
  brain damage, 403
  diagnostic reading, 390
  modality, 390
  oral reading, 389
  reading achievement, 375
  scholastic aptitude, 374
Thorndike, Edward L., 45, 54
Thought unit reading, 124
Tolman, Edward, 77
Type faces, 301

Underlining, 257
Unified Phonics method, 414

Veridicality, 26, 38
Vision:
  acuity, 129
  binocular, 131
  defective, 129
  definition of, 121
  eye-movement research, 122
  refractive errors, 130
  visual readiness, 122
Visual discrimination, 107
Visual field, 123
Vocational subjects (reading in), 327

Watson, John B., 62
Wave frequency, 137
WISC analysis, 386
Word meaning, 240
Word method, 210, 211
Word origins (study of), 251
Word recognition:
  analytic methods of, 210
  emphasis of parts, 215
  emphasis of wholes, 211
  methods of teaching, 24, 202, 208,
    340, 418
  synthetic methods of, 209